AFRICAN WRITERS

AFRICAN WRITERS

C. BRIAN COX
Editor

VOLUME I

CHARLES SCRIBNER'S SONS
Macmillan Library Reference USA
Simon & Schuster Macmillan
NEW YORK

Simon & Schuster Prentice Hall International
LONDON   MEXICO CITY   NEW DELHI   SINGAPORE   SYDNEY   TORONTO

Charles Scribner's Sons
An Imprint of Simon & Schuster Macmillan
1633 Broadway
New York, NY 10019

LIBRARY OF CONGRESS CATALOGING-IN-PUBLICATION DATA

African writers / C. Brian Cox, editor.
    p. cm.
    Includes bibliographical references and index.
    ISBN 0-684-19651-4 (set : alk. paper). — ISBN 0-684-19771-5 (v. 1:
alk. paper). — ISBN 0-684-19772-3 (v. 2 : alk. paper)
    1. African literature—Bio-bibliography—Dictionaries.
2. Authors, African—Biography—Dictionaries. 3. African
literature—Dictionaries.
PL8010.A453 1997
896—dc20
[B]   96-16128
                                         CIP

1 3 5 7 9 11 13 15 17 19   20 18 16 14 12 10 8 6 4 2

PRINTED IN THE UNITED STATES OF AMERICA

The paper used in this publication meets the minimum requirements
of the American National Standard for Information Sciences—
Permanence of Paper for Printed Library Materials, ANSI Z39.48–1984.

ACKNOWLEDGMENTS

Charles Scribner's Sons gratefully acknowledges those publishers and individuals who graciously permitted the use of the following materials in copyright. Every effort has been made to contact copyright holders of significantly quoted materials.

DENNIS BRUTUS. "Erosion: Transkei," from *Sirens Knuckles Boots* by Dennis Brutus. Copyright © 1963 by Dennis Brutus. Excerpt from *Letters to Martha, and Other Poems from a South African Prison* by Dennis Brutus. Copyright © 1968 by Dennis Brutus. "A Simple Lust" and two other poems from *A Simple Lust* by Dennis Brutus. Copyright © 1973 by Dennis Brutus. The prose quotation and ten poems from *China Poems* by Dennis Brutus. Copyright © 1975 by Dennis Brutus. Excerpts from *South African Voices* by Dennis Brutus. Copyright © 1975 by Dennis Brutus. Excerpt from *Salutes and Censures* by Dennis Brutus. Copyright © 1984 by Dennis Brutus. Excerpts from *Airs and Tributes* by Dennis Brutus. Copyright © 1989 by Dennis Brutus. "February, 1990," from *Still the Sirens* by Dennis Brutus. Copyright © 1993. Permission granted by Dennis Brutus.

MOHAMMED DIB. Excerpt from *Formulaires, poésie* by Mohammed Dib. © Editions du Seuil, 1970. Reprinted by permission of the publisher. Excerpt from *Feu, beau feu, poésie* by Mohammed Dib. © Editions du Seuil, 1979. Reprinted by permission of the publisher. Poem extracted from *Omneros* by Mohammed Dib. Copyright © Mohammed Dib. Reprinted by permission of the author.

ES'KIA MPHAHLELE. Excerpt from Es'kia Mphahlele's letter to Guy Butler and excerpt from Es'kia Mphahlele's 1983 interview by Tim Couzens. Reprinted by permission of Es'kia Mphahlele. Extracts from "Exile in Nigeria," "Somewhere," and "A Prayer," from *The Unbroken Song* by Es'kia Mphahlele. Reprinted by permission of Ravan Press.

MEJA MWANGI. Excerpt from Meja Mwangi's 1993 correspondence with J. Roger Kurtz. Reprinted by permission of Meja Mwangi.

AGOSTINHO NETO. Extracts from Agostinho Neto's *Sacred Hope*, translated by Marga Holness. Translation copyright by Marga Holness. Reprinted by permission of Marga Holness.

TANURE OJAIDE. Extracts from Tanure Ojaide, *The Eagle's Vision*. Detroit: Lotus Press, 1987. By permission of the publisher. Extracts from *Children of Iroko* and *Labyrinths of the Delta* by Tanure Ojaide. Reprinted by permission of Greenfield Review Press.

GABRIEL OKARA. Quotations from *The Fisherman's Invocation* by Gabriel Okara. Reprinted by permission of Heinemann Educational Books, publisher.

KOLE OMOTOSO. Excerpt from Kole Omotoso's letter to Uko Atai. Reprinted by permission of Kole Omotoso.

NIYI OSUNDARE. The lines from "Forest Echoes" and "Our Earth Will Not Die," from *The Eye of the Earth* by Niyi Osundare. Reprinted by permission of Heinemann Educational Books (Nigeria) Plc.

ALAN PATON. Excerpts from "Ubi" (originally published in *Eisteddfod Poetry Book*), "The Hermit," "To a Small Boy Who Died at Kiepkloof Reformatory," "Only the Child Is No More," "I Have Approached," "Meditation for a Young Boy Confirmed," and "On the Death of J. H. Hofmeyr" (originally published in *Knocking on the Door*), from *Songs of Africa: The Collected Poems of Alan Paton*. Copyright A. M. Paton. Reprinted by permission of A. M. Paton. Excerpt from the unpublished novel "John Henry Dane" by Alan Paton. Reprinted with permission of A. M. Paton.

WILLIAM PLOMER. Extracts from "Three Pinks," "French Lisette: A Ballad of Maida Vale," "The Playboy of the Demi-World: 1938," and "No Identity," from *Collected Poems* by William Plomer. Reprinted by permission of the Estate of the author and Jonathan Cape, publisher.

OLA ROTIMI. Extracts from *If*, *Kurunmi*, and *Akassa youmi* by Ola Rotimi. Reprinted by permission of the author. Extracts from Ola Rotimi's letter to Martin Banham and from Ola Rotimi's lecture "The Trials of African Literature," delivered at the University of Benin on 4 May 1987. Reprinted by permission of Ola Rotimi.

LÉOPOLD SÉDAR SENGHOR. Excerpts from *The Collected Poetry* by Léopold Sédar Senghor, translated by Melvin Dixon (Charlottesville: Virginia, 1991). Reprinted with permission of the University Press of Virginia.

ABŪ AL-QĀSIM AL-SHĀBBĪ. Excerpts of poems by Abū al-Qāsim al-Shābbī in *Modern Arabic Literature*, edited by M. M. Badawi. Reprinted with the permission of Cambridge University Press.

WOLE SOYINKA. Excerpt from "Dragonfly at My Windowpane," from *Mandela's Earth and Other Poems* by Wole Soyinka. Reprinted by permission of Andre Deutsch Ltd.

Editorial Staff

CONTENTS

ix

WRITERS BY COUNTRY

The authors treated in *African Writers* are here grouped according to the present-day African countries with which they are most frequently associated. This list is intended as a guide to introduce these writers succinctly, to suggest connections between writers from the same country, and to demonstrate the scope of coverage in *African Writers*. It is not meant as a conclusive answer to questions about national identity.

In most cases the countries listed here are the lands in which the writers were born, grew up, and developed their reputations. More than a few of the writers left their native land, whether by choice or by force, and continued their literary careers as expatriates or exiles. Literally or metaphorically, many of these writers can be said to have transcended national — and sometimes continental — boundaries.

In general, the authors from Ghana, Kenya, Nigeria, and South Africa wrote in English; those from Algeria, Cameroon, Guinea, and Senegal wrote in French; those from Angola and Mozambique wrote in Portuguese; and Egyptian authors wrote in Arabic. As noted below, a few authors wrote in indigenous African languages, and some wrote in more than one language.

For explanations of literary and ethnic terms, please refer to the essays.

ALGERIA

ALBERT CAMUS. 1913–1960. Francophone novelist and essayist famed for his existentialist fiction; winner of the 1957 Nobel Prize in literature.

MOHAMMED DIB. 1920– . Francophone novelist and poet whose work offers an existentialist exploration of language, identity, and the alienating effect of modernity.

YACINE KATEB. 1929–1989. Francophone novelist and playwright whose work is characterized by formal innovation and the mythic narrative of the history of the Maghreb people, later career turned to agit-prop drama.

ANGOLA

AGOSTINHO NETO. 1922–1979. Poet of the Generation of 1950 whose work in Portuguese explores themes of the African diaspora, Angolan cultural identity, and Angolan liberation from Portugal; independent Angola's first president.

PEPETELA. 1941– . Writer of Portuguese descent who fought with a Marxist guerrilla group for Angola's independence and who gradually became disillusioned with dogmatic socialism; wrote short stories, plays, and novels that use allegory, myth, and symbols to examine Angolan cultural identity.

JOSÉ LUANDINO VIEIRA. 1935– . Portuguese dissident best known for narratives written while he was a political prisoner of Angola's colonial government from 1961 to 1972; his prose fiction promotes a uniquely Angolan literary form that is deeply influenced by oral tradition.

CAMEROON

MONGO BETI. 1932– . Francophone novelist and essayist whose socially conscious and satirical work was frequently censored and who spent thirty-two years in self-exile.

FERDINAND OYONO. 1929– . Francophone novelist whose work not only criticizes colonial rule but also satirizes native communities; ceased publishing after he became a government official in the conservative postcolonial regime.

EGYPT

TAWFĪQ AL-ḤAKĪM. 1898–1987. Pioneer realist novelist and the founder of the modern Egyptian theater, who produced both intellectual and popular plays in Arabic.

YŪSUF IDRĪS. 1927–1991. Arabic short-story writer, playwright, novelist, and journalist who, foremost in the postindependence generation of writers, abandoned the tradition of sentimental short stories and created a new form of realistic short fiction that portrays the world of the poor; also favored indigenous theatrical forms as opposed to the classic model of Aristotelian drama.

NAJĪB MAHFŪẒ. 1911– . Pioneered development of the Arabic novel in postrevolutionary Egyptian literature with a realist fiction depicting contemporary Cairo between the world wars; winner of the 1988 Nobel Prize in literature.

NAWĀL AL-SAʿADĀWĪ. 1931– . Feminist writer, medical doctor, and political activist whose novels, short stories, and nonfiction explore the injustices faced by women under the oppression of a patriarchal class system, foreign imperialism, and religious authority in a Muslim culture.

ṬĀHĀ ḤUSAYN. 1889–1973. Literary critic and writer who championed western cultural values while asserting the continuing relevance of the Arab-Islamic heritage to Egyptian literature and culture; nominated for the Nobel Prize in literature in 1949.

GHANA

AMA ATA AIDOO. 1942– . Playwright, novelist, and poet who wrote about women in Ghanaian society, expressing her view that freedom for Africa is directly linked to freedom for women; lived in exile from Ghana since 1983 for her radical views.

AYI KWEI ARMAH. 1939– . Novelist, born a member of the elite, whose work struggles to find hope in a pervasive mixture of pessimism and despair in African society.

KOFI AWOONOR. 1935– . Lyric poet, novelist, essayist, and chronicler of African oral literature; served as ambassador to Brazil, Cuba, and the United Nations.

EFUA THEODORA SUTHERLAND. 1924–1996. Playwright and educator who wrote in Akan and English and who was instrumental in the founding of a Ghanaian national theater.

GUINEA

CAMARA LAYE. 1928–1980. Francophone novelist whose autobiographical and allegorical fiction is marked by lyrical evocation and religious vision and expresses apprehension about French modernity and postcolonial Africa; associated with Négritude.

KENYA

MEJA MWANGI. 1948– . Novelist whose fiction draws on the Mau Mau revolt, on contemporary life in the urban ghetto, and on the genre of popular thrillers.

NGŨGĨ WA THIONG'O. 1938– . Dissident writer and activist whose themes and settings in novels, plays, and literary criticism promote indigenous culture and denounce the exploitation of peasants under both colonial and postcolonial governments; wrote in English and Gĩkũyũ.

LESOTHO

THOMAS MOKOPU MOFOLO. 1876–1948. Novelist writing in the Sesotho language about the conflicts between Christian missionary teachings and traditional African culture.

MOZAMBIQUE

MIA COUTO. 1955– . Poet, novelist, and prolific writer of short stories reflecting oral culture and characterized by qualities of myth and magic realism; wrote in Portuguese.

LUÍS BERNARDO HONWANA. 1942– . Pioneer writer of short stories evoking the rural culture of the colonial era; his single published story collection is a classic of African literature in Portuguese.

NIGERIA

CHINUA ACHEBE. 1930– . Igbo novelist, poet, and essayist concerned with political and social issues in postcolonial Nigeria.

JOHN PEPPER CLARK. 1935– . Playwright and poet of royal Ijo and Urhobo descent who draws on both Ijo and western classical traditions.

OBI EGBUNA. 1938– . Igbo writer of polemical novels, short fiction, and plays reflecting concern with tradition and philosophical allegiance to socialist-based Pan-Africanism; leader in the British Black Power movement.

CYPRIAN EKWENSI. 1921– . Igbo novelist with a pan-Nigerian outlook and a journalistic interest in emerging social issues; his populist narratives are intended as entertainment and social commentary.

BUCHI EMECHETA. 1944– . Writer of documentary novels about the immigrant experience in England and the struggles of women in Africa.

FESTUS IYAYI. 1947– . Radical novelist whose realist fiction examines the social decadence of postindependence Nigeria from a class perspective.

TANURE OJAIDE. 1948– . Member of the post–civil war generation of poets who is known for his politically committed populist verse.

GABRIEL OKARA. 1921– . Ijọ poet, novelist, and storyteller concerned with the relationship between language and culture; his work is characterized by parable, stylistic innovation, and linguistic experimentation with English and Ijọ.

CHRISTOPHER OKIGBO. 1932–1967. Igbo poet who played an important role in the development of the modern African literature; killed in the Nigerian civil war.

BEN OKRI. 1959– . Urhobo novelist and short-story writer using mimetic realism and mythology; winner of the 1991 Booker Prize.

KOLE OMOTOSO. 1943– . Yoruba novelist, playwright, and journalist who wrote realistic fiction with detailed caricature of Nigerian social decadence.

FEMI OSOFISAN. 1946– . One of the most prolific Yoruba writers, who furthered the tradition of Wole Soyinka by using drama to bring about social change and political activism.

NIYI OSUNDARE. 1947– . Poet of Yoruba ancestry who strove for accessible themes and language; much of his later verse is strongly grounded in Yoruba cosmology and is intended to be performed orally as songs accompanied by traditional instruments.

OLA ROTIMI. 1938– . Ijọ-Yoruba playwright who exploited the multilingual nature of Nigerian culture to create comic, scathing social criticism.

BODE SOWANDE. 1948– . Yoruba playwright and novelist whose socially committed writing is notable for its humanistic optimism and is framed in the contrast between corruption and utopian ideals.

WOLE SOYINKA. 1934– . Yoruba dramatist, poet, novelist, and essayist whose wide-ranging interests include mythology and agitprop theater, autobiography and cultural theory; winner of the 1986 Nobel Prize in literature.

AMOS TUTUOLA. 1920– . Novelist and short-story writer whose "primitivist" narratives rework traditional oral tales in Yoruba-informed English.

SENEGAL

MARIAMA BÂ. 1929–1981. Francophone novelist who wrote about the plight of women in modern African Islamic society.

SEMBÈNE OUSMANE. 1925– . Francophone novelist and filmmaker whose career spans both colonial and postcolonial periods; themes include postcolonial corruption, the negative influence of religion, and the conflict between Africa and colonialism.

LÉOPOLD SÉDAR SENGHOR. 1906– . Francophone poet and one of the founders of the Négritude movement; the first president of the independent Republic of Senegal.

SOMALIA

NURUDDIN FARAH. 1945– . Multilingual novelist writing in English about poverty and patriarchy in Somalia.

SOUTH AFRICA

PETER ABRAHAMS. 1919– . Colored writer who explored the issues of race and color in novels set in South Africa, "Panafrica," and Jamaica.

ANDRÉ BRINK. 1935– . Afrikaner novelist, writing in English and Afrikaans, whose work draws on South Africa's history as well as its contemporary social ills.

DENNIS BRUTUS. 1924– . Colored poet whose writing style went through several distinct stages; known for his anti-apartheid activities, which kept him exiled from South Africa for nearly thirty years.

ROY CAMPBELL. 1901–1957. White expatriate poet, infamous for his iconoclastic and reactionary views.

J. M. COETZEE. 1940– . Writer of Dutch and English descent whose postmodern novels offer critiques of the social and political state of affairs in South Africa; winner of the 1983 Booker Prize.

ATHOL FUGARD. 1932– . White playwright whose theater in collaboration with black and Colored South Africans dramatizes the hopelessness and oppression of the disenfranchised victims of apartheid; has directed and appeared in his own plays in New York and London.

NADINE GORDIMER. 1923– . White novelist writing about the social and personal consequences of apartheid; winner of the 1974 Booker Prize and of the 1991 Nobel Prize in literature.

BESSIE HEAD. 1937–1986. Colored novelist who wrote about South Africa and village life in Botswana, where she lived much of her life as a refugee; her writing includes autobiographical fiction and anthropological and historical narratives.

CHRISTOPHER HOPE. 1944– . Novelist, poet, playwright of Irish Catholic background whose work often treats the evils of apartheid and racism metaphorically and explores the surreal absurdity of bureaucratic and totalitarian regimes of culture and politics.

DAN JACOBSON. 1929– . Writer of novels, short stories, essays, and travel books; Jewish expatriate who began writing realistic novels with South African settings and

moved to postmodern narratives that continue his preoccupation with the mysteriousness of human behavior.

ALEX LA GUMA. 1925–1985. Colored novelist and short-story writer, expatriate who wrote about how nonwhite South Africans living under apartheid became politically aware.

ES'KIA MPHAHLELE. 1919– . Black writer of autobiography, fiction, poetry, and literary commentary whose work often focuses on the theme of exile; nominated for the Nobel Prize in literature in 1969.

ALAN PATON. 1903–1988. White novelist, essayist, poet, and biographer who struggled to integrate discipline, authority, and Christian compassion; founder of the anti-apartheid Liberal Party.

WILLIAM PLOMER. 1903–1973. White writer of English descent who lived in several countries, wrote in several genres, and was ultimately known as a man of letters within the London literary establishment.

OLIVE SCHREINER. 1855–1920. White fiction and polemical writer and an early feminist who wrote about the lives of white colonial women.

LAURENS VAN DER POST. 1906– . Afrikaner novelist and writer best known for his travel writing, particularly about Africa.

SUDAN

AL-ṬAYYIB ṢĀLIḤ. 1929– . Novelist and short-story writer who often set his narratives in the same fictional Sudanese village and explored the confrontation between the Arab Muslim and Western European worlds.

TUNISIA

ALBERT MEMMI. 1920– . Jewish novelist and essayist writing in French on themes of identity, oppression, dependency, and colonization; an eminent intellectual and sociologist.

ABŪ AL-QĀSIM AL-SHĀBBĪ. 1909–1934. Arab Romantic poet who wrote verse that is both intensely personal and committed to social change; his death at the age of twenty-five has taken on metaphorical dimension.

UGANDA

OKOT P'BITEK. 1931–1982. Cwaa poet and novelist, writing in English and Acholi, who wrote about cultural changes since independence, including urban migration, the move toward a cash economy, and changes in sexual mores.

ZIMBABWE

DORIS LESSING. 1919– . Persian-born writer whose diverse publications range from socialist-realist stories to science-fiction novels, from memoirs about her early life in colonial Southern Rhodesia (now Zimbabwe) to accounts of her visits to that country decades after she had run away from it.

* * *

WOMEN WRITERS

AMA ATA AIDOO, Ghana

MARIAMA BÂ, Senegal

BUCHI EMECHETA, Nigeria

NADINE GORDIMER, South Africa

BESSIE HEAD, South Africa

DORIS LESSING, Zimbabwe

NAWĀL AL-SAʿADĀWĪ, Egypt

OLIVE SCHREINER, South Africa

EFUA THEODORA SUTHERLAND, Ghana

PUBLISHER'S NOTE

Most of the non-English works discussed in this collection are available in English translations. When English translations are available, the published English titles appear in italic type in parentheses following the original titles; for example,

Les Bouts de bois de Dieu (1960; *God's Bits of Wood*).

In the cases of short stories and poems, double quotation marks are placed around the titles of the published English translations; for example,

"A Velhota" (1964; "The Old Woman").

The year that appears inside the parentheses refers to the first publication date of the work in the original language. (Information concerning the publications of translated works can be found in the bibliography at the end of each essay.) The English title is used in subsequent references to the work.

If no English translation of the work has been published, the contributors have given an English equivalent of the original title in roman type and without capitalization; for example,

Fī al-shiʿr al-jāhilī (1926; On pre-Islamic poetry).

In these cases, original-language titles are used in subsequent references. Quotations from such titles, if any, have been translated by our contributors.

INTRODUCTION

C. BRIAN COX, EDITOR

Four writers in this collection have been awarded the Nobel Prize in literature: Albert Camus (1957), Nadine Gordimer (1991), Najīb Maḥfūẓ (1988), and Wole Soyinka (1986). Others such as Chinua Achebe, Bessie Head, Doris Lessing, Ngũgĩ wa Thiong'o, Alan Paton, Olive Schreiner, and Laurens van der Post are well-known to a huge international audience. These writers use many different languages: Arabic, English, French, Portuguese, as well as African languages such as Akan, Yoruba, and Gĩkũyũ (or Kikuyu). This collection offers an introduction to the variety and richness of late-nineteenth- and twentieth-century literature from the African continent. Most of the works discussed in these essays are available in English.

I have chosen writers who were born or spent a good deal of their lives in Africa and who have made significant contributions to the literature of their countries. I have perhaps controversially included Camus, but I have encouraged John Fletcher, the contributor, to concentrate on the early influence of Algeria on Camus. My main criterion has been to choose writers who deserve international recognition for their achievement. I have been fascinated by the way these writers from such different backgrounds treat similar themes, above all the need to create a personal identity free of colonial impositions.

Obviously I could have included additional authors. My choice of sixty-five inevitably leaves out many who might claim equal right to entry. It would be easy to make a list of fifty or more who have considerable achievements to their credit: Lenrie Peters from Gambia; Bernard Binlin Dadié from the Ivory Coast; Chief D. O. Fagunwa and Elechi Amadi from Nigeria; Breyten Breytenbach, Njabulo Ndebele, and Sol T. Plaatje from

South Africa; Taban lo Liyong from Uganda; or Dambudzo Marechera and Charles Mungoshi from Zimbabwe. Correspondents have written to me with enthusiastic recommendations for a host of other names, including some new writers who are just beginning to make a reputation. I hope that this collection of essays will encourage many new readers both to enjoy the works of these sixty-five writers and to realize that my choice by no means exhausts the number of African writers worthy of attention.

THE CURSE OF COLONIALISM

When I was at school and college in the 1930s and 1940s, it was customary for European and North American readers to assume that African civilization was inferior. In the comic books I read so avidly, Arabs were depicted as lazy, irresponsible, and dishonest. My ideas about black Africa were taken from popular novels, such as Captain W. E. Johns's Biggles stories, in which Africans were usually easily duped savages. Joseph Conrad's *Heart of Darkness* (1902) was very influential. The natives on the banks of the Congo take part with the European Kurtz in orgies of promiscuity and violence. Conrad's treatment of the vitality of the "dark continent" is ambiguous, of course, but Kurtz's passionate African mistress, willing to kill for cheap trinkets and colored cloths, seemed to many western readers a representative figure.

In *The Scramble for Africa, 1876–1912* (1991), Thomas Pakenham describes the mixture of Christian missionary zeal and lust for wealth and land that motivated the British, French, Portuguese, German, and Belgian colonists of the second half of the nineteenth century. In 1880, he explains, most of the continent was still ruled by Africans and barely explored by the Europeans. By 1902 these five European powers had grabbed almost the whole continent, giving themselves thirty new colonies and protectorates, ten million square miles of new territory, and 110 million bewildered new subjects. David Livingstone's call for Africa to be redeemed by the three Cs—commerce, Christianity, and civilization—aroused an enthusiastic response in Europe. Soon, as with King Leopold II of the Belgians and his exploitation of the Congo, a fourth C—conquest—became dominant, and the most terrifying atrocities were commonplace. Africans were treated like animals; many whites believed that blacks were genetically inferior. The official racial-segregation doctrine of apartheid in South Africa was enforced until the 1990s.

Much of the literature discussed in this collection is concerned with African reactions to the curse of colonialism. The struggle for freedom was supported by influential writers such as the psychoanalyst and social philosopher Frantz Fanon. In *Les Damnés de la terre* (1961; *The Wretched of the Earth*), Fanon, who was born in Martinique, urged colonized peoples to purge themselves of their degradation in a "collective catharsis," to be accomplished by violence against their European oppressors. Many African writers were subjected to censorship, exile, or imprisonment, including solitary confinement. Revolutionary ideals are found in writings from all over the continent, in Egypt or Tunisia as well as from the well-known independence movements of Angola, Nigeria, and South Africa. The Tunisian poet Abū al-Qāsim al-Shābbī, for example, in his 1933 poem "Desire for Life" is concerned with the awakening of forces that can combat colonialism; this poem is familiar to readers in many Arab countries.

QUEST FOR IDENTITY

Many literary artists were determined to combat colonialism by the rediscovery and celebration of a truly African identity. In Bessie Head's *When Rain Clouds Gather* (1968), Makhaya Maseko, a young Zulu on the run from South African security forces, makes the dangerous crossing into Botswana to find a redemptive purpose for his life. This voyage in search of a true identity is a common feature of much African literature. In Ama Ata Aidoo's *Our Sister Killjoy* (1966), as Shirley Chew explains in her essay in this volume, Sissie reverses Marlow's journey of discovery in Conrad's *Heart of Darkness*. She travels to Bavaria and finds in Europe the heart of racial and class oppression. The pastoral myth of the European village is overlooked by the big castle with its feudal past. She becomes aware of the jingoism of the Europeans and, most horrifying of all, the proximity of the Nazi concentration camps. Sissie's task is to extricate herself from the white man's version of the world and to claim space for herself as an African woman.

Chinua Achebe's aim in his writings is to expose the arrogance of Europeans when they make excuses for their pillage of Africa. The belief that Africa was a Primordial Void, he declared, is sheer nonsense. Africa has a history, a religion, and a civilization, of all of which Africans can be proud. His novels try to reconstruct this history and civilization and to challenge the stereotypes and clichés which dominated western-style schools when he was a boy. His decision to become a writer was influenced by Joyce Cary's novel *Mister Johnson* (1939). He admired Cary but felt that this novel had failed completely to get under the skin of the Africans: "And I felt if a good writer could make this mess perhaps we ought to try our hand." Cyprian Ekwensi, also from Nigeria, similarly wants as a writer to achieve the "reinstatement of the dignity and pride which the black man lost through slavery in the New World and colonialism in the Old." Many African writers, such as Mongo Beti from the French-speaking Cameroon, were helped to escape from colonial stereotypes by reading black American writers such as Richard Wright.

Since the 1980s many authors, such as Achebe in the novel *Anthills of the Savannah* (1987), have responded bitterly to postcolonial dictatorships. In his autobiography *Aké* (1981), Wole Soyinka attacks political intimidation and repression in Nigeria's second republican government. The campaign for freedom, equality, and justice continues in postcolonial societies.

The search for identity is expressed powerfully by women writers such as Olive Schreiner, Buchi Emecheta, and Nawāl al-Saʿadāwī, who are particularly concerned with patriarchal oppression. Schreiner's writings convey the embattled feminism of the late Victorian period, the rebellion of intelligent women against the dictates of the conventional marriage. In recent years the rise of feminism has led to renewed interest in her work. Emecheta inveighs against the grinding exploitation of women by African men across the ages, the burden of a seventeen-hour working day that has sent many African women to an early grave. Al-Saʿadāwī, who was imprisoned under the rule of the Egyptian president Anwar al-Sādāt, writes with passionate anger about the oppression of women in the Arab world; she describes with horror the experience of clitoridectomy. Her aim as an artist is to unveil the mind, for a veil over the mind is more dangerous than a veil over the face. Ama Ata Aidoo believes that freedom for Africa is directly linked to freedom for women. For these female writers literature can be used to make women's lives more visible and significant.

CHOICE OF LANGUAGE

A common question for African writers is what language to choose for their writings. Aidoo is typical in choosing English so she can communicate with other Africans outside Ghana. The language of the imperial masters, particularly English, gives access to a wide international audience, but the English language, with its structures, rhythms, and vocabulary, is deeply involved with a value system which can be seen as European rather than African. In *Decolonising the Mind* (1986), Ngũgĩ wa Thiong'o makes a strong case for writing in indigenous languages and explains his reasons for turning from English to Gĩkũyũ. When he was at school children were beaten for speaking Gĩkũyũ; an English identity had to be imposed.

In his perceptive analysis of African writings, *Chronicles of Darkness* (1989), David Ward says that reading African literature written in English or French is like looking through a tunnel to try to understand the mountain around it: "Even confining oneself to the written literature is distortive. African culture remains firm in its foundation upon a complex of oral cultures: the supervention of the printed word gives the impression that African literature is Anglophone, Francophone, Lusophone, with quaint ethnic outliers like Swahili" (p. 2). Ward praises Ngũgĩ's decision to write in his first language as "a return to the real foundations of discourse and intelligence, an opportunity for the vigour of the oral culture and the energy of the written word to refresh each other" (p. 2).

This tension between the English language and the search for a truly African identity is often also reflected in an uncertainty about what is the appropriate literary form for an African writer. Straight documentary realism is common, but many writers feel the need to experiment in new forms, to find new ways of adapting western realist traditions to nonwestern surroundings. Sol T. Plaatje's early *Mhudi* (1930), the first work of fiction by a black South African to be published in English, mixes fantasy and epic battle scenes. The author seems unwilling to fix a frame on the future; he does not wish to limit himself to the value systems implied in one set of conventions. More recently we have Wole Soyinka's adventurous experiments in a variety of genres, or J. M. Coetzee's use of postmodern techniques. In his essay in this volume, James Harrison shows how Coetzee's fascination with contemporary, postmodern techniques in fiction accompanies—and at times seems to conflict with—a stubborn determination that his writings should be accessible to a wide enough readership for his strong views on South African politics to be heard: "If some of his readers were deeply moved by *Life & Times of Michael K* [1983], baffled by *Foe* [1986] and reassured by *Age of Iron* [1990], others who saw *Foe* as a victory for postmodernism feel betrayed by *Age of Iron*" (pp. 178–179). The breakdown of traditional forms is also a central concern for Doris Lessing; her experiments are examined in detail by Lorna Sage in her essay in this collection. Experiment has taken place particularly in the theater; dramatic performance has been used by playwrights such as Ola Rotimi, John Pepper Clark, and Wole Soyinka as a means of subverting oppressive regimes.

Those African writers who use English have many obvious parallels with those who have to come to terms with colonial languages such as French or Portuguese. In his essay on the Cameroonian novelist Ferdinand Oyono in this collection, Chris Dunton describes how the African novel in French has a slightly longer history than its English-language counterpart. West African writers had begun to produce novels in French some 30 years before Chinua Achebe's *Things Fall Apart* (1958). The tenor of this early francophone African writing, Dunton tells us, was essentially assimilationist, sympathetic to the westernization of African cultural, social, and political life. In *L'Esclave* (1929; The slave), the Dahomean (Beninese) Félix Couchoro suggests that the colonial regime is a benevolent influence, while in *Force-bonté* (1926; Benevolent force), the Senegalese novelist Bakary Diallo asserts his belief in the great goodness of the white man. In the 1950s, with the work of writers such as Mongo Beti, Sembène Ousmane, and Bernard Dadié, the whole tenor of the African novel took a dramatic shift, with fierce critiques of French colonial practice. Writing in Portuguese, both Mia Couto, from Mozambique, and José Luandino Vieira, from Angola, were faced with the same desire to escape from colonial models. As with works by some African writers in English, Couto's writings have adapted well to the stage, where the influence of oral culture provides its own linguistic vitality.

Writers in Arabic face different problems. Many would not wish to be called "African," and they inherit an Arabic literature of great variety and richness. In his essay in this collection Philip Sadgrove describes how al-Ṭayyib Ṣāliḥ shares the belief, prevalent in classical Arabic literature, that writing is, in essence, a moral act: "For him the literary person is, in some way, a historian and a thinker who should shed light on social problems.... Most of his stories have the flavor of the popular and fabulous tales of the traditional Arab storyteller, the *ḥakawātī*" (p. 734). Writers such as Ṣāliḥ and Najīb Maḥfūẓ brought new vitality to the Arab novel. In his essay Roger Allen tells us that the career of Maḥfūẓ, who was born in 1911, "coincides with and indeed represents the complete integration of the novel genre into contemporary Arabic cultural life" (p. 451). The earliest examples of the novel in modern Arabic literature date back to the middle of the nineteenth century. Allen describes how nineteenth-century fiction writers chose to revive the early narrative types, "especially the *maqāmah*, a kind of short, picaresque tale that made use of all the elaborations of traditional Arabic prose style while sardonically commenting on the foibles of contemporary society and its mores" (p. 451). Although African writers in Arabic are born to a very different cultural inheritance, they share with other Africans their hatred of colonialism.

AFRICAN TRADITIONS AND NÉGRITUDE

Many writers in this collection have found inspiration in African tribal cultures, different but not necessarily inferior or superior to European traditions. In his discussion of "Femme noire" ("Black Woman"), one of Léopold Sédar Senghor's best-known poems, Abiola Irele writes: "Senghor appropriates classical western and biblical references and turns them to his account in his conflation of the female figure addressed in the poem with the African landscape, evoked as a symbolic presence and represented as the incarnation of the enduring qualities of the black race in its organic bond with the life of the universe" (p. 781). His verse, Irele says, is infused with the quality of African orality. Oyekan Owomoyela's *African Literatures: An Introduction* (1979) draws attention to the vitality of African oral traditions, the folklore that carried forward from generation to generation in black communities a great tapestry of myths, legends, tales, chants, and incantations. In her introduction to the collection of African praise-poems *Leaf and Bone* (1994, updated edition), Judith Gleason explains that the major form of verbal expression distinctively and pervasively African—that is, a form of oral literature in which continental similarities outweigh ethnic differences—is praise-poetry, regularly performed in households and public spaces in all African languages. Praise-poems may be composed to honor a generous patron's courage or the author's own valor in battle; in some regions highly refined literary-rhetorical skills, plus the ability to compose and deliver praise-poems, were part of the speech training of young boys of good families. Gleason writes: "Implicit in the act of praising is the assumption throughout Africa that every person, human group, tutelary spirit, animal, plant, or body of water, as well as certain manufactured things, has a praiseable core that words can elicit, revitalise, and nudge toward behavior beneficial to the human community" (p. xxiv).

Crucial to African oral literature is the celebration of human community. In *The Rape of Shavi* (1983), Buchi Emecheta contrasts the sickness of European materialistic civilization with the communal sense of fulfillment experienced by villagers in a sub-Saharan region. They are poor in material terms, but their networks of kinship and power are as complex as those of the so-called more advanced societies. The bonds of obligation, of shared culture, create a living community. Famous short stories by Ngũgĩ celebrate the life-affirming contact with the land, a bond to nature that is common to many African tribes; the symbolism often recalls that of D. H. Lawrence. In Senghor's poem "Congo," the African river represents natural energies, an essential vitalism. The same respect for precolonial cultures is found in such writers as Ṣāliḥ, who responds enthusiastically to the myths and legends that gave the village its special enduring identity, the intangible human and spiritual values expressed in common village routines. For all these writers the European settlers violently destroyed rich cultures whose virtues will be difficult to recover.

There is always a danger of sentimentality and nostalgia in such reverence for past traditions, and this is why many black writers rejected the romantic idealization of Africa expressed through the Négritude movement. This movement was launched in June 1932 by young French West Indians in Paris with the publication of the journal *Légitime défense* (Self-defense). Only a single issue appeared; in it writers extolled the African way of life and attacked a number of targets, not only colonialism but also the middle-class capitalist conventions assumed by many West Indians. The movement grew apace in the 1930s and 1940s and became an important driving force for writers such as Aimé Césaire from Martinique, who wrote the long poem *Cahier d'un retour au pays natal* (1939; *Return to My Native Land*). Négritude writers who glorified the African past associated Africa with nonintellectual feeling in contrast to Greek reason and logic; many black authors condemned this as nonsense. In his essay on Senghor, Irele quotes Wole Soyinka as describing Négritude as "this magnitude of unfelt abstractions" (p. 775). Many critics, Irele tells us, have found the declamatory style of Senghor's poetry the expression of a gesture unrelated to the urgent pressures of real experience. Irele disagrees with this view and writes sympathetically of the close friendship between Senghor and Césaire. He describes how they read and discussed together the writings of the new anthropology, whose revision of the conventional image of Africa as a continent devoid of cultural attainments lent the two renewed confidence in their own efforts for the revaluation of the black race. Both Senghor and Césaire played major roles in destroying the white man's myth of superiority.

White settlers in Africa have to face their own problems in defining an appropriate identity. In a 1958 review in the *New Statesman* of van der Post's *The Lost World of the Kalahari*, Doris Lessing wrote that all white African literature is the literature of exile: not from Europe, but from Africa. She recounts how an African had once told her that beyond the white man's more obvious crimes in Africa, there was another unforgivable one: even the best used Africa as a peg to hang their egos on. In *Chronicles of Darkness*, David Ward examines the ways in which writings by whites in Africa become a literature of exile, a literature of egoism. Van der Post catches very well "the kind of excitement which members of a highly literate culture feel when they discover the richness and energy of a culture which is primarily oral" (p. 41). His writings thus reflect his own personal sense of both belonging and not belonging to Africa. Such writers risk romanticizing Africa as "old," a lost culture, with the implicit assumption that Europe is superior and more advanced.

The western novel-reading public often knows little of black African writers such as Ngũgĩ and Bessie Head. The problem of apartheid is seen by such readers as the problem of how a liberal-minded white African should react to it as well as the conflicts it causes between personal problems and public duty. White writers such as Doris Lessing and Nadine Gordimer understand the danger of a concept of "integration," in which utopian whites work to "improve" blacks so that they can be assimilated into white society. There is a danger that white South African writers will indulge in a voyeurism that implicitly downgrades blacks by treating them as observed objects rather than as human beings. André Brink is well aware of such dangers. In *A Dry White Season* (1979) the compassion of the white protagonist seems impotent, and young blacks prefer revolution.

White civilization, from Inquisition to Holocaust, has perpetrated its own horrors. The experiences of Africans who fought in the war against Hitler proved a major turning point in the revolt against paternalists such as Albert Schweitzer, who in the 1960s was severely criticized for his assumption of white superiority. Senghor fought in the French army in 1939 and witnessed at first hand the barbarity of the "civilized." He connects the savagery of the European war to the violations of colonialism. By the 1990s exposing the falsity of the white myth of superiority has become commonplace in the works of writers all over the world. In *Culture and Imperialism* (1993), Edward Said talks of the need to mediate between western and nonwestern worlds, on the overlapping experience of westerners and nonwesterners. He opposes nationalist narratives of any kind and challenges all static concepts of national identity, the barren dogmatism of "us" and "them" that still vitiates so much political discourse everywhere. I hope this collection of essays will contribute to what Said calls "global consciousness," a growing twentieth-century awareness of the need to respect the rich and disparate cultures of the world. This aim has been at the heart of the writings of Africans such as Achebe. My belief is that enjoyment and understanding of African writings may help to further Achebe's great desire for reconciliation.

CHRONOLOGY

1830 — France occupies Algeria, except for the inland regions.

1834–1836 — Boers from the Cape of Good Hope in South Africa immigrate to Transvaal and what is later called the Orange Free State to escape British policies in the Cape.

1841 — The French settle in Gabon.

1844 — By defeating combined Moroccan and Algerian forces at Isly, Morocco, France establishes control over Morocco.

1847 — Liberia, founded in 1817 by freed black slaves from the United States under the aegis of the American Colonization Society, is established as the Free and Independent Republic of Liberia. France extends its control over Algeria to the inland regions.

1849 — The coastal region of Guinea is declared a French protectorate.

1855–1920 — **Olive Schreiner** of South Africa

1857 — The separate republic of Maryland, founded in 1833, is united with Liberia.

1860 — Spain invades and conquers northern Morocco with France's approval.

1861 — Britain annexes the island of Lagos and eventually extends its dominance to the mainland of Nigeria.

1868 — Basutoland (later known as Lesotho) becomes a crown protectorate of Britain.

1869 — The Suez Canal, connecting the Red Sea with the eastern Mediterranean Sea, opens in Egypt.

1870 — Moshoeshoe I (1786–1870), founder of the Basotho nation (in what later becomes Lesotho), dies.
Diamonds are discovered along the Orange and Vaal Rivers in South Africa, attracting foreigners and bringing prosperity to the area.

1870–1900 — France occupies Senegal.

1871 — Basutoland is annexed to the Cape Colony in South Africa.

1874 — Coastal areas of Ghana become a British crown colony, known as the Gold Coast Colony.

1875 — A dispute between the British and the Portuguese over the Delagoa Bay region of Mozambique is decided in Portugal's favor.

1876–1948 — **Thomas Mokopu Mofolo** of Lesotho

1877 — Members of the Church Missionary Society of Great Britain arrive in Buganda (later Uganda).
Britain annexes Cape Colony in South Africa, which has been granted indepen-

dence through the Sand River Convention of 1852.

1878   King Leopold II (1835–1909) of Belgium forms the International Association of the Congo with the intention of developing the Congo region.

1879–1882   Britain and France share control of Egypt's government.

1880   War breaks out between the Basotho and Boers in Basutoland (later Lesotho). The French begin efforts to conquer Mali. Representatives from Britain, France, Spain, Portugal, Belgium, and Germany convene at the Madrid Conference of 1880. The conference is originally organized to address complaints put forth by the government of Morocco that the French-Moroccan agreement of 1863 is not being honored. As a result of the conference, the major provisions of the 1863 agreement are upheld, and the way is paved for the European powers, particularly Britain and Germany, to extend their influence in North Africa.

1880–1881   The Boers defeat the British in the Transvaal of South Africa, returning the area to independence after four years of British annexation.

1881   Swaziland in South Africa achieves independence from Britain. In an attempt to assert its claims to the area over those of Italy, France invades Tunisia and establishes a protectorate over the country.

1882   Britain seizes control of Egypt's government Malagasy (later Madagascar) is declared a French protectorate but resists subjugation through wars in 1883 and 1894–1896.

1883   A Sudanese revolt under Muḥammad Aḥmed (1844–1885), the self-proclaimed Mahdī, defeats evacuating Egyptian forces.

1884   Germany establishes the protectorate of Kamerun, which includes areas later to become British Cameroons and French Cameroun. Basutoland (later Lesotho) is separated from Cape Colony and made a British colony.

1884–1885   Representatives of all major European powers, the United States, and the Ottoman Empire, but not of Africa, meet at the Congress of Berlin, which is called by the German chancellor Otto von Bismarck (1815–1898) to consider rival claims to Africa and the internationalization of the Congo region under Leopold II of Belgium. The congress passes a general act that establishes freedom of navigation on African rivers and free-trade areas. The congress also extends German influence in East Africa to include Ruanda and Urundi (later Rwanda and Burundi) and recognizes the independent State of the Congo with Leopold II of Belgium as autonomous sovereign.

1884–1886   Britain signs treaties with Somali chiefs establishing protectorates in Somalia.

1885   Mahdists in Sudan overrun and destroy the city of Khartoum. General Charles George Gordon (1833–1885) of Britain, a soldier and colonial administrator, is killed. The Mahdists seize complete control of Egyptian Sudan.

1886   Gold is discovered in Witwatersrand in Transvaal, South Africa, attracting many foreigners to the area. Angola acquires the Cabinda exclave, north of the mouth of the Congo River, through an agreement with Belgium.

1887   The German East Africa Company forms.

1889   Italy establishes protectorates in the eastern territories of Somalia. Through the Treaty of Uccialli, Italy claims Ethiopia as a protectorate.

1889–1973   **Ṭāhā Ḥusayn** of Egypt

1890   Italy annexes Eritrea in northern Ethiopia. An Anglo-German agreement on East Africa establishes British control over Uganda and Kenya, and German control over Tanganyika (later part of Tanzania).

1891   Germany establishes a protectorate over Tanganyika (later part of Tanzania).

1893   Guinea, formerly administered with Senegal as Rivières du Sud by France, is established as a separate colony. Malawi becomes a British protectorate.

1895   Britain takes control of the East African protectorate in Kenya after the Imperial

British East African Company has failed to administer it properly.
Guinea becomes part of French West Africa.

1895–1897   France establishes a protectorate over Upper Volta (later Burkina Faso).

1896   Led by Menelik II (1844–1913), Ethiopia defeats an advancing Italian army at Adwa in northern Ethiopia.
France annexes Malagasy (later Madagascar) and makes it a French colony.
Britain extends its protectorate over Buganda, which was established in 1894, to include Bunyoro and most of what is later Uganda.

1897   France abolishes monarchy in Malagasy (later Madagascar).

1898   France conquers Mali.

1898–1987   **Tawfīq al-Ḥakīm** of Egypt

1899   Joint Egyptian and British rule over Sudan begins.

1899–1902   South African War, also known as the Boer War, in which the Boers unsuccessfully fight the British and lose their independence in Transvaal and the Orange Free State.

1899–1920   Sayyid Muḥammad ibn ʿAdb Allāh Ḥasan (1864–1920) of Somalia wages a holy war that thwarts Britain's attempt to rule the country.

1901   The northern territories of Ghana become a British protectorate.
The construction of a railroad between Mombosa in southern Kenya and Lake Victoria in western Kenya is completed and leads to an influx of European and Asian settlers.

1901–1957   **Roy Campbell** of South Africa

1902   Portugal begins building the Benguela railway in Angola.
Following the Boer War, Swaziland is administered by the British governor of Transvaal.

1903   Mauritania is made a French protectorate, and Gabon becomes a territory of France.

1903–1973   **William Plomer** of South Africa

1903–1988   **Alan Paton** of South Africa

1904   Mauritania and Niger are made part of French West Africa.

1906   Control over Swaziland passes to the British high commissioner.
Italy, France, and Britain recognize the territorial integrity of Ethiopia.

1906–   **Léopold Sédar Senghor** of Senegal
Laurens van der Post of South Africa

1907   Mozambique is organized as a colony, one part of which is under Portuguese administration, the other part of which is controlled by the Mozambique Company.

1908   In response to growing criticism of the treatment of the African population, the Belgian parliament annexes the Congo Free State and renames it the Belgian Congo (later Zaire).

1909–1910   The South Africa Act unites Transvaal, the Orange Free State, Natal, and the Cape into the Union of South Africa.

1909–1934   **Abū al-Qāsim al-Shābbī** of Tunisia

1910   The State of the Congo, Chad, and Gabon are made part of French Equatorial Africa.

1911   Italy invades Libya, which is controlled by the Ottoman Turks.
Because of bankruptcy and internal disorder in 1909, Liberia is put under U.S. protection.

1911–   **Najīb Maḥfūẓ** of Egypt

1912   Peace treaty between Turkey and Italy places Libya under Italian control, despite Libyan opposition.
France imposes a protectorate over most of Morocco, and Spain establishes a protectorate over the northern coast of Morocco.

1913   The Union of South Africa government passes the Bantu Land Act, which sets aside 22 million acres of land for blacks and bans them from owning land outside these Bantustans, or homelands; this land is supplemented in 1936 with 15.6 million acres through another parliamentary act.

1913–1960   **Albert Camus** of Algeria

1914	Britain establishes the Colony and Protectorate of Nigeria, which combines the administrations of British protectorates in the region, including the Oil Rivers Protectorate, the Niger Coast Protectorate, and the Protectorate of Northern Nigeria. Egypt is declared a British protectorate. The German protectorate of Kamerun is invaded by Anglo-French forces. Italy occupies Libya.
1917	Liberia declares war on Germany.
1919–	**Peter Abrahams** of South Africa **Doris Lessing** of Zimbabwe **Es'kia Mphahlele** of South Africa
1920	Most of the East African protectorate in Kenya is declared a crown colony of Britain. Chad is made a colony separate from French Equatorial Africa. Senegal changes its status from a protectorate to a colony of France.
1920–	**Mohammed Dib** of Algeria **Albert Memmi** of Tunisia **Amos Tutuola** of Nigeria
1921	Mauritania becomes a French colony— one of the eight territories of the French West Africa Federation—though its capital, Saint-Louis, is in Senegal.
1921–1926	Morocco unsuccessfully fights France and Spain for independence in the Rif War.
1921–	**Cyprian Ekwensi** of Nigeria **Gabriel Okara** of Nigeria
1922	The United Kingdom nominally recognizes Egypt's sovereignty but maintains many restrictions. After several decades of successful resistance to French occupation, Niger is made a French colony.
1922–1979	**Agostinho Neto** of Angola
1923	Belgium is awarded a mandate by the League of Nations over Ruanda-Urundi (later Rwanda and Burundi), which it has occupied since 1916. Ethiopia joins the League of Nations.
1923–	**Nadine Gordimer** of South Africa
1924–1996	**Efua Theodora Sutherland** of Ghana
1924–	**Dennis Brutus** of South Africa
1925–1985	**Alex La Guma** of South Africa
1925–	**Sembène Ousmane** of Senegal
1926	The Firestone Tire and Rubber Company of the United States is granted a concession of one million acres to set up rubber plantations in Liberia.
1927–1991	**Yūsuf Idrīs** of Egypt
1928–1980	**Camara Laye** of Guinea
1929–1981	**Mariama Bâ** of Senegal
1929–1989	**Kateb Yacine** of Algeria
1929–	**Dan Jacobson** of South Africa **Ferdinand Oyono** of Cameroon **al-Ṭayyib Ṣāliḥ** of Sudan
1930	Ras Tafari Mekonnen (1892–1975) of Shewa is crowned Emperor Haile Selassie I of Ethiopia.
1930–	**Chinua Achebe** of Nigeria
1931	Italy captures and executes ʿUmar al-Mukhtar (1862?–1931), a leader of the Sanūsī, a Muslim religious brotherhood in Libya.
1931–1982	**Okot p'Bitek** of Uganda
1931–	**Nawāl al-Saʿadāwī** of Egypt
1932–1967	**Christopher Okigbo** of Nigeria
1932–	**Mongo Beti** of Cameroon **Athol Fugard** of South Africa
1934	Moroccans submit the Plan of Reforms to the French government, and a nationalist movement develops in Morocco. The provinces of Cyrenaica and Tripolitania, in what later becomes Libya, unite.
1934–	**Wole Soyinka** of South Africa
1935	Italy uses Eritrea as a base for its invasion of Ethiopia.
1935–	**Kofi Awoonor** of Ghana **André Brink** of South Africa **John Pepper Clark** of Nigeria **José Luandino Vieira** of Angola
1935–1936	Italy conquers Ethiopia after the League of Nations fails to settle an Italo-Ethiopian clash at Walwal in southeastern Ethiopia.

1936   Blacks in South Africa lose the right to vote.
Army chiefs led by General Francisco Franco (1892–1975) revolt in Melilla, a Spanish presidio and commercial city on the northern coast of Morocco, sparking the Spanish civil war.

1936–1941   Eritrea, Ethiopia, and Italian Somaliland are made part of Italian East Africa.

1937–1986   **Bessie Head** of South Africa

1938–   **Obi Egbuna** of Nigeria
Ngũgĩ wa Thiong'o of Kenya
Ola Rotimi of Nigeria

1939   Libya is formally incorporated into Italy.

1939–   **Ayi Kwei Armah** of Ghana

1940   Despite its neutrality in World War II, Egypt is invaded by Italy.

1940–   **J. M. Coetzee** of South Africa

1940–1945   The production of goods and services in the Belgian Congo (later Zaire) is greatly increased to finance the Belgian effort in World War II. Large-scale social and economic changes occur as many rural Africans relocate to urban areas.

1941   Eritrea is conquered by British forces. Ethiopia regains independence from Italy after being liberated by Britain.

1941–   **Pepetela** of Angola

1941, 1942   Germany invades Egypt.

1942   American-British invasion of North Africa. The Mozambique Company's charter over a territory in Mozambique expires, and the territory reverts to Portugal. Britain occupies Malagasy (later Madagascar).

1942–   **Ama Ata Aidoo** of Ghana
Luís Bernardo Honwana of Mozambique

1943   German troops surrender in North Africa.

1943–1951   Libya is administered by British and French military governors.

1943–   **Kole Omotoso** of Nigeria

1944   Liberia declares war on Germany and Japan.

1944–   **Buchi Emecheta** of Nigeria
Christopher Hope of South Africa

1945   Egypt, Ethiopia, and Liberia join the United Nations as charter members.

1945–   **Nuruddin Farah** of Somalia

1946   The Fourth Republic begins in France and lasts until 1958. The new constitution reorganizes France's colonial empire as the French Union, confers citizenship on inhabitants of French territories, including Senegal, the State of the Congo, Mali, Guinea, Malagasy, Mauritania, Niger, Chad, and Gabon, and provides for gradual decentralization of power and limited participation in indigenous political life.
Ruanda-Urundi (later Rwanda and Burundi) becomes a UN trust territory under Belgian administration.

1946–   **Femi Osofisan** of Nigeria

1947   Upper Volta (later Burkina Faso) is reconstituted as an overseas territory within the French Union.

1947–   **Festus Iyayi** of Nigeria
Niyi Osundare of Nigeria

1948   The National Party ascends to power in South Africa and enforces the policy of apartheid, or racial segregation.

1948–   **Meja Mwangi** of Kenya
Tanure Ojaide of Nigeria
Bode Sowande of Nigeria

1949   UN General Assembly votes that Libya become an independent state.
Britain rejects the Union of South Africa's request for control over Swaziland.
Ṭāhā Ḥusayn is nominated for the Nobel Prize in literature.

1951   Angola, Guinea-Bissau, and Mozambique are made overseas provinces of Portugal. Libya gains independence as the Kingdom of Libya.
South African–born American scientist Max Theiler (1899–1972) wins the Nobel Prize for medicine for his discoveries on yellow fever and how to combat it.

1952   The Society of Free Officers leads a coup in Egypt and overthrows King Farouk I (1920–1965).

The United Nations makes Eritrea a semiautonomous part of Ethiopia with its own constitution.

1952–1958   Legal reforms in the Belgian Congo (later Zaire) permit Africans to own land and give them free access to public establishments and the right to a trial in a court of law.

1952–1959   A state of emergency is declared in Kenya, largely precipitated by the Mau Mau movement, which was formed as a means of resistance against European social and political control.

1953   Egypt proclaims itself a republic.
Sudan achieves independence from Britain.

1953–1963   Despite severe African opposition, Nyasaland (later Malawi) is joined by Britain to Northern Rhodesia (later Zambia) and Southern Rhodesia (later Zimbabwe) in the Central African Federation.

1954   Gamal Abdel Nasser (1918–1970) seizes power in Egypt.
The National Liberation Front (Front de Libération Nationale, or FLN) launches a guerrilla war in Algeria, initiating seven years of nationalist revolt.
A constitution establishes the Federation of Nigeria, which includes Lagos, the Eastern, Northern, and Western Regions, and part of the British mandate of Cameroons.

1955   Libya joins the UN.
The African National Congress in South Africa proclaims a Freedom Charter for a just and democratic country.

1955   **Mia Couto** of Mozambique

1956   Gamal Abdel Nasser is elected president of Egypt and proclaims the nationalization of the Suez Canal and his intention to use it to finance construction of the Aswan dam, which prompts Britain, France, and Israel to intervene in Egyptian affairs.
The African Party for the Independence of Guinea and Cape Verde is formed by Cape Verdeans looking to free themselves from Portuguese rule.
Morocco signs accords with France and Spain and thereby gains independence; Tangier is included as part of Morocco.
South Africa's Coloreds, or persons

of mixed-race origins, lose the right to vote.
The new Republic of Sudan is proclaimed under a parliamentary government.
Tunisia achieves independence from France.
The French government passes *Loi-Cadre*, which dissolves French West Africa and French Equatorial Africa and eventually leads to self-government for many of France's African colonies.

1957   All Muslims in Algeria become French subjects.
The Gold Coast, under the name of Ghana, achieves complete autonomy from Britain, becoming the first country in colonial Africa to gain independence.
Universal adult suffrage is granted in Guinea.
The first direct elections of Africans to the Legislative Council in Kenya are held.
Representatives from France's African colonies attend the Bamako Conference in the French Sudan and express their desire both to govern themselves and to continue their special relationship with France.
Tunisia abolishes monarchy.
Albert Camus wins the Nobel Prize in literature.

1958   The people of France and its overseas territories vote on the constitution of the Fifth French Republic. This new constitution proposes a French Community, in which member states are loosely joined and self-governing, to replace the French Union, which has previously been in force. All of the French colonies approve the new constitution except French Guinea. The following countries become republics within the French Community: Madagascar; French Sudan, which becomes known as the Sudanese Republic (later Mali); Niger; Senegal; Upper Volta (later Burkina Faso); Malagasy; Chad; Mauritania; the State of the Congo; and Gabon.
Guinea gains independence from France, and Ahmed Sékou Touré (1922–1984) becomes president.
Ruben Um Nyobé (1913–1958), leader of the nationalist Union of Cameroon Peoples (Union des Populations du Cameroun, or UPC), is assassinated by French security forces.
Tunisia joins the Arab League.

1959   A state of emergency is declared in Malawi because of the sharply negative reaction to the Central African Federation.
Representatives of the Sudanese Republic (later Mali) and Senegal draft a constitution of the Federation of Mali.
A Hutu revolution against Tutsi begins in Rwanda in protest over social and political inequality.
South Africa passes the Bantu Self-Government Act, which allows limited self-rule in the Bantustans, or black homelands.

1959–   **Ben Okri** of Nigeria

1960   Belgian Congo, Upper Volta (later Burkina Faso), Chad, Gabon, Madagascar as the Malagasy Republic, Mauritania, and the Republic of Niger all achieve independence from France.
The nation of Ghana becomes a republic with Kwame Nkrumah (1909–1972) as its first president.
The Basutoland National Council is created in what later becomes Lesotho.
The Federation of Mali becomes a sovereign state within the French Community. Later in the year, Sudan breaks off relations with Senegal, adopts the name the Republic of Mali, and leaves the French Community.
The Legislative Assembly of Senegal proclaims Senegal's national independence from France, and the poet **Léopold Sédar Senghor** is elected the first president.
Nigeria becomes an independent member of the British Commonwealth and is admitted to the UN.
Italy and Britain relinquish control over their respective stakes in Somaliland, allowing for the independence of the Somali Republic.
In Sharpeville, South African police massacre unarmed black demonstrators protesting against pass laws. The African National Congress is banned in South Africa.
The Republic of the Congo (later Zaire) achieves independence from Belgium.
Albert John Luthuli (1898–1967), president of the African National Congress, wins the Nobel Peace Prize for maintaining a policy of nonviolence and cooperation between whites and blacks.

1960–1963   Culminating a period of postindependence unrest, Katanga (later Shaba Province of Zaire) secedes from the Republic of the Congo.

1961   The Popular Movement for the Liberation of Angola (Movimento Popular para a Libertação de Angola, or MPLA) launches a series of attacks against Portuguese rule in Angola.
South Africa becomes a republic.
The UN Security Council authorizes UN soldiers to use force if necessary to prevent civil war in the Congo, the first time such permission is granted.
Libya begins exporting oil.
Egypt dissolves its union with Syria, which has been formed in 1958.
Tanganyika (later part of Tanzania) achieves independence from Germany.

1962   Algeria gains independence from France.
The National Front for the Liberation of Angola (Frente Nacional de Libertação de Angola, or FNLA) sets up a revolutionary government in exile in Zaire.
Rwanda and Burundi gain independence from Belgium as separate entities.
Ethiopia annexes Eritrea and abolishes its constitution, prompting Eritreans to begin fighting for independence.
Liberation groups in Mozambique unite to form the Mozambique Liberation Front (Frente de Libertação de Moçambique, or FRELIMO).
Uganda achieves independence from Britain.

1962–1967   Egypt intervenes in support of a republican regime in Yemen.

1963   France and Algeria end seven-year civil war, and Ahmed Ben Bella (b. 1916) is elected the first president of independent Algeria.
Ethiopia is a founding member of the Organization of African Unity, which Liberia also joins.
Kenya gains independence from Britain.
Nigeria becomes a republic.
Twelve thousand Tutsi in Rwanda die when Hutu take punitive measures in reaction to an unsuccessful Tutsi invasion from Burundi.

1963–1966   Mauritania develops important mineral deposits.

1964   Kenya becomes a republic within the Commonwealth of Nations, and Jomo Kenyatta (1894?–1978) is elected president.
Nyasaland becomes an independent Commonwealth country and adopts the name Malawi.
Fighting breaks out in Mozambique between Portuguese forces and anti-Portuguese nationalists.
Somalia and Ethiopia engage in a boundary dispute.
President Léon Mba (1902–1967) of Gabon is overthrown in a coup but is immediately reinstated with the help of French troops.
Nelson Mandela (b. 1918), Walter Sisulu (b. 1912), and other members of the African National Congress in South Africa are given life sentences and imprisoned.
Tanganyika merges with Zanzibar to form Tanzania.

1965   President Ben Bella of Algeria is overthrown in a coup and replaced by Colonel Houari Boumedienne (1927–1978).
King Hassan II (b. 1929) of Morocco declares a state of emergency, which lasts until 1970, after a series of student riots.

1966   The Republic of Botswana is created.
President Kwame Nkrumah of Ghana is overthrown after numerous unsuccessful assassination attempts.
Burundi abolishes monarchy.
Guinea expels the U.S. Peace Corps, accusing it of a plot to overthrow President Ahmed Sékou Touré.
Guinean expatriates in Senegal and Ivory Coast form the National Liberation Front of Guinea (Front de Libération Nationale de Guinée, or FLNG).
Basutoland gains independence from Britain and changes its name to the Kingdom of Lesotho. Moshoeshoe II (1938–1996) is proclaimed king.
Malawi becomes a republic.
A military coup in Nigeria results in the death of several government ministers and the ascension to power of Major General Johnson Aguiyi-Ironsi (1924–1966), commander-in-chief of the army. A military countercoup results in the death of Ironsi and the ascension of Lieutenant Colonel Yakubu Gowon (b. 1934).

Uganda abolishes the federal system of government, suspends the 1962 constitution, and adopts a new one, which creates the post of president and commander-in-chief. Prime Minister Milton Obote (b. 1924) is elected president. Obote declares a state of emergency when protestors of the new constitution clash with police.

1966–1972   Cities with European names in Zaire are given African names.

1967   Malawi becomes the first black African country to establish diplomatic relations with white-ruled South Africa.
Egypt and Israel engage in war, and Israel occupies the Sinai Peninsula.
The French discover high-grade uranium ore in Niger, which provides a source of income for Niger through the 1980s because of the demand for uranium in nuclear power plants.
The Eastern Region of Nigeria rejects Yakubu Gowon's proposed division of the country into twelve states and declares itself the independent Republic of Biafra with Lieutenant Colonel Chukwuemeka Odumegwu Ojukwu (b. 1933) as head of state. The poet **Christopher Okigbo** is killed in the ensuing civil war.
Uganda becomes a republic.
Tanzania, Kenya, and Uganda form the East African Community.

1967–1970   Over one million Biafrans die in the civil war between the central government of Nigeria and the secessionist Biafran state.

1968   A military coup in Mali overthrows the government, which had adopted a socialist program, and leads to the Military Committee for National Liberation taking control of the country, returning Mali to the franc zone, and accepting both socialist and nonsocialist investment in the country.
Mauritania and Swaziland gain independence from Britain.

1968–1974   Severe drought devastates countries south of Sahara.

1969   Civilian government is restored in Ghana under Kofi A. Busia (1913–1978).
A coup led by the Free Unionist Officers in

Libya deposes the king, Sīdī Muḥammad Idrīs al-Mahdī al-Sanūsī, and declares the country a republican regime.
Morocco withdraws its claims to Mauritanian territory.
President Abdi Rashid ʿAli Shermarke (1919–1969) of Somalia is assassinated. Army commanders seize power, dissolve parliament, suspend the constitution, arrest cabinet members, and change the name of the country to the Somali Democratic Republic. Major General Muhammad Siyad Barre (1919–1995) is named president.
President Milton Obote of Uganda is shot and wounded in Kampala, leading to the declaration of a state of emergency in the country.
Es'kia Mphahlele of South Africa is nominated for the Nobel Prize in literature.

1970   President Gamal Abdel Nasser of Egypt dies, and Anwar al-Sādāt (1918–1981) succeeds him.
Guinea charges Portugal with attempting to overthrow the Guinean government.
The civilian government in Libya resigns, and a new cabinet is formed under Colonel Muʿammar Muḥammad al-Gadhafi (b. 1942), chairman of the Revolutionary Command Council.
Algeria and Morocco settle a boundary dispute.
President Muhammad Siyad Barre proclaims "scientific socialism" the guiding ideology of Somalia.
Severe flooding in Tunisia causes major economic problems.

1971   Egypt forms a confederation with Libya and Syria, known as the Confederation of Arab Republics.
While President Milton Obote of Uganda is out of the country, Major General Idi Amin (b. 1925) leads a military coup in Uganda and overthrows the civilian government. Amin becomes president of the Second Republic of Uganda.
The Congo changes its name to Zaire.

1972   A Hutu-led coup attempt leads to civil war in Burundi and results in the deaths of many Hutu and Tutsi.
A new constitution creates the United Republic of Cameroon, which in 1984

changes its name to the Republic of Cameroon.
A military coup in Ghana ousts Kofi A. Busia and establishes Colonel Ignatius Kutu Acheampong (1931–1979) as leader of the military government.

1973   Amilcar Cabral (1924–1973), leader of the African Party for the Independence of Guinea and Cape Verde, is assassinated.
Colonel Muʿammar al-Gadhafi, head of Libya, calls for a cultural revolution in the country. Libya annexes the Aozou Strip in Chad.
Zaire proclaims the policy of Zairianization, which includes expropriating foreign-owned businesses and property and distributing them to Zairian government officials; economic chaos ensues.

1974   The exposure of a governmental cover-up of widespread famine and drought in parts of Ethiopia leads to Haile Selassie's deposition.
Guinea-Bissau gains independence from Portugal.
Nadine Gordimer of South Africa wins the Booker Prize for *The Conservationist*.

1975   Angola, Cape Verde, and Mozambique gain complete independence from Portugal.
The poet **Agostinho Neto**, the MPLA leader since 1962, becomes independent Angola's first president.
Comoros, off the coast of southeastern Africa, gains independence from France.
Monarchy in Ethiopia is officially abolished.
Haile Selassie of Ethiopia dies.
Yakubu Gowon is overthrown as leader of the military government in Nigeria because of his slowness in returning Nigeria to civilian rule.
Zaire returns much expropriated property to foreign owners.

1976   Angola becomes a member of the UN.
Riots break out in Soweto as a result of black South Africans' opposition to the compulsory use of Afrikaans (a language developed from seventeenth-century Dutch and spoken by white Afrikaners) in schools.

1977   Steve Biko (1946–1977), a leader of the
        black liberation movement in South Africa,
        dies in police custody prompting the
        UN Security Council to impose an arms
        embargo on South Africa, the first
        time such a mandate is passed against a
        member nation.

1978   Egyptian president Anwar al-Sādāt and
        Israeli prime minister Menachem Begin
        (1913–1992) receive the Nobel Peace Prize
        for their efforts to orchestrate peace
        between their countries.
        Military coup in Ghana ousts Ignatius
        Kutu Acheampong and replaces him with
        Lieutenant General Frederick Akuffo
        (1937–1979).
        President Jomo Kenyatta of Kenya dies
        and is succeeded by Daniel arap Moi
        (b. 1924).

1979   Colonel Chadli Bendjedid (b. 1929),
        secretary-general of the National
        Liberation Front, is elected president of
        Algeria.
        In the Camp David talks, President Anwar
        al-Sādāt of Egypt and Prime Minister
        Menachem Begin of Israel agree to end the
        thirty-one-year war between their
        countries.
        A military coup in Ghana, led by Jerry
        Rawlings (b. 1947), brings the Armed
        Forces Revolutionary Council to power.
        Ignatius Kutu Acheampong, Frederick
        Akuffo, and six other former government
        leaders are found guilty of corruption
        and executed. Following nationwide
        elections, the Armed Forces Revolutionary
        Council hands power over to civilians.
        Armed Libyan forces, under the command
        of Colonel Muᶜammar al-Gadhafi,
        try to save Idi Amin's regime in Uganda.
        Tanzanian forces, in reaction to a
        Ugandan military attack, invade Uganda
        and successfully rout out President
        Amin's troops. Amin is deposed.

1980   Returning from exile in Tanzania, Milton
        Obote is reelected president of Uganda.
        Talks held in Lagos, Nigeria, between
        Ethiopia and Somalia to end war in the
        Ogaden region lead to a lull in the conflict.
        Economic difficulties in Zambia result
        in strikes, led by the Zambia Congress of
        Trades Unions, and calls for multiparty
        democracy. In response, the Zambian

        government imposes a curfew.
        Rhodesia is renamed Zimbabwe, achieves
        independence from white minority
        rule, and converts to majority rule.

1981   Egyptian president Anwar al-Sādāt is
        assassinated by Muslim fundamentalists,
        allegedly for his tactics in quelling religious
        extremists, and succeeded by Husni
        Mubārak (b. 1928).
        Jerry Rawlings leads another coup in
        Ghana and overthrows the civilian
        government.
        Two Libyan jets are shot down by the
        United States over the Gulf of Sidra in the
        Mediterranean Sea.
        The Somali National Movement begins
        antigovernment guerrilla activities in
        Somalia.

1981, 1983   South Africa bombs Maputo,
        Mozambique, for harboring members of
        the African National Congress.

1982   A coup attempt in Kenya led by air-force
        officers leads to the dissolution of the
        air force and the temporary closing of
        Nairobi University.
        The United States bans oil imports from
        Libya and U.S. technology exports to
        Libya, charging that Colonel Muᶜammar
        al-Gadhafi supports international
        terrorism.
        Senegal suppresses an attempted military
        coup in Gambia, and the two countries
        join to form the Confederation of
        Senegambia with Abdou Diouf (b. 1935),
        the president of Senegal, as head of the
        new state.
        South Africa raids an African National
        Congress base at Maseru, Lesotho.
        Tunisia allows Yāsir ᶜArafāt (b. 1929),
        chairman of the Palestine Liberation
        Organization (PLO), and other Palestin-
        ians to enter the country after the PLO is
        evacuated from Lebanon. In response,
        Israel bombs PLO headquarters near
        Tunis.

1982–1984   Devastating drought and famine strike
        northern Ethiopia.

1983   In South Africa, the United Democratic
        Front comes into existence in league with
        the African National Congress.
        Léopold Sédar Senghor of Senegal becomes
        the first black African to be elected as
        a life member to the Académie Française.

J. M. Coetzee of South Africa wins the Booker Prize for *Life & Times of Michael K*.

1983–1986 South Africa imposes economic and food sanctions on Lesotho, which the South African government accuses of harboring members of the African National Congress.

1984 Under President Thomas Sankara (1949–1987), Upper Volta is renamed Burkina Faso.
Severe famine strikes Ethiopia.
President Ahmed Sékou Touré of Guinea dies, and the armed forces stage a coup, establishing their leader, Colonel Lansana Conté (b. 1934), as president.
South Africa and Mozambique sign the Nkomati Accord, in which each government agrees to stop harboring guerrillas that oppose the other's regime.
Pieter Willem Botha (b. 1916) is elected South Africa's first executive state president.
Desmond Mpilo Tutu (b. 1931), secretary-general of the South African Council of Churches from 1979 to 1984, receives the Nobel Peace Prize for his efforts against apartheid.

1985 Severe drought in Ethiopia forces two hundred thousand Ethiopians to resettle in refugee camps in Sudan.
Economic recession provokes strikes in Zambia. In response, President Kenneth David Kaunda (b. 1924) bans all strikes in essential sectors.
A military coup in Uganda leads to the ouster of President Milton Obote and the ascension of Lieutenant General Tito Okello (1914–1996), who is overthrown in 1986 by Yoweri Kaguta Museveni (b. 1944), the leader of the National Resistance Movement.

1985–1986 Mali and Burkina Faso engage in armed conflict over the Agachar Strip, which is subsequently divided evenly between the two countries by the International Court of Justice.

1986 Botswana promises South Africa not to harbor members of the African National Congress.
A volcanic eruption in Cameroon kills two thousand people and poisons twenty thousand more.

The United States orders all Americans out of Libya, bombs Colonel Mu'ammar al-Gadhafi's headquarters, and severs economic ties with the country on account of Libya's involvement with Palestinian attacks on airports in Rome and Vienna in December 1985.
King Hassan II of Morocco meets with Prime Minister Shimon Peres (b. 1923) of Israel, marking the first official meeting between an Arab and Israeli leader after the assassination of Egyptian president Anwar al-Sādāt in 1981 and leading to the dissolution of a federation between Morocco and Libya, which denounces Hassan's action.
President Samoro Moises Machel (1933–1986) of Mozambique and thirty-three other passengers die in a plane crash over South Africa, which the Mozambique government charges is orchestrated by the South African government but an international commission attributes to the negligence of the Soviet crew flying the plane.
The South African government declares a state of emergency in response to increasing unrest in black townships.
Wole Soyinka of Nigeria wins the Nobel Prize in literature.

1987 In a military coup in Burundi, President Jean-Baptiste Bagaza (b. 1946) is overthrown and replaced by Major Pierre Buyoya (b. 1948).
Severe famine strikes Ethiopia.

1988 Over 150 Algerians are killed in the country's worst riots since independence.
Najīb Maḥfūz of Egypt wins the Nobel Prize in literature.

1989 Algeria's constitution is revised to allow for a multiparty system.
President José Eduardo dos Santos (b. 1942) of Angola and Jonas Malheiro Savimbi (b. 1934), the founder and president of the National Union for the Total Independence of Angola (União Nacional para a Independência Total de Angola, or UNITA), sign the Gbadolite Declaration, calling for a cease-fire in the Angolan civil war.
Civil war begins in Liberia when Charles Taylor (b. 1947) leads his rebel army in an invasion against the dictatorship of

President Samuel Doe (1952–1990).
The United States shoots down two
Libyan aircraft.
In a bloodless coup in Sudan, Sadiq
al-Mahdi (b. 1936) is deposed and
Brigadier Omar Hassan al-Bashir (b. 1944)
becomes head of state.
President Botha of South Africa retires for
health reasons and is succeeded by
Frederik Willem de Klerk (b. 1936). Walter
Sisulu and five other African National
Congress members jailed for life in 1964
are set free.
The Senegambian Confederation between
Senegal and Gambia ends.

1990   President Samuel Doe of Liberia is
assassinated.
Kenya experiences the worst
prodemocracy, antigovernment riots since
independence.
Namibia achieves independence from
South Africa.
President Frederik Willem de Klerk of
South Africa legalizes thirty-three
opposition groups and releases Nelson
Mandela, an African National Congress
(ANC) member who has been imprisoned
for twenty-six years. The South African
government begins talks with the ANC; the
state of emergency is lifted; and the
ANC ends its armed struggle against the
government of South Africa.
Four thousand rebels from Uganda invade
Rwanda.

1991   A state of emergency is declared in Algeria
after clashes between the government
and the Islamic Salvation Front, which
won municipal elections in 1990.
Egypt provides military support to the
United States in the Gulf War.
After thirty years of war, Eritrea is
liberated from Ethiopia.
Protestors demonstrate against the
socialist government in Madagascar. In
response, a transitional government
is formed, and multiparty democracy is
promised.
Nigeria officially moves its capital from
Lagos to Abuja.
Antigovernment protestors riot in Zaire.
The Mozambique National Resistance
(Resistência National Moçambicana,
or RENAMO) and FRELIMO agree to a
partial cease-fire.

The South African government admits to
the Namibian government that it
has been funding parties in opposition to
the South-West Africa People's
Organization (SWAPO).
South Africa ends apartheid legislation.
Nelson Mandela becomes president of the
African National Congress.
Nadine Gordimer of South Africa wins the
Nobel Prize in literature.
Ben Okri of Nigeria wins the Booker Prize
for *The Famished Road.*

1992   The military-backed government in
Algeria cancels legislative elections that the
Islamic Salvation Front is expected
to win, sparking an Islamic insurgency.
The MPLA wins free elections in
Angola. UNITA believes the elections are
rigged and resumes the civil war.
Jerry Rawlings is elected president of
Ghana.
Mali holds its first free elections and votes
Alpha Oumar Konare (b. 1946) president.
The Islamic fundamentalist group Nahda
is banned in Tunisia.
President Muhammad Siyad Barre of
Somalia flees from rebels, and Ali Mahdi
Mohammed becomes the interim
president. UN peacekeeping forces, led by
the United States, arrive in Somalia
to administer humanitarian aid.
Voters in South Africa approve a plan to
move toward majority rule. The African
National Congress (ANC) drops out
of the Convention for a Democratic South
Africa in response to the Inkatha
Freedom Party, which is made up of Zulu
nationalists in South Africa, and the
police killing thirty-nine ANC supporters
at Boipatong.

1993   In Eritrea, 98 percent of the electorate
votes for independence from Ethiopia, and
Eritrea officially becomes an independent
state.
Civilian rule begins in Ghana under
President Jerry Rawlings, leader of the
National Democratic Conference.
Niger holds its first democratic election,
and Mahamane Ousmane becomes
president.
Nelson Mandela and President Frederik
Willem de Klerk of South Africa
receive the Nobel Peace Prize for their
efforts to end apartheid and bring about a

peaceful transition to nonracial democracy in South Africa.

Civil war breaks out in Burundi after Tutsi paratroopers assassinate the first democratically elected Hutu president.

1994 Liamine Zeroual is appointed president of Algeria to lead the country's transition to democracy.

Cyprien Ntaryamira (1955–1994), a Hutu, is installed as the first democratically elected president of Burundi. Two months later, he and President Juvenal Habyarimana (1937–1994), the Hutu president of Rwanda, are killed in a plane crash in Kigali, Rwanda. Hutu murder Tutsi in retaliation, and Tutsi stage a counterattack. U.S. peacekeeping forces withdraw from Rwanda.

Nelson Mandela is elected president of South Africa.

1995 Ken Saro-Wiwa (1941–1995), a Nigerian author and advocate for the rights of the Ogoni people of Nigeria, and eight other Nigerians are executed by the Nigerian government of the self-enthroned president, General Sani Abacha (b. 1943), prompting international bans on the Anglo-Dutch oil company Shell, which is accused of condoning the government's act.

1996 President Mahamane Ousmane of Niger is ousted in a coup.

Civil wars reignite in Liberia and Somalia. UN withdraws its peacekeeping mission from Rwanda.

Tutsi-led military coup in Burundi ousts the Hutu president.

AFRICAN WRITERS

Peter Abrahams
1919–

ANDREW PEEK

PETER ABRAHAMS is the first black African author to produce a considerable body of work that synthesizes African and western narrative traditions in a distinctively modern idiom. He deals with themes that writers like Chinua Achebe, Ngũgĩ wa Thiong'o, and others have returned to time and again: the impact of western culture and modernization on traditional Africa, tribalism and the tribal psyche, the role of education, and the Christian church in Africa. Abrahams treats these issues within the context of black discourse in postcolonialism. In many ways modern African fiction in English began with Abrahams.

Abrahams would not, in fact, describe himself as a black writer, but as a "Colored" one, which in his native South Africa means of mixed-race origins. Writing primarily between the early 1940 and the mid 1960s, he considered "the problems of race and colour" to be "perhaps the key problems of our century" (*Jamaica: An Island Mosaic*, p. 261). South Africa consists of many tribal groupings, including the aboriginal Khoisan peoples; major tribes, notably Zulu, Ndebele or Matabele, and Tswana; and whites, broadly divided into Afrikaners, who trace their origins to Dutch settlement, and Anglo–South Africans. Among the Colored peoples are the Cape Colored, descended from blacks and the ear-

liest white settlers at the Cape. All of Abrahams' books address the issue of relations between peoples in multiethnic societies, first in South Africa, then in the rest of Africa, and finally in Jamaica. His writing acknowledges the history of white oppression in these places and attempts to establish a contemporary basis for liberation from this history. This fact, together with his extensive travel and diversified experiences, has given his writing unique perspectives and an enduring relevance.

Abrahams' fiction, published over a period of more than forty years, has had mixed reception. Writers like Nadine Gordimer, Cyprian Ekwensi, and the Caribbean novelist Andrew Salkey have praised it, but academic commentators talk of a writer "not particularly gifted with imagination" (Ogungbesan, p. 120) and "in the middle range, . . . skilful, if flawed" (Wade, 1972, pp. 4–5). As our perceptions of narrative genre and of "imagination" change, it seems likely that the pioneering scope and vision of Abrahams' fiction will maintain and expand his reputation.

BIOGRAPHY

Peter Henry Abrahams was born in Vrededorp, a slum in Johannesburg, on 19 March 1919. The autobiography *Tell Freedom* (1954)

I

notes that Abrahams' father, James, came from a family of erstwhile landowners and slave owners in Ethiopia and had apparently traveled widely around Europe before moving to South Africa. He worked in the mines and gave his son an extensive if increasingly vague lineage. He was "Peter Henry Abrahams Deras, son of James Henry Abrahams Deras whose name at home was Karim Abdul, son of Ingedi(e) of Addis who was the son of somebody else who fought in some battle who was the son of somebody else, who was the son of somebody else who was with Menelik when he defeated the Italians . . . " (p. 11). James Henry Abrahams died when his son was very young, and the family was plunged into poverty. Abrahams' mother, Angelina, née Du Plessis, was a Cape Colored who had already been widowed once. Abrahams grew up in an extended family, moving between different households in Vrededorp and Elsburg, a settlement on the railway outside Johannesburg.

During this period, the family struggled to maintain some sort of contact and stability. While working for white employers, Abrahams' mother was injured and suffered periods of ill health, and Abrahams watched his elder brother, Harry, fall into alcoholism. Maggie, his elder sister, offered the most guidance and sustenance. Street life was lively and dangerous, with the police never far away, but Abrahams managed to survive, earn money at various jobs, and eventually go to school.

At school he learned to read and to supplement the world of Vrededorp with a very different world, that of Shakespeare and the English Romantic poets, who wrote of love and freedom. A job at the Bantu Men's Social Centre brought him into contact with a second major cultural tradition: black American music and literature. Here Abrahams discovered Paul Robeson, W. E. B. Du Bois — who "might have been writing about my land and people" (*Tell Freedom*, p. 193) — and the writers of the Harlem Renaissance: Countee Cullen, Claude McKay, Langston Hughes, Sterling Brown, and Jean Toomer. This new knowledge was a revelation, but it carried a price: "I was rapidly moving out of this Coloured world of mine, out of the reach of even my dear mother and sister. I saw them with the objective eyes of a stranger" (pp. 197–198).

From the Bantu Men's Social Centre, Abrahams moved on to the Diocesan Training College at Grace Dieu, near Pieterburg, to educate himself, though not in order to become a teacher — a conventional way out of slum life — but to further his long-standing ambition to write. With an Afrikaner teacher Abrahams "discovered the rich body of Afrikaner literature and the beauty of the language itself" and wrote his own Afrikaans verses (p. 222). He was also instructed to "read the Bible if you want to see how good English should be written" (p. 223), and, judging from the biblical resonances in the style of his prose, he took this advice to heart. His first published work, a series of poems, appeared in *The Bantu World* in 1935 and prompted a letter of encouragement from the Zulu poet and playwright Herbert Dhlomo.

Abrahams was confirmed a Christian but felt uncomfortable occupying a place at Grace Dieu because he had no intention of teaching afterward. He also found the protected environment and Christian way of life at odds with the world of racial segregation, oppression, and violence outside. In a secular sense, however, the healing power of love remained a theme throughout his fiction.

After two years Abrahams moved back to Johannesburg. After a short time he enrolled in a famous school for nonwhites, St. Peter's Secondary, just outside the city. During the holidays he worked in the Institute of Race Relations at the University of Johannesburg. In both places he met people who seemed to have discovered ways to counter racism. He was especially impressed by the Marxists he met. Although he eventually became disillusioned with Marxist organizations, Marxist ideas clearly influenced his early fiction. He continued writing, and in 1938, when Abrahams was nineteen, a journalist wrote an article on the "Coloured Boy Poet" for the British *Daily Express*, a fact indicative of his special status.

In "One of the Three," a short story published in 1942, Abrahams' narrator explains how he "was going to wander about the country and learn to know [his] people" (*Dark Testament*, p. 14); in the period after he left St. Peter's and before leaving the country, Abrahams was similarly on the move and meeting people. In Cape Town he became involved with prominent Marxists and the National Liberation League and assisted in an attempt to set up a school in the desolate Cape Flats area. Later he hitchhiked to Durban, where he signed on as a stoker on a ship bound for Britain and eventually took up residence in Britain in 1941.

EARLY WORKS

It is generally agreed that Abrahams' writing breaks down into three periods, beginning with his first three books: a collection of short narratives, *Dark Testament* (1942), and two novels, *Song of the City* (1945) and *Mine Boy* (1946).

These early books are powerful social statements on the poverty, pain, and exploitation of nonwhites in urban South Africa. They emphasize the processes of social and psychological disintegration to which urban blacks and Coloreds are vulnerable. Abrahams portrays how government grading of people according to fine variations in color and ethnic background generates divisions within communities. Powerlessness in the face of arbitrary police brutality encourages the characters in these books to take out their frustrations on each other. Most destructive of all are the psychological rifts caused by urbanization and detribalization. Conflict and the

assertion of brute force characterize transactions, right down to the simple act of greeting. Despondent, characters commit suicide, disappear, or become alcoholic.

The white characters who enjoy the comforts of a bourgeois existence are also undermined by the pervasive racism; it is a central irony of the two novels that only the nonwhites have the ability to resist and to grow as individuals. In *Dark Testament* nonwhites are forced by extreme loneliness, lovelessness, or fear to self-understanding, which can be stark but also reassuring. The main male characters in the novels, Dick Nduli and Xuma, like the writer-narrator in *Dark Testament*, have a resiliency and purposeful good nature a characteristic which implies that there is hope in this grim situation.

Dark Testament

Dark Testament (1942) is divided into two sections: "I Remember . . ." and "Stories." "I Remember . . ." contains fourteen short narratives, presented as autobiographical pieces and observed sketches of friends and acquaintances whom Abrahams had met between 1930 and 1938. In the first narrative, "I Remember . . . ," Abrahams describes announcing at school his ambition to become a writer. He tells his teacher—a beautiful "light-coloured girl, who could pass for white in a dim light" (p. 9)—that he wants to be a writer in order to become famous and rich. Shortly afterward he faints from hunger and is sent to a hospital where he is diagnosed as suffering from starvation and later sent out to starve again. The bringing together of race, suggestions of love and desire, education, poverty, and the burning drive to be a writer makes this an archetypal Abrahams text.

Other sketches in the first section describe women struggling to care for their children and lonely men dealing with broken love affairs and discussing service in World War I. The stories "Brother Jew" and "Jewish Sister" evoke intimacy between the Colored narrator and Jewish characters fostered by their shared subjection to racial discrimination. In "Lonesome" and "Saturday Night," Abrahams documents his rejection of the role of "promising young writer" for the Communist movement (p. 59).

The narratives in the second section, "Stories," are longer and more ambitious but lack the terse impact of the earlier ones. "'From an Unfinished Novel'" is set in a Christian teachers college in the Transvaal Province and describes the consequences of the seduction of a black student by a white man who abandons her when she becomes pregnant. The narrative is framed by references to the historical leaders Chaka and Mzilikazi (spelled "Mzilikatsi" in the story) and concludes with an observation by a young black man who loves the girl and angrily exclaims to himself: "So this is Christianity! They were not satisfied with stealing our land and cattle. They most steal our women with sweet words" (p. 127).

Like later works, *Dark Testament* paradoxically repudiates racism and at the same time is dominated by racial hierarchies. However, it was a unique collection when published in Britain and anticipated the short fiction of *Drum* writers Can Themba and Bessie Head and of later writers like Miriam Tlali.

Song of the City

Set shortly after the outbreak of World War II, *Song of the City* (1945) ironically views the looming destruction of the "great European monument, personal liberty" from a South African perspective (p. 43). Anglo–South African characters talk about the necessity for "room for all people and for all ideas" in Europe without recognizing how they deny this to the vast majority of their own nonwhite compatriots (p. 14). Afrikaner characters argue for nonparticipation by South Africa in the war, and extremist Afrikaners

identify with the Nazis. Communist commitment to racial equality and the long-term struggle for a Marxist society fail to meet the immediate needs of the black proletariat (laboring class). Black politicians who advocate separate homelands or a gradualist policy of change appear equally irrelevant.

These positions are dramatized in *Song of the City* by a dozen or so representative characters who mix, debate, and interact with each other. Like the later *Wild Conquest* (1950), Abrahams' first novel uses a particular historical moment to focus on the broad flow and development of South African society.

More significant than any of these characters is Nduli, who leaves his traditional life in the country, with its communality and oral history, to find work in Johannesburg. *Song of the City* traces his path to modern consciousness. This journey involves the shift from a romantic ideal to the dangers, as well as the possibilities, of urban life. In the final chapter Nduli explains, "I want to understand things. And I can only understand in the big city" (p. 178). Although he has just been beaten by passing whites and discovered his sister caring for the illegitimate child of a white man, the novel ends with lines celebrating the "song of the city":

> Oh sing then the song of the city,
> Sing it when your heart is in pain,
> For you are a son of the city
> And the song will lighten your pain;
> To-day there is pain—but to-morrow
> The song will be gay—rich with hope.
> (p. 179)

Mine Boy

Mine Boy (1946) is primarily set in Malay Camp, a nonwhite slum in Johannesburg, with some scenes in the gold mines and the small rural township of Hoopvlei (or Valley of Hope), which was established by whites to encourage urban depopulation among Coloreds and blacks. Abrahams' second novel does not offer a parallel portrayal of white and nonwhite characters in South Africa, although it concludes by suggesting that significant links can be forged between them.

Like Nduli, Xuma "from the north" arrives in Johannesburg looking for a job and becomes involved with a group of people living in Malay Camp (p. 12). Leah is the head of a communal household that includes a live-in lover, Dladla; an alcoholic, Daddy; an old woman, Ma Plank; and a teacher, Eliza. A character named Johannes helps Xuma get a job working deep underground in a gold mine; at the mine, Xuma develops a relationship with his Irish boss, Paddy, and Paddy's girlfriend, Di.

Although dances and storytelling offer moments of relief, *Mine Boy* is dominated by physical, verbal, and psychological violence, which turns almost all the nonwhite characters into schizoid self-torturers. Xuma falls in love with Eliza, who tells him, "I am black. I cannot help it. Inside I am not black and I do not want to be a black person. I want to be like [whites] are" (p. 89). Eliza eventually disappears from the city, although she is still in love with Xuma. Leah, who is one of the few nonschizoid characters, is eventually caught with illicit brewing equipment and sent to prison. Johannes is killed in a mine accident. At the close Paddy and Xuma protest illegally against conditions, defying the racist system and exemplifying the novel's epigraph by Rudyard Kipling:

But there is neither East nor West, Border, nor Breed nor Birth,
When two strong men stand face to face,
Though they come from the ends of the earth!

Writing about Abrahams' early fiction, Ngũgĩ has commented on his "broken vision, broken, that is, because his realism in depicting the social conditions of workers in South Africa fortunately negates his romantic, sentimental vision of a society without colour" (1972, p. 43). Certainly *Mine Boy* carries Marx-ist concepts of the power of labor and the development of an urban proletariat that would meet with Ngũgĩ's approval. However, there is nothing inherently sentimental either in the idea of a society without color or in constructing possibilities for hope and change amid circumstances of social oppression. What is unconvincing is the sexist and macho vision of male strength and bonding that the close of *Mine Boy* proposes as the means to bring about this change. More credible are the relationships and networks set up by the tough, realistic Leah, a precursor of the indomitable women in Bessie Head's *The Collector of Treasures* (1977).

THE SECOND PHASE OF ABRAHAMS' CAREER

One of Abrahams' basic aims in moving to Britain in 1941 was to show a British audience what conditions were like for blacks and Coloreds in South Africa, with the possibility of bringing moral and political forces to bear in his native country. With the completion and publication of *Mine Boy*, Abrahams had certainly created a graphic account of city life from a nonwhite point of view, one less prone to sentimentality and closer to the rhythms of urban life than Alan Paton's comparable 1948 novel, *Cry, the Beloved Country*. It was time for new directions in his fiction, and the second major phase of Abrahams' career involved him in a series of narratives that looked back in time and one that looked into the future.

During the first part of this period, Abrahams wrote two novels, *The Path of Thunder* (1948) and *Wild Conquest* (1950), which in different ways investigate the roots of South Africa's racist establishment. Then, in 1952, he accepted a commission by the London newspaper *Observer* to visit South Africa and write a series of articles about it. By this time Abrahams had been in Europe for eleven years. He had married his first wife, Dorothy, in 1942. The first part of the marriage was spent in France, where Abrahams felt race was less of an issue, although the couple later returned to Britain. This marriage was dissolved in 1948, and he married his second wife, Daphne Miller, an artist, in the same year. Having worked as a journalist, novelist, and spokesman on race issues, Abrahams felt he had come to terms with his own feelings on the subject, but the 1952 visit to South Africa and Kenya was a disturbing reminder of what he had left behind. *Return to Goli* (1953), the book that came out of this trip, renewed Abrahams' credentials as a commentator on South Africa and race relations and led to a venture into his personal history in the form of *Tell Freedom* (1954), the autobiography covering the first twenty years of his life. Many still consider *Tell Freedom* his best book.

Since arriving in Britain, Abrahams had come acquainted with Africans from all over the continent who were living and studying in London, and he helped to organize the 1946 Pan-Africanist Conference in Manchester. He knew Jomo Kenyatta, later president of Kenya, and Kwame Nkrumah, who led Ghana when it became the first of a series of independent African states. In the last novel of the middle phase of his career, *A Wreath for Udomo* (1956), Abrahams presents a pessimistic view of the coming era of independence, addressing issues of race, color, and development in the context of Pan-Africanism and the modernizing impact of western technology.

The Path of Thunder

The Path of Thunder (1948) takes place almost entirely in northern Cape Karroo in South Africa and has a modern setting. After seven years of education in Cape Town, Lanny Swartz returns to the Colored settlement of Stilleveld, where he was raised. He plans to set up a school to repay the community, which, he believes, has supported his education. As soon as he gets off the train,

Lanny is subjected to racial vilification by whites at a coffee stall. The location of Stilleveld and Mako's Kraal, the adjacent black settlement—beneath the house of the Afrikaner Villier family on the hill—remains throughout the novel a graphic image of racist segregation and hierarchy.

Lanny becomes friendly with Issac, the son of the local Jewish shopkeeper, and Mako, a young black teacher who runs his own school in Mako's Kraal, and they spend time discussing the politics of race and nationalism. Lanny's school is successful in the Colored community, but when he meets and falls in love with Sarie Villier, a foundling adopted by the Villier family, he threatens the racist hierarchy. The couple plans to escape to Portuguese East Africa and keep their relationship secret. However, they are ambushed by Gert Villier and his overseer, Viljoen, and eventually die in a shootout in which, according to the pro-Afrikaner local newspaper, a young Colored teacher ran amok in an escapade that exemplified the dangerous policy of "educating black people" (p. 279).

This event gains significance as it becomes clear that the same thing happened years before between another educated Colored, Samuel du Plesis, and a white woman, also called Sarier Villier. In addition, it turns out that Lanny is himself a member of the Villier family, whose money paid for his education.

With its violence and sexuality, a mysterious past throwing a long shadow over the present, and a delving into the dark workings of the psyche, *The Path of Thunder* constitutes what might aptly be termed South African gothic. Like Abrahams, Lanny Swartz loves the English Romantic poetry of William Blake and Percy Bysshe Shelley, but a poem by American Countee Cullen about a black boy and a white boy walking arm in arm and enduring a "path of thunder" provides the title and predominant tone.

Although *The Path of Thunder* has been popular enough to be translated into twenty-six languages—perhaps because Lanny and

Sarie make a Romeo-and-Juliet pair — Abrahams obviously uses passages of dialogue to broadcast his position on the subject of race that sound strained and uncomfortable. Mako, for instance, observes:

> I do not object to the Coloureds grading upward, or trying to, because it is toward the whites. I do so because it shows the way in which he [*sic*] is not free.... If it is compensation for not being white then I will fight it with all my strength. If it is the business of a man and a woman who love and have stepped above and beyond colour then it is their business.
>
> (p. 91)

In this psychological novel romantic escape is not possible, and it would be false to imagine that Lanny's and Sarie's passion is entirely removed from racial and cultural contexts.

Wild Conquest

Wild Conquest (1950), Abrahams' first historical novel, is much more ambitious in scope and complexity than any of his previous works. This novel is divided into three extended sections: "Bible and Rifle," "Bayete," and "New Day."

"Bible and Rifle" begins in 1835 as news filters through from the Cape that British legislation has freed all slaves. The Jansen family quickly decides that without slave labor their farm is no longer viable, so they head north as part of the Great Trek of Afrikaners to the Transvaal. They join other groups and are periodically attacked by Africans whose land they are invading. The "Trekkers" lead a communal life, and couples in the group like Paul Van As and Elsie fall in love and get married. Paul begins to learn the language of the blacks and eventually grows to loathe and distrust the murderous and dehumanizing way the Trekkers live, though he is very much the exception in doing this.

"Bayete" (the royal salute of the Matabele people), which switches the setting to the Matabele empire of Mzilikazi during the same period, presented Abrahams with a number of technical challenges. Unlike the majority of Afrikaner characters in the first section, who could be modeled freely to meet the needs of the narrative, Mzilikazi and others are historical figures, and to some extent the narrative had to be adapted to accommodate them. In addition, Abrahams was reconstructing a period of considerable intertribal turmoil in the history of southern Africa and trying to present all the tribal groupings, including the Matabele, Barolong, Basuto, and Afrikaners, in a dispassionate and objective way.

The result is an elaborately patterned epic narrative containing some of Abrahams' best characterizations, especially in the figure of Anna Jansen, and in the case of the Matabele characters, some of his worst. Particularly problematic are passages of Matabele dialogue, which, as has often been noted, are terribly reminiscent of Rider Haggard's African fiction. For example, Abrahams writes, "It is not only our people who are in darkness, who are bewitched by false medicine men.... It is not only our people who are stirred to a frenzy of madness by the tom-toms" (Penguin edition, p. 236). To add insult to injury, Ogungbesan accuses Abrahams of relying "almost to the point of plagiarism" on the 1930 novel *Mhudi* by Sol T. Plaatje (1979, p. 84), though this "plagiarism" could alternatively be described as an affectionate tribute by Abrahams to the first published novel by a black South African writer.

Wild Conquest ends with the pointless, inevitable clash of arms between Afrikaners and Matabele in "New Day," a title that symbolizes the establishment of the future white hegemony. It is a tragic though not nihilistic moment: the spectacle of individuals on both sides being acted on by historical forces larger than they are, but not so large as to deny the possibility of redemptive love and shared humanity. At the same time the evocation of racial hatred in this novel rather than the treatment of love, stimulates Abrahams' best prose, as, for instance, in the remarkable passage when Kasper Jansen is forced to recognize his former slave, Old Johannes, as a free man.

Return to Goli and Tell Freedom

Goli is the Zulu name for Johannesburg (from the gold mined there), and *Return to Goli* (1953) has been called Abrahams' most bitter book. Certainly it offers little hope for future change, as *Song of the City* and *Mine Boy* do, nor does it generate the tragic humanism of *Path of Thunder* and *Wild Conquest*. Abrahams found on his return to Johannesburg that under the Nationalist government's official policy of racial segregation, or apartheid, the situation in South Africa had become significantly worse for nonwhites in general and Coloreds in particular.

Abrahams has described *Return to Goli*, which offers valuable insights into his life and feelings, as his "declaration of independence, my deliberate revolt against both white and black. For years I have found the burden of oppression by both wearisome and stifling. Now I would be rid of it" (p. 19). However, this work represents an extreme instance of his highly racialized way of presenting a situation. Although the book is committed to human values and individuality, its very structure, with chapters divided into "The Coloureds," "The Indians," "The Blacks," and "The Whites," tends to reinforce the racist mentality that counters these values.

Tell Freedom (1954) is a classic modernist account of the developing consciousness of a young artist impelled by and generating a quest for liberation and freedom. Abrahams' trip from Durban is like Stephen Dedalus' from Dublin at the end of *A Portrait of the Artist as a Young Man* (1914–1915); like James Joyce's novel, Abrahams' portrait presents a deceptively elaborate account of the relationship between autobiography and narrative impulse. It also dramatizes the interaction between oral and written narrative and, as Stephen Gray has shown in an article entitled "The Long Eye of History," carefully constructs the parity between text and reader that is vital to the genre of autobiography.

With stories like the one about the difficulties of a man who decides to move to the city, *Tell Freedom* will be most widely remembered as a dignified repudiation of apartheid. This man discovers he needs a Trek pass identification pass and six-day special pass. Having secured a place to live, a job, and a girlfriend, he also requires a monthly pass, traveling pass, day special pass, location visitor's pass, lodger's permit, and night special pass. Then he runs into difficulties with his employer, ends up in jail, and watches helplessly as his new life disintegrates. He is left, as he started, with nothing.

A Wreath for Udomo

Abrahams' fifth novel, *A Wreath for Udomo* (1956), continues the tragic note on which *Wild Conquest* ends. At the beginning of the novel Udomo has just arrived in London to complete a doctorate and, more particularly, to acquire the authority attached to the title of "Doctor" in order to have the political power to work for the freedom of his native country, "Panafrica," upon his return. Udomo's is a convincing portrait of a man with passion, energy, and the power to lead; it draws on Abrahams' acquaintance with Kwame Nkrumah, "the quintessential symbol of that great African dream of freedom," as Abrahams described the Ghanaian leader in the novel *The View from Coyaba*.

Udomo quickly makes contact with a number of expatriate Africans, including Tom Lanwood, a Panafrican who for years has written in support of political independence; Michael Mhendi, leader of a recent failed uprising in Pluralia (a fictionalized state suggestive of South Africa); Paul Mabi, an artist; and Adebhoy, a medical doctor from Panafrica. Returning to Panafrica much earlier than planned, Udomo meets Selina, a market trader who has great power over her fellow traders; he also begins working as a journalist, successfully engineers the political revolution, and obtains the leadership position, which had been his aim.

The majority of the novel deals with the inevitable failure that awaits Udomo as leader of Panafrica. Udomo believes unequivocally in the need to modernize Panafrican society through western technology. In practical terms this involves relying on advisers and aid from the racist Pluralian regime, and Udomo eventually betrays Mhendi to this regime. This betrayal plays into the hands of Selina and Adebhoy, who see modernization as a threat to their tribalistic power, and they have Udomo ritually murdered. He emerges as a flawed and tragic figure, and Panafrica is left at the novel's end with modernizing forces threatened by a return to tribalism, compounded by the attendant "stifling and destroying of the human personality" (p. 216).

Michael Wade has called this novel a "chillingly accurate paradigm of events to come" in Africa after its publication in 1956 and "the best thing Abrahams has ever done" (1972, p. 152). Ogungbesan sees it as the first of the phase of "overtly political novels" with which Abrahams has completed his career to date (p. 6). Certainly it was bold and provocative statement at the time, appearing a year before Ghana, the state on which Panafrica was loosely modeled, achieved independence. Although *A Wreath for Udomo*, like *Wild Conquest*, carries a commitment to African independence, there is a hard-edged objectivity in the presentation of black and white characters. It is difficult to imagine anyone but a Colored writer treating tribalism so harshly and having a character compare Udomo's Panafrica with his own Pluralia/South Africa, as Mhendi does: "My people are at least a century ahead of his. My God! I wouldn't be in his shoes for anything. The whites have done us so much good" (p. 217).

In spite of its political dimensions, *A Wreath for Udomo* is finally memorable for its portrayal of individuals grappling with personal commitments, compromises, and betrayals.

What haunts Udomo until the moment he dies is the failure of his relationship with an English woman, Lois, whom he meets as the novel commences.

LATER WORKS

In 1955 Abrahams went to Jamaica on a commission from the British Colonial Office for its Corona Library series on dependent territories. He was extremely impressed by what he found there, and *Jamaica: An Island Mosaic* (1957) concludes by contrasting the island with his early memories of South Africa, where "the problems of race and colour, perhaps the key problems of our century, were so riddled with fear and hate that they seemed beyond any but the most terrible and bloody solution" (p. 261). Jamaica, on the other hand, provided the example of a state whose inhabitants "had lived out the multi-racial problem and were now reaching a stage where race and colour did not matter, only a person's worth as a person. In this they are far ahead of most of the rest of the world; have much to teach the rest of the world" (p. 261).

In 1956 Abrahams returned to settle in Jamaica. He subsequently worked as a broadcaster on Jamaican radio, wrote for *Holiday* magazine, edited the *West African Economist*, and published three more novels, the first set in South Africa and the other two wholly or partially set in the Caribbean.

In all three novels Abrahams continues his preoccupation with colonization, multiracial society, and color, but without the tragic overtones that characterize his middle period. The use of Caribbean settings involves another change of some consequence to the texture and characterization in Abrahams' fiction. For the first time in his career, Abrahams was engaging with the political process in the region where he was presently living. Whereas his expatriate lifestyle and physical distance from the country led to a stark narrative outline and a concern with relatively complex characterization in the South African fiction, the Caribbean settings drew Abrahams into his journalistic role of sociopolitical commentator. The result in *This Island Now* (1966) and parts of *The View from Coyaba* (1985) is what could be termed "applied fiction," in which dialogue is used to debate contemporary political issues.

Jamaica: An Island Mosaic

Abrahams' goal for *Jamaica* (1957) was to "fill the place between official Blue Books on the one hand and the writings of occasional visitors on the other, to be authoritative and readable, and to give a vivid yet accurate picture" (introductory note, p. v). Since Her Majesty's Stationery Office was the publisher, it is not surprising that the result was very different from V. S. Naipaul's *The Loss of Eldorado: A History* (1969), which covered some of the same territory in a more powerful and disturbing way. But *Jamaica* still offers a pleasant ramble through historical periods that caught the imagination of the author, including Henry Morgan's time as buccaneer and then governor of Jamaica, the slave period, and the establishment of the Maroon people in the hills (who figure prominently in *The View from Coyaba*). In the text Abrahams shows particular interest in the consequences of the British abolition of slavery in 1834 (the stimulus for events in *Wild Conquest*) and in contemporary slum kids and the urban poor, with whom the author readily identifies.

Ogungbesan complains, rather harshly, about "embarrassing . . . purple passages" in praise of the island and its people, but is probably justified in his opinion that "most black Jamaicans" would reject Abrahams' notion of Jamaica as a world leader of multicultural integration (p. 7).

A Night of Their Own

A Night of Their Own (1965); the last of Abrahams' novels to use a South African set-

ting, is a type of political thriller. At the front of the text Abrahams identifies and typecasts all the characters, including, for instance, "Captain Stikkelund, a seafaring man who has lost the capacity to believe." The narrative is punctuated by set pieces: the arrival of the central character off the Natal coast in a submarine, his negotiation of police checkpoints, and his escape on a freighter in the final chapter. Richard Nkosi's task is to smuggle in a large sum of money and deliver it to Indian members of a resistance organization. When South African security gets wind of this, Richard Nkosi has to go underground. This character's real name is Richard Dube, and his survival is crucial to the continuation of the Richard Nkosi myth (a name used by a series of resistance fighters).

Dube becomes sexually involved with an Indian woman called Dee Nunkhoo, and their love affair is ironically contrasted with the moribund one between Mildred Scott, "Headmistress of Coloured Girl's School," and Karl Van As, the main white South African character, a security officer. Dube is black, and the affair with Dee provides an opportunity for Abrahams to consider interracial relationships in a new context. More generally, Dube is a source of acute danger to the Indians who look after him. If, as Ogungbesan suggests, much of the detail in this novel derives from "copious use of [Abrahams'] notes from his visit of 1952" (p. 128), as well as his reflections on the South African government's successful incursions into the underground in 1963–1964, then the political, moral, and ethical questions that Dube addresses survive as the novel's enduring feature.

This Island Now

This unsettling novel, published in 1966, describes what happens when the neocolonial dictator of a Caribbean island is succeeded by a black leader who becomes trapped in his own tyrannical order. Moses Joshua, dominant in the island's politics for half a century, had become alienated from the needs of the majority of his people, who nevertheless adulated him, and served his own interests and those of old settler families and mercantile concerns instead. Following news of Joshua's peaceful death at the beginning of *This Island Now*, Albert Josiah, "a man of the people," establishes himself as president and sets out systematically to dismantle the old power structures and install a regime to liberate and empower the black majority. He manipulates the mercantile interests of the Isaacs family, though not before they have transferred funds offshore; dismisses the country's senior servant, a member of the island's "old coloured aristocracy"; has the white editor of *The Voice of the Island* summarily removed; and detains the chief justice for his refusal to obey orders.

Abrahams uses point of view to great ironic effect. Initially he presents the changeover to Josiah's new regime through the eyes of characters adversely affected by it, though he also conveys the failure of the old order to provide for poor urban and country dwellers. However, macroeconomics is not subject to the political will of leaders of small island states, nor can these leaders rely on the voluntary labor of the people to support their policies. When two hundred rioters are killed in widespread unrest, Josiah suspends the democratic process by delaying elections.

This Island Now addresses a familiar issue for Abrahams: how to reconcile an absolute commitment to freedom with a deterministic view of history where race and color continue to dominate affairs. For the general reader the novel's principal interest is documentary, for it describes an agonizing phase of postcolonialism through which many states have passed and which others may continue to encounter. It is also interesting to compare Moses Joshua with the almost identical role that Ngũgĩ in *Detained: A Writer's Prison Diary* (1981) ascribes to Jomo Kenyatta as president of Kenya, although the neocolonial regime of *This Island Now* presents ambi-guities and conflicts with which Ngũgĩ's Marxist readings have little concern.

The View from Coyaba

If Abrahams' first historical novel, *Wild Conquest*, was epic, then his second, *The View from Coyaba*, must be termed panoramic. This 1985 novel moves from the early sixteenth to the twentieth century following a route from Jamaica to the southern United States, Liberia, Kenya, and Uganda in the 1950s, to Nigeria and Guinea, back to Uganda during the time of Idi Amin, and returning to Jamaica in 1980.

These settings offer a composite of the consequences of western colonialism for the colonized and enslaved from the Renaissance onward. For the Arawaks, the indigenous inhabitants of Jamaica, Spanish colonization means extinction. For black slaves imported to labor on the sugar plantations, life is brutal and inhuman, though some escape to become the Maroons living in tiny groups in the inaccessible Jamaican hills. The section of the novel set in Georgia portrays W. E. B. Du Bois working to promote black consciousness and dignity. The African settings during and after political independence document the pervasive control exercised by the west and the way its materialist values destroy the cohesiveness of indigenous societies. The final section in Jamaica describes what Andrew Salkey terms "the heroic failure of the socialist government of that island nation" (1985, p. 647).

In the thirty years since *A Wreath for Udomo*, Abrahams' attitude toward the usefulness of western technology and modernization changed greatly, and at the close of *The View from Coyaba* an authoritative character talks of the need to "separate ourselves from this destructive Westernism" (p. 437). In the novel's opening dialogue between two Arawaks, two crucial means of survival are established and recur throughout the narrative: the need to struggle actively to preserve one's cultural identity and the importance of having one's own gods. Later sections of the novel envisage a form of Christianity that is controlled indigenously and therefore free from the cultural and political imperialism of former mission Christianity. This is a new development in Abrahams' fiction, from which the redemptive possibilities of religion had previously been absent.

Narrative structure in the novel is provided by the Maroon family, and *The View from Coyaba* may be called a family saga, a feature that particularly impresses Andrew Salkey: "I will long remember Samson, the Maroon leader; Sarah, the militant grandmother of Jacob, the first missionary to Liberia and afterward Bishop of Uganda; and David, Jacob's son, the doctor and revolutionary" (p. 647). Perhaps the family as a developing and cohesive source of unity through time represents a third means to retain cultural identity. Certainly the family-saga element of *The View from Coyaba* takes us back to the elaborate lineage that had been instilled into Abrahams when he was still very young, "Peter Henry Abrahams Deras, son of James Henry Abrahams Deras whose name at home was Karim Abdul, son of Ingedi(e) of Addis who was the son of somebody else. . . ."

CONCLUSION

Midway through his career, Abrahams wrote: "I felt that if I could see the whole scheme of things with the long eye of history I might be able to fit the problems of my own group into the general human scheme and, in doing so, become a writer" (*Return to Goli*, p. 17). *The View from Coyaba* triumphantly accomplishes this objective. It has been justly described by Stephen Gray as the "summation of his creative career" (p. 100). It offers the most successful resolution to the conflict in his writing between the need for a clear recognition of the historical consequences of "race and colour"

and the search for personal and imaginative freedom from them.

The View from Coyaba encountered many familiar criticisms when it was published. Derek Wright wrote in the *Times Literary Supplement*: "As a philosophic and humane survey of the history of black emancipation since the British abolition of slavery, his book may be recommended: as a novel, not" (p. 326). However, Wright's approach is based on an overly precriptive view of the novel form. Salkey offers a better description of the book as "not only a composite novelistic picture, but also a reverberating metaphor" (p. 647). Abrahams' best writing fuses his reading in the Harlem Renaissance poets, W. E. B. Du Bois, and the English Romantic poets with his own rich life and international view of the world and its peoples. For this reason it will always remain open to bold metaphorical and symbolic extensions of the type Salkey has in mind.

Selected Bibliography

SELECTED WORKS

A Black Man Speaks of Freedom. Durban, South Africa: Universal Printing Works, 1941.

Dark Testament. London: G. Allen and Unwin, Ltd., 1942; Nendeln, Liechtenstein: Kraus Reprint, 1970.

Song of the City. London: Dorothy Crisp, 1945.

Mine Boy. London: Dorothy Crisp, 1946; London: Faber and Faber, 1946; New York: Collier Books, 1970; London: Heinemann Educational Books, 1989.

The Path of Thunder. New York: Harper, 1948; London: Faber and Faber, 1952; Chatham, N.J.: Chatham Bookseller, 1975. Intro. by Richard Rive. Cape Town, South Africa: David Philip, 1984.

Wild Conquest. New York: Harper, 1950; London: Faber and Faber, 1951; Harmondsworth, U.K.: Penguin, 1966; Walton-on-Thames, U.K.: Nelson, 1982.

Return to Goli. London: Faber and Faber, 1953.

Tell Freedom. New York: Knopf, 1954; London: Faber and Faber, 1954. Publ. as *Tell Freedom: Memories of Africa.* New York: Knopf, 1961, 1966; New York: Collier Books, 1970; Boston: Faber and Faber, 1981.

A Wreath for Udomo. New York: Knopf, 1956; London: Faber and Faber, 1956, 1965. New ed. New York: Collier Books, 1971.

Jamaica: An Island Mosaic. London: Her Majesty's Stationery Office, 1957.

A Night of Their Own. New York: Knopf, 1965; London: Faber and Faber, 1965.

This Island Now. London: Faber and Faber, 1966; New York: Knopf, 1967. Rev. ed. London: Faber and Faber, 1985.

The View from Coyaba. London: Faber and Faber, 1985.

Here, Friend. Privately printed, n.d.

ESSAYS

"The Conflict of Cultures in Africa." In *International Affairs* 30 (July 1954).

"The Blacks." In *Holiday* 25 (April 1959). Repr. in shortened form in Langston Hughes, ed., *An African Treasury.* London: Gollancz, 1961.

"Manifesto from Johannesburg." In *Saturday Review* 42 (1 August 1959).

"The Meaning of Harlem." In *Holiday* 27 (June 1960).

"The Real Jamaica." In *Holiday* 33 (March 1963).

"We Can Learn to Be Colour-Blind." In *New York Times Magazine* 38 (11 April 1965).

CRITICAL STUDIES

Abrahams, Cecil. "The Long Journey Home: A Portrait of Peter Abrahams." In *South African Review of Books* 2 (1989).

Anderson, Susan. "Something in Me Died: Autobiographies of South African Writers in Exile." In *Books Abroad* 44 (summer 1970).

Cartey, Wilfred G. *Whispers from a Continent.* New York: Random House, 1969.

Case, Frederick. "Littérature traditionnelle et forme romanesque: Analyse du conte comme procédé littéraire romanesque." In *Éthiopiques* 4, nos. 3–4 (1987).

Gakwandi, Shatto Arthur. *The Novel and Contemporary Experience in Africa.* London: Heinemann Educational Books, 1977.

Gordimer, Nadine. "The Novel and the Nation in South Africa." In *Times Literary Supplement* (11 August 1961).

Gray, Stephen. "The Long Eye of History: Four Autobiographical Texts by Peter Abrahams." In *Pretexts* 2 (summer 1990).

Guerard, Albert. "Le Roman neo-africain: Peter Abrahams." In *La Revue nouvelle* 28 (1963).

———. "Peter Abrahams et la littérature sud-africaine." In *La Revue nouvelle* 45 (1967).

Hamilton, Cynthia. "Work and Culture: The Evolution of Consciousness in Urban Industrial Society in the Fiction of William Attaway and Peter Abrahams." In *Black American Literature Forum* 21 (spring–summer 1987).

Harris, Michael. "South African Past and Future in Peter Abrahams' *Wild Conquest.*" In *World Literature Written in English* 28 (spring 1988).

Heywood, Christopher. "The Novels of Peter Abrahams." In Christopher Heywood, ed., *Perspectives on African Literature: Selections from the Proceedings of the Conference on African Literature Held at the University of Ife, 1968.* New York: Africana Publishing Co., 1971.

Lewis, Primila. "Politics and the Novel: An Appreciation of *A Wreath for Udomo.*" In *Zuka* 2 (May 1968).

Lindfors, Bernth. "Exile and Aesthetic Distance: Geographical Influences on Political Commitment in the Works of Peter Abrahams." In *International Fiction Review* 13 (summer 1986).

Maduka, Chukwudi. "Limitation and Possibility: The Intellectual as a Hero-Type in Peter Abrahams' *A Wreath for Udomo*" (in Polish and French). In *Zagadnienia rodzajow literackich: Woprosy literaturnych Zanrov/Les Problèmes des genres littéraires* 2 (1981).

Maes-Jelinik, Hena. "Race Relationship and Identity in Peter Abrahams' 'Pluralia.'" In *English Studies* 50 (February 1969).

Menager, Serge. "Peter Abrahams, Icare Metis." In *Commonwealth Essays and Studies* 12 (spring 1990).

Miller, George Morey, and Howard Sergeant, eds. *A Critical Survey of South African Poetry in English.* Cape Town, South Africa: Balkema, 1957.

Mphahlele, Ezekiel. *The African Image.* London: Faber and Faber, 1962.

———. "Variations on a Theme: Race and Color" (in French). In *Présence africaine* 83 (1972).

————. *Voices in the Whirlwind, and Other Essays.* London: Macmillan, 1972.

Ngũgĩ wa Thiong'o. *Homecoming: Essays on African and Caribbean Litterature.* London: Heinemann Educational Books, 1972.

————. *Moving the Centre: The Struggle for Cultural Freedoms.* London: James Currey, 1993.

Ngwarsungu, Chiwengo. "The Text in Search of Identity: Freedom in Peter Abrahams' Novels." In *Griot* 5 (fall 1986).

Nkosi, Lewis. "Fiction by Black South Africans." In *Black Orpheus* 19 (March 1966).

————. *Tasks and Masks: Themes and Styles of African Literature.* Harlow, U.K.: Longman, 1981.

Ogungbesan, Kolawole. *The Writings of Peter Abrahams.* New York: Africana Publishing Co., 1979.

Parasuram, A. N. *Minerva Guide to Peter Abrahams'* Mine Boy. Madras, India: Minerva Publishing House, 1977.

Philipson, Robert. "Images of Colonized Childhood: Abrahams, Wright and Laye." In Jonathan A. Peters, Mildred P. Mortimer, and Russell V. Linnemann, eds., *Literature of Africa and the African Continuum.* Washington, D.C.: Three Continents Press, 1989.

Povey, John. "The Political Theme in South and West African Novels." In *African Quarterly* 9 (April–June 1969).

Rive, Richard. "The Liberal Tradition in South African Literature." In *Contrast* 14 (July 1983).

Salkey, Andrew. Review of *The View from Coyaba.* In *World Literature Today* 5 (fall 1985).

Scanlon, Paul. "Dream and Reality in Abrahams' *A Wreath for Udomo.*" In *Obsidian* 1–2 (1980).

Shava, Piniel. *A People's Voice: Black South African Writing in the Twentieth Century.* London: Zed Books, 1989.

Wade, J-P. "*Song of the City* and *Mine Boy*: The 'Marxist' Novels of Peter Abrahams." In *Research in African Literatures* 21 (fall 1990).

Wade, Michael. *Peter Abrahams.* London: Evans Bros., 1972.

————. "The View from Pisgah: Peter Abrahams at Seventy." In *South African Review of Books* 5, no. 2 (1989).

Wright, Derek. "Colonizing the Mind." In *Times Literary Supplement* (22 March 1985).

Chinua Achebe
1930–

G. D. KILLAM

CHINUA ACHEBE describes art as a celebration that encompasses the "remembering of blessings or happy events," in his 1990 essay "African Literature as Restoration of Celebration." More importantly, from his Nigerian/Igbo (or Ibo, one of three major ethnic groups in Nigeria) perspective, this celebration "deliberately sets out to include other experiences—indeed, all significant encounters which man makes in his journey through life, especially new, unaccustomed and thus potentially threatening, encounters" (pp. 2–3). For Achebe celebration takes place within a political context. He is devoted to understanding the effect and legacy "especially for Africa, for black people, for all deprived peoples" of the terrible disaster that proceeded from "Africa's meeting with Europe" in the period of high imperialism in the late nineteenth century. Furthermore he is devoted to conveying his understanding of the consequences of this disaster to Nigerians and to others who choose to contemplate his offerings.

Achebe's life and art encompass the essential duality of human experience as embodied in the aphorism drawn from Igbo cosmology that "wherever something stands, something stands beside it." His art represents a continuing effort to reconcile the disparate elements, essentially political, that alter and shape perception and therefore reality. Along these lines, Achebe has said:

> I had to tell Europe that the arrogance on which she sought to excuse her pillage of Africa, i.e. that Africa was a Primordial Void, was sheer humbug; that Africa had a history, a religion, a civilization. We reconstructed this history and civilization and displayed it to challenge the stereotype and the cliche. Actually it was not to Europe alone that I spoke. I spoke also to that part of ourselves that had come to accept Europe's opinion of us.

Before he could achieve this public task through his art, Achebe had to reconcile the dualities inherent in his personal experiences. These experiences were shaped by his birth during the colonial period and his exposure and attraction to both African and European cultures through education, political institutions, and, most especially for the writer, language.

More precisely, his fiction, poetry, and prose—starting with the publication of the modern classic *Things Fall Apart* in 1958—sum up his religious experience, both traditional Igbo and Christian; his experience of language, both Igbo and English; his education, both formal and acquired; and his purposes as a writer, both aesthetic and educative.

LIFE

Achebe was born Albert Chinualumogu Achebe on 16 November 1930 in Ogidi, in eastern Nigeria. His father, Isaiah Okafor Achebe, was a pioneer Igbo-Christian catechist, trained at the Teacher Training College at Awka in 1904. His mother, Janet Ileogbunam, was educated at St. Monica's in Ogbunike. Achebe was named after Albert, Queen Victoria's consort, and the Igbo name Chinualumogu, "may God fight on my behalf." In 1909 his parents were married by G. T. Basden in a Christian ceremony. Achebe was later to challenge Basden's comprehensive studies of the customs and beliefs of the Igbo people—their marriage and burial rites; arts, crafts, music, trade, and currency; ways of making war; and religious beliefs and sacrificial rites—which were published in two widely respected volumes, *Among the Niger Ibo* (1920) and *Niger Ibos* (1938).

Achebe had his primary education at Ogidi (his father's village, where Achebe now resides) and Nekede, Owerri, where he won the Owerri Province scholarship to study at Government College, Umuahia, one of the premier secondary schools in colonial Nigeria. Among his classmates were Christopher Okigbo (a poet and Achebe's close friend, who gave his life in the Nigerian civil war), Okey Achike, Bede Okigbo, Chukwuemeka Ike, and Chu Okongwu, all of whom became prominent figures in Nigerian public life.

In 1948, Achebe entered University College, Ibadan, then a constituent college of the University of London, as a member of the first group of students to attend the newly founded college. (The school is now the University of Ibadan.) Originally he was intent on reading science and medicine, but he soon changed to literary studies and received his bachelor of arts in English with honors in 1953. He then held various positions in the Nigerian Broadcasting Corporation—as talks producer in Lagos from 1954 to 1957, as controller in Enugu from 1958 to 1961, and as director of the Voice of Nigeria in Lagos from 1961 to 1966.

While employed full-time as a broadcaster, Achebe was writing with his "left hand," figuratively speaking, as were most of his Nigerian contemporaries who aspired to literary careers. Achebe said in a 1962 interview with Marjorie Whitelaw that his interest in becoming a writer was confirmed when he encountered Joyce Cary's novel *Mister Johnson* (1939) as a student at University College, Ibadan:

> one of the things that probably finally decided me was a novel set in Nigeria by Joyce Cary. I regard him as one of the outstanding British writers of the first part of this century. Now he was in this country as an Administrative Officer during the First World War and he wrote this novel called *Mister Johnson,* which is quite famous, and I feel that it's not—in spite of this man's ability, in spite of his sympathy and understanding, he could not get under the skin of his African. They just did not communicate. And I felt if a good writer could make this mess perhaps we ought to try our hand.

In 1957 he went to London to attend the British Broadcasting Corporation staff school. One of his teachers there was the British novelist and literary critic Gilbert Phelps. Phelps recognized the unique quality of *Things Fall Apart* and recommended it for publication. Achebe has remarked that he never had the experience of the struggling artist. With the publication of *Things Fall Apart* in 1958, Achebe achieved a preeminent position, which he has never relinquished, on the Nigerian literary scene.

His writing, therefore, first received attention because of the social purposes he assigned to it and to himself as writer. *Things Fall Apart* was published two years before Nigerian independence. The timing was superb. For while Africans—Nigerians in this case—looked forward with excitement and optimism to political freedom after more than half a century of colonial rule, Achebe understood the necessity of showing Nigerians the role of their own cultures in the task of nation building. To Achebe this role, as described in his 1964 essay "The Role of the Writer in the New Nation," if not completely lost, had been greatly diminished by the imposition of an alien culture:

> As far as I am concerned the fundamental theme must first be disposed of. This theme — put quite simply — is that African people did not hear of culture for the first time from Europeans; that their societies were not mindless but frequently had a philosophy of great depth and value and beauty, that they had poetry and, above all, they had dignity. It is this dignity that African people all but lost during the colonial period, and it is this that they must now regain. The worst thing that can happen to any people is the loss of their dignity and self-respect. The writer's duty is to help them regain it by showing them in human terms what happened to them, what they lost. . . . Perhaps what I write is applied art as distinct from pure. But who cares? Art is important but so is education of the kind I have in mind.
>
> (p. 160)

For Achebe, *Mister Johnson* represented the worst kind of portrayal of Africans by Europeans. The portrayal was all the more disheartening because Cary was working hard to achieve an accurate depiction, unlike many British authors during the imperial-colonial period who deliberately, often cynically, exploited stereotypes of Africans and African society. It was precisely because Cary was a liberal-minded and sympathetic writer, as well as a colonial administrator, that Achebe felt the record had to be set straight.

Achebe's purpose then is to write about and for his own people. His first five novels form a continuum over one hundred years of Igbo civilization. Europeans have not yet penetrated Umuofia, the setting of the first novel, when *Things Fall Apart* begins. When the novel ends colonial rule has been established, significant change has taken place, and the character of the community — its values and

freedoms — has been substantially and irrevocably altered. *Arrow of God* (1964), the third published novel, has much the same setting as *Things Fall Apart* except that colonial rule has been consolidated and the lives of the villagers are completely circumscribed by it. The action of *No Longer at Ease* (1960), the second published novel, takes place in the period immediately before independence from British colonial rule in Nigeria. *A Man of the People* (1966) is located in an unspecified African country that strongly resembles Nigeria in the immediate postindependence period. *Anthills of the Savannah* (1986) examines the consequences of dictatorial military rule in a post–first-republic African country that closely resembles Nigeria, but also suggests the state of affairs in other countries in Africa and in the world.

The novels form the imaginative history, from the perspective of a Christian Igbo, of a group of people in what eventually became Nigeria. At various times Achebe has said that his Christian upbringing was important in his evolution as a writer. In "Named for Victoria, Queen of England," reprinted in *Hopes and Impediments* (1988), he writes:

> I was born in Ogidi in Eastern Nigeria of devout Christian parents. The line between Christian and non-Christian was much more definite in my village 40 years ago than it is today. When I was growing up I remember we tended to look down on the others. We were called in our language "the people of the church" or "the association of God." The others were called . . . the heathen or even "the people of nothing." . . . We lived at the crossroads of cultures. We still do today. . . . On one arm of the cross we sang hymns and read the Bible night and day. On the other my father's brother and his family, blinded by heathenism, offered food to idols. . . . What I do remember was a fascination for the ritual and the life on the other arm of the crossroads. And I believe two things were in my favour — that curiosity, and the little distance imposed between me and it by the accident of my birth. The distance becomes

not a separation but a bringing together like the necessary backward step which a judicious viewer may take to see a canvas steadily and fully.

(p. 23)

Achebe describes the duality in his experience of the religious traditions of his people, viewed from a "little distance." He later detected in the Igbo religion the Christian rituals that shaped his upbringing. This recognition has shaped his art and might be said to be its controlling metaphor. He writes in his essay "The Igbo World and Its Art" (1988):

> The Igbo world is an arena for the interplay of forces. It is a dynamic world of movement and flux....In some cultures an individual may worship one of the gods or goddesses in the pantheon and pay scant attention to the rest. In Igbo religion such selectiveness would be unthinkable. All the people must placate all the gods all the time! For there is a cautionary proverb which states that even when a person has satisfied Udo completely he may be killed by Ogwugwu! The degree of peril propounded by this proverb is only dimly apprehended until one realises that Ogwugwu is Udo's loving consort.

(p. 42)

Given Achebe's purposes as an artist—his duty to the art and the social purposes he intends it to serve—his sensibility is distinctly Igbo, despite any correspondences one might identify between his sensibility and that of artists in other places and cultures. His art reflects the endless permutations of the essential duality of Igbo life. The connection between this worldview and artistic irony is apparent. Achebe's art is essentially ironic; his irony, which ranges from simple to profound, stems from the ambiguities implicit in the duality of Igbo culture and thus differs from that of writers from purely literary cultures. While their uses of irony are cultivated, Achebe's is instinctive: it is generated from the substance of the culture and inseparable from it.

THINGS FALL APART

Things Fall Apart (1958) displays a complex irony, which has exercised its critics and therefore ensures its enduring character. Conceived first as a story of the lives of three men in a family over three generations—of Okonkwo, Nwoye (who becomes Isaac), and Obi Okonkwo—the novel was to be divided into three parts. Eventually, two of the parts were expanded into two novels to tell Okonkwo's story (in *Things Fall Apart*) and Obi Okonkwo's (in *No Longer at Ease*). Nwoye's story has never been told, although interesting speculative articles on that life have been published by literary critics and scholars.

Achebe has spoken of the problems he faced while writing *Things Fall Apart*. There was the purely practical obstacle of finding time to write in the midst of a busy professional life. But there were also more profound difficulties. To set straight the record propounded about Nigerian life by Europeans and to establish in fictional form the validity of Africa's cultural heritage and what he described in "The Role of the Writer in the New Nation" as its "philosophy of great depth and value and beauty" (p. 160), he had to find out in more detail what that philosophy was, and of what consisted its depth, value, and beauty. His most difficult and elusive goal, however, was to discover the appropriate form and language for his fictional evocations.

As Achebe admits in "Named for Victoria, Queen of England," he largely "picked up" the history of his society: "This was the life that interested me, partly the life I lived and the life that was lived around me, supported by what I heard in conversation—I was very keen on listening to old people—and what I learned from my father, so it was sort of picked up here and there" (p. 22). It is very likely, as Robert Wren has shown in *Achebe's World* (1980), that Achebe had read the writing of colonial administrators and missionaries. He had certainly read the quasi-anthropological treatises of Basden. Basden's opinions were widely known and accepted—even by some of Achebe's own people, including his father. As a result, Achebe felt the need to absorb these opinions into his conception of his role as an artist. Like Cary's, presumably, Basden's heart was in the right place, and because he was sincere and earnest his woefully wrong-headed interpretations of Igbo customs could not go unchallenged. He was, ineluctably, one of those writers who contributed to the "almost complete disaster for the black races... the warped mental attitudes of both black and white...the traumatic experience [that] possesse[d] the sensibility," which was the legacy of Africa's long encounter with Europe.

But while Achebe conceived his role as partly that of teacher—"perhaps what I write is applied art as distinct from pure. But who cares?"—he is not a preacher. In an unpublished interview with Arthur Ravenscroft, Achebe said:

> I'm very fully aware and fully conscious of the dangers of idealization. . . . I bend over backwards to paint in all the unsavoury, all the unfavourable aspects of that culture. Because what I think I am is a kind of witness and I think I would not be doing justice to my cause if I could be faulted on the matter of truth.

In this passage Achebe reconciles two impulses: his authorial methods and craftsmanship belie the nonchalance of his comment on applied as distinct from pure art, and the implied paradox—that for the application to be fully effective the art must be consummate—is resolved.

Things Fall Apart tells the tragic story of the rise and fall of Okonkwo and the equally tragic story of the disintegration of Igbo culture, symbolized by the agrarian society of Umuofia, under the relentless encroachments of British Christian imperialism. Okonkwo embodies the qualities most valued by his people, if in exaggerated form—energy, a strong sense of purpose, and a sense of communal cooperativeness, which at the same time is marked by strong individuality. Both Okonkwo and his society are also marked by a degree of rigidity and inflexibility, which ultimately accounts for their destruction.

In portraying the complexities of the psychological makeup of Okonkwo and of the mores of the clan, Achebe is able to show at the same time the civility, dignity, and orderliness of the society and the rigidity that make it impossible for the clan to adapt to the inevitable changes wrought by the more powerful imported culture. *Things Fall Apart* is therefore both an apostrophe to and a lament for the past as well as a fictional evocation of the inevitability of historical change.

Achebe works out the ontological meaning of his story through the life of Okonkwo. Okonkwo's life is "dominated by fear, the fear of failure and weakness" (p. 9). He has achieved wealth and fame, a household of wives and children, and membership in the highest council of the clan by the strength of his will, his back, and his arms. When the novel begins his fame is at its zenith, and having survived calamities that would have broken lesser men, he believes he can survive anything. In metaphysical terms, and in accordance with the beliefs of the clan, Okonkwo's success is attributed to his *chi*. In the concept of the *chi* Achebe secures the philosophical basis of the novel and reveals the essential duality of Igbo beliefs. The *chi*, as described by the Ghanaian writer and critic Kofi Awoonor in *The Breast of the Earth* (1975), "is a personal god or man's deital expression, the ultimate mission brought by man from the creator's house, a deity that makes each man's unique personality or being" (pp. 256–260). But the *chi*, while a dominating force, is also an ambiguous one. The *chi* embodies the duality of Igbo belief: the *chi* can say "yes" and it can say "no," and the success or failure of a person's life is seen in the ways in which the *chi* responds to his or her actions. Okonkwo's rise and fall are seen in the significant way in which he challenges his *chi* to battle.

Things Fall Apart is in three parts. The first part reveals a homogeneous society, not without its inner tensions and conflicts, both personal and communal, but one that conducts its affairs according to codes of religious and political beliefs supported by custom. The thirteen chapters of the first part present the Umuofian agricultural year: the planting and harvest, the celebrations at the harvest's close, the affairs of prominent citizens and their families, and especially the life in Okonkwo's compound—the relations between Okonkwo's son, Nwoye, and the young hostage, Ikemefuna, who is eventually sacrificed to the gods and murdered by Okonkwo. The conclusion to the first part focuses on the crisis in Okonkwo's life, which is brought about by his accidental shooting of a clansman and culminates in his seven-year banishment to his mother's village.

The second part takes place in Mbanta and describes the coming of the white man. Colonial government and the Christian religion establish themselves, bringing about major changes. On a personal level, for example, Nwoye defects to the Christians. Furthermore, the introduction of a cash economy destabilizes the traditional balance between the acquisitive and spiritual aspects of society. Okonkwo witnesses but is unable to rationalize the inevitable processes of historical change.

In the third part Okonkwo returns to Umuofia, and Achebe brings the novel swiftly to a close. When a python, the embodiment of a sacred spirit, is killed by a Christian convert, the villagers burn the Christian church in reprisal. The district officer summons Okonkwo and other village elders on the pretext of wanting to find a way to settle the differences between the opposing factions. Instead he puts them in jail in irons. For Okonkwo there is nothing left to do but fight. He kills a government messenger, and when he sees that he is not supported by his clansmen, he hangs himself, ironically achieving what he had sought all his life to avoid: an abominable death.

The final paragraph of the novel reveals an irony of a different kind. The dangling body of Okonkwo is merely an "undignified detail" (p. 147) to the district officer who is planning to write a book called *The Pacification of the Tribes of the Lower Niger*. In this book Okonkwo's story will make only an incidental detail.

ENGLISH LANGUAGE

Achebe sustains meaning in the novel through his consummate control over the material. His use of the English language is appropriate to all of the moods and modes of the story and makes it completely convincing. Achebe demonstrates his thesis in his essay "English and the African Writer" (1965):

> The price a world language must be prepared to pay is submission to many different kinds of use. The African writer should aim to use English in a way that brings out his message best without altering the language to the extent that its value as a medium of international exchange will be lost. He should aim at fashioning out an English which is at once universal and able to carry his peculiar experience.
>
> (p. 29)

Achebe's opinions, and those of other African writers, most notably Wole Soyinka and Ngũgĩ wa Thiong'o, have occasioned a continuing controversy on the problems related to the choice and use of non-African languages for African literature, what the Nigerian literary scholar and critic Abiola Irele calls a "radical anomaly" (1981, pp. 54–57). The controversy has its origins in the opinions expressed by a 1962 gathering of a group called African Writers of English Expression at Makerere University College located in Kampala, Uganda. In response to these opinions the Nigerian critic Obiajunwa Wali published in the year following the gathering a provocative article titled "The Dead-End of African Literature" (*Transition*, Kampala, September 1963), in which he contends that African literature as defined and understood by the delegates to the Makerere conference would lead nowhere. African writing in English, Wali believes, would "[lack] any blood and stamina and [have] no means of self-enrichment." An outward-looking approach to an internal phenomenon represents "a dead end, which can only lead to sterility, uncreativity, and frustration." In Wali's view, "any true African literature must be written in African languages" (pp. 13, 14). Wali's views have retained currency, although Wali himself has long since disappeared from the literary scene.

Achebe acknowledges the importance of a writer's mother tongue—and has demonstrated in print and public readings of his Igbo verse the power of his mother tongue—and the contradictions inherent in writing African literature in non-African languages. He admits in "African Literature as Restoration of Celebration" that "writing in the language of my coloniser" might be "acquiescing in the ultimate dispossession" (pp. 7–8). But he argues that, given the arbitrary nature of present-day African countries as defined historically by the colonizing powers, African literature cannot be defined monodimensionally because it is the sum total of all the national and ethnic literatures of Africa. Early in his career Achebe wrote in "English and the African Writer" that "there are not many countries in Africa today where you could abolish the language of the erstwhile colonial powers and still retain the facility for mutual communication" (p. 28). Later in his career his position remained the same:

My position is that anyone who feels unable to write in English should of course follow his desires. But he must not take liberties with our history. It is simply not true that the English forced us to learn their language. On the con-

trary British colonial policy in Africa and elsewhere emphasised again and again its preference for native languages.... We chose English not because the British desired it but because having tacitly accepted the new nationalities into which colonialism had grouped us, we needed its language to transact our business, including the business of overthrowing colonialism itself in the fullness of time.

("African Literature as Restoration of Celebration," p. 8)

Things Fall Apart, like Achebe's third novel, *Arrow of God*, is an account of colonial history told in the language of the colonizer, but from the point of view of the colonized: the perspective is African ontology instead of Eurocentric historiography. That ontology led to a novel that explores the philosophical principles of an African community, unique and autonomous at the outset. The discussion, direct and inferred, does not have the depth of *Arrow of God*, for which reason Achebe returned to the theme in his third book.

NO LONGER AT EASE

Achebe's second published novel, *No Longer at Ease* (1960), is the personal story of Okonkwo's grandson, Obi Okonkwo. Obi is the first from his village to achieve an overseas education, with help from the village and its representatives, the Umuofia Progressive Union, in Lagos, which was then Nigeria's capital. The villagers have taxed themselves to provide Obi's education and expect repayment in various forms, including cash and the influence Obi will be able to wield in a government job. That Obi has studied English in London is a disappointment to the village seniors, who had hoped he would study law, but they are mollified to some extent when he obtains an appointment as secretary to the government's scholarship board. He sets out with high principles and resolves not to succumb to the burgeoning corruption in administrative and political circles in the country. But very quickly he falls into debt: he must repay his loan to the Umuofia Progressive Union; he must send money to his parents to meet some of their expenses; he must provide school fees for his younger siblings; he indulges in an extravagant lifestyle; he rents a flat that reflects his social and professional status, and he buys a car that is more expensive than he can afford.

His life is further complicated by his love for Clara, who is an *osu*, or an outcast, because she is a descendant of cult slaves within the Igbo community. His friends and the Umuofia Progressive Union disapprove of this liaison. His mother threatens to kill herself if he marries Clara.

Pressures mount on Obi. As his intellectual and moral opposition to bribery collapses, he succumbs to the corruption he once despised. He is charged with accepting bribes and put on trial.

This is where the novel begins, and it becomes an examination of the question posed at the outset of the book: "How a young man of your education and brilliant promise could have done this?" (p. 2). Obi's story, told as flashbacks from Chapter 2 onward, is set in the years immediately before Nigeria gained independence from British colonial rule. One would have expected that optimism would be in the air and that someone with Obi's youth, education, and professed idealism would represent that spirit. To some extent this is the case, as revealed in discussions among Obi and his friends, Christopher and Joseph, to consider the implications and possibilities inherent in the impending transfer of political power.

The story of Obi is worked out, however, in terms of a contemporary tragedy described by Obi himself with ironic foreshadowing: "Real tragedy is never resolved. It goes on hopelessly forever. Conventional tragedy is too easy. The hero dies and we feel a purging of the emotions. A real tragedy takes place in a corner, in an untidy spot, to quote W. H. Auden. The rest of the world is unaware of it" (p. 36).

Achebe examines a number of related problems in the novel, which are encompassed in the implications of the title of the novel, taken from T. S. Eliot's poem "The Journey of the Magi":

> . . .
> We returned to our places, these Kingdoms,
> But no longer at ease here, in the old
>   dispensation,
> With an alien people clutching their gods.
> I should be glad of another death.

The quotation suggests Obi's deracinated state. But in fact everyone in the novel suffers in some degree from a confusion of values as they try to accommodate themselves to a new, material culture where traditional verities have given way to the complexities of modern life.

Obi's problem is that he approaches everything from an intellectual position; he is given to discourse and relies heavily on western literary allusions to define his position and to account for phenomena he observes. In choosing allusions from western literature to describe local Nigerian circumstances, Obi distances himself from aspects of his society that he claims to be concerned about. Because of this attitude, his moral positions are incapable of withstanding the pressure of being tested. While he takes intellectually defensible positions with reference to corruption, to Clara and his parents' response to his determination to marry her, and to his various professional and personal obligations, he is not able to follow through. He is alienated from tradition and unable to reconcile the contending forces in the modern world.

The fragmented world in which Obi and the other characters find themselves is a result of the process initiated in *Things Fall Apart*. There are contradictions everywhere. The spiritual duality of traditional Igbo life has been replaced by a crass and debased form. With *Things Fall Apart*, Achebe aims to show his society what it had lost as a result of colonial rule. In *No Longer at Ease* he shows his society what it has gained.

The gain, however, turns out to be a terrible loss, as the story of Obi Okonkwo reveals. Through Obi's experiences—with the examinations board, Clara, his parents, and his friends (Christoper, Joseph, and the Honorable Sam Okoli)—Achebe examines the concerns that make up the new Nigeria on the eve of its independence. The story is of Obi's tragedy, but it is also about the tragedy of the society. It is a story of accommodation to materialism, bribery, and moral confusion. The society strives to discover a new modus vivendi. Only individual contracts are struck in this self-interested world. The duality of the Igbo world assumes a new and discredited form in the secular, not the spiritual, world. There is no attempt to accommodate the forces of the spiritual world by recognizing that every moral position has its implied opposite. Rather, the new secular recognition posits that an action may be wrong, and by participating in this action one may discredit oneself, but only if one is caught in the act.

The revelations of the book proceed from Obi's discussions with his friends, his experiences in his job and social life, and his introspections. The focus of the book and its structure is on Obi in thought and action (or inaction). The topics discussed include politics and the possibilities of independence; morality, with bribery at the center of the discussion; religion, or at least the influence of Christianity in a modified form, which determines and undermines Obi's relations with Clara; and materialism as opposed to morality and in connection with bribery. Meditation on these issues not only shapes Obi but also destroys him.

What stands out in this confusion of values is the certitude with which each representative member of the society holds a particular view. The harmony characteristic of the councils of Umuofia is no longer apparent, particularly not in the heterogeneous society of Lagos.

Talk, which produced collective decision and agreement in Okonkwo's time in *Things Fall Apart*, is now merely talk for its own sake.

On his return from London, Obi is expected to use impressive speech when he addresses the Umuofia Progressive Union; substance does not matter. Talk among the Umuofian elders, whom Obi meets on his first visit home from abroad, is invidious: it consists of comparisons between Obi and his illustrious grandfather, a specious comparison as it turns out. When Obi and Christopher discuss the question of the morality associated with accepting bribes, their conversation is intellectual: "If the applicant is getting the job, anyway, there is no harm in accepting money from him. . . . No man wants to part with his money. If you accept money from a man you make him poorer. But if you go to bed with a girl who asks for it, I don't see that you've done any harm" (p. 111).

Moral compromise is everywhere. The president of the Umuofian Progressive Union says, "I am against people reaping where they have not sown. But we have a saying that if you want to eat a toad you should look for a fat juicy one" (p. 5). The proverbs cited to support conventional morality have become debased and reflect how far collective morality sustains current corruption.

The irresoluteness of society is reflected at a more elevated level in Obi's musings on questions of leadership:

"Where does one begin? With the masses. Educate the masses?" He shook his head. "Not a chance there. It would take centuries. A handful of men at the top. Or even one man with vision—an enlightened dictator. People are scared of the word nowadays. But what kind of democracy can exist side by side with so much corruption and ignorance?" When Obi's reasoning reached this point he reminded himself that England had been as corrupt not so long ago. He was not really in the mood for consecutive reasoning. His mind was impatient to roam in a more pleasant landscape.

(p. 40)

Obi's irresoluteness — which accounts, in a more profound form, for his ultimate disgrace — is a reflection of the society at large and of his refusal or inability to face up to the issue, as these musings suggest. One cannot look to the nonchalant intellectual or, if the Honorable Sam Okoli is typical, to the new breed of politicians for much help, caught up as they are with personal enhancement in a material world.

All of Achebe's novels are ironic, but their narrative mode depends on the effect he wishes to create. Okonkwo's and Ezeulu's stories in *Things Fall Apart* and *Arrow of God*, respectively, are linear narratives that move patiently forward in time despite Achebe's use of analysis to flesh out past actions that affect the narrative at specific points. The ironic effect is cumulative, and no final solutions are recommended to the problems posed in the books. That is Achebe's point. History does not offer solutions. Whatever happens to individual characters — and Achebe has said that he is primarily interested in the life that fails, because a certain grandeur is possible in the individual's response to an event that overtakes and overwhelms him — history demands adjustment in forms ranging from the quiescent to the cataclysmic.

In *No Longer at Ease*, however, there is a final solution: Obi's damnation. The ironic effect is achieved through retrospective narration. The novel begins with Obi on trial for crimes committed, and the trial ends with Obi's conviction on the charges. Furthermore, the crimes with which Obi is charged are recounted late in the novel, and the last four pages bring about a swift conclusion. Achebe is concerned with showing how it is that a young man of such brilliant promise could waste his chances so blatantly. All of the events in the novel lead up to and then away from Obi's crucial recognition that "his mind was troubled...by the discovery that there was nothing in him with which to challenge...honestly" (p. 124) the moral dilemmas in which he finds himself.

In part this recognition grows out of his relationships with Clara and his parents. Because Clara was born into a family of traditional cult slaves, she is unacceptable as a wife to Obi. Joseph warns Obi that he will offend the traditions and beliefs of the clan if he marries her. Obi attempts to brazen it out and believes that he might gain his mother's approval. But his mother states that if he marries Clara she will kill herself. Despite the rationalized hopes he has entertained to this point, when Obi hears this his resolve collapses. He sees Clara through a nasty abortion and then deserts her. Ironically, his mother dies at about the same time. He now sees his life as "sheer humbug" (p.141) and has nothing to sustain him. His life becomes the tragedy worked out "in an untidy spot." He is consigned to ignominy.

Moreover, with the death of his mother Obi discovers that the literary formulas of his life are insufficient. He no longer finds consolation in the poetry of A. E. Housman, which had formerly sustained him. He symbolically abandons his ideals by destroying the nationalistic "Hymn to Nigeria," which he had written in London. Obi is in new moral territory. At once he begins to abandon the practical expression of those ideals. The chief result of the crisis in Obi's life is that it makes him examine critically for the first time the mainspring of his actions. In doing so he uncovers a good deal that he could only regard as "sheer humbug."

Obi's tears, which betray him at the outset of the novel as the trial begins, remain the sole remnant of his moral awareness. Not everything is "sheer humbug" as he thought he had found out. While his tragedy may lack grandeur, it is more than merely untidy. The tears indicate an awareness of personal potential greater than has been realized, and Obi, because of that awareness, is left to live with his abnegation forever.

The significance of the title of the novel, taken from Eliot's "Journey of the Magi," has been noted by many critics. In this poem Eliot expresses his belief that the past is defined not only by its pastness, but also by its present-ness. Achebe annexes this notion and exemplifies it in the story of Obi: the inevitable and inexorable historical forces set in motion in *Things Fall Apart* continue into the present; awareness of the past helps not to resolve ambiguities and anomalies but rather to complicate them further. The anarchy that is unleashed upon the earth becomes more anarchic. Moreover, the dim possibilities for resolution in the future, as illustrated by the fate that overtakes Obi or that he brings upon himself through his failure to resolve these anomalies, suggest that this anarchy will compound itself in the future.

ARROW OF GOD

Achebe returns, however, to the past in his third novel, *Arrow of God* (1964), which is possibly the consummate fictional depiction of the colonial period in Nigerian history because all of the novelistic elements are supremely integrated. Here Achebe evokes a world much like that of Okonkwo's in *Things Fall Apart*, but more dynamic and comprehensively detailed. It is a world redolent of the complexities of daily domestic, social, political, and religious life, but further complicated by the religious and political proscriptions that the colonial force has introduced to and institutionalized in Igbo society. *Arrow of God* "goes back to the past, not as remotely as [*Things Fall Apart* because] I've learned to think that my first book is no longer adequate. I've learned a lot more about these particular people...my ancestors" (interview by Nkosi, p. 20). The dynamics of the lives of the people of Umuaro are rendered in vivid detail to display the tragedy of Ezeulu, the chief priest of Ulu and the spiritual and political leader of his people.

The novel is a meditation on the nature and uses of power and on the responsibility of the person who wields it. Ezeulu engages in a power struggle with both the people of his village and the officers of the British Political Service. Always sensitive to the source of his power because of the reasons it was given to him, Ezeulu must try to reconcile the contending impulses in his nature, on the one hand, to serve the needs of his own people as their protecting deity and, on the other, to attain greater personal power by pushing his authority to its limits. His tragedy arises from an attempt to reconcile these contending impulses.

The novel is situated at a moment in which Ezeulu must attempt to resolve this dilemma between public service and personal ambition. Ezeulu is jailed at the British administrative headquarters because he has refused a position in the colonial administration as a warrant chief. During his period of imprisonment two new moons pass and the two sacred yams remain uneaten. The eating of the yams is the event that determines the rhythm of the seasons and announces the harvest. Despite the warm welcome accorded him on his return to the village, Ezeulu decides to wait to eat the two yams and thus delays the harvest. New yams rot in the ground, and the clan is faced with a famine. Ezeulu wrestles with his conscience, seeking to respond to his people's need to harvest their annual food supply and yet determined to honor his god by observing and defending absolute custom. He makes the wrong choice. Achebe displays the social and psychological processes that bring down the priest-leader and his god.

Ezeulu is regarded by the clan as half-man, half-god, but as Achebe has said, "we make the gods we worship." Ezeulu recognizes this and has persistent cause to meditate on the nature of his power:

> Whenever Ezeulu considered the immensity of his power over the year and the crops and, therefore, over the people he wondered if it was real. It was true he named the day for the feast of Pumpkin Leaves and the New Yam feast; but he did not choose the day. He was merely a watchman.... No! the Chief Priest of Ulu was more than that. If he should refuse to name the

day there would be no festival—no planting and no reaping. But could he refuse? No Chief Priest had ever refused. So it could not be done. He would not dare.

(pp. 3–4)

As well as offering a statement of the ambiguous nature of the priest's powers, this passage presages the way in which the events in the novel will unfold. Ezeulu's consideration of his powers becomes more than mere speculation. With the presence of the white man, which Ezeulu recognizes as an influence that will alter and reshape his society, Ezeulu is determined that he will understand this influence and turn it to his own profit (and that of the villages). One of the ways he seeks to achieve this is by sending his son Oduche to the Christian mission school. Although his motives are misconstrued by Chief Nwaka and Ezeulu's rival priest, Ezidemili, Ezeulu is acting out of concern for the clan, and his motives are political: "I want one of my sons to join these people and be my eye there.... My spirit tells me that those who do not befriend the white man today will be saying *had we known* tomorrow" (p. 55).

Nevertheless, his motives are not entirely disinterested. For while he seeks to understand and accommodate the power of the new, imposed regime in order to understand and convert it to the use of the clan, he also seeks to exploit the knowledge for personal use. Likewise, although he delays his eating of the ceremonial yams ostensibly to serve the injunctions of his religion, in fact he does so to castigate his community and bring it to heel. His clearheaded judgments about the changing nature of the political climate in which the clan exists—his assessment of the broader perspective—are compromised by his personal bitterness. His anger supersedes his judgment and prevails despite the warning he receives that the will of the clan—who had created Ulu in the first place—was greater than the will of the god, that when a god gets out of hand the people can "show him the wood he is made of." The community ex-

presses its will: "I said go and eat those yams today, not tomorrow; and if Ulu says we have committed an abomination let it be on the heads of the ten of us here" (p. 260).

Ezeulu ignores their injunction. He is curiously—and ironically—unresponsive to the characteristic flexibility of his people in adjusting to new situations, despite his own announced intention of calculating and adjusting to the effects of the new religion and system of government that have been imposed. The antagonism between factions within the clan is exacerbated by Ezeulu's seeming alliance with the colonial authority, which he has established for purposes of increasing his power over the clan. The irony is that the renewed rivalry between the two priests that threatens to divide the clan is rendered obsolete by the consequences of Ezeulu's decision to castigate the clan by refusing to announce the harvest. In the face of a famine the clan turns to the Christian mission for succor and large numbers of the villagers defect to the Christian fold.

Ezeulu's eventual madness results from his own rationalization of his responsibility, the nature of his power, and his decision to follow the wrong course of action. He is the author of his own destiny, but the British authority is an agent in his destiny. Achebe explores the relationship between the Africans and Europeans in various ways. The crisis in the novel is set up when Ezeulu is perceived by both the people of his village and by Captain Winterbottom, a colonial administrator, to support the British administration in a dispute over a piece of land. As a result of this perception, when Winterbottom is compelled by his masters in administrative headquarters to appoint a warrant chief he decides to appoint Ezeulu. Ezeulu refuses the offer, angering the British and confusing his own people. Ezeulu is incarcerated and released two months later only after colonial policy is changed and warrant chieftaincies are abandoned. His villagers are confused because Ezeulu has repudiated his assumed friendship with "Winterbotta." Thus they fear reprisals, which materialize when Ezeulu does not eat the sacred yams and his tragedy unfolds.

Ezeulu fails because his action jeopardizes the welfare of his community through starvation. Personal motives become entangled with public, political, and religious motives. The Igbo aphorism "No man however great can win a judgment against the clan" is proven true in Ezeulu's destruction. In other words, he fails to integrate the present circumstances with his traditional priestly role. In the end the collective will, the villagers' determination to survive, prevails. Survival is more important than ritual. The god created to secure the tribe against threats to its existence is abandoned when he becomes, paradoxically, a threat to the clan's existence. Ezeulu, the carrier of the clan's burdens, is now seen as the cause of the famine. Where he once walked proudly at the head of his clan, he now walks alone. To the end he is convinced that he has followed the will of his god: "Why, he asked himself again and again, why had Ulu chosen to deal thus with him, to strike him down and cover him with mud? What was his offence? Had he not divined the god's will and obeyed it?" (p. 286).

In a statement that explains the wide and profound implications of the common theme in his novels, Achebe said in a 1971 interview with Robert Serumaga:

In the society we have been looking at in the story you do not do things in the name of the son but in the name of father. The legitimacy is with the ancestors, with tradition and age. We now have a new dispensation in which youth and inexperience [gain] a new legitimacy.... They are going to go to school, to go to church, and will tell their fathers what it is. This almost amounts to turning the world upside down. I think that Ezeulu himself sensed it coming.... This was confirmed the first time he was interviewed by the English administrator Clarke, and Ezeulu looked up and the image in his mind was that of a puppy, something unfinished, half-baked, too young; and yet there

was authority. Now, this reversal itself is tied up with the colonial situation. There is no other situation in the world where power resides with inexperience and young people.... But in the colonial situation [a young man] is given power and he can order a chief around. In a very deep sense this reversal is the quintessence of colonialism. It is a loss of independence.

A MAN OF THE PEOPLE

The consequences of the loss of predictable political power in a village are one thing; at the national level, they are quite different. Achebe turns to this latter issue in his fourth novel, *A Man of the People* (1966), which is set in the postcolonial period in an unnamed independent African country. The governance of the country is, nominally, in the hands of the people. The quality of the leadership and the response of the people to that leadership are the central theme. There is neither collective will in the people nor responsible leadership. Moreover, a collective voice at the village level, through which agreement is articulated in *Things Fall Apart* and *Arrow of God*, no longer exists.

Chief Nanga—the "man of the people"—and his colleagues, senior ministers of government, and their rivals in other political parties have produced what Achebe describes as a "fat-dripping, gummy, eat-and-let-eat regime." The novel depicts an atmosphere of material acquisitiveness unrestrained by traditional religious concerns in the midst of political corruption, where there is no national voice but only (we infer) a confusion of competing village voices. The novel is a first-person retrospective narrative by Odili. At first wholly cynical about the political leadership of the country, Odili, a schoolteacher in his own village, keeps a scornful distance from any political activity. Odili had once placed his faith in university-trained public-minded leaders who believed that through their education and actions they would develop an economically viable and politically stable unified nation in the postcolonial period. But political opportunists, of whom Nanga is a prominent example, have ensured that high-minded, disinterested, well-educated leaders are discredited in order to increase their personal fortunes at the expense of the public purse.

Odili's sole motive is to win a scholarship for study abroad and to abandon his country. But Nanga, his former teacher at the same school, pays a visit, remembers Odili, and offers him assistance in obtaining the coveted scholarship. Odili is swept away by Nanga's charisma and for a time sits at the feet of the political master. Achebe exhibits his narrative control, which allows Odili's current experience and retrospective account to meld perfectly:

> I had felt, like so many other educated citizens of our country, that things were going seriously wrong without being able to say just how. We complained about our country's lack of dynamism and abdication of leadership to which it was entitled in the continent, or so we thought. We listened to the whispers of scandalous deals in high places — sometimes involving sums of money that I for one didn't believe existed in the country. But there was really no hard kernel of fact to get one's teeth into. But sitting at Nanga's feet I received enlightenment; many things began to crystallize out of the mist — some of the emergent forms were not nearly as ugly as I had suspected but many seemed much worse. However, I was not making these judgments at the time, or not strongly anyhow. I was simply too fascinated by the almost ritual lifting of the clouds, as I had been one day, watching for the first time the unveiling of the white dome of Kilimanjaro at sunset.
>
> (p. 45)

This is the first stage in the reeducation of Odili. Under Nanga's sway he reexamines some of his attitudes toward the uses of political power and begins to question the reactions between political idealism and the practical application of political beliefs. However, Odili's amicable relationship with Nanga comes to an end when Nanga steals Odili's mistress, Elsie. The hostility between the two characters that results moves the novel into its second part. Odili plans to seduce Edna, Nanga's "parlour wife," to avenge his manhood. He joins a new political party, the Common People's Convention Party, founded by his friend Max Kumalo. Initially Edna is the primary target, and politics is a secondary concern: according to Odili, politics "would add a second string to my bow." But as Odili engages in an election struggle, prompted by a political-economic scandal that brings down the government, his motives gradually shift. He probes more deeply into the political reality in relation to his own motives and into the possibility of creating a just system of government within the heterogeneous groupings of ethnic interests that make up the nation.

Achebe examines this possibility in various ways and through sometimes seemingly disconnected scenes. A leitmotiv that displays the erosion of communal values in the novel is the story of Josiah, a village trader. Josiah is so corrupt that early in the novel he steals a blind beggar's walking stick. The villagers scorn him, and a boycott ruins his store. Collective communal will is asserted to right a wrong because, in the words of a proverb, "Josiah has taken away enough for the owner to notice." Josiah reappears at a critical juncture in Odili's campaign against Nanga. Odili has scorned Josiah's offer of support, and when Odili appears at Nanga's election rally in the village in order to denounce the latter's corruption, Josiah, who is now acting as a supporter of Nanga, denounces Odili. As a result Odili is beaten by Nanga's bodyguards and is in the hospital when civil order breaks down entirely. Political leaders are assassinated, fighting breaks out between the bodyguards of various contending political factions, and the prime minister appoints a new cabinet. Finally thuggish anarchy becomes so extreme that the military intervenes and locks up the government.

Accounting for the fall of the regime, Odili's father says: "Koko [a political leader] had taken enough for the owner to see." But for Odili this is not satisfactory:

> My father's words struck me because they were the very same words the villagers of Anata had spoken of Josiah, the abominated trader. Only in their case the words had meaning. The owner was the village, and the village had a mind; it could say no to sacrilege. But in the affairs of the nation there was no owner, the laws of the village became powerless.
>
> (p. 166)

The strength of the book's argument — that mere anarchy has replaced the laws of the village — stems from the growing tension in the relationship between Odili and Nanga. Nanga is an engaging and credible character: this is what makes his apostasy so terrifying. Achebe leaves the novel open-ended: an impasse in the political system has been reached and military intervention is plainly not a viable solution to the problems of political governance.

However, the novel is about more than public political life in a postindependence African state. It is also about Odili's self-analysis within the public political context. Fresh out of university Odili sought to become "a full member of the privileged class whose symbol was the car" (p. 122). As he engages in political activities, aware that by hiring bodyguards and using party funds to buy a car he is in danger of compromising his idealism, he begins to sort out his real motives. First he recognizes that he wants Edna for herself and not as some avatar of revenge. He then comes to the conclusion regarding his election battle that "although I had little hope of winning Chief Nanga's seat, it was nonetheless necessary to fight and expose him as much as possible" (p. 155). Odili's self-analysis is complete when he faces Nanga at the rally. His stance is the reverse of the one he subscribed to at the beginning of the novel. After his political transformation Odili vows "never to be corrupted by bourgeois privileges of which the car was the most visible symbol" (p. 122).

Selfless public dedication has replaced cynical distanced disillusionment.

A Man of the People completes a tetralogy of novels that reveal the changes wrought in Nigerian life during the twentieth century. Against a background of changing and evolving social and political realities, Achebe reveals his concern with individual humanity and with the responses of his characters to the social problems in which they become enmeshed. His interest is in failure, for out of his character's responses to failure new possibilities arise. This is why *A Man of the People* is open-ended. At the close of the novel Odili begins to have a sense of what needs to be done. Odili's discoveries allow for the possibility that a new political attitude will emerge.

A Man of the People is a prophetic novel. Its publication in January 1966 coincided almost exactly with the first military takeover in Nigeria. The worsening political situation in Nigeria led to the persecution of the Igbo people, most notably in Northern Nigeria, where a series of massacres took place. Achebe, who had been director of external broadcasting for the Nigerian Broadcasting Service since 1961, resigned from his appointment and returned to his homeland. The Eastern Region declared itself an independent state, Biafra, in 1967, and shortly after a thirty-month civil war began. Throughout the war Achebe traveled widely to Europe and North America on Biafran affairs. He had neither the time nor inclination to write long fiction during this period. Rather Achebe produced most of the poems that appear in the 1971 volume *Beware, Soul Brother and Other Poems* (later revised and enlarged for its 1973 publication in the United States as *Christmas in Biafra and Other Poems*).

ANTHILLS OF THE SAVANNAH

No one has exposed the dangers of the new imperialism to which Africa seems particularly susceptible more tellingly than Achebe. *Anthills of the Savannah*, published in 1987, takes up the inquiry initiated by *A Man of the People*. The novel is set in the fictional West African country of Kangan, which is ruled by a military governor and a cabinet of civilian ministers, and takes place two years after the military regime has replaced the corrupt civil regime of the earlier novel. Things have gone from bad to worse; political chaos has been replaced with anarchy; cynical self-interested leadership has been replaced with military megalomania.

Achebe's chief concern in this novel, as in some facet of all his writing, is with leadership, with what kind of leaders will best serve the general good, and, more particularly, with the dangers to which leaders expose themselves. Sam/HE the current governor and aspiring president-for-life of Kangan is a creation of other people—"His major flaw was that all he ever wanted to do was what was expected of him" (p. 49). Sam/HE is not qualified to be the head of state; even so he is better than some African tyrants who exhibit a joyless passion for power. As the novel opens Sam is not headed in the direction of Idi Amin (the brutal Ugandan dictator) or Colonel Jean-Bedel Bokassa (the dictator who declared himself emperor of the Central African Republic) and subject to those influences and inducements that shaped them, but he is surrounded by "court jesters" and advised by "mesmerised toadies." After attending a meeting of the Organization of African Unity in Addis Ababa, Ethiopia, where he meets an unnamed character modeled on Haile Selassie, the Ethiopian monarch, and the fictional though archetypal president-for-life, Ngongo, Sam's megalomaniacal dreams of ultimate and enduring power begin; he "sees for the first time the possibility of his drama in the role of an African Head of State and withdraws to prepare his own face and perfect his arts" (p. 53).

Sam/HE and his boyhood friends, Ikem Odosi and Chris Oriko, are prominent in the affairs of the military regime during its closing months. Their friendship of twenty-five years dissolves when HE becomes distrustful of Ikem and Chris because of the advice given to him by President-for-Life Ngongo, which is furthered by HE's attorney general: "Your greatest risk is your boyhood friends, those who grew up with you in your village. Keep them at arm's length and you will live long" (p. 23). Ikem is accused of plotting to overthrow the government after he makes a snide remark before a large public audience about HE's intention to have his face minted on the Kangan currency: "My view is that any serving President foolish enough to lay his head on a coin should know he is inciting people to take it off; the head I mean" (p. 162). Ikem is arrested in the dead of night and murdered by his captors. Chris, who to this point in the narrative has sought a mediating role, reveals the causes of Ikem's murder and is forced into hiding. When fleeing the city, Chris tries to stop a soldier from raping a young woman but is shot and killed by the soldier. He dies as the news of Sam's overthrow is announced to the nation.

References and allusions to "story"—to storytelling, to art, and to writers and writing—are presented in various voices and registers throughout the novel. Furthermore, three of the main characters are writers. Chris writes a "detailed diary of what's happening day to day" and defends the fact that he remains in HE's corrupt cabinet by saying: "I wouldn't be writing this if I didn't hang around to observe it all" (p. 23). At this point his writing is private, and his attitude is cautious. He advises Ikem to adopt a similar stance and publish superficial, distorted, and therefore dishonest accounts of the political issues and events in the *Gazette*. But Ikem, while recognizing the possible futility of his crusading editorials, feels a moral imperative to continue publishing them. For Ikem the role of the writer is "not to marshall facts" but to marshall passion—"Passion is our hope and strength" (p. 160).

When he speaks at the university and engages in a heated question-and-answer session with the students, when he insists that the moral imperative of the writer is to ask questions and to cause questions to be asked, when he asserts that the writer's role is "to give headaches," and when he calls for a "new radicalism" in public life, Ikem provokes HE to fire him as editor of the *Gazette*. Ikem's words inspire the students to question HE's corrupt regime. In another example of how writing drives the action of the novel, Chris uses his connections with the international press to have Ikem's murder reported and to expose HE as his murderer.

Beatrice, Chris's fiancée, is the third writer in the novel. She holds an honors bachelor's degree in English and she writes short stories that Ikem, himself a respected poet, praises for their "muscular" and "masculine" style. Beatrice pieces together, with difficulty, the story of the "unbelievable violences we went through" that appears in the retrospective Chapter 7. Achebe's most powerful female figure, Beatrice is also the central character in the novel. She is closely linked to HE, Ikem, and Chris, and she lives to tell the story of their involvement in—and in the case of Ikem and Chris, their sacrifice to—contemporary history.

Through her association with the legendary Idemili, the daughter of the Almighty who was sent to earth to temper man's power, Beatrice is a link with the past and a protector of its values and concerns. Achebe tells us that Beatrice "did not know these legends and traditions of her people because they played but little part in her upbringing" (p. 105). However, Beatrice is intuitively aware of her dual mythic identity and she undergoes a transformation, indeed transportation, when the goddess possesses her for divine purposes. Beatrice's power as Idemili's avatar is revealed when HE invites, or rather commands, her to attend a dinner at the presidential retreat. Among the guests—"the new power-brokers around his Excellency"—is a special guest, Lou Crandfield, an American journalist who presumes, after several drinks, to tell the president how to run his country. Beatrice assumes the role of avenging goddess and is determined to remind HE of his power but also to prevent him from abusing it:

> I did it shamelessly. I cheapened myself. God! I did it to your glory like the dancer in the Hindu temple. Like Esther, oh yes like Esther for my long suffering people.
>
> And was I glad the king was slowly but surely responding! Was I glad! The big snake, the royal python of a giant erection began to stir in the shrubbery of my shrine as we danced closer to soothing airs, soothing our ancient bruises together in the dimmed lights. Fully aroused he clung desperately to me. And I took him then boldly by the hand and led him to the balcony railings to the breathtaking view of the dark lake from the pinnacle of the hill. And there told him my story of Desdemona. Something possessed me as I told it.
>
> (p. 81)

Achebe, in his recounting of the parable of Idemili's coming to earth—in which she took the form of a pillar of water that fused "earth and heaven at the navel of the dark lake"—equates HE with "a certain man handsome beyond compare but in randiness as unbridled as the odorous he-goat." The man so angers Idemili by flouting her injunctions that she sends her royal python to bar the way to his village. The man, proving himself unworthy of possessing power, soon dies. Achebe presents these myths of the ancestors as having sustaining power in the present. The scene that leads to Achebe's telling of the parable is the last meeting between Beatrice and Ikem. He arrives at her apartment soaking wet: "It was literally like barging into a pillar of rain, you know" (p. 93). Ikem has brought with him a prose poem that he reads to Beatrice. Their conversation then turns to the rights and lives of women in their society and extends further to a discussion of the means and impediments to achieving freedom. Through Ikem, Achebe conveys his beliefs about the complex and often paradoxical elements that shape individual destinies.

Ikem, like Beatrice, is identified with Idemili, the avenger of man's misuse of power. Chris Oriko—his name echoes that of Christopher Okigbo, Achebe's close friend, a poet, and a priest of Idoto (the river goddess and offspring of Idemili), who was killed in the Nigerian civil war—recognizes the mythic dimension of Beatrice's character and her connection with Idemili and Idoto:

> Chris saw the quiet demure damsel whose still waters nonetheless could conceal deep overpowering eddies of passion that always almost sucked him into fatal depths. Perhaps Ikem alone came close to sensing the village priestess who will prophesy when her divinity rides her abandoning if need be her soup-pot on the fire, but returning again when the god departs to the domesticity of the kitchen. . . . He knew it better than Beatrice herself.
>
> (p. 105)

Chris, like Ikem, is found worthy when he puts his life on the line for Ikem's sake. Yet he does not survive; Idemili blesses or destroys without explanation. No man, whatever his earthly power, can feel secure.

Achebe believes in the importance of the traditions and beliefs of the past and the ways in which these may be valuable in tempering the excesses of the present. Circumscribed by a mythic structure, *Anthills of the Savannah* is a political novel and is preeminently about contemporary Nigeria. Achebe's position regarding political ideologies is neither doctrinaire nor simplistic. The core of his analysis of the Nigerian situation is found in Ikem's answers to the questions raised by students at the university meeting, and the targets Ikem identifies as impediments to the creation of a just society are various. Admitting that external factors have a bearing on the conduct of public affairs, Ikem says that "to blame all these things on imperialism and international capitalism as our modish radicals want us to do is, in my view, sheer cant and humbug. . . . It is like going out to arrest the village black-smith every time a man hacks his fellow to death" (p. 159).

The novel ends at an impasse. According to Beatrice's account, the new regime is no better than the one it replaced. History repeats itself once more. But the novel also ends on a note of hope as Ikem's ideas live on through the voice of Emanuel, the disaffected student leader who was with Chris when he died: "It wasn't Ikem the man who changed me. I hardly knew him. It was the ideas he set down on paper. One idea in particular: that we may accept a limitation on our actions but never, under no circumstances, must we accept a restriction on our thinking" (p. 223). Ikem's child, born after his death to his girlfriend, Elewa, and named Amaechina, which means "may the path never close," is another sign of hope at the close of the novel.

A number of the first critical responses to the novel note Achebe's deepening understanding and discipline of skill that confirm his place in the forefront of contemporary writers. However, some felt that Achebe's adoption of a structure more complex than found in his earlier writing and his increased use of pidgin English caused him to lose a part of his international audience. To judge thus is to miss the complexities of the earlier writing and perhaps to miss the point that Achebe is seeking a means, through his use of pidgin, to close the gap between those readers who are educated and those who are not. One problem with leadership that Achebe identifies in *A Man of the People* and reiterates in *Anthills of the Savannah* is that leaders' contact with the people has been all but lost. Achebe's language serves to reestablish that connection.

OTHER WRITINGS

Achebe's other writings include two volumes of short stories, a volume of poetry, four stories for children, and six volumes of critical commentary.

Most of his poems were published in *Beware, Soul Brother and Other Poems* (1971). The poems reveal the physical and spiritual horror of the civil war. The final stories in *Girls at War and Other Stories* (1972) also deal with the obscenities, both physical and spiritual, that accrue from the civil war. Achebe writes, in the preface to the thirteen-story volume, that "it was with something of a shock that I realised my earliest short stories were published as long ago as twenty years in the Ibadan student magazine, *The University Herald*" and that "a dozen pieces in twenty years must be accounted a pretty lean harvest by any reckoning" (p. iii).

Perhaps Achebe is correct in suggesting that the harvest of stories is small. But it is not lean. The stories display his full range as a writer—from the humor and wit of "Uncle Ben's Choice," to the irony in "The Madman," "The Voter," "Akueke," and "Dead Man's Path," to the scathing assault on the final follies of people in the political sphere.

Morning Yet on Creation Day: Essays (1975) contains fifteen essays, written between 1962 and 1973, on various literary and political subjects. The collection is divided into two parts: the first part has eight essays dealing specifically with the role of the African writer in society. The essays in the second part are more personal, although they also have a public application to the conclusions drawn. Of special interest is the essay "*Chi* in Igbo Cosmology" because it helps to explain the *chi* in Achebe's first and third novels. This volume has been superseded by *Hopes and Impediments* (1988), which includes some essays from the earlier volume as well as essays and addresses from the intervening years. Of special note are "The Truth of Fiction" and "What Has Literature Got to Do with It?" The latter is Achebe's address on receiving the Nigerian National Merit Award in 1987 for the second time; he was also, in 1979, the first-ever recipient of this award.

Achebe has been recognized at home and abroad with honorary degrees and visiting academic appointments. He has also been involved in literary activities in Nigeria and abroad. He has continued to comment on the political life of Nigeria in the press and in journals. The question of the kind of leadership that would best serve the country is his primary concern. In 1983, in the face of an impending federal election, he published *The Trouble with Nigeria*, which expounds the thesis that the leadership of Nigeria has failed: "There is nothing basically wrong with the Nigerian character.... Nigerian land or climate or water or air or anything else. The Nigerian problem is the unwillingness or inability of its leaders to rise to the responsibility, to the challenge of personal example which are the hallmarks of true leadership" (p. 1).

Before the election could be held, the military intervened and seized power, and it has been suggested that Achebe's words in part prompted the coup. Whatever the truth of these assertions, he said in an interview with Peter Gzowski:

> You must remember that the book we are talking about was actually published before the election. It was intended to be a kind warning. We are now looking at it as a postmortem, but it was not initially intended to be that. At that point in time I was appealing to this generation of educated Nigerians, the younger Nigerians, to get out of the rut, not to follow what I call the "old performers"...those [who] have by and large decided that it would perhaps take too long to set up their own political structures and that perhaps the quickest thing would be to make use of existing structures through the old masters of the game, and so perhaps change the system from the inside. Now I think we must think again.

CONCLUSION

Achebe continues to be involved in the quest to determine a just system of governance for Nigerians and to focus his thoughts on the role of literature in serving society's needs. In his Nigerian National Merit Award acceptance speech in 1987, he acknowledges that "the comprehensive goal of a developing nation like Nigeria is, of course, development or its somewhat better variant, modernization" and that literature is central to the quest of achieving this goal:

> Literature, whether handed down by word of mouth or in print, gives us a second handle on reality; enabling us to encounter in the safe manageable dimensions of make-believe the very same threats to integrity that may assail the psyche in real life; and at the same time providing through the self-discovery which it imparts, a veritable weapon for coping with these threats whether they are found within our problematic and incoherent selves or in the world around us. What better preparation can a people desire as they begin their journey into the strange, revolutionary world of modernization?
>
> (*Hopes and Impediments*, p. 117)

The nineteenth-century French writer Gustave Flaubert, in one of his letters to Ivan Turgenev, wrote that there was nothing new for the writer to say, but there had to be new ways of saying the old things. Such is not the case with Achebe: the old things that were said about Africa throughout history, things predicated on racism, were not worth saying again; indeed they had to be refuted. Achebe has new and important things to say. And he has found a new way of saying them. He sets the record of history straight: no one can think about Africa in the terms that applied before his first novel was published. He restores his people's faith in themselves and provides a context in which they can express their values and define their goals. Achebe dominates the African novel and has a central place in contemporary literature because he, more than any of his peers, reflectively and unobtrusively has modified the traditions of fiction and derived forms that are distinctively his own for the purpose of envisaging and conveying experience in a deeply convincing

way. Deceptive profundity, discriminating insight, mental and moral fastidiousness, and elegance and lucidity are the hallmarks of Achebe's art.

Selected Bibliography

BIBLIOGRAPHIES

Hanna, S. J. "Achebe: A Bibliography." In *Studies in Black Literature* 1 (1971).

McDaniel, Richard B. "An Achebe Bibliography." In *World Literature Written in English* 20 (1971).

Severac, Alain. "Chinua Achebe: I. Notes biographiques; II. Bibliographie." In *Annales de la faculté des lettres et sciences humaines, Université de Dakar* 2 (1972).

NOVELS

Things Fall Apart. London: Heinemann, 1958; New York: Astor-Honor, 1959; New York: Anchor Books, 1994.

No Longer at Ease. London: Heinemann Educational, 1960; New York: I. Obolensky, 1961; New York: Anchor Books, 1994.

Arrow of God. London: Heinemann, 1964; New York: John Day, 1967; New York: Anchor Books, 1989.

A Man of the People. London: Heinemann, 1966; New York: John Day, 1966; New York: Anchor Books, 1989.

Anthills of the Savannah. London: Heinemann, 1987; New York: Doubleday, 1989.

SHORT STORIES

The Sacrificial Egg and Other Stories. Onitsha, Nigeria: Etudo, 1962.

Girls at War and Other Stories. London: Heinemann Educational, 1972; Garden City, N.Y.: Doubleday, 1973; New York: Anchor Books, 1991.

"Sugar Baby." In *Okike* 3 (1972).

POEMS

"There Was a Young Man in Our Hall." In *University Herald, Ibadan* 3 (1951–1952).

Beware, Soul Brother and Other Poems. Enugu, Nigeria: Nwankwo-Ifejika, 1971. Rev. and enlarged ed. London: Heinemann, 1972. Repr. as *Christmas in Biafra and Other Poems.* Garden City, N.Y.: Anchor/Doubleday, 1973.

"Flying." In *Okike* 4 (1973).

"The Old Man and the Census." In *Okike* 6 (1974).

ESSAYS

"The Role of the Writer in the New Nation." In *Nigeria Magazine* 81 (June 1964).

English and the African Writer." In *Transition* (Kampala) 4, no. 18 (1965).

Morning Yet on Creation Day: Essays. London: Heinemann Educational, 1975; Garden City, N.Y.: Anchor/Doubleday, 1975.

The Trouble with Nigeria. Enugu, Nigeria: Fourth Dimension, 1983; London: Heinemann, 1984.

Hopes and Impediments: Selected Essays, 1965–1987. London: Heinemann, 1988; New York: Doubleday, 1990.

"African Literature as Restoration of Celebration." In *Kunapipi* 12, no. 2 (1990).

CHILDREN'S LITERATURE

Chike and the River. Cambridge, U.K.: Cambridge University Press, 1966, 1981.

How the Leopard Got His Claws. With John Iroaganachi. Enugu, Nigeria: Nwamife Publishers Ltd., 1972, 1979; New York: Third Press, 1973.

OTHERS

The Insider: Stories of War and Peace from Nigeria. Coeditor. Enugu, Nigeria: Nwankwo-Ifejika, 1971.

INTERVIEWS

Duerden, Dennis, and Cosmo Pieterse, eds. "Chinua Achebe." In *African Writers Talking: A Collection of Radio Interviews.* London: Heinemann Educational Books, 1972; New York: Africana Publishing Co., 1972.

Gzowski, Peter. Interview. Canadian Broadcasting Corporation, 23 June 1985.

Nkosi, Lewis. Interview. In *Africa Report* (July 1964).

Serumaga, Robert. Interview. London: Transcription Centre, 1971.

Whitelaw, Marjorie. Unpublished interview with Chinua Achebe. Nigerian Broadcasting Corporation, Lagos, 23 May 1962.

CRITICAL STUDIES

Carroll, David. *Chinua Achebe.* New York: Twayne, 1970.

Colmer, Rosemary. "The Start of Weeping Is Always Hard: The Ironic Structure of *No Longer at Ease.*" In *Literary Half-Yearly* 21 (January 1980).

Enekwe, Ossie. "Chinua Achebe's Novels," "Chinua Achebe's Short Stories," and "Chinua Achebe's Poetry." *Perspectives on Nigerian Literature.* Vol. 2. Lagos, Nigeria: Guardian Books Nigerian, 1988.

Gikandi, Simon. *Reading Chinua Achebe.* London: James Currey, 1991.

Innes, C. L. *Chinua Achebe.* Cambridge, U.K.: Cambridge University Press, 1990.

Irele, Abiola. "The Tragic Conflict in Achebe's Novels." In *Black Orpheus* 17 (June 1965). Repr. in Ulli Beier, ed., *Introduction to African Literature: An Anthology of Critical Writing from Black Orpheus.* Evanston, Ill.: Northwestern University Press, 1967; London: Longman, 1979.

———. "African Literature and the Language Question." In his *The African Experience in Literature and Ideology.* London: Heinemann, 1981; Bloomington: Indiana University Press, 1990.

Iyasere, Solomon O. "Narrative Techniques in *Things Fall Apart.*" In *New Letters* 3 (1974).

Killam, G. D. *The Novels of Chinua Achebe.* London: Heinemann, 1969; New York: Africana Publishing Co., 1969.

———. "Chinua Achebe's Novels." In *Sewanee Review* 79 (1971).

———. "Notions of Religion, Alienation and Archetype in *Arrow of God.*" In Rowland Smith, ed., *Exile and Tradition: Studies in African and Caribbean Literature.* New York: Africana Publishing Co., 1976; London: Longman and Dalhousie University Press, 1976.

Lindfors, Bernth. "The Palm Oil with Which Achebe's Words Are Eaten." In *African Literature Today* 1 (1968). Repr. in his *Folklore in Nigerian Literature*. New York: Africana Publishing Co., 1973.

———. "Chinua Achebe and the Nigerian Novel." In Pal Paricsy, ed., *Studies on Modern Black African Literature*. Budapest: Center for Afro-Asian Research of the Hungarian Academy of Sciences, 1971. Repr. in *Lotus: Afro-Asian Writings* 15 (1973).

Maxwell, D. E. S. "Landscape and Theme." In John Press, ed., *Commonwealth Literature: Unity and Diversity in a Common Culture*. London: Heinemann, 1965.

Ojihmah, Umelo. *Chinua Achebe: New Perspectives*. Ibadan, Nigeria: Spectrum Books, 1991.

Post, K. W. J. Introduction to *A Man of the People*. Garden City, N.Y.: Doubleday, 1967.

———. Introduction to *Arrow of God*. Garden City, N.Y.: Doubleday, 1969.

Ravenschroft, Arthur. *Chinua Achebe*. Essex, U.K.: Longmans, Green, 1969.

Riddy, Felicity. "Language as a Theme in *No Longer at Ease*." In *Journal of Commonwealth Literature* 9 (1970).

Soile, 'Sola. "Tragic Paradox in Achebe's *Arrow of God*." In *Phylon* 37 (1976).

Wilkinson, Jane. "Chinua Achebe." In *Talking with African Writers*. London: James Currey, 1992.

Wren, Robert M. "Achebe's Revisions of *Arrow of God*." In *Research in African Literatures* 7 (1976).

———. *Achebe's World: The Historical and Cultural Context of the Novels of Chinua Achebe*. Washington, D.C.: Three Continents Press, 1980; Harlow, U.K.: Longman, 1981.

Zell, Hans, and Helene Silver. "Chinua Achebe." In *A Reader's Guide to African Literature*. New York: Africana Publishing Co., 1971, 1983; London: Heinemann Educational Books, 1972.

Ama Ata Aidoo
1942–

SHIRLEY CHEW

AMA ATA AIDOO was born Christina Ama Aidoo in 1942 in Abeadzi Kyiakor, in the south central region of Ghana. Her father, an admirer of the educator James Emman Kwegyir Aggrey, regarded formal education as important for all Africans and especially for women. Aidoo attended Wesley Girls High School in Cape Coast and the University of Ghana in Legon, where she enjoyed considerable success as an undergraduate. She worked with the influential Ghanaian dramatist Efua Sutherland in the Ghana Drama Studio, was a prizewinner in a short-story competition organized by Ibadan's Mbari Club, and had her first play, *The Dilemma of a Ghost*, staged by the Students' Theatre. After graduating with a degree in English in July 1964, she took up a research fellowship at the university's Institute of African Studies; later, she received a creative writing fellowship at Stanford University in California. Her travels in the two years that she spent abroad took her to many parts of the United States as well as to London and East Africa. She returned to Ghana in 1969.

As an academic, Aidoo has taught at various universities in Africa and the United States. She was Ghana's minister of education under the ruling Provisional National Defense Council from January 1982 to June 1983. Forced to resign and leave the country because her views were considered too radical by the regime, she has since 1983 lived in Harare, Zimbabwe, and in the United States.

Aidoo publishes in English, the language she learned at school. She explains that this gives her "the chance to communicate with other Africans outside Ghana. Even in Ghana alone, if you are writing in English you are more able to carry yourself over" (Zell, p. 121). Her first language, however, is Fanti. A subgroup of the Akan people, the Fanti had a reputation among the British for "their recalcitrance, their rudeness, their contempt for the imperial set-up, and for the white man" (Aidoo, "Male-ing Names in the Sun," 1993, p. 31). Being no exception to this characterization of his people, Aidoo's paternal grandfather was arrested for his anti-British activities and later killed. As she recalls, the punishment consisted in making the prisoners pass cannonballs among themselves as though they were playing volleyball. Aidoo recalls in the article "Male-ing Names in the Sun": "Within a week, they were dead, each and everyone of them, including my grandfather. No beatings, no bruising. Very gentlemanly, very civilised" (p. 32).

Aidoo's family history—"I come from a long line of fighters" (interview by James, p. 13)—was part of Ghana's struggle for freedom, and she grew up amid the optimism and sense of purpose that attended the country's newly gained independence in 1957. Since then, political and economic disasters have followed, but she has kept faith: "What I am basically interested in has not changed. I wish that Africa would be free and strong and organised and constructive, etc. That is basic to my commitment as a writer" (interview by Chetin, p. 25). Just as basic to that commitment is her belief that freedom for Africa is directly linked to freedom for women. A major concern in her writing, therefore, is to make visible and significant women's lives, work, and stories; she intends her art to serve as a force for change. Significant for both their ambitious subject matter and their innovative experiments with form, Aidoo's published works include two plays, two novels, a collection of short stories, two volumes of poetry, and children's literature.

DRAMATIC WORKS

The Dilemma of a Ghost

In *The Dilemma of a Ghost* (1965), Aidoo's first play, the male protagonist, Ato, returns home from the United States with Eulalie, his African-American wife, and becomes entangled in a conflict of cultures. On the one hand, he must readjust to the traditional ways of his family, who are appalled by his marriage to a woman bearing the double stigma of "a stranger and a slave" (p. 18). On the other, he is eager to retain the lifestyle he has grown used to while living abroad and with Eulalie. The cultural conflict, conveyed through the design of the family house, images of food, and distinctive levels of language, is exacerbated by the couple's decision not to have children for the time being. When Eulalie shows no sign of becoming pregnant, his people assume she is barren. The core of the problem, however, lies in Ato's inability to bring about any meaningful reconciliation between his ancestral and adopted cultures. Just

as Eulalie's response to Africa swings between nostalgia and angry recoil, so too Ato is divided in himself. He strikes his wife for insulting his people, yet he is secretly convinced that Ghanaian society has not caught up with "these days of civilisation" (p. 48). At the moment of crisis, his mother, Esi, lays bare his folly. She also puts aside her prejudices and takes her distraught daughter-in-law with her into the family house. As the lights dim, only Ato is left in the middle of the courtyard, irresolute and lost:

> Shall I go to Cape Coast
> Shall I go to Elmina?
> I can't tell
> Shall I?
> I can't tell
> I can't tell
>
> (p. 50)

As an early work in Aidoo's career, *The Dilemma of a Ghost* shows a number of weaknesses. For example, the characterization of Eulalie borders on caricature, and the reconciliation between the women at the end feels contrived. But the main preoccupations of Aidoo's writing are already foregrounded here: the urgent claims of the past to be remembered; the problems related to the traditionally sanctioned roles of women as wives and mothers; and the significant parts women must be expected to play in the remaking of African society.

Ato's "dilemma," as figured in the ghost song that ends the play, seems at first to be the choice between Elmina, inscribed with the history of the Akan people, and Cape Coast, a fashionable modern city important today as an educational center. In other words, he seems to be torn between traditional and contemporary ways and values. The problem, however, is a little more complicated, given that Elmina also recalls the first European fort built on Akan land by the Portuguese, while Cape Coast was the British administrative capital until the mid 1870s when, with the consolidation of British rule, it was replaced by Accra. Taken together, the two place-names signal critical moments in Europe's penetration of the Gold Coast and summon forth a history of greed and exploitation that spans the tribal past, the arrival of the white men, and an era of foreign domination. They are calls to confront the past that Ato, stranded like the "ghost at the junction" (p. 24), finds impossible to answer.

While Ato hangs back, the reconciliation between Esi and Eulalie, though abrupt, is a positive gesture. To a large extent, this is due to Aidoo's assured and versatile representation of the African women. Nana, Esi Kom, Mansa, First and Second Woman Neighbors —each of them is a distinct character in her own right, while collectively they have a strength and wisdom gained from a knowledge of concrete realities, a history of suffering, and a place in a rooted community. Their voices—lithe, intelligent, undeceived—convey the impression that it is here, in the conversations, arguments, and questions of women, where answers crucial to the society and culture are found.

Anowa

In an interview with Adeola James, Aidoo points out that "the whole question of how it was that so many of our people could be enslaved and sold is very very important. I've always thought that it is an area that must be probed. It probably holds one of the keys to our future" (pp. 20–21). Her second play, *Anowa* (1970), grapples powerfully with this question. In its keen reading of history as well as in its unflinching recognition of the importance of social responsibility, *Anowa* ranks as "one of the major plays to have come from the contemporary African theatre" (Banham, p. 8).

The play, according to Aidoo, is "a weaving together of many tale motifs" (interview by Chetin, p. 24). Like the heroine of a popular African folktale, Anowa refuses the suitors selected by her parents and marries the man

of her choice, with disastrous consequences. The form the disaster takes is based on a regional Ghanaian story, an account of a domestic quarrel that deteriorates into "a public washing of dirty linen" and breaks up the marriage. The playwright's imagination, it seems, was teased by "the notion that you have to watch what you say publicly and even privately to people" (interview by Chetin, p. 24).

But *Anowa* does not simply teach the virtues of filial obedience or of decorum in speech. As the old tales are placed in new contexts and reworked, they are transformed into ways of speaking about contemporary realities. Behind Aidoo's achievement is a gift for making the ordinary fully expressive; her unerring ear for dialogue, besides staying true to the portrayal of characters, resonates with a timeless quality. She combines this flair for language with a firm grasp of dramatic patterns and structure.

Two years separate the events of phase two from Anowa's quarrel with her mother in phase one and her subsequent departure from the village. As she and her husband, Kofi Ako, make their way to the coast to sell their supply of skins, their conversation ranges freely from the weather to work, and from a new wife for Kofi to the future. But when Kofi speaks of his intention to buy and own slaves, the relationship begins to show signs of strain. While he resorts to euphemisms—"I think the time has come for us to think of looking for one or two men to help us"—Anowa is direct in her refusal—"We shall not buy men" (p. 89). While he is glib in his reasons for wanting slaves—"they are cheap," "everyone does it," "things would be easier for us"—she speaks her mind plainly: "I shall not feel happy with slaves around.... Kofi, no man made a slave of his friend and came to much himself. It is wrong. It is evil" (p. 90). Her objections, however, make little impression on his well-padded ego.

Mixed in with their argument are comments on Anowa's independence that slide insidiously into criticism of her barrenness. What is "strong" in her is made to chime with "strange," and her spirited ways are dismissed as a "restlessness" brought about by the absence of family ties. Even Anowa begins to feel at odds with herself, her uneasiness communicating itself through a delicate sounding of words and their doubleness.

Defining "wayfarer," for example, poses special problems for her:

> People can be very unkind. A wayfarer is a traveller. Therefore, to call someone a wayfarer is a painless way of saying he does not belong. That he has no home, no family, no village, no stool of his own; has no feast days, no holidays, no state, no territory.

> (p. 97)

Shying away from this desolate vision, Kofi points out that "a wayfarer belongs to other people." But the ambiguity of "belongs," in its two senses of being enslaved and being part of a community, is not lost on Anowa. She then proposes a third possibility: "Oh no, not always. One can belong to oneself without belonging to a place." As things turn out, Anowa's tragedy is that she is not permitted to belong to herself. Having fled her mother's world—in which fulfillment for women is restricted to the roles of wife, mother, and, if one is exceptional, priestess—and having declared her hatred of Kofi's cruel and exploitative world, she finds herself at once barren and bare, with no other place open to her.

In phase three, the rift between husband and wife widens. Kofi, now "the richest man, probably, of the Guinea Coast" (p. 104), decides to banish Anowa to her village on the ground that she is unable to give him a child. In retaliation, she accuses him publicly of impotence; the corruption of wealth, she claims, has eaten away his manhood. Then, to drive home the point, she calls him a woman and, in so doing, destroys them both. The larger, tragic implications of this act rest with her decision to fight Kofi on his own terms.

For, in this case, resistance merely endorses the norms and values upon which traditional society is built, and this failure signals the defeat of Anowa's earlier hopes for change.

A "fierce allegory on the contemporary exploitation of man by man" (Banham, p. 8), *Anowa* derives much of its power from Aidoo's skillful interweaving of several strands of history. According to the choric pronouncement of the Old Man in the prologue, Anowa's departure from her mother's village takes place around 1874, the year the Ghanaian city of Kumasi fell into British hands. In other words, while Anowa finds her world closing in steadily, British power continues to expand and consolidate itself in the Gold Coast. The complicity of the local people in their own subjugation is made plain. For example, back in Anowa's village, the talk is full of the trade she and Kofi are doing with "the white men" and "how they are buying men and women" (p. 93), and in the big hall in Kofi's house, a portrait of Queen Victoria sits cheek by jowl with one of Kofi himself.

The play's anachronistic treatment of the slave trade, which was abolished in 1807, is obvious. As obvious, too, is that even without the practice of "buying men and women," the exploitation of Africa persists undiminished under colonial rule. But the play's bleakest statement is directed at postindependence Ghana. In 1969, the year before *Anowa* was published, the ban on political activity, which was imposed by the military after the overthrow in 1966 of President Kwame Nkrumah, was finally lifted, and general elections followed. The elections brought to power the Progress Party and established a government, headed by Dr. Kofi Busia, with a vested interest in seeing chiefs restored to preeminence and positions of influence. Viewed in the light of contemporary politics, Kofi Ako's greed and self-aggrandizement, symbolized by the rich furnishings of his room, his gilded chair, and his elaborate processions, become acutely topical. Anowa's fears have come true; the evil, which begins so modestly with the desire for one or two men to help with the family business, has rooted itself in the course of history.

FICTION

No Sweetness Here

In Aidoo's aesthetics, African literature has to be redefined in terms of indigenous standards and forms. She sees, for example, fruitful experiments arising from the interaction of African theater, short fiction, and oral literature:

> If I had my way really what I would be interested in is a form of theatre where you don't only have to produce a play—where you can just sit down and relate a story. They don't have to be folktales only, there are lots of stories going around. In fact I believe that when a writer writes a short story, it should be possible for the writer to sit before an audience and tell them the story of a boy and a girl in Accra, or London, or Paris.
>
> (interview by McGregor, pp. 23–24)

To write not just for readers but listeners also, to evolve a new vehicle for expression out of a synthesis of contemporary material and traditional as well as imported forms: these are the governing principles behind the stories in *No Sweetness Here* (1970).

The world seems a smaller place in these stories than in *Anowa*. Motorways and trucks have narrowed the distances between the villages and cities. Below the surface of change, however, is a drab sameness. We hear still of "big men" whose status is measured by their many wives, children, and material goods; of women for whom survival in the city means prostitution; of the rawness of life in villages where infant mortality continues to be high, the cola crop often fails, trade is bad, and families are split up. Aidoo's stories draw us, as reader-listeners, into the action. Recognitions are forced upon us through the collisions, ambiguities, and reworkings of language.

"In the Cutting of a Drink" is a young man's account of his experiences in the city while searching for his missing sister. The interaction between the storyteller and his village audience is represented in a number of ways typical of oral narrative: the repeated statement, in this case "cut me a drink," which marks the pauses in the story; the storyteller's direct address to several of his listeners; and his reminders to himself and his audience of their shared assumptions of what is strange and what customary. Although we are outside the village circle, we participate in the narrative, too. As reader-listeners, we are positioned somewhere between the village and the city, knowledgeable beyond the rural community in some ways but less clever than we imagine ourselves to be in others.

While in the city, the young villager is prepared to think of his sister Mansa as being attached to a "big man." He is not prepared for the shock of discovering that she earns her living dancing with strange men in return for beer, cigarettes, and money. His conventional notions of "work" overturned, he reacts with self-righteous indignation: "I was unhappy thinking about these women. 'Have they no homes?' I asked myself. 'Do not their mothers like them? God, we are all toiling for our threepence to buy something to eat . . . but oh! God! this is no work'" (p. 36). But another shock is in store for him. It seems that, to someone like his sister, "any kind of work is work" when one is hungry (p. 36). This new idea, which he takes back with him to the village, continues to trouble him. As for ourselves, as reader-listeners, we have never had any doubts as to the nature of Mansa's occupation.

Critics have noted Aidoo's success in creating different levels of language in her plays, so that speech becomes "an index of social class, age and background" (Adelugba, p. 72). The same is true of her art in the short stories. One example is "For Whom Things Did Not Change," which examines the social divide between a generation of foreign-educated and well-to-do professionals and another, older one of illiterates and servants, stuck throughout their lives in badly paid jobs. A young Ghanaian doctor staying at a government rest house makes a self-conscious attempt to treat the keeper of the place and his wife as equals. To some extent, the doctor manages to overcome the old man's embarrassment and reserve. The stages of their relationship are signaled, first, in the way the talk between the two moves from mutual incomprehension to a cordial exchange of personal stories until "gradually the main part of the talking" passes to the old man, Zirigu (p. 23). Shifts in language also mark the stages of the relationship, so that pidgin, used to represent the master-and-servant relationship, is juxtaposed with standard English, the young doctor's language, and with a form of English invented by Aidoo, a transcription of dialect that is the vehicle for Zirigu's life story.

However, the gulf between the two men, it is clear from Zirigu's story, can never be fully bridged. The problem is not, as the doctor has imagined, "that one day, [Zirigu and his wife] will learn that we are all the same" (p. 21). It is the young and privileged Ghanaians who must learn the lesson. Zirigu's experiences include fighting in Burma in World War II, the loss of his small business for which there was no compensation, the departure of the British, the new job at the government rest house first under the colonial government and then under the national government. Yet at the end of the day, he is not considered good enough to enjoy modern amenities such as electric light and a flush toilet in his part of the rest house. When under the postindependence government the building was renovated, all he got in his "boys' quarters" was a new bucket.

Aidoo is at her most animated and inventive in her handling of women's talk. In "Something to Talk About on the Way to the Funeral," the chat between the two speakers — one of them clearly a born raconteur — is beautifully rhythmic and serves also as praise for the deceased. Then there is the wary, understated, and intimate exchanges between the women in "Two Sisters." Finally, there is the village hubbub in "The Message," cleverly crossed with the preoccupied, fearful, ironic, and tragic notes of the old woman whose granddaughter must undergo a cesarean section.

Caroline Cooper has written astutely about the asymmetry in "The Message" between, on the one hand, the impersonal abstractions of medical terms ("the Caesarean case") and their blunt translations into everyday language ("they opened her up") and, on the other, the deeply felt personal meanings that the words have for the old woman. Another feature of Aidoo's art here is the way in which everyday things and events are endowed with new significance, so that a journey on a battered truck to the hospital in the city takes on for the old woman an epic dimension because of its strangeness and arduousness. At once comic and poignant, the journey is a rite of passage for an old person that leads to a rebirth. The grandmother emerges triumphant from her journey, just as her granddaughter does from her operation.

Our Sister Killjoy

> But I know that I am also right. Of course, I agree with you about letting time move. But, My Darling, we have got to give it something to carry. Time by itself means nothing, no matter how fast it moves. Unless we give it something to carry for us; something we value.
>
> (p. 113)

In *Our Sister Killjoy; or, Reflections from a Black-Eyed Squint* (1977), from which the quotation is taken, it is the freight of history that time and the text are made to carry. Written in four parts in prose and verse, the novel is an account of Sissie's travels in Europe in the late 1960s; she visits Germany as the Ghanaian representative of an international group of young volunteer workers, and then moves on to England before returning to Africa. As things turn out, very little is expected of Sissie and her fellow campers in the way of hard, useful labor. In the well-managed countryside of Bavaria, for example, their work amounts to "nursing prospective Christmas trees" under the watchful eyes of the peasants, the real workers (p. 36). In this atmosphere of international cooperation and lazy abundance, Sissie undergoes a crisis of remembering, in the course of which she learns to read the history of postindependence Africa against the mythologizing discourse of European imperialism and racism.

Sissie is aided in her journey to knowledge by her "black-eyed squint," which discloses the shabby and ugly realities passed over by the progressivist tendencies of the times, the "problems of Ignorance/Disease/Poverty" (p. 70); economic exploitation; civil war; and apartheid in an age of moon landings, heart transplants, rising incomes, and universal brotherhood. Then there is her habit of speaking her mind, the many notes of her voice— commonsensical, ironical, angry, imploring, tender, gnomic—embarrassingly pronounced among "reasonable well-informed circles" (p. 101). Finally, there is her capacity for "reflection," enacted in the play of different levels of consciousness and of time, suggested by the novel's repeated phrase "from knowledge gained since."

The brief opening section, "Into a Bad Dream," lays down in broad lines the kind of world Sissie is about to enter, with its empty rhetoric, inequalities of wealth, and tyrannies of power that decide

> Who is to live,
> Who is to die,
>
> Where,
>
> When,
>
> How.
> (pp. 13–16)

Power, however, does not have the last word here, for the text asks to be read in more than one way. In this instance, the typographical layout of the quotation gives a page to each of the last three words and, by separating them from the main statement and each other, renders their syntactic status ambiguous. They can be read as the questions to which only power has the answers. They can also be read as the talismans that Sissie must take with her on her travels, the questions she must continue to ask in order to find her way.

In "The Plums," the second episode, Sissie finds herself in Bavaria, amid a landscape of ease and plenty, complete with happy peasants at work, pretty cottages, and an old castle. For the benefit of the international youth, Europe has constructed itself as a pastoral romance untouched by time. In this setting, Sissie is befriended by Marija, a local German with a husband busy at work and a young son. Marija plies Sissie with luscious fruits, cakes, and attention. Sissie is flattered by Marija's curiosity about her and her country, but, as the days pass, she becomes aware of the sexual overtones of their relationship: "In [Sissie's] imagination, she was one of these black boys in one of these involvements with white girls in Europe" (p. 61). It is a fantasy in which she is prepared to collaborate until she is actually confronted with Marija's attempt to seduce her.

Marija's overweening advances in the chilling splendor of her bedroom thrust Sissie out of a dream turned bad into the waking realities of the European power to decide "where," "when," and "how." As C. L. Innes has pointed out, Aidoo can be said to rewrite and reverse Joseph Conrad's *Heart of Darkness* in *Our Sister Killjoy*. In her travels Sissie rediscovers Europe as the heart of racial and class oppression, the menacing signs of which are evident in the landscape—the big castle with its feudal past, the jingoism of Marija's neighbors, the name Adolf belonging to both Marija's husband and son, the proximity of Nazi concentration camps. Even plums become symbolic in the story, having turned up as canned prunes at many colonial tables.

However, to read this particular incident in terms only of the narrative of European aggression is to replace Europe's allegory of itself with another of our own making. The textual evidence would seem to call for a more complex interpretation. Again, as Innes has pointed out, Sissie's consciousness is expanded in a number of ways through her encounter with Marija. She gains a better understanding of the nature of Marija's need and, by extension—though it is not a matter she feels inclined to dwell upon—the desolation that might even have been the lot of the colonialists "whose only distinction in life was that at least they were better than the Natives" (p. 66). Sissie also comes to know her own temptations to power. Borrowing from the patterns of heterosexual relationships and relying upon her superior command of the English language, she has no trouble putting Marija down. Her polite and cold rejection of Marija's proposal to see her off at the station is a fine piece of mimicry: "Why bother? There's no need to waste your morning sleep.... I hate last minute goodbyes, anyway" (p. 77).

Beyond the politics of race and gender, Sissie's relationship with Marija has a poignancy that springs from her recognition of a common loneliness:

> Marija was crying silently. There was a tear streaming out of one of her eyes.... Suddenly Sissie knew. She saw it once and was never to forget it. She saw against the background of the thick smoke that was like a rain cloud over the chimneys of Europe.
>
> (p. 65)

Narrated some years after Sissie's journey, the passage, like the rest of the novel, clearly benefits from the interaction of "reflection" and "knowledge gained since." But, like many other parts of the narrative, the passage leaves ambiguous what precisely she "knew" and she "saw." The reader can only speculate. To what extent, bearing in mind Sissie's confession in the last section of the novel, "A Love Letter," does the resonance of the passage spring from her own experience of romantic loss? To what extent does it speak to her familiarity with the letters that lonely women in Africa write to their sons abroad? And how much does it have to do with the loneliness of the African exiles themselves?

If "The Plums" subverts the myth of Europe as pastoral, "From Our Sister Killjoy," the third section of the novel, is an attempt to engage critically the progressivist myths of the neocolonial era. Having fought off Marija, Sissie can be said to have fought off the danger of being absorbed into somebody else's story. But Kunle, an African she meets in London, is incapable of extricating himself from dependency upon the white man's version of the world. He reads the news of a heart transplant from a black man to a white man in terms of allegory, a scientific breakthrough that will

> rid us, "African negroes
> and all other negroes" of the
> Colour Problem. The whole of the
> Colour Problem.
>
> (p. 96)

Kunle believes that this breakthrough will also usher in universal brotherhood. On the other hand, Sissie reads the transplant as racial exploitation taken to its logical and horrific conclusion, in which the living heart of a black person is merely a piece of property to be snatched and used for the survival of the white race. Sissie's reading is not disproved by a quick review of the newspaper headlines of the day. In a world dominated still by the notions of progress and white supremacy, Kunle, like the numerous faceless Africans, has no place.

> KUNLE has died,
> Killed by the car for which he had
> Waited so long.
>
> (p. 103)

But what does this signify, compared with the death of the second transplant patient, the undimmed distinction of the transplant surgeon, and the death of the French president Charles de Gaulle? For that matter with the death of African refugees, workers, political prisoners? But perhaps these events are the reasons why his story has to be retold and relocated.

"From knowledge gained since" Sissie puts together the ingredients of Kunle's story: the call of mothers for their sons; age-old expressions of love; the things that have gone wrong; the returnee who wishes he had "the courage to be a coward enough to stay forever in England" (p. 107); the big man traveling in a chauffeur-driven car to his village; the accident, the death, and the insurance policy which, taken out with a "very reliable" company, turns out not to be "absolutely comprehensive" (p. 108). In her unerring manner the "black-eyed squint" has picked up the plain facts and realistic details as well as the wild contradictions and grotesque ironies of Kunle's story. It is at once bizarre comedy and a tragedy of waste. It is one person's history, and it has representative significance. It is a story belonging to Africa that reverberates in Europe.

Travel writing, poetry, pastoral, romance, Gothic fiction, news in brief, autobiography, oral narrative—the borders of literary kinds and literary forms are wonderfully blurred in this novel. At the start of the last section, "A Love Letter," Sissie has pulled out of a situation with a man she addresses as "My Precious Something" (p. 112):

> In fact, all sorts of well-wishers have told me what I should have done in the first place, loving you as much as I claim to, whatever that means. They say that any female in my position would have thrown away everything to be with you, and remain with you: first her opinions, and then her own plans. But oh deliciously naive me. What did I rather do but daily and loudly criticise you and your friends for wanting to stay forever in alien places?
>
> (p. 117)

Sissie has the whole of Africa to return to, unlike Anowa, who could not return to the constricting life of her village. Sissie has the opportunity to write and examine her motives, and the letter is as much an attempt to make her "Precious Something" understand as to understand herself. There is no secret language for love, yet all the resources and powers of language are directed toward the attempt to explain how her love has to be as multifaceted as her self. To speak of love is to speak of social ills and political disasters and family and everything else.

Changes

In an interview with Maxine McGregor in 1967, Aidoo remarked that she could not see herself "writing about lovers in Accra because you see, there are so many other problems" (p. 19). Almost twenty-five years later, the appearance of *Changes* (1991), with its vivid rendering of a woman's tender and thorny relationships with her two husbands, can only entail, as Aidoo confesses in the foreword to the novel, "an exercise in words-eating."

Changes returns to a question posed in *Anowa* and *Our Sister Killjoy*: To what extent, if at all, has self-determination become a reality for women in postindependence Ghana, after so many years of purported reform? The answer is found in the frustrations and dilemmas Esi encounters in her attempts to claim a space of her own as a woman, one that will enable her to bring into play the different aspects of her personality. After the collapse of her second marriage, Esi has only makeshift solutions as to how to carry on with her life. Nevertheless, her intelligent and sustained struggle to be true to herself and to her relationships points to the possibility, if not of change in one "definitive overturning gesture," then of "changes" in the making (Bryce and Darko, p. 14).

Narrating Esi's experiences and those of her family and friends, Aidoo rewrites a number of familiar fictions concerning women's lives in a male-dominated society. When, for example, Ali decides that Esi should marry him and become his second wife, she has no reason to object, given that he has courted her with all the charm, liberality, and eloquence to be found in any romantic best-seller. Given, too, that his decision has the sanction of custom, at least within the mythologized version of traditional society, "wives took turns being wives," the man "was not supposed to" have favorites, and "the serious business of living" was done "with our heads, and never our hearts" (pp. 78, 79). However, romance and myth prove short-lived. Once the wedding is over, Ali's charm begins to bear a certain resemblance to deviousness, his gifts seem like bribes, and his eloquence sounds like deception. The version of womanhood that now lies in wait for Esi is one familiar to her grandmother:

> A woman has always been diminished in her association with a man. A good woman was she who quickened the pace of her own destruction. To refuse, as a woman, to be destroyed, was a crime that society spotted very quickly and punished swiftly and severely.
>
> (pp. 110–111)

Change is not considered impossible, but "what it would take is a lot of thinking and a great deal of doing" (p. 111).

On the surface there appears to be no difference between Esi's situation, once the relationship with Ali stops being a marriage, and that of many other women. Behind her lonely existence, however, are conscious and painful choices made from the combined pressures of "heart" and "head." First, her rejection of Ali's "fashion of loving," in which she is expected to play an acquiescent role, is as strong an expression of her sexuality as her uncommon delight in her own body and its energies. Second, in a novel in which the city is a pervasive presence, teaching herself to live on her own in Accra is an assertion of her right as a woman to the urban environment and the opportunities it offers. The city has to be remade, becoming for Esi not just the streets and bars, the haunts of prostitutes, and the little houses with locked gates that are the

prisons of self-sacrificing wives; but a space for the movement, action, and rest that men like Ali can take so much for granted.

Last, Esi's resolution that it is from "her bone-blood-flesh self, not her unseen soul" that the "answers to some of the big questions she was asking of life" should come makes it unthinkable that she would betray Opokuya, even at a time when an affair with Opokuya's husband, Kubi, would have provided a form of comfort:

> She remembered that there is something called friendship. And hadn't her friendship with Opokuya been, so far, the most constant thing in her life? And that whereas mothers, fathers, grandmothers and other relations are like extra limbs we grow, a friend symbolises a choice? And to maintain a friendship is a choice?
>
> (p. 164)

Thus, as the story of romance draws to a disappointing close, the full weight of that other story, the friendship of Esi and Opokuya, begins to make itself felt. The numerous times that the word "friend" is repeated in the narrative—Esi and Opokuya are "friends"; Esi wonders whether she can ever see herself and Ali's wife as being "friends"; Fusena regrets that, by marrying Ali, she has exchanged a "friend" for a husband; Ali and Esi, their marriage not working, become just good "friends"—point the way to other kinds of alignments for women, new patterns of relationship. As Esi's grandmother reminds us, as long as human beings are prepared to try, "it is very possible for life on this earth to be good for us all" (p. 111).

Selected Bibliography

BIBLIOGRAPHIES

Buck, Claire, ed. *Bloomsbury Guide to Women's Literature*. London: Bloomsbury, 1992.

Lindfors, Bernth, ed. *Black African Literature in English, 1982–1986*. London and New York: Hans Zell Publishers, 1989.

Zell, Hans, Carol Bundy, and Virginia Coulon, eds. *A New Reader's Guide to African Literature.* London: Heinemann, 1983; New York: Africana Publishing Co., 1983.

SELECTED WORKS

The Dilemma of a Ghost. Harlow, U.K.: Longman, 1965. Play.

Anowa. Harlow, U.K.: Longman, 1970. Play.

No Sweetness Here: A Collection of Short Stories. Harlow, U.K.: Longman, 1970; repr. Garden City, N.Y.: Doubleday, 1971.

Our Sister Killjoy; or, Reflections from a Black-Eyed Squint. London: NOK Publishers, 1977. Novel.

Someone Talking to Sometime. Harare, Zimbabwe: College Press, 1985. Poems.

The Eagle and the Chickens and Other Stories. Enugu, Nigeria: Tana Press, 1986. Children's literature.

Birds and Other Poems. Harare, Zimbabwe: College Press, 1988. Children's literature.

Changes. London: Women's Press, 1991. Repr. New York: Feminist Press, 1993. Novel.

An Angry Letter in January and Other Poems. Coventry, U.K.: Dangaroo Press, 1992.

SELECTED ARTICLES

"To Be a Woman." In Robin Morgan, ed., *Sisterhood Is Global.* Garden City, N.Y.: Anchor Press/Doubleday, 1984.

"Male-ing Names in the Sun." In Shirley Chew and Anna Rutherford, eds., *Unbecoming Daughters of the Empire.* Sydney: Dangaroo Press, 1993.

INTERVIEWS

Chetin, Sarah. "Interview with Ama Ata Aidoo." In *Wasafiri* 6/7 (1987).

James, Adeola. "Ama Ata Aidoo." In Adeola James, ed., *In Their Own Voices: African Women Writers Talk.* London: J. Currey, 1990.

McGregor, Maxine. "Ama Ata Aidoo." In Dennis Duerden and Cosmo Pieterse, eds., *African Writers Talking: A Collection of Radio Interviews.* London: Heinemann, 1972; New York: Africana Publishing Co., 1972.

CRITICAL STUDIES

Adelugba, Dapo. "Language and Drama: Ama Ata Aidoo." In *African Literature Today* 8 (1976).

Banham, Martin. Entry on Aidoo. In Mark Hawkins-Dady, ed. *International Dictionary of Theatre.* Vol. 2. Chicago: St. James, 1991.

Brown, Lloyd W. "Ama Ata Aidoo: The Art of the Short Story and Sexual Roles in Africa." In *World Literature Written in English* 13, no. 2 (1974).

Bryce, Jane, and Kari Darko. "Textual Deviancy and Cultural Syncretism: Romantic Fiction as a Subversive Strain in Black Women's Writing." In *Wasafiri* 17 (1993).

Elder, Arlene. "Ama Ata Aidoo and the Oral Tradition: A Paradox of Form and Substance." In *African Literature Today* 15 (1987).

Grant, Jane W. *Ama Ata Aidoo:* The Dilemma of a Ghost. Harlow, U.K.: Longman, 1980.

Innes, C. L. "Mothers or Sisters? Identity, Discourse and Audience in the Writing of Ama Ata Aidoo and Mariama Ba." In Susheila Nasta, ed., *Motherlands: Black Women's Writing from Africa, the Caribbean and South Asia.* London: Women's Press, 1991; New Brunswick, N.J.: Rutgers University Press, 1992.

Kern, Anita. "Ama Ata Aidoo's *Our Sister Killjoy.*" In *World Literature Written in English* 17 (April 1978).

Korang, Kwaku Larbi. "Ama Ata Aidoo's Voyage Out: Mapping the Coordinates of Modernity and African Selfhood in *Our Sister Killjoy.*" In *Kunapipi* 14, no. 3 (1992).

Nwankwo, Chimalum. "The Feminist Impulse and Social Realism in Ama Ata Aidoo's *No Sweetness Here* and *Our Sister Killjoy.*" In Carole Boyce Davies and Anne Adams Graves, eds., *Ngambika: Studies of Women in African Literature.* Trenton, N.J.: Africa World Press, 1986.

Odamtten, Vincent O. *The Art of Ama Ata Aidoo: Polylectics and Reading Against Neocolonialism.* Gainesville: University Press of Florida, 1994.

Ojo-Ade, Femi. "Female Writers, Male Critics." In *African Literature Today* 13 (1983).

Petersen, Kirsten Holst. "Ama Ata Aidoo." In Kirsten Holst Petersen and Anna Rutherford, eds., *Cowries and Kobos: The West African Oral Tale and Short Story.* Århus, Denmark: Department of English, University of Århus, 1981.

Rooney, Caroline. "Are We in the Company of Feminists? A Preface for Bessie Head and Ama

Ata Aidoo." In Harriet Devine Jump, ed., *Diverse Voices: Essays on Twentieth-Century Women Writers in English*. New York and London: Harvester Wheatsheaf, 1991.

————. "'Dangerous Knowledge' and the Poetics of Survival: A Reading of *Our Sister Killjoy* and *A Question of Power*." In Susheila Nasta, ed., *Motherlands: Black Women's Writing from Africa, the Caribbean and South Asia*. London: Women's Press, 1991; New Brunswick, N.J.: Rutgers University Press, 1992.

Taiwo, Odalele. *Female Novelists of Modern Africa*. London: St. Martin's Press, 1984.

Ayi Kwei Armah
1939–

ROSEMARY COLMER

AYI KWEI ARMAH has written: "The question...remains to this day: of what creative use are skilfully arranged words when the really creative work—changing Africa's social realities for the better—remains inaccessible?" ("One Writer's Education," p. 1753). All of Armah's novels focus on the question of how one should live purely in an impure society. From the second novel on they also and more importantly pose the question of what the elite should contribute to the masses. These concerns are why the novels are built around metaphorical references to the bearing of gifts (*Fragments* and *Why Are We So Blest?*), knowing the "way" (*Fragments*, *Two Thousand Seasons*, and *The Healers*), and healing the sick mind (*Fragments* and *The Healers*).

Armah grew up as a member of the elite. Born in Takoradi, Ghana, in 1939, he was educated at Achimota School outside Accra, and left Ghana in 1959 for the United States. At Harvard University, he began studying literature but changed to sociology. In 1963 he traveled to Algeria, where he worked as a translator until a nervous breakdown triggered by malnutrition and stress shattered his health, affecting, he says, "body and soul." Following several months of hospitalization he returned to Ghana to work as a teacher and as a scriptwriter. This seems to have been a difficult time in his personal life, for his brief and reluctant comments suggest he felt pressures from his family to conform to a pattern of social behavior that he considered reprehensibly materialistic. But as a writer it was a fertile period, during which he wrote two novels. He worked as an editor in Paris in 1967, undertook a master of fine arts at Columbia University, and taught at universities in the United States, Tanzania, and Lesotho before moving to Senegal. The facts of his life are known principally from articles he published to correct erroneous assumptions, and his views come through in his journalism rather than in any direct comment on his work.

His first three novels deal with the neo-colonial situation. The fourth and fifth suggest that African people had departed from the "way" before they felt the effects of European colonization: greed and a lust for power established social inequalities, which were then exploited by the colonizers. Armah is a didactic writer whose novels present a schematized political argument, expressed in relentlessly metaphorical language.

Armah's first novel, *The Beautyful Ones Are Not Yet Born* (1968), received critical acclaim in the west and remains his best-known work. It had a mixed reception in Africa, as did his later novels. The objections of African commentators to Armah's novels center on his pessimism, which extends to both his political vision and the terms in which he renders reality, particularly his emphasis on real decay and metaphorical corruption. Yet, paradoxically, these features have also been seen as Armah's strengths. Clearly they are the most striking features of his work, particularly in *The Beautyful Ones Are Not Yet Born*, and are thus the elements most identifiable with Armah's voice.

LIFE ON THE DUNGHILL

The Beautyful Ones Are Not Yet Born

Armah's first novel centers on an unnamed railway worker who worries that his refusal to participate in the general climate of bribery and corruption is denying his loved ones the comforts enjoyed by others, particularly by the family of his old friend Koomson, who is now wealthy, influential, and thoroughly corrupt. In his distress the man is comforted by his friend Teacher. His wife, Oyo, learns to appreciate his stand against corruption when a terrified Koomson has to beg the couple's help to flee the country because of a coup d'état.

Armah has chosen as his main character a man who is inseparable from his community. Although he rejects the moral values of those who try to advance by corrupt means, he does not reject his fellow workers. Like them, he is isolated in his present situation, enduring life from payday to payday, unable to escape because his wife and children look to him for financial support. Yet the man is alienated from the rest of society by his refusal to compromise with corruption. He is thus a social misfit who is seen as deliberately depriving his family of the money that they would like to spend on the beautiful, good, and expensive things of life. After refusing a bribe, the man is struck by his own abnormality, and his steadfast honesty begins to seem a crime:

The man was left alone with thoughts of the easy slide and how everything said there was something miserable, something unspeakably dishonest about a man who refused to take and to give what everyone around was busy taking and giving: something unnatural, something very cruel, something that was criminal, for who but a criminal could ever be left with such a feeling of loneliness?

(p. 31)

The compelling effect of the incantatory phrases "something…something…" is typical of Armah's style. The cumulative phrases, like the cumulative incidents of the man's life, inexorably press home his separation from the rest of society.

Much of the language concerning dirt and decay reaches the reader through the consciousness of the man, who perceives and reflects upon the disgustingly corrupted and corruptible objects around him and notices the few moments of clarity and cleanness. His perception of beauty and ugliness in the world is a complex register of moral consciousness. In this register beauty and the "gleam" belong to desirable things that can only be achieved by corrupt means, and clarity and cleanness are only found amid the dirt of everyday life, and rarely there.

Even if one reacts with disapproval, one cannot escape the power of the densely metaphorical language, particularly Oyo's cruel parable about the chichidodo bird, which loves to eat maggots but hates the excrement in which the fat maggots are found (p. 44). While images of dirt and decay are the most obvious and most important images in the novel, connecting the physical and moral decay of urban Ghana, they are not the only important ones. Images of light are also significant: the "gleam" of the rich life reemerges in other images of light, as when the man, driven from home by Oyo's complaints, walks alone in the dark. The darkness becomes a symbol of ordinary life, and the light of the lamps represents, like the gleam, the easy life of wealth and power that most Ghanaians are striving to reach (p. 46).

The central idea in *The Beautyful Ones Are Not Yet Born* is the cycle of change, from birth through decay to death. This cycle takes many forms. The man cannot think of food without thinking also of the processes of digestion, regurgitation, or excretion. Everything is part of a relentless degenerative movement, and only in rare moments of hope are we shown that the movement is in fact a cycle and that out of the ancient, decayed matter comes new life.

The degenerative movement is both natural and unnatural: it is a part of the ordained nature of things, but its ugliness makes it abhorrent to the man, who sees in its accelerated speed signs of unnaturalness. The man is aware that decay is inevitable, but in a natural world it happens slowly. He fears that even his own desire to remain separate from the cycle, uncontaminated by the decay around him, is an attempt to deny a natural process:

> Was there not some proverb that said the green fruit was healthy, but healthy only for its brief self? That the only new life there ever is comes from seeds feeding on their own rotten fruit? What then, was the fruit that refused to lose its acid and its greenness? What monstrous fruit was it that could find the end of its life in the struggle against sweetness and corruption?
>
> (p. 144)

Yet when the natural process becomes unnatural in its haste, it seems right to resist it. So the man resists the corruption of his times, although by doing so he refuses the luxurious sustenance of his own naturally decayed self to his children, those seeds, those sole excuses for all the corrupt acts, performed "for the children" (p. 144).

Tied in with references to decay are allusions to birth, time, and death. These come together most noticeably in the reference to the "old manchild," a child who was born in hope, aged within seven years, and became "far more thoroughly decayed than any ordinary old man" (p. 62). The "old manchild" represents Ghana. Ghana was born in the hopeful years of independence but decayed into corrupt stagnation with indecent haste.

Only the coming of a new order, a new manifestation of nature, will bring an end to the old order, but the man cannot find even the seeds of such a new flowering in the world that he knows. There are two kinds of new life envisaged in the novel. One is the new life that arises naturally from decay, like a flower, and holds hope of a cycle in which decay and death are inevitable but natural and will in their turn produce natural flowering life. The flower is the man's personal symbol for the good and just life that he hopes will come some day. This symbol is echoed by the flower drawn within the inscription "The Beautyful Ones Are Not Yet Born" on the bus that the man sees at the end of the novel.

The other kind of birth is a violent parturition, an ugly process of producing an offspring that decays unnaturally before its time. Such was the birth of independent Ghana. This kind of birth may appear at the start to hold promise, as Ghana did under its first president, Kwame Nkrumah, but its rapid decay makes its rotten state more horrible than a naturally decayed life. The man's wife had her third child by cesarean section, and his memory of this event fixes in the reader's mind an image of ugly, violent birth, which is set against the flowering of hopeful life: "The last child had had to be dragged out of its mother's womb, and when she left the hospital the long scar was still only a sore underneath all those bandages. The sight of the scar never ceased to provoke an involuntary shudder in the mind" (p. 97). The birth is a process of wounding, not a natural process, and it leaves the mother scarred by pain and ugliness.

Gareth Griffiths has examined the scene in which the man and Koomson escape through the latrine hole as an image of birth; clearly this is another image of the violent, ugly birth that Armah opposes. The food cycles of devouring, digesting, and excreting and the life cycle of birth, aging, and death are linked in this image.

Birth can come only from decay. But what kind of birth can be expected from the premature decay of Ghana and the corrupt sweetness of her citizens? The new birth which the man looks forward to will not spring from such rottenness:

> Someday in the long future a new life would maybe flower in the country, but when it came, it would not choose as its instruments the same people who had made a habit of killing new flowers. The future goodness may come eventually, but before then where were the things in the present which would prepare the way for it?
> (pp. 157–158)

The "beautyful" ones are not yet born.

Armah's political commitment is to analysis rather than to action in *The Beautyful Ones Are Not Yet Born*. The novel diagnoses the sickness of society and offers a prognosis that is not entirely pessimistic. Griffiths points out that even the imagery in the novel is reminiscent of turns of phrase found in the political analysis of Frantz Fanon. Certainly Armah's treatment of the "black-white" men — the new black elite who ape their colonial masters — is comparable with the ideas of the French West Indian psychoanalyst and social philosopher, but while Fanon examines the causes, Armah describes the effects. Most of the political discussion is found in the dialogue between the man and his friend Teacher in the sixth and seventh chapters, where the effects of the war, the movement for independence and Nkrumah's role in it, and the present situation of both men are mulled over; but the whole novel reveals Armah's political interest. *The Beautyful Ones Are Not Yet Born* is a moral fable, but the moral is a political one, and the author is committed to a political stance.

BEARING GIFTS

Fragments

Fragments (1970) presents the plight of Baako, a western-educated Ghanaian who returns from abroad without the wealth his family anticipates and without any desire to take up the social position they expect him to assume. Baako's refusal to supply his family with the vicarious experience of success that they crave distresses his mother, Efua, and his sister, Araba. Baako is consoled by his Puerto Rican psychiatrist, Juana, but during her absence abroad he is persuaded by the unanimity of the criticisms of his stance that he is morally and socially aberrant, and he has a nervous breakdown.

Fragments enlarges on many of the ideas found in *The Beautyful Ones Are Not Yet Born* and on some of its imagery. This second novel focuses on an intellectual rather than a worker; whereas Armah's first novel was concerned only with the struggle to make a living without succumbing to moral contamination, *Fragments* also looks at the spiritual aspirations of the main character. The two central metaphors of the novel, the cargo cult (a cult in Melanesia in which believers expect the arrival by airplane of spirits bearing goods for them) and the Mammy Water (a myth about love and loneliness), involve communication between the spirit world and the mundane world. In *Fragments* the human spirit enters upon the cycle of life, which in *The Beautyful Ones* is limited to physical birth, death, and rebirth for objects in the material world. Death is welcomed by Baako's grandmother as a rebirth into a spirit existence; she sees herself as traveling a "circular way" (p. 5).

Fragments does not depend on one consciousness as *The Beautyful Ones* did. The narrative is brought into focus through Baako's blind grandmother, Naana, through Juana, and through Baako himself. Because consciousness is diffused, there is less of the obsessive concentration of imagery found in the man's vision in *The Beautyful Ones*. When two characters express their perceptions of the world using the same imagery, the imagery increases in moral intensity.

Naana's way of apprehending this world is a traditional one, against which Baako's views can be measured. The novel opens with her expressing her concern for the completion of the proper rituals to create a circle of security that will bring her grandson home from a journey away from Ghana, which she sees as akin to death. Baako, on his return, picks up on this metaphor when he feels like a ghost returning home empty-handed instead of the cargo-laden spirit his family had hoped for. Naana's belief in a natural cycle is opposed to the other family members' cargo-cult materialism and expectations of the ghostly dead. Such crude avarice results in a whole generation losing its genuine connection with the spiritual.

Efua, Araba, and friends demand that Baako prove his status as a "been-to" (that is, a Ghanaian who has "been to" the west for education and has therefore attained a higher social standing) with demonstrations of power and wealth. Baako finds it the most difficult to disappoint his mother. Although Efua eventually, in a process of "soul-cleaning," realizes that her expectations were unfounded and unfair, a curse rather than a prayer, they stay in Baako's mind. When he begins to feel guilty, he hears echoes of his mother's demands.

On the altar of Mammon, Baako becomes one of many sacrificial victims in the novel. Early on Juana witnesses the death of a rabid dog and understands not only the fear of madness and death but also the need for masculine assertion of power over life and death. That primal force draws men, with avid eyes, to form a circle around the suffering animal. The next sacrificial victim is a truck driver named Skido, whose passionate attachment to his job leads him to risk his life to board a truck full of food onto a ferry. After the ferry leaves the wharf, the truck and driver disappear into a watery grave. Baako, in his crazy moments of wanting to be like the other been-tos, calls Skido a cargo bearer who should not have been lost.

The last victim is Baako's sister's first baby, whom Baako refers to as "the child that was to have grown to become him" (p. 258). The child has not yet been in this world eight days when the ceremony of "outdooring" is held to celebrate, prematurely, its complete transition from the world of ghosts to the world of mortals. This untimely action, performed by the child's mother in the hope of monetary gain, leads to the child's death. Naana explicitly refers to the baby as "a sacrifice they killed, to satisfy perhaps a new god" and links it with the coming of slavery (p. 284).

Baako first becomes a sacrificial victim when his family performs rituals on the eve of his overseas trip. These rituals make Naana think of his departure as a death; he is being "killed" so that he may fetch things from the land of the ghosts. His second nervous breakdown is like another death. Like the mad dog, Baako is chased by a mob that at the same time fears his teeth and nails as if he were rabid himself. Trussed up with twine, he is delivered to the acute ward of the mental hospital. He has lost the clarity of his vision in the confusion of expectations imposed upon him. Like the man in *The Beautyful Ones* he feels guilty for denying his loved ones the goods they covet, but unlike that man he sinks under the weight of guilt. When he begins to feel that their way is right, he loses his grip on the key to his own sanity.

The novel deals explicitly with the issues of vision, consciousness, and understanding. Baako is conscious of a need to see his own world clearly and to understand it. The need is so great that he once received medical treatment in the United States for the so-called overexpansion of his consciousness — some may see it as clarity of vision; others call it hypermania. Anxiety, which causes this condition, has left in Baako "a desperation . . . so deep it was beginning to be indistinguishable from hope" (p. 149). His condition is partly alleviated when he finds in Juana a friend who can share his loneliness, but in her absence his despair returns. Baako explains to Juana the myth of the Mammy Water, the spirit who inspires a musician by teaching him the agonies of love and loneliness:

> The singer goes to the beach, playing his instrument. These days it's become a guitar. He's lonely, the singer, and he sings of that. So well a woman comes out of the sea, a very beautiful goddess, and they make love. She leaves him to go back to the sea, and they meet at long, fixed intervals only... the musician is filled with so much love he can't bear the separation. But then it is this separation itself which makes him sing as he has never sung before.... After those nights on the shore, when the woman goes, there's no unhappier man on earth.
>
> (pp. 171–172)

Working as a scriptwriter, Baako communicates his vision to viewers with visual images, but he himself is still groping to understand what he sees. He cannot see some of the things that are clear to Naana in spite of her blindness. She sees that life is part of a cycle. She knows too that an overly rigorous quest for meaning in life can be destructive. Her loss of eyesight offers a welcome release from the attempt to understand what she sees in this world; in her blindness her vision is turned toward the next. Retreating from the living world, she has found knowledge that yet escapes Baako, but in the process she has given up the search for worldly understanding and for that greater understanding that lies beyond. Baako, still trying to understand what he sees around him, may yet win that great understanding and a peace against despair. Naana is prepared to leave this fragmented world and enter again on the wholeness of the cycle, but Baako is still trying to make a whole of this world.

Naana's narrative frames the novel and provides a stability that Baako in his mental anxiety badly needs. When he is at odds with the worldview of his demanding relatives, even when his perceptions seem dislocated or illogical, he is close to Naana's way of feeling.

Why Are We So Blest?

Armah's third novel, *Why Are We So Blest?* (1972), examines the fate of an African intellectual, Modin Dofu, who returns (as Armah himself did in 1963) from the United States to contribute to the revolutionary effort in the fictional state of Congheria. Despite his intentions, his education has separated him, perhaps irremediably, from the people he wants to work with and for, and he brings about his own destruction in the form of a predatory white girlfriend from the United States, Aimée Reitsch. The couple is observed on their arrival in Africa by Solo Nkonam, an erstwhile revolutionary who has succumbed to despair. Although Solo's own anxieties color his analysis of Modin's fate, he is rightly dubious about whether Modin's return to Africa, while a step in the right direction, will lead to a successful outcome.

Why Are We So Blest? contrasts two polar opposites: the blessed and the damned. The blessed are those who smugly congratulate themselves on the distance between them and the rest of the world. The image is drawn from an editorial that Modin reads in a U.S. newspaper in which a complacent writer congratulates himself and his fellow U.S. citizens on this distance: "That distance is grace. And that is the distance between the American commonwealth and the remnant of the world. It is the measure of our blessedness" (pp. 98–99). The damned are Fanon's "damnés de la terre."

This novel exists only for its political argument. Every action, relationship, and verbal image in the novel is designed to take its place in the political schema of the distance and opposition between the blessed and the damned. For Solo and Modin separation from their people is not a matter of blessedness, but a shameful incapacity to share in the fate of the masses with whom they wish to identify. Instead their fate is to remain agonized in their separation on the lonely Olympian heights to which their education has lifted them, like heroes raised to the stature of demigods, no longer able to share the fate of mortals.

Modin is sorrowfully aware that his education has separated him from his people. His life is a kind of cultural suicide. The bureaucrats of the People's Union of Congheria scoff at his desire for a heroic death. They ignore the power of hope that Solo recognizes in Modin and thereby destroy it. Modin had hoped that he, like Prometheus in Greek myth, might descend from Olympus with forbidden gifts from the heavens, but like Prometheus he is punished for the attempt, daily tormented by Aimée and finally mutilated and left to bleed to death. His death is no sacrifice for the people, but a wasted life. His suicidal attraction to Aimée leads him into a situation in which—as in all of his sexual encounters with white women—he becomes the object of primitive fears: a mixture of racial hatred and sexual jealousy that explodes into violence. In a sense, Aimée, rather than the revolution, has become Modin's instrument of destruction, his chosen method of suicide.

If Modin's emasculation is a grotesque version of Prometheus' torture, Solo's metaphor for the non-Promethean hero—tough enough to live without pain in the world from which he is alienated by his education—also reflects the myth. As Solo puts it, "To live well now means to develop as highly as possible the ability to do one thing while saying, and preferably also thinking, another thing entirely. The successful livers are those with entrails hard enough to bear the contradiction and to thrive on it" (p. 14). The pun is probably intentional; Armah is fond of concealed puns and references.

Like Baako and Naana, Modin has vision, but he is even more fatally attracted by the shiny things than is the main character of *The Beautyful Ones*, because in Modin's case, the shiny things take human form. Solo laments Modin's blind attraction to Aimée's gleam: "He was not blind. He saw. These notes are not the scribblings of a feeble mind. His soul was not mediocre. Was it then her exterior glow that drew him? What an assault, this luster. What a multitude of images impinging on our souls, diverting every fluid energy, every force of life, to these shiny artifacts of death" (p. 207).

Aimée must be one of the most unpleasant women in fiction. Even the wife of Bradford George Bentum in Armah's next novel, *Two Thousand Seasons*—who is so hideously negative, "an apparition exactly like a ghost" (p. 186), that she exudes an aura of aloneness that blights all surrounding life—cannot compare with her. Aimée is more positively dangerous. In Armah's view, women have the power either to save or to destroy (see, for instance, *Fragments*, p. 257). Women like Oyo, Efua, and Araba destroy with their love and with expectations that are like a curse. Women like Juana, Araba Jesiwa (in Armah's fifth novel, *The Healers*), and Naana can save. Of those who prophesy the "way" in *Two Thousand Seasons*, more are women than men, and part of the reciprocity of the way is that neither men nor women should rule over one another. But Aimée is a white creature formed for the destruction of her black lover.

Solo sees Aimée in the negative terms that inform the reader's perception: as weapon, destroyer, and predator. But Solo is not the only one to recognize her destructive potential. Modin records that he was warned by a fellow student in the United States: "Blue eyes gon eat you, brother, blue eyes gon eat you dead" (p. 200). Aimée's destiny is to devour and destroy Modin. She is "a daughter of a race of destroyers" (p. 149), an "American child of the tribe of death," and one of the "daughters of our white death" (p. 230). In the final scene, Modin's death at Aimée's hands is a hideously literal realization of his student friend's warning.

While Solo is consumed by despair, Modin's chief pain is his loneliness. All the images Modin conjures up for his position suggest a feeling of isolation from his people. When he sees himself as a "factor"—an African go-between for European slave traders, lurking behind stone walls in the traders' castles to bargain for a good price for selling his own people to the Americas—he adds an element of guilt. Modin uses the word "factor" in this sense interchangeably with its common meaning of "element." At one moment he uses the word in its common sense: "I am here because I am a factor. A factor in our history. A factor in our destruction" (p. 160). At the next moment he slips into using it to mean a treacherous go-between and seller of his own kind, so that all occurrences of the word become invested with negative connotations.

In his interpretation of Modin's demise Solo shows his own life to be a failure and demonstrates his inability to see beyond his own despair. We need not accept Modin's death at Solo's valuation. In *Fragments* we are offered, on the one hand, Naana's acceptance of the limits of her understanding and resignation to the continuation of the cycle and, on the other, Baako's pursuit of understanding in this world and the goal of reaching a higher understanding. Similarly, in *Why Are We So Blest?* we are offered the choice between Promethean imagery and the negative interpretation presented by Solo, who we know is in acute despair.

Solo is an intellectual who has been irredeemably isolated from his people. Worse, he is an artist-writer and tends to see this role as that of a parasite. He exists on the emotions of others. He is attracted by the vitality of hope that he senses in Modin, mainly because hope is so alien to his own life. Although literally he becomes Modin's host, metaphorically he is his parasite, relishing the sense of Modin as a living human being and exploring his private papers after his death. Solo is fully aware that his role as a writer is parasitic. He is "not the maker creating new worlds in place of poisoned worlds, but the bloat-eyed watcher sitting over other people's pain, using it, surviving on account of it" (p. 149). As parasite, he is closer even to Aimée than to Modin:

> To be an African now, and a mere artist: to choose to be a parasite feeding on spilt entrails. It does not matter that I eat into myself, too—a part of the rot, feeding on the rot.
>
> I see myself in the couple; I see them in me. The man in me: the African absorbed into Europe, trying to escape death, eager to shed privilege, not knowing how deep the destruction has eaten into himself, hoping to achieve a healing juncture with his destroyed people.
>
> There still is a part of me, closer to the girl, the consumer of experience, user of people.
>
> (p. 232)

The portrait of Solo as a writer is partly autobiographical, both here and more noticeably in the opening chapter. In this novel, as in *Fragments* and the two novels that follow *Why Are We So Blest?* Armah is deeply concerned with the role of the intellectual, particularly the artist, in African society. The artist is in one sense the most impotent member of society, but is also the one who sees and feels the most.

DESTROYING THE DESTROYERS

From an examination of neocolonial society, Armah turned to investigating the precolonial past. His interest in recovering the history of Africa is expressed in a two-part review on George Lamming, titled "The Caliban Complex," published in *West Africa* on 18 and 25 March 1985, a time when Armah was learning ancient Egyptian in order to access the written record of the African past:

> The germane question, then, is this: True or False? Africa has no *written* history, no *written* literature beyond what the foreign conquerors brought. False.... The evidence is not merely available. It is abundant, beautiful in its truth, and astounding in the recognisable freshness

with which it comes again from the depths of buried ages.

But to reach it the awakened intellectual seeker from the West Indies, from Afro-America and from Africa would have to achieve a knowledge of African history and literature so profound it goes beyond the now well known names of the contemporary scene—Niane, Sembene, Achebe; beyond the voices of the not-so-distant past—Mofolo, Magolwane, Balla Fasseke—to include the names and the work of those who, thousands of years ago, *wrote* down the unforgettable record of African humanity for an ambushed posterity.

(p. 571)

Two Thousand Seasons

In his fourth novel, *Two Thousand Seasons* (1973), Armah reacts against the consciousness that pervades *Why Are We So Blest?*—the consciousness of the inevitability of alienation for the elite, particularly for the contemporary artist, who is trying to record the alienation of others. *Two Thousand Seasons* tells, first, of the migration of the Akan people, whose lands are encroached upon by the Arab "predators" of the north, toward the coastal lands of Anoa, where they then become subject to the influence of the European slave traders, the "destroyers." This part of the novel is a fable-history, told in the style of a griot (traditional musician), in the first person plural. This narrative recognizes the role played in history by named individuals, but as this part of the novel progresses, they blur into one people, and the rise of a particular prophet or leader becomes simply a manifestation of the will of the people, the spirit that keeps them close to the "way."

The second part of the novel is also told in the first person plural, but since it concerns the exploits of a particular band of individuals, the effect is to locate the teller within this group. Now only a small group preserves the spirit of the way, and they oppose the mass of their people who have succumbed to the appeal of false roads.

The novel is partly historical fiction, partly wish fulfillment, and partly a parable for the modern day. The slaves who release themselves from bondage and return home to destroy their destroyers offer a new positive image for intellectuals like Solo and Modin. They are significantly named for the artists, fighters, and thinkers of modern Africa. Armah has overcome the problems that faced his intellectual hero in *Why Are We So Blest?* by setting *Two Thousand Seasons* in a past era in which it is possible to be educated by the people, but the novel clearly advocates revolution in the present day.

Two Thousand Seasons picks up all the images of the earlier novels, but develops none of them fully. Particularly in the second part, it hovers uneasily between a novel of ideas and a boys' adventure story. Issues are, rather literally, reduced to black and white in Armah's novels. Yet the simplicity of the issues, combined with the exotic syntax and the metaphor-laden language, adds up to a novel of some power. In *Two Thousand Seasons*, the way in which fabled distant history blends into fiction about the recent past—the past as it might have been if people had been found to lead the way, but also metaphorically the unshackling of the mental slaves of the present—gives impetus and an aura of authenticity to the latter part of the narrative.

The first part of the novel sets up a background of historical fable, which supports what follows. Armah conveys a sense of people united, remembering the way, even when they have departed from it. They suffer together, travel together, hope and fear together. The individuals who leave the way are deviants, the zombies or ostentatious cripples. A few named ones among the people, prophets and leaders, point the way, and the rest follow.

But the people appear to need movement and change to keep them true to this undefined way. After the escape from the predators and the long exodus to the promised land, the new condition of stasis in Anoa promotes growth of the destructive elements, carried from the desert. Society becomes more and more divided against itself, more fragmented. New kings are tolerated. They completely fail to apprehend that for the people they rule the true way is reciprocity, not the obedience of subjects; these kings consolidate their power and become tyrannical. Their failure leaves them open to all kinds of perversion of the spirit. Eventually, the kings of Anoa are led into a subservient alliance with the white destroyers from the sea, giving their people into slavery in return for rum.

Armah's ideas are at times ambiguous. The reciprocal way is not defined, and it is not clear to what, precisely, society is to be returned. Faced with the difference in approach between those followers of the way who fled from the predators in the first part of the novel and those who fight the destroyers with their own weapons in the second part, the reader is led to wonder whether they still pursue the same way. That Armah approves of the new approach is made clear toward the end of the novel: "Why could they not see that those whose vocation it is to destroy destroyers do not through their work become destroyers but the necessary, indispensable finders of paths to the way again? Why were they so blind to this, that in the triumph of des[t]ruction's whiteness the destruction of destruction is the only vocation of the way?" (p. 316). Why not, indeed? Yet, whatever the way is, and however one is to attain it, it does offer a hopeful note in *Two Thousand Seasons*, a goal toward which to direct one's struggle.

In *Why Are We So Blest?* Armah is acutely aware that the intellectual is painfully alienated from the people's struggle and that a massive, perhaps impossible, change in consciousness is necessary before the intellectual can become a genuine revolutionary. Steeped in Fanon's analysis of colonial societies, with its emphasis on the intellectual as go-between or factor of the colonial power, Armah is unable to see a way in which such characters as Modin and Solo can participate in the

people's struggle. Modin's wish to unite himself with the people is a positive force in the novel, but it is not enough. Clearly, this dilemma haunts Armah, for if Modin cannot be a true revolutionary, neither can Armah. The inaction of the man in *The Beautyful Ones*, which can be seen as a reflection of his creator's engaged but inactive social and moral stance, has given way to a desperate but futile attempt to act, on the part of two intellectual characters who reflect their creator's dilemma. Armah believes that the qualities that make him a contemporary artist also preclude him from active participation in the struggle.

In *Two Thousand Seasons*, Armah escapes this dilemma by writing a semihistorical fantasy in which the artist is not yet alienated from society and the educated elite are closer to the heart of their society's way than their fellows, not further away from it. In this context there is no bar to revolutionary struggle against an alien, imposed political structure. Locating himself as narrator, Armah experiences vicariously all the pleasures of certainty — however vague his expressed goal — and writes of the destruction of the destroyers as a basically regenerative process in society.

The Healers

In *The Healers* (1978), Armah turns to the more recent past, the Asante (Ashanti) wars of the nineteenth century. The novel deals again with the health of society, as seen through the ministry of a group of healers and one young man named Densu in particular. His interest in searching for truth and meaning leads him to Damfo the healer, under whose tutelage he learns a great deal about the society he has left behind as well as about the community of healers he is seeking to enter. Densu, who is brave, strong, and courageous, excels at most sporting pursuits but dislikes competitiveness. In this distaste he is joined by his friend Anan and the prince Appia. Appia's noble mother,

Araba Jesiwa, is also a disciple of Damfo's because she, unlike Densu's uncle, the slimy intriguer Ababio, dislikes the shallowness of court circles. The characterization is deliberately exaggerated: stupid characters are utterly moronic; wicked characters are relentlessly evil; Damfo is a true guru; the Fantse leaders are clownish; and the Asante royal family are steeped in self-interest and suspicion.

The plot is long on drama and short on motivation. Densu is framed for the murder of Appia and the mysterious disappearance of Araba Jesiwa, but escapes in the middle of his rigged trial; Damfo heals the Asante general of a spiritual malaise while Densu spies on the British military leaders; in the train of the Asante general, Densu witnesses the fall of the royal city of Kumase; he is tried again in a white court and acquitted after Araba Jesiwa's eleventh-hour appearance to testify that Ababio was the guilty one. The plot devices are drawn from the tricks of adventure novels: hiding in the river by breathing through hollow tubes; bringing down a night runner by stretching a cord across his path; entering the close personal service of the white leader within minutes by a display of enthusiastic servility and leaving again within days with a head full of military secrets.

Neither the plot nor the characterization matters much. They make the novel an easier read than the plotless turgidity of *Two Thousand Seasons*, and therefore make it appeal to a wider readership, but their chief role is to provide a human framework for the moral analysis of a historical moment. Like most historical fiction, the novel revives history in order to reinterpret it. The corruption, cowardice, vanity, and self-seeking spirit that rule the Asante court are the reasons for the loss of the battle, the city, and the war. The highly schematic design of the novel is intended to demonstrate this view.

The Asante general, Asamoa Nkwanta, is an honest soldier and a true servant of his people, but the Asante queen mother intrigues against him. After publicly promising to back his battle strategy, she ensures instead that he will be left without reinforcements:

> When you had left, the queen-mother asked the king and Nana Asafo Adjei if they were such children as to believe that you, Asamoa Nkwanta, had forgiven them. . . . She asked the king if he would rather be king of a violated kingdom or be nothing in a virgin nation. . . . She said if Asante followed Asamoa Nkwanta's plan and resisted the whites, there would be nothing to stop Asamoa Nkwanta from becoming king of the inviolate nation.
>
> (pp. 290–291)

Such a devious mind as the queen mother's cannot believe in the genuine motives of the bluff soldier. The king and the other leaders concur with her suspicions, and the king is readily persuaded to the ignoble conclusion that it is better to be king of a conquered nation than resist the conqueror and surrender his leadership.

As in *Two Thousand Seasons*, kingship is seen as an inherently vicious system of government in which the worst, most power-hungry, and ungenerous people will accede to power either as advisers or, by foul play, as rulers. Part of the scheme of the novel is that good characters have chosen deliberately against a life of intrigue at court. Densu is of the royal family in his hometown, and Ababio initially tries to tempt him with the position of king if he will fall in with his schemes. Araba Jesiwa is a woman of royal lineage who has chosen to marry a commoner. Asamoa Nkwanta has enough influence over the army to seize power if he wanted. All three are members of a privileged elite who deliberately turn their backs on athletic achievement, wealth, personal power, and social position, preferring to attend extensive counseling sessions with Damfo so that they can live a simple life with psychological peace.

Araba Jesiwa's choice is seen as the direct cause of her ability to conceive her longed-for son. Asamoa Nkwanta's choice alleviates his depression and enables him to return to service in the wars, although he is troubled by his new unease with the warrior life, with his service to a degenerate regime, and with violence as a solution to resolving conflict. Densu begins the novel wanting to become a trainee healer, and at the end of the novel he still maintains an attachment to the scattered members of the community of healers who have survived a treacherous massacre, even though his enthusiastic engagement with the world of military affairs would seem to sit oddly with his teacher Damfo's declared philosophy. Densu seems less bothered than any of Armah's earlier characters by the fear of contamination and more eager to engage with current political events, if only as a spectator.

CONCLUSION

Armah's political commitment in his writings cannot be doubted. As he stated in one of his rare comments on his work as a writer, "I saw and still see the neo-colonial order we're all living with as profoundly destructive, its ruling arrangements incurably parasitic" ("One Writer's Education," p. 1753). Armah's disgust at the present state of affairs is clear, but his pessimism about the future has been overstated.

In *The Beautyful Ones Are Not Yet Born* there is a positive model of birth as well as a negative one. A day may come when the beautiful ones are born, when the process of natural decay nurtures the seed of a new and beautiful flowering. In the meantime the chichidodo bird lives on and has a strangely happy song. In *Fragments* the regenerative elements are much stronger than the pessimism. Baako has friends, a woman, and a teacher who will help him face the terrible problems of understanding the world; and Naana, whose vision frames the novel and thus makes its structure a self-generating circle, enters again upon the cycle of death and birth, contentedly resigned to her inability to reach perfect understanding this time

around. In *Why Are We So Blest?* Modin's death forms a terrible image of unregenerative destruction, but in the context of the Promethean metaphor one can see that his death may not have been entirely fruitless. In *Two Thousand Seasons* Armah turns to a hope in revolution as the regenerative force, which his characters were unable to embrace in the earlier novels. In *The Healers* a medical discipline based on psychological counseling is the greatest hope for saving individuals from contamination and restoring them to health.

Selected Bibliography

BIBLIOGRAPHIES

Lindfors, Bernth, comp. *Black African Literature in English: A Guide to Information Sources.* Detroit: Gale Research Co., 1979.
———. *Black African Literature in English: 1977–1981 Supplement.* New York: Africana Publishing Co., 1986.
———. *Black African Literature in English: 1982–1986.* London: Zell, 1989.
———. *Black African Literature in English: 1987–1991.* London: Zell, 1995.
Wright, Derek, ed. *Critical Perspectives on Ayi Kwei Armah.* Washington, D.C.: Three Continents Press, 1992.

NOVELS

The Beautyful Ones Are Not Yet Born. Boston: Houghton Mifflin, 1968; New York: Macmillan, 1969; London: Heinemann, 1969.
Fragments. Boston: Houghton Mifflin, 1970; London: Heinemann, 1974; Nairobi, Kenya: East African Publishing House, 1974.
Why Are We So Blest? New York: Doubleday, 1972; London: Heinemann, 1974; Nairobi, Kenya: East African Publishing House, 1974.
Two Thousand Seasons. Nairobi, Kenya: East African Publishing House, 1973; London: Heinemann, 1979; Chicago: Third World Press, 1979.
The Healers. Nairobi, Kenya: East African Publishing House, 1978; London: Heinemann, 1979.

SHORT FICTION

"Contact." In *New African* 4 (December 1965).

"Asemka." In *Okyeame* 3 (December 1966).

"An African Fable." In *Présence africaine* 68 (1968).

"Yaw Manu's Charm." In *Atlantic Monthly* (May 1968).

"The Offal Kind." In *Harper's Magazine* 1424 (January 1969).

"Halfway to Nirvana." In *West Africa* (24 September 1984).

ESSAYS AND JOURNALISM

"African Socialism: Utopian or Scientific?" In *Présence africaine* 64 (1967).

"Fanon: The Awakener." In *Negro Digest* 18 (October 1969).

"Sundiata, an Epic of Old Mali." In *Black World* 23, no. 7 (1974).

"Chaka." In *Black World* 24, no. 4 (1975).

"Larsony, or Fiction as Criticism of Fiction." In *Asemka* 4 (September 1976). Repr. in *New Classic* 4 (November 1977).

"Masks and Marx: The Marxist Ethos vis-à-vis African Revolutionary Theory and Praxis." In *Présence africaine* 131 (1984).

"The Lazy School of Literary Criticism." In *West Africa* 3522 (25 February 1985).

"The Caliban Complex." In *West Africa* 3525, 3526 (18 and 25 March 1985).

"Our Language Problem." In *West Africa* 3531 (29 April 1985).

"The Teaching of Creative Writing." In *West Africa* 3534 (20 May 1985).

"One Writer's Education." In *West Africa* 3548 (26 August 1985).

"Writers as Professionals." In *West Africa* 3598 (11 August 1986).

CRITICAL STUDIES

Amuta, Chidi. "Portraits of the Contemporary African Artist in Armah's Novels." In *World Literature Written in English* 21 (fall 1982). Repr. in Derek Wright, ed., *Critical Perspectives on Ayi Kwei Armah*. Washington, D.C.: Three Continents Press, 1992.

Anyidoho, Kofi. "African Creative Fiction and a Poetics of Social Change." In *Komparatistische Hefte* 13 (1986).

Bader, Rudolph. "A Vision of Past, Present, and Future." In Robert L. Ross, ed., *International Literature in English: Essays on the Major Writers*. New York: Garland, 1991; London: St. James, 1991.

Barthold, Bonnie-Jo. *Black Time: Fiction of Africa, the Caribbean, and the United States*. New Haven, Conn.: Yale University Press, 1981.

———. "Ayi Kwei Armah: An Akan Story-Teller." In Hedwig Bock and Albert Wertheim, eds., *Essays on Contemporary Post-Colonial Fiction*. Munich, Germany: Max Hueber Verlag, 1986.

Boafo, Y. S. "The Nature of Healing in Ayi Kwei Armah's *The Healers*." In *Komparatistische Hefte* 13 (1986). Repr. in Derek Wright, ed., *Critical Perspectives on Ayi Kwei Armah*. Washington, D.C.: Three Continents Press, 1992.

Chetin, Sara. "Armah's Women." In *Kunapipi* 6, no. 3 (1984).

Colmer, Rosemary. "The Human and the Divine: *Fragments* and *Why Are We So Blest?*" In *Kunapipi* 2, no. 2 (1980). Repr. in Derek Wright, ed., *Critical Perspectives on Ayi Kwei Armah*. Washington, D.C.: Three Continents Press, 1992.

Evans, Jenny. "Women of 'The Way': *Two Thousand Seasons*, Female Images and Black Identity." In *ACLALS Bulletin* 6 (November 1982).

Fraser, Robert. *The Novels of Ayi Kwei Armah: A Study in Polemical Fiction*. London: Heinemann, 1980.

Gillard, Garry. "Ayi Kwei Armah: Postcolonialism/Space/Postmodernism." In *SPAN* 36 (October 1993).

Griffiths, Gareth. "Structure and Image in Kwei Armah's *The Beautyful Ones Are Not Yet Born*." In *Studies in Black Literature* 2, no. 2 (1971). Repr. in Derek Wright, ed., *Critical Perspectives on Ayi Kwei Armah*. Washington, D.C.: Three Continents Press, 1992.

Izevbaye, D. S. "Ayi Kwei Armah and the 'I' of the Beholder." In Bruce King and Kolawole Ogungbesan eds., *A Celebration of Black and African Writing*. Zaria, Nigeria: Ahmadu Bello University Press, 1975. Repr. in Derek Wright, ed., *Critical Perspectives on Ayi Kwei Armah*. Washington, D.C.: Three Continents Press, 1992.

Lazarus, Neil. *Resistance in Postcolonial African Fiction*. New Haven, Conn.: Yale University Press, 1990.

Kisogie, Bai [Wole Soyinka]. "A Plague on Both Your Houses: Ayi Kwei Armah's *Two Thousand Seasons*." In *Transition* 45 (1974).

Lindfors, Bernth. "Armah's Histories." In *African Literature Today* 11 (1980). Repr. in Derek Wright, ed., *Critical Perspectives on Ayi Kwei Armah*. Washington, D.C.: Three Continents Press, 1992.

Lobb, Edward. "Armah's *Fragments* and the Vision of the Whole." In *ARIEL* 10 (January 1979).

———. "Personal and Political Fate in Armah's *Why Are We So Blest?*" In *World Literature Written in English* 19 (spring 1980). Repr. in Derek Wright, ed., *Critical Perspectives on Ayi Kwei Armah*. Washington, D.C.: Three Continents Press, 1992.

Moore, Gerald. "The Writer and the Cargo Cult." In Anna Rutherford, ed., *Commonwealth*. Århus, Denmark: University of Århus Press, 1971.

Ogede, Ode S. "The Rhetoric of Revolution in Armah's *The Healers*: Form as Experience." In *African Studies Review* 36 (April 1993).

Ogungbesan, Kolawole. "Symbol and Meaning in *The Beautyful Ones Are Not Yet Born*." In *World Literature Written in English* 12 (April 1973).

———. Petersen, Kirsten Holste. "The New Way: Ayi Kwei Armah's *Two Thousand Seasons*." In *World Literature Written in English* 15 (1976).

———. "Loss and Frustration: An Analysis of A. K. Armah's *Fragments*." In *Kunapipi* 1, no. 1 (1979). Repr. in Derek Wright, ed., *Critical Perspectives on Ayi Kwei Armah*. Washington, D.C.: Three Continents Press, 1992.

———. "West African Politics and Politicians from a Literary Point of View." In Dieter Riemenschneider, ed., *The History and Historiography of Commonwealth Literature*. Tübingen, Germany: Gunther Narr, 1983.

Rassner, Ron. "*Fragments*: The Cargo Mentality." In *Ba Shiru* 5, no. 2 (1974).

Stewart, Danièle, "L'être et le monde dans les premiers romans d'Ayi Kwei Armah." In *Présence africaine* 85 (1973).

Wright, Derek. "Motivation and Motif: The Carrier Rite in Ayi Kwei Armah's *The Beautyful Ones Are Not Yet Born*." In *English Studies in Africa* 28, no. 2 (1985). Repr. in Derek Wright, ed., *Critical Perspectives on Ayi Kwei Armah*. Washington, D.C.: Three Continents Press, 1992.

———. *Ayi Kwei Armah's Africa: The Sources of His Fiction*. London: Zell, 1989.

———. "Man and His Teacher: A Note on Double-Narrative." In *World Literature Written in English* 31 (fall 1991).

———. "'Dystropia' in the African Novel: A Critique of Armah's Language in *The Beautyful Ones Are Not Yet Born*." In *Commonwealth Novel in English* 5 (fall 1992).

———, ed. *Critical Perspectives on Ayi Kwei Armah*. Washington, D.C.: Three Continents Press, 1992.

Kofi Awoonor
1935–

DEREK WRIGHT

KOFI AWOONOR is Ghana's most famous poet and a major African literary figure who has worked in many genres. In addition to five books of poetry, he has published two novels, two short plays, three books of political essays, a work of translation, a critical study of African literature, and many essays. He has been a prominent academic, having successfully completed graduate and doctoral studies at the University of London (1967–1968) and the State University of New York at Stony Brook (1968–1972). He has held professorships at the State University of New York at Stony Brook (1968–1975) and the University of Cape Coast in Ghana (1977–1982), as well as a number of visiting professorships.

In addition he has, like many African writers, been a public man of affairs and a committed political and cultural activist. During the 1960s he held the offices of research fellow in the University of Ghana's Institute of African Studies (1960–1964), editor of the Ghanaian literary journal *Okyeame* (1961–1965), and managing director of the Ghana Film Industries Corporation (1965–1967). In these positions he participated directly in the national cultural programs of Ghana's first president, Kwame Nkrumah, which were designed to stimulate the growth of indigenous arts and a specifically African literature. In the

1980s Awoonor was a founding member and then general secretary of Ghana's Action Congress Party and threw his support behind the revolutionary military government of Jerry Rawlings, which he served in the capacities of member of a National Commission on Democracy (1983), Ghanaian ambassador to Brazil (1984–1988), and ambassador to Cuba (1988–1992) and to the United Nations (1992–1994).

Awoonor's political activities have at times exposed him to danger. In 1975 he was arrested for suspected subversion and, after being held in solitary confinement for eight months, was finally brought to trial on charges of harboring a fugitive coup plotter and helping him to escape justice. Though found guilty, Awoonor was not required to serve further time in prison and the charge was formally rescinded in 1979. The full story of this episode is told in Awoonor's book *The Ghana Revolution: A Background Account from a Personal Perspective* (1984) and lies behind many of the poems in *The House by the Sea* (1978), the house of the title being Ussher Fort Prison, where he was incarcerated, in the Ghanaian capital of Accra.

Awoonor was born on 13 March 1935 in Wheta in the then British colony of the Gold Coast and grew up as George Awoonor-Williams, under which name he published his first volume of poetry, *Rediscovery, and Other Poems* (1964). His parents, Atsu and Kosiwo Awoonor, were Ewe (a people residing in Ghana and surrounding areas) of mixed national origin; his father was a trader and tailor of Sierra Leonean stock, and his mother a Togolese from a farming background. When Awoonor was eight years old his family moved to the old coastal town of Keta, where he spent most of his childhood and youth. In Keta he had his primary and secondary schooling at, respectively, the Keta Presbyterian Mission School (1944–1950) and the Anloga Zion College (1951–1954). He then moved to Achimota College in Accra (1955–1956) and to the University College of the Gold Coast in Legon (1957–1960), where he won the university's Gurrey Prize for the best original creative writing in 1959 and graduated with honors in English in 1960.

The sea is heard everywhere in Awoonor's poetry, and the sea and lagoon settings of his childhood home of Keta are enduring lyrical presences throughout his work, though their power goes deeper than mere landscape. "Their world was my real world of consciousness, of growth" (p. 216), Awoonor explains in the afterword to *Until the Morning After: Collected Poems 1963–1985* (1987). This consciousness, he says, "was formed in mysteries about life; it had to do with invisible living phenomena that pertained to every day existence.... The magical and mysterious relationships defining only the very simple and the mundane have, beyond time and place, their anchorage in *words*" (p. 216). The sacred words, in Awoonor's case, were those of Ewe oral poetry, and his poetic model was the Ewe Anlo dirge, or song of lamentation. His grandmother was a singer of dirge songs, and he grew up in a community of drummers, dancers, and dirge singers whose traditional language he adapted for some of the poems in his first volume, *Rediscovery*. This early poetry both drew upon a personal family heirloom and opened up a channel into a broader

African heritage; it was at once a process of nostalgic rediscovery and a new beginning and departure, an exploration of change that returned the searcher to his starting point and to the primal sources of his inspiration.

EARLY POEMS

The pervasive mood of *Rediscovery* and *Night of My Blood* (1971), which reprinted two-thirds of the earlier volume, is one of lyric lament, expressing the western-educated African's drifting sense of loss and anguish at his or her severance from indigenous cultural traditions that have been cut away by a perverting modernization. *Night of My Blood* is permeated by the returning exile's complex mixture of feelings: a wary fatalism alongside nostalgia for childhood joys and lost harmonies, longings as well as forebodings about what he will find. Awoonor's model is the Ewe dirge as performed by the great Anlo dirge singer (or *heno*) Vinoko Akpalu, whose work he was later to translate in *Guardians of the Sacred Word: Ewe Poetry* (1974).

A recurring motif in Ewe dirge poetry is the thwarted or painful return: the ancestral pilgrimage, after sojourns in alien and hostile worlds, leads back to a desolate land of neglected and ruined shrines, eaten by termites. In Awoonor's much anthologized poem "The Weaver Bird," which originally appeared in *Rediscovery*, the rediscovered shrines are defiled by the metaphoric droppings of foreign religions and false political messiahs. The image of the weaverbird, notorious for its colonizing habits and its destructive effects on the host tree, allows Awoonor to open out into the larger theme of Europe's colonial assault on Africa's material and cultural wealth, envisaged in the poem as a process of desecration that leaves contemporary Africa with the task of rebuilding everything anew. Once invited in, the weaverbird returns "in the guise of the owner," the tenant turns landlord, and the invader is indulged by the misplaced gratitude of indigenous hosts: "We did not want to send it away" (*Until the Morning After*, p. 21, ll. 6, 3).

The brooding, sorrowful tone of these poems is offset by pointed satire denouncing corrupt neocolonial traitors who have "abjured the magic of being themselves" ("We Have Found a New Land," *Until the Morning After*, p. 11, l. 16). To the lament for neglected gods and decayed shrines is added grief for the short-lived dreams of African independence movements. The dirge's format of worldly disappointment and frustration is a ready-made vehicle for the expression of the dwindling millenarian hopes of African nationalism and of subsequent postindependence disillusionment.

The persona in these poems undertakes a journey that is both realistic and mythical, leading both outward into society and introspectively into the self. The speaking "I" of an Akpalu dirge is simultaneously the grieving individual singer and the voice of the whole community, plunged into mourning by a death. Though the poet-cantor lives a socially secluded life and is sometimes scorned for his low social and economic status, he carries society's collective memory and conscience as part of his *hadzivodoo*, or gift of songs: in his priestlike role, he is medium and clairvoyant, the vessel and vehicle of primal energies. Thus it is through him that the community—and in Awoonor's adaptation, the nation as a whole—expresses and defines itself. Accordingly, Awoonor's imitative elegiac songs are not isolated outbursts of private melancholy and statements of personal alienation; rather, they function as expressions of a collective desolation and as an elegy for the spiritual death of an entire culture and the passing of an era.

The radial swell of Awoonor's nebulous funeral imagery, though diffuse in effect, makes for a poetry of remarkable range and resonance, full of daring imaginative syntheses and startling superimpositions, though these take place in a realm beyond reality in which there is no differentiation among past, present, and future. The legendary migration of the Ewe people from the upper Niger to their present home in eastern Ghana is tentatively grafted onto the dirge archetype of the soul making its moonlit journey by canoe across the waters of death. (This is the "night" of the poet's "blood" in "Night of My Blood.") Superimposed, in turn, upon this pilgrimage is the modern poet-exile's circular passage of departure and return, rediscovering at last the wisdom of ancestors and ritual poetic traditions and submerging himself in their sustaining communal ethos.

The imagery of these delicate lyrics is a haunting, paradoxical mixture of fertilizing floods and ferryboats crossing the river of death, drums and bells, cooking fires and sacrificial altars, bitter herbs and incense, purification and putrefaction; the constant contextual shifts habitually present the poet-exile in terms of death and rebirth. The dead man journeys to a new life among the ancestors, and the poet travels to the dead—to the origins of his Ewe oral culture—in search of new life for his songs. After the spiritual death of alienation in a foreign culture, the homecoming is a painful initiation, another kind of death that must be endured for a possible new birth. This is sometimes accompanied by the darker perception that the poet's visionary liberation, like the protagonist's in Awoonor's experimental poetic novel *This Earth, My Brother . . .* (1971), can be achieved only by passing through madness and bodily death and then returning literally to his native earth, where his buried birth cord awaits him. The dead man must became an ancestor in order to gain powers that may be used to benefit the community from a position outside it; the poet, by analogy, must leave his society to acquire the power to revitalize it on his return.

The trope of exile, envisaged as a kind of death but also as a mediating agent, is crucial, especially insofar as it insists upon the retention of what is vital in alien influences. Awoonor is no cultural purist bent on the retrieval of pristine, precolonial African art forms. On the contrary, he is a great assimilator and syncretist who combines disparate fragments of experience and poetic styles in collages of images drawn from a multitude of sources. *Night of My Blood* contains many distorted and inverted echoes of the Christian liturgy as well as scraps of Gerard Manley Hopkins and T. S. Eliot. Between the anvil of Africa and the hammer of the west the poet's pains are transformed

> In the forging house of a new life,
> . . .
> Into the joy of new songs.
> ("The Anvil and the Hammer,"
> p. 31, ll. 2, 4)

Even so, the ominous pun on "forging" suggests that some counterfeiting, falsifying agent may be at work. In the same poem the refrain, "Sew the old days for us, our fathers,/That we can wear them under our new garment" (p. 31, ll. 14–15), western images and African forms as separate entities still await combination, giving the impression, as in many of Awoonor's longer and more ambitious poems, of an admixture or juxtaposition rather than a genuine synthesis of influences. Moreover, even the old "garment" of tradition that is worn closest to the poet's skin and heart is the cause of some discomfort and is completely concealed by the borrowed garment.

Though it is a poetry of the speaking (and singing) voice, Awoonor's work is, of course, a print-based approximation and simulation of dirge orature rather than the thing itself—we experience the poet alone on the page, not the singer abroad in the marketplace. The poet, having denied himself both the natural polytonality of his native Ewe tongue and the external reinforcements of western metrics (all the poems are written in free verse), has to reproduce artificially the rhythmic counterpoint of the dirge through the equivalent devices of syntactical parallelism, balanced antithesis, and repetition. Nevertheless, in the best poems of *Night of My Blood*, there is a genuine and powerful sense of a voice coming through from another language and culture, progressing from virtual translation through personal adaptation to the creation of entirely new forms.

The most noticeable weakness of the poems is perhaps an excessive and limiting reliance on the dirge's highly stylized incantatory formulas, producing poems that are sometimes profound but sometimes trite and monotonous. It is perhaps significant that one of the finest poems in the volume is a personal elegy in which the familiar dirge imagery is put to very private use. In "Lament of the Silent Sister," for Christopher Okigbo, the Igbo poet who was killed in the Nigerian civil war, Awoonor presents his poetic self as a female persona, artistically immature and unprepared to be impregnated by Okigbo's uncompromising muse until the moment of the Igbo master's death, when the floods of poetry are released in a state of sexual tumult. The canoe and flood symbolism carried by the poem's rhythmic surge are simultaneously funereal and sexual, telescoping death and procreation, sexual initiations and immolation, ancestral passages and rebirth.

EXILE

After the fall of President Nkrumah in 1966, exile became the fate of most of those who, like Awoonor, had had close association with Nkrumah's government. Thus the theme of exile becomes poignantly personal in Awoonor's next volume, *Ride Me, Memory* (1973), which is based on the first years of his experience in the United States between 1968 and 1975. Here mellow African memories crowd in alongside U.S. anecdotes and larger political statements as Awoonor moves away from the dirge-lament into other oral styles and into literary traditions outside his ancestral heritage. The range of Ewe forms is extended to include the *halo*, the earthy vitriolic song of abuse, and the praise song. Under the first category come jocularly caustic portraits of meddling first-world scholars, under the second earnestly adulatory portraits of black American writers, singers, and jazz musicians. A violent energy coincides with a tightening of the bonds of political commitment in these poems. Awoonor testifies to the sufferings and struggles of victims of the black diaspora, especially under the brutalities and hypocrisies of the modern United States, which keeps breaking into his enjoyment of the company of his American hosts. There is a greater looseness of form and a slighter dependence on hypnotic ritual formulas, and the imagery is more boldly explicit and less dreamlike than in the earlier volumes. Even so, there are still strong continuities with the first two collections, and some African critics, notably Kofi Anyidoho, have commended Awoonor's continued, more sparing use of the dirge (in "African Memories") and his richly comic deployment of the *halo* (in "Songs of Abuse"). Yet the collection as a whole, perhaps because of the preponderance of proper names for people, places, and events, tends toward the diffuseness and breezy thinness of a travelogue.

On his return to Ghana in 1975 Awoonor very quickly found himself in political trouble, detained for alleged collusion with an Ewe coup plot. He recounts the experiences of his period in prison in *The House by the Sea*. The prison poems at the center of this volume, in their remorseless examination of the nature of political involvement and responsibility, reveal a harsh, distilled intensity, a gritty sharpness and brittle clarity that are new in Awoonor's work. This is raw, survivalist poetry (some of it written on toilet paper and smuggled out of his cell), urgently confronting the realities of political repression, torture, and assassination in African and global contexts and posing ultimate questions about the nature of freedom — whether it is best served by the private pursuit of self-fulfillment or by the public service of unromantic revolutionary labors. The volume opens out beyond the merely personal to take in political outrage and injustice over the African continent and throughout human history in the world at large — for example, in South Africa and Latin America, notably poet Pablo Neruda's Chile.

But in the last and most ambitious poem, "The Wayfarer Comes Home" (home is simultaneously Eweland, Ghana, and Africa), the lyric lusciousness returns and the dominant mood is one of affectionate celebration. Awoonor says in the prison poems that the pursuit of political liberty, though it may involve "the possibility of being murdered in a dark cell" ("Revolution: A Chat with Ho Chi Minh's Ghost"), is worth living longer for:

> On such a day
> who would dare think of dying?
>
> So much Freedom means
> that we swear we'll postpone dying
> until the morning after.
> ("In a Prison Yard," p. 52, ll. 8–12)

These lines provide Awoonor with the title for his collected poems, in which nine new poems offer a mixture of undaunted resilience and stoical resignation in the face of the everyday tragedies of economic ruin, destitution, and early death, which continue to devastate modern Africa:

> Do not lose heart,
> have arms, we have shields
>
>   . . .
> Some rivers there are you cannot swim
> some strong rivers there are you cannot ford.
> ("So the World Changes," *Until the Morning After*, p. 204, ll. 15–16, 19–20)

The circle continues to widen in Awoonor's next collection, *The Latin American and Caribbean Notebook* (1992), the harvest of his diplomatic employments and travels in Brazil, Cuba, and Nicaragua. In this volume the poet is by turns self-defensive (of his Nkrumah period and after) and self-accusatory. He presents himself, in the historical present, as "the braggart loudmouth boastful / uncertain diplomat" ("Rio de Janeiro: Fearful and Lovely City," p. 11, ll. 53–54) who has taken "refuge in an inane occupation" ("Of Home Once More," p. 8, l. 15), shunted off abroad to serve another country while his own is being wrecked by fools and criminals. The ambassador-poet then proceeds, from a position of comfort and privilege, to project his own sense of displacement upon victims of the black diaspora in other lands — African gardeners in Middlesex, England; squatter communities in Brasília, Brazil; "the limping habitants of inconsolable *favelas*" ("Rio de Janeiro," p. 10, l. 21). With ironic presumption, he claims doubtful solidarities with those who have fallen from the regal ancestral glories of their African heritage — "down the vast saharas of my history" ("In Memoriam: Return to Kingston," p. 45, l. 83) — to degraded and desperate levels of existence. These self-scrutinizing, self-suspecting poems alternate with celebratory public pieces that indulge a sentimental adulation of the heroes of the Cuban and Nicaraguan revolutions. Thus, a statue of the revolutionary leader Che Guevara is described this way:

> around his head now a halo
> on his face a vision
> in his hand a gun, in his eye a love supreme
>   a love supreme.
>
> ("Cuban Chapters," p. 18)

The poems that carry most conviction in this volume, however, are the nostalgic and delicate love lyrics ("Time Revisited," "Distant Home Country," "Lover's Song," "Dream — Again," "Readings and Musings"), which wrench subtle reflections upon time and aging from hallucinated childhood memories and the casual affairs of the lonely, middle-aged diplomat, condemned to empty beds in alien cities. The most disappointing efforts are the long, rambling prosy pieces in which obliquely personal reminiscences are randomly interspersed with catalogs of political outrages and scandals (the United States' impoverished blacks and Britain's homeless in "Betrayers") and with snapshot newspaper headlines (an Iranian airliner downed by U.S. forces and Arab boys killed by Israeli soldiers in "Of Home and Sea I Already Sang"). These poems are amorphous affairs, each one an obscure "kingdom where I stash / a memory" ("Betrayers," p. 24, ll. 68–69), and the very choice of verb in this line indicates the casual, slapdash manner in which the memories are arranged and the poems composed. Significantly, in the most poignantly moving poem in the collection — about the poet's first diplomatic assignment in Cuba, which involved the death of a nineteen-year-old African girl — Awoonor confines himself strictly to the experience at hand ("The Girl That Died in Havana").

Even some of the best poems in *The Latin American and Caribbean Notebook* are, unfortunately, marred by a bland populist idealism, vented in prosaic clichés of "the wisdom of the people" and "the validity of struggle" ("A Death Foretold," pp. 39–40, ll. 53–55), and by a windy racial chauvinism. There are repeated speculations about the regathering of "our black African people" around new revolutionary foci in the Caribbean and Central America, though how and where this reunion is to take place, except in the poet's wishful imagination, is never clear (" 'As Long as There Are Tears and Suffering,' " "In Memoriam"). The poems are also spoiled by indiscriminate, unfocalized political invective and by the embarrassingly personal naming of unknown and unidentified people ("Maurice," "Neville," "David") whom the reader is apparently expected to recognize. *The Latin American and Caribbean Notebook* is Awoonor's most prosily self-indulgent volume. Bearing out the title, many of the poems read like uncoordinated diary jottings, thinly contextualized anecdotes that have not been imaginatively energized into poetry.

AWOONOR AS NOVELIST

Outside of his poetry Awoonor is best known for his experimental poetic novel, *This Earth, My Brother . . .* (1971). The twin narratives of this ambitious work operate on two different levels of consciousness and reality. The realistic prose narrative carries the protagonist, the foreign-educated lawyer Amamu, through the despairing round of an average working day, during which he encounters both the oppressed—in the form of beggars, criminals, and the unemployed—and their oppressors, the corrupt elite who are now running Ghana. These prose chapters also include, in flashback, vignettes of a typical colonial childhood, the legacy of which is accumulated and stored in the novel's consciousness. But the prose narrative is interspersed with poetic interludes that draw upon the worlds of myth, dream, and ritual. These lyrical passages, in contradistinction to the forward linear movement of the primary narrative, bring Amamu back to the visionary rediscovery of his lost childhood playmate and cousin Dede, who at the deeper level of his subconscious is identified with Africa's legendary precolonial innocence and pre-European mythology—notably, the myth of Mammy Water, the mermaid or woman of the sea, who takes men into her element and returns them to the land with supernatural healing and regenerative powers.

The pattern of Amamu's return to a reborn childhood is complicated, moreover, by being tied to a parallel life-and-death cycle. The visionary liberation achieved by what Amamu refers to as the assumption of the "body" of Dede's death can be purchased, it seems, only in his own passage, at the end of the book, through madness and bodily death—a death that is presented as a rebirth into the spirit world from which the child Amamu arrives in the first chapter. Thus, as in his poetry, Awoonor once again incorporates western linear advancement into a pattern of circular return. Amamu is the bridger of transitional gulfs between the worlds of the living, the dead, and the unborn and is the historical link between the corrupt modern state and a reservoir of lost myths and faiths.

Perhaps the most crucial superimposition upon Amamu's personal return, however, is that of a ritual bearing away of a communal historical burden. Dede's death from malnutrition in 1944 is made to mark the centenary of the colonial incursion into Ghana and is seen as the culmination of a century of theft, pillage, and neglect. Independent Ghana struggles into a horrific birth after a long and violent colonial gestation: "This revolting malevolence is thy mother. She begat thee from her womb after a pregnancy of a hundred and thirteen years. She begat thee after a long parturition she begat you into her dust, and you woke up after the eighth day screaming on a dunghill" (pp. 36–37, the Doubleday edition). The dunghill is contemporary Ghana, blighted at infancy because it was begotten by colonialism. Significantly, Nkrumah rules from the old colonial castle through which slaves were once shipped; in one satiric episode the night soil truck fresh from the dunghill rides at the head of the presidential motorcade, carrying symbolically before it the rottenness of the ruling regime.

This rot and decay may yet, however, develop the fertile, regenerative capacities of manure, for Amamu casts himself metaphorically in the ritual role of carrier in the West African coastal community's annual purification rite; however, his task is to bear away not the accumulated pollution of the past year, as is customary, but 113 years of colonial ills. The antiquity of Ghana's corruption is finely caught in the last part of the book. Amamu, before retracing his forefathers' steps back to the village lagoon and the scene of his childhood dreams, undertakes a harrowing journey through the slums of Nima in search of his houseboy, Yaro, for whom his help comes too late: "[Yaro] suddenly looked old; he wore for the first time an indeterminable age, an oldness that was not time's, an agedness of hills and rivers. . . . It had to do with a doom, a catastrophe, a total collapse of all things" (pp. 222–223). It is Amamu's ritual task to roll back the years on the accumulated, unpurged misery represented by the Nima dunghill: "The centuries and the years of pain of which he was the inheritor, and the woes for which he was singled out to be carrier and the sacrifice, were being rolled away" (p. 227).

This Earth, My Brother . . . is a hauntingly elegiac, richly textured work of great poetic beauty, deserving of its considerable critical acclaim. It remains, however, an overambitious work and leaves an impression of ungathered threads and unrealized purposes. Chiefly, the links between the novel's view of rebirth and social vision, between the posthumous progression of the protagonist's spirit and an implied social regeneration, are tenuously theoretical. Awoonor has said in essays and interviews that Amamu is "liminal, yet central" ("Voyager and the Earth," 1973, p. 92) and that his journey, which is both "realistic" and "mythical," is at once personally redemptive and a venture "into the very entrails of his society" ("Interview with Kofi Awoonor," p. 60). Yet Amamu's completion of a religious cycle through death, though it achieves a supernatural communion with the spirit of his lost childhood love, cannot be construed except in the most marginal terms as an act of communal deliverance that restores some collective loss. At the realistic level his final vision of Dede rising from the waves like a mermaid is pure illusion, the fruit of his madness, and the death that immediately follows is not invested in the renewal of society but is squandered. It is suicidal rather than sacrificial, more narcissistic than altruistic: it is not a public but a personal event, in which ritual mystique has priority over social reality.

Amamu is, in any case, an unlikely, doubtful savior. As a lawyer he carries on his conscience the unprosecuted crimes and unexpiated guilt of his society and identifies with the poor and downtrodden. Yet as his influence over customs and traffic officers illustrates, he also profits from and participates in the general corruption: "A lawyer is next to God. He is the one who gets you out of trouble; he is the one who puts you into trouble" (p. 203). Amamu makes a high-minded stand against the ruling elite's sellout to neocolonial values (though partly to expiate his own complicity). This stand, together with the graphic realism of the account of the Nima slums, infuses the novel with a more militant and socially oriented spirit. But his mission stops at contemplation of Africa's sufferings and is not translated into action. Amamu merely assumes the moral and intellectual burden, the maddening weight of consciousness of Africa's evil legacies, and it is doubtful that his subsequent despair and suicide at the scene of his childhood dreams are necessary stages of a regenerative process that will transform the dunghill into a place of renewed creation.

The problem of contrived rebirth is more acute in Awoonor's shorter and slighter second novel, *Comes the Voyager at Last*, which was not published until 1992, although a long extract appeared in the journal *Okike* in 1975. This novel contains three parallel narratives. The first narrator, a black American from the state of Virginia, undergoes experiences reminiscent of those of Malcolm X (whose bodyguard he eventually becomes) in the 1950s: social deprivation and premature death, wrongful arrest and imprisonment, conversion to black Islam and return to Africa. The second narrator is a garrulous and facetious Ghanaian intellectual and poet-broadcaster cloned from Awoonor's own public life, notably his service to Nkrumah and subsequent demotion after the leader's fall. The two narrators meet in an Accra nightclub, where the American, now called Brother Lumumba, gets into a fight over a woman and knifes a couple of white expatriates. The unnamed Ghanaian manages to spirit the fugitive away to his native village in Eweland where, in a sentimental ending, he is adopted back into the ancestral African fold. Here, in the black

American's dream consciousness, the novel's twin narratives of return—the American Negro's to Africa and the westernized African intellectual's to his native roots—converge and link up with a third narrative, that of a mythic southward journey of a slave caravan from the desert to the coast, which is interspersed with the primary narratives throughout the book in a series of bardic interludes.

After the elegiac beauty and lyrical richness of *This Earth, My Brother . . .*, the second novel's textural thinness is a disappointment. Awoonor's attempt to transfer the first book's black historical consciousness and motif of race retrieval to the American context, but without its enriching poetic mythology, is largely unsuccessful and is not helped by a rather unconvincing rendition of the 1950s black American experience—a derivative potpourri of Richard Wright, Malcolm X, and James Baldwin—through a racy, vernacular jive style.

Awoonor has more success with the rambling narrative of his swish, shallow Ghanaian, and in the nightclub scene he handles well the tensions between the latter's flippant, sophisticated cynicism and the uneducated American visitor's naive racial polemics and advocacy of Fanonian politics of third-world revolution. The very depth of the chasm between the two men, however, makes their sudden assertion of racial solidarity and blood brotherhood in the murder scene hard to accept. Finally, when Brother Lumumba, during his initiation into village life, discovers in his race memory a mystic, instinctive rapport with African ritual behavior and effortlessly embraces his lost heritage—"soon he too joined in singing the words as if he had been familiar with them all his life" (p. 126)—the novel lapses into the kind of sentimental fantasy indulged in by books like Alex Haley's *Roots* (1976). The climactic coincidence of the personal and mythic narratives, and of nuclear and racial family reunions, is too contrived, and the poetic writing of the interludes, which sustain the race narrative, is not of a

very high order; fellow Ghanaian writer Ayi Kwei Armah has used this technique much more successfully in his *Two Thousand Seasons* (1973).

Moreover, Awoonor's narrative is flawed by some crude caricatures of contemporary literary personalities (notably Armah); this sour satiric material, which was published in the 1975 extract and dates from Awoonor's years of exile in Britain and the United States (1967–1975), fails to connect with the African American narrative of the first half of the book, which was clearly added much later. *Comes the Voyager at Last* is an unconvincing and unengaging novel, a rather artificial, patchwork affair that contains some of Awoonor's most flat and tired writing. During his ambassadorial years his fiction, like his poetry, has shown signs of flagging inspiration and waning artistic execution.

NONFICTIONAL PROSE

Awoonor's most substantial work of nonfictional prose is *The Breast of the Earth: A Survey of the History, Culture and Literature of Africa South of the Sahara* (1975), which is based on his 1972 doctoral dissertation. This ambitious work spans a broad historical panorama of African literary forms and traditions, ranging from oral literature and writing in African languages to contemporary literature written in European languages. Its main emphasis, however, is on the fruitful continuity of orature and written forms and on the relationship between the individual poetic genius and the public communal tradition, a relationship that has proved to be dynamic and volatile even where the forms of expression are rigid and conservative. The most valuable chapters of the book are Chapter 7, which discusses the oral poetic practice of the Yoruba, Akan, and Zulu peoples alongside that of Awoonor's native Ewe, and Chapter 12, which demonstrates how contemporary anglophone poets—notably the Zulu poet

Mazisi Kunene, the Igbo poet Christopher Okigbo, and Awoonor himself—consciously ground their work in oral cultural traditions. Awoonor is on less firm ground when he deals with African history, music, and art (there are a few flaws in his dating and stylistic concepts), but his long chapter on oral literature remains one of the most informative and illuminating contributions to the subject by an African scholar and poet, and it has made *The Breast of the Earth* essential critical reading in African literature courses throughout the world.

In the 1980s Awoonor ventured increasingly into the realm of the political essay, an interest that was first nurtured in his privately printed pamphlet *Come Back, Ghana* (1972), devoted to the rebuilding of the country after the fall of Nkrumah. *The Ghana Revolution: A Background Account from a Personal Perspective* (1984) views the military regimes of the 1970s through the prism of his personal experience of political detention, while *Ghana: A Political History from Pre-European to Modern Times* (1990) situates Ghana's current difficulties and search for just forms of government in the context of the nation's cultural and ethnic history. Awoonor's work as a political analyst, which has drawn mixed and often controversial reactions, is revealing both of its subject and of its author, but it is sketchy and uneven work, not on a par with his best imaginative writing.

CONCLUSION

It is as a lyric poet that Awoonor has secured a place in the canon of African literature. Here his critical reputation is firmly based, and his most vibrant criticism is informed by his own poetic practice. During the thirty years of writing poetry, and most conspicuously in his early writings, Awoonor has maintained a special relationship with his native literary tradition, a relationship first fostered by his apprenticeship to masters of Ewe dirge-

orature and from there periodically fueled by his own meticulous researches into African oral cultures. His great achievement, along with that of poets like Mazisi Kunene and the Ugandan Okot p'Bitek, has been the successful infusion of a second, alien language with the distinctive cadences and imagery, the mythological aura and intellectual structures of the first, native language, and the evocation of the culture upon which it draws. In so doing, Awoonor has, in his best work, kept his indigenous Ewe culture alive in English and has given it a place on the map of world poetry. He has turned the process of inheritance into creation, making the traditional fresh and new.

Selected Bibliography

BIBLIOGRAPHY

Amoabeng, Kwaku, and Carroll Lasker. "Kofi Awoonor: An Annotated Bibliography." In *Africana Journal* 13, nos. 1–4 (1982).

COLLECTED WORKS

Until the Morning After: Collected Poems, 1963–1985. Greenfield Center, N.Y.: Greenfield Review Press, 1987; London: Heinemann, 1987; Accra, Ghana: Woeli, 1987.

POETRY

Rediscovery, and Other Poems. Ibadan, Nigeria: Mbari, 1964.
Night of My Blood. Garden City, N.Y.: Doubleday, 1971.
Ride Me, Memory. Greenfield Center, N.Y.: Greenfield Review Press, 1973.
The House by the Sea. Greenfield Center, N.Y.: Greenfield Review Press, 1978.
The Latin American and Caribbean Notebook. Trenton, N.J.: Africa World Press, 1992.

NOVELS

This Earth, My Brother . . . Garden City, N.Y.: Doubleday, 1971, 1972; London: Heinemann, 1972.

Comes the Voyager at Last: A Tale of Return to Africa. Trenton, N.J.: Africa World Press, 1992. Excerpt publ. in *Okike* 7 (April 1975).

SHORT STORIES

"Just to Buy Corn." In *Eastern Horizon* 4 (July 1964).

"The Funeral." In *Eastern Horizon* 4 (May 1965).

"The Reverend." In *Eastern Horizon* 4 (June 1965).

DRAMA

Ancestral Power and *Lament.* In Cosmo Pieterse, ed., *Short African Plays.* London: Heinemann, 1972.

NONFICTION

Come Back, Ghana. Accra, Ghana: self-published, 1972.

The Breast of the Earth: A Survey of the History, Culture and Literature of Africa South of the Sahara. New York: Nok Publishers International, 1975; Garden City, N.Y.: Anchor, 1975, 1976.

The Ghana Revolution: A Background Account from a Personal Perspective. New York: Oases, 1984.

Ghana: A Political History from Pre-European to Modern Times. Accra, Ghana: Woeli and Sedco, 1990.

ESSAYS

"Modern African Literature: A Survey." In *Eastern Horizon* 4 (August 1964).

"Fresh Vistas for African Literature." In *African Review* 1 (May 1965).

"The Changing Role of the African Writer." In *Ghana Guardian* 1 (October 1966).

"Culture, Literature and Arts in Africa." In *New Time* 2 (September 1967).

"Sources of Ghanaian Literature." In *New Time* 3 (October 1967).

"Reminiscences of Earlier Days." In Per Wästberg, ed., *The Writer in Modern Africa.* Uppsala, Sweden: Scandinavian Institute of African Studies, 1968; New York: Africana, 1969.

"Nationalism: Masks and Consciousness." In *Books Abroad* 45 (spring 1971).

"Africa's Literature Beyond Politics." In *Worldview* 15 (March 1972).

"Kwame Nkrumah: Symbol of Emergent Africa." In *Africa Report* 17 (June 1972).

"Voyager and the Earth." In *New Letters* 40 (fall 1973).

"Coming from My Own Tradition." In *Compass* 5/6 (1974).

"Tradition and Continuity in African Literature." In Karen L. Morell, ed., *In Person: Achebe, Awoonor and Soyinka at the University of Washington.* Seattle: African Studies Program, Institute for Comparative and Foreign Area Studies, University of Washington, 1975. Repr. in Rowland Smith, ed., *Exile and Tradition: Studies in African and Caribbean Literature.* London: Longman and Dalhousie University Press, 1976; New York: Africana, 1976.

"The Poem, the Poet and the Human Condition: Some Aspects of Recent West African Poetry." In *Asemka* 5 (September 1979).

"The Imagery of Fire: A Critical Assessment of the Poetry of Joe de Graft." In *Okike* 19 (September 1981).

"The Writer and Politics in Africa." In Robert W. July and Peter Benson, eds., *African Cultural and Intellectual Leaders and the Development of the New African Nations.* New York: Rockefeller Foundation, 1982; Ibaban, Nigeria: Ibadan University Press, 1982.

"A Servant of the Ghanaian Dream." In *South* (June 1985).

OTHER WORKS

Review of Mercer Cook and Stephen Henderson, *The Militant Black Writer in Africa and the United States.* In *Africa Report* 15 (March 1970).

Messages: Poems from Ghana. Ed. with biographical notes by Awoonor and G. Adali-Mortty. London: Heinemann, 1971.

Guardians of the Sacred Word: Ewe Poetry. Trans., ed., intro., and notes by Awoonor. New York: Nok Publishers, 1974.

INTERVIEWS

Bozimo, Willy. "Politics? It's for Scoundrels: Kofi Awoonor." In *Sunday Times* (Lagos, Nigeria) (6 February 1977).

"Class Discussion." In Karen L. Morell, ed., *In Person: Achebe, Awoonor, and Soyinka at the*

University of Washington. Seattle: African Studies Program, Institute for Comparative and Foreign Area Studies, University of Washington, 1975.

Ephson, Ben. "Historical Forces." In *West Africa* (4 November 1985).

"Ghana: Visionary Writer Fights 'Moneybag Politics': An Interview with Kofi Awoonor." In *To the Point* (30 June 1978).

Goldblatt, John. "Kofi Awoonor: An Interview." In *Transition* 41 (1972).

"Interview with Kofi Awoonor." In Bernth Lindfors et al., eds., *Palaver: Interviews with Five African Writers in Texas.* Austin: African and Afro-American Research Institute, University of Texas, 1972.

"Kofi Awoonor on Poetry and Prison." In *West Africa* (17 April 1978).

Munro, Ian, and Wayne Kamin. "Kofi Awoonor: Interview." In *Kunapipi* 1 (November 1979).

"Panel on South African Oral Traditions." In *Issue: A Quarterly Journal of Africanist Opinion* 6, no. 1 (1976).

Serumaga, Robert. "George Awoonor-Williams, Writer, Poet and Director of the Ghana Film Corporation, Interviewed." In *Cultural Events in Africa* 29 (April 1967).

———. "Kofi Awoonor." In Dennis Duerden and Cosmo Pieterse, eds., *African Writers Talking.* London: Heinemann, 1972; New York: Africana, 1972.

Wilkinson, Jane. "Kofi Awoonor." In Wilkinson, ed., *Talking with African Writers: Interviews with African Poets, Playwrights and Novelists.* London: James Currey, 1992; Portsmouth, N.H.: Heinemann, 1992.

CRITICAL STUDIES

Achebe, Chinua. Introduction to *This Earth, My Brother . . .* , by Awoonor. Garden City, N.Y.: Anchor/Doubleday, 1972. Repr. in *Transition* 41 (1972).

Anyidoho, Kofi. "Kofi Awoonor and the Ewe Tradition of Songs of Abuse (Halo)." In Lemuel A. Johnson et al., eds., *Toward Defining the African Aesthetic.* Washington, D.C.: Three Continents Press, 1982. Repr. in Richard Priebe, ed., *Ghanaian Literatures.* Westport, Conn.: Greenwood Press, 1988.

———. "Kofi Awoonor." In Bernth Lindfors and Reinhard Sander, eds., *Dictionary of Literary Biography.* Vol. 117: *Twentieth Century Caribbean and Black African Writers.* First Series. Detroit: Gale Research, 1992.

Chinweizu. "Surfaces of Disillusion." In *Okike* 6 (September 1974).

Colmer, Rosemary. "The Restorative Cycle: Kofi Awoonor's Theory of African Literature." In *New Literatures Review* 3 (May 1977).

———. "Kofi Awoonor: Critical Prescriptions and Creative Practice." In *ACLALS Bulletin* 5 (July 1978).

Duclos, Jocelyn-Robert. "'The Butterfly and the Pile of Manure': A Study of Kofi Awoonor's Novel, *This Earth, My Brother . . .*" In *Canadian Journal of African Studies* 9, no. 3 (1975).

Early, Leonard R. "Kofi Awoonor's Poetry." In *ARIEL* 6 (January 1975).

Egudu, Romanus N. *Modern African Poetry and the African Predicament.* London: Macmillan, 1978; New York: Barnes & Noble, 1978.

Fraser, Robert. *West African Poetry: A Critical History.* Cambridge, U.K.: Cambridge University Press, 1986.

Goodwin, K. L. *Understanding African Poetry: A Study of Ten Poets.* London: Heinemann, 1982.

Haynes, John. "Song and Copy: The Relation Between Oral and Printed in Kofi Awoonor's 'Dirge.'" In *Journal of Commonwealth Literature* 20, no. 1 (1985). Repr. in his *African Poetry and the English Language.* London: Macmillan, 1987.

Killam, G. D. "Kofi Awoonor: *The Breast of the Earth.*" In *Dalhousie Review* 56 (1976).

Knipp, Thomas R. "Myth, History and the Poetry of Kofi Awoonor." In *African Literature Today* 11 (1980).

Mamadu, Ayo. "Kofi Awoonor as Poet." In *Lagos Review of English Studies* 3–5 (1981–1983).

Moore, Gerald. *The Chosen Tongue: English Writing in the Tropical World.* Harlow, U.K.: Longmans, 1969; New York: Harper & Row, 1970.

———. "Death, Convergence and Rebirth in Two Black Novels." In *Nigerian Journal of the Humanities* 2 (1978).

———. *Twelve African Writers.* London: Hutchinson University Library for Africa, 1980; Bloomington: Indiana University Press, 1980.

Mphahlele, Ezekiel. Introduction to *Night of My Blood*, by Awoonor. Garden City, N.Y.: Doubleday, 1971.

Ogunsanwo, Olatubosun. "Awoonor's *This Earth, My Brother*...: A Personal Memoir." In *Kunapipi* 9, no. 1 (1987).

Ojo-Ade, Femi. "Madness in the African Novel: Awoonor's *This Earth, My Brother*..." In *African Literature Today* 10 (1979).

Omotoso, Kole. "The Trial of Kofi Awoonor." In *Afriscope* 6 (November 1976).

Priebe, Richard. "Kofi Awoonor's *This Earth, My Brother*... as an African Dirge." In *Benin Review* 1 (1974). Repr. in his *Myth, Realism and the West African Writer*. Trenton, N.J.: Africa World Press, 1988.

Tucker, Martin. "Kofi Awoonor: Restraint and Release." In *English in Africa* 6 (March 1979).

Utudjian, Elaine Saint-Andre. "Rites of Passage in the Poetry of Kofi Awoonor." In *Commonwealth Essays and Studies* 8 (spring 1986).

———. "Aspects of Myth in Two Ghanaian Novels." In *Commonwealth Essays and Studies* 10 (fall 1987).

Wright, Derek. "Ritual and Reality in the Novels of Wole Soyinka, Gabriel Okara and Kofi Awoonor." In *Kunapipi* 9, no. 1 (1987).

———. "Scatology and Eschatology in Kofi Awoonor's *This Earth, My Brother*..." In *International Fiction Review* 15 (winter 1988).

Yankson, Kofi. "*This Earth, My Brother*...: A Study in Despair." In *University of Cape Coast English Department Workpapers* 4 (1972).

Mariama Bâ
1929–1981

NWAMAKA B. AKUKWE

MARIAMA BÂ was born to Muslim parents in Dakar, Senegal, in 1929. Her mother died when she was very young, so she was brought up by her maternal grandparents in a well-to-do family. Because her father, an educated civil servant, insisted that his daughter have a French education, she attended the École normal, a girls' boarding school in Rufisque, near Dakar. There her literary interests were developed, and two of her essays were published. The school also prepared Bâ for later life as a schoolteacher and an active campaigner and speaker on key women's issues, such as polygamy and female circumcision. These issues remained of foremost importance to Bâ both as a writer and as a woman who saw and experienced the effects of these practices on the lives of women in a male-controlled Islamic culture and society.

Bâ married a Senegalese politician with whom she had nine children, but the marriage ended in divorce. Her own apparent unhappy experience with married life provided the inspiration for her highly acclaimed novel, *Une Si Longue Lettre* (1980; *So Long a Letter*). She wrote a second novel, *Un Chant écarlate* (*Scarlet Song*), but died before its publication in 1981. She had been ill for a long time.

There was an underlying sense of the tragic in Bâ's personal life and in her novels, especially *Scarlet Song*. But there was also great dignity; Bâ gave a quiet grace to her female protagonists, especially Ramatoulaye in *So Long a Letter*, who can be seen as the embodiment and voice of the novelist's personal anguish and experience.

Bâ wrote about women in modern African society. Her novels explore the agony and dilemmas and the pleasures and triumphs of women like herself, who are caught between two diametrically opposed worlds: traditional African and modern societies. The emotional, psychological, and physical consequences of being in this position are captured with sensitivity. In the course of examining these cultural conflicts, the novels focus on the institution on which the survival and propagation of all societies—modern and traditional—rests: marriage. *So Long a Letter* and *Scarlet Song* show the joys, sorrows, and tribulations of modern African marriages in the lives of several couples. The novels also look at how the actions of family members impinge on the main characters' lives, for better or worse.

Bâ's juxtapositions of various marriages highlight the status of women in contemporary African society. These women live in a society that seems to be designed primarily to keep them subjugated. The men enjoy unlimited freedom, choosing and discarding wives as they wish, while the women are expected to keep silent and accept their lot in accordance with the divine will of Allah.

SO LONG A LETTER

In *So Long a Letter* (1980), Bâ's first and major novel, she began what was eventually to become the major theme of her fiction — the plight of women in Muslim societies, such as Ramatoulaye and her friend and confidante Aissatou, who after many years of marriage find themselves relegated or discarded by their husbands for younger brides. The novel focuses on how each of these women tries to cope with the trauma of being cast aside after giving so much, including bearing many children. Ramatoulaye grieves for her husband, Modou Fall, who has just died of a heart attack, while the family makes arrangements for the funeral. The funeral and the activities of her in-laws prompt Ramatoulaye to seek escape through a long letter to Aissatou. When faced with having to cope with a co-wife, Aissatou has decided to divorce her husband, Mawdo, and return to school. Eventually she secures a plum job as an interpreter at the Senegalese embassy in New York.

Ramatoulaye's letter turns out to be a sustained account of the emotional and psychological trauma that she has been through in the years preceding Modou's death. She knows Aissatou will understand because she has gone through a similar experience. So as Ramatoulaye touches on their shared experiences, which are similar to those of other oppressed Senegalese Muslim women, she ends up writing her "so long a letter." That her story is told in the form of a letter makes it possible for the novel to have the intimate tone that only a personal letter can have and at the same time avoid the appearance of a conventional autobiography.

A third woman whose life and stories interweave with those of Ramatoulaye and Aissatou is Jacqueline, who comes from the Ivory Coast but is married to a Senegalese. Unlike their mothers, these three women are educated, a fact that unites them. Whereas the older generation was raised solely with traditional Senegalese-Muslim values, the younger women have had a mixture of the traditional and French educations. So while their mothers accepted, in silence (because they have been led to believe that a beautiful woman is a silent one), the position the traditional society imposed on them, these younger women rebelled. Also unlike their mothers, who were content to have their fathers choose for them, the younger women chose their own husbands. The irony, however, is that having the choice alone does not guarantee them freedom, as events in their respective marriages prove. They yearn for the freedom associated with life in a modern world, and they wish to shake off all of the shackles that restrain women in traditional African customs. But they realize that the traditional practices, especially those associated with male privileges, cannot be discarded overnight because they are at the heart of traditional African society.

In Ramatoulaye's account, she, Aissatou, and Jacqueline choose to marry modern, educated African men — Modou, Mawdo, and Samba, respectively. Stubborn opposition from their parents does not deter the young couples from going ahead with the decision to base their unions on personal choice and reciprocal love. In spite of this, and in spite of years of toiling and sharing their lives together, the husbands end up treating them the way men have always treated women throughout the ages in their society. They are still "despised, relegated or exchanged . . . abandoned like a worn-out or out-dated *boubou*" (p. 41) because of what Ramatoulaye in her rage calls the exclusive right of men to answer natural urges for sexual variety, a right to betray love and the loyalties of so many years. Bâ seems to imply that all men are the same: no matter what circumstances have led to marriage and no matter what pressures are brought to bear on the couples, men are polygamous by nature. Bâ's anger is not directed at the practice of polygamy but at the men who hide behind it to break the contract of faith that a marriage demands. Her disapproval is also directed at the in-laws who stand behind their sons to get back at their uppity daughters-in-law.

The three women no doubt believe that by marrying men of their choice—educated, modern men—they would be spared the trauma of having to share their husbands with new and younger brides. But Modou, Mawdo, and Samba discard their wives like objects when they feel like experimenting with polygamy. The men forget that for their wives, marriage means a union between two and only two individuals to be sustained through caring and sharing. Edris Makward points out in his essay on Bâ:

> Two initially successful marriages, between Mawdo and Aïssatou and [Ramatoulaye] and Modou, ended in failure precipitated by the excesses of polygamy. But while the former couple's failure is partly due to Mawdo's mother's efforts to correct what she considered as her son's misalliance, his marriage with a member of a lower caste, the latter is simply caused by Modou's infatuation with a much younger woman.
>
> (p. 278)

The marriage of Samba and Jacqueline fails in part due to the refusal of Samba's Muslim family to accept their son's wife because she is non-Senegalese and a Christian. But the marriage fails mainly because of Samba's unfaithfulness and inconsiderate behavior and his desire to take full advantage of his traditional right to polygamy.

In addition to the callous behavior of Modou and Mawdo in taking second wives, there is also the issue of family pressure on marriages. Mawdo's mother swears revenge when her son marries a mere goldsmith's daughter, a threat she carries out by grooming a second wife from the right caste for him. This marriage, therefore, is doomed from the start. The union of Samba and Jacqueline is also under pressure because she is seen by society as a foreigner. And Ramatoulaye suffers the destabilizing influence of her sisters-in-law, as she reminds her friend that

> in our different ways, we suffered the social constraints and heavy burden of custom. I loved Modou. I compromised with his people. I toler-

ated his sisters, who too often would desert their own homes to encumber my own. They allowed themselves to be fed and petted. They would look on, without reacting, as their children romped around on my chairs. I tolerated their spitting, the phlegm expertly secreted under my carpets.

> His mother would stop by again and again while on her outings, always flanked by different friends, just to show off her son's social success but particularly so that they might see, at close quarters, her supremacy in this beautiful house in which she did not live. I would receive her with all the respect due to a queen.
>
> (p. 19)

Despite all Ramatoulaye's efforts to please members of her husband's family, Modou still takes a second wife, Binetou. To add insult to injury, after Modou's death, his brother Tamsir expects to take Modou's place as husband to Ramatoulaye and Binetou, in accordance with Senegalese-Muslim custom.

To Tamsir, Ramatoulaye also offers an economically useful alliance. She earns her own living as a teacher, and she has just come into possession of quite a few things as a result of her husband's death. Understandably, Ramatoulaye lashes out at Tamsir: "You forget that I have a heart, a mind, that I am not an object to be passed from hand to hand" (p. 58). In the same vein, young Nabou, whom Mawdo will eventually take as a second wife, is handed over to her aunt, Tante Nabou, by her father with words that clearly indicate her status as an object: "Take young Nabou, your namesake. She is yours. I ask only for her bones" (p. 29). Of course, Tante Nabou, still spiteful toward her daughter-in-law, Aissatou, for being a mere goldsmith's daughter, proceeds to train and use the young girl as her instrument of revenge, and when the time comes she in turn hands her over to her son. Her own words again reinforce this image of an object being passed from hand to hand: "My brother Farba has *given* you young Nabou to be your wife, to *thank* me for the worthy way in which I have brought her up" (p. 30, emphasis added).

Likewise, Binetou's mother sees her daughter as an object with which to secure for herself a future life of plenty. Binetou's marriage to Modou as his second wife is, for her mother, the only gateway to a life of luxury that she has long been denied. She therefore pushes and prods her daughter until the poor girl agrees to marry Modou, a man whom she despises and ridicules, who is too old for her, and who incidentally is the father of her best friend. Binetou's mother sacrifices her daughter's life and future for a life of affluence. And she closes her ears to Binetou's pleas that she is not in love with Modou and would not be happy in a marriage to him. The poor girl's feelings and wishes do not count—after all, she is only a woman.

Finally, during Modou's funeral, his wives have no say in what goes on, how much is spent, and what should be bought and used for the burial. They are simply confined in a place where they are hardly seen or consulted by anyone, all this according to Muslim law and rites for the dead. This means that the in-laws have the liberty to spend generously on the funeral. Very often, as is the case with Ramatoulaye and Binetou, the relatives end up spending so much that the wives and children left behind have nothing to live on. Of even greater annoyance to Ramatoulaye is the fact that all through the funeral the wives are treated as equals, no matter how long they were married to the dead man. This illustrates how women are simply lumped together on the same level, irrespective of age, service, and individual achievement. Ramatoulaye wryly, and very bitterly, comments on this injustice to Aissatou: "Our sisters-in-law give equal consideration to thirty years and five years of married life. With the same ease and the same words, they celebrate twelve maternities and three" (p. 4).

After the betrayals of Ramatoulaye, Aissatou, and Jacqueline by their husbands, each woman responds differently. Ramatoulaye, the author of the letter, chooses not to make a clean break from Modou; instead she stays and forces Modou to leave their matrimonial home. Normally, it is the woman who leaves when a marriage breaks down, while the man stays and enjoys his new wife. But going against tradition, Ramatoulaye stays and tries to piece the shards of her shattered life together and raise her twelve children without Modou's help. Her decision to stay in the marriage, despite her daughters' opposition, is based on a weak assertion that she has never "conceived of happiness outside marriage" (p. 56), and she appears to bow to tradition in her unfailing faith in the institution of marriage. In the end, though, her stubborn determination to carry on without her husband pays off, since Ramatoulaye emerges from this experience both knowing and appreciating herself better.

Aissatou, on the other hand, makes a complete break from Mawdo. She left with her four sons, making a success of her new career and a new life for herself and her children. And Jacqueline, although she suffers a mental breakdown because of the way she has been treated by Samba, is still able to pull herself together before another downturn in her mental health, from which total recovery would be impossible. A doctor with a "soft, reassuring voice" gives Jacqueline the heart to go on living, and she leaves hospital fully understanding "the heart of her illness" and ready to fight against it (p. 45). Thus, out of despair comes hope and renewal for these women. Bâ's optimism in this novel is not surprising, because these women represent aspects of Bâ's own experience—their battles had been hers as well.

SCARLET SONG

Bâ's second and last novel, *Scarlet Song*, has a structure similar to that of the first. *Scarlet Song* also uses juxtaposition of marriages to highlight the position and plight of women in modern African society. However, this novel goes further in dealing with real effects of traditional practices on marriage. *Scarlet Song* does not, like *So Long a Letter*, concentrate on the breakup of the marriages, but rather on the internal tensions within the unions and the resulting psychological trauma and devastation. The novel is also concerned with polygamy and the destabilizing interferences of the extended family that very often lead to the subsequent failure of most marriages.

In *Scarlet Song* Bâ explores the concept of choice and its attendant notion of responsibility. In the previous novel not all the choices made by the characters affect other people the way they do in *Scarlet Song*. The story centers around two young students, Ousmane and Mireille, who are in love and eventually marry in spite of attempts by members of both families to stop them. These two young people — the man Senegalese and the woman French — marry for love just as Ramatoulaye and Modou, Aissatou and Mawdo, and Jacqueline and Samba do in the earlier novel. Mireille's diplomat father whisks her off to France the moment he finds out about her love for Ousmane, despite his avowed open-mindedness about nonwhite people and interracial relationships. But the couple still manage to meet and get married in Paris. For a while all goes well; it is not until they return to Senegal that their problems begin. The idealism of the early years disappears as they come face-to-face with the reality of modern African society, in which all the traditional values are still strong.

As in *So Long a Letter*, the bride in *Scarlet Song* is rejected by some members of the groom's family, in her case because she is white and from another part of the world. Mireille's problem is even greater than the problems of Aissatou and Jacqueline because of the enormous cultural gulf between her and her in-laws. In Paris mixed-race couples enjoy the freedom to be by and for themselves; in Senegal they must face all the problems an interracial marriage may bring. Eventually the marriage deteriorates to such an extent that Ousmane begins to seek fulfillment of emotional and what he calls cultural needs in his childhood flame, Ouleymatou Ngom, whom he eventually marries without his wife's knowledge. And when poor Mireille is informed of this by Soukeyna, the only member of Ousmane's family to befriend and try to understand her, she responds first with disbelief, then with sadness and rage. Finally, she goes mad, and in revenge she kills their only son, Gorgui, whom she sees as a mulatto who can be comfortable neither in her own culture nor in her husband's.

The failure of the marriage and the tragedy it brings about is presented by Bâ as resulting from the inability of the couple to make the necessary adjustments and compromises that a coming together of cultures and races demands. Although Mireille decides to convert to Islam, she cannot accept the traditional customs, such as polygamy and extended families, in the Senegalese society. As a result, she holds strongly to her Frenchness. At the same time Ousmane escapes into a fake search for cultural "authenticity" as a means of establishing his male dominance in the marriage. The outcome of such intransigence can only be disaster. Their stubbornness is further compounded by Yaye Khady, Ousmane's mother, who does not approve of the marriage in the first place. Although she does not go out of her way to wreck her son's marriage, as Mawdo's mother does, by encouraging the relationship between her son and Ouleymatou she achieves her desire to see her son married to a more suitable daughter-in-law.

For Bâ, the problem is not with interracial marriages per se, but rather with the people who enter into them. By providing the enviable example of Lamine, a close black friend of Ousmane's and his European wife, Pierrette, Bâ suggests that this seemingly enormous racial and cultural gulf can be bridged. Lamine, who is able to deal with the conflict, says: "You can't combine two different conceptions of life. If you're to be honest, you've got to make a choice. *You* want happiness without making any sacrifices. *You* won't make any concessions, while demanding concessions from others. Married life is based on tolerance and a human approach" (pp. 98–99). And tolerance seems to be the one ingredient lacking in most of the major characters in *Scarlet Song*.

CONCLUSION

According to Bâ, the essential problem of oppressed and marginalized women in modern Islamic African society can be tackled by a reduction in the influence of the twin marriage destroyers: polygamy and the extended family system. Men use polygamy to satisfy their desire for extramarital sexual relations. Pressures from the extended family make it impossible for a couple to work for and find happiness in their marriage on their own terms. By presenting Mireille's fight and collapse in *Scarlet Song*, Bâ warns that although the women in *So Long a Letter* fight and survive in their individual ways, tragedy could well be the outcome, especially for someone like Mireille who has been brought up in a culture so different from the polygamous, Islamic, communal culture into which she has married.

In portraying the harmonious marriage of Lamine and Pierrette in *Scarlet Song*, Bâ shows that modern marriage in an African Muslim society could succeed—even if the marriage is racially mixed and despite the negative influence of the extended family— with some effort from both parties. Toward the end of *So Long a Letter*, Bâ hints that the lot of women in African Muslim societies may be changing for the better. Daba and Aissatou, Ramatoulaye's two older daughters, represent the future for such women. Their relationships with men are based on openness and compromise, which were lacking in their parents' relationships. With women receiving more education and gaining more independence, certain traditional and Islamic practices—such as a man's claim to his deceased

brother's wife and children—will change. Whereas the older generation of women had no choice, Ramatoulaye chooses to reject her brother-in-law's claim. In Daba and Aissatou's generation, such a claim may never be suggested.

Selected Bibliography

NOVELS

Une Si Longue Lettre. Dakar, Senegal: Les Nouvelles Éditions Africaines, 1980.
Un Chant écarlate. Dakar, Senegal: Les Nouvelles Éditions Africaines, 1981.

TRANSLATIONS

So Long a Letter. Trans. by Modupé Bodé-Thomas. London: Heinemann, 1981.
Scarlet Song. Trans. by Dorothy S. Blair. New York: Longman, 1985.

CRITICAL STUDIES

Busby, Margaret, ed. *Daughters of Africa: An International Anthology of Words and Writings by Women of African Descent from the Ancient Egyptian to the Present*. London: Jonathan Cape, 1992.
d'Almeida, Irene Assiba. "The Concept of Choice in Mariama Bâ's Fiction." In Carole Boyce Davies and Anne Adams Graves, eds., *Ngambika: Studies of Women in African Literature*. Trenton, N.J.: Africa World Press, 1986.
Makward, Edris. "Marriage, Tradition, and Woman's Pursuit of Happiness in the Novels of Mariama Bâ." In Carole Boyce Davies and Anne Adams Graves, eds., *Ngambika: Studies of Women in African Literature*. Trenton, N.J.: Africa World Press, 1986.

REVIEWS

Case, Frederick Ivor. "Mariama Bâ, *So Long a Letter*." In *World Literature Written in English* 21 (fall 1982).

Mongo Beti
1932–

JOHN D. CONTEH-MORGAN

MONGO BETI returned to his native Cameroon on 24 February 1991 after thirty-two years of self-imposed exile in France. This visit by one of Francophone Africa's most prolific and celebrated writers immediately touched off a controversy in the country. The Cameroonian public welcomed the homecoming of their long-lost son. Proud of his literary and intellectual achievements and of his principled and sustained opposition to their country's successive authoritarian governments, they had come to regard Beti as the intellectual leader of the opposition and the conscience of their nation. The government, on the other hand, feared that he would become a rallying point for popular discontent and swiftly moved to discredit him, portraying him in the state-controlled media as a French tourist and "a poor scribbler" (Kom, p. 150) and turning down requests to allow him to deliver public lectures.

Of course, this was not the first time Beti found himself at the center of a controversy. Shortly after its publication in 1956, his corrosively satirical novel on Catholic missionary activity in Africa, *Le Pauvre Christ de Bomba* (*The Poor Christ of Bomba*), was banned by the then French colonial governor at the request of the church. In 1972 copies of his book-length essay *Main basse sur le Cameroun: Autopsie d'une décolonisation* (The plundering of Cameroon: Autopsy of a decolonization) were seized, and the book was banned, in France, where it had been published. The French government attempted to invalidate Beti's legal status in France, expel him from his teaching position in a public school, and deport him to Cameroon. After a four-year legal battle, he won his case and *Main basse sur le Cameroun* reappeared in bookstores.

Beti's experience as a writer has been characterized by endless acts of official harassment—in the form of censorship, seizures of publications, and other prohibitions—which he carefully documented and publicized in several essays, book prefaces, interviews, and articles. The roots of that experience can be found in his life, ideas, and writings.

PORTRAIT OF A NOVELIST

Mongo Beti was born Alexandre Biyidi-Awala in 1932 in Mbalmayo, a small town twenty-five miles south of Yaoundé, Cameroon's capital. His father, Oscar Awala, died by drowning in 1939. Although Beti was only seven then, his father's image remained indelibly etched in his memory. In a 1979 interview with Anthony Biakolo and in a 1981 article, "*Le Pauvre Christ de Bomba* expliqué!"

83

he proudly portrayed his father as a man of short and slender build, but one of great courage who stood up to the colonial authorities when they bullied or beat women in his village.

Beti's declared attachment to his father has led to suggestions that he may have worked it out in the father-son relationship in his 1954 novel *Ville cruelle* (Cruel city). He did not deny this, but he pointed to a more symbolic relationship with his father than the religious one in the novel. Beti explained that it was the memory of his father's courage and a determination to be worthy of him—rather than a belief, like the son's in the novel, in the reality of his invisible presence—that sustained him in the face of difficulties.

Beti seems to have had less of an attachment to his mother, who died in 1992. Not only did he rarely mention her, but he also hinted at a profound disagreement with her that made their thirty-two-year separation not much of an ordeal for him: "My sense of family was very different from hers. We held divergent opinions on the attitude to adopt to the colonial system or the churches. I was then like now deeply at odds with my community of origin" (interview by Célestin Monga, p. 102).

Beti's early schooling was in a Catholic institution, but he was expelled because of his indifference to religion and his resistance to the missionaries' attempts to force it on the pupils. He received the rest of his education in government schools. In 1951 he left for higher education in France on a scholarship and enrolled at the University of Aix-en-Provence. Beti remembers this early period in France not so much for his academic studies but for his crucial discovery of American literature. He has reminisced about listening to a lecture on the sixteenth-century French writer Michel Eyquem de Montaigne with one ear while avidly reading a novel by Mark Twain, William Faulkner, Harriet Beecher Stowe, Chester Himes, or, especially, Richard Wright, who had recently arrived in France and had un-

leashed something of a cult following among French intellectuals.

In the article "*Le Pauvre Christ de Bomba expliqué!*" Beti variously describes the works of these writers as providing him with a "magic lantern" and their discovery as constituting his "road to Damascus" (p. 117). The Institute of English and American Studies, where their works and those of other writers were housed, became his favorite haunt. Not only were the books there more to his taste, but the social atmosphere was also less bourgeois than the French and classical literature sections of the university's library, which he found stodgy. He explains that in those years, the Greco-Roman classics on which he was to become an expert and to build a lifelong career suddenly appeared "distant, pale and obsolescent" (p. 118). In addition to American literature, he also discovered American popular culture in the jazz music of Duke Ellington, Charlie Parker, John Coltrane, and many more, artists whom he wrote about as connoisseur in the 1989 *Dictionnaire de la négritude* (Dictionary of negritude), co-authored with his wife, Odile Tobner.

By 1953 Beti was already formulating his ideas on literature in a series of articles for the cultural journal *Présence africaine*. In an often quoted article of that series, he wrote critically of the Guinean novelist Camara Laye, whose *L'Enfant noir* (1953; *The Dark Child*) he compared unfavorably with Wright's *Black Boy* (1945). In 1954, the same year this article appeared, Beti published his first novel, *Ville cruelle*, under the pen name Eza Boto. He explained his pen name: "In 1953, I knew someone who greatly liked the work of the American poet Ezra Pound. The name sounded dynamic, musical and striking; so I made up Eza Boto which has an Ezra Pound ring to it" (interview by Monga, p. 102).

In 1956 Beti's second novel, *The Poor Christ of Bomba*, appeared, this time under the pseudonym by which he has since been known, Mongo Beti, a name that means "son of the Beti people," his ethnic group. The change of name was necessitated by his desire to distance himself from his first novel, with whose production quality he was deeply dissatisfied. It has been suggested, however, that a more accurate reason would be the less than satisfactory quality of the work's artistry. Nevertheless, Beti's career as a novelist was well under way.

In Paris, where he had moved in 1955, he wrote fiction and took postgraduate courses at the Sorbonne. He lived in ramshackle accommodations near the Porte de Lilas, doing a variety of odd jobs for a living. Although in the article "*Le Pauvre Christ de Bomba expliqué!*" he has compared his upward move to Paris to that of Rastignac in the French novelist Honoré de Balzac's *Le Père Goriot*, he was determined, unlike this famous hero, not to depend on or be exploited by anyone, like the ruthless Vautrin in *Le Père Goriot*, who could help him advance in society. This perhaps is why he called himself a "Rastignac à l'envers" (reverse Rastignac). He did not seek out the nineteenth-century hero's company of the rich or the influential, but "the poor . . . the humiliated, the exiled" (p. 129). Even his female companions of the time were from the broken homes of French working-class or peasant families. Beti's taste for the marginal in society was a matter of both temperament and ideological disposition, a topic to be discussed later.

A mere three years after he arrived in Paris, Beti had published two more works of fiction: in 1957, *Mission terminée* (*Mission to Kala*), which won the Prix Sainte-Beuve, a prestigious French literary award, and in 1958, *Le Roi miraculé: Chronique des Essazam* (*King Lazarus*). With this fourth novel Beti's first creative phase came to an end.

For the next fourteen years, Beti fell silent, tending more assiduously to his studies and life. He obtained his professional teaching qualification in classics in 1959, and in 1963 he married Odile Tobner, a French colleague, with whom he had three children. In 1966 he was successful in one of France's most pre-stigious competitive examinations, the Agrégation de lettres classiques. With this, he quietly settled into a secure job in Rouen in northern France, teaching scholarship preparatory classes for the arts section of the *grandes écoles*, France's elite institutions of higher education.

In 1972 he was dramatically propelled into the public sphere again with the publication of *Main basse sur le Cameroun*, a book that is widely recognized to have inaugurated his second creative phase. This book can be read on two levels. On the more immediate one it is a chronicle of the nationalist phase in Cameroonian history and politics from 1948 to 1972. It documents the emergence in 1948 of the mass nationalist political movement, the Union des Populations du Cameroun (UPC), which from 1952 called for total independence from France; the efforts of the latter to weaken UPC influence by encouraging the formation of rival, more conservative nationalist movements based on ethnicity, regionalism, or religion; the outlawing of the UPC by the French colonial government; and, finally, the assassination in 1958 of UPC's charismatic leader, Ruben Um Nyobé, by French security forces. But it was the trial and execution in 1971, by Cameroon's first independent government, of Ernest Ouandié, the last of the so-called historic leaders of the UPC, that aroused Beti from his slumber.

On a more general level *Main basse* is, as subtitled, "the autopsy of a decolonization." Using his country as a case study, Beti sets out to show that though formally independent in the 1960s, Francophone countries often remain colonies in all but name. He subjects to critical scrutiny, for example, the famous Franco-African treaties of cooperation signed with Francophone countries before independence and argues that behind the rhetoric of aid to the poor inscribed in these treaties lies a calculated French pursuit of self-interest that is incompatible with these countries' development. But the book is equally about the weaknesses of Africa's modern elites. In accents worthy of the French-West Indian psychoanalyst-writer Frantz Fanon, it highlights their nonentrepreneurial spirit and readiness to act as willing accomplices in the dispossession of their countries.

All six novels that Beti published between 1972 and 1994 are in fact fictionalizations of ideas, and sometimes of situations and characters, of *Main basse*: "I wanted to embody in fiction all the ideas I had expressed in essay or pamphlet form in *Main basse*" (interview by Anthony Biakolo, p. 105). This task started as soon as he undertook the fight against the ban on his book in France. The first product of this literary endeavor was the English-titled novel *Remember Ruben* (1974), part of a trilogy that also included, from the same year, *Perpétue et l'habitude du malheur* (*Perpetua and the Habit of Unhappiness*) and, in 1979, *La Ruine presque cocasse d'un polichinelle: Remember Ruben 2* (*Lament for an African Pol*). Beti then wrote three other novels: in 1982, *Les Deux Mères de Guillaume Ismaël Dzewatama: Futur Camionneur* (The two mothers of Guillaume Ismaël Dzewatama: Future truck driver); in 1984, its sequel, *La Revanche de Guillaume Ismaël Dzewatama* (The revenge of Guillaume Ismaël Dzewatama); and in 1994, his tenth novel, *L'Histoire du fou* (The story of the madman).

Beti not only wrote fiction during that period, but he also became more of an activist. In 1978, in attempts to get his ideas across to a wider, nonliterary audience, he founded a journal of which he was director and editor, *Peuples noirs, peuples africains*. Unlike the similar Paris-based African journal *Présence africaine*, founded in 1947, Beti's is not a predominantly cultural publication. In addition to essays in literary criticism and cultural analyses, it devoted abundant space to issues of African politics and economics. In content, orientation, and perhaps even ambition, it is comparable to *Les Temps modernes*, privileging—like the latter, and Beti's fiction itself—the analytical category of class rather than, as in *Présence africaine*, of race.

In 1986 Beti published *Lettre ouverte aux Camerounais; ou, La Deuxième Mort de Ruben Um Nyobé* (Open letter to Cameroonians; or, Ruben Um Nyobé's second death). Part history, part memoir, as he explained, this book is also to an extent a reformulation of *Main basse*. What is new, however, are his more personal experiences, concerned with ruses mostly by Cameroon's second postcolonial government to bring him from the margins of dissidence and, when that failed, to wreck his publishing concern and thus destroy him morally and materially. In this book Beti positions himself as the Victor Hugo of Cameroon, lampooning from his exile in France Cameroon's presidents, one of whom, Paul Biya, he calls "le petit dictateur" (the little dictator; p. 37), "le petit dictateur-stagiaire" (the little apprentice-dictator; pp. 55, 65)—an adaptation of Hugo's celebrated description, from his exile in Guernsey, of Napoléon III, "Napoléon le petit." Given Beti's professed "Hugomania" (*La France contre l'Afrique*, 1993, p. 141) and the climate of opportunism, ambition, and repression that he attributes to the Cameroonian presidents' regimes, it would be surprising if such self-positioning were not cultivated with relish.

In 1989 Beti and his wife published *Dictionnaire de la négritude*, a reevaluation, from a radical African perspective, of figures and events past and present from Africa and the African diaspora. It is an assertion of the right to collective self-interpretation—to speech—seen as a condition of freedom. This book was followed in 1993 by *La France contre l'Afrique: Retour au Cameroun* (France against Africa: A return to Cameroon). Despite its title, there is nothing polemical about this book, which is arguably his best essay. An intellectual diary of his journeys home in 1991 and after, it combines acute sociological observations and reflections on Cameroon—its hospitals, university, teeming cities, rural areas, and so forth—with realistic suggestions for improvements. As usual in Beti's books, this one is full of uncondescending tenderness for the poor and suffering and full of pain at the blocked and squandered potential for the development of his country.

From these disparate details of his life, a coherent portrait of Mongo Beti emerges—one worth sketching because of the light it sheds on his writings. It is that of a man of courage and independence of spirit—an iconoclast even. Throughout his career he has refused, with admirable steadfastness, to be appropriated or "domesticated" by any party, church, or doctrine. Early in his life as a writer, he came to the conclusion that largess from any establishment, the French in particular, "constituted the greatest threat to the African writer: the threat of domestication," as he wrote in "*Le Pauvre Christ de Bomba* expliqué!" (p. 129). In this article he sketches with scarcely concealed contempt the alternative vision of life, urged on him by some, that he could have adopted after the success of his second novel:

> It is true that I could have completed my unexciting studies in a small, gray and cozy provincial town. I would then, no doubt, have caressed ordinary, orthodox dreams. Perhaps I would have returned to pre-independence Africa....
>
> But what would I have become in [the system] of French Cooperation? A domesticated intellectual producing obsequious books on neocolonialism in order to be parsimoniously rewarded by it ... or an uncompromising rebel. (p. 128)

Beti, of course, chose the second option, which is why there were no sacred cows on his list. He freely satirizes institutions such as the French language, the Catholic church, Franco-African economic and political cooperation, and their officially declared roles in Francophone Africa. But he also ridicules, together with their venerated exponents, established Francophone literary doctrines such as negritude, traditional religious beliefs and practices such as gerontocracy (or a system of social organization in which elderly people exert control, and a system against which

Beti's heroes, from Banda in *Ville cruelle* to Mor-Zamba and Abena in *Remember Ruben*, rebel), levirate (marriage, sometimes forced, of a widow to her dead husband's brother), polygyny (the practice of one man marrying many wives), among others.

He also consistently spurned all attempts to be won over by successive Cameroonian governments, or by what he called "the technostructure of the (French) Cooperation establishment and of Francophonie" (interview by Monga, 105). As he proudly asserted in a 1990 interview: "Whatever has been published and said about me, I belong to no political party ... which is why I'll continue the struggle, even when my political friends are in power" (interview by Monga, pp. 108–109).

This fierce assertion of independence (through which lurks an irreducible individualism) and the determination not to lose it to any structure partly explain the tendency observed in Beti to sniff out and sometimes to actually see conspiracies where there are none. Although the often vicious attempts that were used to "normalize" him should in no way be minimized, an intense, almost irrational, fear of being trapped is real and discernible in Beti's nonfictional writings and pronouncements. He is convinced that "[he] remain[s] ... the man to be brought down, no matter the means" ("*Le Pauvre Christ de Bomba* expliqué!" p. 128).

Beti is happiest on the fringe of society. He is the natural outsider who prefers to study the hierarchical structures of authority from a distance so that he can expose their mechanisms and ridicule their pretensions. It is precisely this aspect of his personality that he has projected in his fictional universe.

MARGINALITY, POPULAR CULTURE, AND ARTISTIC VISION

All of Beti's protagonists—Banda in *Ville cruelle*; Zacharie, Sanga Boto, and Catherine in *The Poor Christ*; Jean-Marie Medza, his cousin Zambo, and their village friends in *Mission to Kala*; Mor-Zamba, Joe the Juggler, and Abena in *Remember Ruben*; Perpétue, her brother Essola, and the soccer star Zeyang in *Perpétue*; Ismaël Dzewatama in *Les Deux Mères de Guillaume Ismaël Dzewatama* and its sequel, *La Revanche de Guillaume Ismaël Dzewatama* — are individuals who, because of their youth, gender, or ideas, are, like Beti, marginal characters in their societies. They constantly battle, with varying degrees of success, against oppressive social and political structures of recent or ancient origin.

Against the humbuggery and inflexible spirit of seriousness of the official cultures and figures of their communities, Beti's marginalized characters (at one level the young and the women against tyrannical village elders, and at another all three groups against pompous and authoritarian colonial colonels, governors, missionaries, and their modern African successors) assert the ribald, irreverent humor of their popular cultures. There is a certain peasant vitality in Beti's characters — Zambo and his friends, Zacharie, Dzewatama's relatives in the popular Niagara district, and so on. It is a vitality that the young schoolboy, and African-Frenchman in the making, Jean-Marie Medza, is in danger of losing with his modern official education, but one to which he has the immense and novel sexual pleasure of being quickly initiated by his cousins during his visit to their village.

A certain coarseness and exuberance characterize all of Beti's village protagonists. In spite of their material deprivation and the constraints on their lives, they all enjoy their local gin. Moreover, as Medza is quick to discover and indeed experience, or as Father Drumont sadly has to admit to himself after twenty years of missionary work, they also enjoy sex, uninhibited by any Christian considerations. The old ones, like the chief in *Ville cruelle*, Essomba Mendouga, are prepared to renounce their many wives for one when in the presence of a missionary, especially if there are practical advantages to be gained from the act or penalties for not so doing. But they merrily go about their ancient ways, even ridiculing the missionary as soon as he turns his back.

It is clear in this regard that the omnipresence of the missionary in Beti's fiction has a significance greater than is generally realized. Beyond Beti's specific cultural and political disagreements with missionarism is his rejection of its symbolic function: the cultivation of abstinence and repression of the vitality in man makes the missionary the anti-natural archetype and therefore a favorite satirical target for Beti.

The robustness of Beti's popular characters, their self-deprecatory attitude, their coarse humor have all led to correct suggestions of a Rabelaisian ring to his fiction, especially his first four novels. But like François Rabelais, the sixteenth-century French satirist, Beti did not use popular culture and figures as ends in themselves, although he clearly derives a pleasure from depicting them. They are rather a means of subverting, through the contrast they present, stiff, authoritarian officialdom.

This quality of Beti's literary imagination also explains his aversion to the French literature of school texts, and his attraction for a writer like Mark Twain. He explained in the 1979 interview by Anthony Biakolo in *Peuples noirs, peuples africains*:

> French literature as I knew it was a literature of the bourgeois; of polished people. It only depicted intelligent men. . . . In Mark Twain on the other hand, and this is typically American, all or almost all the characters belong to the popular classes. He depicts drunks, prostitutes, slaves, and in a most engaging way. He is not your intellectual that comes from the city and discovers some strange human fauna.
>
> (p. 100)

In the essay *"Le Pauvre Christ de Bomba expliqué!"* Beti wrote about Twain's achievement:

His unique genius seems to me to lie in those warm and sweet accents of a speech typical of the braggart vagabond who is sensitive to human suffering, and who after having drunk plenty of alcohol with all kinds of people, decides to bequeath his grandchildren with the treasure of his experience, in joyous prose.

(p. 118)

Beti's admiration for Twain was so strong that it is reasonable to believe that an incident in *Ville cruelle*—in which the body of the fugitive Koumé, who has drowned while crossing a river at night with his rescuer, Banda, is fished out by Banda—was actually inspired by a similar incident in *The Adventures of Huckleberry Finn*, where Jim discovers the corpse of Huck's drunken father (p. 118).

While an understanding of Beti's outsider mentality provides certain clues to his work, it would be grossly oversimplifying to see the significance of that work and the passions it generates solely in terms of that aspect of his personality. He himself warned against such psychologism in "*Le Pauvre Christ de Bomba expliqué!*":

Even if one accepts, as Balzac says somewhere, that the artist . . . works under the influence of factors whose total chemistry remain mysterious, does it mean that the writer's project, consciously arrived at at some time in the light of specific needs, and discussed with a third party, should be completely ignored?

(p. 111)

Beti's themes, characters, vision, and style are also the result of consciously formulated ideas on the function of literature. If at university in France he liked Twain and French writers such as Émile Zola and Voltaire, it is in the novels of Richard Wright, especially *Black Boy*, that he experienced something of a shock of revelation: "A scandal for all the fearful Uncle Toms of the new black bourgeoisie, [Wright] was the first fulminating prophet, at least in France, of the revolt of the

ghettoes; the tireless Cicero of their frightful moral and material misery, consequent on their oppression by whites" (p. 117). He was attracted to Zola and Voltaire because their writings witnessed to the misery the French people suffered as a result of social and economic oppression; but for the colonized subject that he then was, it is the specific victims of that oppression in Wright's novels—the black Americans, whom Beti saw as internally colonized—that made Wright's work much more appealing to him. Like Wright, Beti was also determined to become "the fulminating prophet of the revolt" of the African, a revolt then against colonial rule, now against equally dehumanizing postcolonial regimes.

This is the vision that has guided his literary practice throughout his career. And in its name he made a dramatic entry into the world of African letters in 1953, when he roundly denounced Camara Laye, the Guinean novelist who was then emerging, for abdicating his duty as a writer by being silent on colonial rule in his novel *The Dark Child* and for pandering to his European audience's taste for exoticism with tableaux of Africans engaged in endless rounds of drumming and exotic ceremonies. He contrasted Laye's novel with Wright's *Black Boy* in these terms: "Unconcerned with pleasing his public, Wright poses issues in all their stark reality and avoids platitudes. . . . Laye, on the other hand, takes pleasure in the anodyne, especially the picturesque" ("L'Enfant noir," p. 420).

Beti was dissatisfied with the picturesque, which he also called a "literature of folklore," because it projects what is essentially a mythical (that is, a timeless and tension-free) vision of the African past. To him this idealized vision concealed the undeniable social injustices suffered, by those such as women and the young, and removed the need to attend to these injustices. It also failed (a serious shortcoming for Beti, a politically liberal satirist and rationalist in the mode of Voltaire) to acknowledge the irrational nature of many of the beliefs and customs underpinning traditional social and political structures, and the need to sweep them aside. In any case, Beti contends, what is passed off as traditional in this literature are but degraded forms of earlier practices (interview by Biakolo, p. 109). But even if one assumes the truth of this vision, Beti asks, could it, in the mid 1950s when Laye began writing, have remained unaffected by the political reality of colonial domination?

It is clear from these structures of his that Beti, unlike Laye, has a more dynamic and open conception of tradition. He does not subscribe to the static view of it as a set of beliefs, practices, and customs laid down once and for all in some primordial, precolonial, and undifferentiated time, where the happiness of its adherents depends on fidelity to that originary, essential identity. Such a view, apart from being wrong insofar as it negates time and change, is tantamount to creating for free spirits a prison from which there can be no escape.

Traditions are constantly changing, and in the Africa of the 1950s, as Beti maintains, new ones were being forged out of the continent's experience with "political spoliation and phenomena such as the monetarization of exchanges, urbanization, rural exodus, social struggles, and participation in the wars of the metropolitan countries" (quoted by Mouralis, p. 14). The role of the writer then is not to depict idyllic images of Africa in the manner of Laye, but to reflect the tensions and dislocations resulting from the introduction of such changes. One should adopt, to borrow Bernard Mouralis' distinction, a sociological and not an ethnological vision of society: a vision of society in historical context and movement, and not in a state of stasis.

THE NOVELS

The Poor Christ of Bomba

Of the four novels of his early period, *The Poor Christ of Bomba* and *Mission to Kala* are the most representative of Beti's art and ideas. Set in the 1930s in the imaginary central African mission town of Bomba and its environs, *The Poor Christ* is an account of the life and activities of the French missionary Father Drumont. Animated "with the ardour of an Apostle," he has left France for Africa to "extend the Kingdom of Christ" to the "disinherited or those whom [he] was pleased to regard as such" (pp. 143, 153). But he discovers after twenty years of work that he has been a pathetic failure and returns to France embittered and guilt-ridden.

The immediate cause of his disillusionment is a visit he pays to Tala, a parish he had abandoned two years earlier, to punish his parishioners for what he thought were their unchristian ways. He returns, however, to discover not a penitent people "thirsting for him," as he has calculated, but one who has prospered from record harvests of cocoa and has regressed, as he sees it, to its traditional pagan ways. Wherever he goes in Tala, he sees men proudly flaunting their many wives, as well as unmarried women and their children. Equally disappointing to him is the fact that his church buildings are crumbling, and traditional religion and its chief priest, Sanga Boto, are making a daring comeback.

But Father Drumont's anger and bitterness soon yield to reflection. At the prompting of Zacharie, his cook, he starts to wonder whether his enterprise has not been fundamentally flawed from the outset. His self-doubt grows more intense during a conversation with Vidal, the French colonial administrator, to whom he confesses: "I am a failure, a sacred failure. . . . These good people worshipped God without our help. What matter if they worshipped after their own fashion? . . . I've never asked myself this before. Why don't the Chinese devote themselves to converting all Paris to Confucianism?" (pp. 150–151). Also he realizes that his real motivation is not religious but psychological. The exercise of power is what gives him pleasure, which is why he compares himself to Napoléon.

But Father Drumont is not the only character to describe the trajectory from innocence to maturity; Denis, his houseboy, also does. His growth is artistically realized in the diary technique adopted by Beti. When the story begins, Denis, who completely identifies with the point of view of his master, is content to note events, conversations, and activities with no comment. What judgment there is in these notations derives solely from the discrepancy between the matter-of-fact way in which he reports in his diary entries and the gross nature of the events reported. By the time the novel ends, however, Denis' syntax has become more complex and his entries have acquired a more interpretive edge. Denis' evolution from the gullible boy that he was at the beginning to a more critical person is symbolic of that of his people who, after a period of uncritical submission to colonial rule, were able to see the brutal reality behind the rhetoric; the reality, as Father Drumont discovers in the end, of "forced labour . . . floggings, arbitrary imprisonments" (p. 155).

Mission to Kala

Like *The Poor Christ*, *Mission to Kala* is also a first-person narrative of the picaresque adventures of a schoolboy, the sixteen-year-old Jean-Marie Medza. Having just returned home to Vimili on holidays, the young Medza, reeling from failure in his university-entrance exams and apprehensive about the welcome he will receive from his father, finds himself confronted with a serious problem. The wife of Niam, his cousin, has recently abandoned her husband and fled back to her parents in Kala. Convinced that there is no better person than their "son," Jean-Marie, with his western education and city ways, to avenge the affront they have suffered, the villagers entrust him with the responsibility of bringing Niam's wife back, by bullying the "rustic" Kalans into submission if necessary.

Although initially reticent, Jean-Marie finally accepts this mission. He soon begins to enjoy the irony of being a failed student who is transformed into a hero. Recovering his cousin's, and by extension his clan's, wife has become a question of national honor to which he is now fully committed. He starts nursing inflated images of himself as a latter-day Francisco Pizarro (the famous leader of the sixteenth-century Spanish conquest of Mexico and Peru), marching down the Andes mountains to conquer the Incas. He in fact contemplates lengthening his name to Medzaro to give it a Spanish-sounding ring.

But Jean-Marie's self-doubts are reignited the moment he gets to the gates of Kala. There, he is impressed to the point of fear by the sturdy muscles and athleticism of a group of Kalans engaged in sporting activities. Fortunately for him, he is recognized by one of the wrestlers, Zambo, who turns out to be a cousin of his. The rest of his stay is built on a superb misunderstanding. While Zambo and his friends are proud of their city guest and exhibit him all over town, hoping to have some of his prestige rub off on them, Jean-Marie secretly admires their earthiness, sensuality, and uninhibited sense of freedom.

In the mistaken assumption that he is an old hand at pleasure-seeking, his friends take him through countless rounds of drinking and feasting and introduce him to the prettiest girls in town. What they do not realize is that their guest is not only new to all this but also uninitiated in sexual matters. Jean-Marie conceals this fact all the while he is playing the role that has been created for him. Thus he wriggles himself out of embarrassing encounters with women through a variety of pretexts. Of course he does not remain innocent throughout his visit. He manages, with the help of several shots of whiskey, to lose his sexual innocence and even to get married. Although he has scarcely paid any attention to his mission, he succeeds, thanks to the intervention of his uncle and the chief, in taking back Niam's wife. Upon his return to Vimili, he is treated like a hero, his exploits grossly exaggerated by the villagers.

But Jean-Marie's triumph is not unalloyed. Inebriated by his sense of newfound freedom, he is now determined not to submit to the tyranny of his father. He refuses to be contrite for failing his exams, let alone submit to any beating for it. He stays out late and drinks. Although the novel ends on the rather serious note of rupture within family, it is shot through with a self-deprecatory and scabrous humor that makes it not the novel one has thought it to be: that of a conceited boy whose western education has made him contemptuous of rural African values. Such a view misses the entirely ironic thrust of the novel. Medza affects an attitude of superiority only when he realizes that his own community has overestimated his real achievement. But even then he constantly undercuts this heroic image whenever it asserts itself. *Mission to Kala* is a parody of heroism — literally a mock epic.

In the story references to epic action abound. We have already seen the conquistador image. Beti's knowledge of the classics is also evident. Jean-Marie suggests a parallel between the case of Niam's wife and the Trojan abduction of Helen and sees his mission as that of a Vimili Achilles leading the charge to recover Niam's wife. Moreover, the ovations that greet his entry, with his cousin and friends, into the many beer parlors in Kala are compared to those welcoming Caesar home from his Gallic wars.

But Jean-Marie has hardly finished making these comparisons when he proceeds to mock them. The Vimili Achilles has nothing of the physique of his Greek counterpart. He pokes fun at his naïveté and weakness, and at the fact that he shrinks in terror at the sight of the muscles of his rather more Greek cousins of Kala. Also, instead of a mighty army in his charge, he goes alone, ironically adding another reference to the Greek classics: "Menelaus was a far-sighted man, and preferred to go well escorted" (p. 29). Jean-Marie's armor is a bicycle. It is this image of our Achilles-Medza on a bicycle that is the defining characteristic of *Mission to Kala* and of

Beti's vision; a carnivalesque vision in which authority, age, heroism (all symbolized here by the epic) are subverted, made fun of, through juxtaposition with their opposites: the carnal, the popular and the young, the trivial.

Perpetua and the Habit of Unhappiness

With his 1974 novel *Remember Ruben*, the first of a trilogy, Beti started, as has been observed, his second creative phase. But although chronologically it is part of the second set of novels, it is more properly described as transitional. Like that of his first four novels, its action unfolds within the colonial period. But the events depicted—the assassination of UPC leader Ruben and the rise of radical nationalism—has implications that group it with his later novels. Of these later works, the most representative is perhaps *Perpetua and the Habit of Unhappiness*, a detective story.

A young man, Essola, has just been released from a prison camp where he was incarcerated for belonging to a "subversive" group, the revolutionary People's Progressive Party. On his return home to his parents, he discovers that his sister Perpetua has died during his nine-year absence. Because none of his relatives knows or is prepared to tell him the circumstances of her death, he decides to investigate.

After several trips around the country and the piecing together of testimonies from his late sister's friends and neighbors, he discovers the truth: a sordid tale of an intelligent and ambitious girl whose noble dreams of a career in medicine are cut short by a tyrannical and avaricious mother, who forces her out of school and marries her off. The "rich" man whom she marries not only turns out to be very poor but, more importantly, totally unworthy of her, intellectually and morally. As their marriage goes sour, he becomes abusive. She suffers the height of humiliation when her unscrupulous husband forces her to have a relationship with his police boss for a promotion he has been unable to earn through exams. The psychological strain and the lack of proper medical care during her third pregnancy finally lead to her death.

But *Perpetua* is not just a novel of a personal tragedy. The investigation of his heroine's death gives Beti a chance to present the reader with a picture of life in an imaginary postindependence African country. It is an anachronistic picture of traditional marriage customs that sacrifice the happiness of girls like Perpetua for the greed of parents; it is also a picture of venal bureaucrats and of repressive political regimes. The fate of Perpetua is in this sense symbolic of that of her country. Just as she is not consulted about any of the decisions concerning her (Beti uses the words "tied up" and "wrapped up" to denote the way in which her destiny has been decided), so her country has similarly been handed over to be exploited and destroyed. Perpetua's arrested development is like that of her country (a thinly veiled reference to Cameroon) and in a sense that of many of the independent nations of Africa.

While Beti's later novels share with those published before 1972 an acute social consciousness, they are also both more bleak and positive. They lack the ironic detachment and humor of *Mission to Kala* or *The Poor Christ*. Their heroes seem to suffer an unending catalog of misery. They are hunted down, incarcerated, killed—fates that are suffered by none of the heroes of his earlier work. And yet in spite of all this, there is a sense that they are less tragic. Beti's earlier heroes submit to fates they do not understand and against which their only weapons are humor and satire. His later protagonists, on the other hand, have developed a greater awareness of the sources of their own ills. They are consequently less resigned and more prepared to effect change. But they are also, by the same token, too serious. This aspect of their personality, ironically, is vulnerable to the type of parody and self-deprecatory humor Beti used to such sublime effect in his earlier novels.

Selected Bibliography

FICTION

[Eza Boto, pseud.]. "Sans haine et sans amour." In *Présence africaine* 14 (1953).

[Eza Boto, pseud.]. *Ville cruelle.* Paris: Éditions Africains, 1954.

Le Pauvre Christ de Bomba. Paris: R. Laffont, 1956.

Mission terminée. Paris: Éditions Buchet/Chastel, 1957.

Le Roi miraculé: Chronique des Essazam. Paris: Éditions Buchet/Chastel, 1958.

Perpétue et l'habitude du malheur. Paris: Éditions Buchet/Chastel, 1974.

Remember Ruben. Paris: Union Générale d'Éditions, 1974; Paris: L'Harmattan, 1982.

La Ruine presque cocasse d'un polichinelle: Remember Ruben 2. Paris: Éditions des Peuples Noirs, 1979.

Les Deux Mères de Guillaume Ismaël Dzewatama: Futur Camionneur. Paris: Éditions Buchet/Chastel, 1982.

La Revanche de Guillaume Ismaël Dzewatama. Paris: Éditions Buchet/Chastel, 1984.

L'Histoire du fou. Paris: Julliard, 1994.

TRANSLATIONS

Mission to Kala. Trans. by Peter Green. London: Heinemann, 1964.

King Lazarus. Intro. by Oscar Ronald Dathorne. New York: Collier Books, 1971.

The Poor Christ of Bomba. Trans. by Gerald Moore. London: Heinemann, 1971.

Perpetua and the Habit of Unhappiness. Trans. by John Reed and Clive Wake. London: Heinemann, 1978.

Remember Ruben. Trans. by Gerald Moore. London: Heinemann, 1980; Washington, D.C.: Three Continents Press, 1980.

[Eza Boto]. "Without Hate or Love." In Willfried F. Feuser, ed., *Jazz and Palm Wine and Other Stories.* Harlow, U.K.: Longman, 1981.

Lament for an African Pol. Trans. by Richard Bjornson. Washington, D.C.: Three Continents Press, 1985.

BOOK-LENGTH ESSAYS

Main Basse sur le Cameroun: Autopsie d'une décolonisation. Paris: F. Maspero, 1972.

Lettre ouverte aux Camerounais; ou, La Deuxième Mort de Ruben Um Nyobé. Rouen, France: Éditions des Peuples Noirs, 1986; Paris: Diffusion L'Harmattan, 1986.

Dictionnaire de la négritude. With Odile Tobner. Paris: L'Harmattan, 1989.

La France contre l'Afrique: Retour au Cameroun. Paris: La Découverte, 1993.

ARTICLES

A[lexandre] B[iyidi]. "Problèmes de l'étudiant noir." In *Présence africaine* 14 (1953).

A[lexandre] B[iyidi]. "Afrique noire, littérature rose." In *Présence africaine*, special series, nos. 1–2 (April–July 1955).

A[lexandre] B[iyidi]. "L'Enfant noir." In *Présence africaine* 16 (1955).

"Identité et tradition." In Guy Michaud, ed., *Négritude: Traditions et développement.* Brussels, Belgium: Éditions Complexe, 1978.

"Afrique francophone: La Langue française survivra-t-elle à Senghor." In *Peuples noirs, peuples africains*, no. 10 (July–August 1979).

"*Le Pauvre Christ de Bomba* expliqué!" In *Peuples noirs, peuples africains*, no. 19 (January–February 1981).

INTERVIEWS

Biakolo, Anthony. "Entretien avec Mongo Beti." In *Peuples noirs, peuples africains*, no. 10 (July–August 1979).

Monga, Célestin. "Mongo Beti règle ses comptes." In *Jeune Afrique Économie*, no. 136 (October 1990).

CRITICAL STUDIES

Arnold, Stephen H. "The New Mongo Beti." In *Africana Journal* 13, nos. 1–4 (1982).

Battestini, Monique, Simon Battestini, and Roger Mercier, eds. *Mongo Beti: Écrivain camerounais.* Paris: F. Nathan, 1964.

Benot, Yves. "Mongo Beti ou le réalisme contre les colonialismes." In *La Nouvelle Critique*, no. 93 (April 1976).

Bestman, Martin T. "Structure du récit et mécanique de l'action révolutionnaire dans *Remember Ruben*." In *Présence francophone* 23 (fall 1981).

Bjornson, Richard. "Mongo Beti: Counter History and Critical Consciousness" and "The Reemergence of Mongo Beti." In *The African Quest for Freedom and Identity: Cameroonian Writing and the National Experience.* Bloomington: Indiana University Press, 1991.

Brière, Éloise A. "*Remember Ruben:* Étude spatio-temporelle." In *Présence francophone* 15 (fall 1977).

Britwum, Kwabena. "Irony and the Paradox of Idealism in Mongo Beti's *Le Pauvre Christ de Bomba.*" In *Arts and Letters* 6 (fall 1972).

Erickson, John D. "Mongo Beti: *Le Roi miraculé.*" In *Nommo: African Fiction in French South of the Sahara.* York, S.C.: French Literature Publications, 1979.

Gakwandi, Shatto Arthur. "The Illusion of Progress: Achebe's *No Longer at Ease* and Beti's *Mission to Kala.*" In *The Novel and Contemporary Experience in Africa.* New York: Africana, 1977.

Kom, Ambroise. "Mongo Beti Returns to Cameroon: Journey to the End of the Night." In *Research in African Literatures* 22 (winter 1991).

Lambert, Fernando. "Narrative Perspectives in Mongo Beti's *Le Pauvre Christ de Bomba.*" In *Yale French Studies*, no. 53 (1976).

Melone, Thomas. *Mongo Beti: L'Homme et le destin.* Paris: Présence africaine, 1971.

Moore, Gerald. "Mongo Beti: From Satire to Epic." In *Twelve African Writers.* Bloomington: Indiana University Press, 1980.

Mouralis, Bernard. *Comprendre l'oeuvre de Mongo Beti.* Issy-les-Moulineaux, France: Classiques Africains, 1981.

Ndongo, Jacques Fame. *L'Esthetique romanesque de Mongo Beti.* Paris: ABC, 1985.

Palmer, Eustace. "Mongo Beti." In *The Growth of the African Novel.* London: Heinemann, 1979.

André Brink
1935–

RONALD AYLING

ANDRÉ PHILIPPUS BRINK was born on 29 May 1935 in Vrede, a small village in the Afrikaans-speaking province of the Orange Free State in South Africa. Rooted strongly in Afrikaner tradition (Afrikaners are South African people of Dutch settler descent with rural roots), Brink has lived most of his life in various rural environments in his native land, first in the Orange Free State and the Transvaal and later in the eastern Cape. His father, Daniel Brink (1905–1993), was a magistrate, and his mother, Aletta Wilhelmina (née Wolmarans, born in 1907), a schoolteacher. Educated at the high school in Lydenburg, a small town in the eastern Transvaal, and Potchefstroom University, also in the Transvaal — where, in the 1950s, he obtained three degrees in seven years, including master of arts in both Afrikaans and English — he completed his formal studies in France, undertaking graduate work in comparative literature at the Sorbonne in the University of Paris from 1959 to 1961. From 1961 to 1990, Brink lived and worked in Grahamstown, teaching Afrikaans and Dutch literature at Rhodes University in the primarily English-speaking eastern Cape. Since 1991 he has been a professor of English at the University of Cape Town.

Destined for an academic career, Brink had already completed three novels in Afrikaans while a student at Potchefstroom; he wrote another, *Die Ambassadeur* (*The Ambassador*), soon after his sojourn in Paris. All four involve considerable autobiographical content and, as the author has admitted on various occasions, are the work of an immature and in many ways naive young man. At one point, Brink thought of settling in Paris; however, the massacre at Sharpeville in 1960 occurred while he was in France. At least sixty-eight unarmed black people were killed by the police and almost two hundred wounded while engaging in a civil rights demonstration similar to those being held in the United States at this time. This horrendous event with its overt racial connotations had a profound effect upon Brink. Henceforth, he has said, he was committed to returning to South Africa, writing about that country, and helping to change it, politically, socially, and morally.

His polemical essays, collected in two volumes in Afrikaans and in one volume in English (variously called *Mapmakers* in England and *Writing in a State of Siege* — the English edition's subtitle — in the United States), have been preoccupied with ethical and moral issues arising from the application of apartheid — the official policy of racial segregation — in South African society, as well as with problems of censorship and human rights in his native land. Indeed, *Writing in a*

State of Siege (1983) is an apt title for this collection of articles, essays, informal talks, and speeches. The ten novels published since *Die Ambassadeur* (1963) have all been similarly preoccupied, demonstrating a conscious effort on Brink's part to accept full responsibility for everything he writes—not as a member of a relatively small white enclave within a largely black country or as a member of the Afrikaner tribal unit within that white community (although he incorporates both elements of that experience in his imaginative creations), but, rather, as a writer of a country belonging more to Africa than to Europe.

THE SIXTIES

Initially, Brink believed that South Africa needed a gigantic upheaval in cultural and aesthetic life and an opening to changing international perceptions of sex and gender as well as of race. During the 1960s, he became one of the spokesmen for the Sestigers, a group of Afrikaans writers (taking their name from the Afrikaans for "the sixties") who challenged Afrikaner literature's conventional treatment of traditional subjects. A rift developed in the group as Brink, Jan Rabie, and Breyten Breytenbach came to reject the experimental apolitical approach, which most had initially embraced, in favor of an insistence on open and direct political commitment. For these rebels—as they appeared to everyone in Afrikaans circles at that time and long after—it meant straightforward confrontation with the policies of a powerful and entrenched government that became ever more ruthless and oppressive as time went by. Fearlessly, Brink, the movement's major spokesman and theorist, became the editor of the Sestigers' short-lived journal. Increasingly, he was forced to use English as well as his native language as dual weapons in bitter ideological combat.

Facing increased danger of being silenced in his native land as an Afrikaans writer, he turned to writing novels in both languages.

Though his earliest novels in English are mostly straightforward transcriptions from Afrikaans, he soon found new imaginative resources in the adopted language. Brink has remarked that more than half of the many preliminary notes made in the early 1970s before beginning the actual writing of *An Instant in the Wind* (1976) came to him, "quite spontaneously, in English." Since "the novel deals, essentially, with two modes of experiencing Africa," represented in the novel by its two protagonists, he said it was interesting "to see how far the planning of the book could be influenced by thinking in English when dealing with the white character and in Afrikaans when imagining the black slave.... it was remarkable to see to what extent the two languages spontaneously associated themselves with the two spheres of experience represented by the main characters" (*Mapmakers*, p. 114). In this instance, as in subsequent writings, Brink's two versions of his novel are not identical transcriptions of a single narrative but, rather, separate activities within (usually) close approximations to the primary narrative; occasionally, scenes occur in the English version that are not in the Afrikaans text and vice versa. He has certainly worked hard to become a writer in English, rather than remain a straightforward translator into that language; and, though he is the first to admit that he has not managed to write like a native speaker, he can now be looked upon as a genuinely creative artist in English, worthy of attention in his own right in that regard. Indeed, some of his creative writings in English—the novel *States of Emergency*, for instance—have never made an appearance in his native language.

The Ambassador

The first of Brink's major publications in the English language was *The Ambassador*, published in South Africa in 1964, the year after its initial publication in Afrikaans. All the main characters in the novel, set in Paris around 1960, are white South Africans. While the problem of apartheid is not dealt with directly in the book, the moral life of the Afrikaner is. Stephen Keyter, third secretary to the South African ambassador in France, decides to report the ambassador for immoral behavior with a young South African woman named Nicolette Alford. His evidence is circumstantial and, at the time he makes his complaint, the allegations are wholly unfounded, but in time his charges come to reflect the truth. Overcome with remorse for having, as he believes, destroyed the diplomat's career and personal life, Keyter commits suicide. The middle-aged ambassador, a fellow Afrikaner, left alone at the end of the novel awaiting an official inquiry into his conduct, is almost certainly doomed to disgrace and ignominious recall by his puritanically minded superiors.

The Ambassador reveals throughout its author's romantic infatuation with Paris and with Gallic ways of life and culture. Though there are few specific references to, and fewer concrete realizations of, South Africa, that country nevertheless pervades the novel. Most of the private remarks made by the ambassador about his country are negative. When an acquaintance criticizes Paris by saying, "Oh, to be back in South Africa: Paris is such a terribly *profane* city, so Catholic. What a good thing our little group can be together tonight," the ambassador thinks to himself, "*Our little group. Our little group of strangers in this strange, cold world*" (1985, p. 176). The isolation of the South African group in Paris is paralleled by the isolation the ambassador feels from virtually everyone he encounters, whether in France or his native land. The atmosphere of alienation and existentialist angst, strongly conveyed throughout, not only reveals Brink's affinity with the contemporary French literary scene (and his immense admiration for the writings of Albert Camus especially) but undoubtedly reflects his own personal as well as philosophical concerns. The worry and fear that infuse the ambassador's outlook, confused as it is by his newly awoken erotic desires, are aspects of his

troubled life that were assuredly shared by Brink at that time in his life. Brink's struggle to find his place in the world when he was questioning (and on the way to rejecting) officially sanctioned versions of his homeland and many of its dominant political, religious, and cultural values is shown in the thoughts of his fictional protagonist, the ambassador. Less concerned with political questions (even those raised by apartheid) than Brink's subsequent novels are, *The Ambassador* offers a vivid portrayal of the bustling Parisian scene, embodied in the casual and seemingly carefree hedonistic world of Nicolette, as well as in lyrical depictions of the people and the cityscape.

APARTHEID AND SLAVERY

It was ten years before Brink's next novel was to appear—and, as with all his early fiction, that publication was initially in Afrikaans. His prolific literary output (now in English as well as Afrikaans) remained constant, however. This period was taken up by teaching, lecturing, editorial work, writing plays in Afrikaans, and much polemical writing—primarily within Afrikaner cultural circles—in which Brink sought to change the aesthetic climate in South Africa and to introduce a new openness to sexual and racial experiences, until then denied or ignored in Afrikaans literature. *The Ambassador* was criticized in his native land for its treatment of sex, mild though it is in comparison with contemporary European and American literature. To these innovations, which continued the aesthetic crusade he had started in the 1960s, Brink added in the 1970s a stronger and more insistent opposition to the practical workings of apartheid in his society. It is not surprising, therefore, that the novel he completed after *The Ambassador* should run into trouble there.

Looking on Darkness

Kennis van die aand, published in 1973, has the dubious distinction of being the first book written in Afrikaans to be banned in South Africa. Though government spokesmen and pro-apartheid Afrikaner newspapers had for years conducted an organized campaign against the freer spirit in contemporary literature and the more open discussion and realization of sexual matters, only writings in English had actually suffered censorship. Previously, traditional Afrikaner reverence for serious literature in the relatively new language (new for literary purposes, that is) had protected even controversial writings from state interference; indeed, official disapproval —whether by state or church—had often been sufficient to provoke self-censorship by Afrikaner publishers and writers. *Kennis van die aand* changed all that: from that time on, censorship of writings in all languages became a regular practice in South Africa, with a correspondingly huge expansion of appropriate legislation, bureaucratic administration, and police surveillance. Banned in Afrikaans, though not before it had sold out its first print run, *Kennis van die aand* was translated by Brink into a more robust English than he had been capable of for *The Ambassador* ten years earlier; as *Looking on Darkness*, it was published in 1974. This version was likewise banned in his native land, the dual ban being another undesirable "first" there.

The novel is a first-person narrative of the life of Joseph Malan, a Colored actor from the Cape Province. Most likely the book was banned because it portrays a Colored man (in South Africa, a man of mixed-race origins) as having an affair with a white English woman in South Africa. The relentless and detailed descriptions of police brutality and of the routine use of systematic torture in South African prisons—then heatedly disputed by the authorities, though soon to be corroborated by several notorious instances in which political prisoners were beaten to death in police custody—were other possible targets for the state's persecution.

Like Brink's other novels, *Looking on Darkness* moves freely back and forth in time: the

beginning of the novel is really the beginning of the end. Malan is in jail after his trial waiting to be executed. Most of the novel depicts the unfolding of Malan's life, including a memorable historical account of his enslaved ancestors; a portrayal of his own childhood and early interest in drama; and his days in college and his years in England, working in repertory there until he becomes a regular member of the Royal Shakespeare Company. The condemned man's narrative concludes with his return to South Africa, his valiant attempts to run a black theater company there in spite of constant police harassment, and his fatal friendship with a white woman. The novel's details of theatrical life and of Malan's attempts to create a new form of South African drama (mostly by adapting foreign classics to relevant contemporary themes) are especially vivid, presumably drawing upon some of Brink's own experiences in the 1960s, when he himself wrote and adapted several plays for the burgeoning Afrikaans theater.

Initially, Malan thinks that he can leave South Africa for good and make another country his home; like Brink himself when he was living in Paris, however, the actor discovers that he is inextricably bound to his native land, even though it denies him many of the freedoms he enjoys abroad. In Cape Town he founds his own theater company to devise and stage drama with clear social and racial implications; for this he is systematically persecuted. Malan's productions criticize living conditions and racial inequality, thereby provoking critical dissent as well as supportive public disturbances. His professional and private life becomes increasingly difficult, but he nonetheless feels he is trying to do something for his people and getting through to many of them. Ultimately, though, he is destroyed because of his intimate friendship with a white woman, which is not merely forbidden but even criminalized by apartheid legislation. Unable to love each other openly, the lovers decide upon mutual suicide; Malan kills her but then is unable to take his own life, an act which he believes would signal his ultimate defeat.

Looking on Darkness is an honorable and realistic attempt to confront what were, in the early 1970s, the increasing horrors of state tyranny at every level of South African society, in particular their destructive manifestations in interracial relations and in art (in this case, theatrical presentation) that tries to tell the truth about these problems. The novel—Brink's first aesthetic confrontation with such material—can now be seen to be politically flawed, at once confused and self-compromising. Its strengths, however, lie in the detailed, gut-wrenching realization of slavery and cumulative violence that underlie Malan's family history, which in itself implicitly shows apartheid to be the logical and systematic end product of centuries-old state-sanctioned slavery. The narrative depicts an individual's attempts to create a politically conscious South African drama and to find a place for racial issues and black participants on that country's professional stages. The novel anticipates developments that Athol Fugard and a number of black theater groups were to bring to fruition, despite state interference and harassment, in the 1970s and 1980s. In its initial and painful (though brief) emphasis on the ongoing heritage of slavery, the novel is also, in significant ways, a dry run for Brink's next novel, *An Instant in the Wind* (1976).

An Instant in the Wind

After *Looking on Darkness*, which is set in the early 1960s, Brink turned to the middle of the eighteenth century for this next novel, in which the main characters are Elisabeth Larsson, a white woman, and Adam Mantoor, a runaway slave. Elisabeth's husband has died while they are exploring the interior of the Cape; deserted by servants and camp followers, she is left, alone and helpless, until Adam happens to find her. After some initial

awkwardness and antagonism, the two become friends and then lovers, breaking the most intimate cultural taboos of both. At one point, they hope to remain together, alone in the wilderness in an almost idyllic state of nature; but eventually, they come to recognize that they must return to Cape Town. For saving Elisabeth's life and aiding her in the arduous journey back to civilization, Adam hopes that he will be given his freedom; instead, he is tortured and then executed.

The protagonists are presented at the beginning of *An Instant in the Wind* as historical figures about whom the narrator wants to know more: "*Who were they? The names are known*—Adam Mantoor and Elisabeth Larsson—and something of their history has been recorded" (p. 9). That "something" is indistinct and fragmentary, though: mere bits of information gleaned from legal documents in the Cape archives and from Elisabeth's brief, rather dry memoir of her travels (her subsequent history is unknown and probably unknowable). Yet in her journal account are two glimpses beyond history that captivate the narrator's (and our) interest: in words seemingly wrung from her, she exclaims, "*This no one can take away from us, not even ourselves*" (p. 12), and later, "*Such a long journey ahead for you and me. Oh God, oh God*" (p. 15). These two apparent cries from the heart fire the narrator into imagining the strange meeting and subsequent fluctuating relationship between the pair in a wild and hostile environment that is, by turns, dangerous, beautiful, lush, mysterious, barren, and unimaginably harsh.

The reader knows from very early in the narrative that Adam will die cruelly at the hands of the authorities shortly after his return to the Cape, but not until the end is it suggested that he dies because Elisabeth has betrayed him. The vulnerability, tenderness, and mutually supportive sacrifices of the two out in the bush have affected the reader, who, like the pair themselves, tries to hold a number of contradictions in mind at the same time. Once back in Cape Town, their intimacy is impossible. By implication, the corrupting influences of society destroy the clearsighted and unsentimental love that Elisabeth and Adam have managed, painfully, to create for themselves; no matter how strong their mutual passion and indebtedness, that love cannot withstand systematic and long-established racism. Nevertheless, there is a tender human dimension to the novel, which is accentuated by its lyrical descriptions of bush and desert, seascape and inland storms. Intermingled with vivid realizations of the unspoiled wilderness and of the couple's deteriorating conditions are several memorable if plaintive cries and questionings (mostly unspoken) from Adam and Elisabeth. Although there are occasional purple passages and awkward emotional transitions, which are perhaps unavoidable in handling such delicate subject matter, presented as it is in the context of extreme circumstances of hardship and distress, the love story is told with little sentimentality or mawkishness.

POST-SOWETO WRITINGS

Brink's next two novels, *Rumours of Rain* (1978) and *A Dry White Season* (1979), return to the present on, respectively, the eve and the immediate aftermath of the Soweto riots of 1976. Though neither narrative is really about those cataclysmic events—whose deep and abiding significance was quickly grasped by only a few South African intellectuals (Brink and Nadine Gordimer among them)—the radically changed and the newly charged psychic states to which the riots gave rise form the powerfully sensed background in both novels. Each work focuses on a single Afrikaner; their personalities and moral outlooks are vastly different. Martin Mynhardt, in *Rumours of Rain*, is an affluent businessman who wants to maintain the political status quo while Ben du Toit, in *A Dry White Season*, is

a naive but idealistic schoolteacher who is destroyed as he tries to expose social iniquities he never dreamed could exist in the Republic of South Africa.

Rumours of Rain

Rumours of Rain, like *Looking on Darkness*, is a first-person narrative. Martin Mynhardt, in London on a conference stopover that gives him a period of unexpected leisure at a time of acute personal and domestic crisis, is writing an account of his life. Through the use of flashbacks, he recounts significant events in his life, primarily centered on the events of one fairly recent weekend during which he had gone with his son, Louis, to the family farm in the Transvaal in order to make arrangements for its sale. That his mind at such a time should be searching and researching such moments in the past is quite credible; that he should be casting these experiences in the form of a novel, though, seems most improbable. His son has recently returned from fighting with the South African expeditionary forces in Angola as an emotionally scarred, bitter young man; his estrangement from his father and from his father's rightwing politics is exacerbated when he discovers that Mynhardt has failed to help his friend Bernard, Louis's godfather and an Afrikaner lawyer, whose politically progressive activities have run foul of the police and the Special Branch (South Africa's security police).

We soon see how corrupt and vile Mynhardt is and how firmly he believes he is always right. Often, his ideas and attempts at self-vindication are thinly disguised novelistic devices that permit Brink to expose in the most direct manner pro-apartheid ideology and its die-hard grassroots support among rural Afrikaners. Mynhardt's occupation is no accident: a highly successful Afrikaner businessman, he is portrayed as a rising tycoon who exerts considerable influence upon the political party in power. Such men think that they control the government whereas, in actuality, the National Party's ideological concerns dictate their policies. The South African corporate community had traditionally been an English-speaking preserve, but from the 1960s onward Afrikaners increasingly gained a foothold in this financial domain and the international banking community as well. Mynhardt believes that Bernard's quest for social and racial equality is doomed because he is "trying to wage a moral war in a world determined by other, economic, forces" (1979, p. 55). For Mynhardt, material considerations are the be-all and the end-all. We now know in hindsight—with the subsequent dismantling of the apartheid system—that these very forces were in the long run at the mercy of international economic pressures (including sanctions), which eventually toppled the political and social system defended so devotedly by Mynhardt. He is a beastly man, but he is very clearly the result of a particular history. Brink, while displaying Mynhardt's failure and inherent inability to give love, elicits some sympathy for this man who has no sympathy of his own to give to anyone or anything. This difficult effect is accomplished by allowing him to tell his own story.

A Dry White Season

In *A Dry White Season* (1979), Brink takes another Afrikaner for his protagonist and gives him—after a long, hard struggle—the understanding that does not come to Mynhardt. A history teacher at an Afrikaans private school, Ben du Toit is drawn into a series of events that leads him to question police procedures at the time of the Soweto riots and then to probe intently the investigatory actions of the Special Branch (in particular, its methods of interrogation in state prisons); as a result, he is threatened by the authorities, his home is bombed, he loses his job, and he finds himself alienated from colleagues, wife, and daughter, though not his son. Eventually, he loses his life in a hit-and-run car "accident" that clearly has been planned.

At the beginning of the novel, du Toit's moral understanding is very little different from Mynhardt's: he believes that the government and the security police act in a just and democratic manner. It is the mistreatment of a black janitor at his school—a man whom he knows to be neither a criminal nor a political activist—which leads the teacher into a complex and self-perpetuating involvement that results in disillusionment, harassment, and death. Such courageous integrity and relentless truth-seeking—ironically, the tribal virtues usually most often celebrated by du Toit's nationalist colleagues, family, and friends who become his critics and opponents in the course of the novel—make one feel that Brink is making amends, consciously or not, for his ugly portrait of the Afrikaner in *Rumours of Rain*.

The steps in du Toit's heightened awareness of injustice are carefully delineated. Gordon Ngubene, the janitor, comes to du Toit seeking help in gaining information about the detention of his schoolboy son, one of the many children arrested during the Soweto education protests. At first du Toit believes that the security police are merely doing their job to maintain law and order. But by the time Gordon, like his son, is killed in detention, Ben du Toit begins to question what exactly the role and responsibilities of the security police, the notorious Special Branch, are; he comes to realize, unwillingly and reluctantly, that there has been a massive cover-up, which he feels he must expose. Ben du Toit thereby comes to represent those white liberals who question the system but, by a variety of means, are effectively silenced. South Africa—depicted as a massive totalitarian state with an elaborate apparatus of paid or terrorized informers and a highly organized system of torture and intimidation both within and outside the prisons—is revealed to du Toit as a self-perpetuating terror machine. The paranoia and persecutorial mania of its law officers and agents (whether they be judges, policemen, magistrates, or prison doctors) are depicted. Individually and collaboratively, these people are shown conspiring to foil all investigations into abuses of the system and to destroy anyone who questions, let alone criticizes or opposes, government operations and methods. In the process of analyzing this situation, Brink's novel also realizes in agonizing detail the enormous practical and ethical difficulties facing the individuals of conscience in South Africa under apartheid.

Often, one cannot help but respond to the voice of the narrator of *A Dry White Season* (particularly toward the book's end) as though it had become Brink's own voice describing the role of the writer in the post-Holocaust period; this development is particularly marked in the final pages, when the narrator questions his own participation in the shaping of du Toit's painfully assembled notes and affidavits. "Then why did I go ahead by writing it all down here?" he asks, to reply in ever more affirmative terms (especially in the final phrase, which is also the last five words of the novel; emphasis added): "Perhaps all one can really hope for, all I'm entitled to, is no more than this: to write it down. To report what I know. So that it will not be possible for any man ever to say again: *I knew nothing about it*" (1980, p. 316). By telling du Toit's story, the narrator becomes a political being, as does Brink in his work, overtly at times and implicitly throughout. Like the protagonist in *A Dry White Season*, a fellow Afrikaner agonizing over equally urgent social issues, Brink has known what it is like to be harassed and pressured by the powers that be. He has testified that, especially since the publication of *Looking on Darkness* in 1974:

> I've been under constant surveillance: all my mail is opened, and my phone is tapped — those are the sort of bottom-line things that you have to accept, and if you're not prepared to accept them you simply shouldn't write. But I have been called in for interrogation, I've had my

> house searched, I've had notes and things seized, my typewriter confiscated.... So they certainly keep one aware of their existence.
>
> (Davidson, p. 28)

Tenaciously, he has gone on writing, keeping a wider world aware of "their existence"—and of his own, in determined opposition.

HISTORY AND SLAVERY

A Chain of Voices

In his next novel, *A Chain of Voices* (1982), Brink moves back in time to the early nineteenth century to tell the story of an actual slave uprising in the Cold Bokkeveld of the western Cape. He begins and ends the novel with legal documents that outline the bare facts of the episode. The cold, convoluted legal language of the opening's indictments and of the harsh judicial findings at the close contrasts sharply with the varied vibrant voices heard throughout the novel in the personal testimony of all those touched, however minimally, by these events. As with several of his earlier novels, Brink supplies the reader right away with the unvarnished facts of the action; in *A Chain of Voices*, for instance, we learn at the outset that eleven people have been charged for their part in a rebellion that resulted in the deaths of three white men. The indictments describe the immediate events prior to and including the uprising. Monologues by all the characters go back in time and recount, more or less chronologically, the interwoven lives of, and relationship between, Galant, the leader of the uprising, and Nicolaas van der Merwe, who is Galant's master and the man he kills.

Each one of the characters tells his or her story, without interruption, firsthand. This works particularly well, allowing each character to reveal what is important (although what is not said is often as important as what is).

The monologues vary in length from one line to several pages, and the more involved characters provide more than one link in the chain. Ma-Rose, an old Khoin woman, points out that it is the whole chain which tells the real story, not the individualized bits that make up the chain: "And perhaps someone will hear us calling out, all these voices in the great silence, all of us together, each one forever alone. We go on talking and talking, an endless chain of voices, all together yet all apart, all different, yet all the same; and the separate links might lie but the chain is the truth" (1983, p. 441). As Ma-Rose suggests—and Brink presumably believes—true reality emerges from the total consideration of perceived realities. There cannot be any one view: multiple first-person narratives (some mutually contradictory, some even self-contradictory) are therefore imperative. And while many of the statements are intrinsically riveting, their cumulative effect as a whole is the narrative's most powerful feature.

When Ontong and Old Plaatjie, who belong to the older generation of slaves, protest the use of violence by fellow slaves, Galant is adamant that force is the only tool the slaves have: "What if it's the only way to be free?" he exclaims. After the carnage, Galant is still not free and he knows it, but he still seeks to justify the violence: "Only through killing can I, perhaps, be heard. I have no other voice" (p. 508). The appalling situation in which Galant finds himself in 1825 has been (and is still) repeated daily in South Africa. Brink implicitly makes the same point that was realized in *An Instant in the Wind*—that, in his homeland, many agonizing lessons of history have yet to be learned despite their cyclical (and invariably tragic) recurrence.

Brink does not concentrate solely on the inevitability of retaliatory violence against whites on the part of blacks; one of his more important recurrent themes, here as elsewhere, is the violence done to whites by themselves through the system they promote. Brink shows the pain that the system of slavery causes Nicolaas by forcing him to become master to his childhood friend Galant. In Nicolaas' monologues we can see the confusion of the child who does not understand why he and his black friend must live different lives: "I needed Galant. He was the only one around who was prepared implicitly to accept me as an equal. . . . Galant was my mate. Of course we often fought, and competed, and quarrelled: but always as equals" (p. 85). When Galant is forced, like Nicolaas, to assume his place—the one as slave, the other master—both men lose. Dying, Nicolaas admits that the master-slave relationship has destroyed the only real friendship he ever had. A cruel and perverse man, Nicolaas has killed Galant's child, impregnated Galant's wife, and has further humiliated him in hundreds of ways. Yet the only person to whom he can express his unhappiness is this very slave—and it is particularly ironic that Nicolaas should complain to him that he himself is not free.

A Chain of Voices, in its emphasis on the endemic violence of the powers that be in South African society and the persistence of its virulent racism, shows its author's movement toward accepting the regrettable inevitability of violence to topple the apartheid state in the near (rather than the distant) future. Much as Nadine Gordimer, who was increasingly allying herself with ANC (African National Congress), sanctioned armed resistance in the 1980s and 1990s, we can see how Brink for the first time was beginning to believe that only violence could bring about any positive shift in the country's power structure. In the decade following 1982, which culminated in the publication of *An Act of Terror*, we can see that Brink became increasingly preoccupied with the practical realities and moral implications—particularly for whites (and Afrikaners especially) and for Colored people—of possible guerrilla conflict and armed insurrection.

A Chain of Voices gains its power from the simple beauty of its narrative expression and the honesty of its collective political consciousness. Its characters are individuals whose histories combine to form mutually supportive and collaborative links in the chain of history. Brink's prose work can itself be seen as a chain of voices and, indeed, his novels taken together can themselves be envisaged as further links in an ongoing chain. His renderings of various past and present situations show an abiding interest not only in how things are but also in how they came to be so. Brink has tried to see his world from several angles and through several modes of narrative expression. The opening words of Ma-Rose show how necessary the multiple viewpoint is, not only for *A Chain of Voices* but also for Brink's work taken as a whole. Ma-Rose points out: "To know is not enough. One must try to understand too. There will be a lot of talking in the Cape these days, one man's word against another's, master against slave. But what's the use? Liars all. Only a free man can tell the truth" (p. 23).

Brink knew, from history and from his researches into eighteenth- and nineteenth-century Cape colonial archives, that no one was free in South Africa's past; he was also acutely aware from his own experience that no one there was free in his own lifetime. Thus, no individual could tell the truth any better than in the past; yet by putting the pieces of the puzzle or the links together, one can create a chain that gestures toward the truth. That some of the individual links often have an intrinsic aesthetic interest and occasionally a lyrical intensity and literary power of more enduring value is an inestimable gift that we can but seldom hope to savor in a world necessarily dominated by immediate social commitments and pressing political demands.

LIVING IN THE INTERREGNUM

If the 1970s was a decade of escalating violence, with black children in the forefront of the struggle and among its many casualties, it also witnessed a new sense of purpose and resolve in the growth of a black consciousness movement, for which the celebrated activist Steve Biko became a martyr. Greater destruction and confusion, with less tangible evidence of positive gains, made the 1980s an even more dreadful and unstable period in the nation's history. By then, South Africa was, for all intents and purposes, in a state of revolution. Lurching from crisis to crisis, its government seldom if ever appeared to be in command of events. In the mid 1980s a "state of emergency" was proclaimed several times, during which all normal democratic processes were suspended. Engaged in armed struggles within and beyond its borders, isolated by boycotts and sanctions from the world outside, the government responded alternatively with rage and fear. Waves of protest were met, first, by excessive force and other repressive measures and, later, with conciliatory concessions and appeasement. Writers similarly underwent extremes of reaction, from hopelessness to exhilaration: some thought literature an irrelevance; others, a moral duty. Apocalyptic warnings, imagery from the Book of Revelation, and encoded allegories became common. In an essay, "Living in the Interregnum," Nadine Gordimer declared:

> Historical co-ordinates don't fit life any longer; new ones, where they exist, have couplings not to the rulers, but to the ruled. It is not for nothing that I chose as an epigraph for my novel *July's People* a quotation from Gramsci: "The old is dying, and the new cannot be born; in this interregnum there arises a great diversity of morbid symptoms."
>
> (p. 263)

In their introduction to *A Land Apart* (1986), a collection of contemporary South African writings for which Brink chose the Afrikaans selections, he and J. M. Coetzee declared, "Underlying almost everything written in Afrikaans today . . . is an intimation of violence and death." They go on to say, "In one form it emerges as a series of relentless explorations of war, conscription, border skirmishes, incursions into neighbouring territories, the invasion of privacy," but more generally, "it is expressed as an intimation of apocalypse, which implies not just the death of the individual or the end of his hopes, but the destruction of the entire known world or a way of life" (p. 13). The titles of Brink's novels written during this decade are illuminating: reflecting moods of somber introspection and self-doubt about the role of the writer in a totalitarian state and an increasing sense of national urgency, there appeared, in succession, *The Wall of the Plague* (1984), *States of Emergency* (1988), and *An Act of Terror* (1991); there is an admirable breadth of subject matter and technique in the three works, though none of them is a wholly satisfying entity in itself.

The Wall of the Plague

Where *A Chain of Voices* was tied by its subject matter to a particular historical event, limited in time and place, *The Wall of the Plague* is more ambitious in its historiographical scope: it ransacks European history and literature concerned with the various sporadic incursions of the bubonic plague, or Black Death, from the late fourteenth century onward, paying particular attention to its physical manifestations, its horrifying psychological and social repercussions, and continuing psychotic aftermath. As though to free himself, imaginatively as well as geographically, Brink sets his complex narrative (in what is arguably his most highly organized novel) in France, roaming through Provence, with scenes in Paris and flashbacks to the Cape. The psyche of the South African abroad is explored, with portraits of black, white, and Colored exiles in France and England, and, for the first time, he puts a young Colored woman in the forefront of the action.

For a long time, reading the book, we think that this woman, Andrea Malgas, is the narrator; later, after her disappearance (when she has left France and her lover, Paul Joubert, to return to a presumably committed life oppos-

ing apartheid in South Africa), we realize that it is Paul, a writer, who is constructing her story from her notes and journal entries and his own memories. Thus the narrative becomes a much more complicated organism than it at first appears and, at crucial moments, self-reflexive and self-interrogative. An Afrikaner in permanent exile, Paul has made a modestly successful life for himself by cutting himself off from South African life. Hating the regime there, he yet fears being sucked into its political maelstrom were he to live there. "To be a writer in a place like that," he complains, "means that one is dragged into so many other things that in the end you have no time left for the one thing you set out to do, writing. . . . I don't want to have a role forced on me, dammit. I'm not a social reformer or a revolutionary, I just want to be a writer" (1984, pp. 35–36). For a long time, traumatized by her own (and her family's) brutalization by the police there, Andrea agrees with, and shares, this neutral stance; even midway through the book she can say, "I prefer to stay out of history" (p. 225). The major impetus in the novel works to show that no one can (or should) keep out of history; no one can remain beyond the reaches of this world's plagues and infections.

In the fourteenth century the French built a wall in Provence to contain the Black Death but, like the Berlin Wall, it failed in its task. Apartheid is another such wall. Journeying in Provence to research sites for a film on the plague, Andrea learns important lessons about contemporary history—and insidious diseases such as imperialism, colonialism, racism, and gender prejudice, all of which reach farther into her life than she has grasped. In this quest, she is helped by her temporary "research student," Mandla Mqayisa, an activist on the run from the South African Special Branch. Later, in researching her spiritual odyssey and trying to understand her political "conversion," Paul truly if inadvertently finds himself and his vocation: his manuscript eventually becomes the "committed" novel, *The Wall of the Plague*, that he has for so long resisted writing. In the process, he recreates Andrea's story (with some memorable episodes from her youthful life in District Six, the once vibrant Colored quarter of Cape Town turned into a "whites only" area by government decree) and, in Mandla, something of the shadowy figure of the Xhosa warrior too. Mandla is not a member of the opposition ANC party but a trade union organizer whose work has constantly been sabotaged by the police. Through him we see the age-long struggles of the Xhosa people and view the present social and racial conflict as one further battle of the many fought in the eastern Cape, where Mandla grew up.

The Wall of the Plague is much concerned with history, continuing a line of inquiry begun in *A Chain of Voices*. In the better parts of the book, this preoccupation affords a strong backbone to a wide-roaming narrative; too often, however, it degenerates into long passages that read like lecture notes, with heavy-handed symbolism and far too extensive a network of analogies and illustrations. The three journeys that Andrea makes — two by recollection, reenacting them in the third — have a justifiable place as they stand in the narrative, but each is too protracted, and the repetition becomes monotonous as a consequence; the didactic content remains too strident throughout.

If these artistic faults originate in the author's overambitious strivings, some positive results can be discerned in these efforts too. In technique, Brink begins to experiment in ways that look forward to subsequent writings. In his self-interrogation, particularly as a writer with an understandable fear of losing his artistic integrity, Paul reflects a number of Brink's own anxieties. The final introspective section of the book becomes a significant (and sometimes moving) confession by a writer worried that his role as a novelist is an ineffectual, if not downright irrelevant, response to the plague in modern life. In the process he asks a question that Brink leaves open: "What is the weight of a book against the turmoil of history?" (p. 441). Paul also becomes newly aware of certain practical possibilities in writing a spontaneous, self-generative narrative that results in his suggesting (to himself) several alternative openings and more than one ending to his narrative. These theoretical issues reveal Brink's new aesthetic preoccupations, to which he allows greater access in his subsequent novel, *States of Emergency*.

States of Emergency

States of Emergency is not a wholly satisfying novel, yet it affords the reader an intriguing and stimulating encounter with a witty and playful mind whose existence may not have been evident in Brink's earlier books. Brink has an impish sense of fun and a buoyant fund of good humor, characteristics too long withheld from his novels, where irony has had to supply such wit as he found compatible with serious themes. In *States of Emergency*, the upheaval of a chaotic world is reflected in a postmodern narrative (or series of fragmentary narratives) that is, at different times, transitory, provisional, seemingly contradictory, and much of the time highly self-conscious. It is presented as a text being written, canceled out, rewritten, with marginal instructions countermanding textual changes. We are, in other words, in the postmodern worlds of John Fowles and Roland Barthes, where Brink, for much of the time, revels as though in his true element. Despite his intellectual fastidiousness, he allows himself *to play*: the magician-artist is allowed to show some of his tricks as well as to comment on some of the more theoretical concerns he has about the inextricable relationship between artifice and art, illusion and reality, theory and practice. Brink highlights the incompleteness and provisionality of his exercise by starting with what he says are "notes towards a love story" and, after saying, "No, I don't think I shall be writing my book after all" (p. 243), closing proceedings with the words "a story not written" (p. 244). However, for all this apparent inconclusiveness and repudiation of closure, we actually encounter several alternative endings tried out in the text; in the same way, several possible openings are proposed and discussed by the nameless narrator.

One of the narrators in the book — the major character, perhaps, though the narration never encourages the reader to single out individuals in such a manner — is a writer planning a new book by using various opportunities presented by the events in an eastern Cape engulfed in the flames of insurrection and counterterrorism. This writer gives evidence in witty and sometimes subversive footnotes that he may well be the author of *The Ambassador* and encodes in his draft (here called "the emergent text") other echoes of earlier writings by André Brink (pp. 18–19). The basic story that this speaker is intent upon telling is no more (but also no less) than a simple love story, inspired by a manuscript received from Jane Ferguson, a stranger who, like many would-be authors, thinks an established writer has all the time in the world to help her publish a passionate but tragic tale that she has written. The writer is touched by her story. In an uncertain world wobbling on the edge of all-out civil war, where politics seems to intrude into every sphere of life, Jane Ferguson's evidently autobiographical manuscript seems to offer a refuge from politics.

Exploring further, in order to flesh out a promising but rather brief novella, the writer discovers that the love affair was indeed based on actual experience but that the writer's real-life lover — his identity was unknown to her when they first met — had been a disguised revolutionary leader on the state's "most wanted" list. It is as impossible to write a really uncomplicated love story as it is to live one, it seems, and in an increasingly dangerous world, Brink's other quoted epigraph from the South African playwright Athol Fugard ("The only safe place in the world is inside a story") seems as dubious as everything else in life and fiction alike. Juxtaposing this tender relationship with a more

squalid adulterous affair closer to the fictional writer's own experience may be a predictable ploy, but the contrast does bring out the salient features of both.

States of Emergency transmits a charge of energy and a lightness of touch that was new to Brink's writing. It is as though, in response to successive sociopolitical crises in the country, the novelist had for almost three decades voluntarily confined his modes of expression to varieties of realism and his thematic emphases to documentary-like political, racial, and sexual problems. Now, temporarily released from formal restraints, he exults in unfamiliar liberties. There are some subtle language games as well as a brilliant use of fire imagery and analogies to situations in Richard Wagner's *Ring* cycle. Unfortunately, just when the action becomes most heated — literally and figuratively — the writing fails to rise to the occasion: the student protest scenes at the university are particularly implausible. Instead, the diction becomes vague, abstract, and banal, particularly in love scenes toward the end of the narrative. *States of Emergency* may be only a partially successful construct, but it looks forward to subsequent metafictional writings, such as *On the Contrary*, where a more homogenous fable grows out of disparate texts.

An Act of Terror

What *States of Emergency* does not appear to anticipate is its immediate successor, *An Act of Terror* (1991), the longest and most easily accessible of Brink's novels. The latter possesses many of the most obvious attributes of a popular best-seller: it has the plot of a spy thriller and sufficient action and violence to sustain the interest of a popular audience. The story opens at a cracking pace with the attempted assassination of the South African president and turns into a police hunt for the assailants, who, when identified, are engaged in an extended journey across the length and breadth of the country to stay ahead of the security services. The progress of investigation and pursuit is very well paced to culminate eventually in an exciting climax on the border. The psychological closeness of law enforcers and lawbreakers is pursued in a manner worthy of Dostoyevsky and Conrad: here, Kat Bester, the security chief, and Thomas Landman, the anti-apartheid "terrorist," share a common interest in the Afrikaner past. Their relationship, as it develops (at least for Bester, whose twisted mind is delineated with chilling precision), is an absorbing one. Other subplots dovetail skillfully into the major action.

For all this expertise, however, *An Act of Terror* is a flawed work of art. As one might expect with a novel of well over six hundred pages (with an appendix of over two hundred), there are tedious patches and some unwieldiness in handling the background lives of the various members of the multiracial organization, orchestrated by Brink to show how and why these individuals became engaged in terrorism. In stark contrast to the ineffectualness of this often awkward and stilted commentary, too obviously employed for its polemical content, is the practical utility of Landman's profession. Here Brink shows rather than argues. We see Landman working as a photographer in a country where racism and social inequalities are visually apparent to any observant eye everywhere: most of the whites in the book, by contrast, are blind to the world around them.

The lengthy supplement to the novel is in many ways a remarkable document whose narrative power and characterization make it a finer work of art than the novel to which it is appended. It is presented as Thomas Landman's reconstruction of his family's history, about which Brink says, in an introductory note to the novel:

> This supplement should be regarded as a floating presence in the text [of the novel, in which there are concrete references to it], to be read where and when the reader chooses — whether at the beginning, as a background and preparation; or at the end, as reflection; or at any suitable pause in the narrative; or even piecemeal, as certain figures, or places, or events from that history surface in the story.

Landman's family chronicle, extending over thirteen generations from the early seventeenth century to the present, is not only a revisionist view of Afrikanerdom, but also a deeply personal statement. Like his schoolteacher father, Thomas has been collecting data for much of his adult life. His father's history had been highly selective, omitting details of those family members who had been outright rebels or married non-Afrikaners — and there is, from the earliest recorded generation, evidence of slave blood, mixed with Khoin, black, and Jewish, as well as Islamic influences. The son's chronicle is written while he is recuperating from severe wounds received in a border gunfight in which he avoided capture and Bester was killed.

Believing that "one is not simply the result of one's history," but also "a reaction to it, a rebellion against it" (p. 826), Thomas celebrates the persistent existence among the Landmans of those whom his father would have called, in shame, rebels and traitors to their tribe. He also salutes a number of weird, exotic, and eccentric ancestors — such as Fransoois, a towering patriarchal figure who built a huge ship something like Noah's ark in the interior of a desert wilderness — in portraits that often remain vividly present long after one reads them. Trying to fly past what James Joyce has called the nets of nationality, race, and religion, Thomas shows in his family's representative history an Afrikanerdom less united, less conformist, and far more individualistic than nationalist politicians have dared to admit over the past century. It is a vision that Brink has promoted for many years in his effort to redefine the European myth of "Adamastor," in which the inextricably mixed racial component of southern

African history shall be honored. It is his attempt to undo and revise the white man's history in which the landscape (as in his father's chronicle) has "no sign of a black figure anywhere in it. As if they didn't exist, had never existed." To which Thomas adds, in a firm voice that we know to have Brink's imprint all over it: "While I know that the whole direction and texture of his life, as of all our lives, the deepest sense of it, was *determined* by those invisible black multitudes. Their presence has shaped us and defined us. He didn't know. I do. And that has made all the difference" (p. 825).

POSTAPARTHEID WRITINGS

The First Life of Adamastor

Two works of fiction have been published by Brink since the government's repudiation of its apartheid policy: *The First Life of Adamastor* and *On the Contrary*, both appearing in 1993, though the former (more properly a novella) had been projected and partly written several years previously. In these books, Brink can be seen to have taken a decisive new direction in his work. Both texts, like the earlier *States of Emergency* (in which the narrator speaks of being engaged in writing a manuscript about the mythical lives of Adamastor), can legitimately be associated with several of the theories and narrative possibilities embodied in that movement of ideas loosely known as postmodernism. The structure, unpredictable narrative development, and the sometimes puzzling self-reflexive nature of both *The First Life of Adamastor* and *On the Contrary* invoke, or suggest, contemporary metafictional concepts. Though not all of these devices are wholly new or even unconventional in themselves — several could be effortlessly accommodated within the mainstream eighteenth-century English novel tradition — the total linguistic mosaic in both

texts is certainly indebted to postmodernism. Both works are clearly intended for a sophisticated adult readership though readers who are neither can nevertheless enjoy the assorted adventures and fabulous exploits in each of them. *The First Life of Adamastor* makes special use of the particular narrative suppositions and preconceptions that belong to the realm of fairy tales, mythological legends, oral storytelling, and children's literature. We are presented, in other words, with a number of alternative readings and directly informed that there are indeed limitless narrative possibilities.

In Brink's postapartheid fiction, the appropriate literary expectations raised are, roughly: "What if?" "Just suppose?" and, occasionally, "On the other hand" — phrases that permeate storytelling in all cultures from time immemorial. The introduction to *The First Life of Adamastor* begins, "Once upon a time there was and there wasn't," which, for Brink's next work, *On the Contrary*, one might appropriately adjust to something like "Once upon a time there was and, contrariwise, there was also (perhaps)." That *perhaps* exists primarily in the reader's mind; textually, we are presented with parallel and often conflicting accounts of events from which we have to surmise a probable sequence of possible happenings. That is, if anything happened at all. Often, there are two (and sometimes more) enactments, concretely realized and often in tandem, in a proliferating narrative which combines, coerces, and contradicts its narrator's stories and the book's many sources as well as its multiple modes of expression, if anything happened. But, then, it did happen; all the contrary versions happened, concretely, in Brink's text(s) if nowhere else. These concisely realized events are thus actual, and vibrantly real, even though they are surrounded by qualifying, modifying, doubt-provoking declarations. (*The First Life of Adamastor* concludes with these final words by the narrator: "And then I died, the first of my many deaths. As far as I can remember.")

Yet the narrator's cruel, racially motivated murder is vividly evoked by images that, for all the generality of mythic projection, implicitly deny any faultiness of memory or the imagination:

> Through the blood I saw the sun come up, a great eye slaughtered on the horizon. In the farthest distance—but perhaps it was my imagination—the great sea-birds [the European sailing ships] were sailing off proudly and beautifully to wherever they had come from. There was a terrible urge in me to shout: "Khois!" But my voice was like a fistful of old feathers thrust into my throat.
>
> (p. 132)

At one point in his introduction to *The First Life of Adamastor*, Brink quotes a passage from Luis Vaz de Camoens' *The Lusiads*, a sixteenth-century Portuguese saga that describes the enforced metamorphosis of the Titan rebel Adamastor into the mountainous spine of the Cape Peninsular. The latter, portrayed as an ugly and monstrous outcrop of land with inhabitants appropriate to its cursed origins, was known to European mariners as (dependent on whether it was viewed meteorologically or as a gateway to the riches of the Orient) the Cape of Storms and the Cape of Good Hope. Not surprisingly, Camoens' quotation is cast in conventional heroic terms, about which Brink comments: "Rather exaggerated; but that is what happens to the truth when writers get their hands on it" (p. 5).

The author's basic hypothesis is explained in his introduction:

> Suppose there *were* an Adamastor, a model for the giant of Camoens' fanciful history; and suppose that original creature, spirit, or whatever he may have been, had survived through the centuries in a series of disparate successive avatars in order to continue watching over the Cape of Storms: how would *he* look back, from the perspective of the late twentieth-century, on that original experience?
>
> (p. 7)

This is the "leap," as he calls it, that he proposes to take in the novella, choosing as avatar-narrator the chief from a nomadic tribe of Hottentots, the Khoi or "first people" encountered at the Cape by the earliest European sailors. In the course of the action, T'kama becomes the spirit of his race and immortal in that something of his people's adaptable and basically tolerant character, customs, and beliefs still lingers there today, four hundred years later, in the other aboriginal peoples with whom they interacted. The Hottentots, to all intents and purposes exterminated over the centuries, are belatedly but movingly memorialized in *The First Life of Adamastor*; ironically, this act of restitution and retribution is performed in a ribald saga that vividly creates a revisionary heroic trek, in which the travelers are Hottentots in retreat from European incursions. A strange tale for an Afrikaner to tell! Like *An Instant in the Wind*, the myth eventually becomes a celebration of black-white sexuality, edged with a dark acknowledgment of the destructiveness of primal racial fears and taboos.

The First Life of Adamastor embodies a spirit of healing and of reconciliation through suffering as well as a somber warning for a land on the brink of a latter-day but yet newfound meeting of the races, a spirit replete with possible new directions but threatened to be pulled back by past misunderstandings (here realized vividly). The novella is notable for its simple clarity, its imaginative delight in nature and in language, and an inventive ribaldry new to Brink's erotic repertoire. For Brink here, as for Chinua Achebe in *Things Fall Apart* and *Arrow of God*, it is morning yet on creation day and the linguistic clay is still wet and malleable. The advent of the first Europeans is seen in mythic terms, as eggs from enormous seabirds (symbolizing rowing boats launched from sailing ships) hatch into marauding groups of sailors who, on shore, misinterpret the intentions and actions of the natives. Perhaps the most delightful writing is to be found in the primal and unsentimental Garden of Eden love story, recasting the wilderness scenario involving a white woman and a black man of *An Instant in the Wind* in an even more stylized simplicity.

On the Contrary

On the Contrary (1993) is indebted to the exploits of an actual eighteenth-century Cape adventurer and soldier of fortune from France bearing the same name as Brink's protagonist, Estienne Barbier, recorded in extant court documents of his trials as well as in journals and books by a number of his contemporaries. Perhaps the book's outstanding feature, however, is the ingenuity of Brink in synthesizing disparate experiences in a distinctive and resourceful manner. Were *On the Contrary* simply a freewheeling fictional adaptation of actual eighteenth-century Cape exploration, it would still be a comic delight, an enjoyable romp like Voltaire's *Candide* or, in music, Richard Strauss's modernist tone poem celebrating Till Eulenspiegel's merry pranks. The sense of fun and impudent audacity that radiates from a rebellious rogue at odds with a hidebound conformist society is common to both Strauss and Brink, tinged as it is in each case by a sad note because both their protagonists are doomed to undergo a felon's death. Brink goes further, however, in giving not just a new imaginative cast of thought to rather predictable eighteenth-century descriptions of travel in the wilderness, inventing parallel and contradictory versions of the selfsame scenes, juxtaposed with Barbier's real-life adventures. Brink also introduces fantasy figures from European history and literature, including characters and images from Cervantes' *Don Quixote* and from the life of Joan of Arc — characters which we can, if we like, imagine peopling Estienne Barbier's extravagant and multifaceted imagination.

The new creation is a jaunty, lighthearted, and yet violent mosaic of fresh and familiar writings that blossoms into a metafictional allegory of colonial sin and exploitation, racist barbarity and renunciation. It achieves a new level of literary expression with a spiritual theme that has run through many of Brink's writings, sometimes explicitly but usually subliminally, in which one or more figures take on responsibility for the racial prejudices and cruelties of themselves and, more often, of their own people. Many of these figures are victims and scapegoat figures as well as supposed or actual activists. All must suffer and, ultimately, make conscious decisions to seek self-knowledge in bodily torment; they include Mandla and Thomas Landman as well as Joseph Malan, Adam Mantoor, Ben du Toit, and Galant.

More than any of these purgative characters, Barbier consciously humbles himself before the realities of large-scale and institutionalized cruelty, exploitation, and genocide in his world; and he repudiates his part in inhumane actions by his kind, from the highest authorities in Cape Town to the least significant of the inland colonists, the largely Afrikaner farmers and hunters of the western Cape. In the course of *On the Contrary*, Barbier participates in three exploratory expeditions — each pushing farther inland, into the Boland and what is now Namibia, and deeper each time into his own psyche and conscience. When he first arrives from Europe, Barbier tends to identify with and esteem the Cape officials who hate the natives and despise those European settlers who are already beginning to become free-minded, dissident Afrikaners. After living among these farmers and hunters, Barbier comes to appreciate their resolute self-reliance, and he naturally assumes many of their values, especially their contempt for the corrupt administrators, who prefer to live in their own class-conscious, European-fixated ghettos of the mind. His account of having joined a bloodthirsty expedition of these settlers into the interior — where they slaughter everything that moves, be it beast, bird, or indigenous inhabitant — becomes an ever more horrifying indictment of wanton cruelty and inhumanity, all the more powerful for the account's not being presented in either apologetic or censorious terms. That Barbier must have been affected traumatically by the experience is suggested by his third expedition—which most probably is an imaginary journey, incited by nightmares and guilt—in which he goes alone among the Khoikhoin and San of Namibia to seek forgiveness and assuage his conscience.

CONCLUSION

Barbier's experience of protracted torture in prison, like that of Malan in *Looking on Darkness*, eventually takes on some semblance of saintly purgatory, which one is inclined to think represents Brink's own feelings of secular anguish in confronting his homeland. An increased recognition of spiritual and ethical responsibilities in a predominantly nonreligious context, realized in the torments and burdens of the body (always physically apparent in Brink's work) and in a new sense of self-abnegation (both in rejecting the needs of self and possession of goods), is a characteristic of these writings—and, especially, the postapartheid fiction—in ways that similarly distinguish the later writings of fellow South African novelist J. M. Coetzee, particularly in *Waiting for the Barbarians* (1980) and *The Life & Times of Michael K* (1983). While neither artist experienced a religious conversion and their outlook has remained predominantly secular and worldly, it is tempting to see their contemporary literary epiphanies as instinctive personal responses to a time of extraordinary spiritual crisis. The 1980s and early 1990s witnessed the darkest period in South Africa's history, followed by a speedy and hardly credible rebirth. The apparently new order, socially and politically, was pursued in a mood of hope and fear which bordered, at times, on desperation. These were days that many artists and politicians had seen in apocalyptic terms, even before the precipitous collapse of the once seemingly impregnable apartheid system; afterward, ominous apocalypse gave way to a sense of

deliverance charged with the miraculous, though not without a lingering dark edge of anxiety. Brink's two postapartheid fables skillfully reflect each one of these often contrary features in the new South Africa.

Fluent in at least six European languages, Brink has translated novels and plays into Afrikaans to diversify that new and vibrant language's literary resources; in addition, he has also translated some of the more exciting new writings in Afrikaans into English. A prolific writer for almost four decades, Brink shows no signs of slowing down or repeating himself. Having exhibited considerable versatility in realistic modes of expression and a mature command of narrative techniques, he has shown in his most recent work promise of further artistic development in diverse metafictional forms. The conscience of his race and tribe throughout a turbulent career, he seems poised to take an honored place in a country finally acknowledging its full African heritage, a heritage that Brink has done as much as anyone living to try to understand, to honor, and to celebrate.

Brink has received many honors and awards. He has three times been awarded South Africa's leading literary prize, the Central News Agency (CNA) Award: for Afrikaans writing in 1965, for *Rumours of Rain* in 1978, and for *A Chain of Voices* in 1982. Twice he has been a finalist for the prestigious Booker Prize in Great Britain: in 1976 for *An Instant in the Wind* and in 1978 for *Rumours of Rain*. In 1980 he received both the Martin Luther King Memorial Prize in Great Britain and the Prix Médicis Étranger in France for *A Dry White Season*. In France he was made a Chevalier de la Légion d'Honneur in 1982, named an Officier de l'Ordre des Arts et des Lettres in 1987, and was promoted to Commandeur of that order in 1992. He received an honorary doctorate at Witwatersrand University in Johannesburg in 1985 and the Monismanien Award for Human Rights in Sweden in 1993. The novelist has been married four times; he has three sons and one daughter.

Selected Bibliography

SELECTED WORKS PUBLISHED IN AFRIKAANS

Die meul teen die hang. Cape Town, South Africa: Tafelberg, 1958.

Die gebondenes. Johannesburg, South Africa: Afrikaanse Pers Beperk, 1959.

Die band om ons harte. Johannesburg: Afrikaanse Pers Beperk, 1959.

Die eindelose weë. Cape Town: Tafelberg, 1960.

Caesar. Johannesburg: Nasionale Bockhandel, 1961.

Lobola vir die lewe. Cape Town: Human & Rousseau, 1962.

Die ambassadeur. Cape Town: Human & Rousseau, 1963.

Orgie. Cape Town: John Malherbe, 1965.

Elders mooiweer en warm. Cape Town: John Malherbe, 1965.

Bagasie. Cape Town: Tafelberg, 1965.

Miskien nooit. Capt Town: Human & Rousseau, 1967.

Die verhoor. Cape Town: Human & Rousseau, 1970.

Die rebelle. Cape Town: Human & Rousseau, 1970.

Kennis van die aand. Cape Town: Buren, 1973.

Pavane. Cape Town: Human & Rousseau, 1974.

'n Oomblik in die wind. Johannesburg: Taurus, 1975.

Die hamer van die hekse. Cape Town: Tafelberg, 1976.

Gerugte van reën. Cape Town: Human & Rousseau, 1978.

'n Droë wit seisoen. Johannesburg: Taurus, 1979.

Houd-den-bek. Johannesburg: Taurus, 1982.

Die muur van die pes. Cape Town: Human & Rousseau, 1984.

Literatuur in die strydperk. Cape Town: Human & Rousseau, 1985.

Waarom literatuur? Cape Town: Human & Rousseau, 1985.

Die eerste lewe van Adamastor. Cape Town: Saayman & Weber, 1988.

Die kreef raak gewoond daaraan. Cape Town: Human & Rousseau, 1991.

Inteendeel. Cape Town: Human & Rousseau, 1993.

SELECTED WORKS PUBLISHED IN ENGLISH

The Ambassador. Johannesburg, South Africa: Central News Agency, 1964. Repr. as *File on a Diplomat.* London: Longmans, Green, 1965. Rev. trans. London: Faber and Faber, 1985.

Looking on Darkness. London: W. H. Allen, 1974; New York: Morrow, 1975.

An Instant in the Wind. London: W. H. Allen, 1976; New York: Morrow, 1977; New York: Penguin, 1985.

Rumours of Rain. London: W. H. Allen, 1978; New York: Morrow, 1978.

A Dry White Season. London: W. H. Allen, 1979; New York: Morrow, 1980.

A Chain of Voices. London: Faber and Faber, 1982; New York: Morrow, 1982.

Mapmakers: Writing in a State of Siege. London: Faber and Faber 1983. Publ. as *Writing in a State of Siege: Essays on Politics and Literature.* New York: Summit, 1983.

The Wall of the Plague. London: Faber and Faber, 1984; New York: Summit, 1984.

A Land Apart: A Contemporary South African Reader. Ed. by Brink and J. M. Coetzee. London: Faber and Faber, 1986; New York: Viking, 1986.

States of Emergency. London: Faber and Faber, 1988; New York: Summit, 1988.

An Act of Terror. London: Secker and Warburg, 1991; New York: Summit, 1991.

An Act of Violence: Thoughts on the Functioning of Literature. Cape Town, South Africa: University of Cape Town, 1991.

The Essence of the Grape: A South African Brandy Book. Cape Town, South Africa: Saaymand and Weber, 1992.

The First Life of Adamastor. London: Secker and Warburg, 1993. Publ. as *Cape of Storms: The First Life of Adamastor.* New York: Simon and Schuster, 1993.

On the Contrary: Being the Life of a Famous Rebel, Soldier, Traveller, Explorer, Reader, Builder, Scribe, Latinist, Lover, and Liar. London: Secker and Warburg, 1993; Boston: Little, Brown, 1994.

INTERVIEWS

Davidson, Jim. "An Interview with André Brink." In *Overland* 94–95 (1984).

"South African Writers Talking." In *English in Africa* 6 (1979).

CRITICAL STUDIES

Ayling, Ronald. "Literature of the Eastern Cape from Schreiner to Fugard." In *ARIEL* 16 (1985).

Coetzee, J. M. "André Brink and the Censor." In *Research in African Literatures* 21 (1990).

Cope, Jack. "A Driving Ferment." In his *The Adversary Within: Dissident Writers in Afrikaans.* Cape Town, South Africa: D. Philip, 1982; and Atlantic Highlands, N.J., 1982.

Gordimer, Nadine. "Living in the Interregnum." In her *The Essential Gesture: Writing, Politics, and Places.* London: Jonathan Cape, 1988; New York: Knopf, 1988.

Hassall, Anthony J. "The Making of a Colonial Myth: The Mrs. Fraser Story in Patrick White's *A Fringe of Leaves* and André Brink's *An Instant in the Wind.*" In *ARIEL* 18 (1987).

———. "André Brink." In R. L. Ross, ed., *International Literature in English: Essays on Major Writers.* New York: Garland, 1991.

Hope, Christopher. "The Political Novelist in South Africa." In *English in Africa* 12 (1985).

Jacobs, J. U. "The Colonial Mind in a State of Fear: The Psychosis of Terror in the Contemporary South African Novel." In *North Dakota Quarterly* 57 (summer 1989).

MacDermott, Doireann. "A Narrow Beam of Light: A Reading of Two Novels by André Brink." In *World Literature Written in English* 28 (1988).

Peck, Richard. "Condemned to Choose, but What? Existentialism in Selected Works by Fugard, Brink, and Gordimer." In *Research in African Literature* 23 (1992).

Rich, Paul. "Tradition and Revolt in South African Fiction: The Novels of André Brink, Nadine Gordimer and J. M. Coetzee." In *Journal of South African Studies* 9 (1982).

Viola, André. "André Brink and the Writer 'in a State of Siege.'" *Commonwealth* 7 (1985).

Ward, David. "André Brink." In his *Chronicles of Darkness.* London and New York: Routledge, 1989.

Dennis Brutus
1924–

BERNTH LINDFORS

DENNIS BRUTUS was born in Salisbury, Southern Rhodesia (now Harare, Zimbabwe), of South African parents on 28 November 1924. Both his father, Francis Henry Brutus, and his mother, Winifred Bloemetjie Brutus, were teachers. Educated in South Africa at Fort Hare University College in Alice and the University of the Witwatersrand in Johannesburg, he taught English for fourteen years in South African high schools. A Colored person, Brutus participated in many anti-apartheid campaigns, particularly those concerned with sports. (*Colored*, spelled *Coloured* in South Africa, designates a person of mixed-race origin in that country.) The South African government eventually banned him from attending political and social meetings and made it illegal for any of his writings to be published in South Africa. In 1963 he was arrested for attending a sports meeting. When released on bail, he fled to Swaziland and from there tried to make his way to Germany to meet with the world Olympic executive committee, but the Portuguese secret police at the Mozambique border handed him back to the South African security police. Realizing that no one would know of his capture, he made a desperate attempt to escape, only to be shot by the police in the back on a Johannesburg street. On recovery he was sentenced to eighteen

months of hard labor on Robben Island off the coast of Cape Town. When he finished his term in prison, he was permitted to leave South Africa with his wife and children on an exit permit, a document that made it illegal for him to return.

Brutus lived in London from 1966 to 1970, then took a position as a visiting professor at the University of Denver for a year, after which he moved to Northwestern University in Evanston, Illinois, and later to the University of Pittsburgh. He remained active in a number of anti-apartheid organizations, particularly the South African Non-Racial Olympic Committee, which led the movement to have South Africa excluded from the Olympic Games because of its discriminatory sports policies. He was also campaign director of the International Defense and Aid Fund. Brutus is as famous for his political activities as he is for his poetry.

There have been five distinct phases in his development as a poet, each marked by formal and thematic shifts that not only reflect his changing preoccupations and professional concerns but also document profound transformations in his conception of the nature and function of poetry. Each new phase has grown out of a personal experience that made him question his previous attitudes toward verbal art and seek a more satisfying outlet for his energies of articulation. The five phases may be termed complexity, simplicity, balance economy, and variety.

COMPLEXITY

Brutus' first book of poems, *Sirens Knuckles Boots* (1963), contains a variety of lyric forms invested with many standard poetic conventions. There are neatly demarcated stanzas, end rhymes, assonance, alliteration, literary allusions, carefully balanced contrasts, paradoxes, and skillful reiterations and refrains that enlarge rather than merely repeat an idea. These poems include well-reasoned arguments couched in logically connected images and utterances so rich in symbolic suggestiveness that they speak at several levels of significance simultaneously. There are no loose ends in this poetry, no wasted words, no compromises with the reader's dull-wittedness. This is highbrow poetry—tight, mannered, formal, and sometimes formidably difficult. Schooled in Shakespeare, John Donne, Robert Browning, Gerard Manley Hopkins, T. S. Eliot, and other classic English poets of exceptional intellect, Brutus attempted to write poems that would challenge the mind, poems sufficiently subtle and intricate to interest any well-educated lover of poetry. During this period he wrote nearly all of his most complex verse.

Brutus' greatest imaginative achievement in *Sirens Knuckles Boots* is the creation of an ambiguous idiom that allows him to make a political and an erotic statement in the same breath. Some of his poems can be read superficially as straightforward love lyrics, but lurking just beneath the surface is a political undercurrent that turns passion into militant protest. The loved one is not only a particular woman, but also the poet-speaker's homeland. The torments he experiences when contemplating her spectacular beauty, tenderness, and ability to endure great suffering spur him on

to bolder efforts in her behalf, efforts by which he can express the intensity of his love for her. A good example of this kind of double-breasted love lyric is "Erosion: Transkei," where the word "eros," embedded in "erosion," is a deliberate pun. The version reprinted here is from *A Simple Lust* (1973), which is slightly different from the version in *Sirens Knuckles Boots:*

Under green drapes the scars scream,
red wounds wail soundlessly,
beg for assuaging, satiation;
warm life dribbles seawards with the streams.

Dear my land, open for my possessing,
ravaged and dumbly submissive to our will,
in curves and uplands my sensual delight
mounts, and mixed with fury is amassing

torrents tumescent with love and pain.
Deep-dark and rich, with deceptive calmness
time and landscape flow to new horizons—
in anguished impatience await the quickening
rains.

In addition to the double entendre that informs this entire poem, it is worth noting the formal structure the poetic statement takes. Three four-line stanzas, slant rhyming ABCA (scream/streams; possessing/amassing; pain/rains), are peppered with alliteration (for example, "scars scream," "wounds wail") and assonance ("assuaging, satiation," and the deft intermingling of long "a" and short "i" sounds in the last rhythmic line: "in anguished impatience await the quickening rains"). The poem opens with a description of tormented deprivation as old and new injuries ("scars," "red wounds") cry out for comfort and fulfillment. The cries of the ravaged loved one are soundless, lending a "deceptive calmness" to her plea. The poet-speaker responds with his own plea, asking her to submit to his painful and furiously mounting love. Their union promises to bring relief by producing new life, but immediate consummation of their desires is not achieved. The poem ends as it began, with the loved one, the land, waiting in agony and impatience for satisfying change. As in many other poems in *Sirens Knuckles Boots*, the poetic argument is rounded off by a reassertion of the initial idea.

The political thrust of this poem is made more explicit by the title, which identifies the despoiled landscape as the Transkei, the area in the eastern Cape Province of the Republic of South Africa that was designated as the first Bantustan, or homeland for a Bantu people. The erosion of the Transkei is not only a geological reality, but also clear evidence of social injustice and political oppression. But such erosion, such pain, such impatience for revolutionary change is not confined to one area of South Africa. The Transkei also functions as a metaphor for all Bantustans and ghettos created by apartheid and other institutionalized forms of racial discrimination. The poem thus has universal as well as local reverberations.

"Erosion: Transkei" is a fairly uncomplicated multileveled lyric when compared with such poems as "A troubadour, I tráverse all my land" and "So, for the moment, sweet, is peace," upon which Brutus has commented extensively. The troubadour poem, for instance, has lines in which he attempts to make a single image yield different meanings simultaneously. "Weathered strand," for instance, connotes not only a frayed thread but also a beach where the waves break, that beach being on Robben Island, where Brutus, a "cast-off" of his land, anticipated being imprisoned. The word "sweet" in "So, for the moment, sweet, is peace" also has numerous special connotations for him. Indeed, it would be difficult for even the most astute student of literary ambiguity to decipher the full range of significance that such words and images are meant to carry without consulting the gloss that Brutus has provided in discussions of these poems. Some of the symbolism is private, cryptic, and therefore impenetrable to anyone but the poet himself.

SIMPLICITY

While Brutus was in prison in 1964 and 1965, he decided to stop writing super-cerebral poetry. The five months he spent in solitary confinement caused him to reexamine his verse and his attitudes toward creative self-expression. The more he looked at his poetry during this period of forced isolation, the more "horrified" he became, until finally he decided that if he were ever to write again, he would write very differently. He has stated in an interview:

The first thing I decided about my future poetry was that there must be no ornament, absolutely none. And the second thing I decided was you oughtn't to write for poets; you oughtn't even to write for people who read poetry, not even students. You ought to write for the ordinary person: for the man who drives a bus, or the man who carries the baggage at the airport, and the woman who cleans the ashtrays in the restaurant. If you can write poetry which makes sense to those people, then there is some justification for writing poetry. Otherwise you have no business writing.

And therefore, there should be no ornament because ornament gets in the way. It becomes too fancy-schmancy; it becomes overelaborate. It is, in a way, a kind of pride, a self-display, a glorying in the intellect for its own sake, which is contemptible. . . .

So I said, "You will have to set the thing down. You will 'tell it like it is,' but you will let the word do its work in the mind of the reader. And you will write poetry that a man who drives a bus along the street can quote, if he feels like quoting." Very ambitious indeed.

But this is based on the idea that all people are poets. Some are just ashamed to let it be known, and some are shy to try, and some write but don't have the guts to show it to others. But we all are poets because we all have the same kind of response to beauty. We may define beauty differently, but we all do respond to it.

So this was the assumption: don't dress it up; you will just hand it over, and it will do its own work.

(Lindfors et al., 1972, p. 29)

The first poems he wrote after making this resolution are collected in *Letters to Martha, and Other Poems from a South African Prison* (1968). The change in idiom is immediately apparent. The diction is far simpler; rigid poetic devices, such as end rhyme, metrical regularity, and symmetrical stanza structure, have been all but abandoned; conceits, tortuously logical paradoxes, and tantalizingly ambiguous image clusters can no longer be found; ornament of virtually every kind has vanished almost entirely. The result is a flat, conversational mode of poetry that surprised and in some cases alarmed readers who had admired the technical complexity of the poems in his first volume and had expected more of the same. Instead of saying three things at once, Brutus says one thing at a time and says it very directly. In this second volume he has created a poetry of plain statement, a poetry that bus drivers, porters, and cleaning women can understand and presumably appreciate.

This new idiom is evident in the tenth "letter" to his sister-in-law Martha, in which he describes life in prison:

> It is not all terror
> and deprivation,
> you know;
>
> one comes to welcome the closer contact
> and understanding one achieves
> with one's fellow-men,
> fellows, compeers;
>
> and the discipline does much to force
> a shape and pattern on one's daily life
> as well as on the days
>
> and honest toil
> offers some redeeming hours
> for the wasted years;

> so there are times
> when the mind is bright and restful
> though alive:
> rather like the full calm morning sea

(p. 11)

Until the last line, there is not even an image in this poem. Moreover, "the full calm morning sea" enters the poem as a simile, not as a metaphor or symbol with wider connotations. Like the other ideas in the poem, it is there for a specific purpose and has only one meaning. This is Brutus at his simplest.

Not every poem in *Letters to Martha* is this stark. There are some, such as "Longing" and "Abolish laughter first, I say," that actually derive from the earlier *Sirens* period and manifest many of the complexities characteristic of Brutus' early work. Also, several poems are not quite as simple as they seem—"Cold," the poem about Colesberg, for example, the subtleties of which Brutus has explicated at some length. Moreover, one finds certain of the older tendencies—the well-rounded statement, the learned allusion or quotation, the harmonious imagery—resurfacing in several poems and giving an orderly appearance to even the freest-flowing lines. In other words, there is evidence of continuity as well as change as Brutus shifts from complex to simple registers of poetic expression. The transformation is sudden and obvious but not absolute.

BALANCE

In July 1966, a year after being released from prison, Brutus left South Africa on an exit permit that did not allow him to reenter his homeland. His life in exile began with four years of anti-apartheid work in London and continued after September 1970 in the United States, where he taught as a professor of English at the University of Denver, Northwestern University, and the University of Pittsburgh, with occasional visiting professorships at the University of Texas at Austin, Swarthmore College, and the University of Colorado at Boulder. During these years his poetry underwent three modifications: first a minor modulation to a position of balance, then a major shift to a phase of extreme economy, and finally a return to different forms of simple verse that enabled him to achieve variety. Although these successive changes are observable in much of what he wrote after going into exile, there are occasionally new poems that could be categorized as complex or simple. In other words, Brutus retained the capacity to express himself in his earlier poetic modes even when consciously attempting to define a new style. Whereas certain of the poems he composed in exile can be viewed as throwbacks to or lapses into a former habit of articulation, the fresh impulses and newer tendencies are dominant in most of what he has written since July 1966.

The two major thematic preoccupations in Brutus' early exile poetry are, first, his awareness of the personal freedom and mobility he has gained while others remain confined and suffering in South Africa and, second, his recognition of what he has lost in leaving the homeland he dearly loves and traveling restlessly about the world in quest of compelling but sometimes elusive goals. Much of this poetry could be characterized as both nostalgic and plaintive—the unhappy recollections and reflections of a homesick poet. These tendencies can be found in *Poems from Algiers* (1970), which was written while Brutus was attending the first Pan-African Cultural Festival in the Algerian capital in 1969; in *Thoughts Abroad* (1970), which was written piecemeal in various cities throughout the world and published under the pseudonym John Bruin so it could be sold and circulated in South Africa; and in the third part of *A Simple Lust* (1973), which includes some poems he wrote in the United States and England as well as much of the verse published in the two preceding collections.

Perhaps a good place to begin would be with one of the first London poems in *A Simple Lust*:

I walk in the English quicksilver dusk
and spread my hands to the soft spring rain
and see the streetlights gild the flowering trees
and the late light breaking through patches
    of broken cloud
and I think of the Island's desolate dusks
and the swish of the Island's haunting rain
and the desperate frenzy straining our prisoned
    breasts:
and the men who are still there crouching now
in the grey cells, on the grey floors, stubborn
    and bowed.

(p. 102)

The painful recollection of his imprisonment on Robben Island, the contrast between freedom and confinement, the manifold sensory perceptions—all these are typical of Brutus' poetry in exile, but even more noteworthy is the full-bodied texture of the poem. Brutus is no longer writing unornamented verse. The diction is simple, the form irregular, the line length flexible instead of fixed, but there are also traces of alliteration, slanted end rhymes (dusk/dusks/breasts; rain/rains; cloud/now/bowed), and parallelism (in the seven lines beginning with the word "and"). In addition, the rhetorical structure of the poetic statement is carefully balanced to make an effective contrast. The silver and gold ambience of an English dusk is offset by the desolate grayness of South African prison cells. England's "soft spring rain" is placed in opposition to Robben Island's "haunting rain." The poet-speaker walks freely and spreads his hands expansively while the prisoners crouch "stubborn and bowed." The poem is not a bald string of abstract nouns and verbs stretched out into a prosaic statement, but rather a succession of graphic, sentient perceptions that turn poignant when juxtaposed. Because of its rich texture, because it is obviously well wrought without being highly mannered or ambiguous, this poem falls somewhere between the polar extremes of complexity and simplicity, toward which Brutus had gravitated previously. It is a middle-of-the-road poem, neither excessively plain nor unusually fancy. It belongs to the period of balance (or synthesis) in Brutus' poetry.

Another example from *A Simple Lust*, a poem about poetry itself, demonstrates the subtle technique behind Brutus' balanced poetry:

> Sometimes a mesh of ideas
> webs the entranced mind,
> the assenting delighted mental eye;
> and sometimes the thrust and clash
> of forged and metalled words
> makes musical clangour in the brain;
> and sometimes a nude and simple word
> standing unlit or unadorned
> may plead mutely in cold or dark
> for an answering warmth, an enlightening
>   sympathy;
> state the bare fact and let it sing.
>
> (p. 136)

Artful without being enigmatic, the poetic statement is trisected into meticulously counterpoised clauses that onomatopoetically—that is, by linking sense and sound of a word—describes three of the stylistic options available to a poet. The noisy "thrust," "clash," and "clangour" of "metalled words," for instance, contrasts sharply with the "nude," "mute" "simple word." Although the poem yields its meaning easily and with seemingly effortless grace, it is actually more complicated than it appears, depending for its effect on a calculated orchestration of syntax, image, and sound toward the trim finality of the last line: "state the bare fact and let it sing." Such singing is not done effectively without a good score. In the best of Brutus' balanced poetry, his compositional scoring is surreptitious, his art almost invisible.

ECONOMY

Brutus might have remained a well-balanced poet longer had he not been invited to the Peoples' Republic of China in the summer of 1973 to represent the exiled South African Table Tennis Board and the South African Non-Racial Olympic Committee at a table-tennis tournament in which eighty-six countries from Africa, Asia, and Latin America participated. Shortly before taking the trip he discovered Chinese communist leader Mao Tse-tung's poetry in a new translation by Willis Barnstone and Ko Ching-po. Extremely impressed with the classic economy in Mao's poetry, he began to experiment with Chinese modes of poetic expression, attempting to capture in his verse in English the laconic terseness of what he had read in Chinese poetry. In a note to his *China Poems* (1975) Brutus explains his intention:

> Even before my trip I had begun to work towards more economical verse. My exposure to *haikus* and their even tighter Chinese ancestors, the *chueh chu*, impelled me further. The trick is to say little (the nearer to nothing, the better) and to suggest much—as much as possible. The weight of meaning hovers around the words (which should be as flat as possible) or is brought by the reader/hearer. Non-emotive, near-neutral sounds should generate unlimited resonances in the mind; the delight is in the tight-rope balance between nothing and everything possible; between saying very little and implying a great deal. Here are examples, from other sources, of this form.

> Goose-grey
> clouds
> lour

There is an enormous gap to be traversed in the mind between the softness (silliness is also suggested) of "goose-grey" and the thunderous menace of "lour" presaging a storm.

> Exile:
> schizophrenia:
> suicide

Consider the terror of the journey to be made
in the mind from exile to the declension of
suicide.

(p. 35)

The verse in Brutus' *China Poems* is economical to the point of being epigrammatic,
as the following three mini-poems exemplify.

It is to preserve
beauty
that we destroy.
(p.18)

The Chinese carver
building a new world:
chips of ivory in his hair.
(p. 24)

At the Long Wall:
a soldier
holding a flower.
(p. 17)

These poems operate on the principle of
paradox, of unexpected and seemingly illogical leaps of thought or image that give the
impression of being self-contradictory: we destroy in order to preserve; chips of an ancient
art material (ivory) play a part in building
a new world; a soldier holds a flower. The
poems try to balance on the tightrope between sense and nonsense, between premises
at variance with conclusions. The initial images briefly build up expectations, and the
final image knocks them down. The imagination sets out on its journey and is ambushed
at the end. It is the ability of these poems to
astonish and betray us that makes them successful.

There are also several vignettes among the
China poems that gain their strength from
irony, the cousin of paradox.

On the roofs
of the ruined palaces of Emperors
imperial lions snarl
at the empty air.

(p. 10)

The tree in the Emperor's Garden
will not accept
the discipline of marble.

(p. 9)

It is easy to read political messages in these
ironies, but different readers might be inclined
to interpret them in different ways. For instance, the undisciplined tree in the emperor's
garden could have one meaning for a Chinese
mainlander (the meaning being Taiwan,
which China considers a renegade province)
and another meaning (that is, China) for a
Taiwanese. Explication of the image depends
entirely on one's point of view. Here is where
extreme economy backfires on the economist.
Or does it? Perhaps part of the strategy of
generating "unlimited resonances in the mind"
is to create ironies, ambiguities, and contradictions that can never be completely
resolved. A few well-chosen words could
conceivably produce myriad tensions in the
imagination. The poet thus gets maximum
mental mileage with a minimum of verbal fuel.
What he loses in precision by such economy
he certainly regains in amplitude.

Not all of Brutus' China poems achieve
such heady inflation, however. Several fall so
utterly flat that they cannot be resuscitated. A
banal observation such as

Peasants, workers
they are the strength
of the land
(p. 20)

never gets off the ground poetically, nor does

Miles of corn:
it is simple:
life is simple
(p. 21)

which is simply too simple for words. Brutus'
flattest poem, however, is his toast at a sixty-
course banquet in the Great Hall of the
People, the Chinese parliament building in

Beijing. It consists of but six words, one of which is repeated three times:

> Good food
> good wine
> good friendship.
>
> (p. 12)

To which one is tempted to add, "but *not* good poetry."

In 1974–1975, during a year as visiting professor of English and ethnic studies at the University of Texas at Austin, Brutus continued to experiment with economical poetic forms, adapting the Chinese idiom he admired to suit new subject matter and new emotions. One of these poems, still unpublished, was dashed off after a discussion with friends about the care and preservation of his manuscripts:

> Bach's wife, they say
> made curlpapers
> from his manuscripts.

He wrote many other mini-poems equally flippant in tone, making jokes in terse verse. These short poems represent the lighter side of his interest in Chinese poetry.

A more serious side is visible in poems concerned with his relationship to South Africa. He wrote homesick verse occasionally, focusing on the disquieting reminders of South Africa that intruded upon his awareness at odd moments, forcing him to contemplate his existence in exile. His six-poem "Sequence for South Africa" in *South African Voices* (1975) sounds a familiar plaintive note, but the individual poems tend to be shorter, pithier, more like his Chinese model:

> Golden oaks and jacarandas
> flowering:
> exquisite images
> to wrench my heart.
>
> (p. 31)

Another sample:

> At night
> to put myself to sleep
> I play alphabet games
> but something reminds me of you
> and I cry out
> and am wakened.
>
> (p. 32)

Economy remains the defining principle of these poems.

VARIETY

It would be misleading, however, to suggest that Brutus gave up writing longer poems entirely and never returned to former habits of composition after visiting China. At times it was necessary for him to make an extended statement, especially when he wanted to underscore a specific political point or convey a personal message to a particular individual. But even in these instances, the longer poems he wrote after his Chinese phase tend to be simpler and freer than those he wrote during his phase of balanced poetry. If he periodically swings away from austere economy, he does so in the direction of extended simplicity rather than of increased complexity. Thus he achieves variety without sacrificing directness and accessibility.

Some examples of his increased flexibility and eclecticism in choosing suitable poetic vehicles for his extended meditations can be found in *Salutes and Censures* (1984) and *Airs and Tributes* (1989), which bring together statements applauding allies and condemning enemies in the struggle against injustice and oppression. In a sardonic poem in *Salutes and Censures*, for instance, Brutus adopts the unusual tactic of ironically lauding the world-class efficiency of apartheid:

> You may not see the Nazis
> in our streets—
> certainly, no coal-scuttle helmets

or jackboots;
the swastikas are few and far between
drawn clumsily, mostly by pranksters;
no greasy tarpaulins of flesh-soured smoke
drag lazily across our roofs
(Cleanliness!)

But are the men any less efficient
for being uniformed like cops?
(the girls, the coveralled shopgirls,
how they love 'em!)
if our millions die less spectacularly—
malnutrition
instead of extermination—
is it really so inferior?

There are more people
in Meadowlands than Belsen
(make no mistake
the place is pretty thoroughly occupied
or, as we would say, "policed")
The death-rate is really quite high;
and if you listen carefully
you will hear the faint cries from the prison
of people who have not been charged with any
   crime.

Really, we are not doing too badly.

(p. 35)

The use of highly personalized diction to make a direct or implied comparison between conditions in South Africa and inhumane situations elsewhere in the world is characteristic of this phase of Brutus' work. In this volume he speaks against social and political barbarities in Nicaragua, Chile, the United States, Angola, Zimbabwe, Germany, and England as well as South Africa. His concerns are truly international even when his focus remains fixed on his homeland. The analogies he draws often require a greater amplitude of expression than was available to him in the Chinese forms he exploited earlier.

However, he did not entirely abandon his former strategies. In *Airs and Tributes* there are many brief poems celebrating resistance to oppression or commenting philosophically on lasting public or personal problems. For instance, another haiku was prompted by his memory of West Lake, China:

Even nightingales
by West Lake cannot silence
the wail of exile.

(p. 5)

Some of the longer poems in the collection also retain an austere simplicity of diction, as in this tribute to Kwame Toure, the African-American activist formerly known as Stokely Carmichael:

He does not die
who lives in the consciousness
of his people

he does not die
whose works endure
in the society
of his people

his spirit lives
when the memory
of his people
preserves his work
and his words
and when his deeds
continue to march forward
to shape the future.

(p. 16)

Brutus' impulse to salute those who have inspired others by resolutely opposing injustice is manifest again in *Still the Sirens* (1993), which contains many poems, short and long, praising heroes of the world's political struggles. Typical of this honorific verse is "February, 1990," his paean to Nelson Mandela:

Yes, Mandela—
some of us admit embarrassedly
we wept to see you step free
so erectly, so elegantly
shrug off the prisoned years
a blanket cobwebbed of pain and grime:

behind: the island's seas and,
harsh, white and treacherous
ahead: jagged rocks and krantzes
bladed crevices of racism and deceit.

In the salt island air
you swung your hammer, grimly stoic
facing the dim path of interminable years.
Now, vision blurred with tears
we see you step out to our salutes
bearing our burden of hopes and fears
and impress your radiance
on the grey morning air.

(p. 24)

Similar tributes are offered to Oliver Tambo, Martin Luther King, Jr., Arthur Ashe, Indira Gandhi, Pablo Neruda, and other political leaders, prisoners, victims, and martyrs. Brutus' verse takes on a commemorative air, congratulating those who triumphed over adversity and honoring those who sacrificed their lives in pursuit of a noble ideal. The rhetoric in these panegyrics is not flowery and verbose but simple, direct, and elegant.

CONCLUSION

Throughout much of his career the hallmark of Brutus' most mature poetry has been a consistently resonant lucidity couched in a variety of expressive forms. He has also remained a steadfast opponent of social injustice and political oppression, speaking out against the evils of apartheid and other institutionalized forms of racial discrimination. The title poem of *A Simple Lust* serves both to sum up and to illustrate his achievement as a poet committed to voicing the grievances of suffering people in memorable terms:

A simple lust is all my woe:
the thin thread of agony
that runs through the reins
after the flesh is overspent
in over-taxing acts of love:

only I speak the others' woe:
those congealed in concrete
or rotting in rusted ghetto-shacks;
only I speak their wordless woe,
their unarticulated simple lust.

(p. 176)

In the mid 1990s, Brutus still lived and worked in the United States but traveled frequently to the postapartheid South Africa, where he took part in conferences and literary events and continued to speak out in behalf of the downtrodden masses in his society.

Selected Bibliography

COLLECTED WORKS

A Simple Lust: Selected Poems Including Sirens Knuckles Boots, Letters to Martha, Poems from Algiers, Thoughts Abroad. London: Heinemann Educational Books, 1973; New York: Hill and Wang, 1973.
Stubborn Hope: New Poems and Selections from China Poems *and* Strains. Washington, D.C.: Three Continents Press, 1978; London: Heinemann Educational Books, 1978. 2d. ed. Washington, D.C.: Three Continents Press, 1983; Oxford: Heinemann, 1991.

POETRY

Sirens Knuckles Boots. Ibadan, Nigeria: Mbari, 1963.
Letters to Martha, and Other Poems from a South African Prison. London: Heinemann Educational Books, 1968.
Poems from Algiers. Austin: African and Afro-American Research Institute, University of Texas at Austin, 1970.
[John Bruin, pseud.]. *Thoughts Abroad.* Del Valle, Tex.: Troubadour Press, 1970, 1975.
China Poems. Austin: African and Afro-American Studies and Research Center, University of Texas at Austin, 1975. Includes Chinese translations by Ko Ching-po.
South African Voices. Ed. by Bernth Lindfors. Austin: African and Afro-American Studies and Research Center, University of Texas at Austin,

1975. Collection of poems by seven South African writers.

Strains. Ed. by Wayne Kamin and Chip Dameron. Austin, Tex.: Troubadour Press, 1975; Chicago: Troubadour Press, 1982.

Salutes and Censures. Enugu, Nigeria: Fourth Dimension Publishers, 1984; Trenton, N.J.: Africa World Press, 1990.

Airs and Tributes. Ed. by Gil Ott, intro. by Samuel Allen. Camden, N.J.: Whirlwind Press, 1989.

Still the Sirens. Intro. by Lamont B. Steptoe. Santa Fe, N.M.: Pennywhistle Press, 1993.

ESSAYS

"Childhood Reminiscences." In Per Wästberg, ed., *The Writer in Modern Africa: African-Scandinavian Writers' Conference. Stockholm 1967.* Uppsala, Sweden: Scandinavian Institute of African Studies, 1968; New York: Africana Publishing Co., 1969.

"Protest Against Apartheid: Alan Paton, Nadine Gordimer, Athol Fugard, Alfred Hutchinson and Arthur Nortje." In Cosmo Pieterse and Donald Munro, eds., *Protest and Conflict in African Literature.* London: Heinemann, 1969; New York: Africana Publishing Co., 1969.

"Poetry of Suffering: The Black Experience." In *Ba Shiru* 4, no. 2 (1973).

"English and the Dynamics of South African Cretive Writing." In Leslie A. Fiedler and Houston A. Baker, Jr., eds., *English Literature: Opening Up the Canon.* Baltimore, Md.: The Johns Hopkins University Press, 1981.

INTERVIEWS

Berger, Renato. "Interview with Dennis Brutus." In *Genève-Afrique* 18, no. 2 (1980).

Duerden, Dennis, and Cosmo Pieterse, eds. *African Writers Talking: A Collection of Radio Interviews.* London: Heinemann, 1992; New York: Africana Publishing Co., 1972.

Lindfors, Bernth. "'Somehow Tenderness Survives': Dennis Brutus Talks About His Life and Poetry." In *Benin Review* 1 (June 1974).

Lindfors, Bernth, et al., eds. *Palaver: Interviews with Five African Writers in Texas.* Austin: African and Afro-American Research Institute, University of Texas at Austin, 1972.

Miller, E. Ethelbert. "An Interview with Dennis Brutus." In *Obsidian* 1, no. 2 (1975).

Thompson, William E. "Dennis Brutus: An Interview." In *Ufahamu* 12, no. 2 (1983).

CRITICAL STUDIES

Chipasula, Frank M. "A Terrible Trajectory: The Impact of Apartheid, Prison and Exile on Dennis Brutus's Poetry." In Abdulruzak Gurnah, *Essays on African Writing: A Re-evaluation.* Oxford, U.K.: Heinemann, 1993.

de Meester, Ria. "An Introduction to Dennis Brutus' Prison Poems." In *Restant* 8 (spring 1980).

Egudu, Romanus N. "Pictures of Pain: The Poetry of Dennis Brutus." In Christopher Heywood, ed., *Aspects of South African Literature.* London: Heineman, 1976; New York: Africana Publishing Co., 1976.

Elimimian, Isaac. "Form and Meaning in the Poetry of Dennis Brutus." In *Literary Half-Yearly* 28 (January 1987).

Gardner, Colin. "Brutus and Shakespeare." In *Research in African Literatures* 15 (fall 1984).

JanMohamed, Abdul R. "Dennis Brutus." In Bernth Lindfors and Reinhard Sander, eds., *Twentieth-Century Caribbean and Black African Writers*, vol. 117 of *Dictionary of Literary Biography.* Detroit: Gale Research, 1992.

Lindfors, Bernth. "Dennis Brutus and His Critics." In *West African Journal of Modern Languages* 2 (September 1976).

———. "Dialectical Development in the Poetry of Dennis Brutus." In Alastair Niven, ed., *The Commonwealth Writer Overseas: Themes of Exile and Expatriation.* Brussels, Belgium: Didier, 1976.

McLuckie, Craig W., and Patrick J. Colbert, eds. *Critical Perspectives on Dennis Brutus.* Colorado Springs, Colo.: Three Continents Press, 1995.

Nkondo, Gessler Moses. "Dennis Brutus and the Revolutionary Idea." In *Ufahamu* 10 (spring 1981).

———. "Dennis Brutus: The Domestication of a Tradition." In *World Literature Today* 55 (winter 1981).

Ogundele, Wole. "The Exile's Progress: Dennis Brutus' Poetry in the First Phase of His Exile."

In *Commonwealth Essays and Studies* 10 (spring 1988).

Ogunyemi, Chikwenye Okonjo. "The Song of the Caged Bird: Contemporary African Prison Poetry." In *ARIEL* 13 (October 1982).

Ojaide, Tanure. "The Troubadour: The Poet's Persona in the Poetry of Dennis Brutus." In *ARIEL* 17 (January 1986).

Onuekwusi, Jasper A. "Pain and Anguish of an African Poet: Dennis Brutus and South African Reality." In *Literary Criterion* 23, nos. 1–2 (1988).

Povey, John. "Three South African Poets: Dennis Brutus, Keorapetse Kgositsile, and Oswald Mbuyiseni Mtshali." In *World Literature Written in English* 16 (November 1977).

Ssensalo, Bede M. "The Autobiographical Nature of the Poetry of Dennis Brutus." In *Ufahamu* 7, no. 2 (1977).

Theroux, Paul. "Voices Out of the Skull: A Study of Six African Poets." In *Black Orpheus* 20 (August 1966).

Wylie, Hal. "Creative Exile: Dennis Brutus and René Depestre." In Carolyn Park et al., eds., *When the Drumbeat Changes*. Washington, D.C.: Three Continents Press, 1981.

RECORDING

"Dennis Brutus, Exiled Black South African Playwright [*sic*]." Washington, D.C.: National Public Radio, 1986, FA-860225.

Roy Campbell
1901–1957

JOHN FLETCHER

FAMOUS, EVEN NOTORIOUS, in his own day, Roy Campbell is now largely forgotten. His much anthologized poem, "Horses on the Camargue," from his finest volume, *Adamastor* (1930), is probably all that most readers know of his work. To Rowland Smith, one of the few academic critics to have written at any length about him, Campbell is an enigmatic figure whose frequent changes of loyalty are confusing and contradictory. This is hardly surprising, Smith points out, since Campbell's literary career was built around shifting allegiances, which were publicly proclaimed and usually accompanied by a change of country of residence.

Throughout his life, in fact, Campbell was on the move. Born in South Africa, he left at the age of seventeen with the aim of securing admission to Oxford University. When his plan did not work out, he led an irregular bohemian life in London and wrote his first major work, the long poem *The Flaming Terrapin* (1924), which brought him instant acclaim and a standing rarely enjoyed by novice poets. He married romantically, without parental consent and was still living with the same woman when he died.

He returned to South Africa in 1924. Although he remained at heart a member of the "white tribe" of Africa all his life, admired the work of South African writer Olive Schreiner,

and formed close friendships with other writers, such as Alan Paton, William Plomer, and Laurens van der Post, it was not long before he found himself at loggerheads with the colony's cultural establishment. His own wild, "African" personality had been a useful attribute in Europe, but once back in Africa he felt alienated. He stayed only three years, and after returning to England he published poems harshly critical of South African culture. But he soon fell out with the English literary establishment, too, and moved with his family to neutral ground in the south of France.

This move to France was, as Smith points out, a major change that brought with it a new sense of values. Up to this point Campbell had shared many of the progressive views of the English intellectuals with whom he was mixing. After leaving England, however, he became increasingly reactionary at a time when English literary life was entering the 1930s with a growing social conscience. What isolated him more decisively, however, was the publication in 1931 of *The Georgiad: A Satirical Fantasy in Verse*, a satire on the English intelligentsia.

After writing this book Campbell was ostracized from literary circles, and his conservative voice became increasingly strident as he commented on the worsening political situation in Europe. He moved to Spain and became a Roman Catholic. When the Spanish civil war broke out, his passionate advocacy of General Francisco Franco's Fascist rebellion further alienated him from the vast majority of English writers who supported the Spanish Republic. He was pronounced a fascist, and his increasingly bitter attacks on British democracy only served to confirm the accuracy of the label. On the other hand, he did not take to the British Fascist leader Oswald Mosley, whom he felt to be on his side for all the wrong reasons.

Like so much else in his personality, the issue of Campbell's racism is complex. At home in Durban, South Africa, while assuming, as virtually all of his generation did, that the white man's right to rule was part of the natural order, he never shared the uglier prejudices of his fellow Europeans. If anything, he was sympathetic to black South Africans because those of his own race looked down on them. All his life, in fact, he espoused views that were embraced by people whom he admired or views that were opposed by people whom he despised. Even a taboo subject like love and marriage between white and black—the theme of Plomer's first novel, *Turbott Wolfe* (1926)—did not shock Campbell because he liked Plomer.

More positively, he had no time for the color bar with its mean and petty segregation and foresaw that apartheid, far from resolving racial tension in South Africa, would exacerbate it. Indeed, he considered the policy of institutionalized racism suicidal because it gave rise to such pent-up resentment that the state risked being swept away and with it the "beloved country" that he, like Alan Paton, could never bring himself to disown.

Similar contradictions are evident in his attitude toward Jewish people. Campbell was anti-Semitic, but his anti-Semitism, like his flirtation with fascism, was that of a simpleton in public affairs. He was a man for whom political theory was merely the sum total of his current likes and dislikes, that is to say more emotional than rational. John Povey speaks of his "crude lack of competent political insight" (p. 152). His adored wife had reason to believe herself partly Jewish, and in East Africa he greatly enjoyed the company and conversation of a group of Jewish refugee intellectuals with whom he shared housing.

In fact, the outbreak of World War II saw a complete about-face in his loyalties. He enlisted in the British army and wore the king's uniform with pride. Accepted once more on the English scene, he stayed on for several years after the war. He never felt he truly belonged in England, however, and in the early 1950s moved to Portugal, where he died in 1957, still cantankerously at odds with the prevailing intellectual climate.

Smith's verdict is that these changes in allegiance and outlook had a deleterious effect on Campbell's writing. He never fully realized his early promise. The lyric power of his first volumes of verse became increasingly diverted into polemical and satirical writing as he grew older and his political and personal feuds multiplied. His distinctive lyrical gift was for capturing inward reactions to the power and beauty of the natural world, exemplified in the justly popular poem, "Horses on the Camargue," about the wild horses that inhabit the Camargue, a delta salt marsh in southern France. "Theirs is no earthly breed," the poet suggests, so it must surely have been "the great white breakers [that] gave them birth" (*Adamastor*, p. 77). The poet then proceeds, in a long bravura passage, to imagine a Camargue horse transported far inland from his native sands, until one day he catches "some far-off fragrance of the wave" (p. 77):

Many have told the tale
Of how in fury, foaming at the rein,
He hurls his rider; and with lifted tail,
With coal-red eyes and cataracting mane,
Heading his course for home,
Though sixty foreign leagues before him sweep,

Will never rest until he breathes the foam
And hears the native thunder of the deep.

(pp. 77–78)

Such magnificent wild creatures, the poem concludes, "spirits of power and beauty and delight,"

out of hardship bred,
...
Have ever on such frugal pastures fed
And loved to course with tempests through the night.

(p. 78)

Campbell's later obsession with argument could only lead him away from such vivid expression of subjective values and into statements and comments that are open to more damaging objective assessment. There is no doubt, Smith concludes, that Campbell's colonial background and resulting sense of being an outsider when he moved to England had a profound impact on his work. Once his unhappy return to South Africa seemed to cut him off from his native culture as well, his feeling of isolation grew even more intense. Most of the positions that he subsequently took up were the inevitable result of his steadily increasing alienation throughout the 1930s. Furthermore, his need to justify himself and the values that he had adopted became more acute and their expression more strident. As a result, Glyn Pursglove finds a "deficiency of human sympathy in too much of Campbell's work" (p. 60).

According to Smith, Campbell's isolation affected his work in two ways. First, it drove him into self-justifying polemic and predictable, public response. Second, it gave his writing remarkable intensity when he used his lyrical gift to communicate the personal tensions and values that lay behind his less successful public poems. But once he was finally accepted, albeit as an eccentric, on the English literary scene, his lyrical impulse deserted him. He published his last volume of original poems, *Talking Bronco*, in 1946.

Between 1946 and his death eleven years later he published several volumes of verse translations, for most of which he won great acclaim, and four prose works. In his favorite role as rugged individualist, he was likely to appear on public occasions dressed in an army bush hat or as an Iberian cattleman. His repertoire of tall stories seemed inexhaustible. But his distinctive lyrical power had gone, and his later poetry shows none of the burning intensity that characterized his finest work, which was produced during the long period of isolation when Roy Campbell the colonial was kept at arm's length by the English literary establishment.

LIFE

Ignatius Roy Dunnachie Campbell was born in Durban, in the Natal Province of South Africa, on 2 October 1901. His family came originally from Scotland and was strictly Presbyterian and teetotalist. His father, Samuel George Campbell, was a doctor of great energy and ability who tended black and white patients alike, a color blindness that endeared him to the Zulu people and that his son inherited. Although he treated the poor free of charge, his practice was so extensive that he became wealthy; he used his fortune to establish Durban's social services and to found the University of Natal, among other things.

The young Roy was brought up a Scot, like his siblings Ethel, Archibald, George, Neil, and Bruce: he wore a kilt despite the humid climate and learned traditional Scottish ballads from his mother, Margaret Wylie Dunnachie Campbell. At the same time, he had a Zulu nurse, Catherine Mgadi, and became fluent in Zulu. In the former British Empire, it was common for children born in the colonies to enjoy a double inheritance: the language and culture of their parents on the one hand, and the language and culture of their nurse on the other. This made them different from first-generation colonists: they felt as much African or Indian as they did British, and they looked upon the country of their birth as home. When the time came to leave they suffered homesickness, and Roy Campbell was no exception. As his biographer Peter Alexander makes clear, Campbell always thought of the Africa of his childhood as a paradise lost.

Another early influence on his personality, and a less happy one, was A. S. Langley, the bullying tyrant who ran the Durban Boys' High School, which Campbell attended from 1910 to 1917. Alexander argues convincingly that the young Campbell's fear and loathing of his headmaster gave rise to a deep-rooted contradiction in his character because he unconsciously associated Langley with his own adored but feared father.

Hatred of one father-figure and love of another, Alexander believes, made Campbell both detest authority and long to be subjected to it, which helps to explain three paradoxes in his life: his natural anarchy and attraction in the 1930s to the autocratic orderliness of European dictatorships, his early anticlericalism and later adherence to the authoritative teachings of the Roman Catholic Church, and his loathing of what he saw as the regimentation of modern life and happiness serving under military discipline in the British Army.

What is more, Campbell associated all that he hated at Durban Boys' High School with book learning and idealized instead the free life of the wild, which he experienced in the African bush. And yet, as a born writer, his natural impulse was to venerate the life of the mind. He never managed to resolve the contradiction between his bookish temperament and his distaste for the literary world. Like the American poet Ezra Pound, the French writer Pierre Drieu la Rochelle, and other intellectuals of the 1930s, he despised his own kind and instead worshiped rather masochistically the virile man of action, the strong leader, the tough authoritarian—precisely the kind of politician who held in contempt people living

by the pen, like Campbell himself. True to type, Campbell admired Franco, a brutal philistine who had no time for the values held dear by the South African writer.

As a young man that writer, Alexander demonstrates, fell under the influence of William Wordsworth, Percy Bysshe Shelley, and the early William Butler Yeats and never lost his admiration for the great Romantic poets. He soon began to feel restless in Natal, conscious that his identity lay elsewhere and that his dedication to a life of art was going to require a break with many of his family's values.

He had by now become a complex person, indeed, a mass of contradictions. He combined a host of incompatible feelings: a hatred of discipline with a keen need for it; hypochondria (he suffered from a succession of psychosomatic ailments) with a fine physique (he was six feet two inches tall, broad shouldered, slim, and muscular); a delight in solitude with a longing to be accepted by his fellows; a contempt for bookishness with an addiction to poetry; a deep-rooted respect for his puritanical upbringing with a bohemian inclination (especially bisexuality and alcoholism, both of which would have horrified his Scottish forebears); and, last but not least, a pride in his African background with a feeling of alienation from it.

In late December 1918 he sailed for England with the intention of becoming a student at Oxford. He failed to meet the entrance requirements, however, and settled in London, where he was soon moving in exalted circles. He became friendly with the composer William Walton, the poet T. S. Eliot, the novelist Aldous Huxley, and the painter Augustus John. He lost his colonial timidity and played up his African background for all it was worth, telling gripping tales of adventure in the bush and speaking in a strong Natal accent sprinkled with Zulu words and phrases. At this time he discovered the French symbolist poets; he was later to translate the work of Charles Baudelaire.

Campbell also became an enthusiastic supporter of futurism, the artistic movement that exalted color, violence, and speed, and he formed a close association with its leading figure in England, Wyndham Lewis, about whom he wrote a book in 1931. In Italy, where the movement was born, the futurists were sympathetic to fascism, which embodied the same values in the political arena as they propounded in the aesthetic sphere. Campbell's advocacy of futurism arose in violent reaction to what he saw as the effete versifying of the dominant Georgian poets, so it comes as no surprise that both he and Lewis later became keen admirers of Franco and the Spanish Nationalists. There was a decided streak of authoritarian illiberalism in both writers.

As a result of his disenchantment with the state of English letters, Campbell soon became restless in London. He was homesick for the light and vigor of Africa, for the simplicity of life spent, as he liked to put it, under corrugated iron, the standard roofing material in the colonies. In 1920 he moved to Provence in the south of France because, with its bright colors, harsh sunlight, and wild, empty landscapes, it reminded him of Africa. He stayed for eighteen months.

On his return to London he met and immediately fell in love with Mary Garman. They married on 11 February 1922 and embarked on a hippie lifestyle long before the term was invented. They were living in a remote part of Wales when their first child, Teresa, was born in November 1922 in a converted cowshed, lit only by an oil lamp. There, too, Campbell completed his first major work, a long poem entitled *The Flaming Terrapin*, which appeared in Britain and America in May 1924 to great critical acclaim.

The royalties Campbell earned from the poem, however, were not enough to support the family, so he returned to South Africa, where he was feted as a homegrown genius. To earn money he began writing for the local papers and was invited to edit a new literary journal, *Voorslag* (Whiplash), but he soon quarreled with the proprietors and resigned. In spite of this and other distractions, some of his finest poems were written at this time.

In March 1926 his second daughter, Anna, was born, but his wife did not take to life in South Africa, so in December the family returned to England. Campbell was never again to reside in the land of his birth. His return to his roots, Alexander points out, had been a chastening experience: not only had his hopes of an easy life in the subtropical paradise of his childhood been dashed, but he had acquired a reputation in South Africa for holding dangerously radical views, and his sense of being an outsider had intensified. Even at home, therefore, he felt like a foreigner. From then on he was to be a foreigner indeed, and often an unhappy one.

His marriage went through an almost fatal crisis when Mary fell in love with the lesbian poet Vita Sackville-West, on the grounds of whose stately home the Campbells were living. Sackville-West soon tired of her lover, however; eventually Mary accepted this and rejoined Campbell in Provence, where he had fled in despair in April 1928. They stayed in the south of France until November 1933; here he wrote, among other poems, "Horses on the Camargue." Of this turbulent period Pursglove comments: "the poems written . . . in Provence . . . contain much of his best work," revealing a "quality of static inward illumination" (pp. 62, 67).

Before long the family was on the move again, this time to Spain: first to Barcelona, then to Valencia, and finally to Altea, where they were received into the Roman Catholic Church. Campbell's new faith made him happier and more stable. The family moved on to Toledo, where they lived from 1935 to 1936. Driven out by the fighting in the Spanish civil war, they returned briefly to England; after much wandering, they returned to Toledo when hostilities ended in the spring of 1939.

The outbreak of World War II aroused Campbell's patriotism, especially the sight of the British aircraft carrier *Ark Royal* being greeted by wild cheering as it limped, badly damaged after an engagement, into Gibraltar harbor. He returned to London in August 1941. His younger brother, Neil, was killed in action in North Africa soon afterward, which made Campbell even keener to fight the Germans. He joined the British army in the spring of 1942 and was made a sergeant in the King's African Rifles. Much to his regret, Campbell had a quiet war, mainly in East Africa, and a hip injury and malaria led to his discharge on medical grounds in 1944.

In postwar London Campbell first found work on the War Damages Commission and then in 1946 joined the British Broadcasting Corporation as a radio talks producer. A frequent drinking companion during this period was the great Welsh poet, Dylan Thomas. But Campbell could not be happy in England for long. He and Mary moved to Portugal in 1952. Apart from lecture tours in North America in 1953 and 1955 and a last visit to South Africa to receive an honorary doctorate of literature at the University of Natal in 1954, he lived in Portugal in ever declining health. He was killed in an automobile accident on 23 April 1957 and buried at Sao Pedro, not far from Lisbon. Mary Campbell, who survived the crash, died in February 1979 and was laid to rest next to her husband's grave.

PRINCIPAL WRITINGS

Roy Campbell was above all a poet. In other genres his work was less significant, although his outstanding translations from Saint John of the Cross and from Federico García Lorca (in *Collected Works,* vol. 2, 1985), deserve special mention. His translations of Baudelaire, on the other hand, "are less consistently convincing, and do less than justice to the sophistication of their originals" (Pursglove, p. 69).

His prose works are equally uneven. *Broken Record: Reminiscences* (1934) is an autobiography written hastily for money, and its sequel, *Light on a Dark Horse* (1951), is, in Alexander's opinion, "the product of imagination. He drew upon his former autobiography, retelling the tales and embroidering them until they bore scarcely any resemblance to the original event" (p. 217). Alexander points out that Campbell gives himself a heroic role in the stories, boasting in such a way that not even the most credulous reader would believe him.

Moreover, the autobiography is disingenuous and, in its selectivity, actually dishonest. For instance, Campbell directs such venom at Vita Sackville-West—without mentioning her affair with his wife—that the uninformed reader might well be puzzled by an apparently unprovoked display of ferocity, especially in the description of his host's stately home as "something between a psychiatry clinic and a posh brothel" (*Light on a Dark Horse*, p. 256). But Campbell was profoundly humiliated at "being cuckolded by a woman," as an acquaintance tactlessly reports him to have said (Alexander, p. 83), so he simply suppressed all reference to the true reason for his hatred of Sackville-West and of the entire literary circle known as the Bloomsbury set. But this hatred did induce him to write *The Georgiad*, a long poem which finalized his break with the English literary establishment.

Other prose compositions include a study of García Lorca in 1952 or, more precisely, an "appreciation of his poetry" as the subtitle makes clear, largely made up of Campbell's translations linked by a not very searching commentary; a spirited essay on his friend Wyndham Lewis, the British painter and writer; a chatty travel book on Portugal; and *The Mamba's Precipice* (1953), a story for children that powerfully evokes the Zululand of his youth.

Campbell wrote poetry from an early age, but his earliest work was heavily influenced by the English Romantic poets and is of historical interest only. His first work of significance was *The Flaming Terrapin*, a poem embodying "the young poet's reaction to the violent contrast between the postwar Europe which he encountered in 1919 and the African wildness of his previous eighteen years" (Smith, p. 19).

The importance of this contrast can hardly be exaggerated. John Povey, a British writer who made the journey in the opposite direction, points out that what strikes the newcomer to Africa

> is its excess, the dazzle of its beauty, the almost unimaginable brilliance of color, of the birds, of the myriad of animals. There is so much to comprehend beyond the bland expectations of experience that it inevitably appears intellectually and emotionally indigestible, . . . [which] suggests that when Campbell occasionally appears exaggerated in his descriptions, he may perhaps be more deliberate and accurate than can be recognized by those who have not witnessed the regions about which he writes.
>
> (p. 167)

All critics agree that *The Flaming Terrapin* is a remarkable achievement for a writer of only twenty-three. However, "to stress excessively the youth is to miss those qualities of the poem which are valid and mature," writes Povey, who lists these as "a brilliance—a glitter of color unmatched by perhaps any other poet in English"—and a dazzling energy that nevertheless "leaves the intellectual muscles of the reader finally unresponsive, too exhausted by the continuous fire and drive of the poet's intentions" (p. 41). Campbell's fiery emotionalism was fully present in his early verse, which left little room for development and change.

Change could have manifested itself in an increasing maturity—measured by a tighter control of the lavish, too freely moving force—and in an intellectual depth capable of sustaining the brilliance of the surface imagination, but this never happened. At the age of twenty-three Campbell seemed as gifted as T. S. Eliot or W. H. Auden were at the same age. What Campbell lacked, however, was their intellect. As it was, they went on from strength to strength in their verse, so that as mature poets, though recognizably the same people as the brilliant beginners, they surpassed their youthful achievements by an order of magnitude never attained by Campbell.

All the essential qualities of Campbell's most characteristic verse are already present in *The Flaming Terrapin*: words of color, violent verbs of movement, classical allusions, metaphors extending over several lines, iambic pentameters with exact rhymes in end-stopped lines, and a "sense of tension, of charged throbbing" (Povey, p. 44).

The opening and closing lines exemplify this perfectly:

> Maternal Earth stirs redly from beneath
> Her blue sea-blanket and her quilt of sky,
> A giant Anadyomene from the sheath
> And chrysalis of darkness; till we spy
> Her vast barbaric haunches, furred with trees,
> Stretched on the continents, and see her hair
> Combed in a surf of fire along the breeze
>
> . . .
>
> It is the silent chanting of the soul:
> "Though times shall change and stormy ages
>   roll,
> I am that ancient hunter of the plains
> That raked the shaggy flitches of the Bison:
> Pass, world: I am that dreamer that remains,
> The Man, clear-cut against the last horizon!"
>
> (pp. 3, 83)

The poem addresses the issue of the imposition of humankind's rule upon the world. The terrapin, a kind of giant tortoise, tows a newly launched Noah's ark on a voyage of discovery. The ark represents the world created by humankind. This ark is brought to the point where it can be present at a whole series of apocalyptic events. These incidents threaten the ideal civilization that can be constructed if the benign and rational ideology of the terrapin is allowed to sustain the world. People are able to determine the triumph of the terrapin's will, but humanity's potential is threatened by a trio of personified attitudes designated as Corruption, Anarchy, and Mediocrity. Civilization triumphs, fortunately, in this symbolic vision of human history.

The poem's strengths have already been enumerated: energy, color, brilliance, and fire. Impressive too is the stress on the African background, not only as the source of imagery (the Zambezi River is personified in much the same terms as the Mississippi is in the lyrics of "Ole Man River" by Oscar Hammerstein II, for example), but also as the rationale for the vehemence of the language.

The countervailing weaknesses are categorized by Povey all the more tellingly because he is a sympathetic critic of Campbell's work. The poem, he says, is "too long both in totality and in individual sections," which total six. "Many metaphors," his indictment continues, "establish their impact in a single incisive line and are then repeatedly developed, swollen, until the point seems excessive and belabored," so that "the effect of the poetry is lost, because the apparent intention appears to be less to convey meaning through metaphor [than] to create and extend metaphors. . . . [A]lthough the lines are regularly end-stopped," the stop is rarely a period, so that the "average sentences stretch across ten or even twenty lines. It is a style," Povey concludes, that "matches Campbell's thought"; it becomes monotonous and repetitious in its "determination to pile intensity upon intensity and thus create the culminating impact of a generated ecstasy of effect" (p. 47).

Four years later Campbell published *The Wayzgoose: A South African Satire* (1928), a lively piece in imitation of, and in homage to, John Dryden and Alexander Pope, two representatives of the English literary heritage for which Campbell had the highest regard. The poem, about literary life in Natal, avoids the sterility of past battles and retains its cutting edge. Attacking general follies and foibles, it has a much wider application than South Africa: it ridicules the cultural pretensions of any pompously self-satisfied or aggressively chauvinistic community.

A wayzgoose in this context is an annual literary convention or vast corroboree of journalists held annually in "Banana Land," Campbell's sardonic name for South Africa — the "garden colony" in more flattering official parlance — "Where *weeds* in such variety are found / And all the rarest *parasites* abound" (p. 9). This joke sets the tone for the portrayal of the fundamental dullness of colonial culture in Campbell's wittily imagined competition to decide who can produce the most boring single piece of writing. This hilarious contest is won by someone reading names and addresses straight out of a directory.

Campbell's most significant achievement followed two years later. *Adamastor* (1930) is "the one volume upon which must rest any justification he may have for being considered a major poet" (Povey, p. 59). Apart from "Horses on the Camargue," the collection contains the often anthologized African poems, "The Serf," "The Zulu Girl," and "The Zebras." "These three poems describe the African scene with an accuracy that equals love. It is impossible [for Campbell] to be so intensely aware of these African places and animals and not demonstrate that [he] is bound to that continent in some close emotional reaction" (Povey, pp. 59–60).

"The Zebras" indeed is the most powerful and evocative poem of Africa that he ever wrote. A dazzling "use of color is reinforced by [carefully] chosen verbs of action and of movement" to describe the zebras that "wander in their striped herds across the . . . high veldt" (Povey, p. 62): "Harnessed with level rays in golden reins, / The zebras draw the dawn across the plains" (p. 62).

The vision that Campbell "had as he recapitulated the Africa of his youth, the Africa of his intense feeling" (Povey, p. 90), is well captured in a poem of farewell to the great continent, "Rounding the Cape." In it he speaks of "all that I have hated or adored" (p. 28). There is freedom in escaping to the extensive literary opportunities in Europe, but there is also agony at leave-taking. Campbell knew that the "stimulation which the violence and color of Africa lent to his verse [was] the source of his genius. When these were withdrawn, there was no equivalent to take their place in European life. The passion and fire he later pretended to have found in Spain were nothing but a dim reflection of the true tropical fervour . . . [of] the Natal of his . . . youth" (Povey, pp. 93–94). Once the link with Africa was severed there was "vigor without control, a directness without intellectual balance, and the vivid sense of natural beauty flar[ing] to mere colorfulness" (Povey, p. 94).

Not all the fine poems in *Adamastor* are about Africa. "Mass at Dawn" is an effective poem, set in Provence, that compares to a sacrificial Eucharist the arrival of the poet's daughters bearing food and drink to meet him on his return from an overnight fishing trip:

> My arms were tired and I was heavy-eyed,
> But when . . .
> The children met me at the water-side,
> Never was wine so red or bread so white.
>
> (p. 79)

In Povey's opinion this powerful celebration of the "tenderness of total physical delight" shows that Campbell possessed a vivid lyric gift "unmatched in the contemporary English tongue," at this, the poetic climax of his career (pp. 87–88).

"Georgian Spring" manages in a single page of *Adamastor* to make most of the points that Campbell chose in his next volume, *The Georgiad*, to spread across forty pages of monotonous rhyming couplets lampooning, in a pastiche of *The Dunciad* (1728) by Alexander Pope, the bloodless intellectuals of literary London. This was followed by *Flowering Reeds* (1933), a slender gathering of poems, and *Mithraic Emblems* (1936), a collection linking his newfound Catholicism with a long-held belief in the supposed mythic dimension of bullfighting. Tauromachy was first explored in his prose study of the art of bullfighting in southern France, *Taurine Provence* (1932), which is not just a "slender

enthusiastic travelogue . . . [but] a kind of credo" (Povey, pp. 111–112).

The poems about bullfighting, however, show "strain and overtension" (Povey, p. 140), as do those about the war in Spain in *Mithraic Emblems* and the next volume, *Flowering Rifle* (1939). About this body of work all that needs to be said is that the Falange (the Spanish Fascists) had only one international figure prepared to celebrate their victory, and that was Roy Campbell.

He had his reasons. He loved the old Spain, his substitute for Africa, and he believed that the Republicans, whose power base lay in the proletarian industrialized cities, were bent on destroying the virile peasant fraternity that the icon of the plain-living man with a horse between his legs represented for Campbell. Moreover, his newfound Roman Catholic faith led him into uncritical acceptance of Falangist propaganda about indiscriminate Republican church burning and priest killing. Finally, there was a cantankerous streak in his nature, and he was certainly not displeased by the fact that "the liberals, the Nancy-boys, the Bloomsburyites" (Povey, p. 154), whose ridicule he had found so hard to bear and whom he had fully repaid in kind in *The Georgiad*, were virtually all supporters of the Republic.

Talking Bronco (1946) is Campbell's last collection of verse, containing his reactions to World War II in grim disillusioned tones that are curiously reminiscent of the English writer Siegfried Sassoon's to World War I. Otherwise the contents show Campbell "wandering [further and further] from any possibility of sober, considered belief" or rational system of thought (Povey, p. 178). All that is left is what Povey calls "a kind of quixotic grandeur" (p. 178). This admirably just critic puts his finger on what is wrong with all the later verse. It is, he says, Campbell's lack of ability to distinguish between poetry and doggerel: "not being able to recognize what was characteristic of his best work, he could not discover and eliminate those qualities which made it degenerate into spleen and silliness" (p. 194).

It would not, however, be fair to judge Campbell's overall literary reputation solely on his last works. Before his work declined with the waning of the influence of Africa, Campbell wrote in "The Zulu Girl" perhaps the finest lines—certainly the most sympathetic—devoted by a colonial to an indigenous laborer, a woman who breaks off from hoeing to suckle her child:

> She takes him to a ring of shadow pooled
> By thorn-trees: purpled with the blood of ticks,
> While her sharp nails, in slow caresses ruled,
> Prowl through his hair with sharp electric
>   clicks,
> His sleepy mouth, plugged by the heavy nipple,
> Tugs like a puppy, grunting as he feeds:
> Through his frail nerves her own deep languors
>   ripple
> Like a broad river sighing through its reeds.
>   (*Adamastor*, p. 36)

This is Campbell at his best: strong, simple, vivid writing that is truly universal and genuinely humanitarian in its sympathies. His feeling for people in this poem, for animals in "Horses on the Camargue" and "The Zebras," and for the landscapes of Africa, Provence, and Spain, expressed in powerful, unobscure, strongly rhythmical verse, shows that in his twenties and early thirties he could—and did—write great poetry.

Selected Bibliography

COLLECTED WORKS

Collected Poems. 3 vols. London: The Bodley Head, 1949; Chicago: Henry Regnery, 1957, 1960.
Collected Works. 4 vols. Craighall, South Africa: Ad. Donker, 1985, 1988.

POETRY

The Flaming Terrapin. London: Jonathan Cape, 1924; New York: Dial Press, 1924; St. Clair Shores, Mich.: Scholarly Press, 1970.
The Wayzgoose: A South African Satire. London: Jonathan Cape, 1928.
Poems. Paris: The Hours Press, 1930.
Adamastor. London: Faber and Faber, 1930; Westport, Conn.: Greenwood Press, 1971.
The Georgiad: A Satirical Fantasy in Verse. London: Boriswood, 1931.
Flowering Reeds. London: Boriswood, 1933.
Mithraic Emblems. London: Boriswood, 1936.
Flowering Rifle. London: Longmans, 1939; New York: Green and Co., 1939.
Sons of the Mistral. London: Faber and Faber, 1941, 1943, 1948, 1960.
Talking Bronco. London: Faber and Faber, 1946; Chicago: Henry Regnery, 1956.

PROSE

Wyndham Lewis. London: Chatto and Windus, 1932.
Taurine Provence. London: Desmond Harmsworth, 1932; Paris: Alyscamps Provencal Library, 1994.
The Mamba's Precipice. London: Frederick Muller, 1953; New York: J. Day Co., 1954. Children's story.
Portugal. London: Max Reinhardt, 1957; Chicago: Henry Regnery, 1958.

AUTOBIOGRAPHIES

Broken Record: Reminiscences. London: Boriswood, 1934; St. Clair Shores, Mich.: Scholarly Press, 1978.
Light on a Dark Horse. London: Hollis and Carter, 1951, 1969; Harmondsworth, U.K.: Penguin, 1971.

TRANSLATIONS BY CAMPBELL

The Poems of St. John of the Cross. London: Harvill Press; New York: Pantheon Books, 1951; New York: Grosset and Dunlop, 1967.
Baudelaire, Poems: A Translation of Les Fleurs du mal. London: Harvill Press, 1952.
Lorca: An Appreciation of His Poetry. Cambridge, U.K.: Bowes and Bowes, 1952; New York: Haskell House, 1970.

CRITICAL STUDIES

Alexander, Peter. *Roy Campbell: A Critical Biography.* Oxford, U.K.: Oxford University Press, 1982.

Kershaw, Alister, ed. and trans. *Salute to Roy Campbell.* Francestown, N.H.: Typographeum, 1984.

Lyle, Anna Campbell. *Poetic Justice: A Memoir of My Father, Roy Campbell.* Francestown, N.H.: Typographeum, 1986.

Povey, John. *Roy Campbell.* Boston: Twayne, 1977.

Pursglove, Glyn. "The Poetry of Roy Campbell: The Bull and the Crystal." In James Hogg, ed., *Outsiders: Roy Campbell, Peter Russell, William Oxley, Anthony L. Johnson.* Salzburg, Austria: Universitat Salzburg, 1989.

Smith, Rowland. *Lyric and Polemic: The Literary Personality of Roy Campbell.* Montreal: McGill-Queen's University Press, 1972.

Wright, David. *Roy Campbell.* London: Longmans, Green, 1961.

Albert Camus
1913–1960

JOHN FLETCHER

ONE OF THE most influential twentieth-century writers, Albert Camus was born in Algeria of French parents. He was thus what the French call a *pied noir* (black foot), a European settler in a predominantly Arab and Berber country. After a bitter struggle, Algeria won its independence from France in 1962. By then Camus was dead, but the conflict in his homeland cast a dark shadow over his final years. Even at the height of his international fame, he never forgot his origins: he remained a *pied noir* all his life. Although as a person of liberal political opinions Camus would have accepted Algerian independence, there is no doubt that he also would have regretted it and would have wished that such an outcome could have been avoided.

The attitude was condemned in his lifetime as cowardly ambivalence, but since his death opinions have changed. It is now widely agreed that independence was not the unalloyed triumph of justice over injustice but, rather, the substitution of a lesser injustice, the uprooting of the *pieds noirs*, for a greater injustice, the harsh treatment of the indigenous population. It is clear, too, that Algeria has had more than its fair share of problems as a sovereign state. The revolutionary oligarchy that came to power in 1962 pursued economic policies that made this potentially wealthy country, with its large reserves of natural gas, one of the poorer nations of North Africa, condemned to rely on emigration to siphon off excess labor. In France, the resulting increase in the number of Algerians led to severe racial tension and the rise of the Front National, a neofascist party that advocated the forcible repatriation of immigrants.

Camus, a man of the Left all his life, would have deplored the success of the Front National in France, just as he would have regretted the advance of its mirror image in Algeria, Islamic fundamentalism. Such polarization, in which intolerance and fanaticism have threatened human rights on both sides of the Mediterranean, would have appalled the liberal, humanist democrat that Camus was in every fiber of his being. During the Algerian War he felt sympathy for the motive common to the rebels and the *pieds noirs* — the desire for a homeland — but he underestimated the political nature of the conflict and its resulting bitterness. His perspective limited by his universalist humanism, he believed — or perhaps wished desperately to believe — that if only Algeria's underdevelopment, poverty, and lack of educational opportunity were tackled through systemic reform, then French, Arab, and Berber could live together in a confederation modeled after the German-French-

Italian union of Switzerland, with proportional representation in a parliament made up of members drawn from all sections of the community.

However, it was unrealistic to hope that Europeans and indigenous North Africans could live together as neighbors. French Algeria was a society of unofficial apartheid. Although in law all races were held to be equal—that is why Meursault is executed for murdering an Arab in *L'Étranger* (1942; *The Stranger*, also known as *The Outsider*)—the two communities lived separate lives. Integration had never been attempted; perhaps it was never a serious possibility. Thus, when the war of independence broke out, it could end in only one of two ways: in the defeat of the rebellion or in the expulsion of the *pieds noirs*.

It was the second of these possible outcomes that prevailed. Once the Algerian War passed into history, however, even if not every wound had been healed by the passing of the decades, intellectuals and writers on both sides of the Mediterranean agreed that the reinstatement of Camus the Algerian into North African life was overdue. The time had come, they believed, to consider renaming one of the thoroughfares in the capital city of Algiers "Albert Camus Avenue." Even if Camus did not find the "right" answers, they felt, he was nevertheless an idealist and a moralist who persistently asked the right questions. As Conor Cruise O'Brien has put it, "Camus both flinched from the realities of his position as a Frenchman of Algeria, and also explored with increasing subtlety and honesty the nature and consequences of his flinching" (p. 105).

LIFE

Albert Camus was born on 7 November 1913 at Mondovi near Bône (now Annaba) in eastern Algeria. His father, Lucien Auguste Camus, whose family originally came from Bordeaux in southwestern France, was working as a stock clerk for an Algiers wine shipper. The family of Albert's mother, Catherine Sintès Camus, had emigrated from the Spanish island of Minorca, which was once occupied by Moors from North Africa, so it is quite possible that Camus had Moorish (that is, Arab-Berber) blood. When Albert was born, Lucien and Catherine already had one son, also called Lucien, then aged three. Albert never got to know his father, who was drafted soon after his birth and died of wounds sustained at the Battle of the Marne in the early weeks of World War I.

As long as his father was able to support the family, they were not poor; they were respectable working-class people. Yet Catherine Camus was illiterate; she was also partially deaf and had a speech defect, which made her withdrawn and seem inarticulate. Albert Camus's feelings about her were complex. Later, in the context of the terrorist atrocities that racked Algeria, he said that if he had to opt between his mother and justice, he would choose her—in other words, if any harm came to her at the hands of the freedom fighters, he would back the forces opposing the independence movement. His remark, made to an Arab journalist at the Nobel Prize ceremony in Sweden, was at once misunderstood: it was claimed that his feelings about Algerian independence were hostile, whereas in fact they were more ambivalent than that. In this reference to his mother, he was merely stating the obvious, that blood is thicker than water.

At the same time, however, he was rather ashamed of her and carefully avoided bringing school friends to the house. In later life he was made all too aware by other members of the Paris intelligentsia that, unlike them, he was not of middle-class origin. The root of Camus's famous 1952 quarrel with the philosopher-writer Jean-Paul Sartre, for instance, lay in the fact that Sartre came from a comfortable background, whereas Camus had known real hardship: his widowed mother took on house-cleaning to support the family. Sartre, for example, would sermonize about poor whites in the Deep South of the United States on the basis of secondhand knowledge derived from American novels read in translation; Camus knew firsthand what it felt like to be the French equivalent of "white trash" and found Sartre's ignorant condescension patronizing.

Fortunately, by doing well at elementary school, he was able to escape the environment in which he was reared; he won a scholarship to the local *lycée* (elite high school). He was a keen soccer player and swimmer, but the onset of tuberculosis, a disease from which he never entirely recovered, curbed his sporting activities from 1930 onward. In 1933, he went on to study philosophy at the University of Algiers; he worked his way through college doing a variety of jobs. On 16 June 1934 he married Simone Hié, an upper-class woman about his own age, but the marriage failed, largely due to Simone's morphine addiction. They divorced in 1940, and she spent the rest of her life in and out of private clinics and rest homes.

In 1936, Camus submitted his master's thesis on the links between Christianity and Hellenism in the works of a fellow North African, Saint Augustine, and of the Alexandrian thinker Plotinus, but he failed the medical examination that would have allowed him to enter for the *agrégation*, an annual competition for a teaching post in the French higher education system. This missed opportunity was a major setback; he particularly wanted the job, since it would have left him sufficient free time for his writing.

As it was, he had to make a living in less convenient ways. He worked as a newspaper reporter by day and as a semiprofessional actor and theater director by night. In this capacity, he took a leading role in setting up the Workers' Theater movement in Algiers and with three friends wrote a play about a

Spanish miners' strike, *Révolte dans les Asturies* (1936; *Revolt in the Asturias*). It was banned by the authorities, who were fearful that parallels could be drawn between the treatment of workers in Spain and the exploitation of Arabs in Algeria.

The Workers' Theater proved to be of great importance in Camus's life. It revealed to him his true vocation, that of a writer-actor-manager. From then onward, he always felt happiest rehearsing a play and adjourning afterward to a café for supper with the company until late into the night. Unlike most French writers, he was not comfortable in the society of other intellectuals: he preferred the sickly odor of sweat and greasepaint backstage to the choking fug of pipe smoke in rented rooms.

At the outbreak of World War II in 1939, Camus tried to enlist but was turned down again on medical grounds. In 1940 he married Francine Faure; they were soon afterward separated because of the war, and they remained apart for much of this period. Their twin children, Catherine and Jean, were born on 5 September 1945. While Francine stayed behind in Algeria, Camus was living in German-occupied France, working first for the daily *Paris-Soir* and then joining the resistance as editor and leader-writer of the clandestine newspaper *Combat*. It was dangerous work; anyone connected with illegal publishing was liable to be deported or even summarily executed by the Germans.

Fear did not stop Camus from writing, though. On the contrary, he had already published two volumes of essays, *L'Envers et l'endroit* (Betwixt and between) in 1937 and *Noces* (Nuptials) in 1939. In 1942 *The Stranger* brought him instant fame. It caught the spirit of the times, yet it remains relevant to this day. It has become one of the most influential novels of all time and a worldwide best-seller; by 1992, the fiftieth anniversary of its publication, it had sold a staggering six million copies.

After the liberation of France in 1944, Camus continued to write for *Combat* but left it three years later to work as a reader for the publishing firm of Gallimard in Paris. In 1947 *La Peste* (*The Plague*) appeared; it too became a best-seller. At the same time, Camus was doing well in the theater; his play *Caligula* had been a runaway success in 1945. He also proved to be a brilliant stage adapter of the works of others; his version of William Faulkner's *Requiem for a Nun* was the hit of the 1956 Paris drama season. It was through the theater that he met the great love of his life, the actress Maria Casarès. She ended their affair when his second wife rejoined him in October 1944, but it resumed in June 1948 and continued until his death.

Much has been written about Camus's attitude toward the opposite sex. He had many female friends with whom his relations were platonic, but he also had many lovers. He wrote about the legendary seducer Don Juan and was aware of his own tendency to womanize. Like Don Juan, he was very attentive to women; but, also like his hero, he could be selfish, predatory, exploitative, and manipulative. Insofar as Camus seems to have loved any woman, that woman was Maria Casarès.

He was enabled by his growing international reputation to travel widely on lecture tours, making a major visit to the United States in 1946. His fame reached a peak in 1957 when he was awarded the Nobel Prize in literature, the youngest French writer ever to receive it. In some ways, the prize did him a disservice. Paris intellectuals who envied him his literary, theatrical, and amatory successes were quick to sneer at the "lay saint" that they claimed he was turning into.

The 1956 publication of *La Chute* (*The Fall*), the fictional confession of a man whose act of self-accusation licenses him to sit in judgment on others, had given some credence to the charge. Stung by a whispering campaign that he had "sold out" to reactionary capitalism by embracing the sort of flabby humanism that the Nobel Prize was thought by many to reward, Camus started work on a major project, an epic novel about French Algeria to be called *La Premier Homme* (*The First Man*). It was, he said, to be his *War and Peace*, the work that would prove to his detractors that he really was the great writer that the Nobel committee had judged him to be.

He never completed the work (although the unfinished draft was published by his daughter Catherine in 1994). On 4 January 1960 he was on his way back to Paris from the country, where he had been working on the book. The car in which he was traveling swerved off the road and hit a tree; he was killed instantly. With an irony that this least stuffy of men would have savored, he had in his pocket the return half of a round-trip rail ticket; but because of a date with a new girlfriend, he had accepted the offer of a lift in order to be in Paris with her twenty-four hours earlier than his wife expected him. That he did not make it to the secret rendezvous would have struck Camus as grimly comic. Women had literally been the death of this inveterate womanizer; he might well have thought it served him right.

He was buried at Lourmarin in southern France, where he had bought a house with the Nobel Prize money. His Nobel winnings marked the first time in his life he had possessed a large enough sum to buy a house. The poor boy from a working-class district of Algiers had come a long way; it is a pity that he did not live to enjoy the rewards of his achievement.

ESSAYS

Most of Camus's nonfiction writing about Algeria is contained in the collections of essays already mentioned, *L'Envers et l'endroit* and *Noces*, and in *L'Été* (*1954*; *Summer*) and *Actuelles III: Chroniques algériennes, 1939–1958* (*1958*; Algerian journalism). His essays reflect a lost world, French Algeria, and if nothing else are of considerable historical interest for analyzing the dilemmas of liberal-minded intellectuals settled in the colony, living astride what O'Brien calls "the cultural frontier" (p. 27).

As O'Brien points out, Camus's position after the rebellion broke out in 1954 was "one of extreme intellectual and emotional difficulty and tension." In his philosophical writings, he had meditated upon

> freedom, justice, violence, and revolt in abstract terms, and had asserted principles that he presented as both of fundamental importance and of universal application. He never altogether abandoned this language and he continued to write about politics in the tone of a severe moralist. Yet, his actual positions were political and partisan.
>
> (p. 91)

While there is no doubting the genuineness and sincerity of Camus's liberal views on the Algerian question, the trouble was that once the rebellion broke out and atrocities of ever increasing savagery were committed on both sides, liberal measures were no longer a solution to the conflict — if they ever had been.

The radical solution to Algeria's ethnic conflict would have been very hard for Camus. The victorious Algerian rebels massacred many thousands of *harkis* (Muslims serving in the French forces), expelled the *pied noir* population, and changed place names so that only the settlers' family tombs and ornate cemeteries remained to show that Algeria had once been French. While his own relations with members of the indigenous population were excellent, he never forgot that his forebears lay in those cemeteries. He felt closer, he said, to an Arab farmer or a Kabyle shepherd than to a shopkeeper of northern France. He believed that there was a specific North African–French culture and that its "particular contribution," as Camus's friend Roger Grenier explained, was "a sense of spareness, of reserve, and also the sense of friendship, of human brotherhood" (Lottman, p. 410).

He was always willing to write in defense of Muslims being tried in French courts, to protest against police brutality, and to denounce what he called in 1953 "this ancient conspiracy of silence and of cruelty which uproots Algerian workers, keeps them in miserable slums, and makes them desperate to the point of violence" (Lottman, pp. 526–527). The remark turned out to be prophetic: a year later pent-up resentment against oppression led to armed insurrection.

Camus's position in the essays and journalism about Algeria can be summed up in a remark he made to a publishing colleague in December 1958, shortly before his death.

> I am suspect to the nationalists of both sides. I am blamed by one side for not being sufficiently ... patriotic. For the other side I'm too much so. ... What too many Arabs don't understand is that I love [Algeria] as a Frenchman who loves Arabs, and wants them to be at home in Algeria, without himself having to feel a stranger there because of that.
>
> (Lottman, p. 639)

It was not an ignoble aspiration. Unfortunately for Camus and his fellow *pieds noirs*, it was not an option that was available in 1958 and probably never had been. Tragically, as is so often the case in human history, no amount of goodwill and generous sentiment — and Camus's Algerian essays are full of both — could disguise the fact that there was no possibility for two different ethnic groups to continue sharing the same territory. There was no question of the majority indigenous population leaving, so it was the minority *pieds noirs* who had to go. It was the lesser evil; France and the whole community of nations came to terms with it. But Camus was a man of absolutes; he would never have accepted such a compromise. It was therefore just as well, perhaps, that he was never asked to try. The volumes of Algerian essays, however, remain, "because they are not relics of a dead culture but the raw material of Camus's inspiration ... depict[ing] his vision in its stark simplicity — the mother, the sea and the desert" (McCarthy, p. 329).

THE STRANGER

Perhaps the greatest of all novels to come out of Africa, *The Stranger*, begun sometime in 1938 and finished in May 1940, was published in 1942. The narrator, Meursault, works as a clerk in an Algiers shipping office. Of French descent, he had once been a student and lived in Paris, he tells us, but after he dropped out he realized "none of it really mattered" (p. 41): all he is now concerned about is living the life of the senses to the full, especially by swimming in the warm sea and sunbathing on the wide sandy beaches near the city. In order to understand the novel, however, it is important to appreciate that Meursault is an intellectual, albeit one who claims to be no longer interested in things of the mind.

When his story begins, he learns that his mother has died at an old people's home, some fifty miles inland from Algiers, and he gets permission from his boss to attend the funeral. He borrows a black tie and armband from a friend and has to run to catch the bus. As a result of the heat and the glare from the sun, he sleeps most of the way. When he arrives, he is expected to follow local French custom and watch over the body all night. From this point on, he commits a number of social blunders that will later be remembered and used in evidence against him in a murder trial. He refuses the janitor's offer to unscrew the coffin lid so that he can pay his last respects to his mother. During the vigil he accepts a cup of coffee and lights a cigarette. Later he dozes off. The next day at the funeral he cannot remember his mother's age. He sheds no tears for her; on the contrary, suffering greatly from the heat and the glare, he is anxious to get back to Algiers as quickly as possible.

After returning home and sleeping soundly for twelve hours, he goes to the beach (it is Saturday), where he runs into Marie, a typist who once worked in his office but with whom he had lost touch. They play about in the water together; when they get dressed, she notices his black tie and is taken aback that he was so recently bereaved. However, she agrees to accompany him to the movies, where they see a funny film. They cuddle and kiss, and she goes back with him to his place.

So far, Meursault has done nothing more reprehensible than showing a lack of concern over his mother's death. Now, however, he gets involved in something considerably more serious: his neighbor, a pimp called Raymond, asks him to write a letter to an Arab girlfriend, whom Raymond has beaten up because he suspects her of having cheated on him. Meursault is an educated person to whom letter writing comes easily, whereas Raymond finds it difficult. Meursault is not sure why he agrees to do the pimp's dirty work for him; it just seems to Meursault that he has no particular reason to refuse. He says repeatedly that because nothing matters anyway, there is no compelling reason why he should do one thing rather than another. But his claim is hardly convincing. Leaving aside the question of morality, it is the merest common sense that in such a society it is dangerous to side with a pimp in a quarrel with a woman of another ethnic community. At the very least, Meursault should have realized that the girl would have brothers or cousins and that Arab men do not take insults to their womenfolk lightly.

Ever since the novel was published, critics, misled perhaps by the utterly convincing first-person narrator, have tended to confuse Meursault with Camus. But if Meursault seems careless of Muslim susceptibilities, Camus was not. He knew only too well that one humiliates Arab women at one's peril. By agreeing to write in his own hand a letter to Raymond's girlfriend, Meursault was being launched — by Camus, that is — upon a collision course with destiny.

Matters come quickly to a head. When Raymond's girlfriend, enticed by the letter, returns to Raymond, he so savagely attacks her that a neighbor calls in the police; they let Raymond off with a warning after Meursault testifies in his favor. He invites Meursault to bring Marie to join him and friends for lunch the following Sunday at the friends' chalet. Before hanging up, he warns Meursault that a group of Arabs, one of whom is the battered woman's brother, has been shadowing Raymond and that Meursault should be on his guard.

The Arabs follow Meursault and Raymond to the beach. A fight breaks out, and Raymond is slashed with a knife. After having his wounds dressed, Raymond, armed with a revolver, returns with Meursault to the beach. Meursault takes the revolver from Raymond to prevent Raymond, who is in an ugly mood, from shooting first; together they confront the Arabs, who retreat behind a rock. Seeming satisfied, Raymond talks of catching the bus home as he returns to the chalet with Meursault.

Meursault does not rejoin the others, however. The terms in which he explains this act are significant: "To stay or go, it amounted to the same thing" (p. 57). In claiming that it does not matter much what he decides to do, he tries to convince us that the outcome turns on something as contingent as the throw of a die. This is of course nonsense. He could have gone back to town with the others. He chooses instead—chooses, because the action is not automatic—to walk back to the rock. This time he finds only one Arab, who draws his knife.

Throughout this scene on the beach, Meursault has stressed how intense the glare was and how much the heat tormented him. Now he seeks to lay the blame for what happens next not on himself, naturally, nor even on the Arab, but on the North African sun, whose light "shoots off the steel" and is "like a long flashing blade cutting" at his forehead (p. 59). At the same time the moisture trapped in his eyebrows pours down into his eyes, and the salty sweat blinds him: it was, he says, "a scorching blade that slashed at my eyelashes and stabbed at my stinging eyes" (p. 59). Then "the trigger gave"—the impersonal construction is revealing—and before he knew what was happening, he says, he had fired four times more into the Arab's lifeless body. Those four unnecessary shots were, he says, "like knocking four quick times on the door of unhappiness" (p. 59).

Far from feeling that he was in any way at fault, Meursault presents the whole incident as a ghastly accident. But at his trial the prosecution has no difficulty in securing a conviction for murder in the first degree, for which the penalty, in French dominions at that time, was public execution by guillotine. The novel ends as Meursault, defiant as ever, hopes that people will turn out in large numbers and greet his death with "cries of hate" (p. 123).

It is sometimes said that the novel is unrealistic, because in colonial Algeria no European would have been executed for killing a member of the indigenous population, just as formerly in the Deep South no white would have been hanged for the death of a black person. This is true, up to a point, but Meursault makes things difficult even for a racially biased criminal justice system.

He is shown to be a thoroughly bad sort: first, he fails to shed tears at his mother's funeral. Worse, at her wake he smokes and drinks coffee (not black, to keep him alert, but coffee with cream, for pleasure); the very next day he sees a funny film with a girl with whom he then goes to bed. Second, he befriends a member of the criminal fraternity and condones the man's savage attacks on a defenseless woman. Third, he consciously takes possession of the crook's gun and, having returned to the scene of an earlier confrontation, shoots a man dead—admittedly an Arab—who is armed only with a knife.

Thus far Meursault might have been able to argue that he was provoked or had acted in self-defense, the usual plea in racist murders. But he undermines any plausibility that a claim of provocation might have had by his final and worst offense: he empties the revolver into his victim, and only a sadist does that.

Even in French Algeria, where few Muslims had the right to vote, the authorities could not turn a blind eye to a premeditated, callous murder, even if the victim was an Arab. After all, the French Republic's motto, "*Liberté—Egalité—Fraternité*" was carved over the portal of every public building. Even if the philosophy behind the motto was honored more in breach than in observance, it could not simply be ignored. There is thus nothing unrealistic about the outcome of Meursault's trial: he is properly convicted on the evidence.

And yet the reader feels very sorry for him. It is clear that Camus has a lot of sympathy for him, too. Meursault, in Camus's portrayal, refuses to lie. He does so because even though lies make life simpler, he does not wish to make life simpler; at the risk of getting into difficulties, he prefers saying what he thinks and doing just what he feels like doing. So when, for example, Marie asks him if he loves her, he replies that he doesn't think so, even though a noncommittal reply would have upset her less. Or, to take another example, since he finds chatting with Raymond interesting, he does not see why he ought to shun him as the other tenants in the building do.

Society, Camus shows, feels threatened by people who refuse to conceal their true feelings. During the investigation Meursault is asked to declare, in time-honored fashion, that he regrets his crime. He replies, honestly, that he feels more annoyance about it than true regret. What he means is that he wishes it had not happened—because it brought to an abrupt end a life in which he had been happy—and that he was so annoyed at himself for doing such a stupid thing he fired those damning four extra shots. This candor tilts the judgment against him: it is, in fact, the shade of difference between "annoyance" and "regret" that sends him to the scaffold.

It is a tribute to Camus's artistry that generations of readers have cried "not fair!" as they close the book. But a cool assessment must conclude that it is perfectly fair that Meursault be found guilty on the evidence laid before the court. Instead of remaining silent, he could have spoken up in his own defense. He could have declared that he was sorry; he could have offered compensation to the victim's family. Any of these actions might have saved him, but he is too stiff-necked to undertake them. It is a young man's novel—Camus was not yet thirty when he wrote it—and young readers the world over respond instinctively to it, because people of that age do not, on the whole, enjoy apologizing either. So thanks to Camus's literary skill in deflecting attention from the gravity of the crime, Meursault has become a kind of hero to them.

But this alone would not explain the book's phenomenal success. A deeper reason, as O'Brien suggests, is that the story probes the increasing anguish in the minds of western people over the west's relations with the third world. The choice of an Arab as victim is deliberate, because one symbolically kills—that is, one seeks through metaphor to eliminate—what makes one feel guilty. In shooting the Arab, and even more in firing four shots more into his already lifeless body, Meursault is expressing the unconscious urge of westerners to blot out the cause of their bad conscience. A similar psychological trait is found in child abusers, who beat all the more viciously the infant whose screams exacerbate their self-loathing. Camus's short story "L'Hôte" ("The Guest") takes up again the theme of the Arab as living reproach to the colonist.

THE PLAGUE

Like *The Stranger*, *The Plague* (1947) is set in Algeria, this time in the city of Oran, hometown of Camus's second wife. Whereas *The Stranger* presents a realistic picture of Algiers as a hot, bustling capital blessed with sandy beaches close at hand, the setting of the next novel is largely incidental. Oran had a large Arab population, but Arabs are absent in the book. Their curiously deserted streets, and even the fronts of their houses, do appear, but more in the nature of a backdrop. The story and its characters are exclusively European, and the action could just as plausibly have been set in Argentina, for instance. Camus knew Oran from visiting his wife's family.

The story of *The Plague* is simple. The admirably understated opening sets the tone: "When leaving his surgery on the morning of 16 April, Dr. Bernard Rieux felt something soft under his foot. It was a dead rat lying in the middle of the landing" (p. 7). The janitor in his building is outraged; there are no rats in his well-maintained premises, he insists, so some youngster must have brought this one in from the street to play a trick on him. But it is no schoolboy prank. That evening, Dr. Rieux sees another rat. This time it is still alive — barely:

> It moved uncertainly, and its fur was sopping wet. The animal stopped and seemed to be trying to get its balance, moved forward again towards the doctor, halted again, then spun round on itself with a little squeal and fell on its side. Its mouth was slightly open and blood was spurting from it.
>
> (pp. 7–8)

Rats are soon dying in large numbers, and at first the inhabitants of the town are glad to see the back of them. But when several humans — all Europeans, since no Arabs are depicted — fall ill and die, the terrible truth dawns: their city is being visited by that scourge of humankind from time immemorial, bubonic plague.

Oran is sealed off to prevent the plague from spreading to other towns and cities, as used to happen routinely in the Middle Ages until medical science identified the carrier, a flea that feeds on both rats and human beings. In addition, the townspeople are required to practice extreme cleanliness, in particular to

destroy as many fleas as possible with insecticide and to disinfect sickrooms thoroughly. Thanks to measures such as these, the plague gradually abates and the quarantine can at last be lifted. There is, understandably, great rejoicing at this deliverance. But the novel ends on a note as eloquently restrained as that of the beginning:

> And, indeed, as he listened to the cries of joy rising from the town, Rieux remembered that such joy is always imperiled... that the plague bacillus never dies or disappears for good; that it can lie dormant for years and years in furniture and linen-chests; that it bides its time in bedrooms, cellars, trunks, and bookshelves; and that perhaps the day would come when, for the bane and the enlightening of men, it roused up its rats again and sent them forth to die in a happy city.
>
> (p. 278)

It is obvious that a tale as plain and straightforward as this must have a deeper meaning. *The Plague* is a fable: Oran's bubonic fever epidemic is a metaphor for the occupation of France by the Germans between 1940 and 1944. As the citizens of Oran suffered from the plague, French people were oppressed by the Nazi invader, but in both cases, Camus suggests, they were made wiser and better by the experience — ennobled indeed, with the dignity of their humanity enhanced. They had merited what the novel calls "the proud egoism and the injustice of happy people" (p. 268), and "it was only right that those whose desires are limited to man and his humble yet formidable love should enter, if only now and then, into their reward" (p. 271). On this level the novel is undoubtedly convincing, a "sermon of hope," in the words of Conor Cruise O'Brien, conveying a "deep sense of the joy of life," a tale in which "the almost unremitting grimness of the narrative is subtly transformed by a current of dry, crisp gaiety in the prose" (p. 58).

But, as O'Brien goes on to point out, a mere seven years after the publication of *The*

Plague, the "rats came up to die," metaphorically speaking, "in all the cities of Algeria" (p. 59). The armed insurrection that had been lying dormant for decades erupted from the very quarter never mentioned in the novel, the slums inhabited by the indigenous population. "The realization of this adds a new addition to the sermon," O'Brien concludes; "the source of the plague is what we pretend is not there, and the preacher [Camus] is already, without knowing it, infected by the plague" (p. 59).

In other words, Camus may have intended consciously to write a sermon in fable form about the way the French bore their sufferings at the hands of the German invaders, but unconsciously he was writing the obituary of French Algeria. Far from limiting his achievement, to discern his unconscious project is to see the enhanced impact of his novel.

THE FALL

The last novel to be published in Camus's lifetime is set not in sunny North Africa but in foggy Amsterdam. As befits a book with such a gloomy setting, it is about guilt. Clamence, a retired Paris attorney, corners strangers in the Mexico-City, a sleazy bar in a run-down district of Amsterdam, and pours out his confession to them. His underlying purpose is to solicit their indictment, secure in the assurance that his act of self-accusation licenses him to sit in judgment upon others. He does all the talking: his interlocutors' rare answers can only be surmised from his summaries of and response to them. His technique is always the same: he practices public confession at length and in depth, accusing himself first and foremost. Not, he makes clear, in a histrionic manner — there is no vulgar beating of the chest — but subtly, insidiously, so that when his self-portrait is complete, he springs a surprise on his interlocutor (with whom the reader inevitably identifies): the portrait is turned around and suddenly becomes a mirror in which the hapless drinker on the neighboring bar stool no longer sees Clamence, but rather himself.

The reader is reminded more than once of Samuel Taylor Coleridge's Ancient Mariner (in his *Lyrical Ballads*, 1798), who buttonholes the unfortunate wedding guest and forces him to listen to the haunting recital of the disasters caused by the Mariner's reckless killing of the albatross. It is unlikely that Camus drew on this source, but his novel does have a disturbing archetypal quality and offers proof — if proof is needed — that he was a restlessly innovative genius who was by no means limited in his choice of subject matter to the land of his birth.

THE FIRST MAN

Camus's last novel was left tantalizingly incomplete at his death, but enough of it survives to show that in this book he was working at the height of his powers. It is set, like all his major fiction, in the North Africa of his youth, and indeed the principal theme is the nature of autobiography. It tells the story of a fatherless boy — obviously Camus himself — growing up in a poor, white suburb of colonial Algiers, who is picked out for special attention at primary school by a devoted teacher, and wins a scholarship to the lycée. This success opens the door to his escape from poverty but spells the end of innocence and the carefree happiness of childhood.

Another theme is the boy's search for the father he had lost in World War I, although the teacher replaces the father to some extent. When the boy becomes a man, he goes in pilgrimage to Saint-Brieuc in northwestern France. In the town's cemetery he finds his father's grave and is shocked to realize that the soldier buried there was actually younger when he died than the hero is now.

The most significant theme, however, is the march of history. The "first man" of the title is the settler who becomes so rooted in the land he farms that he loses his original identity. He belongs to a new race, no longer wholly European and not yet fully African. The tragedy the book intimates is the expulsion of this new tribe from its adopted homeland, just as the first man, Adam, was driven from the Garden of Eden. One of the most powerful passages tells of a farmer who has been ordered off his landholding by the French army for his own protection because the rebels control the district. Before he goes, he drives his tractor for days up and down his vineyard systematically uprooting the vines he has tended so lovingly in the past. Having, as he sees it, made a desert bloom, he is determined to leave a desert behind him.

Such people, Camus makes clear, do not hate the Arabs. If anything they are closer to them than they are to the French administration, which they feel has betrayed them. There is solidarity between people of both races who have endured the heat of Algeria's summers and the drenching rain of its winters. When the hero of the novel is born, the father (who later dies in a military hospital) takes shelter outside with an old Arab:

> He could feel [the Arab's] shoulder against him, and he smelled the smoke given off by his clothes; he felt the rain falling on the sack over their two heads. "It's a boy," he said. . . . "God be praised," answered the Arab. "You are a chief."
>
> (p. 15)

As the baby's first cries reach the men outside in the rain, the "immense almost uninhabited land" casts its spell indiscriminately over both of them. European and Arab are — however briefly — united in awesome contemplation of the miracle of human birth, which has just been enacted behind them, and in male solidarity over the arrival of a boy child ("you are a chief" would be better translated "that means you are a real man").

Camus's last book is brilliantly written, with all the spontaneity and freshness of his earliest works. It is also a glowing tribute to North Africa, where the light and warmth of the climate make childhood unforgettable and even poverty bearable and where — if things had turned out differently — the "first men" could have gone on living in peace and harmony with their neighbors, the native population.

SHORT STORIES

Camus saw all his works as so many "efforts at depersonalization" (Lottman, p. 458), none more so than the stories collected in *L'Exil et le royaume* (1957; *Exile and the Kingdom*). Those short stories set in Algeria are particularly fine.

"La Femme adultère" ("The Adulterous Woman") takes place in the Sahara Desert, in an oasis town 270 miles south of Algiers called Laghouat, which Camus visited in the winter of 1952. The heroine of the story, Janine, is traveling with her boor of a husband. He feels uncomfortable in this territory where few Europeans penetrate, and when he retires to bed early, she goes off to explore the town by herself. Janine has no hostility toward the indigenous population; in fact, her feelings are quite the reverse. But it is not with a local man that she commits adultery; it is with the terrible beauty of the African night, which gathers her up in its arms and makes love to her as she has never been made love to before:

> Each time Janine opened a little more to the night. . . . Her whole belly pressed against the parapet as she strained toward the moving sky; she was merely waiting for her fluttering heart to calm down and establish silence within her. The last stars of the constellation dropped their clusters a little lower on the desert horizon and were still. Then, with unbearable gentleness, the water of the night began to fill Janine, drowned the cold, rose gradually from the hidden core of her being and overflowed in wave after wave, rising up even to her mouth full of moans. The next moment, the whole sky was stretched out over her, fallen on her back on the cold earth.
>
> (p. 31)

This remarkable story encapsulates Camus's own love affair with Algeria, expressed in overtly erotic terms but skillfully depersonalized by the device of ascribing the experience to a female character. Camus's essays put great stress on the physical beauty of the country, its mountains, desert, farmland and vineyards, beaches and sea. Reading "The Adulterous Woman" in light of the essays shows that when Camus said he loved Algeria, he was not using the word lightly.

A more disturbing, less upbeat story in the *Exile and the Kingdom* collection is "L'Hôte" ("The Guest"). Daru, a French schoolteacher in the Algerian interior, acquires an unwelcome guest when the local French police chief brings an Arab accused of murder to stay at Daru's house overnight, with orders that the prisoner be sent on to jail the next day. Playing the role of the "good" colonist who respects local customs (hospitality is a sacred duty in the Islamic world), Daru gives the Arab food, but at the same time he feels annoyance that his guest has placed him in a dilemma. Should Daru carry sympathy with the indigenous population to the extent of helping the man escape? Or should he behave like a good official—teachers are public servants in France—and deliver the prisoner to the authorities? In the end he sits on the fence. He leaves the decision to the Arab, who, conditioned by generations of colonial obedience, does not make a dash for it, but dutifully tramps off to prison.

The story ends with Daru returning to his classroom, where he finds scrawled on the blackboard a death threat, "You handed over our brother: you will pay" (p. 109). His well-meaning gesture has not been understood by the guerrillas, who see it simply as treachery. Camus himself was familiar with the situation of the intellectual who wants to do the right thing but who ends up assailed on all sides, at best being upbraided for sitting on the fence, and at worst being accused of betraying the cause.

Turning from this chilling inscription, Daru takes a last look "at the sky, the plateau, and beyond, the invisible land stretching all the way to the sea" (p. 109). The last sentence is especially poignant: "In this vast country which he had loved so much, he was alone" (p. 109). Camus chose the past perfect "had loved" in the story's last sentence after some hesitation—he first wrote "which remained his only *patrie*" (native land, mother country). It shows that the final version was, as Roger Quilliot has argued, both "a renunciation and a farewell" (O'Brien, p. 86). Like Daru, Camus could not throw in his lot with either the indigenous or the *pied noir* communities, so, just like his hero, found himself rejected by both sides, a man without a *patrie*.

CONCLUSION

Although not entirely devoid of personal happiness, Camus's existence was on the whole a tragic one. He came from a background that in material terms was poor, even deprived. It was also largely loveless. There has been considerable speculation about Camus's relations with his silent, illiterate mother. He continued to visit her at regular intervals, even though he lived in Paris and she in Algiers, so in that sense he loved her in a dutiful way. Although Camus should never be confused with his heroes, there are moments when the fiction clearly conveys his own feelings. This is nowhere more true than in *The Stranger*, when Meursault explains why his mother was, "all things considered," better off being looked after in an old people's home than living with him:

When she was at home with me, Maman used to spend all her time following me with her eyes, not saying anything. For the first few days at the home she cried a lot. But that was because she wasn't used to it. A few months later and she would have cried if she'd been taken out. She was used to it. That's partly why I didn't go there much this past year. And also because it took up my Sunday. . . .

(p. 5)

This may seem callous, but in fact Meursault is, as usual, being honest. He and his mother had little in common, and she needed a nurse, something that on his modest salary he could not afford. In the home, on the other hand, not only did she receive proper medical attention, she even formed new friendships and felt able to start life again. "Nobody," says Meursault, and Camus probably thought so too, "nobody had the right to cry over her" (p. 122).

What effect Camus's relations with his mother had on his marriages and love affairs later is a matter for speculation, but it is difficult to avoid the conclusion that his compulsive womanizing and two failed marriages were somehow connected with his inability to share with Catherine Camus his interest in literature, philosophy, and art. It is revealing that Meursault refers to his mother as *maman*, a child's term corresponding to "mummy" or "mom" in English; clearly, he had never rejected her. He had merely grown apart from her; but at the end, when he himself faces death, he feels close to her again.

As Patrick McCarthy explains, given the emotional and material poverty of his childhood, and the unsatisfactory nature of his adult relationships (with the exception of the affair with Maria Casarès), Camus's life after the initial triumph of the publication of *The Stranger* has been "seen as an exile from Algeria and as a string of failures" (p. 7). Algeria was a particularly painful subject for him: it "remained present, as a lost dream of innocence and as an insoluble and tragic problem," says McCarthy, who goes on to point out that "Camus never went beyond Algeria: however much he changed, he remained an unrepentant *pied-noir*" (p. 163).

He was trapped between the terrorists of the independence movement and the torturers of the French army, both up to their necks in what McCarthy calls "the monotony of cruelty," which, as someone committed to nonviolence, Camus found completely abhorrent (McCarthy, p. 291). As a result, McCarthy

observes, "French Algeria, which had offered him instincts, passions and happiness, however tangled with poverty and prejudice, almost destroyed him along with itself" (p. 328).

If Camus was at odds with the French intellectual establishment over Algeria, he was a loner even in the way he looked. In appearance—and appearances matter a lot in literary Paris—he did not look the way an author is supposed to look; if anything, he struck people as being more like a rather charming, handsome garage mechanic. No wonder that his closest friends remained the men he had known in adolescence, and no wonder that, however unrealistically, he looked back from the complicated Paris of the 1950s to the Algiers of the 1930s as a golden age, the paradise—celebrated lyrically in the Algerian essays—that he felt he had lost beyond recall.

So what remains of the great African writer Albert Camus? If nothing else, an African novel that never grows old. *The Stranger* reaches two hundred thousand new readers every year among people whose parents were not even born when the book was published; this continually renewed interest is unlikely to flag in the years to come. What McCarthy and others have seen as the novel's "irony, ambiguity, and understatement" (p. 329), along with Camus's admirably terse style, have established it as a classic for all time.

Summing up the importance of this author can best be left to another great writer who had quarreled with him. When news reached a stunned Paris that Camus had been killed on the northbound main highway to the city, Jean-Paul Sartre set aside any lingering feelings of resentment he might have been harboring and penned this magnificent tribute:

He represented in this century, and against History, the present-day heir of that long line of moralists whose works constitute what is perhaps most original in French letters. His stubborn humanism, strict and pure, austere and sensual, delivered uncertain combat against the massive and deformed events of the day. But inversely, by the unexpectedness of his refusals, he reaffirmed, at the heart of our era, against the Machiavelians [*sic*], against the golden calf of realism, the existence of the moral act.

(*France-Observateur,* 7 January 1960)

Selected Bibliography

BIBLIOGRAPHY

Roeming, Robert F. *Camus: A Bibliography.* Madison: University of Wisconsin Press, 1968.

COLLECTED WORKS

Théâtre, récits, nouvelles. Paris: Gallimard, 1962.
Essais. Paris: Gallimard, 1965.

SELECTED WORKS

L'Envers et l'endroit. Algiers, Algeria: Charlot, 1937.
Noces. Algiers, Algeria: Charlot, 1939.
L'Étranger. Paris: Gallimard, 1942.
La Peste. Paris: Gallimard, 1947.
La Chute. Paris: Gallimard, 1956.
L'Exil et le royaume, nouvelles. Paris: Gallimard, 1957.
Actuelles III: Chroniques algériennes, 1939–1958. Paris: Gallimard, 1958.
Le Premier Homme. Paris: Gallimard, 1994.

TRANSLATIONS

The Stranger. Trans. by Stuart Gilbert. New York: Knopf, 1946. Trans. by Joseph Laredo. New York: Knopf, 1988. Publ. as *The Outsider.* London: Hamish Hamilton, 1982.
The Plague. Trans. by Stuart Gilbert. New York: Knopf, 1948.
The Fall. Trans. by Justin O'Brien. New York: Knopf, 1957.
Exile and the Kingdom. Trans. by Justin O'Brien. New York: Knopf, 1958.
The First Man. Trans. by David Hapgood. New York: Knopf, 1995.

BIOGRAPHICAL AND CRITICAL STUDIES

Ellison, David R. *Understanding Albert Camus.* Columbia: University of South Carolina Press, 1990.
Fitch, Brian. The Fall: *A Matter of Guilt.* New York: Twayne, 1995.
Girard, René. "Camus's Stranger Retired." In *PMLA* 79 (December 1964).
Goldstein, R. P. Jacques. "Camus et la Bible." In *Albert Camus,* no. 4 (1971).
Guérin, Jeanyves, ed. *Camus et la politique: Actes du colloque de Nanterre, 5–7 juin 1985.* Paris: L'Harmattan, 1986.
King, Adele, ed. *Camus's* L'Étranger: *Fifty Years On.* Basingstoke, U.K.: Macmillan, 1992.
Lottman, Herbert R. *Albert Camus: A Biography.* London: Weidenfeld and Nicolson, 1979; New York: Doubleday, 1979.
McCarthy, Patrick. *Camus: A Critical Study of His Life and Work.* London: Hamish Hamilton, 1982.
O'Brien, Conor Cruise. *Albert Camus of Europe and Africa.* London: Fontana/Collins, 1970.
Rhein, Phillip H. *Albert Camus.* Revised ed. Boston: Twayne, 1989.
Suther, Judith D., ed. *Essays on Camus's* Exile and the Kingdom. University, Miss.: Romance Monographs, 1981.
Tarrow, Susan. *Exile from the Kingdom: A Political Rereading of Albert Camus.* University: University of Alabama Press, 1985.
Thody, Philip. *Albert Camus: 1913–1960.* London: Hamish Hamilton, 1961; New York: Macmillan, 1962.

John Pepper Clark
1935–

OSITA OKAGBUE

JOHN PEPPER CLARK was born John Pepper Clark-Bekederemo in 1935 in Kiagbodo in the western Niger Delta region of Nigeria. His father, Chief Clark Fuludu Bekederemo, was an Ijọ, and his mother, Poro Amakashe Adomi Clark, was an Urhobo princess. Educated at Government College in Ughelli, he went on to study English at University College, Ibadan (now University of Ibadan), where he earned a bachelor of arts with honors in 1960. After university, Clark became a Parvin fellow at Princeton University and a research fellow at the Institute of African Studies at Ibadan. He later taught at the University of Lagos and retired as a professor of English in 1980. In 1964, Clark married Ebun Odutola, an Ijebu Yoruba and a professor at the University of Lagos. They have three daughters and a son. In 1982 Clark set up the PEC (Pepper and Ebun Clark) Repertory Theatre in Lagos and was still its artistic director in the mid 1990s.

Clark, who was born of an interethnic marriage and is himself married to a Yoruba, seems to be the ideal Nigerian. This may partly explain his support for the Nigerian state to remain united while the country approached a civil war in the mid 1960s. The crises began with riots in the wake of the elections in the Western Region of Nigeria; the rioting, combined with the corruption and graft of the central and regional governments, brought the nation to the brink of catastrophe. This state of unrest, it is believed, led five majors to stage the first military coup d'état on 15 January 1966. The coup was only partially successful but established Igbos (or Ibos, one of three major ethnic groups in Nigeria) as leaders. However, following the ascension of Lieutenant Colonel Yakubu Gowon to the head of state, what appeared to be a planned and systematic killing of army officers of Igbo origin began all over the country. Furthermore, Igbo civilians were massacred in the north, which the federal government did nothing to stop and actually tacitly endorsed. People of Igbo origin returned en masse to the east, the only place where they could feel safe. In May 1967, the Eastern Region seceded from the federation and formed the Republic of Biafra, headed by Chukwuemeka Odumegwu Ojukwu. The civil war broke out.

Clark is one of the foremost writers in Africa and a contemporary of Chinua Achebe, Wole Soyinka, and Christopher Okigbo, who published Clark's early poetry. Clark has written poems in which he laments Okigbo's tragic death in the Nigerian civil war, many of which appear in his collection *Casualties* (1970). A controversy surrounds both Clark's ambivalent stance during the crises and his friendship with Okigbo and Emmanuel Ifeajuna, one of the young Igbo army officers responsible for the coup of January 1966. All this notwithstanding, he remains one of the great writers on the African literary and theatrical scene, bestriding the whole spectrum of literary activity from poetry to playwriting, from journalism to literary and dramatic theory and criticism. He is, however, best known as a poet and playwright.

EARLY POEMS

Clark's first four collections of poetry— *Poems* (1962), *A Reed in the Tide* (1965), *Casualties*, and *A Decade of Tongues* (1981) — not only reflect his developing poetic sensibility, but also point to an emerging social vision and voice. *Poems* contains most of his early poetry previously published in *The Horn*, a literary magazine for new creative writing that Clark cofounded and edited while an undergraduate at Ibadan. Some of the poems also appeared in *Black Orpheus*, Nigeria Magazine, and *Ibadan*. Clark's mastery of poetic diction and experimentation with the English language, evident in this collection, established him as a talented poet. The second collection, *A Reed in the Tide*, contains most of the key poems from the first collection and nearly all his poems about the United States. It is remarkable for its central image of people as both children and victims of nature. Structurally, it contains the first intimations of Clark's emerging vision and voice as a public poet with segments from "Ivbie," which first appeared in *Poems*, at the middle of the collection, after a series of very private poems and before a group of public ones including the American poems. This poem marks his transition from a private to a public consciousness, which culminates in his later collections. "Ivbie" is significant also because it moves the poems from the personal experience, delta landscape, and metaphors of "For Granny (from Hospital)," "Night Rain," "Agbor Dancer," and "Streamside Exchange" to

images of postcolonial Nigeria and onto the American poems, which first appeared in *America, Their America* (1964), Clark's not very flattering response to the United States. The collection reflects a progression as well as a widening of experience from his traditional landscape, through the wider Nigerian environment that he laments in "Ivbie," to the international stage of his American experience.

A Decade of Tongues is a comprehensive collection of ten years of Clark's poetry. It contains the major pieces from *Poems*, including a full version of "Ivbie," and all the American poems from *A Reed in the Tide*. But more significantly, it contains the whole of *Casualties* plus "Epilogue to *Casualties*," which is absent from the original publication; the inclusion of *Casualties* allows the reader to witness the private sensibility of the poet of *Poems* and *A Reed in the Tide* as he grapples with the trauma of a national and therefore public catastrophe. *A Decade of Tongues*, consequently, provides a full sweep of Clark's poetry, containing poems of differing tempers and sentiments and displaying a maturing sensibility. In the acknowledgments to *A Decade of Tongues* Clark describes *Poems* as works "of a first love"; the poetry is very personal, making frequent use of the first-person voice of the poet. Even third-person narrative poems like "The Imprisonment of Obatala" and the ever popular "Abiku" reflect the poet's presence as he recreates personal experience. Clark might be neither the *abiku*, a child-spirit who delights in tormenting a mother by its repeated births and deaths, nor the tired mother, who is the victim of the *abiku*'s wicked pranks, but the poem suggests that the mother's agony is his too.

Poems

Clark is a private man, and the poems in *A Decade of Tongues* are sensitive expressions of an individual experience. They are personal images of a world through which the poet has passed from his early days in his native Kiagbodo. Clark conveys the innocent wonder of the child in the newness of everything, a novelty of experience, through the inquisitive tone of "Streamside Exchange":

> River bird, river bird
> Sitting all day long
> On hook over grass,
> River bird, river bird,
> Sing to me a song
> Of all that pass
> And say,
> Will mother come back today?
>
> (p. 20)

An atmosphere of peace pervades the entire landscape of *Poems* with an occasional hint that nature can be capricious and the world an unkind place. In the second part of "Streamside Exchange," for instance, the bird reveals that the child's mother is never coming back. This theme is also present in "Abiku," where the born-to-die child persists in tormenting the unfortunate mother, and "Night Rain," where even through the child's innocent fascination at the waterdrops "Falling like orange or mango / Fruits showered forth in the wind" (p. 6), one is aware that not only the poor family's sleep is threatened but also their home and lives are at risk of being washed away by the rain.

Clark's strengths as a poet are his lyricism and his mastery of the potent image. When these strengths combine with his remarkable ability to capture the texture and rhythm of the delta landscape, he produces the pulsating picture of a dancing girl in "Agbor Dancer" or the sprawling rusty city of "Ibadan." In these, as in other poems in the collection, Clark establishes the water imagery and nature metaphors that are a central feature of his writing; a key metaphor in his poetry and drama is the powerless reed carried along by the tide.

The long poem "Ivbie," which closes *Poems*, deserves special attention because it is different from the other poems in so many respects. "Ivbie" is "a hand-over-head signal and cry by women at a time of great loss or wrong for which there can be no remedy or justice," (glossary, *Poems,* p. 56). The only poems with which it has any affinity are "Abiku" and possibly "Streamside Exchange." But its position as closure is not fortuitous because it introduces the hopelessness and despair that dominate Clark's later writings. The underlying theme of the six meditative poems that make up "Ivbie" is the agony of European devastation of Africa from slavery to colonialism. Clark calls it "a song of wrong," the subtitle he added to the version that appears in *A Decade of Tongues,* and its tone is one of regret; it laments and accuses the communal gods for their inability to protect their own people. It ends with a tired plea to be left alone in a "sleep of the ages" (*A Decade of Tongues,* p. 32). For the wrong done, there can be no remedy, only anguish and "ivbie."

A Reed in the Tide

Clark includes thirteen poems from *A Reed in the Tide* in *A Decade of Tongues,* and they reflect a continuum of experience with *Poems.* "Flight Across Africa" records the journey away from home toward this new experience of another culture brought about by the catalytic events of "Ivbie." The structure of *A Decade of Tongues,* as well as the allusions and metaphors, reflects the poet's widening experience and consciousness. From *A Reed in the Tide* onward Clark moves out of his native Ijọ environment and begins to reflect on the larger Nigerian context in poems like "Emergency Commission," which deals with the political disturbances and state of emergency in the Western Region of Nigeria, and "The Leader," which is about Obafemi Awolowo:

Who unannounced home from abroad
Wrestled to a standstill his champion
Cousin the Killer of Cows.

(p. 36)

The "killer of cows" is Dr. Nnamdi Azikiwe, the first president of Nigeria, whom Clark also discusses quite critically in "His Excellency the Masquerade." After acknowledging the political landscape of Nigeria and its simmering crises, Clark uses an ironic tone to criticize western civilization and its technology for going too fast and too far in "Boeing Crossing":

pray
We have the common sense to tell
When we hit either ceiling or floor
Please pray before we all
Lose our heads in the clouds.
(*A Decade of Tongues*, pp. 41–42)

"Cuba Confrontation" (a reference to the 1962 Cuban missile crisis between the United States and the Soviet Union), "I Wake to the Touch," and "Home from Hiroshima" express Clark's reaction to the nuclear weapon argument, with Hiroshima used as a chilling reminder of the dangers of nuclear war. Through a mask of irony, Clark directs his rage at the fact that the superpowers are playing god with the life of the entire human race in their game of territorial control. "Home from Hiroshima" is a particularly well-wrought poem, sinewy and powerful in its statement and imagery. Together with most of the other poems in the collection, it provides an appropriate context for Clark to make, as Thomas Knipp says, "the distilled observations of a sardonic outsider determined not to be impressed by America and not to be fooled" (p. 138).

America, Their America

Whether Clark was determined not to like the United States is not clear, but the general tone of *America, Their America* suggests that his experience was not a very pleasant one. Such incidents as when he was told to bathe more often or when he was told that he was an embarrassment to the entire group on a tour to the Parvin Center show the extent of the fractious relationship which he had with his hosts. Finally, the hasty manner of his departure from the country—he was actually asked to leave—could not have endeared the United States to a man who was told he had a chip on his shoulder. His American poems go beyond the fact that he did not like the United States or that his hosts found him a difficult guest; they are Clark's way of saying that the land of glory is just a decadent morgue, "Whose keepers/play at kings" (*America, Their America*, p. 185).

On the whole the American experience marks a turning point in Clark's career; from then on he was no longer the private romantic concerned with expressing his personal experience in poetry that is sometimes very intimate and privately allusive, but always lyrical. Following his visit to the United States, Clark began writing very public poems.

SONGS FOR THE MARKETPLACE

Casualties

Casualties (1970) and *State of the Union* (1985) are the public poems of a very private man. Maintaining a measure of insularity, Clark directs his gaze at social ills, which impinge on his imagination because he also is part of the madhouse. *Casualties* chronicles the events of the Nigerian crises that led to the bloody civil war of 1967–1970 and the war itself. In these events, according to Clark, "we are all casualties" as well as participants: some, like Okigbo and Soyinka, by a hotheaded rush into danger; and some, like Achebe, as "wandering minstrels" and "emissaries of rift" who are

> So smug in smoke-rooms they haunt abroad,
> They do not see the funeral piles
> At home eating up the forests.
>
> ("The Casualties,"
> *A Decade of Tongues*, p. 84)

But some, like Clark, were complicit by their ambivalent silence during the war. The poems in *Casualties* are, according to Robert Wren, "a mask for the poet" (p. 129), because "the state of mind that produced the poems is not innocent. The poems are an *apologia*, a vindication" of Clark's attitude and position in the crises (p. 130). (Although ostensibly Clark did not get involved in the crises, later it emerged that he in fact was an active federalist who supported Gowon. Soyinka in *The Man Died* disparagingly refers to Clark as Gowon's poet laureate.)

Casualties is structured like a historical narrative; it begins with the lament of "Song" and ends with the restated lament and hope of "Night Song." Between these two are poems that chronicle the causes and aftermath of the Nigerian crises. The two poems provide a tragic frame and indicate the poet's anguish. "Song" is powerful, and its lament seems genuine enough for the poet's friends who died in the war — Okigbo, Ifeajuna, and Sam Agbam — and for the friendship of the living, which he has also lost because of his controversial silence. Clark has been vilified for his retreat to "the edges of both conflict and ideology" (Knipp, p. 139) during those dark times of the Nigerian disturbances, which he acknowledges in "Epilogue to *Casualties*." But "Song" is one of the best poems in *Casualties* with its evocation of a sense of loss and emptiness:

> I can look the sun in the face
> But the friends that I have lost
> I dare not look at any.
>
> (*A Decade of Tongues*, p. 52)

This lament takes the reader into the desolate atmosphere of the killing fields and unmarked graves of "Skulls and Cups" for a gruesome census of the dead:

> "Look, JP,
> How do you tell a skull
> From another?"...
> "That this, could you find where he fell,
> Was Chris, that Sam, and
> This there in the sand
> Of course Emman.
>
> (p. 53)

These were the friends whom the poet had "held ... in my arms" ("Song," p. 52), but who are now only empty "skulls and cups" on the hills of "Akwebe,/A place not even on the map" ("Death of a Weaverbird," p. 79). There is no denying the sadness and sense of rage for such waste of talents like those of Okigbo, the weaverbird who dies with an unfinished song in his throat in "Death of a Weaverbird." In "Skulls and Cups," as in "Conversations at Accra," Clark displays his sense of drama by having the poem unfold as a graveside dialogue between the poet and another friend, both survivors visiting the deserted war plains where their fallen friends lie unsung. He conveys the futility of the attempt to identify which skull or cup belongs to whom through the tentative and questioning tone of the exchange.

The next eight poems in *Casualties*, from "Vulture's Choice" through "Leader of the Hunt," deal with the coming of the military rule, and in doing so establish a sense of inevitable doom. More importantly, Clark introduces the essential animal and savage metaphors that run throughout the narrative in *Casualties*. It is almost as if he is suggesting that the principal actors have reduced themselves to a level of bestiality that only animals can manage. The title of the poem "The Burden in Boxes" refers to the dead bodies of the politicians who lost their lives in the January 1966 coup. The vulture who wants a child in "Vulture's Choice" is the Nigerian state; Major-General Aguiyi-Ironsi, the first military head of state, is

> The high priest of crocodiles who skipped
> Over hedge in the dark, then leapt back
> Into sharp sunlight.
>
> ("The Burden in Boxes," p. 55)

"The Usurpation" describes how Ironsi hijacks the coup led by Major Chukwuma Kaduna Nzeogwu and Ifeajuna; and Nzeogwu may be identified with the animal in the title of "The Cockerel in the Tale," which hints at the one-sided nature of the coup—most of the plotters were Igbos, and, significantly, no Igbo politicians lost their lives. "The Reign of the Crocodile" exposes Ironsi's inadequacies and his incompetent six-month tenure, during which he failed to control the government and bring the country out of its dangerous stasis.

Clark casts Ironsi as the most guilty villain in the first army takeover. The majors who started the coup may have had cause, but from Clark's point of view Ironsi exacerbated the situation by not comprehending the enormity and deep-seated antagonism of the ethnic politics that were wracking the country and that had prompted the idealistic young majors to strike.

"Seasons of Omens" is a chanted catalog of all that Clark believes had gone wrong in Nigerian society, where "calabashes held petrol and men / turned faggots in the streets" (p. 60); looting, arson, corrupt ministers, and election fraud, all prompt the "five hunters" to the rescue. Despite its attempt to employ a narrative structure and a complex network of metaphors and imagery, "Seasons of Omens," like most of *Casualties*, is not successful. Technically, most of the poems pass as highly crafted but dispassionate chronicles of a momentuous and emotionally charged period in a nation's history. That Clark could stand outside of this moment and clinically dissect it is beyond

the understanding of most Nigerians, who had been irrevocably touched and traumatized by the events. For this reason *Casualties* drew much criticism from across the country when it first appeared: Achebe referred to it as "a terrible book," the poet Michael Echerus called it a "disaster" and "sheer journalism," while Kalu Uka, another poet, dismissed it as "rubbish."

It has received praise from other critics, however, and Abiola Irele believes that in it Clark has written his best poetry. It has its fine parts like "Song," "The Cockerel in the Tale," the short "August Afternoon" with its ironic metaphor of a column of rats scaling roofs in pursuit of cats, and "Night Song" with its haunting echoes and undying memories:

> The night for me is filled with faces,
> Familiar faces no season
> Of masks can cover....
>
>   ...
> Now winds gallop through the gates
> Of their eyes. In pots their mouths make
> In fields already forgotten....
>
> (*A Decade of Tongues*, p. 86)

It also succeeds as a narrative developed along a fairly complex series of animal, vegetable, and landscape metaphors. The choice of animals as major characters in the unfolding drama appears well thought out and in some cases easily accessible: for example, the metaphors of Ironsi as crocodile and of Okigbo as the weaverbird that sings from the threshold of dreams only to die with an unfinished note in his throat.

That said, one can only wonder at what *Casualties* would have been, given the poet's unquestionable technical ability, had he been physically and psychically involved in the crises and the civil war. *Casualties* is a journey through madness and hell, but in spite of its bleak outlook, it ends in hope. The hope begins with the plea for the combatants on all sides of the conflict to forgive and forget because

in
The daze of noon the song rises,
Burns down the old ramparts
Of the heart, and before
Smoke seal our eyes, mud our mouths,
Firm upon the ground appears the house
Of our dream, with a mansion
For them who followed ghosts
Into the forests of the night.
("Night Song,"
A Decade of Tongues, p. 87)

"Epilogue to *Casualties*," which was not in-cluded in the original *Casualties* and first appeared in *A Decade of Tongues*, is an after-thought; even though it structurally rounds off the narrative, it does not help the sequence. Instead, its almost unpoetic detached reflec-tion on the devastation the war left behind breaks the beautiful lyricism and spell that "Night Song" provides as closure. It is an addition that the collection could do without, an addition that desperately struggles to be poetry, but does not quite succeed.

State of the Union

The progression from *Casualties* to Clark's next volume, *State of the Union*, is especially marked by his attempt to pare down his poetic language to an almost barren and lazy prose. This development seems to reflect his disil-lusionment with the sorry state of affairs in a nation that, as he points out in "The Sover-eign," had no business coming into being in the first place. Reading *State of the Union*, one finds nothing dignifying about this monstrous political "alchemy" called Nigeria ("The Sov-ereign"). Clark's indirect and weary irony is appropriate for presenting the unwholesome picture of a country where nothing works; this is the subject and title of the first poem, "Here Nothing Works." Even the meager and con-trolled passion, the rich allusions, and com-plex metaphors that give *Casualties* a depth of emotion and intensity of language seem mark-edly absent from *State of the Union*.

In spite of the starkness, some of the poems achieve a brilliance and potency of image that one has come to associate with Clark's poetry. No one can miss the powerful irony of "The Cleaners," with its indirect reference to the military who come into office on the pretext of sweeping clean the national polity, but

are themselves so full
Of muck nobody can see
The bottom of the pool
For the mud they carry
And cast so freely at a few.
(p. 5)

There is also the scathing irony of "Return of the Heroes," which refers to two bitter ene-mies, Ojukwu and Gowon, who had once been political self-exiles (the former a failed se-cessionist leader, the latter an overthrown head of state) but returned to a hero's wel-come. These two are also the colonels in the postscript, "The Playwright and the Colonels."

"Other Songs on Other States" is much closer to Clark's poetry in the earlier phase and is quite removed in temper and theme from most of the poems in *State of the Union*. Instead of the innocent exuberance and emo-tive tone of *Poems* and *A Reed in the Tide*, however, the poems in "Other Songs on Other States" convey the detached, experienced, and essentially brooding voice of a man who mourns the passing of time, which is the theme of the section. "The Wreck," "Last Rites in Ijebu," "Autumn in Connecticut," "The Coming of Age," and especially the very short "Harvest" capture this mood of despair for a lost time:

In time, even leaves on
The ground in a garden
Are gathered home.
Where do I find the basket
To gather in my gone years?
("Harvest," p. 43)

The resigned irony in this poem is unmistakable; Clark captures the irretrievable finality of the passing years in an elegiac tone and melancholic grandeur here and in the closing lines of "The Coming of Age."

State of the Union and *The Bikoroa Plays* (1985) remind one of Sophocles' *Oedipus at Colonus*, where the raging and impatient Oedipus of *Oedipus Rex* gives way to a mature, somber, and deeply reflective man who accepts his fate with a stoicism that even the implacable gods admire. These later works of Clark's reflect a mature man and writer who takes stock of life from his retreat at Funama and in observing the playing herons only wishes

> To walk, swim and fly
> like you, oh, herons
> At play on my waterfront!
> ("Herons at Funama," p. 49)

Mandela and Other Poems

Mandela and Other Poems (1988) continues in the brooding reflective mood and language of "Other Songs on Other States." The book has three parts, a division significant for the way in which the last two sections, "Ceremonies for Departure" and "Departures," cast a "recessive light" on the controlled rage of "Mandela." More significantly, these sections are the reflections of a poet who uses the context of the deaths of friends and relatives to measure and pass commentary on life.

The first section, entitled "Mandela," deals with the liberation struggle in South Africa, which the poet believes is taking too long to conclude. The title poem, "Mandela," looks at the life of Nelson Mandela as he wastes away in the Robben Island prison and at the huge sacrifices that the struggle entails for all its leaders. This section also celebrates great freedom fighters like Samora Machel of Mozambique and the heroic children of Soweto who,

> afraid to live
> In the concentration camp
> He has made of their land,
> Stampede barb-wire and bullet.
> ("The Beast in the South," p. 9)

But nothing in "Mandela" comes close to the haunting beauty of the poetry of "Ceremonies for Departure" and "Departures." The two are made up of a series of elegies on the subject of death, a brooding sense of loss of close friends and relatives to this "vagrant guest" whom no one wants but everyone must entertain someday ("Homecoming," p. 33). The mood is somber, the pace idle and sedate, as in a long recessional in a personal vespers for the dead. Its tone is meditatively relaxed, and the slow tempo and sleepy cadence of poems like "Leaves Falling" and "The Last Wish" suggest a feeling of slowly approaching dusk. Because of either the highly emotive nature of the subject of death or a higher level of maturity and mastery of poetic technique, the poems in *Mandela and Other Poems* are exceptionally moving. In them Clark finally achieves a unique fusion of emotion, imagery, and language to produce poetry that is part elegiac, part nostalgic, and part resigned rumination on the passing of time: "All under spell of day / Moves on into night ("The Coming of Age," p. 47).

But *Mandela and Other Poems* does not end quite so hopelessly, for its last poem, "The Order of the Dead," promises a life after death:

> The dead of this land, praising God,
> May come again into town as children,
> If at their first coming,
> They went away with a sign of great wrong.
> (pp. 36–37)

This modification of Clark's tragic vision provides the hope that rescues the volume from its pervasive sense of resignation to the finality of death, a view that is not particularly African. For the poet, and happily for his readers, this is not the end of the road, for there is life and poetry after middle age.

A THEATER OF TRAGIC ANGUISH: *THREE PLAYS* AND *OZIDI*

It is difficult to say whether Clark is better known as a poet or as a playwright. His first collection of plays, *Three Plays* (1964), contains *Song of a Goat*, which established his reputation as a playwright. Together with the other two plays in the collection, *The Masquerade* and *The Raft*, *Song of a Goat* constitutes a manifesto of Clark's tragic vision, glimpses of which had appeared in his poems. Critics have been quick to point out what they see as his imitation of Greek models in his three tragedies, especially *Song of a Goat* and *The Masquerade*: a chorus of villagers, serious action that happens offstage, and a reliance on the notion of culpable inevitability.

In spite of this closeness to Greek models, Clark portrays life in his delta Ijọ homeland as he knows it. Each play therefore deals with an aspect of life that is important to Ijọ people—traditional practices, like marriage and procreation, and socioeconomic practices, like fishing, trading, and lumbering. In each play Clark presents characters who, in spite of their shortcomings, confront harsh laws of nature that pose difficult situations. But none of them is able to master fate or triumph; they all come to grief. In *Song of a Goat* the brothers Zifa and Tonye perish while Ebiere, Zifa's wife, suffers a miscarriage and subsequently bleeds to death; Tufa and Titi in *The Masquerade* are shot to death by Titi's irate father while her mother goes mad; and the four lumbermen in *The Raft* perish in spite of their efforts to bring their stricken raft safely into port. This working out of unstoppable tragedy is an indication of Clark's tragic vision, which leaves no room for any of his major characters to escape. In other words, as Wilfred Cartey concludes, Clark simply "cuts his characters adrift and watches them move, powerless to steer their own course" (p. 341).

Clark's early plays have none of the "final optimism" that one often finds in Soyinka, whose characters defy fate in order to break the recurrent cycle of history and bring to an end an inherited tragic destiny (Cartey, p. 340). *Song of a Goat* poses the moral question of who is responsible for the tragedy that befalls the house of Zifa. It deals with Zifa's sexual impotence, which is responsible for his wife's adulterous relationship with Tonye, and the subsequent passions aroused by the adultery. Essentially, the notion of culpable inevitability is present because each character in some way helps to set off the time bomb of a curse that hangs over the household. Zifa's impotence results from his having broken a taboo; Ebiere, acting on the Masseur's advice, seduces Tonye; and Tonye's abomination is that he succumbs to the seduction. The three fail not only because of the flaws in their personalities but also because of the curse on the family. In the final analysis, they are powerless to stop the design of forces outside themselves.

In his essay "Two African Playwrights," published in *Black Orpheus* 19 (March 1966), Martin Esslin calls *The Masquerade* Clark's most successful play, a play of immense emotional power written in a language that is remarkable for its "highly sophisticated simplicity" (p. 36). In *The Masquerade*, also a family tragedy, Clark dramatizes a popular legend of the village belle who, after refusing all eligible suitors, falls for a handsome stranger whom she meets in the market. Tufa arrives on the last day of Titi's stately ritual pageant through the market, the chemistry between them is instant, and everybody knows immediately that Titi's search and "long waiting for her man was over" (p. 59). Their union is fraught with danger because of the mystery surrounding the groom. Clark handles this mythic archetype very well in this moving story of love and death. At the height of the wedding festivities, word gets around about Tufa's background. His mother, impregnated by her husband's brother, died giving birth to Tufa. (Tufa is the problematic link from *Song of a Goat* to *The Masquerade*: he is supposed to be the child from the adulterous affair between Ebiere and Tonye, but we already know that Ebiere had a miscarriage.) Titi, like her archetype, would have her chosen groom, warts and all. But her father, Diribi, will have none of it and kills Tufa during a scuffle.

In an essay entitled "Diribi's Incest: The Key to J. P. Clark's *The Masquerade*" in *World Literature Written in English* 18 (November 1979), William Connor suggests a subliminal incestuous motive behind Diribi's insane rage, and there is evidence in the play to support this. Connor argues that Titi had rejected all former suitors because they could not measure up to the standard set by her father in the amount of gifts that he showers on her. Furthermore, Diribi appears jealous of and angry with Tufa because Tufa surpasses him in gifts to Titi. It is therefore inevitable that he takes advantage of any excuse to call off the wedding in order to avoid giving Titi to another man. But he clearly underestimates his daughter's love and will, which results in the haunting tragedy that Clark so beautifully creates in *The Masquerade*.

The last play, *The Raft*, follows the tribulations and eventual deaths of four lumbermen adrift on a raft heading downstream as if under the impulse of an implacable malevolent force. The four men are on the raft in order to make a living, and their being adrift, although under mysterious circumstances, happens to be a hazard of the trade. Adrian Roscoe suggests that "the waters of life and the river of life are being alluded to" (p. 208), but such a reading overloads the significance of this simple play. Clark creates meaning by placing the men in a twilight zone—a wide expanse of water that is suggestive of the beginning of the world—which, despite their history and individual identity, leaves them liminal and thereby increases their universal suggestiveness. In spite of their names—Olotu, Kengide, Ogro, and Ibobo—the drifters are four ordinary lumbermen caught in a perilous situation from which they struggle futilely to escape. We feel for them because they could be us, which is why Clark's play is so successful. *The Raft* yet again illustrates the hopelessness of the human condition central to Clark's tragic vision. That Kengide and Ibobo manage to survive the whirlpool and shipwreck only to drift on to the small port of Burutu to die is further evidence of this hopelessness.

Ozidi: A Play (1966), set in the delta, is a retelling of a well-known Ijọ folk legend of the house of Ozidi, often told and performed as a communal play or storytelling performance. Clark first recorded this story as *The Ozidi Saga*, which was not published until 1977. The play has a three-part structure corresponding to key moments in the unraveling of the epic saga of the Ozidi household. In the first part, the father, Ozidi, a general of Orua, is set upon and slain by his war colleagues— Ofe, Azezabife, Oguaran, and Agbogidi— who spitefully present his severed head to Temugedege, his idiot brother and king of Orua. Unbeknownst to them Orea, Ozidi's young bride, is pregnant, and their first mistake is to spare her life. She escapes to her mother, Oreame, the powerful witch of Dodama, who takes care of her until her baby boy, named after his father, is born. In the second part of the play, Oreame prepares young Ozidi for revenge, and in the third part the revenge is carried out.

The epic scope of events in the play, which expands over twenty years, is such that the seemingly sacred unities of Clark's first three plays disappear. The younger Ozidi's fight with his father's killers takes place over days, weeks, and "moons" in the human and spirit worlds. *Ozidi* is by far the most successful of Clark's early plays because he has found an authentic voice and form that are uniquely African and capable of accommodating the complex realities and forces that Ozidi's revenge brings into play. Structurally, it is an accomplished and performable play despite its numerous scenes. Clark succeeds in holding this seemingly seamless piece together through deft use of song and dance, the way a traditional master storyteller would by getting the audience to help with choric interludes.

As in his other plays, Clark displays his mastery of language and a keen ear for the sound and density of words that only an accomplished poet has. Again, the rich flora and fauna of his Ịjọ homeland provide him with appropriate metaphors for expressing the bizarre but essentially human experience of the Ozidi story. The metaphor of the reed that is powerless to resist the drift of the tide, which Clark used in poems like "New Year" to depict the poet-persona and a lover as "two reeds swaying on / The banks with the wind of world-blight" (*A Decade of Tongues*, p. 15), returns in this play as the unmistakable image of the younger Ozidi as one who controls neither his destiny nor his actions in fulfilling that destiny. His destiny is chosen for him before he is even born; he simply follows the wind of his preordained life, which is constantly fanned and directed by his magically resourceful grandmother. Even when he wants to stop he cannot, because the choice to act or not to act is never really his own. It is difficult to agree with Lewis Nkosi when he says of Clark's work, and especially of *Ozidi*, which he sees "as a very loose and rambling play":

> There is a more serious problem which applies with equal force to everything Clark has written. Clark's *oeuvre* is, I would say, less satisfying because of a lack of controlling idea or philosophy of society behind it; his work always seems to lack an organising principle: nothing gives it personal stamp; no obsession, no psychic wounds, no vision of society beyond a tepid humanism, gives us a perspective from which to judge his writing.
>
> (p. 187)

This seems an unfair assessment of Clark. If he is guilty of anything, it is his ability always to maintain a distance from his subjects and events, no matter how emotional these may be. Admittedly, this posture sometimes smacks of an unfeeling arrogance. But then not every writer can be expected to have a wounded or tortured psyche, wearing his or her injuries like eloquent banners in the battlefield of life. Clark's other problem is that, unlike Soyinka, he fails to give his heroes or antiheroes the courage to intervene positively and change the course of destiny. For Soyinka, the individual can and must sometimes act in order to break the cycle of human folly and the often capricious designs of the gods and nature. Clark, however, seems to accept that people are powerless and that it is futile to try to stem the tide of tragic fate; for example, in *The Raft* the drifting lumbermen's attempt to make a mast to help them out of the terrible whirlpool ironically generates the force that breaks the raft in two. Where Soyinka is concerned with the active individual who can deny the gods, Clark is content with the person who accepts and suffers his or her fate. This seems to be the central theme of Clark's theater, from the serene passivity of *Song of a Goat* to the tempestuous energy of *Ozidi*.

RETURN TO SOURCE: *THE BIKOROA PLAYS*

In *The Bikoroa Plays* (1985), which was published nineteen years after *Ozidi*, Clark shows himself to be a mature playwright no longer concerned with his precious "Elizabethan blank verse" and echoes of Gerard Manley Hopkins and other models. The plays in this trilogy are about simple people and are written in a simple everyday language, and therein lies their power. Again Clark traces a family tragedy that spans three generations. However, his tragic view undergoes a remarkable shift as characters are no longer wholly powerless to intervene and stop the flow of history.

The Boat, The Return Home, and *Full Circle* tell the story of a family in the Niger delta. Unlike the trilogy in *Three Plays, The Bikoroa Plays* seems a more unified attempt to explore the notion of the tragic from a purely African perspective. Clark's return to the theme of domestic tragedy, treated in part in *Song of a Goat* and *The Masquerade*, gives *The Bikoroa Plays* a simple but powerful story outline. In the introduction to *Collected Plays and Poems, 1958–1988*, Irele quite rightly suggests that "their triadic scheme virtually makes them into a single play in three extended movements, not only linked thematically . . . but also unified by a reflective point of view" (p. xlix).

Clark creates an effective structure for the trilogy in which the intense atmosphere of *The Boat*, the first play, and *Full Circle*, the third play, is balanced and mediated by the subdued serenity of *The Return Home*. The middle play acts as "a bridge from one moment of intensity in the cycle to another" (Irele, introduction to *Collected Plays and Poems*, p. l), from the explosive rivalry of Bradide and Biowa in the first play to the equally tense jealousy of Ojoboro and Kari in the third play. Clark displays maturity in his dramatic technique and in the remarkable shift in his vision of tragedy.

In *The Boat* Clark examines the stormy and disastrous relationship between two brothers, whose shared ownership of a boat creates tension and conflict that eventually lead to tragedy. Biowa, the younger brother, is prosperous from his ventures in Lagos and therefore the toast of the town and the darling of their mother, Umuto Diakohwo, who unwittingly fuels the rivalry between her sons. She reads jealousy in every move that Bradide, the older brother, makes, so when he suggests carrying out repairs on the boat, Umuto suspects a ruse to deprive her favorite son use of the boat. Peletua, Biowa's friend and later a town spokesman, calls her "the fierce mother-hen who'll fight owner and hawk alike, protecting her brood, while trampling on the chicks in the process" (p. 27). That is exactly what she does in the end; her meddling pushes Biowa to shoot his brother, and he in turn is condemned to death by the community.

In *The Return Home* Clark explores the ritual cleansing that is needed to recall the spirits of the dead brothers wandering rest-lessly because of the manner of their deaths. The cosmic disruption caused by the original tragic incident of Biowa's murdering Bradide must be contained so that its threat to the family can be removed. The sons of the dead brothers quarrel over a slight misunderstanding, and it appears that the family's tragic history is about to repeat itself. But fortunately, what starts out as a dangerous clash between the cousins is gently turned by Maika (another of Biowa's peers) and the long-suffering Emonemua (sister of Bradide and Biowa) into a joint ritual to bring home the spirits of their wandering dead.

The Return Home is a festival play sandwiched between two tragedies. Structurally it is similar to a ritual, opening with a crisis that the Bikoroa community resolves by bridging the tragic gulf and eventually breaking the tragic cycle of the family. The pace of events has a deliberate, repetitive, ritualistic rhythm that controls the action and characters. The language too is rich in ritual metaphors of blood and sacrifice, water and purification. Although written in prose, the ritual intensity of the moments comes through the language, which acquires the poetic splendor of an incantation, as in this farewell from Emonemua: "You have been called home; you have been washed; you have been robed; you have been feted as princes; how beautiful you are, my brothers, oh my brothers, and now all the state is escorting you to your kindred, oh, my brothers, may you go in peace, may you bring us peace!" (p. 104). Whether or not this cleansing has occurred is difficult to say because an overwhelming aura of tragedy still hangs over the household and eventually reappears in *Full Circle*.

The events in the last play complete a full circle as it again returns us to the disaster of *The Boat*. The tragic impulse and its aftermath, which was narrowly averted in *The Return Home* and was intentional in the first play, becomes an accident in the third play. Ojoboro accidentally kills his younger brother, Kari, while trying to stop him from beating their mother. In a sense, Kari deserves no sympathy because he brings tragedy on himself by being unnecessarily vicious toward his brother and mother. He blames his mother for his failures in Lagos and at the same time envies Ojoboro's success at home. This is almost a replay of *The Boat*, only this time the roles are reversed—the older brother kills the younger one—and the methods different; the result, however, is the same—one brother causes the death of another brother. Within the moral universe of the plays this action is wrong, and no one realizes this better than Ojoboro himself in his anguished cry: "I didn't kill him! Do you hear me? I didn't kill him! My own brother, born after me, how could I kill him?" (p. 124). The genuineness of his lament is unquestionable, which perhaps explains why the community decides that no crime has been committed and decides against declaring mourning. Maybe in refusing to acknowledge this tragedy, the community hopes to have put an end for all time to the recurring cycle of tragic fate of the Bradide-Biowa clan.

In an interview in the *New York Times* of 20 December 1985 Clark said that he is concerned with the "business of people living together and squabbling over common property." The trilogy is his attempt to explore this idea in as natural a setting as possible and in a language that is as close as possible to that thought and spoken by the fishermen, traders, and lumbermen of the riverine community. In *The Bikoroa Plays* he seems to have resolved the dilemma that every African writer, given the colonial heritage, confronts in the choice of the language in which to address his or her audience. The language here is that of the creeks and fishermen; the pleasantries and salutations reveal much about the speakers and their environment. In *The Bikoroa Plays* Clark comes closest to creating a theatrical language that is genuinely African and a landscape that is authentically riverine and Ijọ, and in doing so he again shows that he is an accomplished dramatist who is comfortable in both prose and verse. Although his earlier plays succeed theatrically in poetic and dramatic intensity, they represent only a partial success—for which one must give Clark credit—in transplanting Greek and Shakespearean models onto an African setting. *The Bikoroa Plays* are more successful for the simple reason that they are firmly rooted in an African setting, from which they draw inspiration and strength, thus providing the playwright with the appropriate metaphors and cultural symbolism to express what is essentially an African view of tragedy.

Selected Bibliography

COLLECTED WORKS

A Decade of Tongues. London: Longman, 1981.
Collected Plays and Poems, 1958–1988. Intro. by Abiola Irele. Washington, D.C.: Howard University Press, 1991.

POETRY

Poems. Ibadan, Nigeria: Mbari Publications, 1962.
A Reed in the Tide. London: Longman, 1965, 1970.
Casualties. London: Longman, 1970; New York: Africana Publishing Co., 1970.
State of the Union. London: Longman, 1985.
Mandela and Other Poems. Ikeja: Longman Nigeria, 1988.

PLAYS

Three Plays. London: Oxford University Press, 1964, 1970. Contains *Song of a Goat*, *The Masquerade*, and *The Raft*.
Ozidi: A Play. Ibadan, Nigeria: Oxford University Press, 1966.
[John Pepper Clark-Bekederemo]. *The Bikoroa Plays.* Oxford, U.K.: Oxford University Press, 1985. Contains *The Boat*, *The Return Home*, and *Full Circle*.

TRANSLATION

The Ozidi Saga. Collected and trans. from the Ijọ of Okabou Ojobolo. Ibadan, Nigeria: Ibadan University Press, 1977; Ibadan, Nigeria: Oxford University Press, 1977.

OTHER WORKS

America, Their America. London: A. Deutsch, 1964; London: Heinemann, 1968; New York: Africana Publishing Co., 1969.

The Example of Shakespeare. London: Longman, 1970; Evanston, Ill.: Northwestern University Press, 1970.

The Hero as Villain. Lagos, Nigeria: University of Lagos Press, 1978.

CRITICAL STUDIES

Banham, Martin. *African Theatre Today.* London: Pitman Publishing, 1976.

Beier, Ulli, ed. *Introduction to African Literature: An Anthology of Critical Writing.* London: Longman, 1979.

Berney, K. A., ed. *Contemporary Dramatists.* 5th ed. London: St. James Press, 1993.

Cartey, Wilfred. *Whispers from a Continent: The Literature of Contemporary Black Africa.* New York: Random House, 1969.

Dathorne, O. R. *African Literature in the Twentieth Century.* Minneapolis: University of Minnesota Press, 1975. Originally pub. in expanded form as *The Black Mind: A History of African Literature.* Minneapolis: University of Minnesota Press, 1974.

Duerden, Dennis, and Cosmo Pieterse, eds. *African Writers Talking: A Collection of Radio Interviews.* New York: Africana Publishing Co., 1972; London: Heinemann, 1972.

Egudu, Romanus N. *Modern African Poetry and the African Predicament.* London: Macmillan, 1978; New York: Barnes and Noble, 1978.

Elimimian, Isaac Irabor. *The Poetry of J. P. Clark Bekederemo.* Ikeja: Longman Nigeria, 1989.

Knipp, Thomas. "'Ivbie': The Developing Moods of John Pepper Clark's Poetry." In *Journal of Commonwealth Literature* 17, no. 1 (1982).

Nkosi, Lewis. *Tasks and Masks: Themes and Styles of African Literature.* Harlow, U.K.: Longman, 1981.

Ogunba, Oyin, and Abiola Irele. *Theatre in Africa.* Ibadan, Nigeria: Ibadan University Press, 1978.

Roscoe, Adrian. *Mother Is Gold: A Study in West African Literature.* Cambridge, U.K.: Cambridge University Press, 1971.

Taiwo, Oladele. *An Introduction to West African Literature.* London: Thomas Nelson, 1967.

Wren, Robert. *J. P. Clark.* Lagos, Nigeria: Lagos University Press, 1984; Boston: Twayne, 1984.

J. M. Coetzee
1940–

JAMES HARRISON

DAVID ATTWELL, a remarkably sympathetic and perceptive critic of South African novelist J. M. Coetzee's work, begins his introduction to *Doubling the Point* (1992), a selection of Coetzee's critical prose, by referring to his subject's computer analysis of Samuel Beckett's short prose piece, "Lessness." In it Coetzee shows how all the phrases that make up the first half reappear, in a different order, to form the second half. Similarly, when Coetzee was asked to contribute to an anthology (*Momentum*) devoted to writers' role in South African society, he submitted "A Note on Writing," which consisted of two pages on the role of a middle voice between the active and the passive. (In the same volume, thirty-three thoughtful pages by three thoughtful academics are devoted to the social, historical, and political implications of Coetzee's first three novels.) Despite appearances, neither of these two pieces was an instance of pedantic insensitivity; Coetzee was in fact analyzing with great subtlety how style is an integral component of whatever is said or written.

Coetzee's novels have increasingly been seen both at home and abroad as penetrating if sometimes oblique critiques, in literary form, of the social and political state of affairs in South Africa. This recognition has taken the form of numerous awards to Coetzee: South Africa's Central News Agency (CNA) Literary Award for both *In the Heart of the Country* (1977) and *Waiting for the Barbarians* (1980), the latter also winning Britain's Geoffrey Faber Award and the James Tait Black Memorial Prize; yet another CNA as well as Britain's premier literary award, the Booker-McConnell Prize, and France's Prix Femina Étranger for *Life & Times of Michael K* (1983); and Israel's Jerusalem Prize in 1987, awarded to the author who best expresses the ideal of freedom in his or her work. Yet by many, and even by as sincere an admirer as Nadine Gordimer (p. 6), his work has at times been found overly intellectual, lacking in compassionate realism, and politically suspect.

ANCESTRY AND EDUCATION

John Maxwell Coetzee was born in Cape Town in South Africa on 9 February 1940. His mother, Vera Wehmeyer, was a schoolteacher, and his father, Zacharias, an attorney. There have been Coetzees in South Africa since the earliest Dutch settlers arrived there. As Dick Penner reports him as saying, he is one of "a huge clan of Coetzees who have been part of the history of [the] country for three hundred years" (p. 1). Yet because his mother was of English stock, he grew up speaking English at home and Afrikaans— the local language of people of Dutch descent—to more distant relatives, and he attended an English-speaking Catholic boys' school. Coetzee is therefore fluently bilingual but much prefers to write in English, considering it a far richer, more flexible language than Afrikaans, which he finds "dull" (interview by Sévry, p. 2).

In addition, Coetzee is deeply aware of the need to free both blacks and whites from the crippling effects of apartheid—until the early 1990s South Africa's official policy of racial segregation—as is clear from his "Jerusalem Prize Acceptance Speech" (Coetzee, *Doubling*, pp. 96–99). His very chromosomes embody a historic clash of cultures within the white community in South Africa—on the one hand, the stern paternalism and puritanic Calvinism of the original Dutch settlers, on the other, the opportunistic materialism of the British traders who followed.

Coetzee's postsecondary education began at the University of Cape Town with an honors bachelor's degree in English in 1960 and in mathematics in 1961. A year later he sailed for London, where in 1963 he married Philippa Jubber and, for his master's degree from Cape Town, wrote a thesis on the English writer Ford Madox Ford while working for IBM, the computer giant. In 1965 he began a doctoral program in linguistics at the University of Texas at Austin; he completed it in 1969.

Coetzee acknowledges that he has always felt more at ease teaching language than literature, and his early published papers confirm this bias. His doctoral dissertation, "The English Fiction of Samuel Beckett: An Essay in Stylistic Analysis," brought together the critical, mathematical, and computing skills he had been acquiring, and sharpened his stylistic awareness.

During his time at Austin he also discovered a wealth of original manuscripts, not just those written by Beckett while hiding from the Germans in France during World War II, but also others by and about travelers and explorers in southern Africa from the seventeenth to the early twentieth centuries. These latter included a remote ancestor of his own, one Jacobus Coetzee, whom he would later flesh out into the ruthlessly rapacious protagonist of "The Narrative of Jacobus Coetzee" in *Dusklands* (1974).

Awarded his doctorate in 1969, Coetzee took his first teaching post at the State University of New York at Buffalo, where he also wrote the other novella in *Dusklands*, "The Vietnam Project." This is a study of twentieth-century imperialism that, as a South African, he could not help but associate with an earlier, cruder, but no less brutal imperialism in his homeland. He left the United States with regret in 1971, to continue lecturing and to complete *Dusklands* in Cape Town, where he still taught as professor of general literature in the mid 1990s.

DUSKLANDS

Coetzee's first novel of fiction consists of two separate novellas whose similarities are of much greater interest and significance than their differences. They deal with acts of imperialist aggression in the twentieth and seventeenth centuries; the aggressor in both cases, whether victorious or not, is left feeling dissatisfied.

"The Vietnam Project" is narrated by Eugene Dawn, a bundle of tics and twitches who works in the mythography section of a psychological warfare unit in Washington, D.C. It soon becomes clear that his manifold inadequacies, his taste for sado-erotica, and his rapidly disintegrating marriage are of a piece with his plan for winning the war in Vietnam. The Vietcong, he argues, see the war in terms of a myth in which sons, in league with Mother Earth, overthrow a patriarchal god of the sky—the United States—by emasculating him. This god is replaced, since there must always be heaven as well as earth, father as well as mother; but the master-myth of history, claims Dawn, has superseded the archetype of a symbiotic heaven and earth. We no longer live by tilling the earth; we devour her in order to manufacture—to breed out of our own heads. This updated myth of a sterilized feminine earth instead of an impotent masculine sky prompts Dawn to advocate exclusive reliance on spraying with PROP-12, a fictional herbicide that could change the face of Vietnam in a week, as the way to win the war.

The epigraph to "The Vietnam Project" is a quotation from Herman Khan's introduction to *Can We Win in Vietnam?* a collection of studies of tactical options in Vietnam. Nowhere in it is there even a mention of Agent Orange, the herbicide that was used in the war. Even those accounts of the war that refer to defoliation do so as one of many linked strategies. That Dawn sees it as the consummate form of future attack—that is, the destruction of Mother Earth and her progeny from the air—confirms his deep-seated misogyny. This is borne out when his proposal is rejected and he attacks his wife by kidnapping his young son and hiding in a remote motel. When the police enter the room with his wife, his chief concern is not to be humiliated in front of her. He uses the boy as a hostage, wounds him with a fruit knife, and is promptly knocked down. "Now I am beginning to be hurt," he records in an astounded and astounding present tense (p. 43).

In the final pages, Dawn describes his response to therapy in a mental institution. For the first time in the story he is happy—happy in his own room with his own window, door, and walls. It is a simple place, he tells us, for men in need of simplicity—an all-male institution where he wants and receives no visits. He submits scrupulously to the routine prescribed by his doctors and he says, "I have high hopes of discovering whose fault I am" (p. 49).

Intensely critical of the war in Vietnam, this novella is by an author and about characters who have never set foot in the place. In sharp contrast to "The Narrative of Jacobus Coetzee," the imperialism satirized here is entirely cerebral and theoretical. And this is precisely what becomes the chief source of our horror: that this sorry travesty of an all-American hero—who is incapable of relating to wife, child, and fellow workers other than by offering or demanding total submission, and who seethes with repressed hostility toward a wife who is a constant reproach and reminder of his inadequacies—is employed to devise ways of making life intolerable for half a nation half a world away. In Eugene Dawn's pathetic ruthlessness, Coetzee strips imperialism of any imperial quality and leaves it sounding shrill and peremptory. Moreover, by reallocating mythic roles so that it is Mother Earth who is left sterile, he links the evils of male chauvinism and environmental irresponsibility to those of imperialism.

Eugene Dawn's supervisor is named Coetzee. Not a common name in the United States, it serves to suggest the fictional nature of the narrative. In "The Narrative of Jacobus Coetzee," the other novella in *Dusklands*, the Coetzees proliferate more wildly. The narrator and protagonist is an ancestor of the novelist; the supposed editor of the narrative and author of notes and an afterword is a Dr. S. J. Coetzee; the translator is his son and bears the name J. M. Coetzee. Metafiction—that is, fiction concerned with its own structure and meaning, thereby calling attention to its fictional nature—is alive and well.

Yet by adding, as an appendix, the "Deposition of Jacobus Coetzee (1760)"—a transcript of the brief oral account given by Jacobus to the political secretariat at the Cape of Good Hope of his hunting expeditions northward from that early Dutch colony—Coetzee seems to be striving for authenticity. His version of archaic bureaucratic speech patterns, as translated into English, enables us to accept the novella as a realistic account of life in eighteenth-century southern Africa. This in turn helps to legitimize Jacobus' highly anachronistic meditations on the nature of exploration and the mythic properties of the gun. As Stephen Watson points out in an interview, few readers find these meditations plausible, spoken as they are by an eighteenth-century frontiersman who cannot even sign his name. In response, Coetzee merely states that Jacobus is not an eighteenth-century frontiersman but a figure in a book.

There, in a nutshell, is the tension to be found in all Coetzee's work. On the one hand, he claims postmodernist freedoms to take liberties with narrative voice and historical verisimilitude—in short, with straightforward realism. Only thus can he avoid "straightforwardizing" the complexities of life to the point of simplism. On the other hand, he refuses to take refuge from reality and claim that literature is a self-sufficient game with no relevance to or bearing on the business of living.

Jacobus' first-person narration begins with background comments on the Hottentots and Bushmen, two native peoples of southern Africa. "A bullet is too good for a Bushman," he tells us (p. 60), and "a Bushman girl . . . is nothing, a rag you wipe yourself on and throw away" (p. 61). On his first expedition he takes six Hottentot servants and an ox wagon. They encounter a band from a Namaqua village— "wild" Hottentots carrying spears. Jacobus offers to pay well for water, grazing, and fresh oxen. However, he is unable to prevent the wagon from being plundered by the villagers, so Jacobus orders a retreat until sickness forces him to return to the village, where his Hottentot servants revert to savagery. Recovering and bathing in a stream, he sees some young boys steal his clothes, and in the struggle to regain them he bites off an ear. Shocked by such a savage act, the villagers expel him.

On the long walk home he ponders his treatment by the Namaquas. Assuming their capacity for persistent hostility is as well developed as his own, he finds the punishment they gave him sadly deficient. Savagery, by definition, places no value on human life and takes sensual pleasure in the pain of others. Yet these savages, he admits reluctantly, seem not to know what it means to be a savage.

He himself knows more about savagery than they do, as he demonstrates in the second, brief section of the narrative, which tells of a punitive expedition by Jacobus and a small group of native soldiers. He remembers and describes in revolting detail the execution of the four servants who had "deserted" him, and records the eradication of the village. Yet once again he is disappointed: "There was nothing that could be impressed on these bodies, nothing that could be torn from them or forced through their orifices, that would be commensurate with the desolate infinity of my power over them" (pp. 101–102).

A complaint often heard concerning Coetzee's fiction—that he offers no social or economic diagnosis for the state of affairs with which he finds fault—seems justifiable in the case of these two early novellas; emphasis is so clearly placed on psychological factors at work in the case of each narrator-protagonist. Yet the very lack of mundane realism in their presentation—the strongly psychotic nature of their personalities—suggests that they are playing allegorical roles. Coetzee is able to imply a great deal about the societies capable of producing such personalities without committing himself, politically, to any of the diagnostic methodologies available.

IN THE HEART OF THE COUNTRY

Both halves of *Dusklands* were narrated in the first person by the protagonist, a typical device in almost all Coetzee's fiction. In none of his novels, however, is this device more crucial than in *In the Heart of the Country* (1977). Everything that happens in the novel is filtered through and colored by the consciousness of Magda, our sole source of information. In addition, a great deal that does not (or that may or may not) happen is similarly transmitted to us, as when Magda kills her father twice and is still caring for him in the closing pages. The narration is so subjective, with no warning markers distinguishing fact from fantasy, the deed from the dream, that a stream of consciousness plunges at times into one of unconsciousness.

At the outset, an unmarried daughter keeps house for her father on a lonely South African farmstead, her mother having died many years earlier. We witness the return of the father with a new, young bride, sense the daughter's resentment, watch as she murders both of them on the bridal bed, then see the father return to the farm without the bride he set out to win. All this is set down in numbered paragraphs or short pieces of dialogue ranging from a single line to two or three pages in length, somewhat like a journal but in a continuous present tense, as if Magda were recording a commentary on what she sees and hears and does.

Shortly after his second return, the father starts an affair with Anna, the black bride of the black farmhand Hendrik. Magda threatens and accidentally kills her father with his rifle, and in the process of disposing of the body she tries to establish a relationship of equals with Hendrik and Anna. History, however, both personal and social, is against her. She is unable to pay Hendrik's wages and is compelled to submit to his nightly visits, whether real or imagined. When neighbors call to see the father and ask questions, Hendrik and Anna leave, afraid they will be blamed if the truth comes out.

Left to herself, Magda starts to hear voices speaking gnomic nonsense in Spanish issuing from flying machines. In the closing four pages, she turns her back on her Spanish-speaking sky-gods and resumes caring for her invalid father. Finally, in the closing sentence, she seems to choose to be reconciled to the barren landscape and life her days have consisted of: she is ready to lie in death beside her father's bones.

First-person narration in *Dusklands* is by men, reflecting two very different forms of imperialist aggression, each relevant in some way to South Africa in the late twentieth century. The first-person narration in *In the Heart of the Country* presents a parody of the Afrikaner ideal of womanhood. This, as Susan Gallagher makes clear in her analysis of Coetzee's work, reached its acme during the Anglo-Boer War (1899–1902), in which Afrikaner women and children were interned in British-run concentration camps where the casualty rate from disease and hunger was almost double that among the husbands and sons fighting the British. Only the women's stubborn courage made possible the survival of the Afrikaner tribe. As a result, the two most famous war memorials depict the Afrikaner woman, in her roles of wife and mother, as the true hero of the struggle. In total contrast to Magda, she is the embodiment of racial purity, of fecundity for the sake of the race, and of self-sacrifice for the sake of her children and husband. (The self-sacrifice is important because the husband remains the source of all authority, despite having such a paragon for a wife.)

Most of the actions in both "The Vietnam Project" and *In the Heart of the Country* are narrated in the present tense. The effect of the present tense can be astonishing, as when Dawn describes stabbing his son while doing so. On the other hand, it is natural that Jacobus should tell his story in the past tense, since he recounts what has already happened to someone who is transcribing his words. It is equally natural that Magda uses the present tense, since for much of the novel what we hear are her thoughts. Magda's style is also even more shot through with anachronisms and other incongruities than Jacobus'. As Coetzee reminds us in his interview with Watson, a character in a novel is not a person in real life.

WAITING FOR THE BARBARIANS

Coetzee's third volume of fiction is viewed by many as pivotal in his career and as his most important work yet. In many ways less adventurous with respect to narrative voice, *Waiting for the Barbarians* (1980) is the most ambitious of his first three works of fiction in its presentation of a sizable social unit and the forces at work on and within it.

The action takes place at an unspecified time in a town on the frontier of a nameless empire. Vehicles are horse drawn, primitive firearms are in common use, and winters are severe. The narrator is the local magistrate, an aging, easygoing, live-and-let-live, epicurean bachelor. Colonel Joll of the Third Bureau (the intelligence arm of the military) has just arrived to investigate rumors of increased barbarian activity on the frontier. Against his better judgment, the magistrate concerns himself with the human wreckage left by the colonel's interrogation of those local aboriginal fisherfolk, plus a few stray barbarians from the hills, whom his soldiers succeed in rounding up. Once Joll has gone in search of barbarians worthier of his mettle, the magistrate ensures that the fisherfolk return to their village.

There remains a young barbarian woman, however, whose father was killed and whose own ankles were broken and eyes almost blinded in the colonel's quest for truth. Out of pity, guilt, and other mixed motives, the magistrate installs her in his household, finding work for her in the kitchen and room for her in his bed. To their mutual frustration, though, all that ever happens is an elaborate expiatory washing of her feet, night after night. Finally, he decides to return her to her people. Nearing the end of the arduous journey, the magistrate is at last able to make love to her and asks her to go back with him. Wisely, she declines the offer.

On his return he finds the Third Bureau in charge of everything, and he is accused of treasonously consorting with the enemy.

Elated at first to nail his colors to the mast, he finds it hard to remain heroic when subjected to the daily discomforts of imprisonment. At temporary liberty when the colonel returns with barbarian prisoners, the magistrate protests loudly the cruel public humiliation they suffer. From that point on, harsh physical punishments and public humiliations become his daily lot, climaxing in a mock execution.

However, the authorities have more important things to concern themselves with. A second expeditionary force rides out, and the magistrate heals slowly and begins to put on weight. When rumors of disaster overtaking the expedition are confirmed and the remainder of the garrison scramble after those who have already left for the capital, the magistrate reclaims his office and begins to take the lead in seeing that what must be done is done. The novel ends with life returning to a crippled normality, though whether on a semipermanent or very temporary basis is left open.

The work is far richer than any mere summary can indicate. For instance, Susan Gallagher, who considers *Waiting for the Barbarians* Coetzee's most powerful work, sees the chilling emphasis on methods of interrogation and torture as a response by Coetzee to the death of the South African dissident Steve Biko and to the treatment of others like him. Similarly, Colonel Joll's arrogant certainty that he needs to learn nothing more about the barbarians—that there is nothing more to be learned—is typical of most European colonizers of Africa. Symbolic of this arrogance are the dark lenses of the glasses the colonel continually wears—a voluntary blindness that contrasts with the involuntary blindness he inflicts on the young barbarian woman, who nevertheless sees much more than the magistrate. Coetzee also makes an attempt to contrast seasonal time in which barbarians live, like fish in the water and birds in the air, with historical time of the empire, perpetually fearful of its end.

The core of the book, however, is the relationship between the magistrate and the young barbarian woman, and the ineptitude of the well-meaning white liberal that it illustrates. Late in the book, the magistrate diagnoses his feelings for her as pity masquerading as desire and tells himself what he wishes she had been able to tell him: to take lessons either from Joll on how to hurt her or from someone else on how to love her. Finally, he sees his earlier, easygoing, pleasure-loving, liberal self as condoning the dark side of empire by his complicitous acquiescence—summer to Joll's winter, but part of the same climate. It is a hard truth for white, middle-class liberals to learn: that sometimes, for all their best intentions, they help to perpetuate what they deplore.

This learning process, from imprisonment and torture and most of all from his relationship with the barbarian woman, is a learning process for the reader also, in part because it is conveyed through present-tense narration. The magistrate's running commentary on an agony that makes him bellow almost incoherently is as extraordinary as Eugene Dawn's description of stabbing his young son. However, few readers are aware of and still fewer disconcerted by the incongruity of action and narration occurring simultaneously. On the contrary, narration in the present tense compels us to share the magistrate's experiences instead of viewing them from a later, detached point in time.

The importance of the link between the magistrate and the young barbarian woman is further emphasized in a series of dreams that reflect the stages and changing aspects of their relationship. After he has returned her to her people and has suffered for so doing, for instance, he dreams that she bakes him bread that he takes at her hand. The dreams also recapitulate the formal unity that the novel derives from its single seasonal cycle. The first three dreams are wintry; the barbarian woman and some children are building a snow castle. Later dreams change the scene, the final one confirming the freedom of magistrate and barbarian, man and woman, from

each other. At the end of the novel, the magistrate actually watches children build a snowman—"not a bad snowman" (p. 156).

LIFE & TIMES OF MICHAEL K

Michael K's speech and features are disfigured by a harelip, his mind works slowly, and he grew up in a residential school for the handicapped. In every way, he is the least articulate of Coetzee's protagonists. Presumably because Michael K cannot adequately explain himself and those events surrounding him, more than three-quarters of *Life & Times of Michael K* (1983) is narrated in the third person. Yet Coetzee apparently finds the impersonal third-person voice insufficient to compose the whole work. Part Two of the book's three sections is narrated by a much more articulate character, a medical officer, whose role is to discover and analyze what has happened to Michael for the first two-thirds of the story. Yet at the same time the medical officer is unable to fathom some hidden depth to Michael's being. Like the magistrate, he understands yet does not understand.

The book is also the most overtly political of Coetzee's novels up to the time of its writing. In some ways, as David Attwell points out, it was a response to the South African government's attempt to establish a government by three minorities (roughly 4.5 million whites, 2.5 million "Coloreds" of mixed racial descent, and 0.8 million Asians) through a complex arrangement of three racially determined separate legislative bodies. Enfranchising Coloreds and Asians for the first time, this proposal would have permanently excluded 19 million black Africans from any say in government except in a handful of impoverished, backward Bantustans or "reservations," set aside as their share of their original homeland but too small to hold them.

Not surprisingly, Coetzee and other writers —most notably Nadine Gordimer in *July's People* (1981)—wrote novels at this time depicting a state of civil war in South Africa. Through a landscape torn by such a conflict, Michael K sets out to push his mother in a handcart the two hundred or so miles from Cape Town to the small town of Prince Albert, where she hopes at least to be able to die in peace. She dies before they get there, but Michael is able to scatter her ashes on the fields around the farmhouse where she was born.

Here, while living in the deserted building, he embarks on his vocation as a gardener by planting pumpkin seeds. Forced to move on, he is arrested and sent to a labor camp, from which he escapes and returns to the farmhouse to resume cultivating pumpkins. His solitude is now invaded by guerrillas from the hills, whom he considers accompanying when they leave. He decides, however, that "enough men had gone off to war saying the time for gardening was when the war was over; whereas there must be men to stay behind and keep gardening alive, or at least the idea of gardening; because once that cord was broken, the earth would grow hard and forget her children" (p. 109; the Viking edition). He is arrested again, as an accomplice of the guerrillas, and sent to a rehabilitation camp, where the medical officer takes over the narration.

The officer's first priority is to get nourishment into a wasting body that will not accept food. Though at wit's end about what to do with Michael, the doctor is in awe of something peculiar to him. After Michael escapes, the officer talks to himself about how he should have gone with him, and then imagines himself talking to Michael as he envisions pursuing him. He tells Michael of his sense, watching him sleep, of "a thickening of the air, a concentration of darkness, a black whirlwind roaring in utter silence above [his] body" (p. 164).

The final section of the book, roughly fourteen pages long, serves mainly to reestablish Michael K as the controlling if limited consciousness of the novel. All other characters are new—strangers on a beach whose foot-

steps the next tide will erase. They feed him bread and honey and a little wine, a man steals some of his pumpkin seeds, and a woman performs fellatio on him. He finds the room under the stairs where he and his mother used to live—now a storeroom for furniture, but clearly someone still sleeps there from time to time. He imagines this to be a little old man with a stoop, a bottle, and a beard. Remembering with pride his vocation as gardener, he fantasizes taking him back to Prince Albert, both of them with pockets full of seeds.

Coetzee says of the final section, in an interview with Tony Morphet, that "it would be a cop-out for the book to end after Part Two. It is important that K should not emerge from the book as an angel" (p. 457). Coetzee's statement appears to be an embarrassed disavowal of the "black whirlwind" above Michael's bed. Yet at the end of *Foe* (1986), Coetzee creates a similar, even more strongly symbolic "slow stream" from Friday's mouth that moves north and south "to the ends of the earth" (p. 157).

In fact, it is hard not to sense that Michael K is symbolic from start to finish. Gordimer describes the book in "The Idea of Gardening" as "a marvelous work that leaves nothing unsaid . . . about what human beings do to fellow human beings" and thus makes amends for its other, more negative, comments (p. 6). However, for sheer viciousness nothing in the novel touches *Waiting for the Barbarians*; compared with Colonel Joll, the commanding and medical officers of the rehabilitation camp are the "angels." *Age of Iron* (1990), too, is far more unrelentingly pessimistic in its portrayal of human behavior. Michael K's plight is due as much to what he is as to what others do to him—and what he is is a nostalgic symbol of innocence in a garden, an innocence and a garden that have never existed except as a mythic ideal and to which modern man would not welcome a return, even if it were possible.

This is not to deny the power of the novel, but merely to acknowledge the understandable impatience that prompted a black reviewer, as quoted by Attwell, to write: "The absence of any meaningful relationship between Michael K and anybody else ... means that in fact we are dealing not with a human spirit but an amoeba, from whose life we can draw neither example nor warning" (*J. M. Coetzee*, p. 92).

FOE

At a first reading, Coetzee's next novel, *Foe*, is a complete change, with little or no relevance to South Africa. What Coetzee has done, as Attwell has noted in *J. M. Coetzee*, is to rewrite Daniel Defoe's *Robinson Crusoe* (1719), reverting to Defoe's original name before he added the aristocratic prefix *De* to his own, and to the original spelling of the protagonist's name he borrowed from his friend Timothy Cruso. In Coetzee's version, a woman castaway, Susan Barton, joins Cruso and Friday on the island. Cruso is a morose individual who spends most of his time terracing the island's slopes, although he has no seeds to plant there. Unlike Defoe's Friday, who is a handsome Carib, Coetzee's is a Negro who has had his tongue cut out. Just how he or Cruso arrived on the island is a mystery (Cruso tells a different story every time). It seems likely, however, that when Friday ceremonially scatters petals off the coast, he does so where the ship that brought one or both of them lies wrecked.

After all three of them are rescued by a passing ship, Cruso dies on the voyage home. Barton, finding herself responsible for Friday as well as herself, writes an account of her time on the island—which forms the first section of the novel—and seeks out Foe as the author likely to be able to rewrite it in marketable form. The second section is a journal kept by Barton of her adventures while trying to track down Foe and her manuscript, for he has vanished in order to escape creditors. A puzzling but important feature of this section is the pursuit of Barton by her self-styled daughter, also named Susan Barton. The older Barton had a daughter, who was abducted by an English trader and carried off to Bahia in Brazil. (It was from an unsuccessful search for her that her mother was returning when the crew of her ship mutinied, killing the captain and marooning his mistress.) However, the older Barton does not recognize as her daughter this girl haunting her threshold and is convinced that the girl has been sent into her life—which is to say, written into her story—by Foe.

The third section is a first-person present-tense account (but not in the form of letters or a manuscript written by Susan Barton, as the first two were) of the encounter between Susan Barton and Daniel Foe, once she has tracked him down. Two important themes emerge. First, Foe refuses merely to rewrite the story of life on the island, as Barton has related it; instead, he wants to start with a mother's quest for a daughter, continue with a daughter's quest for her mother, and end with a final meeting in London. Barton was clearly right that the daughter who haunts her was sent by Foe—indeed, was fathered by Foe rather than mothered by Susan Barton. To that extent, therefore, this is a feminist rather than a postcolonial novel for it addresses male appropriation of, and attempts to assert hegemony over, a woman's reading of her own life story.

The second theme is Friday's silence. Barton is quite willing to admit that there is a blank, a silence, in the story she tells, and that this gap is the story that Friday cannot tell—or, more accurately, will not tell. When Foe suggests that Barton teach Friday to write his story, beginning with "a," or alpha, Friday subverts the whole enterprise by proceeding straight to "o," or omega, the last letter of the Greek alphabet.

The very choice of *Robinson Crusoe* as a text to be rewritten makes a political statement, since Defoe's novel has long been seen as an early embodiment of colonialism. To this Coetzee adds a Cruso who imposes on the island his own barren concept of what an island should be. He adds as well a Friday who is totally silenced, unlike Defoe's, who is restricted to a crude pidgin version of English (despite only ever having heard Crusoe speak the language). Moreover, when Friday finds he can express himself by dancing in one of Foe's robes and does so with such abandon that the robe flies high in the air around him, Barton admits to seeing the naked Friday but is strangely silent as to whether the missing tongue is a kind of euphemism for a more radical dismemberment.

Thus, though the novel is overtly about the silencing or disempowerment of Susan Barton by Daniel Foe — that is, of woman by man — it is even more strikingly about the silencing of Friday. Presumably, the mystery of who silenced (and possibly emasculated) him — slave traders or even Cruso himself — implies that it is not Afrikaners or white South Africans or capitalist plutocrats or any other single group who are to blame for the plight of black Africans or third-world citizens in general. Rather, everyone who benefits from their exploitation is to blame.

Friday gains in power as his story unfolds, much as the young barbarian woman and Michael K (that is, the inarticulate characters) in the preceding two novels do. Moreover, the fact that Friday and his need of empowerment must share the novel with Susan and her need should not be seen as weakening the case for either of them; both feminism and post-colonialism have need of allies rather than rivals.

In the brief, enigmatically symbolic final section of *Foe*, "the faintest faraway roar ... of waves in a seashell" (p. 154), like "a slow stream, without breath, without interruption," flows from Friday's mouth "to the ends of the earth" (p. 157). Both this stream and the black whirlwind over Michael K's bed are intimations of a power that as yet remains untapped, but soon will be. As Salman Rushdie in *Shame* (1983) uses magic realism to enable his child-like, powerless heroine, Sufiya, to exact a terrible revenge on the sources of sadness in her own life and of corruption in the life of the nation, so Coetzee uses Michael K and Friday to suggest, much less melodramatically, the inevitability of a similar day of reckoning.

AGE OF IRON

Rushdie also describes how Sufiya's immune system, whose role is to defend her body from disease, treacherously becomes the enemy — that is, the autoimmune disease that attacks her body. He uses her disease as a metaphor for the corruption of those who forsake their role as guardians of the social and economic health of Pakistan by using their power to enrich themselves at the country's expense. Similarly, Coetzee in *Age of Iron* (1990) chooses a narrator and protagonist who is dying of cancer to report on the state of affairs in South Africa during the troubled years in which Coetzee was writing the novel.

One of the book's most striking features, in fact, is the directness with which social and political realities in that country are described. Elizabeth Curren, a retired university teacher of Latin and Greek, witnesses casual police brutality toward Bheki (the teenage son of her domestic servant Florence) and his friend John, but she is ignored when she protests it. She witnesses living and dying conditions in the township of Guguletu, which resembles Soweto, outside Cape Town. She watches blacks setting fire to the shanties of other blacks, identifies Bheki as one of five youths shot by the police, and hears them shoot John when he takes refuge in her house. She also responds vituperatively to the politicians she sees on the television screen. This novel is no mere allegory of evil: as Attwell observes, "Coetzee seems far less chary in *Age of Iron* about using representational discourse" (1993, p. 120).

Another marked departure is the articulate anger of the downtrodden. Florence will not listen when Elizabeth finds fault with her son for staying away from school. She and people like her are proud of their youngsters' insistence on "liberation before education," proud of their willingness to risk death in support of each other. When Elizabeth, shocked by living conditions in Guguletu, is too taken aback to find the right words to express her feelings, her plea for more time is dismissed by bystanders as "shit." The Michael Ks and Fridays of the world are no longer silent; Gordimer cannot say of this novel, as she did of *Life & Times of Michael K*, that Coetzee "does not recognize what the victims, seeing themselves as victims no longer, have done, are doing, and believe they must do for themselves" (p. 6).

The narrative takes the form of a journal or long letters to Elizabeth's daughter in the United States—a letter begun the day she learns that cancer has renewed its attack, but not to be mailed until after her death. On that same day, the beginning of the end of her life, she returns from the hospital to see that a drifter has taken up residence in the alley beside her garage. Like an angel of death, he haunts her remaining days, yet increasingly is the one to whom she turns and on whom she relies.

As with Michael K, Coetzee does not identify the drifter's race. It seems likely that Michael is Colored or black, since he is automatically assumed to be in league with the guerrillas, even though the use of "K" as his name indicates that a Kafkaesque nonspecificity is intended. But "Vercueil" is presumably the name of a white or Colored descendant of the 180 or so French Huguenot immigrants who arrived in 1689, only to be assimilated by the original Dutch settlers. That Bheki and John do not mention his color when berating him for being a drunk, coupled with the fact that Coetzee keeps him away from any blacks other than Florence and the two boys, intimates that Vercueil's role is not a racial one.

What factors, then, prompted Coetzee to incorporate within the same novel an edu-

cated, articulate woman dying of cancer, a homeless and largely silent "good for nothing" who nevertheless becomes increasingly indispensable to her, her African servant and the servant's son, a distant daughter who will read this account of her mother's slow death when it is too late to help her, and a country torn by civil strife? On the simplest level, cancer may, as already suggested, be seen as analogous to the something that is so clearly rotten in the state of this particular Denmark. Elizabeth even sees cancer, or the body cannibalizing itself, as an instance of self-loathing—an apt metaphor for the South African body politic. When, sleepless, she lies listening to Florence and her children sleeping and breathing in harmony with each other, she muses, as many white South Africans must fear having to do: "Once I had everything, I thought. Now you have everything and I have nothing" (p. 37). Where, however, do the daughter and the drifter fit into the scenario?

In this novel as in none of the others it may be helpful to take autobiographical factors into account. As Gallagher points out, the book is dedicated to V.H.M.C. (1904–1985), Z.C. (1912–1988), and N.G.C. (1966–1989)— that is, to Coetzee's mother, father, and son, all of whom died while he was writing *Age of Iron* or the final stages of *Foe*. That he should have chosen a dying woman as his narrator is therefore understandable, and that a novel he completed in the year his son was killed in an accident should deal so extensively with parent-child relationships bespeaks a cruelly prescient irony. What these personal tragedies have the most obvious bearing on, however, is a tentative, exploratory, undogmatic tone to the whole novel.

For instance, although the magistrate in *Waiting for the Barbarians* achieves self-knowledge only after prolonged and painful trial and error, in the end he can reassure himself that he has it right—that his condemnation of imperialism was insufficiently grounded in a genuine, emotional commitment. He took pity on a young barbarian girl he could not love. It takes Elizabeth much less time to perceive that while her concern for Bheki is a loving one, she cannot feel the same way about his friend, John. However, this prompts her to write to her daughter, "Not wanting to love him, how true can I say my love is for you?" (p. 126, the Secker & Warburg edition). Only paragraphs later, moreover, in her drug-induced hallucination, she has become a dog lost in a maze, unable to seek help from God, who also appears as a dog. God can scent her, since she is in heat, but cannot find her because God is lost in another maze. Even allowing for the effect of the pills she takes to deaden the pain, this is powerful imagery for Coetzee to let her use, unless he intends her self-knowledge to be much less stabilizing than the magistrate's.

Similarly, her arguments with Florence and Mr. Thabane, a teacher, about the violent role of children in the struggle for equality end inconclusively. In both the public and the private sphere there are no longer any certainties, and though this may also be true of his earlier novels, it is much more apparent in this one that Coetzee is using the writing of fiction to carry out rather than merely to record his explorations.

Whether intentionally or not, Coetzee's emphasis on an incident that happened to Elizabeth's mother — and one that Elizabeth sees as key — may do more than anything else to clarify the link between the public and private sectors of the novel, between the travail of a bitterly divided nation and her own painful and lingering death. A childhood memory of her mother's was of how, on the family's annual trek to the seaside for Christmas, the children used to sleep under the wagon and their parents in the wagon. One night, when they had camped at the top of a mountain pass, she lay awake watching the stars between the spokes of the wheels and it seemed that either the stars or the wheels were moving. Terrified lest her parents be carried down the mountainside in a runaway wagon, yet afraid to say anything and appear foolish, she

fell asleep and told the story to no one until her own daughter was old enough to understand.

This incident, as Elizabeth recounts it to Vercueil and writes it down for *her* daughter to read, is where she feels her own identity to have begun. Neither she nor Coetzee offers any explanation as to how or why this came to be, but in a curious way the novel's divergent foci are mirrored in the alternatives that faced the child under the wagon: either the stars or the wagon wheels were slowly but inexorably moving; either the whole (society) or a part thereof (the individual) is in a spin. By choosing a dying narrator to report on a sick society, Coetzee creates a similar ambiguity of relative movement, with the very real possibilities that everything is turning and that there is no still point to such revolutions.

In such a universe of relatives rather than absolutes, Elizabeth Curren struggles to hold on to what there is left for her to believe in. Even at those times we think she is wrong — whether when she lectures Florence on her parental duties, or when she ignores Vercueil's advice either to tell her daughter she needs help now or to refrain from telling her at all — we respect the steadfastness, the stability of her stubborn courage. We are reminded that societies are made up in part of people who are wrong (whom we nevertheless admire) and of people who are right (whom we nevertheless dislike), of superfluous overachievers and indispensable drifters. We recognize that novelists too have private as well as public lives and preoccupations, and their works reflect and do not always reconcile them.

Thus, as becomes increasingly apparent the longer he writes, Coetzee is an author whose private preoccupations include a fascination with contemporary, postmodern techniques in fiction, but who stubbornly insists on his novels remaining sufficiently accessible to a wide enough readership for his strong views on South African politics to be heard. If some of his readers were deeply moved by *Life &*

Times of Michael K, baffled by *Foe*, and reassured by *Age of Iron*, others who saw *Foe* as a victory for postmodernism feel betrayed by *Age of Iron*. As in *Age of Iron* itself, so in his oeuvre as a whole, incompatibles aspire to compatability.

THE MASTER OF PETERSBURG

By *Age of Iron* it must have become apparent to readers of Coetzee that, however varied his novels are one from another, there is an enduring quality to them that is quintessentially Coetzee. At the same time, however, unforeseen surprises lie in wait for them in every new novel he writes, and those lurking in his seventh novel, *The Master of Petersburg* (1994), are more unexpected than ever. For the first time in a Coetzee novel the narration is entirely in the third person, the story is set in nineteenth-century Russia, and its protagonist, Fyodor Dostoevsky, is a well-known historical figure. Reassuringly familiar, however, is the start-to-finish present-time narration, even if combining it with a third-person narrative voice can sound a little strange.

The great novelist returns from Dresden, Germany, where he has taken refuge from his creditors, to St. Petersburg. He returns because, in the novel, his stepson has either killed himself or been killed, whether by the police or by fellow revolutionaries. In life Pavel, the stepson, outlived his stepfather by a couple of decades, and Dostoevsky remained in Dresden with his young wife for several more years. In fiction, however, Dostoevsky becomes politically involved with Nechaev (a revolutionary whom in real life Dostoevsky never met but whose murder of a fellow conspirator helped spur him to write *The Possessed*, 1872), and emotionally involved with Anna Sergeyevna (Pavel's former landlady) and her young daughter.

A search for parallels with Coetzee's earlier novels turns up instances that are initially promising but ultimately not always enlight-

ening. A correct but menacing tone to exchanges between Dostoevsky and Councillor Maximov of the police recalls those between the magistrate and Colonel Joll in *Waiting for the Barbarians*. But we neither witness nor are told of brutality that remotely matches the colonel's. And a long, heated dispute between Dostoevsky and Nechaev echoes in abstract terms much of what the earlier novels enact directly. Clearly the intent is to throw light on the inconsistencies and blind spots of both advocates rather than to convince us of the validity of one or the other's case.

Another link to an earlier Coetzee novel is the presence of the two novelists, Defoe and Dostoevsky, in *Foe* and *The Master of Petersburg*, respectively. Admittedly the role of Dostoevsky as protagonist is much more overt and central, and that of Defoe more implied and peripheral. Admittedly, also, the intertextuality of *Foe* and *Robinson Crusoe* is far more integral and extensive than that between *The Master of Petersburg* and Dostoevsky's *The Possessed*. In the former case the impact of Coetzee's novel depends to a large extent on questions raised by his radical rewriting, from a postcolonial and feminist viewpoint, of Defoe's original text. In the latter case, however, the two novels are linked more loosely and more straightforwardly by similarities of incident and personality. Most obvious of these are the death in each book of a young revolutionary, killed in the original version certainly and in Coetzee's version possibly by his fellow conspirators, and the hostility (unequivocal in his own novel, ambivalent in Coetzee's) of Dostoevsky toward the godless young rebels in question.

Much of the strangest and most striking correspondence, however, originates in the chapters of *The Possessed*, which the initial publisher refused to print. In them Nicholas Stavrogin, an aging roué, admits to having raped a ten-year-old girl. But he is not the only such lecher in Dostoevsky's novels. Indeed, his portrayal of such characters as Stavrogin and Svidrigailov (in *Crime and Punish-*

ment) contributed in no small way to rumors that Dostoevsky himself had similar tastes. So it is plausible for Coetzee to have Anna Sergeyevna accuse Dostoevsky, during their most frenetic night of lovemaking, of using her as a "route" to her daughter, Matryona. This chapter then closes with Matryona discovering her mother and Dostoevsky still in bed together in the morning.

Significantly titled "Stavrogin," the final chapter shows us Dostoevsky at work composing a few erotic paragraphs about two young lovers. The young man remembers Svidrigailov saying, in *Crime and Punishment*, "Women like to be humiliated" (p. 244). At the same time he compels his partner to specify, more and more loudly and excitedly, precisely what it is she wants him to do to her in the course of their lovemaking. Their assignations become a regular Wednesday feature. And on each occasion the young man is well aware, and is excited by the thought, that his landlady's young daughter is watching their performance through a door left slightly ajar. While Dostoevsky is still at work, Matryona enters his room and talks to him briefly. When he has finished the piece he places it open on the table, clearly intending her to read it, and leaves the house. "It is an assault upon the innocence of a child," says the narrator. "It is an act for which he can expect no forgiveness" (p. 249).

As early as in *In the Heart of the Country*, less ostentatiously in *Life & Times of Michael K*, again in *Foe*, and now in the closing chapters of *The Master of Petersburg*, Coetzee infuses a basically realistic style with intimations of symbolism. It seems as if he is searching in desperation for a way—almost a magic realist way—to reach some kind of conclusion. Yet the reader is always conscious of great power in the writing, a great poetic power.

Throughout the novel, moreover, but particularly toward its mysterious close, the reader cannot avoid a sense that Coetzee is escaping from a South African setting and choosing one with an equally troubled but less prejudged past and present. It may be that he feels better placed, in a fictional czarist Russia, to help readers apply his insights to their own circumstances than when he wrote about a nation that gave the world cause for so much self-satisfaction and enjoyably righteous indignation. Or is may just be that, writing in a South Africa in process of reforming itself, he feels a need to insist that evil is still alive and well.

Unlike Percy Bysshe Shelley, therefore, whose *Defence of Poetry* (1821) claims on behalf of the artist that "Poetry is the record of the best and happiest moments of the happiest and best minds," Coetzee's Dostoevsky offers the writer a choice of responses to the worst and unhappiest perversions of the unhappiest and worst minds:

> He can cry out in the midst of this shameful fall, beat his arms like wings, call upon God or his wife to save him. Or he can give himself to it, refuse the chloroform of terror or unconsciousness, watch and listen for the moment which may or may not arrive—it is not in his power to force it—when from being a body plunging into darkness he shall become a body within whose core a plunge into darkness is taking place, a body which contains its own falling and its own darkness.
>
> (p. 234)

It is necessary, that is, if the novelist is to be true to his or her vision and if that vision is to be true to life, that he or she know the best and the worst—that he or she encompass the best and the worst, but especially the worst. And the most unthinkable form of evil by which Dostoevsky has been tempted or can conceive of being tempted is "an assault upon the innocence of a child." In no other novel has Coetzee been so preoccupied by evil.

Yet unlike those of Eugene Dawn, Jacobus Coetzee, Magda, the magistrate, Susan Barton, or Elizabeth Curren, the tone of voice the reader hears behind the printed word of *The Master of Petersburg* reveals nothing and conceals nothing inadvertently. It is the voice of a novelist creating the life of a novelist, with as much or as little candor or irony as he pleases. This is a new Coetzee.

Selected Bibliography

BIBLIOGRAPHY

Goddard, Kevin, and John Read, eds. *J. M. Coetzee: A Bibliography*. National English Literary Museum Bibliographic Series 3. Grahamstown, South Africa: NELM, 1990.

FICTION

Dusklands. Johannesburg, South Africa: Ravan Press, 1974; London: Secker & Warburg, 1982; Harmondsworth, U.K.: Penguin, 1983; New York: Penguin, 1985.

In the Heart of the Country. London: Secker & Warburg, 1977; New York: Harper (retitled *From the Heart of the Country*), 1977; Johannesburg, South Africa: Ravan (bilingual ed.; spoken dialogue between Magda and the servants written by Coetzee in Afrikaans), 1978; repr. under original title, New York: Penguin, 1982.

Waiting for the Barbarians. London: Secker & Warburg, 1980; Johannesburg, South Africa: Ravan, 1981; New York: Penguin, 1982.

Life & Times of Michael K. London: Secker & Warburg, 1983; Johannesburg, South Africa: Ravan, 1983; New York: Viking, 1984.

Foe. London: Secker & Warburg, 1986; Johannesburg, South Africa: Ravan, 1986; New York: Viking, 1987.

Age of Iron. New York: Random House, 1990; London: Secker & Warburg, 1990.

The Master of Petersburg. New York: Viking, 1994; London, Secker & Warburg, 1994.

COLLECTED ESSAYS AND ARTICLES

White Writing: On the Culture of Letters in South Africa. New Haven, Conn.: Yale University Press, 1988. Essays by Coetzee on South African landscape, race, and language in South African novels; important background to Coetzee's treatment of such themes. This and the following collection reprint the important Coetzee articles not listed below.

Doubling the Point: Essays and Interviews. Ed. by David Attwell. Cambridge, Mass.: Harvard University Press, 1992. Linked groups of wide-ranging essays by Coetzee are introduced by deeply thoughtful conversations (rather than interviews) between editor and Coetzee.

ESSAYS, ARTICLES, AND REVIEWS

"Statistical Indices of 'Difficulty.'" In *Language & Style* 2, no. 3 (1969).

"The Comedy of Point of View in Beckett's *Murphy.*" In *Critique* 12, no. 2 (1970).

"Alex La Guma and the Responsibilities of the South African Writer." In Joseph Okpaku, ed., *New African Literature and the Arts.* Vol. 3. New York: Third Press, 1973.

"Samuel Beckett and the Temptations of Style." In *Theoria* 41 (1973).

"Samuel Beckett's *Lessness*: An Exercise in Decomposition." In *Computers and the Humanities* 7, no. 4 (1973).

"Surreal Metaphors and Random Processes." In *Journal of Literary Semantics* 8, no. 1 (1979).

"Art and Apartheid." Review of *Notebooks 1960–1977* by Athol Fugard. In *New Republic* (9 April 1984).

"How I Learned About America—and Africa—in Texas." In *New York Times Book Review* (15 April 1984).

"Listening to the Afrikaners." Review of *Waiting: The Whites of South Africa* by Vincent Crapanzano. In *New York Times Book Review* (14 April 1985).

"Tales of Afrikaners." In *New York Times Magazine* (9 March 1986).

"A Prisoner of the Thought Police." In *New York Times Book Review* (31 May 1987).

"The Novel Today." In *Upstream: A Magazine of the Arts* 6, no. 1 (1988). Keynote address (and key Coetzee document) at *Weekly Mail* Bookweek, 9–13 November 1987.

"The Taint of the Pornographic: Defending (Against) *Lady Chatterley's Lover.*" In *Mosaic* 21, no. 1 (1988).

"André Brink and the Censor." In *Research in African Literatures* 21, no. 3 (1990).

"Too Late the Liberal." Review of *Save the Beloved Country* by Alan Paton. In *New Republic* (8–15 January 1990).

EDITING AND TRANSLATING

Posthumous Confession, by Marcellus Emants. Trans. with intro. by J. M. Coetzee. Boston: Twayne, 1975.

A Land Apart: A Contemporary South African Reader. Coedited with André Brink. New York: Viking, 1986; London: Faber & Faber, 1986.

INTERVIEWS

Morphet, Tony. "Two Interviews with J. M. Coetzee, 1983 and 1987." In *TriQuarterly* 69 (1987).

Rhedin, Folke. Interview in *Kunapipi* 6, no. 1 (1984).

Sévry, Jean. "An Interview with J. M. Coetzee." In *Commonwealth Essays and Studies* 9, no. 1 (1986).

Watson, Stephen. "Speaking: J. M. Coetzee." In *Speak* (Cape Town) 1, no. 3 (1978).

CRITICAL STUDIES

Attridge, Derek. "Oppressive Silence: J. M. Coetzee's *Foe* and the Politics of the Canon." In Karen Lawrence, ed., *Decolonizing the Tradition: New Views of Twentieth-Century "British" Literary Canons.* Urbana: University of Illinois Press, 1992.

———. "Trusting the Other: Ethics and Politics in J. M. Coetzee's *Age of Iron*." In *South Atlantic Quarterly* 93, no. 1 (1994).

Attwell, David. "The Problem of History in the Fiction of J. M. Coetzee." In Martin Trump, ed., *Rendering Things Visible: Essays on South African Literary Culture.* Athens: Ohio University Press, 1990.

———. *J. M. Coetzee: South Africa and the Politics of Writing.* Berkeley: University of California Press, 1993. Comprehensive, but with a clear line of argument. Theoretical but not impenetrably so. Indispensable.

Barnard, Rita. "Dream Topographies: J. M. Coetzee and the South African Pastoral." In *South Atlantic Quarterly* 93, no. 1 (1994).

Begam, Richard. "Silence and Mut(e)ilation: White Writing in J. M. Coetzee's *Foe*." In *South Atlantic Quarterly* 93, no. 1 (1994).

Bishop, G. Scott. "J. M. Coetzee's *Foe*: A Culmination and a Solution to a Problem of White Identity." In *World Literature Today* 64, no. 1 (1990).

Brink, André P. "Writing Against Big Brother: Notes on Apocalyptic Fiction in South Africa." In *World Literature Today* 58, no. 2 (1984). Important statement by one of the Gordimer-Coetzee-Brink triumvirate.

Cantor, Paul A. "Happy Days in the Veld: Beckett and Coetzee's *In the Heart of the Country*." In *South Atlantic Quarterly* 93, no. 1 (1994).

Castillo, Debra A. "The Composition of the Self in Coetzee's *Waiting for the Barbarians*." In *Critique* 27, no. 2 (1986).

Dodd, Josephine. "Naming and Framing: Naturalization and Colonization in J. M. Coetzee's *In the Heart of the Country*." In *World Literature Written in English* 27, no. 2 (1987).

Donoghue, Denis. "Her Man Friday." Review of *Foe*, in *New York Times Book Review* (22 February 1987).

Dovey, Teresa. "Coetzee and His Critics: The Case of *Dusklands*." In *English in Africa* (Grahamstown, South Africa) 14, no. 2 (1987).

———. "Allegory vs. Allegory: The Divorce of Different Modes of Allegorical Perception in Coetzee's *Waiting for the Barbarians*." In *Journal of Literary Studies* (Pretoria) 4, no. 2 (1988).

———. *The Novels of J. M. Coetzee: Lacanian Allegories.* Johannesburg, South Africa: Ad. Donker, 1988. Shrewdly perceptive; too exclusively Lacanian.

———. "Introduction" to Kevin Goddard and John Read, eds., *J. M. Coetzee: A Bibliography.* Grahamstown, South Africa: National English Literary Museum, 1990.

Gallagher, Susan VanZanten. *A Story of South Africa: J. M. Coetzee's Fiction in Context.* Cambridge, Mass.: Harvard University Press, 1991. Lives up to its title; places the novels in a historical context.

Gardiner, Allan. "J. M. Coetzee's *Dusklands*: Colonial Encounters of the Robinsonian Kind." In *World Literature Written in English* 27, no. 2 (1987).

Gillmer, Joan. "The Motif of the Damaged Child in the Work of J. M. Coetzee." In M. J. Daymond et al., eds., *Momentum: On Recent South African Writing.* Pietermaritzburg, South Africa: University of Natal Press, 1984.

Glenn, Ian. "Nadine Gordimer, J. M. Coetzee, and the Politics of Interpretation." In *South Atlantic Quarterly* 93, no. 1 (1994).

Gordimer, Nadine. "The Idea of Gardening." In *New York Review of Books* (2 February 1984).

Harrison, James. "Point of View and Tense in the Novels of J. M. Coetzee." In *Journal of Commonwealth Literature* 30, no. 1 (1995).

Jolly, Rosemary Jane. "Territorial Metaphor in Coetzee's *Waiting for the Barbarians*." In *ARIEL* 20, no. 2 (1990).

Knox-Shaw, Peter. "*Dusklands*: A Metaphysics of Violence." In *Contrast* 4, no. 1 (1982). Repr. in *Commonwealth Novel in English* 2, no. 1 (1983).

Lindfors, Bernth. "Coming to Terms with the Apocalypse: Recent South African Fiction." In Britta Olinder, ed., *A Sense of Place: Essays in Post-Colonial Literatures*. Göteborg, Sweden: Göteborg University Press, 1984. An important overview.

Maes-Jelinek, Hena. "Ambivalent Clio: J. M. Coetzee's *In the Heart of the Country* and Wilson Harris's *Carnival*." In *Journal of Commonwealth Literature* 22, no. 1 (1987).

Marais, Michael. "Interpretative Authoritarianism: Reading/Colonizing Coetzee's *Foe*." In *English in Africa* (Grahamstown, South Africa) 16, no. 1 (1989).

———. "'Omnipotent Fantasies' of a Solitary Self: J. M. Coetzee's 'The Narrative of Jacobus Coetzee.'" In *Journal of Commonwealth Literature* 28, no. 2 (1993).

Martin, Richard G., "Narrative, History, Ideology: A Study of *Waiting for the Barbarians* and *Burger's Daughter*." In *ARIEL* 17, no. 3 (1986).

Moore, John Rees. "J. M. Coetzee and *Foe*." In *Sewanee Review* 98, no. 1 (1990).

Moses, Michael Valdez. "Solitary Walkers: Rousseau and Coetzee's *Life & Times of Michael K*." In *South Atlantic Quarterly* 93, no. 1 (1994).

Olsen, Lance. "The Presence of Absence: Coetzee's *Waiting for the Barbarians*." In *ARIEL* 16, no. 2 (1985).

Penner, Dick. *Countries of the Mind: The Fiction of J. M. Coetzee*. Westport, Conn.: Greenwood Press, 1989. Comprehensive, clear, an excellent introduction.

Post, Robert M. "Oppression in the Fiction of J. M. Coetzee." In *Critique* 27, no. 2 (1986).

———. "The Noise of Freedom: J. M. Coetzee's *Foe*." In *Critique* 30, no. 3 (1989).

Rich, Paul. "Tradition and Revolt in South African Fiction: The Novels of André Brink, Nadine Gordimer and J. M. Coetzee." In *Journal of Southern African Studies* 9, no. 1 (1982).

———. "Apartheid and the Decline of the Civilization Idea: An Essay on Nadine Gordimer's *July's People* and J. M. Coetzee's *Waiting for the Barbarians*." In *Research in African Literatures* 15, no. 3 (1984). An important comparison of two major South African novelists.

Rody, Caroline. "The Mad Colonial Daughter's Revolt: J. M. Coetzee's *In the Heart of the Country*." In *South Atlantic Quarterly* 93, no. 1 (1994).

Strauss, Peter. "Coetzee's Idylls: The Ending of *In the Heart of the Country*." In M. J. Daymond et al., eds., *Momentum: On Recent South African Writing*. Pietermaritzburg, South Africa: University of Natal Press, 1984.

Vaughan, Michael. "Literature and Politics: Currents in South African Writing in the Seventies." In *Journal of Southern African Studies* 9, no. 1 (1982). Important statement by a hostile critic.

Watson, Stephen. "Colonialism and the Novels of J. M. Coetzee." In *Research in African Literatures* 17, no. 3 (1986). Astutely clarifies the intellectual, social, and cultural sources of Coetzee's creativity.

Wood, W. J. B. "*Waiting for the Barbarians*: Two Sides of Imperial Rule and Some Related Considerations." In M. J. Daymond et al., eds., *Momentum: On Recent South African Writing*, Pietermaritzburg, South Africa: University of Natal Press, 1984.

Mia Couto
1955–

DAVID BROOKSHAW

MIA COUTO is the pen name of António Emílio Leite Couto. He was born on 7 July 1955 in Mozambique's second-largest city, Beira, of parents originally from the north of Portugal. From an early age he came to be known by the nickname Mia. His father, Fernando Couto, worked as an administrator for the railways but also wrote poetry and served as editor of the local newspaper, *Notícias da Beira*. Couto spent his youth in Beira, but after finishing his secondary education in 1971, he left for the capital, Lourenço Marques (now called Maputo), to study medicine at Lourenço Marques University (called Eduardo Mondlane following independence). Following the 1974 coup in Portugal, which brought an end to the forty-eight-year-old dictatorship and reestablished a democratic government, which in turn ushered in Mozambique's independence the following year, Couto interrupted his medical studies to take up a career in journalism. In 1977, he was appointed director of the Mozambican Information Agency, and later served as general editor of the weekly magazine *Tempo* (1978–1981) and of the daily newspaper *Notícias* (1981–1986). In 1985, while still working on the newspaper, he returned to his studies at Eduardo Mondlane University, completing a degree in biology in 1989. After graduating, he began working as a lecturer and researcher at the university, with a special interest in the ecology of coastal areas.

Even after resuming his studies in biology, Couto continued to write a column for *Notícias*, for which he was awarded a prize by the National Journalists' Organization in 1988. His first volume of poetry, *Raiz de orvalho* (Root of dew), was published in 1983. Several of his poems were later published in reviews and anthologies in Mozambique, Brazil, Portugal, and other European countries. But he became internationally recognized for his fiction. His first collection of short stories was published in Maputo in 1986 under the title *Vozes anoitecidas*. The success of the collection prompted the Lisbon publisher Caminho to put out a slightly expanded edition of it in 1987. *Vozes anoitecidas* went on to win Mozambique's first ever national prize for literature in 1990. In 1991, another collection of stories, *Cada homem é uma raça*, was published in Lisbon. In the same year, Caminho also published *Cronicando*, a collection of Couto's chronicles written for *Notícias*, a shorter version of which had been published in Maputo in 1988. In 1992, his long-promised first novel, *Terra sonâmbula* (A sleepwalking land) was published by Caminho. In 1994, Couto's status as a writer of short fiction was reconfirmed when Caminho published the collection of stories *Estórias abensonhadas* (Dream-blessed stories).

The English translation of *Vozes anoi-tecidas* was published in London in 1990 under the title *Voices Made Night*. This translation was based on the Lisbon edition, but contained two additional stories that were subsequently published in Portuguese in *Cada homem é uma raça*. The English translation of this latter collection was published in 1994 as *Every Man Is a Race*. Six shorter sketches from the Lisbon edition of *Cronicando* were added to the English edition to make up for the two stories previously published in *Voices Made Night*. Couto's poems and stories are featured in a number of anthologies, including *Contemporary African Short Stories* (London: Heinemann, 1992), and have been translated into other European languages. His work is studied at Mozambican schools as well as at schools and universities in South Africa and neighboring countries.

ORAL CULTURE AND THE FANTASTIC

Comparisons are often made between Couto's work and that of José Luandino Vieira, the trendsetting Angolan writer whose stories were influential in the 1960s and 1970s. Both writers have sought to create a literary language based on the way Africans have transformed spoken Portuguese. This has meant the cultivation of oral storytelling techniques and an attempt to capture the expressiveness of speech untrammeled by the constraints of conventional syntax. Couto's playful treatment of language is manifested in his abundant use of neologisms, an example of which can be found in the title of his 1994 collection of stories, *Estórias abensonhadas*, in which the invented adjective of the title is derived from two existing adjectives, *abençoada* (blessed) and *sonhada* (dreamed). One indication of the success achieved by Couto in expressing the orality of Mozambican Portuguese has been the excellent adaptation of his stories to the stage by the Maputo theater group Mutumbela Gogo, a sign that a written work inspired by oral culture has in a very real sense repaid its debt to that culture.

In *Voices Made Night* Couto began to develop characteristic themes derived from the oral tradition of storytelling. Some of the tales in that collection, for example, feature elements of the macabre, such as the physical distortion of the young girl in "A menina de futuro torcido" ("The Girl with a Twisted Future") and the torture of the supposed witch in "Afinal, Carlota Gentina não chegou de voar?" ("So You Haven't Flown Yet, Carlota Gentina?"). In several tales, Couto also explores the relation between the world of the spirits and the world of the living, a theme that he further develops in later books. The jealousy and obsession with honor that shape "Saíde, o lata de água" ("Saíde, the Bucket of Water") and the natural calamity central to "De como o velho Jossias foi salvo das águas" ("How Old Jossias Was Saved from the Waters") likewise reveal the thematic influence of oral culture. Last but not least, Couto incorporates certain aspects of the storytelling technique into his narrative; in particular, he will often use the statement of a truth to introduce a tale designed, in turn, to illustrate that truth. For example, "O ex-futuro padre e sua pré-viúva" ("The Ex-Future Priest and His Would-Be Widow"), in *Voices Made Night*, begins in the following way: "Life is a web weaving a spider. Whether the creature believes himself a hunter in his own home or not, it matters little. The instant turns round and he becomes the quarry in the intruder's trap. This will be proved in the following tale which occurred in real though humble surroundings" (p. 95).

On the other hand, *Voices Made Night* is a self-consciously integrated work, a quality that points to its purely literary intentions. Two threads bind the stories in the collection into a coherent whole. One is the concern to express some sort of integrated Mozambican identity, which Couto does by paradoxically invoking the country's cultural and ethnic diversity. The presence in the stories of the

Goan, the Muslims, and the Chinese, along with the black Mozambicans and those of mixed descent, recalls attempts by other Mozambican writers, such as Luís Bernardo Honwana and José Craveirinha, to depict the range of human society contained within the country's borders. This sense of a diverse but unified Mozambicanness is also expressed in Couto's use of language, in particular his exploitation of the transformations that the colonial language has undergone in the mouths of those for whom it is not a mother tongue. This process becomes even more marked in the otherwise more disparate collection of stories, *Every Man Is a Race.*

The second thread that runs through *Voices Made Night* is encapsulated in the author's introductory note, which explains that the stories derive from a preoccupation with the power of fantasy and its ability to rule the lives of those who are all but destitute. Fantasy becomes a compensatory mechanism, but it is equally a destructive force, as Couto explains in the foreword: "There exists in nothingness that illusion of plenitude which causes life to stop and voices to become night."

Couto presents us with a world in which belief in the supernatural, or the impulse to reenact age-old myths, can overwhelm the individual's ability to act in the cause of good and to achieve genuine solidarity with others. The illusions that preoccupy Couto's protagonists take different forms, but their effects are always similarly destructive. In "A fogueira" ("The Fire"), the source of an old man's illusion is the flame that he thinks warms his hearth. Yet this fire exists only in his imagination. It is an imaginary fever that gives him life while at the same time gnawing away at his body. Convinced that his wife is going to die before he does, he concerns himself with digging her grave. In order to render the prophecy true, he even decides to kill her — with her compliance. But the energy expended in the fulfillment of this obsession kills him first. Paradox and tragic irony are the upshot

of the old man's illusion, an illusion that is, in turn, the product of his poverty.

Similar ravings are responsible for the downfall of Temba, the fisherman who devotes his life and stock of food to a pair of birds that he believes are envoys of God destined to end the drought afflicting his village. His wife abandons him, the villagers burn the birds, and Temba kills himself. An obsession destroys its creator but, in an ironic twist, the rains begin to fall at the end of the story, suggesting that the birds have perhaps fulfilled their purpose after all.

In some stories in *Voices Made Night*, Couto's characters are conscious of their fantasy and exploit it for material gain. Such is the case in "O último aviso do corvo falador" ("The Talking Raven's Last Warning"), in which the rakish Zuzé supplements his income with a raven that supposedly has visionary powers, while the barber, Firipe Beruberu, in "Sidney Poitier, na barbearia, de Firipe Beruberu" ("The Barber's Most Famous Customer"), uses the advertising gambit that he had once cut the hair of Sidney Poitier. Elsewhere, illusion takes on more brutal characteristics, as in "The Girl with a Twisted Future," in which a man kills his daughter by keeping her tied over a barrel in the hope of turning her into a circus contortionist. The story illustrates one of Couto's primary concerns in the collection, namely, cruelty is not necessarily the work of wickedness but can also be the result of poverty, ignorance, and cultural alienation.

FANTASY AND SOCIAL CRITICISM

The setting of Couto's stories is, generally speaking, timeless: the landscape is stylized and symbolic, and natural phenomena such as drought and flood are evoked with a biblical overtone. In practically all the stories in *Voices Made Night*, an overriding presence of death, violence, and indifference to suffering is paradoxically coupled with instances of love and solidarity, usually emanating from the feminine world of the mother or spouse. Likewise, fatalistic resignation alternates with bouts of illusion, while alcoholic indulgence brings on further violence. Some of the stories contain historical and sociological references that nevertheless do not detract from the author's characteristically abstract view of reality. "Patanhoca, o cobreiro apaixonado" ("Patanhoca, the Lovesick Snake Catcher") is the tale of a reencounter, an attempt to recapture a brief, happy love affair between a black snake catcher and a Chinese widow. The circumstances behind the violence responsible for their original separation are built up obliquely in an atmosphere of mystery and tension, but the overall impression is of a couple brought together by the universal myth of temptation and love but driven apart by the shame and prejudice of a man whose snakes symbolize the poison that surrounds their relationship. In this highly symbolic story, Couto comments gravely on the prejudice from which no one is shielded during colonial times, whether as an agent or as a victim.

"De como se vazou a vida de Ascolino do Perpétuo Socorro" ("How Ascolino do Perpétuo Socorro Lost His Spouse") is the story that focuses most clearly on the predicament of a particular ethnic group, in this case the Goan, who can trace their ancestry to the former Portuguese enclave of Goa on the western coast of India. As in Couto's other tales, there are two levels of reality, but here the two levels correspond to the Indo-Portuguese cultural dualism within Ascolino and tend to manifest themselves simultaneously during his bouts of drunkenness.

Ascolino's spouse, Epifânia, is, as her name suggests, the epitome of Catholic sobriety. Her abandonment of the family home, while Ascolino is at the local bottle store drinking himself into oblivion and alternately proclaiming his Portuguese identity and his allegiance to India, is an allegory of decolonization. Although Ascolino attempts to catch up with the reality of decolonization, we are led to understand that he will remain in Mozambique, nursing the illusion of his former grandeur as the head of his household without the protection of a wife. As for Epifânia, she is the long-suffering woman who appears in different guise in Couto's other stories, but she is also the myth of moral perfection and security to which Ascolino is wedded. Like the divine apparition suggested by her name, Epifânia disappears, leaving Ascolino to a lonely and dissolute future. She, like the birds or the old man's fire in the other stories mentioned, is the cause of Ascolino's fantasy and self-destruction.

POSTINDEPENDENCE MOZAMBIQUE

Three of the stories in *Voices Made Night* relate directly to the situation in postindependence Mozambique. In "O dia em que explodiu Mabata-bata" ("The Day Mabata-bata Exploded"), the death by explosion of a prized bull belonging to Uncle Raul is explained by his nephew Azarias, the cowherd responsible for the bull, as being the work of the "ndlati," or bird of lightning. Are we to believe the child's supernatural interpretation, his integrated mythical vision of the world, or are we to understand simply that the bull strayed into a minefield laid by the guerrillas, an explanation that pertains to the adult world of violence and disunity? Couto leaves the question open. Yet the central symbol of the story is the bull, which embodies Raul's accumulated wealth as well as representing his power over his orphaned nephew, whom he deprives of an education. Furthermore, because the bull is being kept as a bride-price for Raul, it also represents the power of traditional culture over more progressive, egalitarian social aspirations. When Azarias, lured by Raul's promise to send him to school, leaves the place where he has been hiding from his uncle's wrath, only to step on another land mine, the message of the story becomes clear:

the youth of the country has been betrayed by the greed of an older generation.

In "As baleias de Quissico" ("The Whales of Quissico"), abundance is symbolized by the whale, in this case not a real creature but the product of the hysterical imagination of a hungry peasant, Bento. Convinced that the whale will disgorge the consumer products lacking in Mozambique, Bento is drawn by his fantasy toward the coast in some private messianic urge and wades feverishly off into the sea and to his death in pursuit of his obsession, the whale. The tale illustrates in striking fashion the forsaking of the spirit of independence for a neocolonial alternative of material comfort. Here again, the counter-revolutionary theme is touched on. Bento's friends give his fantasy a political explanation, that he is in league with the counter-revolutionaries, right-wing "bandits," supported by South Africa and some former Portuguese settlers, who claimed to be for democracy and free elections but employed extremely brutal tactics. Their supposition is incorrect, but not totally so, because Bento's fantasy unconsciously resembles an anti-revolutionary myth of a submarine disgorging arms for the rebels. Thus word of mouth transforms the whale into a submarine. In the final paragraph, whale and submarine merge in the popular imagination, and we are invited to wonder whether Bento's fantasy of abundance did not in fact provide the excuse for the proliferation of far more sinister rumors.

The direst warning against the dangers facing postrevolutionary Mozambique is provided in "A história des aparecidos" ("The Tale of the Two Who Returned from the Dead"), in which two villagers who were assumed drowned in a flood come up against the inflexibility and corruption of local bureaucracy in their efforts to be reinstated among the living. With the help of the village schoolteacher and a journalist from the city, the authorities eventually accept that the two are truly alive and therefore have a right to rations. As in all the stories in the collection,

a symbolic element underpins the message. In this case, the flood serves as a symbolic catalyst for Mozambican society's transformation from colonial to independent, and the two returnees perform a quasi-mythical function because they provide a means by which the new society's integrity can be tested. The story contains a condemnation of those who would create new hierarchies or maintain old ones, a theme that will become a constant one in Couto's subsequent fiction. Society's conscience is represented by the intellectuals: Samuel, the teacher who shelters the two victims and urges them not to give in to the dictates of the local bureaucrats, and a journalist, who threatens to expose the corruption of officials.

THE DIVIDED SELF AND REINTEGRATION

The title of Couto's second collection of stories, *Cada homem é uma raça* (Every Man Is a Race), is explained by the epigraph at the beginning of the book: the supposed declaration to the police of John the Birdman, the bird-seller in "O embondeiro que sonhava pássaros" ("The Bird-Dreaming Baobab"), that each individual is his or her own race. The title also confirms Couto's commitment as a writer to focus on the individual's relationship to the community rather than on collective values.

These stories examine in a more complex way some of the themes of Couto's first collection. We can discern the same binary view of human nature, in which characters have somehow become detached from — or have never been attached to — their opposing half. These stories are full of fragmented characters, social outcasts who are either orphans or widows, deprived in some way of the "other" with which their personalities might be completed. Yet Couto suggests that orphanhood or widowhood can occur outside of actual physical bereavement. Death, as the epigraph to "Rosalinda, a nenhuma" ("Rosalinda's Journey to Neverness") states, is not a complete rupture with life: the dead are not absent but continue to dwell among the living. The dead are half of the dichotomy by which all of human existence is made up; thus widowhood can also occur before the death of the partner, as in "Rosalinda's Journey to Neverness" and "The Ex-Future Priest and His Would-Be Widow." (The original Portuguese version of "The Ex-Future Priest and His Would-Be Widow" was published in *Cada homem é uma raça,* although it appeared in English in *Voices Made Night.*) This attention to the theme of the interpenetrability of life and death reflects Couto's increasing interest in the traditional African cosmovision with its emphasis on the close links between the world of the living and the spirit world of the dead.

The inability of characters to complete themselves and each other is given particular poignancy in the stories that are most clearly set against the backdrop of contemporary Mozambican history, such as "O apocalipse privado do tio Geguê" ("The Private Apocalypse of Uncle Geguê") and "Os mastros do paralém" ("The Flagpoles of Beyondwards"). Both of these stories extract tragic ironies from an individual's experience of the war of independence (1964–1974) and the counter-revolutionary (or contra) insurgency that followed (1978–1990). The contras erased the original socialist program of the postindependence government, and the utopian optimism of the early years was replaced in these stories by an apocalyptic vision.

Just as he did in *Voices Made Night,* Couto experiments with language in *Every Man Is a Race* in his continuing attempt to capture Mozambican authenticity and to convey the flavor of oral culture. Strange and fantastic incidents abound, and the author frequently provides an unexpected twist at the end of the tale. As in the previous collection, the almost mythical quality of the stories is conveyed through the presence of socially marginalized figures whose actions have a profound and sometimes disastrous effect on the communities and individuals who come into contact with them.

In "A Rosa Caramela" ("Rosa Caramela"), the outcast, a female hunchback who talks to statues, is an object of fascination to the boy narrator. Her madness, according to the local gossips, stems from her having been abandoned at the altar by her lover. A statue of an old colonial hero that sits in the square in front of the narrator's house is her favorite, and because of her apparent admiration for a colonial hero, she is briefly imprisoned by the new regime. Upon her release, she appears at the funeral of Jarvane, a local male nurse, and undresses on his grave, leading the reader to assume that Jarvane was the lover who abandoned her. However, the narrator later witnesses an encounter on the steps of his house between Rosa and his own father, the indolent and sickly Juca, in which Juca calls her his sweetheart. Juca may have been the lover, or may simply be accepting the role of the deformed woman's beloved. This act, which occurs in sight of the half-demolished colonial statue, points to a reconciliation between two divided halves and suggests the rehumanization of Rosa. The symbolic reintegration of Mozambique is implicit in the story's conclusion, as Juca and Rosa head off into the night together.

A similar conciliatory message is implied in "O pescador cego" ("The Blind Fisherman"). Maneca, far out at sea in his little boat and having no luck with his catch, decides to gouge out his eyes and use them as bait in order to survive. After catching fish and satisfying his hunger, he feels his way back to shore, having lost "the windows of his soul." Once back among his family, his macho pride will not allow him to let his wife go out to fish. Instead, he goes off and lives by himself in his beached boat. More and more convinced that this, his last refuge, will be taken from him, he sets fire to it and is abandoned by his despairing family. Eventually, a mysterious old woman who never speaks in the story takes him in. Is it his returned wife? We are not told, but, in spite of Maneca's blindness, he succeeds in building another boat, which he allows her to use while he remains on the shore, "seeking the rest of his face among the generations of waves" (p. 57). This story again describes loss as a type of orphaning of the soul that leads to an apocalyptic act of self-destruction but is followed by some sort of redemption and the search for a lost identity.

In "The Private Apocalypse of Uncle Geguê," the narrator is an orphan raised by his uncle, who gave him "lessons of hope when the future had already grown feeble" (p. 11). The central symbol of the story is a remnant of the war of independence, an old guerrilla army boot that the narrator at first rejects, then forgets about, and finally gives an honorable burial to. The boot comes to represent the young narrator's idealistic inheritance, his long-lost conscience. Meanwhile, Uncle Geguê becomes head of the governing party's local vigilantes and uses his position to exercise tyranny, employing the narrator as a robber and bully. The narrator's rediscovery of the boot reminds him of Zabelani, a young female refugee from north of Mozambique who had awakened his sexual interest and been sent away by the uncle. He sets off to find Zabelani, only to be told that his uncle had turned her over to the bandits. The narrator returns home and shoots his uncle, realizing that, by so doing, he is "firing at that whole lapse of time, killing the belly inside us, where the dead shadows of this old world are born" (p. 24). As in the story of the exploding bull in *Voices Made Night*, we witness the abuse by an older generation of the orphaned young. This theme once more seems to symbolize, in a broad sense, the emergent nation itself, held hostage by ignorance and authoritarianism.

"The Flagpoles of Beyondwards" also has war and social instability as its backdrop, but in this case it is the colonial war. The scene is a settler's plantation on the frontier between Portuguese-controlled Mozambique and the high mountains that provide a neutral ground between it and the guerrilla territory. Bene, a black plantation guard, lives with his two children, João and Chica, who, like many of Couto's young characters, are semi-orphans. As in "The Private Apocalypse of Uncle Geguê," the parental figure attempts to shield his offspring from the contemplation of freedom, symbolized by the mountains, though Bene himself is aware of the constraints of colonial rule. As the cathartic figure in the story, a city mulatto passes through in the direction of guerrilla territory and camps nearby. With his revolutionary ideals and a flag of the emergent Mozambican nation inside his haversack, he becomes a focus of attraction for brother and sister. Soon Chica becomes pregnant and gives birth to a lighter-complexioned child. Bene assumes the father to be the mulatto and sets off to exact vengeance. Bene attacks the mulatto with a cutlass and leaves him for dead, taking with him the contents of the haversack. But Bene is later told that the father of his grandchild is none other than Tavares, his white boss. Dispatching his children toward the mountains, Bene returns to the plantation; in an atmosphere of mounting anarchy, he sets the plantation on fire and at the same time raises the flag he took from the mulatto.

Like most other figures in Couto's tales who serve as mythical presences, the mulatto simply disappears, after he has been severely wounded. The mulatto, with his utopian program and his flag, affects the attitudes and actions of those whose political consciousness is only half formed. Although Bene is stirred to rebellion in order to defend his honor, it is ironic that his illegitimate grandchild, as Chica confides to her brother, was not the fruit of rape, but of love. Thus, Couto suggests the ambiguous motivations that propel people toward political revolt. Yet for all this, one suspects that Couto has greater fellow feeling for Bene in his revolt than for those whose motivations belong to the realm of utopian ideology. These ideologues are summed up in the story's cryptic epigraph: "All we want is a new world, one which has everything new and nothing of the world" (p. 73).

THE MYTHICAL FUNCTION
OF THE OUTSIDER

The theme of the relationship between the individual and the community is also central to "A lenda da noiva do forasteiro" ("The Legend of the Foreigner's Bride") in *Every Man Is a Race*, whose title underlines the mythical quality of the story. A stranger and his dog encamp in the vicinity of a closed, isolated rural community. After various individuals who go to ask him to leave fail to return, the stranger enters the community's folklore as the reincarnation of Amangwane, a Zulu warrior and former oppressor, "the author of much bloodshed and many a massacre" (p. 65). Eventually, following the prophecy of the local medicine man, a young woman named Jauharia is sent to the stranger to save the village from death and destruction. After a while Nyambi, a village youth to whom Jauharia is betrothed, succumbs to jealousy and goes after her, killing the stranger and releasing the previous captives back into life in the process, only to discover that Jauharia had fallen in love with her captor. She gives Nyambi the choice of following her out into the world or returning to the village alone, and he chooses the latter.

According to Jauharia, the stranger was a much travelled man who sought a paradise far from human society: "So he had given himself a mission: to seek out a distant place, an earthly island, and protect its solitude, fighting the arrival of time" (pp. 71–72). As a mythical presence, the stranger, like the mulatto in "The Flagpoles of Beyondwards," tests the closed structure of the community, but because he functions as a sort of prototype he loses his individual humanity. In addition, as in that tale, an unexpected revelation gives the story an ironic twist.

In "The Bird-Dreaming Baobab," the mythical presence is a bird-seller who lives in a baobab tree and plays a harmonica. His appeal to the children of the settlers causes concern among their parents, for, as in the legend of the Pied Piper, the children seem to be abandoning their parents' control for a world that is beyond the comprehension of the community and that arouses the community's prejudices. The children are kept indoors, but when strange things begin to happen, the settlers decide to teach the old man a lesson. He is beaten up and carted off to the local jail. However, one of the children, Tiago, finds the old man's harmonica and goes off to hide in the baobab. When the settlers awaken the following morning to find the jail doors open and the air filled with birdsong, they march off to the baobab and set it on fire, mistakenly killing Tiago, who is still inside. The bird-seller, like the mulatto of "The Flagpoles of Beyondwards," has disappeared.

Here, Couto writes of a world and an epoch remembered from his childhood: the latter years of colonial rule. This story addresses implicitly the question of cultural loyalty and Mozambican identity: Tiago and the other locally born children, unaffected as yet by prejudice, are more integrated into the traditional culture of their country than are their parents. The children are Mozambicans in the making.

FEMALE CHARACTERS

In a number of stories female characters serve a mythical function. "A princesa russa" ("The Russian Princess"), in *Every Man Is a Race*, takes the form of a confession to a priest by a cripple, the former servant of a Russian gold miner whose enigmatic wife, Nádia, had treated the servant as her confidante and soul mate. Far from the town, in the midst of the violence and exploitation of colonial Mozambique, Nádia's metaphorical fever directs her desire toward the fulfillment of her romantic imagination, the wished-for arrival of a long-lost lover from Russia. She represents the merciful, spiritual side of the human duality. Her relationship with the servant is ambiguous, for it goes beyond that of a mistress and her houseboy to something that borders on a type of platonic love between two outcasts: he as a physical cripple, she as a psychological cripple. Significantly, when she dies of her fever, she enters his body and lives on in his conscience.

In its examination of the binary relationship between male and female, "The Russian Princess" is similar to another story in the same collection entitled "Mulher de mim" ("Woman of Me"). This story consists of the ramblings of a man afraid of a mysterious woman who visits him in semidream states. Is she, he asks himself, the jealous soul of one not yet born or the spirit of a dead person? In the end, she explains that she has come not to take him over but to complete him, to be to him "the woman of me" rather than "my woman."

Couto's most audacious treatment of the male/female dichotomy occurs in two of the stories in *Estórias abensonhadas.* "Sapatos de tacão alto" (High-heeled shoes), set in colonial times, is the tale of Zé Paulão, a white docker who is abandoned by his wife and takes to wearing women's clothes in the privacy of his house at night, as if to compensate for his loss. "Joãotónio no enquanto" (John Antonio for now) relates a husband's ploys to make his frigid wife respond to him. After sending her to the local prostitute for some training, she returns to assume the dominant sexual role he might have expected for himself. However, this, like the first story, is a tale of the unexpected; the male narrator finally confesses that he enjoys his new passive bedtime identity: "Each day I wait only for night, the gentle storms in which I'm both John Antonio and Joanna Antonia, male and female, in my wife's virile arms. For the time being, brother, I'm still John Antonio. Ever so slowly, I'm taking leave of my true name" (p. 126).

A third story in the collection, "Lenda de Namarói" (The legend of the Namarói), dealing with this theme of male/female dichotomy, recounts a matriarchal myth of origin as told by the wife of a chief in Zambézia, central Mozambique: The world was first peopled by women. Men appeared as a result of a process of initial self-fertilization by women. Ashamed of their physical difference, men crossed the stream to live on the other side of the mountain. Looking back, the men saw that the stream had widened to a river. The abyss had been created. Thereafter, men lived in a state of internal conflict, crossing the river only to mate, but for the rest of the time resenting the female ability to engender life.

All of Couto's stories reflect his ability to combine his own experience of Mozambican African culture and recent history with more general observations of the dramas and motivations behind human existence. A central and recurring motif in all his work is the lost cohesive force enshrined in the female figure. She stands in opposition to the male, the surrogate father, who is all too often revealed as violent and prone to destructive fantasy.

At the same time, through characters like Zé Paulão and John Antonio, Couto is questioning the fixed nature of gender identity and accepting the commonly held notion that human beings are made up of both masculine and feminine qualities. In the specific case of Mozambique, with its experience of colonial brutality and postcolonial civil war, the melding of male and female values symbolizes the reconciliation of all Mozambicans. He invites Mozambicans to reject those aspects of their historical and cultural legacy, including inherited Latin machismo, and perhaps even the biblical myth of Adam and Eve, that have assumed the female of the species to be inherently inferior and certainly posterior to the male.

THE NOVEL OF THE CIVIL WAR

Terra sonâmbula elaborates on some of the themes already present in Couto's short stories: the quest for reunion with a divided half, the destructiveness but also the beauty of fantasy, the proximity of the spirit world of the dead to the world of the living, and woman as symbol of permanence and victim of violence and exploitation. However, the energy of the novel is very clearly provided by contemporary events: the war from 1975 to 1990, the abandonment of the revolutionary ideal, petty corruption, and the rise of a native middle class. The novel is not conventionally structured, but rather consists of short stories woven together within a loose two-plot structure; at the end of the novel, the two plots merge.

The first plot revolves around the experiences of an old man, Tuahir, and a young boy, Muidinga, who emerge from a war-torn landscape to seek shelter in a burned-out bus that was recently attacked by bandits. Muidinga discovers eleven notebooks among the effects of a dead man lying by the roadside and begins to read their contents to Tuahir. The notebooks tell the story of Kindzu, the dead man, who had taken to sea in a rowing boat in order to seek out the "naparamas," a sect in northern Mozambique who, according to popular lore, were immune to the effects of bullets and successfully repelled the bandits from their villages. Before Kindzu can find them, however, he encounters a beautiful young woman named Farida, who has been abandoned by some looters on a wrecked provision ship. Falling in love with her, he sets off on a quest to find her son, Gaspar, who has been lost in the turmoil of war.

The two stories combine to create an effect of movement throughout a country that is on the verge of self-destruction. Kindzu's journey begins at sea and ends on land, where he is shot down. His story crosses over into that of the old man and the boy, for as Kindzu lies dying, he glimpses Muidinga in the distance and imagines him to be Gaspar. For their part, Tuahir and Muidinga also set out on a journey. However, their journey belongs more closely to the realm of metaphor. Sitting in the wrecked bus, they do not move, but as Muidinga narrates the landscape of Mozambique rolls past them. The effect is multiple: we are given the idea of a country on the move, but we must not forget that Muidinga, the storyteller, is instrumental to the journey. Their journey is also temporal: Muidinga matures while Tuahir grows old. When they eventually reach the sea, the old man, now in the throes of a mortal fever, has himself put in a rowing boat, the very one used by Kindzu, and pushed out into the waves. As if in death's cradle, Tuahir is lulled by the sound of his adopted son's voice reading the last chapter of Kindzu's story.

The proximity of the world of the dead and of the living is a cornerstone of Couto's magic realism. In *Terra sonâmbula*, this proximity not only echoes traditional African belief, but also serves as a metaphor for the relationship between the dead world of the colonial past and the living world of postcolonial and postrevolutionary Mozambique. Thus, a Portuguese trader named Romão Pinto dies around the time of independence and is abandoned in his coffin but reemerges fifteen years later to seek a business partnership with an official of the new generation.

Loss of the utopian ideal of equality and national integration has been dealt with in Couto's previous stories. Likewise, the exposure of the rigid and cynical use of political dogma by officialdom features prominently in his work, nowhere more so than in some of the shorter pieces published in *Cronicando*. In *Terra sonâmbula*, Couto shows us how the prejudices of a previous era have survived the socialist years. Surendra, the Indian storekeeper who had sought to reconcile his adopted country with his ancestral land by suggesting to Kindzu a common Indian Ocean identity, has now been forced into a partnership with a member of the new black bourgeoisie. The black partner needs Surendra's money and business acumen to further his own ends while preferring to consign Surendra to social invisibility on the grounds that he is a *Monhê*, a derogatory term for an Indian.

This new black bourgeoisie is the inevitable child of petty corruption and the abuse of power. Kindzu encounters a panoply of officials who are on the make—from Assane, who is crippled as a result of being tortured as a class enemy for looting a provision ship and who now rents out the wheelchair given to him in return for his silence about diverted funds, to Estêvão Jonas, the new administrator, who prevents aid from being distributed to the refugee camp until he is there, so that he can strengthen his political support.

One of the constant themes in Couto's depiction of postindependence Mozambique is that the chaotic process of the country's first fifteen years of independence has produced a nation of orphans in search of some integral wholeness. His Mozambicans look to some sort of utopian ideal that was alive at independence but has been lost under the weight of civil war, of self-interest, and of timeless traditions that never sat easily with the imported European political model.

Kindzu and Farida are two such orphans, and though their contact is brief, their relationship casts a shadow over the whole book. They represent a generation that came of age with independence but had their ideals submerged in the struggle to survive the ensuing civil war. Kindzu is essentially a figure of witness to violence and change. Farida, like most of the women in Couto's stories, is a victim of her ancestral culture (she is cursed for being a twin, a traditional sign of evil); of the lasciviousness of her employer, Romão Pinto, who raped her; and of the lust of the new administrator. Her portentous end as she gazes out to sea—she is accidentally incinerated in the lighthouse that she has made her abode—somehow symbolizes the sacrifice of her generation, as does the subsequent murder

of Kindzu himself. Farida, in her search for freedom, has become something of a moral embarrassment to the local officials, and her death is hardly mourned. More than anything, perhaps, Farida and Kindzu represent the romantic notion of noble love, and their inevitable separation is symptomatic of a Mozambique that has failed to join its two halves.

Equally, the sense of dislocation felt by Farida and Kindzu is a product of their cultural duality. Brought up within a system of traditional, rural cultural values, they have also been affected by the colonial educational system. In the words of Kindzu, "Our memory was peopled by the ghosts of our village. These ghosts spoke to us in our native languages. But, by now we were only able to dream in Portuguese" (p. 102). Caught between an old world, partially destroyed by the war, and a new world, as yet barely formed, Kindzu and Farida are the sacrificial victims of the time in which they live.

If there is any hope to be found in *Terra sonâmbula,* it must be found in the figure of the boy, Muidinga/Gaspar, a member of a new generation of victims, but a generation that may survive the war. Muidinga has a memory of school but no memory of colonial rule. His innocence has not been sullied. He has the power of the word and a pliable, imaginative mind that gradually exercises its influence over his surrogate father, Tuahir, thus reconciling the two generations. The stories Muidinga reads are the saga of Mozambique since independence, of a land and people struggling to survive and create beauty against all odds.

CONCLUSION

In reviewing the career of Mozambique's most prolific fiction writer, it is clear that certain aspects of his narrative technique that were present from the beginning, such as the strong influence of oral culture and the emphasis on linguistic experimentation, become even more marked in his later work. Similarly, Couto's flair for subtle political satire, already noted in a couple of the stories in *Voices Made Night*, achieves its most cutting expression in some of the pieces in *Cronicando* (see, for example, "The Swapped Medals" and "The Secret Love of Deolinda," both first published in Portuguese in the Caminho edition of *Cronicando* but appearing in English translation in *Every Man Is a Race*) and resurfaces in his novel, *Terra sonâmbula*. Couto, along with other writers of his generation, has grasped a complicated reality that his predecessors, particularly those who had been active in the independence campaign, could not readily account for. Independence delivered a utopian ideal that sought to wipe the slate clean and impose itself on the timeless customs and cultures of rural Mozambique. Couto has turned his back on the pamphleteering tendencies of the early years of independence, preferring instead to derive his art from the stories of popular culture that form the mythical underbelly of Mozambique's contemporary experience and that, for him, are the stuff of an emergent literary identity.

Selected Bibliography

POETRY, FICTION, AND CHRONICLES

Raiz de orvalho. Maputo, Mozambique: Edições Tempo, 1983.
Vozes anoitecidas. Maputo, Mozambique: A.E.M.O., 1986, 1989; Lisbon, Portugal: Caminho, 1987, 1992.
Cronicando. Maputo, Mozambique: Edições Notícias, 1988; Lisbon, Portugal: Caminho, 1991.
Cada homem é uma raça. Lisbon, Portugal: Caminho, 1991, 1992.
Terra sonâmbula. Lisbon, Portugal: Caminho, 1992.
Estórias abensonhadas. Lisbon, Portugal: Caminho, 1994.

TRANSLATIONS

Voices Made Night. Trans. by David Brookshaw. London: Heinemann, 1990.
"How Ascolino do Perpétuo Socorro Lost His Spouse." Trans. by David Brookshaw. In *Third World Quarterly* 12 (January 1990).
"So You Haven't Flown Yet, Carlota Gentina?" Trans. by David Brookshaw. In *Southern African Review of Books* (February/May 1990).
"The Talking Raven's Last Warning." Trans. by David Brookshaw. In *Critical Quarterly* 33, no. 1 (1991).
"The Birds of God." Trans. by David Brookshaw. In Chinua Achebe and C. L. Innes, eds., *Contemporary African Short Stories.* London: Heinemann, 1992.
"The Barber's Most Famous Customer." Trans. by David Brookshaw. In *Being Here: Modern Short Stories from Southern Africa.* Cape Town, South Africa: David Philip, 1994.
Every Man Is a Race. Trans. by David Brookshaw. London: Heinemann, 1994.
"The Lesson of Old Skeleton." Trans. by David Brookshaw. In *Passport to Portugal.* London: Serpent's Tail, 1994.
"In the Waters of Time" and "The Stain." Trans. by Richard Zenith. In *Trafika* 4 (winter 1994).
"From *A Sleepwalking Land.*" Trans. by David Brookshaw. In *Literary Review* (Fairleigh Dickinson University) 38, no. 4 (1995).
"Grandma's Blood Is Staining the Carpet." Trans. by Peter Bush. In *Literary Review* (Fairleigh Dickinson University) 38, no. 4 (1995).

INTERVIEWS

d'Oliveira, Teresa Roza. "Mia Couto entrevistado." In *Letras & letras* 6, no. 90 (3 March 1993).
Morris, Patricia. "*Voices Made Night.*" In *Africa Events* (May 1990).

CRITICAL STUDIES

Brookshaw, David. "Mia Couto: A New Voice from Mozambique." In *Portuguese Studies* 5 (1989). Includes bilingual versions of two stories published in *Voices Made Night*.
Daniel, Mary L. "Mia Couto: Guimarães Rosa's Newest Literary Heir in Africa." In *Luso-Brazilian Review* 32 (summer 1995).

Laranjeira, Pires. "Mia Couto: Sonhador de lembranças, inventor de verdades." In *Letras & letras* 6, no. 100 (September 1993).

Leite, Ana Mafalda. "A sagração do profano: Reflexões sobre a escrita de três autores moçambicanos: Mia Couto, Rui Knopfli e José Craveirinha." In *Vértice* 55 (July/August 1993).

Lepecki, Maria Lúcia. "*Vozes anoitecidas*, o acordar." In *Sobreimpressões: Estudos de literatura portuguesa e africana.* Lisbon, Portugal: Caminho, 1988.

Medina, Cremilda de Araújo. "No rastro da expressão mestiça." In her *Sonha mamana África.* São Paulo, Brazil: Edições Epopeia, 1987.

Mohammed Dib
1920–

CHARLES BONN

TRANSLATED BY JOHN FLETCHER

IT IS WIDELY agreed that Mohammed Dib is the greatest indigenous North African writing in the French language, yet public awareness of his work falls far short of its significance. He is best known for his first three novels, written during the early years of the Algerian war for independence, but his most important writings were not published until after the war ended in 1962.

Over the years this demanding writer has on occasion changed his style. Furthermore, for many years after Algeria became independent, French critics in particular found it difficult to approach the texts of Algerian writers straightforwardly as works of literature, especially when, as in Dib's case, the writers had made no secret of their political militancy.

Mohammed Dib was born in Tlemcen (now Tilimsen) in western Algeria on 21 July 1920. He was educated there and in Oujda, Morocco. His father, a carpenter and merchant, died in 1931. After holding various jobs (including that of French interpreter with the Allied army in North Africa, 1943–1944), he worked in Algiers (1950–1951) as a journalist on the major communist newspaper, *Alger Républicain.* In 1951 he married Colette Bellissant. The following year he moved to France.

EARLIEST NOVELS

La Grande Maison (1952; The big house), *L'Incendie* (1954; The fire), and *Le Métier à tisser* (1957; The loom) form a trilogy set in colonial Algeria that depicts the gradual increase of radical political awareness. These early works are far from being the most personal. Their relatively limpid and largely descriptive style, together with their subject matter (the childhood and adolescence of a youth of humble background), has made them popular in school textbooks and in ideologically based literary studies.

The odyssey of the young hero, Omar, serves as a useful means in all three novels for showing urban squalor, the first peasant uprisings in the countryside, and the political apprenticeship of the new industrial labor class. But these three novels are not as black-and-white as the use to which they have been put may suggest. A closer reading shows that Dib was already fascinated by the power of words, a fascination that came to haunt him increasingly as his writing matured. Underlying Dib's whole output is the power of the word to determine the status not only of the writer but of all humanity in relation to reality, the world, and indeed life itself.

La Grande Maison and *L'Incendie* complement each other, since the first describes extreme poverty in the cities and the second deals with one of the earliest violent protests in the rural areas. Historically, the Algerian revolution was essentially a peasant phenomenon, just as colonialism was characterized by extensive landed estates. In *La Grande Maison*, Omar's mother, a widow named Aïni, is driven to various expedients, including smuggling, to feed her children. Omar discovers the unofficial racial and class apartheid of two sections of the same city largely unaware of each other. Influenced more by how his schoolmaster and a communist named Hamid Saraj (who reappears in *L'Incendie*) behave than by what they say in lessons, Omar begins asking political questions.

L'Incendie, too, uses the child to record the injustices of the world, but a closer reading shows that the realism sought is not realism at all, since the abuses of colonization are described exclusively in highly metaphorical — and highly poetic — peasant language, which Hamid Saraj cleverly allows to follow a peculiar logic that seems to have nothing to do with realism. Hamid Saraj himself talks as little as possible, but he listens to the peasants even when what they say does not seem to be — but in reality is — political. The novel is essentially an illustration of the way in which peasant speech, normally least affected by politicization (largely an urban phenomenon), becomes politicized of its own accord.

Transcribing this phenomenon into another language — French, in this case — would have been impossible, and Dib does not attempt it through tricks of realism. Instead, he shows, in the context of a novel in French, the essentially artificial nature of peasant discourse. He does so in order to create in the reader a tension that will raise his or her consciousness. Some might be tempted to call this an alienation effect, pioneered by German dramatist Bertolt Brecht, but it is more a meditation on the political efficacy of language, in particular of the kind of ideological discourse that Dib was using at the time.

This meditation on language is all the more true because other discourses come to light in *L'Incendie*: that of the women through whom politicization necessarily occurs and that of the adolescents Omar and his female cousin Zhor, the language of whose bodies challenges all ideology. The love play with which the novel ends so poetically invests the fire metaphor of the title with a much more complex meaning than any it could be given by ideological language, the limits of which are thereby highlighted.

Indeed, from the outset and in parallel with the politically motivated writing found chiefly in *Le Métier à tisser*, the last volume of this trilogy, Dib was engaged in a more covert enterprise whose central theme could be described as scrutiny of the power of the word. This theme had already been illustrated in the dialectical novel *L'Incendie*, in which the raising of the peasants' consciousness is depicted, above all, through the evolution of their language. At the same time Dib was writing less-known texts in a more personal manner. This personal manner became dominant when, following his expulsion on political grounds from Algeria in 1959 (to take up permanent residence in France), he published collections of verse that made increasing demands on the reader.

Although Dib is best known for his novels, he was first and foremost a poet; well before the trilogy appeared, he had published "Vega" (1947), a long poem in the style of the French poet Stéphane Mallarmé. He has always acknowledged having poured his deepest inspiration into his verse. To use his own terms, poetry is the most striking "nomination" — the act of naming — of the combined glory of language and love, bordering on madness and death. Death constitutes the basic preoccupation of Dib's work.

VERSE

Every venture involving nomination is fraught with mockery, but that does not detract from nomination's absolute necessity, even where the necessity is one of disaster. It is on this uncomfortable margin that Dib's poems are located, and it is there that the most profound currents in his work are exposed. And, paradoxically, it is in these regions, denuded of vegetation and generally life, that the word is revealed as the guardian, a guardian celebrated in a fine early poem that gives its name to the 1961 collection, *Ombre gardienne* (Guardian shade).

The very title of the 1970 volume of verse, *Formulaires* (Formularies), announces that explicit reflection upon the power of the word will be its chief concern; the last part of the collection, titled still more explicitly "Les Pouvoirs" (The powers), is devoted to it entirely. The last poem in the volume reveals "the almost human face of the word":

> waiting between the nails
> frozen beneath a huge fire
>
> and feeding upon space
> sleeping on its bleeding mouth
> keeping still
>
> from afar and even further afar
> (*Formulaires*, p. 107)

Later verse collections—*Omneros* (1975), *Feu, beau feu* (1979; Fire, fine fire), and *Ô vive* 1987; Oh live)—celebrate the hidden face of the vertiginous marriage of love, nomination, madness, and death. This ever changing relationship is also the subject of the novels from *Habel* (1977) to *Le Désert sans détour* (1992; The detourless desert).

Omneros is first and foremost a celebration of love and death, for, as the author says in the introduction, "The clearest side of life, the visible side, is certainly the most obscure. It is but the shadow cast by Eros; it, and we in it,

are but the project of Eros, even in the instances where it hardly seems to be the case." When all is said and done, this play upon the right and the wrong side of reality is the same as the one to which the author has accustomed the reader in his long reflection on the powers of the word. But the collection progresses from a celebration of the body of woman and of sexual desire, as in this example:

> she-wolf in a hollow of desire
> all within these arms secluded
> constantly claws away
>
> plaint urging from afar
> all with a conch smitten
> constantly stretches out
>
> umbral umbel at the forests' edges
> walled only by the fire's incandescence
> (p. 59)

The collection ends with the final journey into the beyond of death itself, toward the "fire's edges":

> as childhood blossoms
> in the hands of scarlet night
> dawn having survived a sheet
> faces up to death
> (p. 149)

The declared aim in *Feu, beau feu* is to "pursue as chance allows / writing that espouses the body's contours" (p. 94) but the collection extends its celebration of woman— "eye that names me / hail me!" (p. 166)— toward a perhaps more intimate encounter with the elements. There is profound serenity in the images of "Natyk of the fine fire," but appearances can be deceptive:

> because it falls
> this drop of blood
>
> because it splits
> time in two
>
> the snow hides
> its face in a scream
> (p. 172)

This celebration of the elements connected with the female body and with the word is also the theme of the collection *Ô vive*: "word, water, woman who makes all empty around her, and then emptier still to reach out and touch us, love us, and quench our thirst." It almost seems as if, while the novels from *Habel* on betray increasing anxiety, Dib's verse adds to the instability by the celebratory nomination, under an extreme economy of means, of the "body inexhaustible glory" of her "whose name is life." Nevertheless, both the snow in *Feu, beau feu* and the "last great white wing" in *Ô vive* serve in their different ways to remind us that the greatest glory is that which lives only through its exhaustion and its loss and which derives from them a kind of ontological serenity.

NOVELS OF THE 1960s

In 1962 Dib's novel *Qui se souvient de la mer* (*Who Remembers the Sea*) was published. Its depiction of the Algerian conflict deliberately chooses fantasy over realism to suggest the horror of war. Dib himself compared the work to Picasso's *Guernica*. In both cases, he asserts, describing atrocity realistically would be to fall into the trap of staleness and triteness that realism mockingly lays for the artist. Only suggestion, by way of the fantastic, can enable writing to rival horror itself.

Who Remembers the Sea is the story of a quest and an initiation. The narrator's pursuit of the unattainable woman he loves, through cities that are juxtaposed and superimposed but always hostile, leads him progressively to shed his self and accept his transfer to the "other side." An ideological reader would be satisfied to interpret this journey as a metaphor for the recruitment of the narrator into the resistance.

The reader is invited to dig deeper by the next work, *Cours sur la rive sauvage* (1964; Course on the savage shore). Perhaps Dib's most obscure novel, it depicts the "other side" in terms of a "savage shore" on which one finds oneself after agreeing to lose everything, including one's self. On the shore only the uncontrollable laughter of Hellé—the hero's guide in the perilous search for Radia—echoes "from one end of the world to the other."

The power to name engenders meaning, both in the individual and within the group. The quest for this power is a spiritual one, but it is no less political, since the major question raised by decolonization is that of identity, and therefore of memory. In *La Danse du roi* (1968; The king's dance), Rodwan and Arfia are former resistance fighters. Their interconnected accounts lead to a stunned realization that the new city prefers to forget the violence that has brought it into being and to expose the heroes to mockery as they act out mad tales of derring-do.

Rodwan and Arfia are subject to ridicule because neither has recovered from the deaths he has caused and because neither is capable of love, which cannot be dissociated from death. Their interwoven accounts strive in vain to conquer a huge, unspeakable sense of guilt. At the end of the novel, all that is left is the mockery of the ludicrous exhibition suddenly played out in front of them; beyond the exhibition there is only emptiness—the same emptiness that lurks behind all speech, behind the act of writing, and derives ultimately from loss. "Disaster," the critic Maurice Blanchot called all literary and poetic writing; in Blanchot's idea of "writing of disaster," writing is an experience of losing oneself. The terrible mockery arising from the impossibility of expressing the reality of war through the medium of words is a challenge already encountered in *Who Remembers the Sea*. The king parodied in the closing spectacle is also the cleric arriving too late at the banquet (if one actually took place) given by the rich citizen Chadly.

Identity, even when mocked, continues to be the central issue in the two succeeding novels, which are explicitly devoted to newly independent Algeria and to its tragic inability to find the answer, on which its very existence depends, to the question, "Father, why have you abandoned us?" It is asked by Arfia's close friend in *La Danse du roi*, the crazed peasant Lâbane, who has been cast adrift by the armistice in a town where he cannot get his bearings.

NOVELS OF THE 1970s

In *Dieu en Barbarie* (1970; God in Barbary) and in *Le Maître de chasse* (1973; The huntmaster), the characters in their quests for identity come up with answers that are as hollow as they are contradictory. *Dieu en Barbarie* centers, in a retrospectively prophetic manner, on the loneliness of Kamal Waëd, a political leader who sincerely seeks his country's good but is able to achieve this only by eclipsing its memory and very identity. Much closer, paradoxically, to that reality is French aid worker Jean-Marie Aymard, who has joined the Mendicants of God in their search for a true (and nonreligious) identity, an identity predating civilization, including even splendid Roman ruins to which a poverty-stricken peasant woman, riding through on her donkey, pays absolutely no attention.

Kamal seeks symbolically to find out who paid for the education that enabled him to obtain the high position he now occupies. The answer is as laughable as the one given to the hero of *Cours sur la rive sauvage*; this novel, too, ends on "his big shrill laugh which echoed and re-echoed in the lonely night."

In *Le Maître de chasse*, the Mendicants of God have gone to seek an answer in the poorest and most remote village, far from all "civilization." The mission ends in tragedy when the army sent by Kamal to put down the resulting disorder opens fire. But the violence is without purpose, because the Mendicants of God fail to find the answer they seek. Indeed, it is doubtful whether any answer can be given in words. The village people, at one with the stony ground on which they live, have refused the assistance this band of city folk has come to bring them, and ultimately the answer the Mendicants receive is no answer at all. It boils down to the word *nothing*, as Tijami, one of the Mendicants, finds out:

> *Nothing.* That fills me with joy. An answer that boils down to the word "nothing," who could ask for more? *I'm* happy with that; I want nothing else. It's now the turn of the pupil of the daytime, dilated on these mountains, to speak. It's the turn of the wind and light sweeping their emptiness. It's the turn of the afternoon—an afternoon that won't do any longer.
>
> (*Le Maître de chasse*, p. 73)

These two novels thus question modernity in a particularly anguished manner; first and foremost to be questioned is the modernity of an Algeria in the throes of an identity crisis. The questions raised in *La Danse du roi* are whether memory can be uttered and how those inhabited by an invasive past in an amnesiac and counterfeit present can hope to come to terms with their maladjustment. In *Dieu en Barbarie* and *Le Maître de chasse*, the doubt surrounding the legitimacy of a technocratic modernity is made extreme. This is not political denunciation, but it does constitute a questioning of the powers of speech and action, even those filled with good intentions. *Habel* (1977) goes even further, introducing a subtle variation on exile in a large European city and on living at the edge, where madness beckons tantalizingly.

Habel can on one level be read as the story of Habel, a young North African immigrant in Paris. Like the whole of Dib's output, the novel is a meditation on modernity and the violence associated with it. There is the violence of exile and separation, with whose victims Habel often identifies himself. These victims include the individual beaten and left lying on the urine-soaked floor of the men's room of a café and the youth who mutilates himself before a select audience in a strange ceremony, to which Habel is invited by the "Old Man" Eric Merrain, alias "The Lady of Mercy." Merrain then debauches Habel before dying.

The novel cannot be read on this level alone, however. Pleasure scrambles meaning and admits ambiguity. As the place where meaning and identity are divided in two and turned upside down, the city also represents the doubling of word and the splitting of time: each place in the city reminds of another place, and words, such as *exile*, are endowed with other meanings. Habel conducts a dialogue with a brother who has stayed behind in the home country. He talks to him from the intersection at the Saint Michel Fountain on the Left Bank in Paris, where he has seen death face-to-face and where death divides in two in the person of Lily, the ever changing inverse double of Sabine, doubled in her turn by the Lady of Mercy. Habel is in love with both Lily and Sabine.

Because Habel has seen the Angel of Death, however uncouth he may seem in other respects—for instance, when he steals Eric Merrain's papers and throws them in the toilet—he becomes the one responsible for "giving everything a very precise name"—that is, he becomes a writer. His madness, separation from Sabine, and pursuit of Lily (who is just as ever changing) can thus also be read as a fresh metaphor for the "writing of disaster," just as Eric Merrain's pleasure-death is also a metaphor for writing. This time the disaster is that Habel has become the keeper through his encounter with the Old Man, a well-known writer whose pleasure-death will pursue him and whose stolen papers have in a way become his means of redemption.

Thus the meaning of exile is overturned: exile—that of the writer and that of the character—is a privileged position because it enables Habel, from the Saint Michel intersection watched over by the Angel of Death, to appreciate the abandonment of his brother left at home and to appropriate the famil-

ial and also political power. The Angel of Death, the writer-harlot Eric Merrain/Lady of Mercy, and Lily, swept along by the insanity in which Lily will ensnare Habel at the end, are all further manifestations of the tragic "savage shore" on which he—whose role it is to name things—finds himself. Love, madness, and writing are three different aspects of the fearsome power that can be acquired only at the expense of life and being.

NOVELS OF THE 1980s AND 1990s

Dib chose the "savage shore" of *Cours sur la rive sauvage* as the setting of the novels of the 1980s and 1990s, up to and including *Neiges de marbre* (1990; Marble snows), with its stark sobriety and almost autobiographical directness, and *Le Désert sans détour* (1992; The detourless desert). These are probably the finest texts in a body of work of the highest quality. Love, madness, and writing often go hand in hand in these works, even to the point of hallucination, in the poetry and in *Habel*, Les Terrasses d'Orsol (1985; The Orsol terraces), and *Le Sommeil d'Ève* (1989; Eve's sleep), whereas *Le Désert sans détour* can be read to some extent as a comment on the Gulf War between the United States and Iraq and the traumatic effect it had on relations between the west and the Arab world. But it is in no way a polemical novel, instead stressing the war's deep existential resonance.

The "Nordic" novels (to distinguish them from the "Algeria" trilogy of the 1950s)—*Les Terrasses d'Orsol*, *Le Sommeil d'Ève*, and *Neiges de marbre*—can be read as Habel's deliberate entry into madness, following Lily at the end of *Habel*. In *Les Terrasses d'Orsol* the reader first encounters an initiation quest that in some respects harks back to *Who Remembers the Sea* and *Cours sur la rive sauvage*. Eïd has been sent—or has he?— from Orsol to Jarbher, a rich city supposedly in northern Europe, to investigate the inexpressible nature of this ideal society: a pit to which mysterious beings are relegated. He will leave Jarbher and find love during an excursion to a nearby island only when he has agreed to abandon a quest that is perhaps all the more pointless for the fact that the answer might seem to be obvious: "Of course! What else has been at issue from the outset? This surely, and only this: the poor from everywhere redeeming the world, and we have been given neither the chance of brushing the question aside, nor the hope of eluding it" (p. 176).

Once again the quest serves only to unveil something so self-evident that it has been concealed by its very enormity, like the identity of Kamal Waëd in *Dieu en Barbarie* or something obvious that has a largely political meaning, like the identity of Kamal in the same novel or the hero's prostitution in *Habel*. This political meaning becomes straightforwardly obvious once it is no longer expected — when, as if by chance, a character gives every appearance of being an immigrant.

But it would serve no useful purpose to limit oneself to this possible meaning. Otherwise, there would be no reason for all this playing with names that, like Orsol and Jarbher, have no precise meaning and therefore indicate their gratuitous nature, or even names that, like Eïd's, change gradually until (in his case) it becomes almost indistinguishable, phonetically speaking, from his female partner's. Once again behind the name is the very being of the investigator who in love will find a glory in the face of which the initial inquiry is mere illusion.

The question then arises of whether love itself really exists, for otherwise it is difficult to understand the sacrifice of the investigator Eïd (now Ed). Back in town where Aëlle is living, Ed is symbolically violated in an infernal ballet of leather-clad women motorcyclists who drive over his body. This sacrifice, which leads to his loss of memory, has analogies with that of the hero and of the individual beaten in the men's room in *Habel*. One also must ask what meaning to attach to Ed's final stupor, a kind of absence comparable in some

respects with that of the narrator at the end of *Who Remembers the Sea*, and in other respects with that in *La Danse du roi* (indeed, a detailed study needs to be made of the last pages of Dib's novels as a whole).

After being left for dead on the deserted square by the motorcyclists, Eïd/Ed is taken in by Aëlle. In the passage that ends *Les Terrasses d'Orsol* he tells her:

> "You know what, miss? As soon as I leave here, I'll go and live in Jarbher.... I'll find Aëlle again, too."
> "Ed, you're in Jarbher. I am Aëlle."
> "Aëlle. Ah, Aëlle.... She's over there, in Jarbher."
>
> (p. 214)

And yet the whole being is involved in love: that is how *Le Sommeil d'Ève* reveals the insanity of Faïna, possessed by the Wolf of Norse legend (a story equally well known in Dib's native North Africa). The wolf (or she-wolf) was encountered earlier in the "hollow of desire" in *Omneros*, where it was much more than a simple metaphor, indicating precisely what, in passion and in the unleashing of the senses, transcends all reason. The wolf figure is also found in the metaphor of the Hunter that gives *Le Maître de chasse* its title and is echoed in that novel's ending. It is also, by a happy coincidence, echoed in the author's own name, *dhib* meaning "wolf" in Arabic.

In *Le Sommeil d'Ève* there is a further reversal. Solh, the narrator, appears on first reading to have nothing in common with the wolf that Faïna loves in him. "Does one ever know who one is?" he wonders. "The wolf...does it know it's a wolf?" At this point, the wolf, if it is a metaphor for madness, concerns Faïna more than Solh. But there is another reversal: the real madness is perhaps that of reason. Here, too, division occurs, between the word and what it is supposed to say, and between one person's version and another's, because the novel is built on two stories, the first titled

"I who am called Faïna," and the second, "I who am called Solh."

Neiges de marbre may at first seem like an unexpectedly prosaic sequel to the final separation of Solh and Faïna in *Le Sommeil d'Ève*, the last sentence of which, while remaining ambiguous, sternly challenges the course taken: Solh tells Faïna, "You will, I hope, refuse to listen any more to those who call you she-wolf" (p. 222). There is no ambiguity in *Neiges de marbre*. This work gives the impression of leaving "literature" behind altogether, assuming that the word still means something. It is the story — no longer a novel — of separation and, above all, of its most tragic and most prosaic consequence: the loss of the child born of this Nordic love affair. The child reappears in *L'Infante maure* (1994; The Moorish princess).

In *La Danse du roi*, each of Rodwan's narratives consists of describing the faces of women or girls, and beneath each narrative the subsequent story reveals another face, and so on to the last face, that of the dead woman. Dib's entire work can be read as the successive peeling off of all the superimposed masks of literature as pretense, right up to the discovery of a verso side, of a world this side of madness that this story-reality might constitute. A common thread running throughout Dib's work could be this mockery, the very essence of the text's literary tension, of words' constant loss of reality.

If that is the case, then *Neiges de marbre* can be situated at the level of reality itself, well on the other side of literature. This mundane reality is still that of loss, no longer the loss of reality as object of literature but, more prosaically, the loss of a child. It makes no difference if this child is called Lyyl (recalling, among other things, Lily in *Habel*): this text invites not literary analysis but biographical wiretapping. Or it could be a new, painful way of indicating the limits of literature and of the loss that is consubstantial with it.

So these Nordic novels are — along with *Habel*, which in part heralds their arrival — among the most intense in a body of work that can hardly be said to be bland. They also are the ones that have most disconcerted critics, who lose their bearings for dealings with Maghreb (North African) writing. But perhaps the term "Maghreb literature" no longer has much meaning, assuming it ever had any; certainly, confining the Maghreb writer, or more generally the African writer, within a specific geographical category amounts, on closer inspection, to imprisoning him or her in a kind of ghetto or gilded cage. This may result in the writer's work being read largely for its politics or anticolonialist stand, rather than being judged as literature on the basis of an intrinsic aesthetic quality, or the lack of it.

As a general rule, the Maghreb writer who abandons North Africa as an exclusive point of reference is heavily penalized by the critics; atypical works are simply ignored. This was the case with the "Canadian" novels of Driss Chraïbi and with *L'Ange aveugle* (Blind angel) by Tahar Ben Jelloun, the Maghreb writer whom the critics held in highest esteem. It was certainly the case with the later novels of Mohammed Dib, including the Nordic novels. Moreover, as if to emphasize their marginalization, these works were published from 1985 on by Sindbad, a much less prestigious imprint than Dib's previous publisher. By a supreme irony, Sindbad normally specialized in literature translated from the Arabic, whereas Dib wrote in very fine French.

Le Désert sans détour is the novel of a world beyond cataclysm. The desert in which two grotesque characters, Hagg-Bar and Syklist, lose their way during a war can be read as the desert of the Gulf War, the trauma of which was felt far beyond the confines of the Arab world (a fact that perhaps is not fully appreciated). In that sense, reality imitated art, since Dib wrote the book before the war broke out; but it is perhaps also a new mischievous game played by literature and reality.

In any event, if retrospectively the Gulf War gave unexpected meaning to this novel, it ought to be read primarily as a fresh stripping down to basics and as a new desertification, in the strict sense of the term, of the game of literature. The glory of Hagg-Bar is comparable with that of the king whose mime show ends *La Danse du roi*. The great portal reappears as before, opening suddenly onto the void that precedes and engulfs every word, since the meaning still has to be grasped; but meaning stays, as mockingly as ever, just out of reach. The desert, here, is more that of meaning, over which the unruffled Hagg-Bar is posted as lookout:

> But I never cease being a wandering soul, both where I am and where I am not. Wandering soul, soul in search of its memory, my fingers clinging to the wire mesh, I seem, just by following my gaze, to hear and understand everything with my eyes. So who is asking me in a murmur: "Where do you come from?" Space itself without beginning or end seems to take up the question and run with it. Torrid the sky, torrid the earth, torrid the air between them. Uncertain the horizon and dry the smell of stone consumed by its own fire. A world: a desert, and the fever of the desert. "Where do you come from?"
>
> Where do I come from? The other toneless voice answers, emerging from somewhere beyond myself. From all that space. A reply, I soon realize, that neither does justice to the question nor brushes it aside. As if there were still one, a reply, still others, to give. And the question stays asked. I see only stone and dust. I see only this flame; it ruins the eyes; it alone is true. I can be true in my turn only if I come from it, if I am haloed by it. . . . One and unique, the light cleanses the earth, scrubs it white. It would not be light if it did something else.
>
> It would not be light if it did not also leave your soul ravaged by nostalgia. But why this wound? Why does that which could be beautiful, and definitely is, take shape simultaneously as abomination?

(pp. 72–73)

Selected Bibliography

VERSE

Ombre gardienne. Paris: Gallimard, 1961.
Formulaires. Paris: Seuil, 1970.
Omneros. Paris: Seuil, 1975.
Feu, beau feu. Paris: Seuil, 1979.
Ô vive. Paris: Sindbad, 1987.

NOVELS

La Grande Maison. Paris: Seuil, 1952.
L'Incendie. Paris: Seuil, 1954.
Le Métier à tisser. Paris: Seuil, 1957.
Qui se souvient de la mer. Paris: Seuil, 1962.
Cours sur la rive sauvage. Paris: Seuil, 1964.
La Danse du roi. Paris: Seuil, 1968.
Dieu en Barbarie. Paris: Seuil, 1970.
Le Maître de chasse. Paris: Seuil, 1973.
Habel. Paris: Seuil, 1977.
Les Terrasses d'Orsol. Paris: Sindbad, 1985.
Le Sommeil d'Ève. Paris: Sindbad, 1989.
Neiges de marbre. Paris: Sindbad, 1990.
Le Désert sans détour. Paris: Sindbad, 1992.
L'Infante maure. Paris: Albin Michel, 1994.

TRANSLATION

Who Remembers the Sea. Trans. by Louis Tremaine. Washington, D.C.: Three Continents Press, 1985.

BIOGRAPHICAL AND CRITICAL STUDIES

Bonn, Charles. *Lecture présente de Mohammed Dib*. Algiers, Algeria: ENAL, 1988.

Chikhi, Beida. *Problématique de l'écriture dans l'oeuvre romanesque de Mohammed Dib*. Algiers, Algeria: Office des Publications Universitaires, 1989.

Déjeux, Jean. *Mohammed Dib: Écrivain algérien*. Sherbrooke, Canada: Éditions Naaman, 1977.

Khadda, N. *Mohammed Dib, romancier: Esquisse d'un itinéraire*. Algiers, Algeria: Office des Publications Universitaires, 1986.

Obi Egbuna
1938–

GARETH GRIFFITHS

OBI BENUE EGBUNA was born on 18 July 1938 at the village of Ozubulu near Onitsha, in the East Central State of Nigeria. In 1961 he went to England to study law and remained there after completing his studies. A follower of the Pan-African philosophy of Ghana's first president, Kwame Nkrumah, he edited the Nkrumanist journal *The Voice of Africa* and was the president of the Universal Coloured People's Association, an organ of the radical British Black Power movement, in the mid 1960s.

An Igbo (or Ibo), Egbuna remained in Britain during the period of the Igbo-led secession of the Republic of Biafra from Nigeria and the ensuing civil war, which ended in 1970 in Biafra's defeat. The pamphlet *The Murder of Nigeria: An Indictment* (1968) describes his view of the politics leading to the war and outlines his demand for a committed socialist, nontribal political system for Nigeria. The pamphlet is a powerful indictment of the collusion of interests between the new ruling elite, the former colonial powers, and the neocolonial interests of the United States, then still very much in cold war mode and at its most "interventionist" in countries such as Nigeria and the Congo. It was later reprinted in the essay collection *Destroy This Temple: The Voice of Black Power in Britain* (1971).

For Egbuna the only effective model for African independence is the socialist-based Pan-Africanism. In his view Nigerian independence served only to usher in a new elite class. Although Egbuna's analysis is strikingly similar to the later indictments of Kenyan independent governments by Ngũgĩ wa Thiong'o in the novels *Matigari ma njirũũngi* (1986; *Matigari*) and *Caitaani mũtharaba-inĩ* (1980; *Devil on the Cross*), it is worth noting that analysis of postindependence politics in black Africa is not as successfully integrated into Egbuna's creative work as it is for Ngũgĩ. Nevertheless, Egbuna must be given credit for speaking out strongly against the uncritical adoption of tribalism as a basis for political formations in the Africa of the late 1960s.

As Egbuna sees it, only a consciously ideological stance can expose the false loyalties implicit in tribalist political formations and can clearly address the urgent need of the subclass of Nigerians ignored by the politics of the new Nigerian elites. His ideal figure is the young Major Chukwuma Nzeogwu, the leader of the openly socialist coup of January 1966, to whom *The Murder of Nigeria* is dedicated. Portrayed as the only person who had sought to expose the British colonial government's policy of installing compliant puppet rulers, Nzeogwu promoted instead a genuinely socialist and democratic revolution.

Egbuna, in the middle of a bitter civil crisis that had overwhelmed most of Nigeria's intellectuals and caused them to divide along tribal lines, perceived that such divisions are not likely to address the common problems of the Nigerian people.

On the negative side, it is a pity that Egbuna singles out for criticism in the pamphlet compatriots such as Wole Soyinka, whose record of opposing knee-jerk tribal response was at least the equal of Egbuna's. By dismissing Soyinka with such characterizations as "the literary wonder-boy on the Western pop-literature chart" (p. 9), Egbuna anticipated the many later "leftist" attacks on Soyinka, who would accuse him of being detached from social realities and overconcerned with the mythic past. In retrospect, Soyinka's lengthy imprisonment for his opposition to the policies of the federalist leader, Colonel Yakubu Gowon, and to the war might have garnered more sympathetic consideration from Egbuna, especially in the light of Egbuna's acknowledgment that his own advice was given from the safety of London. He blames this self-imposed exile on Biafran leader Chukwuemeka Odumegwu Ojukwu's "purges" of socialist opposition from the Biafran side; otherwise, he asserts, "instead of hibernating and writing revolutionary literature in this dingy tenement in London, [I] would be right there in the 'jungles of Biafra,' converting my philosophy into reality" (p. 125).

In *The Murder of Nigeria*, Egbuna emphasizes the idea of "negritude," or black consciousness, and the attendant notion of the essential "African personality." This may explain, in part, the vehemence of his dismissal in that text of Soyinka's rejection of the essentialist dangers of Négritude, the movement among francophone writers such as Léopold Sédar Senghor and Alioune Diop in the 1940s and 1950s that sought to characterize and classify those elements which made black Africans and their culture distinctive and different from Europeans and their culture.

Soyinka rejected Négritude because of the way in which it was used crudely to characterize features of black African culture as essential and fixed by racial features and not historically and culturally determined. For Egbuna, however, Soyinka's rejection of Négritude is synonymous with a denial of Africanness, since for him this is inextricably bound up with the concept of an African personality and linked to a worldwide vision of black consciousness. The degree to which this essentialist idea of Négritude continued to permeate Egbuna's work made him most unusual among the anglophone writers of this period, who mainly followed Soyinka in rejecting the ideas that underlay the movement in favor of a more specific and more historicist view of what gave the many African cultures their distinctive features.

During the late 1960s Egbuna became a leading figure in the British Black Power movement, a loose association of radical black groups influenced by the philosophy of black Americans who rejected a compromise with white society and advocated a separate development of black society. In 1970 he was arrested on a charge of conspiracy to murder police officers and held without bail in Brixton Prison in London for six months. At the trial that followed he was found guilty but given a suspended sentence. In *Destroy This Temple*, Egbuna writes about this episode and about his visit to the United States in the late 1960s, where he met American leaders of the Black Power movement, including Elijah Mohammed, the leader of the American black Muslims.

During this period Egbuna helped found the Black Panther movement in Britain while also managing to write a series of short novels, stories, and plays. After his release from prison he returned to Nigeria, where he worked as director of programs for the state television and as director of the state writer's workshop. He also worked as a columnist and recorded his observations on the Nigeria to which he had returned. These commentaries were issued in the 1976 volume *Diary of a Homeless Prodigal*, which also reprinted "Letter from Brixton Prison" from *Destroy This Temple* as "Letter to a Sister (from London Prison Diary)," a letter to an African-American prostitute named Dolores in which Egbuna recorded his sharp observations on black culture in Britain and the United States. During this time he continued to produce longer fiction and stories. In 1976 he came to the United States, where he participated in the International Writing Program at the University of Iowa, obtaining his master's degree there in 1977. In 1980 he completed his doctorate at Howard University in Washington, D.C., and published three new works, *The Madness of Didi*, *The Rape of Lysistrata*, and *Black Candle for Christmas*.

Egbuna has been among the most controversial of the new African writers in English. His first novel, *Wind Versus Polygamy* (1964), reissued in 1978 under the title of *Elina*, provoked extreme and contradictory criticism. As the critic Reinhardt Sanders notes in his introduction to *Diary of a Homeless Prodigal*, contemporary reviews were violently divided in their judgments: Cameroonian novelist Mbella Sonne Dipoko referred to it as "an extraordinary novel with world-wide implications" while the West Indian critic O. R. Dathorne called it "the worst African novel I have ever read." Controversy and divided opinion have followed Egbuna ever since. Sanders sums up this attitude as follows:

> Obi Egbuna arrived in Britain on a scholarship from Nigeria. He quickly won success as a novelist, playwright and political writer. Just as quickly, he grew frustrated and incensed on seeing how Black people were treated, not only in Britain, but over much of the world, compelling the young writer to pause and ask himself the question: To whom does my talent belong?... [T]his uncharacteristic and unsubmissive departure from the traditional approach to African literature did not endear this "cheeky"

new generation author to the publishing élite in the Western world and, as might have been expected, it soon earned him the reputation among critics as the bad boy of Nigerian literature.

(p. 5)

Certainly, Egbuna's work has attracted little critical attention, and much of what exists in the form of brief and passing references in other work is negative in tone.

It is impossible to separate Egbuna's polemic work from his more strictly literary output. Time after time elements from the former are incorporated into the latter, even in the form of direct quotation. But more importantly, the work as a whole challenges the assumptions of western constructions of the literary; Egbuna forces us to question the possibility of separating literary aims and values from the social effects and purposes of writing.

WIND VERSUS POLYGAMY

In the short novel *Wind Versus Polygamy*, Egbuna tackles the issue of the relative merits of polygamy and monogamy, a question that formed the basis for a number of African works in the 1960s (Soyinka's *The Lion and the Jewel*, for example). As in the Soyinka piece, the struggle in *Wind Versus Polygamy* is in part an allegory of the struggle between the forces of "modernization" in contemporary Africa and the need to maintain traditional African culture, with its established values and its claim to continuity in the light of cultural neocolonialism.

The central figure is a paramount chief, the wily and powerful Chief Ozuomba. The heroine, the beautiful Elina, is the victim of Nigerian tradition, which has been corrupted and distorted from its effective purpose by the "winds of change," which the British Prime Minister Harold Macmillan had noted in his 1960 Cape Town speech were sweeping the African continent. Although Macmillan was referring to the move to political independence, the phrase became a catchall for the change and modernization of Africa, and it is in this latter sense that Egbuna used it as the novel's subtitle (dropped after the first edition): *Where "Wind" Is "Wind of Change" and Polygamy the "Change of Eves."* Elina is caught between an inherited debt to the hunter Okosisi Ojukwu, which was converted to a bride-price by her dead father, and pressure from her father's brother, Maza Ofodile, to marry the corrupt Councillor Ogidi. The archvillain of the novel, Ogidi represents only the desire to use tradition to accomplish his destructive, moneymaking goals. In the conflict that follows, Chief Ozuomba acts as the traditional authority and appears to resolve the dispute by getting Elina to agree to marry the chief himself. The chief knows that in so doing he is laying himself open to charges under the new antipolygamy law.

The main part of the novel is a detailed account of the trial in which, although represented by counsel, the chief defends not only his actions but the practice of polygamy. In a series of polemic speeches, he castigates western societies for hypocrisy in insisting on monogamy, a practice which they can neither sustain nor justify in terms of the profound negative social effects to which it has given rise. For Chief Ozuomba, the real defendant of the trial is the right of African cultures to their own values and social practices. His arguments range from the convincing—"You want facts? All right, I will give you facts. In the United States of America alone, ten thousand homes break up every day. Ten thousand monogamous homes between every sunrise and sunset" (p. 67)—to the absurd. "An average man is capable of having three thousand children in his lifetime," the chief says in one of his more bizarre arguments. "But the lifetime capacity of the average woman is ten only.... From each man according to his ability, distribution among women according to their needs. Sex democracy must prevail" (p. 68).

It is hard to judge whether Egbuna is successful in distancing the reader from Ozuomba's more extreme views or even whether he intends to do so. Elements of the chief's presentation as a character are clearly satirical, but overall he emerges as a figure of strength and dignity, whose rootedness in his own culture—symbolized significantly by his resistance to the written word—means neither a loss of wisdom nor a loss of verbal and logical skill. In this uncertainty of tone lies the main problem critics have had in assessing all of Egbuna's writing: it is difficult to determine whether polemic is successfully employed to further the satire or whether it merely alienates the reader. On balance, in *Wind Versus Polygamy* the satire does seem to carry the reader into the camp of Chief Ozuomba, distancing the chief from the more solemn, humorless characterizations of the thoroughly westernized characters, such as the prosecutor, Mr. Azodo. The reader does not have to accept all the chief's polemical arguments in order to see the force of his general stand against cultural neocolonialism.

Readers who may have found the arguments less than fully convincing are reassured when a surprise ending reveals that Chief Ozuomba has not married Elina at all. Instead, he has bribed Elina's uncle to pretend to have witnessed the wedding so that the chief would get his day in court. To make all right in this allegorical tale, the chief's western-educated son, Jerome, and Elina have fallen in love. At the end, the young couple lives happily ever after. The rather cloying sweetness of the resolution is relieved by the figure of the young couple's old Jesuit priest and confidant, Father Joseph. His final triumph when the young couple is married in a monogamous ceremony illustrates how the chief's victory is a partial and temporary one, since it is clear that Jerome and Elina represent the new ways (they are both sincere Catholic converts) and that their romantic and monogamous westernized union represents the likely future for marriage in modern Nigeria.

Nevertheless, Egbuna's attitude remains ambiguous to this ending, which sees the couple "happily married" in a "white" wedding ceremony. The book's final image reinforces this: "'Ah!' she whispered. 'It is going to be a white wedding.' Up on the tree top, two little black birds were making love" (p. 128). This sardonic final image undercuts the "happy ending."

THE ANTHILL

In 1965, Egbuna wrote a play script, *The Anthill.* Most of the play consists of fairly unhumorous banter between Bobo, an African student of art, and his English roommate, the medical student Nigel. The banter centers on Nigel's aversion to a permanent relationship with his girlfriend, Elizabeth, who is beautiful but whom he characterizes as too intelligent and "cold." This is tagged on to a more serious, though hardly more convincing, main plot, in which Tommy, the young soldier son of Bobo and Nigel's landlady, dies of fear when he is confronted first by Bobo's painting of an anthill and then by Bobo himself. In a flashback scene Tommy is revealed to have been the instigator of a cruel hoax, in which a young African dies of fright after being subjected to a mock trial and execution at the site of an African anthill of the kind Bobo paints obsessively. In a scene set in the coroner's court, it is revealed that the young African is Bobo's twin, although Bobo knew nothing of the circumstances of his brother's death until now. Its plot unconvincing to the point of absurdity, the play also features hardly credible dialogue. For example, at one point a coroner remarks that "the moral lesson of this case is there for all to see. All young British soldiers must behave like English gentlemen at home and abroad. Under no circumstances —and I repeat—under no circumstances must you kill a man to whom you are not properly introduced. The case is closed" (p. 57).

The play has an oddly haunting and affective air in the horrifying scene of the murder of Bobo's twin, with the hint of a supernatural link between the twins through which vengeance is effected. The second half of the play replaces this structure of supernatural melodrama with a low-level parody of English comedy of manners. The haunting effect built up in the first half is lost in this change of tone, and the comedy element in the second half is also weakened by the fact that it never makes a clear satirical point.

DAUGHTERS OF THE SUN

The collection of short stories *Daughters of the Sun* appeared in 1970. The opening story "Divinity," which tells of the conflict between two generations, more successfully focuses the concerns that had permeated Egbuna's previous work, including the overtly polemic *The Murder of Nigeria.* The father, Thomas, an old Catholic catechist who adheres to the religion of the colonizer, seeks to live by this faith and is moved to kill the "juju," an African ritual figure, which in his opinion binds his fellow villagers to outdated superstition. His son, David, and David's friend Daniel are university students who have both been raised as good Catholics but who at the university are drawn into the African Cultural Society and persuaded to join the traditional cult Ozo-Ebunu, servants of the juju. Participating in a ceremony in order to become an initiate of the society, David is made to wear the masked costume of the juju. Unaware of the identity of the person behind the mask, David's father, acting on the instructions of the Catholic priest, shoots the masked figure to expose what he sees as its superstitious claim to be an immortal god. When he returns to find David, whom he has locked in a hut a mile away from the ceremony, he discovers his son dead from bullet wounds. The father begins to believe in the supernatural power of the juju himself.

The mysterious circumstances surrounding David's death in the locked hut is explained away by Daniel, who tells how David's being locked up was part of the ploy to demonstrate the power of the juju by making it seem as if he could not have been the one who carried the mask of the god. After he was shot, his body was smuggled back into the "locked" hut to confirm the juju's power. In telling this to the Catholic priest, Daniel seals his own fate, in accordance with the society's law that says traitors of the secrets of the society die within an hour of their betrayal.

"Divinity" confirms the power of the juju and the validity of the African religion the juju represents. The story exposes the idea of the juju as a superstition but at the same time confirms the importance of the African adhering to his or her own mysteries rather than those imported by outside forces such as the Catholic church. Daniel tells the Catholic priest at the end: "The youth of Africa has become like a pendulum, oscillating between Europe and Africa through turbulent cyclones of dissimilar beliefs and contradicting philosophies" (p. 46).

Egbuna was to rework this story later in dramatic form; in 1980 it was issued as a script accompanying a radio broadcast. The plot bears some resemblance to the better-known play by Soyinka, *Death and the King's Horseman*, insofar as it shows the conflict between tradition and change within two generations. The two plays also share the irony that the young are forced to defend tradition and to sacrifice their lives to ensure its continuity when the older generation fails to perform its task of preserving and handing on the past. The plays are thus much closer in their views than Egbuna's implacable public opposition to Soyinka in this period might suggest was possible.

Similarly, in the story "The Scarecrow of Nairobi" the clash of a white settler and a Black Power leader is resolved in a strangely amicable way, given Egbuna's uncompromising political position. This story undermines

the arguments of those who contend that Egbuna's writing always reproduces the Black Power perspective of the polemic texts in a simplistic way. The story concerns the supposed rape of a nun by a black man who turns out to be blind. The settler's wife, the only fair-minded figure in a story otherwise populated with bigoted characters (including the black activist who opposes the racist settler), points out that their prejudiced views of the world have prevented them from seeing the truth. The nun has unconsciously created the incident when her buried fantasies of black sexuality made her perceive the stumbling of the blind man as an angry "pursuit." More in sorrow than in anger, the wife tells the nun: "It's not your fault. It's all those sensational stories in the papers...making you read a nightmare into the harmless movements of a blind man" (p. 54).

"The Medics," which concerns the power of a traditional healer challenged by an overconfident young peace corps doctor, is tinged with gentle humor. Although the story presents a solid endorsement of the "irrational" traditional African value system, it is not just a polemic but develops a narrative and characters who have a valid life in their own terms. Its humorous tone embraces the young doctor, who narrates the story and is drawn into an understanding of traditional African values and culture by example rather than mere exhortation. The wisdom of the old African healer is shared by Dr. Williams, a white British doctor, who helps the young peace corps doctor to appreciate the value of another culture and point of view. "The Medics" shows a new breadth and tolerance in Egbuna's writing.

The final and title story, "Daughters of the Sun," is a simple but effective endorsement of traditional African fables and their value to society. The narrator tells an old woman, when he offers to carry her pot, that he collects "legends" and that he will pay her for them. He realizes at the end that the value of the tale that she tells him lies not only in its intrinsic charm but also in the way it has rewarded him for his help in assisting the woman in her task of bringing water from the river. This fable, one of the most subtle of Egbuna's short narratives, directly takes on the issue of the revaluation of traditional culture in the modern world.

In Egbuna's next collection of short stories, *The Emperor of the Sea and Other Stories* (1974), the title story uses the same narrator and old woman. She again tells him a traditional legend, but the subtlety of the earlier ending is missing, as is the larger narrative purpose of depicting the potentially fruitful interaction of traditional wisdom and contemporary practices. The theme is taken up again when Egbuna employs the same figures for a third time in the 1980 collection *Black Candle for Christmas.*

THE EMPEROR OF THE SEA AND OTHER STORIES

Egbuna's second story collection consists of three tales. The first, "Rivers Can't Speak," picks up the theme of *Wind Versus Polygamy* in telling of an encounter between a young man (the narrator) and an old man. Watching a beautiful maiden at the river, the old man offers advice on life and women to the young man, advice that includes a spirited defense of the traditional ways, and polygamy in particular. It ends with the revelation that the young woman is the wife of the old man.

Egbuna's accounts of the cultural importance of polygamy seem rather dated when compared with the more complex analyses of the practice offered by writers such as Isidore Okpewho and Festus Iyayi, not to mention the powerful indictments of the effects on women of polygamy by contemporary African women writers such as Buchi Emecheta. These later writers have tended to deal with the phenomenon as a sociocultural construct; they show us that its virtues or inadequacies as a practice depend on changing social con-

ditions. It is not polygamy as such that they find lacking, but its decay as an effective social form when it is forced to meet the changed social and economic conditions of modern Nigerian life. Thus, for example, later writers argue that the practice does not survive as an effective social structure when it is coupled with modern, urban, wage-earning life conditions.

The psychological consequences for women in polygamous marriages, analyzed with some detail by writers such as Iyayi and Emecheta, is rather glossed over by Egbuna, whose insight into female sexual psychology here and elsewhere is lacking. Egbuna's primary goal of reasserting the validity of African custom in order to vindicate the concept of a distinctive African personality prevents him from presenting polygamy as a practice subject to social pressure and change. This failure is peculiar in light of Egbuna's stress elsewhere in texts of the same period (for example, in *The Murder of Nigeria*) on a socialist ideology. In the pamphlet *The ABC of Black Power Thought* (1973), Egbuna had indicated that he was aware that many people felt there was an irreconcilable clash between Marxism and Black Power ideology, and he devotes much of that pamphlet to arguing that the two can coexist. But outside this brief text, the seeming incompatibility between the essentialist tendency of black consciousness/ negritude and the historicist, materialist basis of socialist ideology is never properly resolved by Egbuna. This conflict powerfully affects the ways in which the traditional past and its survival into the present are represented in many of his literary works.

Egbuna's sharp sense of the material conditions of contemporary Nigerian life is made clear in the middle section of the three-part story "A Tale of Three Souls." This section, titled "Soul in a Creek," captures with more force than most writing of its time the real conditions for ordinary Africans in colonial and neocolonial Africa. It was not until the work of the new generation of writers such as

Iyayi (*Violence*, 1979; *Heroes*, 1986) that accounts as powerful as Egbuna's were written of conditions among ordinary Africans. Even Ayi Kwei Armah (*The Beautiful Ones Are Not Yet Born*, 1968) had restricted his work to the lower middle class of clerks and office workers. In "Soul in a Creek," Egbuna presents with real force the conditions of life for the servant class—or the "shit class," as he refers to it, with characteristic directness, in his polemic writing—demonstrating how this class needs to be given a voice if Black Power is to be really effective. The following extract gives an idea of how powerful his descriptive writing is:

> My room was at the back, close to an open-drainage gutter, and the smell always churned my stomach, and made sleep impossible. And if this wasn't enough, there was a public water-pump right outside our house, and the noise of people coming to fetch water at night to avoid the day-time rush, singing when they were happy, drumming on their buckets when they were drunk, screaming when they were fighting for queues, on and on until the early hours of dawn made sleep impracticable. Especially when your room was on the groundfloor of our house, like mine was.
>
> (pp. 41–42)

In stories like "Soul in a Creek" Egbuna addresses specific living conditions without sentimentality, in sharp contrast with his romanticized discussion of traditional practices such as polygamy:

> Working men...assembled out here for a little relaxation after slogging all day at work. Sneaking out of their tiny, rented rooms, they had lied to themselves they were coming to their favourite lamp-posts to munch a few oranges. But the real truth was that they had come here to recapture echoes from their peasant past, to regain...if only in one fleeting hour every night...that spirit of community-belonging which they had left behind in their surrounding villages.
>
> (pp. 42–43)

The young narrator in "Soul in a Creek" meets a girl who is abused by her rich master, with whom she refuses to sleep. The master, who is a powerful politician, puts pressure on her through threats to her family. Unable to help her in any way against her master, the narrator strangles her, with her acquiescence, and throws her body in the creek. Although a trifle melodramatic, this short story presents the urban world as a world complete in itself and illustrates how that world has created new and damaging conditions for the workers brought in from the villages and for the young women who are brought in by the middle-class employers to work as servants. It bears some resemblance to the urban fiction of South Africa and may have been influenced by the work of realist writers such as Ezekiel Mphahlele (*Down Second Avenue*, 1959) and Alex La Guma (*A Walk in the Night*, 1962). Earlier Nigerian fiction dealing with town life emphasizes the "high life" worlds of the night-club and prostitution bars (for example, Cyprian Ekwensi's *Jagua Nana*, 1961). Egbuna is one of the earliest Nigerian writers to record the living conditions and struggles of the ordinary worker.

"Soul Come Home," the final section of "A Tale of Three Souls," does not work as well, largely because it uses the narrative merely as a cover for political arguments; in fact, the section in which Leroi, the African American organizing the workers in the town of Inosha to strike against the oil company, describes the horrors of American slavery is taken word for word from *Destroy This Temple*. The real problem with the piece, though, is that its political solutions are so unbelievable. The oil company's manager gives in to the workers' demands in a speech that has absolutely no credibility as a response from a neocolonial industrial executive. His collapse in the face of the strike, indeed, his abject surrender to all the workers' demands, is more a case of wish fulfillment than a convincing political account.

The story works best in the satirical allegory of the final episode. The old Papa Duru, the strike leader, bathes his mule in the lake belonging to the oil company, as he has done every Sunday. For weeks the new young Dutch engineer in charge of the company has tried unsuccessfully to stop him. In the end the engineer draws his gun and fires it off near the old man to intimidate him. The old man waits until the gun is empty and then produces his own rusty gun, which he uses to force the engineer to kiss the old mule. In this final episode, which has real satirical force, it is possible to see how, stripped of the excessive and largely unnecessary direct polemic, "Soul Come Home" could have been turned into an effective political satire, communicating its message of the need for the black world to stand up and demand its rights more effectively.

What emerges clearly from an overview of Egbuna's work as a whole is that two impulses struggle to coexist, sometimes more and sometimes less successfully, in all of it: the impulse to polemic and the impulse to satire, a less direct form of political commentary. This is not to demand that art function independently of social message, but rather to point out that the two modes used to deliver Egbuna's message, polemic and satire, have been mixed in ways that do not always further Egbuna's aims.

THE MINISTER'S DAUGHTER

In Egbuna's second novel, *The Minister's Daughter* (1975), the balance between polemic and satire is more successful than in his earlier works. Nevertheless, from time to time polemic still intrudes too directly into the text, sometimes edging out the satire altogether. This is especially so in the final chapters — in which accounts of the historical ill treatment of slaves, in the form of direct quotations from earlier work such as *Destroy This Temple*, are found — and in an analysis of the Biafran war that is identical to what had appeared in *Destroy This Temple* and *The Murder of Ni-*

geria. But overall a satiric tone prevails, as in the scene where the servant Boniface turns the tables on the Minister Arima and — in the presence of Major Okoye, the leader of an antigovernment coup, and the young officers who support him — forces the corrupt and self-centered minister to bite his pimpled bottom, strip, and to watch Boniface enjoy his European mistress, Muriel, in his place. This Plautian turning of servant on master achieves the bite of effective satire and yet retains its political point about the corruption of the current government, the weakness and sycophancy of its "strong men," and the approval of ordinary people like Boniface for the coup, which offers them a chance to turn the tables on these false leaders. The major is bemused by the idiotic antics of the minister. The tone of the dialogue is not realistic but satirical and is deliberately exaggerated:

> "Are you sure he doesn't mind doing these things?" asked the major.
> Boniface smiled and replied:
> "Why don't you ask him Major?"
> The major turned to the Minister and said: "Well?"
> The Minister looked at Muriel helplessly and she nodded her head encouragingly.
> "Er...er...these tricks are nothing to me, Major, I can do them."
>
> (p. 74)

The announcement with which this chapter ends, "Major, the coup has failed," signals a change in mood from satire to tragedy. This switch in part justifies the more openly polemic tone employed in the novel's final section. Major Okoye reverts from satiric "plain-dealer" to being the leader of a serious coup; indeed, it is clear in this final section that he is modeled quite closely on the leader of the 1965 coup, Major Nzeogwu, whom Egbuna had hailed as the hero of the struggle for ideological revolutionary change in *The Murder of Nigeria*. Major Okoye's call for the coup to resist the intervention of the Major-General (clearly meant as a portrait of the real traitor of the 1965 coup, Major-General Johnson Aguiyi-Ironsi) and to become a revolutionary struggle leads to his execution by his supposed best friend and most trusted officer, Captain Duru. The ending of the novel—which reminds us that this failed coup, labeled a "tribalist" coup by its opponents, will open the way to segregation and secession along tribal lines—reinforces the novel's construction of a direct political allegory of contemporary Nigerian politics. *The Minister's Daughter* closes on an ambivalent note: although the failure of the coup is mourned, the coup itself is presented as beyond reproach. We are reminded that in an early scene Major Okoye had ordered the brutal murder of a seven-year-old boy to ensure the coup's success: "In a neighbouring village, the body of a seven-year-old boy lay strangled at the bottom of the river. And in a little while, the body of a young major would be buried in the same valley" (p. 96).

Although not completely successful in integrating its diverse narrative modes, *The Minister's Daughter* succeeds in presenting a powerful and eloquent dramatization of Nigeria's need for broad-based popular opposition rather than coups executed by elite factions. At the same time the novel effectively satirizes the greed and corruption of the new civilian elite.

THE MADNESS OF DIDI

In 1980, after completing his doctorate at Howard University, Egbuna returned to Nigeria, where he took the initiation rites of the Ozo system, the traditional system of social ranking in Igbo society, achieving the title of Aklunnie. One might speculate that Egbuna's action was intended to indicate a commitment to Igbo society and to its traditional values and a desire to take up a role in that world. His commitment and desire are reflected in the novel written at that time, *The*

Madness of Didi (1980), which deals with the return of an activist similar to Egbuna himself and with his search for a role in his own society after years spent abroad. *The Madness of Didi* is perhaps the most accomplished of Egbuna's works in its complexity and narrative development. Egbuna often weaves autobiographical elements into his fiction, frequently appearing as a character under his own name, in situations and places with which he has been associated in life. In *The Madness of Didi*, traces of Egbuna's life experience can be found in the story of the return of Didi, a Black Power activist, to his native village.

The novel examines Didi's relationship with the local community, and then with the larger world of modern Nigeria. A "been-to" (the colloquial term used by Nigerians for those who return from abroad), Didi challenges the locals' expectations of the behavior of a been-to by mingling with the ordinary locals. He finally falls afoul of the local elite and is blamed for radicalizing and alienating an elite's daughter in his class at a local technical college.

The narrator, a young boy called Obi (which is also Egbuna's first name), is drawn to Didi and through him is awakened to the inadequacies of the society in which he lives. Obi realizes the corruption of leaders such as Chief Ndumezay, a been-to who causes Didi's death, and the traditional ruler, the ironically named Chief Jesus Osisioma, who uses his position to brutalize young girls such as Nkechi, who lives with Obi and his mother and who has been like a sister to Obi.

Didi's life as a Black Power activist draws on Egbuna's own experience. Thus Egbuna's experience of six-month *remand* in Brixton for "uttering a threat" to murder becomes in the novel a *sentence* for killing six whites chosen at random as part of a bizarre plot in which Didi seeks to demonstrate by example to white society its illogical and vicious treatment of blacks throughout history. Didi's reasoning gives rise to long digressive passages, the rhetoric of which is again drawn from the polemic texts from the 1970s such as *Destroy This Temple* and *The ABC of Black Power Thought*.

The novel ends dramatically with an attempt by the formerly cynical and self-serving village cripple Oputa to rescue Didi from a fire set by Ndumezay's henchmen. Didi dies, but through his friends the young Obi is sent to England to study. He chooses librarianship, preferring pure knowledge to the kind of social power associated with the usual choices of medicine and law. The length of the narrative and the complexity of its story line make *The Madness of Didi* an ambitious undertaking, and in this novel Egbuna succeeds in maintaining the structure and developing it with more success than in the other longer fiction he had written since *Wind Versus Polygamy*.

THE RAPE OF LYSISTRATA

Egbuna published two more books in 1980. *The Rape of Lysistrata* is also labeled a novel, but it is so interwoven with actual events in Egbuna's life—featuring not only the writer as his own character but also a passage from *Destroy This Temple* as a crucial feature in the plot—that it ends with a disclaimer that "the narrative itself, and all the incidents in it, are entirely fictitious" (p. 192). The work deals with an accusation of rape made against a black Brazilian writer named Moses Camillo by a white student at the University of Iowa, who is about to marry him. It turns out that the student has been manipulated by a psychotic white female friend into attributing the authorship of a violent written account of the nature of black-white sexual relations to Camillo. The student is so horrified by the account that she cries rape as a vengeance on what she sees as Camillo's betrayal, since she believes no one who had written this "racial poison" could be capable of "Black or white

love." Bizarrely the piece in question is actually Egbuna's own writing, a section of *Destroy This Temple* called "The Little Boy of Brussels." The excerpt is a diatribe against the possibility of love between black men and white women except as a conscious or unconscious act of racial retribution by the black against the white. The identity of the author is revealed to the student—now a nun suffering from alcoholism—by Egbuna, who appears as himself in the story. The student, we are told, "forgives" Egbuna, who excuses the piece on the grounds that he was "revising that book" at the time (does he mean retracting it?) and that it was the anger of an imprisoned man that accounted for the appalling sexism and aggressive racism and misogyny of the piece. One can't help suspecting that this whole bizarre "novel" is an elaborate justification a decade later for this earlier piece. If so, it fails both as a justification of the earlier diatribe against black-white sexual relations and as a piece of fiction, since its justifications for the content of the sexist diatribe is unconvincing and labored and the fictional framework in which this justification is cast is highly contrived and finally implausible at the level of characterization and plot.

BLACK CANDLE FOR CHRISTMAS

The collection of short stories *Black Candle for Christmas* (1980) is also very uneven. The stories range from a description of a homosexual encounter leading to social betrayal ("Da Vinci's Curtain"), through a brief autobiographical sketch of an incident in Egbuna's early life ("Pearl"), to a long, rambling story ("The Execution of Dr. Echidime") that indicts the notorious summary executions of "criminals" by the Nigerian government at Bar Beach, Lagos, in the late 1970s. The potential force of this last tale, which has some excellent descriptive passages and analyses (notably an acute account of the possibility of effectively appropriating English as a vehicle to record African experience), is lost in a narrative that is disjointed and unfocused. The title story, however, redeems the collection. It completes the trilogy of stories about the legend collector and the old woman started in "Daughters of the Sun." Here the legend collector turns the tables on the old storyteller by telling her a story of exploitation and cruelty toward a young black British worker. In the story the young man, who has been forced to clean stinking toilets, enters a church and meets an old black woman. He asks her to excuse his smell, and she replies that he smells not of excrement but of social "fear...weakness...castration" (p. 166). The legend collector concludes: "this old woman was translating into the language of my generation the eternal verities of the ages" (p. 167). This final story in the trilogy of tales begun in 1970 unifies Egbuna's three collections of short stories and unifies the impulse underlying the diversity of his work by bringing together his basic political drive to make the values of traditional African culture effective in the contemporary world. Egbuna refuses to accept that contemporary Nigeria must mean a Nigeria that turns its back on its own traditions and past and that looks to the outside world for its solutions. At the same time, as the three versions of this collecting of traditional stories and legends (the stuff of traditional wisdom) indicate, the process is not a static one—the past must be transformed and made relevant to the present, not simply accepted unchanged.

Black Candle for Christmas may hold a clue to the silence of Egbuna, at least in English, since 1980. In the story "The Execution of Dr. Echidime," the young boy Obi is told by his teacher, who is Welsh, that

All the great masters of world literature write in their own language. And I do not mean a studied language. I mean their own language. Unless you learn this lesson, Obi, the fear of foreign language is going to rob gifted young people like yourself of the courage to be and give from yourself. And what they'll be churning out as African literature will continue to be hard-covers of artless verbiage and fatigued images, tailored into series of so-called African literature, by the new type of invaders who arrive with publishing machines, for the same reason as their invading predecessors came: profit.

(pp. 96–97)

It is notable that Egbuna's last work in English to be published abroad was *The Madness of Didi*, which deals with the return of a disenchanted intellectual and his attempt to reintegrate himself into his own society. As we saw, this mirrored Egbuna's own life at that time. The other two books published in 1980 were both issued by a Nigerian press, Fourth Dimension, in Enugu. This may be indicative of a desire of Egbuna to resist being absorbed by the machinery of "African" literature publishing, which he so eloquently condemned in "The Execution of Dr. Echidime." This short story suggests that Egbuna may have switched to writing in Igbo, but no further texts by Egbuna since 1980 can be traced.

CONCLUSION

If not always successfully, Egbuna has sought throughout his work to speak across the gap between traditional African culture and the experience of being black in the modern world—in Nigeria and in the rest of the black diaspora. His best work is informed by a raw and uncompromising honesty and a sharp emotional content. For Egbuna, the only place in which African culture of the past and of the present can meet effectively is in the living experience of black people, whether presented as polemic autobiography or as "fiction." His unique and sometimes disturbing attempt to demonstrate this belief marks his special contribution to the development of African writing in English.

Selected Bibliography

FICTION, PLAYWRITING, AND NONFICTION

Wind Versus Polygamy. London: Faber & Faber, 1964. Subsequently adapted for the stage under the same title, and then reissued as a novel under the title *Elina* by London: Fontana/Collins, 1978.

The Anthill. London: Oxford University Press, 1965.

The Murder of Nigeria: An Indictment. London: Panaf Publications, 1968.

Daughters of the Sun and Other Stories. London: Oxford University Press, 1970.

Destroy This Temple: The Voice of Black Power in Britain. London: MacGibbon & Kee, 1971.

The ABC of Black Power Thought. Lagos, Nigeria: Di Nigro Press, 1973.

Emperor of the Sea and Other Stories. London: Fontana/Collins, 1974.

The Minister's Daughter. London: Fontana/Collins, 1975.

Diary of a Homeless Prodigal. Enugu, Nigeria: Fourth Dimension, 1976.

Divinity: A Radio Play. Stuttgart, Germany: Ernst Klett, 1980.

The Madness of Didi. London: Fontana/Collins, 1980.

The Rape of Lysistrata. Enugu, Nigeria: Fourth Dimension, 1980.

Black Candle for Christmas. Enugu, Nigeria: Fourth Dimension, 1980.

INTERVIEWS

Lindfors, Bernth, ed. *Dem-say: Interviews with Eight Nigerian Writers.* Austin: University of Texas Press, 1974.

CRITICAL STUDIES

Brucac, Joseph. "Obi (Benedict) Egbuna." In James Vinson, ed., *Contemporary Dramatists.* London: St. James Press, 1973.

Coussy, Denise. *Le Roman nigérian.* Paris: Éditions Silex, 1988.

Ihekweazu, Edith. "The Return: Educated or Alienated? The Problems of Re-integration of Africans Trained Abroad as Reflected in West-African Novels in English." In Edith Mettke, ed., *Tensions Between North and South: Studies in Modern Commonwealth Literature and Culture.* Würzburg, Germany: Königshausen und Neumann, 1990.

Klima, Vladimir. *Modern Nigerian Novels.* Prague: Oriental Institute in Academia, Publishing House of the Czechoslovakian Academy of Sciences, 1969.

Lindfors, Bernth. *Five Nigerian Novels.* In *Books Abroad* 39 (1965).

Rameswamy, S. "Obi B. Egbuna's *The Anthill*: An Appreciative Note." In *Explorations: Essays on Commonwealth Literature.* Bangalore, India: M.C.C. Pubs., 1988.

Taiwo, Oladele. *Culture and the Nigerian Novel.* New York: St. Martin's Press, 1976.

Tejumola, Olaniyan, ed. *Perspectives on Nigerian Literature: 1700 to the Present.* Lagos, Nigeria: Guardian Books, 1988.

Cyprian Ekwensi
1921–

CHIDI OKONKWO

CYPRIAN EKWENSI has been writing fiction since the end of World War II. An Igbo born on 26 September 1921 in Minna, Northern Nigeria, he was educated in the Northern and Western Regions of Nigeria and in England. At the end of his formal education, he took up full-time employment in the federal civil service in Lagos, first as head of features in the Nigerian Broadcasting Corporation and from 1961 as director of information in the Federal Ministry of Information. Consequently, Ekwensi did not become immersed in Igbo culture until 1966, when a floundering federal government was overthrown by an Igbo-led military coup d'état. (The Igbo are one of the three major ethnic groups in Nigeria, the other two being the Yoruba and the Hausa.) This event provoked a Hausa-Fulani countercoup and massacre of Eastern Nigerians, mainly Igbo, and led to the secession of the Eastern Region as the short-lived Republic of Biafra (1967–1970) and the ensuing civil war, which ended in Biafra's defeat. Ekwensi's writing career manifests the two-phase (pre- and post-Biafra) development seen in the work of many major Igbo authors who started writing in mid century, including Chinua Achebe and Christopher Okigbo.

As a pioneer of modern African literature written in European languages, Ekwensi had no indigenous models. His professional training in forestry, pharmacy, and radio journalism provided no counterbalance to the literary fare of a colonial education, which included an overdose of eighteenth- and nineteenth-century European fiction, westerns, detective thrillers, Oriental fantasies, and what has come to be known as the European novel of Africa, such as the Africa novels of Joseph Conrad and H. Rider Haggard. In *The Masks of Conquest*, Gauri Viswanathan convincingly argues that, contrary to conventional perceptions of English literature as a discipline created for British students and then exported to the colonies, it was actually an ideological Trojan horse fashioned in early-nineteenth-century India by colonial administrators to subvert Indian political assertion. From India it was then introduced to England for analogous purposes.

From the beginning of his career, Ekwensi had very clear ideas about the nature of African literature and his own writing. In the 1964 essay "African Literature," he defined African literature as based on African character, psychology, and living heritage for the "reinstatement of the dignity and pride which the black man lost through slavery in the New World and Colonialism in the Old" (p. 299). In an interview with Lewis Nkosi in *African Writers Talking*, he described himself as "a writer for the masses" to whom style is "just incidental" (p. 79). Almost ten years later, he told Lee Nichols that he had achieved his ambition "to be a populist writer": "My audience consists of the ordinary working man. I don't pretend to aim at any intellectuals.... The literary writer communicates with the intellectuals who are in the universities, in government, in executive positions and so on but who are not really living their life for the people." Ekwensi's list of populist writers includes "Charles Dickens, the Russian writer Dostoevsky, Hemingway in America, even Shakespeare." Such a writer "writes about life and death, truth and fiction, justice and injustice, corruption and the virtues of life — this is a man who touches the elements of life and everyone understands these elements" (p. 44).

To reach out to a broad audience, he has been "exploring all means of increasing [his] productivity, including the use of a word processor" (Ekwensi, "Random Thoughts on Clocking Sixty-five," p. 88). As a populist writer, he prides himself on understanding the taste and psychology of his audience:

> The Nigerian loves a good story. He loves spectacle. You only need to stand in a street corner where there has been a motor accident or something and everybody leaves whatever he's doing and is on the street. We like to see things. We like to hear scandalous things about people. We like to see how all these rich men are coming to a soggy end.... We want to see how we can acquire the wealth to build twenty-story buildings. And we also like to see those who have twenty-story buildings being impeached for getting their wealth in a corrupt way. So it's all part of the ebullience of life ...[and] the joy of living in the Africa of today.
> (interview by Nichols, p. 46)

Ekwensi clearly identifies with this world, participates in it, and distrusts the western image of the artist as a hypersensitive soul surrounded by philistine humanity. The result is fiction written in refreshingly accessible language, with plots predominantly fashioned from everyday reality and stories designed to serve simultaneously as entertainment and social commentary. Although he borrows heavily from foreign literary models, he is sensitive to the vitality of local oral traditions. The narratives proceed like the performance of a raconteur, with episodic plots, stock motifs, settings, and language, and the random introduction of incidents as they occur to the narrator rather than in response to causal demands of plot or theme.

He is a narrator of vivid stories rather than a meticulous craftsman or coherent thinker. From the fiction published in the mid 1940s to that published in 1992, there are contradictions in details of time, incident, characterization, attribution of dialogue, and management of point of view that careful revision would have refined, despite his censuring such lapses in other people's works. There are also contradictions between his advocation of public nationalism and the apolitical vision in his pre-Biafra work, between his critiques of urban chaos and the absence of any consistent vision of order, between his espousal of an African ethos in literature and an uncritical imitation of foreign models, for which he has justly been described as "an accomplished literary *assimilado*" (Lindfors, p. 3).

CHRONICLER AND CRITIC

Ekwensi started writing seriously in 1947 with a collection of Igbo folktales in English translation, *Ikolo the Wrestler and Other Ibo Tales*, followed by *When Love Whispers* (1948), the romance novella of cultural conflict that popularized him among Southern Nigerian youth for a decade. By 1966 he had published five full-length novels, seven storybooks for children, four collections of folklore, and two collections of short stories. During the post-Biafra period he published four full-length novels and several more books for children. Together, these works chart

Nigeria's postcolonial social experience from the last days of colonial rule in *People of the City* (1954), to the Nigerian civil war in *Survive the Peace* (1976) and *Divided We Stand* (1980), to the blight of self-perpetuating tyrants in *King for Ever!* (1992). The actual night of independence, on 1 October 1960, is described in "Night of Freedom," a short story anthologized in 1967 in Ezekiel Mphahlele's *African Writing Today* but probably written earlier.

The writing reveals a heightened awareness of sociological realities, highlighting, in the 1940s and 1950s, subjects that did not engage mainstream African literature until the 1960s and 1970s. An early short story, "The Cup Was Full," published in *African New Writing* (edited by Cullen T. Young, 1947), handles the historical event treated nearly thirty years later by Wole Soyinka in *Death and the King's Horseman* (1975): a colonial administrator's disruption of a Yoruba ritual during which an Alafin chief minister should have committed suicide upon his master's death to help him cross to the ancestral world. Whereas Soyinka probes this incident for the repercussions on the community's well-being of the white man's meddling and the minister's failure, Ekwensi sees only a conflict between primitive past and enlightened present.

"Land of Sani" and the comic "Deserter's Dupe," also published in *African New Writing*, are set during World War II and successfully evoke the crisis of a transitional society under colonial rule, the transformation of peasantry into urban labor class and petty middle class, and the impact of economic change on traditional land tenure. In its story of a soldier who wants to become a sugar manufacturer through the help of a talisman, "Deserter's Dupe" reflects the tension between the strong influence of the past and the longing for material gain in the future. *Burning Grass* (1962) inserts into the collective odyssey of a nomadic Fulani family a similar vision of incipient urbanization and industrialization, through Hodio's move to the emerging urban

center of New Chanka to manufacture sugar rather than follow the traditional occupation of cattle rearing. The end product of this transformation is revealed in such works as *People of the City*, *Jagua Nana* (1961), and *Lokotown and Other Stories* (1966). In children's stories like *The Drummer Boy* (1960), *Trouble in Form Six* (1966), and *Motherless Baby* (1980), Ekwensi demonstrates his ability to identify social problems before they become part of public awareness. These stories highlight issues facing contemporary Nigerian society, where the material and psychological support offered by traditional family structures is crumbling: the need to rehabilitate juvenile delinquents and the handicapped, the problems of teenage pregnancy and illegitimate children, and the question of discipline in schools.

Ekwensi's journalistic interest in incorporating topical events into his fiction frequently recalls the original meaning of the word *novel* as "news." This emerges clearly in the vaguely conceived and technically flawed *Beautiful Feathers* (1963), the more competently structured *Iska* (1966), and the two novels inspired by the Nigerian civil war, *Survive the Peace* and *Divided We Stand*. The plot of *Beautiful Feathers* is essentially an extended anecdote based on a skewed interpretation of an Igbo proverb: "However famous a man is outside, if he is not respected inside his own home he is like a bird with beautiful feathers, wonderful on the outside but ordinary within." Ekwensi has misapplied this proverbial motif, intended to caution against vanity, to the issue of the conflict between public duty and private interest.

In *Iska* Ekwensi demonstrates a clear understanding of the constant threat posed to Nigeria's unity by tribalism, political opportunism, and the absence of a viable national political culture. Its plot is based on the recurrent phenomenon of tribal and religious killings, which have characterized relationships between Northerners and the Southerners in their midst. Nevertheless, the novel introduces a new problem for critics, for the author has given more than he intended but not what he has led readers to expect. Ekwensi claims:

> *Iska* is just the story of a girl whose life is very short. In the African context we have a belief there are certain people in this world who do not live long.... They come into the world and they die very early but they come again.... Now these people have certain characteristics. They are very kind. They don't take things very seriously. They are out to despise the things that other people value very dearly because they know they are not going to live long in this world. So this is *Iska*. Iska happens to be a Hausa word meaning wind. And then this girl's life just fleets like that.
>
> (interview by Nichols, p. 42)

Ekwensi's explanations do not tally satisfactorily with what happens in the novel, for the symbolism is not clear and often seems accidental. Consequently, critics have labored in vain, scrutinizing *Iska* for the wind-of-change symbolism latent in the title and in the social convulsions depicted.

Of the post-Biafra fiction, *Survive the Peace* explores the material, psychological, and sociological ravages of war beyond the duration of hostilities. Every rifle discarded by defeated Biafrans in the opening scene is an evil lying in ambush against the so-called peace. Ekwensi portrays this continuing threat of violence through the tragic death of James Odugo, a journalist who survives the war only to be murdered in peacetime by a robber armed with one of those rifles. The next war-inspired novel, *Divided We Stand*, is, like John Munonye's *A Wreath for the Maidens* (1973), a fictionalized documentation of the war, its causes, its prosecution, and the massive suffering caused by the Nigerian government's terror bombing of Biafra's civilian populations. *Divided We Stand* shares with Buchi Emecheta's *Destination Biafra* (1982) the inherent difficulties of documenting history as fiction, especially when the events are so recent that many readers have a partisan view of them.

Nevertheless, both *Survive the Peace* and *Divided We Stand* show a definite advance in Ekwensi's ability to formulate a coherent vision of history, suggesting that although the Biafran experience did not transform him into a great prose stylist, it did sensitize him to the need to impose imaginative order on the flux of life. Thus, sociopolitical events are presented not as random occurrences, but as products of historical and geopolitical forces in postcolonial states. Compared with his previous fiction, the story of *Divided We Stand* is not as dependent on commentary from the narrator and works more through the interplay of events and character. The reign of unreason and the poisoning of sacred human bonds are eloquently revealed in Selina Chika's anguished recognition in *Divided We Stand* that her Northerner fiancé, Garuba Zaria, is one of the army officers leading the genocide against her people. Ekwensi's tendency to send protagonists on cross-country or even intercontinental journeys remains; but whereas in earlier novels the journey is primarily an artifice for stitching yet more incidents onto a ritualistic plot, in the war novels it is part of an attempt to re-create history as saga. Running in undercurrents from beginning to end of *Divided We Stand* are the linked issues of imperialism, neocolonialism, and black Africans' historical complicity in their own destruction:

> Isaac had by now begun to recognise the familiar debris of bombing: broken cement walls, the grains of powdered concrete...splashes of blood, fragments of gut and bone, sinew and hair, above all, the horror of sudden death, the desolation, bereavement. There was the black man's self-delusion of being all powerful and righteous, whereas he was merely being used to kill his brothers by the hundred thousands...to further the economic interests of the super powers.
>
> (pp. 169–170)

King for Ever! is a logical development from this new sensitivity. Though written as a story for children, it addresses the core of Africa's postcolonial crises, namely, the meretricious path to power and the megalomaniacal quest for godhead that transform many African leaders into a curse on society. Taken from innocuous beginnings to the rank of army colonel, not by special merits but by fortuitous events, the villainous protagonist Sinanda makes himself king through a coup d'état. Sinanda is a composite of military leaders, tyrants, and rulers for life who have haunted postcolonial Africa since the 1960s, perverting the dreams of decolonization struggles into waking nightmares in the neocolonial present for nearly half a billion Africans. The portrayal of his moral and psychological disintegration is a sickeningly familiar personification of the cure that becomes the disease: fake messiah, paranoid megalomaniac, murderous buffoon. Of equal importance is the way in which the novel transforms history into myth and then moves into fable making—a strategy that links *King for Ever!* with such adult novels as Ngũgĩ wa Thiong'o's *Devil on the Cross* (1982), Ayi Kwei Armah's *Two Thousand Seasons* (1973), and Achebe's *Anthills of the Savannah* (1987).

THE OLD AND THE NEW: NEOCLASSICISM AND RECYCLING

Ekwensi's plots tend to move in circles, from village to city and back to village. This tendency reflects the influence of oral narrative traditions and Ekwensi's inclination toward a neoclassical theory of art. In rebuking a Nigerian undergraduate who had dismissed *Jagua Nana* as "obscene artifice," Ekwensi repeats the neoclassical theory of art, properly adapted to his own position as a novelist— "The function of a novelist. At least ONE of them: To hold a mirror up to nature" (Emenyonu, 1974, p. 25). What Chris Nnolim in "Cyprian Ekwensi: His Comic Vision" de-

scribes as a pedagogical "straining after a happy ending for his protagonists" and "the home-coming of the prodigal son" accompanies an insistence on a definite closure to the plot in the tradition of the classic realist text (Emenyonu, ed., 1987, p. 81).

Moreover, composition for Ekwensi frequently means stitching together earlier stories, as in *People of the City*; he revealed to Nichols that this novel was composed during a thirteen-day ship voyage in 1951 by putting together several short stories dating from the last days of World War II and all depicting "a pattern of city life" (p. 40). Composition for Ekwensi also means recycling old materials, as in *Jagua Nana*, which evolved from the earlier story "Fashion Girl," and *For a Roll of Parchment* (1986), which was actually written around 1951. "Fashion Girl" itself comprises two plots that are mirror images of each other: the protagonists exchange roles as savior and villain in a repeated pattern that involves the heroine's being helped by a man who subsequently attempts to rape her but is thwarted by the providential arrival of a savior. The combat between Jagua and Nancy in *Jagua Nana* is reenacted in almost the same words twenty-five years later by Liza Nene and Tamuno pitted against Saka Jojo's wives in *Jagua Nana's Daughter* (1986).

Although it was written in Ekwensi's post-Biafra period, *Jagua Nana's Daughter* is a throwback to his pre-Biafra practice, a cheap exploitation of the popularity of *Jagua Nana* through a sequel in which Jagua and her just-revealed daughter vaguely search for each other. Technically, the novel is a compendium of Ekwensi's old flaws augmented by new ones. Many details introduced to harmonize it with *Jagua Nana* are actually contradictory. These include details that Ekwensi could easily have verified by rereading the earlier work, such as the heroine's father's profession and her early life. Forgetting that the heroine of *Jagua Nana* did not earn the nickname "Jagua" until her thirties, Ekwensi uses it as her proper name right from childhood in *Jagua Nana's Daughter*. The novel is so chaotically executed that it fully merits its dismissal by Adewale Maja-Pearce as "an unmitigated disaster" (p. 159). In a footnote to her essay in *The Essential Ekwensi*, edited by Ernest Emenyonu, Helen Chukwuma reports that Ekwensi was contemplating yet another sequel, tentatively titled "Jagua Nana's Mother."

THE CITY: PICAROONS, FRONTIERS, AND RITES OF PASSAGE

Ekwensi has described the city as "a terribly corrupting influence, a den for Ali Baba where forty thieves have stored all their gold, and anyone who has the magic words can go and help himself. And sometimes greed traps the sesame and the thieves come back and stab the intruder to death as they did to Ali Baba's brother" (Emenyonu, ed., 1974, p. 29). The emergence of a client-centered market economy, a corresponding decay of the traditional agrarian economy, and the concentration of development projects in emerging urban centers combined to provoke a massive population shift from villages to urban areas, with a consequent outbreak of juvenile delinquency, prostitution, syndicated crime, environmental squalor, political chicanery, and violence. More farsighted than most, Ekwensi recognized the ugliness of the African present when others were celebrating the beauty of the past. His journalistic training and instinct for the newsworthy have enhanced his ability to identify as problems what most people see merely as incidents.

However, it is sometimes unclear whether what one is reading is a conscious critique of social evils or a noncommittal presentation of "the ebullience of life." Ekwensi's city emerges as novelist V. S. Naipaul's "picaroon" society, "where it is felt that all eminence is arrived at by crookedness" (Naipaul's *The Middle Passage*, 1969, p. 79), and Ekwensi is occasionally seduced by his picaresque heroes' antics into losing his own moral perspective. Often, the difference between hero or heroine and villain is one of degree rather than kind, determined principally by the amount of instinctive sympathy the author has chosen to invest in each, as in the characterizations of Freddie Namme and Uncle Taiwo in *Jagua Nana*. "Glittering City" in *Lokotown and Other Stories* (1966) introduces a further variation. Essi's mission to join her fiancé is ruined by the "Brainer" (confidence trickster) called Fussy Joe. In her last appearance, she is ushered out with this comment: "Her mission to Lagos had failed. But she had enjoyed her time, thanks to her uncle" (p. 151). This statement could be read either literally, as ebullience, or ironically, as naïveté succumbing to the fatal lure of the tinsel city, with a faint echo of Ernest Hemingway (one of the "populist writers" Ekwensi so admired) whose protagonists rarely indulge in self-pity.

Confronted with this ambiguity, critics frequently insert their own moral schemes into Ekwensi's fictive world. They scrutinize it for a profound and unified vision of urban culture despite the circumstances of the novel's composition and the postcolonial client culture of the portrayed city. Thus, Emmanuel Obiechina, who argues in his essay "Cyprian Ekwensi as Novelist" that *People of the City* fails because "it attempts to do too much" (Emenyonu, ed., 1987, p. 10), is evaluating it against his own theory of urban culture rather than Ekwensi's artistic intentions. Ekwensi's city, which is usually Lagos, is remarkable for lacking a cultural identity or background against which the dynamics of transition can be measured. Although located in Yorubaland, it is neither a Yoruba society undergoing urbanization nor a virile mosaic of ethnic cultures.

Strictly speaking, there is little rural-urban clash in Ekwensi's writing, for the extreme atomism of the picaroon city has not created an organic culture and the rural culture lacks the dynamism to exist in conflict with the city. Although Ekwensi's rural settings do not have the cultural inchoateness and atomism of the city, they are hardly more than stylized sketches of society: either a city dweller's romanticizing of a village, like Ogabu, or inconsequential spots with little real interaction with the city, like Bagana and Krinameh, in the Jagua Nana novels. For example, there is something hollow in Ekwensi's attempt to project a sense of cosmic harmony between Bagana people (as represented by the canoeists) and their rural environment: "The birds and crocodiles never attacked them for they were part of the habitat" (*Jagua Nana*, p. 74). Birds rarely prey on humans and the docility of crocodiles is also implausible. The most appropriate model for these fictions is the frontier-cum-spiritland of mythology, where intrepid adventurers deploy their wits in search of "the Golden Fleece" (Ekwensi's own metaphor).

At the level of narrative, the movement from village to city and back to village corresponds to the pattern of "separation — initiation — return" identified by Joseph Campbell in *The Hero with a Thousand Faces* as the archetype of a folk hero's sacred journey. The hero "ventures forth from the world of common day into a region of supernatural wonder," combats and defeats "fabulous forces," and returns home "with the power to bestow boons on his fellow man" (1988, p. 30). The frontier of cowboy stories or westerns and the spiritland of Igbo folktales are functional equivalents. A character like Jagua Nana is thus not just a prostitute, she is also a quest heroine; she is the beautiful but vain girl of the Igbo folktale, who will not marry just any man and so is thrust into dangerous adventures by her search for the ideal hero. The model adventurer is Ikolo, the hero of the title story in *Ikolo the Wrestler and Other Ibo Tales*, who is a variant of the Ojadili archetype in Igbo myth (obliquely referred to by Ezeulu in Achebe's *Arrow of God*, 1964).

In heroic myth, the quest hero or heroine who survives ultimately returns home. In the more tawdry reality of the city, the picaroons rarely do so, except when the novelist's pedagogical impulse manifests itself as a hand of God to snatch them out of their meaningless existence. Ekwensi has not advanced any theory of existential absurdism, but there is much of Algerian-born French writer Albert Camus's absurd man in Ekwensi's picaresque characters, especially in their lust for life intensely and variously lived. Fussy Joe in "Glittering City" puts it succinctly: "Life is short and must be enjoyed" (*Lokotown*, p. 112). This "philosophy" reduces characters' lives to ritualistic orgies of drinking, dancing, and whoring in stories like "The Cup Was Full," "Lokotown," "Fashion Girl," *People of the City*, *Jagua Nana*, and *Jagua Nana's Daughter*. One can understand this philosophy in the context of Camus's words: "There is thus a metaphysical honor in enduring the world's absurdity. Conquest or play-acting, multiple loves, absurd revolt are tributes that man pays to his dignity in a campaign in which he is defeated in advance" ("Absurd Creation," in *The Myth of Sisyphus and Other Essays*, 1955, p. 69).

ATTITUDE TOWARD RACE IN CHILDREN'S STORIES

A major source of conflict in Ekwensi's work is the vaguely conceived universalism arising from a conjunction of his personal and professional background with the realities of British colonial policy in Nigeria. As early as 1964, Ekwensi saw himself as living in "these modern times when the most travelled man in the world is the educated African" ("African Literature," p. 295). This image of the modern African has so fascinated his imagination that he amplified it a decade later:

[The] new man of today is living in the computer age, he's living in the nuclear age — the new African who's far out in front...the technological and...electronic African. He's an executive and he's like his counterpart throughout the entire world except that he just happens to be an African. He's internationally travelled.... And he's trying to find his way in the international context with all the problems of the economy and fuel shortage and energy crisis and so on around him.

(Nichols, ed., pp. 45–46)

In these respects, modern Africans are an extreme expression of the delayed cultural awakening of British-protected persons, in sharp contrast to their counterparts in the French colonies. The consequent lack of anger and political thought is easily seen in a typical product of the era: *African New Writing* (1947), an anthology sponsored by the British Council and made up of fourteen stories (five of them Ekwensi's) by six English-speaking West Africans and one South African. One has only to compare these English-speaking West Africans' stories with Négritude work of the same period from the French colonies. Indeed, in the same 1964 essay cited earlier, Ekwensi explicitly disapproves of the prominence of racial issues in African American fiction up to the early 1950s (as he dated it) and black South African fiction in the 1960s.

Ekwensi's attitude toward race issues colors the adult novels and the children's stories written in the pre-Biafra phase, but it is more startling in the children's stories. Collectively, these stories, as indigenous alternatives to culturally subversive texts from abroad, are important contributions to the national quest for education. Because these stories are designed to stimulate children's faculties for wonder and love of adventure, their protagonists are usually schoolchildren. Some of these works are boys' adventure stories with plots modeled on cowboy stories, detective thrillers, Oriental fantasies, or European-traveler-in-Africa books; examples include *The Passport of Mallam Ilia* (1960), *Yaba Roundabout Murder* (1962), *Juju Rock* (1966), and *Samankwe and the Highway Robbers* (1975). Others offer serious discourses on the problems of Nigerian children, like *The Drummer Boy, Trouble in Form Six*, and *Motherless Baby*.

Yet nowhere are the conflicts in Ekwensi's art more apparent than in this genre. His thrillers and adventure stories are infiltrated with the idioms, imagery, and other constructs that are denigrating to black peoples. An extreme case is *Juju Rock*; the plot combines a treasure hunt with a search for a missing philanthropist. By having Rikku, the Nigerian schoolboy "hero," lead two Europeans, Ekwensi reenacts the familiar motif of, in the words of Bill Ashton, Gareth Griffiths, and Helen Tiffin, "the journey of the European interloper through unfamiliar landscape with a native guide." The adventure quickly degenerates into a domesticated composite of Conrad's *Heart of Darkness* (1902) and Haggard's *King Solomon's Mines* (1912) and *Allan Quatermain* (1913), with African savages characterized in typically Conradian epithets and slaughtered in set-piece, novel-of-Africa battles. Rikku emerges as a dedicated slave exerting himself fully to please the master. This early passage sets the tone of the novel:

> At that very moment one of the most formidable men I have ever seen rushed past me. In one short glimpse of him I saw his huge hairy black chest. His hands were enormous and hairy too. His arms hung down to his knees like a gorilla's. He ran with a kind of lurching hop....
>
> I was still gazing after this horrible man when another, and a very different-looking man, came out of the house. He was a tall Englishman in clean white shirt and trousers, and his hair was golden like sunshine.

(p. 16)

Confronted with Ekwensi's curious contrasts, the reader hardly suspects that the angelic European is one of the villains of the story while the simian African is merely his servant. This is mimicry of the same order as the pseudo-industrialization policies of postindependence African states. Ekwensi must have realized this, for the revised edition in 1971 reveals a serious but unsuccessful attempt to remove some of the more offensive passages.

Even the color symbolism in much of the pre-Biafra fiction is an undisguised valorization of whiteness. Ekwensi uses whiteness as a standard for beauty and a moral ideal. "Glittering City" opens on the image of Essi, who has "the fair skin that went with most beautiful Nigerian girls" (p. 107). Of Fatimeh, the heroine of *Burning Grass*, Ekwensi emphasizes that the extra beauty contributed by her Europeanness qualifies her to be a heroine. Conversely, villains are grimacing "dark-faced," "very black," or, in moments of neoclassical influence, "dark-visaged" figures in "Deserter's Dupe," *The Passport of Mallam Ilia*, *An African Night's Entertainment* (1962), *Samankwe and the Highway Robbers*, and *Burning Grass*. Evil medicine is "black magic" practiced by "black magicians." Even the stock European duality of positive white heroine and evil dark heroine is scrupulously observed in the contrast between Fatimeh and Kantuma, the dark temptress who is constantly "dressed in Oriental fashion" and "beautiful in a dark way" (*Burning Grass*, p. 110).

CONCLUSION

In the inverted values of these works, Ekwensi comes perilously close to Naipaul, the Trinidadian Indian who has written novels of Africa in the European tradition. Two qualities rescue Ekwensi's works, however: an absence of self-contempt and an optimism that, creating yet another tension, transforms the misguided domestication of alien themes into a quest for national harmony. In this context, Ekwensi's advocacy in "Wazobia, Esperanto, or Mother Tongue?" (1992) of a lingua franca for Nigeria, created through legislation if necessary, merely reaffirms a principle that has been running as an undercurrent in his creative works (p. 9). More pan-Nigerian than any other Nigerian writer, past or present, he has striven since the beginning of his career to create a genuinely Nigerian literature, reflecting Nigerian realities in plot, characterization, and language, in sharp distinction to ethnic literatures that pose as parables of the Nigerian or African experience. In *Jagua Nana*, the "All Languages Club" was founded by a man working for universal harmony, as was "Harlem Club" in "Glittering City," the picaresque hero of which speaks "all Nigerian languages." In the Ebun stories of *The Rainmaker and Other Stories* (1965), the leading characters are chosen from Nigeria's three major ethnic groups.

Such nationalism partly accounts for the typically unwieldy picaresque plots that traverse the length and breadth of Nigeria and are enacted by characters from a variety of ethnic cultures. Displaying a visionary's tendency for wish fulfilment, Ekwensi consistently attempts to achieve in his fiction the elusive ideal of national integration. Even the Biafran war could neither dim his optimism nor lessen his commitment to what has become a political and artistic cause. *Survive the Peace* displays a remarkable faith in a fundamental harmony that transcends Nigeria's ethnic rivalries, as demonstrated both in the perfect amity between the Biafran central character, James Odugo, and his professional colleagues in Lagos after Biafra's defeat. The decidedly pro-Biafra *Divided We Stand* ends with an epilogue that balances bitterness toward African governments with a gesture of reconciliation in Isaac Chika's handshake with "some Foreign Correspondents who had lived in this basement room with him" (p. 235).

Considering that Ekwensi's nationalism and universalism are integral to his concept of populist writing, it is tempting to conclude that they are responsible for the flaws in his artistic achievement. This conclusion would be untenable, however, for they are not inherently antagonistic to art. Ekwensi's problems arise from his fundamentally flawed identification of artistic populism with indifference to aesthetic demands. Consequently, even as a populist writer, he is still not a great one. He is an important writer nevertheless.

His importance lies in the clarity with which he identified and foregrounded social problems whose enormity still lay in the future, ensuring that even his earliest works will retain some currency when the works of many greater artists will have dated.

Selected Bibliography

NOVELS

People of the City. London: Dakers, 1954; London: Heinemann, 1968.

Jagua Nana. London: Hutchinson and Co., 1961; London: Heinemann, 1961, 1975.

Burning Grass. London: Heinemann, 1962, 1990.

Beautiful Feathers. London: Hutchinson and Co., 1963; London: Heinemann, 1978.

Iska. London: Hutchinson, 1966; Ibadan, Nigeria: Spectrum Books, 1981.

Survive the Peace. London: Heinemann Educational, 1976, 1979.

Divided We Stand. Enugu, Nigeria: Fourth Dimension Publishers, 1980.

For a Roll of Parchment. Ibadan, Nigeria: Heinemann Educational Books, 1986.

Jagua Nana's Daughter. Ibadan, Nigeria: Spectrum Books, 1986.

CHILDREN'S STORIES

When Love Whispers. Lagos, Nigeria: Chuks Bookshop, and Onitsha, Nigeria: Tabansi Press, 1948.

The Leopard's Claw. London: Longmans, Green, 1950.

The Drummer Boy. Cambridge, U.K.: Cambridge University Press, 1960; Nairobi: Heinemann Kenya, 1991.

The Passport of Mallam Ilia. Cambridge, U.K.: Cambridge University Press, 1960, 1977.

Yaba Roundabout Murder. Lagos, Nigeria: Tortoise Series Books, 1962.

Juju Rock. Lagos, Nigeria: African Universities Press, 1966; Nairobi: Heinemann Kenya, 1990.

Trouble in Form Six. Cambridge, U.K.: Cambridge University Press, 1966.

Coal Camp Boy. Lagos, Nigeria: Longman, 1973.

Samankwe in the Strange Forest. Lagos: Longman Nigeria, 1973, 1981.

Restless City and Christmas Gold. London: Heinemann, 1975.

Samankwe and the Highway Robbers. London: Evans Brothers, 1975.

Motherless Baby. Enugu, Nigeria: Fourth Dimension, 1980.

Gone to Mecca. Ibadan, Nigeria: Heinemann Educational Books, 1991.

Masquerade Time. Oxford, U.K.: Heinemann, 1991.

King for Ever! Oxford, U.K.: Heinemann, 1992.

FOLKLORE

Ikolo the Wrestler and Other Ibo Tales. London: Nelson, 1947.

An African Night's Entertainment. Lagos, Nigeria: African Universities Press, 1962, 1977; Nairobi: Heinemann Kenya, 1990.

The Great Elephant Bird. London: Nelson, 1965.

The Boa Suitor. London: Nelson, 1966.

COLLECTIONS OF SHORT STORIES

The Rainmaker and Other Stories. Lagos, Nigeria: African Universities Press, 1965; London: Ginn, 1971.

Lokotown and Other Stories. London: Heinemann, 1966.

The Rainbow-Tinted Scarf and Other Stories. London: Evans Brothers, 1975.

ARTICLES, REVIEWS, AND EDITIONS

"Outlook for African Writers." In *West African Review* (January 1950).

"The Dilemma of the African Writer." In *West African Review* (July 1956).

"What Mr. Ekwensi Thinks About Himself." In *Nigerian Teacher* (September 1961).

"Ezunaka: The Legend of Nkwelle" and "Problems of Nigerian Writers." In *Nigeria Magazine* 78 (September 1963).

"Literary Influences on a Young Nigerian." In *Times Literary Supplement* (London) (4 June 1964).

"African Literature." In *Nigerian Magazine* 83 (December 1964).

"Statists and Federalists." In *Spear* (September 1971).

Review of *The Calabash of Wisdom and Other Stories*, by Romanus Egudu. In *Okike* 7 (April 1975).

Festac Anthology of Nigerian New Writing. Lagos, Nigeria: Federal Ministry of Information, 1977.

"Random Thoughts on Clocking Sixty-five." In Ernest Emenyonu, ed., *The Essential Ekwensi: A Literary Celebration of Cyprian Ekwensi's Sixty-fifth Birthday*. Ibadan, Nigeria: Heinemann, 1987.

"Wazobia, Esperanto, or Mother Tongue?" In *West African Association for Commonwealth Literature and Language Studies Lecture Series* 1 (April 1992).

INTERVIEWS

Lindfors, Bernth. "Interview with Cyprian Ekwensi." In Bernth Lindfors, ed., *Dem-Say: Interviews with Eight Nigerian Writers*. Austin: African and Afro-American Studies and Research Center, University of Texas at Austin, 1974.

Nichols, Lee, ed. *Conversations with African Writers: Interviews with Twenty-six African Authors*. Washington, D.C.: Voice of America, 1981.

Nkosi, Lewis. "Interview with Cyprian Ekwensi." In Dennis Duerden and Cosmo Pieterse, eds., *African Writers Talking: A Collection of Radio Interviews*. London: Heinemann, 1972.

Ogbeide, Mike. "Ekwensi Speaks on Mankind." In *Sunday Observer*, Nigeria (15 August 1971).

CRITICAL STUDIES

Abrahams, Peter. "A Literary Pioneer." In *West Africa* (16 October 1954).

Ashcroft, Bill, Gareth Griffiths, and Helen Tiffin. *The Empire Writes Back: Theory and Practice in Post-Colonial Literatures*. London and New York: Routledge, 1989.

Cook, David. "A Good Bad Heroine: A Study of Cyprian Ekwensi's *Jagua Nana*." In his *African Literature: A Critical View*. London: Longman, 1977.

Emenyonu, Ernest. "African Literature: What Does It Take to Be Its Critic?" In *African Literature Today* 5 (1971).

——. *Cyprian Ekwensi*. London: Evans Brothers Ltd., 1974. Contains a short select bibliography of Ekwensi's writing and writing on Ekwensi up to 1972. It derives considerable authority from Emenyonu's personal interviews with Ekwensi as well as from access to the writer's library, on the basis of which it dates Ekwensi's *When Love Whispers* as 1948 instead of 1947 as other bibliographies have stated. Emenyonu's citation of the publisher as Tabansi Press, Onitsha, appears to conflict with Ekwensi's own statement to Lee Nichols: "I don't know if [*When Love Whispers*] was sold in Onitsha Market because it was published in Lagos." The pamphlet was certainly sold in Onitsha under the imprint given by Emenyonu.

——. "Cyprian Ekwensi." *Guardian* (Lagos, Nigeria) (17 August 1985).

——. "Cyprian Ekwensi." In Yemi Ogunbiyi, ed., *Perspectives on Nigerian Literature, 1700 to the Present*. Vol. 2. Lagos: Guardian Books Nigeria, 1988.

——, ed. *The Essential Ekwensi: A Literary Celebration of Cyprian Ekwensi's Sixty-fifth Birthday*. Ibadan: Heinemann Nigeria, 1987. Updates to 1986 the select bibliography appended to Emenyonu's *Cyprian Ekwensi*.

Hawkins, Loretta A. "The Free Spirit of Ekwensi's Jagua Nana." In *African Literature Today* 10 (1979).

Ibitokun, B. N. "Prostitution or Neurosis: A Note on Cyprian Ekwensi's *Jagua Nana*." In *Nsukka Studies in African Literature* 3 (October 1980).

Inyama, N. F. "Language and Characterization in Cyprian Ekwensi's *People of the City* and *Jagua Nana*." In *African Literature Today* 17 (1991).

Killam, Douglas. "Cyprian Ekwensi." In Bruce King, ed., *Introduction to Nigerian Literature*. Lagos, Nigeria: University of Lagos, 1971; London: Evans Brothers Ltd., 1971.

Laurence, Margaret. "Masks of the City: Cyprian Ekwensi." In her *Long Drums and Cannons: Nigerian Dramatists and Novelists*. London: Macmillan, 1968.

Lindfors, Bernth. "Cyprian Ekwensi: An African Popular Novelist." In *African Literature Today* 3 (1969).

Mackay, Mercedes. "People of the City." In *Venture* 6 (February 1955).

Maja-Pearce, Adewale. *A Mask Dancing: Nigerian Novelists of the Eighties.* London: Hans Zell Publishers, 1992.

Nganga, Bernard. "Cyprian Ekwensi, romancier de la ville?" In *Asemka: A Bilingual Literary Journal of the University of Cape Coast* 4 (September 1976).

———. "Ekwensi and the 'Something New and Unstable' in Modern Nigerian Culture." In Donatus Nwoga, ed., *Literature and Modern West African Culture.* Benin City, Nigeria: Ethiope Publishing Corporation, 1978.

Okonkwo, Juliet I. "Cyprian Ekwensi, *Survive the Peace.*" In *Okike* 13 (January 1979).

Palmer, Eustace. "Cyprian Ekwensi." In his *The Growth of the African Novel.* London: Heinemann, 1979.

Povey, John. "Cyprian Ekwensi: The Novelist and the Pressure of the City." In Edgar Wright, ed., *The Critical Evaluation of African Literature.* London: Heinemann, 1973.

Sesay, Kadiatu. "Ekwensi and Okpewho on the Nigerian Civil War." In *African Literature Today* 9 (1978).

Shelton, Austin, Jr. "'Rebushing' or Ontological Recession to Africanism: Jagua's Return to the Village." In *Présence africaine* 46 (1963).

Viswanathan, Gauri. *The Masks of Conquest: Literary Study and British Rule in India.* New York: Columbia University Press, 1989, 1992; London: Faber, 1990.

Buchi Emecheta
1944–

CHRISTOPHER SMITH

BUCHI EMECHETA has always proclaimed that much of her fiction is based on her own life. She could well echo the words of Johann von Goethe, who said not only that nothing would be found in his writings that he had not experienced himself, but also that nothing in them was in exactly the form in which he had experienced it. Emecheta's early years spent in Nigeria and England have given her material for her most successful novels. The realism of her writings—with the notable exception of *The Rape of Shavi* (1983), which is perhaps her best novel—has led critics to categorize her as a documentarist. Although she sometimes overreaches when she departs from imaginatively transposing formative experiences, her most impressive achievements owe as much to her creative imagination as to the often harrowing conditions and situations of her life. This combination of imaginative and documentary writing is evident in her autobiography, *Head Above Water* (1986), but it is possible that Emecheta may have depleted her fictional creativity with this work.

Writing has given Emecheta standing both in England, where she has resided since the early 1970s, and abroad. In her autobiography she speaks of the therapeutic benefits she has derived from writing. No doubt these have come from her growing sense of self-awareness and self-confidence as she has found expression for inner tensions. For most readers, however, Emecheta's fiction is of interest primarily for its portrayal of the predicament of the individual—often a woman—under pressure in uncaring, if not cruel, situations.

In her introduction to and comments throughout *Our Own Freedom* (1981), a volume of black-and-white photographs by Maggie Murray, Emecheta evokes the lot of African women with a compelling combination of accuracy and compassion. A quotation from an International Labour Organization report sets the scene: "Women and girls, [though constituting] one-half of the world population, ... perform nearly two-thirds of work hours, but ... receive only one-tenth of the world's income and less than one-hundredth of world property." In words and pictures, *Our Own Freedom* documents the seventeen-hour day that African women work, toiling in the fields, fetching water and gathering firewood, bartering in the village marketplaces, tending their children, preparing meals, and generally waiting on their menfolk. In addition to documenting the grinding exploitation of women by African men across the ages, the photographs suggest that there has been little improvement under western influences. Within traditional societies, women exerted some influence, but even this power has been undermined by the spread of Christianity, which in its less sensitive missionary forms tends toward androcentricity and reinforcing male-dominated hierarchies as norms. There are indeed signs of change, but women are still fortunate if they can even aspire to being second-class citizens.

What *Our Own Freedom* depicts graphically about woman's lot in Africa, Emecheta presents in her novels with accounts of what women experience not only in her homeland of Nigeria but also in her adopted home of England.

Before we begin to explore her documentarist fiction, however, we will look at *The Rape of Shavi*, which is in many ways the most outspoken expression of her ideals and, in the opinion of some, her most successful artistic achievement.

THE RAPE OF SHAVI

The Rape of Shavi is perhaps best categorized as what French critics call a "philosophical tale." It stands, despite many differences in tone, content, and purport, in the tradition of such works as Voltaire's *Candide* (1759) and *L'Ingénu* (1767). Describing Emecheta's novel as a fable is unsatisfactory, for its characters are human beings, not animals, and though her manner owes something to the parables with their evocation of patriarchal rural society in order to convey a moral lesson, *The Rape of Shavi* is more extended than anything that might be considered its counterpart in the Bible. Although Emecheta probably was not directly influenced by Voltaire, the parallel with the "philosophical tale" is well worth pursuing.

In *The Rape of Shavi*, Emecheta provocatively juxtaposes western values and the lifestyle of an idyllic African community, in a way that sets it apart from both her immigrant and African novels. The narrative tone is dispas-

sionate, and from the outset it is clear that events have been contrived to bring certain problems in western and African culture into sharp focus. No sustained attempt is made to engage our sympathies by making the story realistic. As in Voltaire's tales, the object is to draw attention to abstract issues by presenting them in contrived situations. What is surprising, given these circumstances, is that *The Rape of Shavi* takes on human warmth and moves us to compassion.

The setting of the novel is the imaginary sub-Saharan kingdom of Shavi, where time seems to have stood still. Untroubled by other tribes and nations and so far spared contact with western civilization, the people lead an existence that many outsiders might regard as harsh. By western standards, the people of Shavi are poor, with few material possessions, and women generally have a more difficult life than men. All the same, there is a good deal of contentment: King Patayon feels that he is well provided for, and his subjects do not consider themselves impoverished. Generally, there is enough to satisfy their wants and allow for the occasional celebration. The people accept drought and famine as part of the natural order of things. Emecheta rejects the type of anthropology that interprets communities like that of Shavi as simple and uncomplicated. She points instead to the networks of kinship, influence, and power within the village and to social divisions by sex, status, and age-group, implying that these structures and stratifications are no less complex or significant than those in what are considered more advanced societies. The pattern may well be a hierarchy, but it is not simplistic.

At the beginning of the novel, a mechanical object comes crashing down from the sky and bursts into flames. White figures emerge. Are they albino human beings? Are they humans at all? These questions haunt the rest of the novel. These representatives of an alien civilization view their involuntary hosts with puzzled curiosity and are in turn regarded with a mixture of awe, scorn, inquisitiveness, and suspicion. One tiny detail epitomizes the attitude of the Shavians toward the newcomers: why do they carry things in their hands when any sensible person would balance them on his or her head?

The new arrivals are, in fact, men and women fleeing Europe to escape an expected thermonuclear holocaust, which in itself is a scathing comment on western values and the perverted use of science. They have come in an aircraft of revolutionary design called the Newark (best pronounced "new ark," like Noah's Ark, to make the allegory plain). Parallels with the book of Genesis, however, are not developed very far.

The novel is concerned with an issue that preoccupies Emecheta in all her works: the integration into one society of representatives of another. She explores this problem to a large extent by portraying relationships between the sexes. From the outset the Europeans are nervous and uncomfortable. Scared when they find themselves in an unexpected predicament, they quarrel among themselves and expect to be butchered by people they regard as savages. The Shavians, by contrast, soon overcome their own initial fright and treat the new arrivals with kindness. They give them shelter, let them rest, and effectively treat their injuries with folk medicine. For a while pride and prejudice hamper the Europeans' response to this humane treatment from people they tend to despise, but gradually nearly all of them are won over. A high point in what might be called their education comes when a European gynecologist offers her help at a difficult delivery. She is gently but firmly pushed aside and is amazed to discover that natural childbirth takes place without her skills and services.

This is a great lesson for a highly trained professional of considerable intellect and is symbolic of the general point that Emecheta is making. In this novel she stages not a clash between an advanced society and a primitive one, but rather a clash between two highly evolved cultures, each producing significant values and skills of its own. As their first fears and worries evaporate in response to kindness, some of the Europeans start to adopt an African lifestyle, taking part in village celebrations, enjoying the pleasures of home-brewed alcohol, and engaging in less-inhibited sexual relations. They gradually cast aside western worries and turn toward what might be regarded as natural.

Trouble comes with Ronje, one of the Europeans who most stubbornly refuses to be taken in by the Shavians. Like many a colonialist, he dreads what might happen if he were to "turn native." His scorn of Africans takes a form that may also be categorized as typical of the colonialist attitude: he is convinced that he is at liberty to gratify his sexual desires with any girl or woman who takes his fancy. Thoughtlessly, brutally, he rapes young Ayoko; his genuine surprise at learning she is a virgin reveals much about his outlook. He never suspects that she is a person of importance in the kingdom, for the long-laid plan had been that she should become King Patayon's ninth wife.

Ronje's crime is a clear and shocking symbol of the havoc wrought in Africa by colonialism. All that is worst in Europe has unthinkingly, indeed unknowingly, violated and destroyed what was best in Africa, and Emecheta neatly underlines the wider significance of this devastation by calling her book not "The Rape of Ayoko," but *The Rape of Shavi*. Although Ronje's crime marks the pivotal point of the novel, its importance is more emblematic than structural. Emecheta resists turning the novel into a tale of crime and punishment. She portrays the worldly wisdom of the Shavian women in dealing with the problem. They are aware that to raise a hue and cry will only make the wretched Ayoko's position worse in the male-dominated society. Instead, they take Ronje captive, truss him up, and leave him to die in the bush, but Ayoko steals out to give him a chance to escape. Her magnanimity is not rewarded, however, as she learns later that he has infected her with syphilis.

The next phase of the novel opens with the Europeans' succeeding in repairing the Newark and leaving Shavi for their homeland, which has emerged from the thermonuclear crisis. It is anything but a happy return. One of the white women who had conceived with a Shavian insists on having an abortion, which is presented as a commentary on western mores that is all the more scathing because it involves the use of advanced medical technology. Equally unsettling is the treatment of Asogba, a Shavian who insists on accompanying the Europeans. In Africa he is a prince, but in England he is treated as an undesirable alien of limited intelligence.

Finally Asogba returns to Shavi with white men who have come to collect hard stones that are believed to be valuable but are in fact worthless. In a few pages Emecheta sketches the familiar story of the pillaging of Africa's mineral riches for the benefit of western economies, and before long oversupply brings the market crashing down. In the meantime Asogba becomes hungry for power, convinced that with the help of European technology he can crush neighboring tribes. Brutality follows excess and results in disaster. Drought sets in, and when Asogba marries Ayoko, he contracts syphilis from her, passes it on to two more wives, and dies childless.

His half brother, who becomes king of a grievously reduced kingdom, speaks the epilogue to this tragedy. Perhaps the "albinos" have a civilization, but the Africans have one, too. Technology and westernization, like dreams of conquest, threaten a way of life that has developed over the centuries. To abandon it is folly, destroying the harmony between humankind and nature and between the members of society, leading to an imbalance that can have dire psychological consequences. The grim lesson is presented in uncompromis-

ing terms. Such is the power of the story, so frightful is the account of what happens after the arrival of Europeans fleeing their sick civilization, that it is impossible not to respect Emecheta's values.

In many ways *The Rape of Shavi* is her most accomplished literary work, but it is not her most characteristic; generally, she relies less on her imagination and develops stories from life experiences.

LIFE

Emecheta was born in Yaba, near Lagos, the teeming then capital of Nigeria, on 21 July 1944, toward the end of World War II, in the aftermath of which the British empire was to break up. These few facts are clues to some of the major polarities in her fiction. Often Emecheta depicts the contrast between the observed strain and squalor of bustling urban life and an idealized nostalgia for the village where age-old social structures still governed everyday life and people lived harmoniously with one another and with nature. It may not have been an earthly paradise, for physical conditions could be severe and underlings, especially women, were often treated harshly. But hierarchies gave stability, a sense of social belonging, and a sense of a shared culture bound up with the natural environment.

The lack of these social structures was sorely felt by urbanized Nigerians whose family ties were often stretched to the breaking point and who had lost most meaningful contact with wider village social networks. Not only did they suffer a feeling of exile from their past, but they had further cause for dissatisfaction. The British colonial adminstration, though under severe strain as the war dragged on, offered glimpses of a far more privileged lifestyle. Further away lay Britain, which seemed to offer great material benefits to those determined enough to leave home. Vague notions of an easier life in Britain became more sharply focused when reports filtered through of the welfare state that had been set up by Clement Attlee's Labour government, which held power from 1945 to 1951. Social security benefits appeared to offer an insurance against poverty that made setting out for Britain in search of a better future—to fill the gaps in the labor market and, if possible, to train for a profession at the public expense—seem far less of a gamble. Like the idyll of the village, the mirage of Britain bred dissatisfaction, and for many Nigerians, as for most immigrants from Commonwealth countries, immigration to Britain was a traumatic experience. Furthermore, if colonialism seemed baleful—since Britain could not afford to make any worthwhile investment in Nigeria and yet demanded troops and other support from the country—independence, when at last it came, was no better, because it failed to usher in a period of contentment and economic progress.

Personal circumstances in the first thirty years of her life brought all these factors home to Emecheta. Her family was by no means rich, and her father, Jeremey Emecheta, who had worked as a molder on the railways, was killed while serving with the British army in Burma. He died far away from home in a war that was hardly his business, and the fact that the family was never given any details about his death adds to a feeling that his fate was a matter of indifference to callous white officers. Left fatherless at an early age, Emecheta was fortunate to be educated in the Methodist Girls' High School in Lagos, but this experience also bred a sense of alienation. Kindly and well-meaning, but strict and conservative, her teachers introduced her to old-fashioned aspects of British culture. The teaching of the English language could itself be regarded as an even more insidious means of separating the child from her background, obliging her to imbibe habits of mind and thought that were essentially foreign. Emecheta's comment in her autobiography that her mother "permitted Christianity to tighten the knot of enslavement" (p. 3) is a savage indictment of

what missionary endeavor could do to human psychology.

During these years Emecheta was also learning that men, whether old or young, were the privileged members of the family. Not surprisingly, the young Emecheta, whose intelligence had had some opportunity to develop, decided to break out and seek freedom. She did so in the only way open to a Nigerian girl. At the age of sixteen she married Sylvester Onwordi, a student to whom she had been engaged since she was eleven, and the couple emigrated to London, where she had five children before separating from him in 1966. She worked in the library at the British Museum and then, between 1970 and 1974, was a student at the University of London taking an honors degree in sociology. Her course of study helped to provide her with analytic tools that she would use to structure her observations and insights.

At this time too she began to write. Her career as an author was launched when passages that were subsequently gathered into the novel *In the Ditch* were printed in the *New Statesman*, a British left-wing magazine. From then on Emecheta was launched on a dual career as a writer and a social worker, serving on public committees and becoming a respected voice on feminist and integrationist issues. Her fiction dates largely from the 1970s and early 1980s, and she has scored some notable successes with both critics and the general reading public. She added further dimensions to her literary career by founding the Ogwugwu Afor, a publishing company based in London and Nigeria that concentrates on African literature, and by taking posts as a visiting lecturer and professor at a number of universities in the United States and Africa. Her status in Britain has been confirmed by her membership in the Home Secretary's Advisory Council on Race and in the Arts Council of Great Britain, which exercises considerable power and discretion in the allocation of public funds for support of the arts.

IMMIGRANT NOVELS

Adah's Story

In the Ditch was published in book form in 1972, and *Second-Class Citizen* came out two years later. The two novels were republished in a single volume entitled *Adah's Story* in 1983. *Second-Class Citizen* tells of the early years of Adah, the young woman whom we meet at a later stage of life in *In the Ditch*. The theme of the two novels is that discrimination threatens to destroy individual liberty, hampering the development of innate talent at every turn. Emecheta portrays women in particular as the victims of a heartless society. There is, however, a countervailing force: the great wellspring of energy, creativity, and idealism within individuals that enables them to overcome grueling ordeals and come through victorious.

In Nigeria, Adah is a strong-minded little girl. She has to fight against the prejudices of a male-dominated society in order to gain a western education, and it is not long before she decides that her best hopes for a fulfilling future lie in England. She is quickly disabused of this notion, however. Life in London proves more difficult than it was in Lagos. Emecheta presents, through the experiences of the characters in her immigrant novels, a perceptive analysis of the socioeconomic problems that had arisen in Britain, and in London in particular, in the second quarter of the twentieth century, a period when issues were immensely complicated by the destruction caused in World War II and then by the economic crisis that followed. As an immigrant Adah is the victim of color prejudice, which had always been endemic in England, especially in the capital, but escalated during the postwar years when the British government encouraged large-scale immigration from Commonwealth countries in order to alleviate what was perceived as a shortage of labor for manual jobs. Paradoxically, competition for employment was one of the major factors that led to racial friction, and there was a great deal of resentment about immigrants with no record of contributions or tax payments drawing social security benefits from the recently established welfare state. Difficulties also arose over housing. Slum clearance had begun in the 1930s, but progress, which had never been rapid, stopped during the war when many houses were destroyed by air bombing in the Blitz. Peace did not bring plenty to Britain, and a decline in the quality of the housing stock, especially in London, was a clear indication of the country's economic decline.

Private landlords did not hesitate to profiteer from the situation, charging immigrants exorbitant rents for substandard accommodations. In an effort to solve the problem local boroughs built council houses (public housing). Difficulties arose, however, because insufficient attention was given to social factors: families were uprooted and relocated to anonymous housing estates, and high-rise apartment buildings suited neither old people nor young couples with children. Few were happy with the situation, and the word *alienation* was often used to describe the characteristic reaction. For immigrants matters were even worse. As there was a shortage of council housing, many British felt it was unfair that immigrants be given priority in allocating accommodations, and when they were, they found themselves in an environment in which they were ill at ease. Successive governments had to tackle problems that were alarming the electorate, and there were hard-fought battles in Parliament over legislation designed to place strict limits on immigration from Commonwealth countries, which had previously been largely unregulated, and over measures aimed at improving the lot of the immigrants who had already arrived by prohibiting racial discrimination.

Adah experiences all the problems associated with inadequate housing. Everyday life becomes more and more difficult, and she is soon caught in a dangerous downward spiral.

Confronted with this situation she turns to the social services, as many in Britain at that time complained that women in her position always did. Some might protest that Emecheta's portrayal of the administration of the welfare state is harsh because Adah's encounters with officialdom are usually bruising. Her needs are great, and her benefits are not only meager but delivered in a condescending and demeaning way.

There is, however, a factor that makes every aspect of life in Britain, including the notoriously depressingly wet and chilly weather and the food that Adah finds unappetizing, even worse for her. Her hopes of freeing herself from sexual tyranny, now that she is away from Nigeria, are dashed. Indeed, Emecheta's characterization of Adah's husband is a virulent attack on the black man. Lazy, greedy, and sexually demanding, Francis is a perpetual student who demands quiet and leisure so that he can prepare for examinations that he does not pass. Less intelligent than his wife, he nonetheless expects to dominate every aspect of her life and interprets any initiative on her part as a threat to his ever declining superiority, a gradual loss of status of which he is dimly aware.

In one domain in particular he insists on what he considers his rights, and Adah may be seen as the victim of his uncontrolled sexual demands. It is perhaps facile to suggest that he is looking to compensate for his frustration, boredom, and failure in other spheres. For Adah, however, as one pregnancy follows another and he leaves her all the responsibility for rearing a growing family in cramped conditions with little money to pay for food, clothing, and other necessities, sex in marriage is not very different from rape. Francis strengthens that impression when he turns violent and begins to beat her.

At the end of *Second-Class Citizen*, Adah begins to find a new life for herself by writing fiction. Her breach with Francis occurs when he discovers the manuscript that she has been working on and burns it. In *In the Ditch*,

Emecheta portrays the next phase of Adah's development as she gradually recovers from the initial disasters of a Nigerian woman's life in England. She is first seen in the Pussy Cat Mansions, a public housing estate for what are designated problem families. It is presented as an essentially female society where women depend on the social security benefits that are grudgingly handed out by unsympathetic officials. Gradually, however, Adah begins to assert herself. She knows that she has an intellect and is determined to make use of the training she received in Nigeria. As a consequence this second episode of Adah's story might be considered misnamed as *In the Ditch* for its heroine largely succeeds in extricating herself by showing a strength of character that allows her to benefit from her natural gifts.

The narration of *In the Ditch* and *Second-Class Citizen* is straightforward, and the depiction of situations is always vivid, with clear-cut characters and lively dialogue. Both novels have a refreshing directness, and the unpretentious narrative style endorses the honesty and reliability of the testimony about intolerable conditions.

Gwendolen

Gwendolen was not published until 1989, after Emecheta had turned away from writing immigrant fiction in the documentarist tradition in order to concentrate more on women's experiences in Nigeria and then appeared to have given up writing fiction. But this thought-provoking novel should be considered alongside the two early novels that make up *Adah's Story*. Although the storytelling is more complex, *Gwendolen* shares their qualities of passionate protest against accurately portrayed contemporary problems and makes some important points as it explores anew the problems of immigrant communities in Britain.

The first two sentences of the novel bring the issue of alienation into sharp focus: "She was christened Gwendolen. But her Mammy could not pronounce it, neither could her Daddy or his people" (p. 9). The girl suffers a constant reminder of the gap between the reckless overreaching that led her parents to choose a complex name with European cultural overtones and their embarrassing inability to get their tongues around it. She cannot even be sure herself what her name is, and her identity seems reshaped each time the question of her name arises. The English schoolteacher who pronounces her name correctly hardly knows what to make of a twelve-year-old child who does not realize she is being addressed. A miniature tragedy occurs when an attempt to establish a little friendly contact by shortening the name to Gwen is greeted with blank incomprehension. The theme of a linguistic barrier, which is both real and symbolic, is taken a stage further by Emecheta's portrayal of Londoners, who tend to equate poor language skills with a lack of intelligence. What is equally disturbing is the reminder that immigrants from different origins, such as Africa and the Caribbean, find it difficult to communicate in the version of English they have learned before coming to Britain. That one of the major characters aspires to be an eloquent preacher yet suffers from a marked stammer is one more example of the problem highlighted here.

In the United States, *Gwendolen* was published in 1990 as *The Family*. Although this title deemphasizes the theme of communication, it points up the fact that in this novel problems within the family always exacerbate cultural difficulties. This is not a novel that blames the host country for all the problems that arise over immigration. Gwendolen is still only a little girl when her father, Winston, like many West Indians of his generation, leaves Jamaica to seek a better life in London and after a while asks his wife to join him. Left with her grandmother, Gwendolen is denied a decent education; instead she is condemned to the traditional round of household chores that old-fashioned people think ought to be her only concern.

To make matters worse, she is sexually assaulted by her uncle. She has not recovered from the trauma, which leaves her in a state of shock and leads to a degree of introversion, when her parents tell her to come to London. They make clear that they want her there to look after her younger brothers. Her first impressions of England bring to life the familiar concept of culture shock. In the account of Gwendolen's schooling Emecheta shows how easily educational opportunities can be squandered and how immigrant children may experience difficulties in a new environment. Though an unsympathetic observer might argue that she was given every chance, Emecheta successfully conveys why a girl like Gwendolen cannot take advantage of what she is offered and how every attempt to make allowances for differences can be interpreted as further evidence of discrimination.

Emecheta gives her depiction of the plight of immigrants, and particularly women, two important extra dimensions. Not only does she see the issue from the Caribbean angle, but she also contrasts it with the experience of Nigerians who have come to London. They too are underprivileged victims of discrimination, but they possess an ancient African culture that gives them standards and a sense of pride. This is made particularly clear when a Nigerian workmate is disgusted to find that Winston is tempted to have sexual relations with his daughter. Winston does commit incest and makes Gwendolen pregnant. Matters are made worse for her by the treatment she receives from the social services and by her fear of denouncing her father. His death in a horrific accident on a building site smacks of poetic justice, and Gwendolen recovers some self-respect as she comes to accept her baby. From the Nigerian viewpoint, the experience of slavery has left West Indians culturally and morally diminished, and the novel concludes with Gwendolen's rediscovery of her African roots. This is neatly symbolized when she decides to give her child an African name, Iyamide.

REALIST NOVELS OF AFRICA

Emecheta's homeland, Nigeria, is the setting of several other novels in the second phase of her fiction. Her major concerns in these stories are the unequal struggle that women have to wage in a male-dominated society and the need for attitudinal changes in order for women to have the opportunity to fulfill their potential.

The Bride Price

The Bride Price (1976), like the novels set in London, is a straightforward, third-person narrative. The title of the book, as is so often the case with Emecheta's fiction, is highly significant. A "bride-price" is the considerable sum of money that a bridegroom pays to the male head of the bride's family, and it is believed that if the bride-price is not handed over, she will die in childbirth.

We first meet Aku-nna, whose name means "my father's wealth," in a typical African extended household in Lagos in the period following World War II. When her father dies, her mother decides to take the family back to rural Ibuza. There Aku-nna's mother becomes, as custom demands, one of the four wives of Okonkwo, her late husband's brother. Though Aku-nna is not treated unkindly, she feels something of a misfit in this old-fashioned community. Only because an educated girl will command a higher bride-price is she allowed to continue with her schooling. Trouble comes when she falls in love with her teacher, Chike, a young man of ability and a little wealth. Despite his obvious merits, the older generation in Ibuza regards him as inferior because he descends from slaves. Emecheta shows prejudice to be as virulent in Nigeria as in London. After attempts are made to force Aku-nna to marry another young man with a physical handicap who is considered a more suitable husband, she runs away with Chike. The couple is happy together, and to bring matters to a satisfactory conclusion Chike's father tries to win over Okonkwo by offering a great deal more than the traditional bride-price. He refuses; though he may not seem to have great social status himself, nothing will reconcile him to the idea of his stepdaughter marrying beneath herself.

In the final phase of *The Bride Price*, Aku-nna dies during childbirth in a westernized hospital. Modern gynecology is powerless against the force of deeply ingrained superstition, though there is hope in her last words, a request that the child be called Joy.

The Slave Girl

The Slave Girl (1977) takes us back to an earlier period in the development of Nigeria. It is set toward the beginning of the twentieth century in the countryside near Ibuza. A couple with two sons is delighted at the birth of a daughter, Ojebeta, who has a pampered childhood. But when her parents die in the 1916 flu epidemic, everything changes for her. One of her brothers decides to migrate to Lagos, while the other decides to raise the cash needed for his coming-out celebrations by selling her into domestic slavery. She is taken to Onitsha to work in a large household fetching and carrying, minding the children, and serving meals. Conditions improve when her mistress converts to Christianity, and the slaves are sent to the church to learn to read and write. Ojebeta eventually leaves the household and marries; her husband redeems her from slavery by paying the sum for which she was originally purchased. Throughout the novel there is, however, a strong sense that a woman is never truly free.

The Joys of Motherhood

The Joys of Motherhood (1979), with its ironic title, is perhaps Emecheta's most successful realist African novel. This is a tale of women's lives in Nigeria from the 1930s to the eve of independence, a period of titanic political, economic, and social change. For the men in the Igbo immigrant society in Lagos these were traumatic times, but for women matters were yet worse: the yoke of tradition weighed all the more heavily on them as their menfolk sought to compensate within the household for their increasing loss of status in the wider world. From the outset Emecheta describes the strains Nnu Ego endures as she copes in a society where maternity is the only way for a woman to achieve any real status. Emecheta acknowledges the difficulties that arise from the transformation of a village community into an urban one where the men have no choice but to become a laboring class, but also stresses that men's attitudes toward their wives in a society that permits and indeed institutionalizes polygamy need considerable revision. Nnu Ego's attitudes, especially those toward her daughters, are developed in contrast to those of Adaku, her co-wife, who is prepared to consider more radical means of securing some degree of economic freedom in order to achieve greater personal autonomy in a male-centered society. Emecheta describes the sexual mores of Nnu Ego's circle with unembarrassed frankness as an essential component in its social life, and she shows her powers of rapid description and characterization in a story that ends, after all the anguish, on a note of hope.

Destination Biafra

The background to *Destination Biafra* (1982) is the civil war between the federal government and the breakaway republic of Biafra, which threatened to rend Nigeria apart over a period of two and a half years. Between midsummer 1967 and January 1970 the country was plunged into what Emecheta calls the bloodiest carnage ever seen in Africa. The situation was exacerbated by the ambiguous attitudes of western powers, especially Britain, and their refusal to intervene. African officers trained in the west deployed the destructive weaponry of modern warfare, and matters were made worse when traditional intertribal animosities were reawakened. Atrocities became commonplace, and starvation decimated the population. The impact was felt particularly in the Nigerian midwest, Emecheta's homeland; in her dedication and foreword to *Destination Biafra* she writes with emotion of her relatives and friends who died in the course of the hostilities. She also notes that her editors insisted on considerable cuts in the original manuscript. What remains, however, is still one of her longest texts.

Destination Biafra is historical fiction in that it gives a vivid and circumstantial account of events that actually occurred, but it sees them largely through the eyes of an imaginary character who symbolizes the suffering that Nigeria underwent in the Biafran War. Although Emecheta changes the names of politicians and army officers, the disguise is transparent. Emecheta uses her documentarist skills to great effect in descriptions of horrors, atrocities, and the interplay of different types of people in situations of great tension as she details the start of the war and its operations. She creates too an impression of the swirling confusion that enveloped the country.

Emecheta creates an intelligent young woman character, Debbie, to serve as the focus of our attention in the maelstrom of action and as an involved spectator of the civil war. Debbie Ogedemgbe is the grown-up daughter of a wealthy businessman who has risen to some prominence in postcolonial Nigeria and is soon to be punished for profiteering from his position. Sending his daughter to Britain to study at Oxford was one of the many luxuries that he has been able to lavish on his family. When she returns home shortly before the coup that initiates this tragic civil war, she finds that many in Nigeria treat her with a distrust mingled with envy, and she cannot rid herself of feeling like an outsider. That this modern, emancipated woman has sympathies with both sides in the conflict and feels obliged to try to effect a resolution adds complexities to the plot. In her descriptions of Debbie's travels across the country, Emecheta reminds us that women and children are the saddest victims of war. Sexual aggression serves as a literal and figurative expression of appalling violence in a bitter civil war.

Deeply felt and evocative in descriptions that always have a personal dimension, *Destination Biafra* is a powerful account of historical events that failed to capture the attention of the international community. But Debbie's personal development is not satisfactorily combined with the exploration of an internecine conflict with unfamiliar intricacies that demand careful attention if they are to be unraveled. Writing *Destination Biafra* meant a great deal to Emecheta. In her preface she comments that this book "is one that simply had to be written" (p. vii), and she expresses her regrets that the economics of publishing forced her to reduce her manuscript to half its original size. It seems likely that writing *Destination Biafra* was her way to contribute to momentous events in which she could play no direct part; she was in London at the time and could only participate in protest demonstrations in Trafalgar Square. All the same, the attempt to work on a larger canvas than that in her novels of family life has not been entirely successful.

Double Yoke

Writing *Double Yoke* (1982) may, to some extent, be seen as another attempt by Emecheta to widen her range and develop her narrative technique, but again the results are not entirely convincing. From 1980 to 1981 she was a senior research fellow and visiting professor of English at the University of Calabar, which had been founded five years earlier. Although *Double Yoke*, which is dedicated to her students there, is a novel of campus life in Nigeria, it is also a reflection on the difficulties women encounter in changing circumstances. It is a struggle for them to fulfill traditional roles and maintain old standards of personal conduct while pursuing the new opportunities offered by education in a postcolonial society that sets a high value on university degrees and professional qualifications.

The structure of the novel, though not very complex, is more ambitious than some of Emecheta's earlier fiction, but it is not entirely successful because the changes of perspective are not convincingly motivated. In the opening Emecheta introduces Ete Kamba, a young male student. He is attending a creative writing course and decides, as an exercise in composition as well as an effort to exorcise the past, to relate his experiences when he lost his girlfriend, Nko. This scenario involves a flashback, and the early chapters, narrated from his point of view though in the third person, are a sensitive account of a couple of young people getting to know one another and falling in love. Upon Nko's arrival at the university, Emecheta changes the narrative stance to provide a disturbing account, again in the third person but from Nko's angle, of the problems that confront female students. Already she has had to cope with men's double standards in sexual matters, for Ete has unwittingly made it clear that women are expected to be more virtuous than men. Now she finds herself preyed upon by a libidinous professor whose behavior is all the more reprehensible because he hides his lust under a cloak of religion. She quickly learns that avoidance will not solve the problem and yields to him, but decides to blackmail him into awarding her a first-class degree. *Double Yoke* presents a singularly depressing picture of material and moral decline in the Nigeria of the early 1980s. It ends by returning to Ete and his creative writing tutor as they discuss Ete's work. They conclude that male attitudes need to be reformed if women are to have a chance in modern Africa.

FICTION FOR THE YOUNG

Emecheta's ability to enter the minds of other people is evident in her fiction for children. *Titch the Cat* (1979) and *Nowhere to Play* (1980) are short tales with pictures that are set in London. As well as offering fairly undemanding entertainment, these stories help to create in young minds tolerance between people from different ethnic groups and people who pursue different lifestyles. The same can be said of her short novels for young teenagers — *The Wrestling Match* (1980), *The Moonlight Bride* (1980), *Naira Power* (1982), and *A Kind of Marriage* (1986) — which are set in Nigeria. Description and dialogue, not narrative construction, are the strengths of these slightly sententious books, which, though they add nothing significant to an understanding of Emecheta, serve their intended function.

CONCLUSION

In the mid 1990s, a summing up of Emecheta's work would reveal stages marked by shifts in style and approach. Her early documentarist work caused a great stir, both for its distinctive tone and because it touched a sensitive nerve in the more liberal sections of the British reading public. Then her novels about women's experiences in Nigeria marked a significant development. If *Double Yoke* and *Destination Biafra,* despite the author's commitment, were less impressive, *The Rape of Shavi* suggested that Emecheta had hit upon a fresh approach to the writing of thoughtful and persuasive fiction. After a long hiatus, Emecheta wrote *Gwendolen*, which, for all its qualities, cannot really be interpreted as evidence of a further stage in its author's evolution. It was hard to guess the direction of her future work, but many of her readers hoped that this passionate author would continue writing humane fiction to advance the causes in which she believes.

Selected Bibliography

NOVELS

In the Ditch. London: Barrie & Jenkins, 1972; Oxford, U.K.: Heinemann, 1994. Reprinted, with *Second-Class Citizen,* as *Adah's Story.* London: Allison & Busby, 1983.

Second-Class Citizen. London: Allison & Busby, 1974; Oxford, U.K.: Heinemann, 1994.

The Bride Price. London: Allison & Busby, 1976; New York: G. Braziller, 1976; Oxford, U.K.: Heinemann, 1995.

The Slave Girl. London: Allison & Busby, 1977; New York: G. Braziller, 1977.

The Joys of Motherhood. London: Allison & Busby, 1979; New York: G. Braziller, 1979; London: Heinemann, 1994.

Destination Biafra. London: Allison & Busby, 1982; New York: Schocken, 1982; Oxford, U.K.: Heinemann, 1994.

Double Yoke. London: Ogwugwu Afor, 1982; New York: G. Braziller, 1983, 1991.

The Rape of Shavi. London: Ogwugwu Afor, 1983; New York: G. Braziller, 1985.

Gwendolen. London: Collins, 1989; Oxford, U.K.: Heinemann, 1994. Published in the United States as *The Family.* New York: G. Braziller, 1990.

CHILDREN'S FICTION

Titch the Cat. Illus. by Thomas Joseph. London: Allison & Busby, 1979. Based on a story by Emecheta's eleven-year-old daughter Alice.

Nowhere to Play. Illus. by Peter Archer. London: Allison & Busby, 1980; New York: Schocken Books, 1980.

TEENAGE FICTION

The Wrestling Match. Oxford, U.K.: Oxford University Press, 1980.

The Moonlight Bride. Oxford, U.K.: Oxford University Press, 1980; New York: G. Braziller, 1983.

Naira Power. London: Macmillan, 1982.

A Kind of Marriage. London: Macmillan, 1986.

AUTOBIOGRAPHY

Head Above Water. London: Ogwugwu Afor, 1986; Oxford, U.K.: Heinemann, 1994.

PHOTOGRAPHIC PRESENTATION

Our Own Freedom. With photographs by Maggie Murray. London: Sheba Feminist, 1981.

CRITICAL STUDIES

Brown, Lloyd W. *Women Writers in Black Africa.* Westport, Conn.: Greenwood Press, 1981.

Davies, Carole Boyce, and Anne Adams Graves, eds. *Ngambika: Studies of Women in African Literature.* Trenton, N.J.: Africa World Press, 1986.

Jones, Eldred Durosimi, Eustace Palmer, and Marjorie Jones, eds. *Women in African Literature Today,* special issue of *African Literature Today,* no. 15 (1987).

Lindfors, Bernth, ed. *Critical Perspectives on Nigerian Literatures.* Washington, D.C.: Three Continents, 1976.

Petersen, Kirsten Holst. "Unpopular Opinions: Some African Women Writers." In *Kunapipi* 7, nos. 2–3 (1985).

Solberg, Rolf. "The Woman of Black Africa, Buchi Emecheta: The Woman's Voice in the New Nigerian Novel." In *English Studies* 64 (June 1983).

Taiwo, Oladele. *Female Novelists of Modern Africa.* London: Macmillan, 1984; New York: St. Martin's Press, 1985.

Ward, Cynthia. "What They Told Buchi Emecheta: Oral Subjectivity and the Joys of 'Otherhood.'" In *PMLA* 105 (January 1990).

Nuruddin Farah
1945–

ROBERT McDOWELL

NURUDDIN FARAH'S novels, stories, and plays for the theater and radio present the most vivid depiction of Somalian life and culture since World War II. Born in 1945 in Baidoa, a town in southern Somalia, to a merchant, Hassan Farah, and a poet, Aleeli Faduma, Farah became fluent in three languages as a child: Somali, Amharic, and Arabic; later, he attained proficiency in Italian and English.

From his earliest years, Farah seemed destined to follow the life of a writer. In childhood he was tutored in an oral literary tradition in which poetry was an honored, essential activity. Somalis recognize Farah's mother, Aleeli Faduma, as a master composer and speaker of verse. Exposure to his celebrated mother's literary contacts, the frequently shifting borders of his home region, the volatile upheavals of Somalian politics, and a wanderlust that is inspired and sustained both by necessity and by the nomadic lifestyle of his tribal forebears instilled in Farah's consciousness and later art an expansive worldliness that transcends his Somalian settings.

This worldliness enabled Farah to write powerfully about the most grinding problems of his time. With Somalia as his focus—"my country in my mind," he has said—Farah's writing assumes the challenging shape of passionate, analytical explanations of political repression and exposés of the dynamics of traditional domestic abuse. In this latter context, especially, Farah has created a potent body of feminist work that attacks the patriarchal assumptions on which so many forms of world oppression are based. In "In Praise of Exile," an essay he wrote in 1988, Farah offered an acute description of his work up to that time: "My novels are about states of exile; about women shivering in the cruel cold in a world ruled by men; about the commoner denied justice; about a torturer tortured by guilt, his own conscience; about a traitor betrayed."

Although Farah is not a native speaker of English, all his novels were written in English with the exception of an unfinished work he began in Somali in 1973 after the creation of an orthography for the Somali language. In a 1992 interview with Feroza Jussawalla and Reed Way Dasenbrock, Farah stated that his decision to write in English was pragmatic rather than political: "Because I could find a typewriter in English, as you can see a practical thing that has nothing to do with the politics of language. To me, to this day it doesn't really matter what language I write in" (pp. 47–48). His use of English, however, does have an effect on the style of his works. Virtually all his novels contain examples of awkward phrasing and construction: for example, from *Sweet and Sour Milk* (1979), "Mother ... *knows not how to throw* anything away" or, from *Sardines* (1981), "a car came out from *out* a blind curve" (emphasis added). If composing in English detracted from Farah's performance as a stylist, it also afforded him the opportunity to reach directly an international audience. The novelist Doris Lessing noted in her review of *Close Sesame* (1983): "There is another pleasure, English is not Farah's first language; and some of the most dingy of our cliches seem to get fresh life when put in unexpected contexts, reminding us that the English language is now a house of many mansions" (p. 244). Particularly in academic circles, a growing number of critics and readers have embraced and followed Farah's books. It is rare when a writer's subject is sufficiently powerful to overcome noticeable shortcomings in style, but this has always been the case with Farah.

Farah's first book, the novella *Why Die So Soon?*, appeared in Somalia in 1965, when the author was only twenty years old. This apprentice work, which served as a promising debut and not much more, gained for Farah only modest attention in his home country. Hardly discouraged by the book's reception, Farah attended the University of Chandigarh in India (1966–1970), where he wrote his first significant novel.

FROM A CROOKED RIB

From a Crooked Rib (1970) is an allegorical tale of a young country girl, Ebla, who flees her tyrannical grandfather and the unwanted marriage he has arranged for her. Joining a caravan (the caravan, itself a symbol of nomadic life, literally becomes a lifeline), Ebla's journey toward enlightenment, independence, and a measure of freedom involves a temporary layover in a small town, then her arrival and life in Mogadishu, capital of Somalia. In the key stopover between her rural origin and her urban destination, Ebla stays with her cousin Gheddi and his wife, Aowralla.

Ebla arrives at the small, dirt-floor house of her relatives in a moment of high domestic drama. Aowralla is in labor, and Gheddi is unwilling, or unable, to assist her. The task falls to Ebla, whose appearance releases Gheddi from obligation and responsibility, allowing him to return to his shop. The scenes of the birth of Aowralla's daughter are superb in their gritty, understated realism. Though the women hardly speak to each other, Farah evokes the immediate and the deeper ties that bind them together. Through their interaction Farah exposes the blunt and bestial patriarchal oppression against which all Somali women struggle to survive. For a brief period Ebla remains with her relatives, caring for Aowralla and her child, preparing meals, and tending livestock. She also receives subtle instruction in the ways of men and cities from a character identified only as the widow—an attractive, mysterious neighbor in her thirties who effortlessly moves in and out of scenes, bringing with her the atmosphere and authority of moral conscience.

These lessons serve Ebla well, for the longer she remains with her relatives, the more antagonistic her cousin becomes. After his initial obligatory extension of hospitality, Gheddi reveals himself to be arrogant, pompous, selfish, cruel, and ridiculous. His sexist attitudes are not included in this list because they are the basis of the condition that brands him and virtually all male characters created by Farah. As Ebla's visit draws to a close, we discover that Gheddi is also dishonest and incompetent. Engaged in smuggling illegal goods, he is betrayed by an associate and awaiting the rough judgment of the authorities. His betrayal offers a microcosmic glimpse into how the Somalian government conducted its business through bribes, informants, and acts of intimidation.

As Ebla's relationship with her cousin deteriorates, her bond with Aowralla grows stronger. Here (and elsewhere in Farah's stories) women come together as if under siege, confiding in each other, consoling, managing a household and family, and resisting constant domestic and political pressure. Yet even this relationship cannot overcome Gheddi's increasing enmity toward his cousin, whom he blames at one point for his changing fortunes. Inevitably, Ebla must continue her journey, her awakening, and with the widow's encouraging guidance she completes her journey to Mogadishu accompanied by the widow's nephew, who lives in the city. From a traditional small-town beginning, Ebla fully enters modern Somalia and takes charge of her own destiny. In the novel, Farah composes remarkably insightful passages dealing with Ebla's sexual and political awakening.

Having arrived in Mogadishu, Ebla withholds sex from her protector, the widow's nephew, until he agrees to marry her. Once that promise is made, her sexual initiation is far from satisfactory; it is one she endures by thinking of it in political-historical terms. After the perfunctory wedding ceremony, Ebla becomes acquainted with her husband. This period of adjustment and discovery is surprisingly brief. Her husband, who works in a government office, announces that he has been posted to Italy and will depart within a few days. Ebla is left alone in his apartment in the care of his landlady.

The introduction of this older woman provides another opportunity for female bonding in response to the brutish bumbling of men. Ebla, at first a loyal wife awaiting her husband's return, loses the last vestiges of her rural naïveté when she accidentally discovers a photograph of her husband and a white woman embracing on an Italian beach. Her solution, inspired by the landlady, is to take another husband. The landlady introduces Ebla to Tiffo, a fat, wealthy suitor who is already married to a woman with a legendary

temper. A similarly perfunctory wedding ceremony takes place, and Ebla sleeps with Tiffo whenever he can get away from his domineering first wife. In exchange, he gives Ebla money to cover her expenses.

Elements of a bedroom farce are clearly evident, but they are tempered by the serious flaws in Somalian matrimony. The novel's twenty-seventh chapter consists of a monologue (echoing Molly Bloom's in James Joyce's *Ulysses*) in which Ebla lies on her bed and meditates on her life. Already she has rejected one of the linchpins of Somali faith: "I wonder if it is true that God has said that 'a woman's prophet and second-to-God is her husband.' If this is true, then life is not worth living" (pp. 151–152). She speculates further, as a believer, on her current lot and her relationship to God. "I am a naturally confused person," she thinks, "but though the Creator is responsible for his creation, I am responsible for my actions" (p. 158). Her resolution suggests that she has learned well from experience. "Let me analyse my men" (p. 158), she concludes, and she proceeds to catalog their faults and weaknesses, their responsibilities to her, and hers to them. Furthermore, this evaluation takes place without an assumption of closure. Ebla will go on with these men and with others (or without them), but she will always take responsibility for her actions and circumstances. The message is clear: Somali life may have a patriarchal structure, but its moral authority is matriarchal.

This key assertion receives comic emphasis in a late scene in the novel. Tiffo's first wife, the notorious husband beater, and two cohorts arrive at Ebla's apartment with the intention of punishing not only Tiffo but Ebla as well. Ebla and the landlady present a formidable, united front, and the three visitors turn away resolved to vent their anger only on Tiffo.

Alone again, Ebla prepares for her first husband's return from Italy, and the novel concludes with their reunion. Rather than desert the man—an option she has considered—Ebla takes him back as a parent would reclaim a long-absent, erring child. Now nobody's fool, Ebla possesses the courage to confront and articulate internal conflicts brought on by external circumstances. From this point on, she will control the tenor and set the terms of her relationships with men.

From a Crooked Rib, though not widely reviewed after its publication, has stayed in print and remains one of Farah's most successful, readable novels. Its simple structure and effective evocation of scene, qualities not always present in his later works, as well as the memorable characterization of the peasant girl, Ebla, make this a story worth rereading.

SWEET AND SOUR MILK

The 1970s proved to be one of great turmoil and hardship for Somalia and for Farah. A coup in 1969 saw the rise to power of the military dictatorship of Siad Barre, whose antagonism toward Farah's hypercritical depiction of Somali life was eventually translated into law. While teaching in a secondary school, Farah completed his second novel, *A Naked Needle*, which probed the effects and aspirations of the revolution among Somalia's urban elite. As a result of the country's volatile political situation, the publisher delayed releasing the novel until 1976. This censorship may have contributed to Farah's eventual rejection of the book, though he also indicted it for failing to confront effectively the abuses of Barre's corrupt regime. Farah's disdain resulted in his refusal to have *A Naked Needle* reprinted.

A second major development of this decade occurred in 1972 when the Somali language was officially transcribed, creating from a shared oral speech a written literary language. Farah considered this a great moment and in 1973 began the serialized novel "Tolow Waa Talee Ma ...!" The series began to appear in *Somali News* but was quickly censored. While traveling out of the country, Farah received word from home that he would be well advised to take no more risks. Correctly interpreting this information as a serious threat, Farah decided to remain abroad, living in exile. Ironically, against his wishes, he found himself adopting the nomadic lifestyle of his ancestors. He also discovered that the country he wrote about became more vivid the longer he was away from it. Farah lived for a time in the United States and throughout Europe and Africa, making his living through his writing and occasionally supplementing his income by teaching.

During this period he also completed the novel *Sweet and Sour Milk* (1979), the first book in a trilogy he would call "Variations on the Theme of an African Dictatorship." In *Sweet and Sour Milk*, Farah builds on the achievement of *From a Crooked Rib* to tackle head-on Somali life under military dictatorship. This story of institutional hardship and personal betrayal is heavy with symbolism. Each chapter, for instance, begins with a poetic description of the natural world—sunrise, sunset, heat, weather—that wraps characters and circumstances in a shroud of dramatic hostility. At the center of this thriller is the dentist Loyaan, whose twin brother Soyaan's mysterious death launches the tale. In a country "where rumor rules," Loyaan takes it upon himself to investigate the cause of his brother's death. In the process, he also searches for the content and truth of Soyaan's life.

That life, unlike Loyaan's, was wholly linked, by opposition, to the emerging regime of Siad Barre. While holding a government post, Soyaan belonged to a small but effective underground group committed to overthrowing General Barre. Suddenly Soyaan falls seriously ill, lingers for a brief period, and dies while his brother sits alone at his bedside. Incredibly, the government wastes no time in its well-orchestrated efforts to co-opt not only Soyaan's death, but his life as well. Within hours the deceased revolutionary is declared a hero of the official revolution by the state-controlled media. One of the government's highest-ranking officers, representing the general, will officiate at Soyaan's state funeral. Even the dead man's last words are revised and fabricated. The official story declares that Soyaan died praising General Barre and his revolution, a lie authoritatively supported by the state's most chilling collaborator, Keynaan, the twins' own father. This betrayal of a son by his father seems less shocking only when one remembers that the Somalia Farah describes is a land of informers, where on the radio the country's most famous actress must "sing the psalms of the General's praise-names" (p. 15), where even a trusted family friend, Dr. Ahmed-Wellie, is eventually exposed as an informer.

Against the sad weight of the moment, and the crushing momentum of the state's revision of everything leading up to that moment, Loyaan must struggle for some degree of truth. In the process, he discovers that his brother had written an important insurrectionist tract that has disappeared. He meets Soyaan's lover and their young son. He interviews his brother's friends and associates, all of whom talk reluctantly. Increasingly he measures the slowly emerging picture of Soyaan's secret, activist life against his own and finds his own life lacking. He finds his country increasingly lacking, too, and he faces fully, for the first time, its stifling tribal affiliations, its subjugation of women (who, for example, are not allowed to learn how to read), and its mandatory two-year national service for all citizens. Loyaan comes to the realization that in the general's Somalia "once in a while the police gather these beggars as if they were a season's pick" (p. 13). Even worse, the government can be expected to "humiliate the living; make claims on the souls of the dead" (p. 81).

In such an environment Loyaan's striving to discover anything beyond a private truth is doomed to failure. His father's collaboration becomes increasingly vocal and belligerent. Despite discovering enough information to clarify, in his own mind, his late brother's true

political beliefs and activities, Loyaan understands that he is powerless to counteract the revisionist machinery of the state. Even as he imagines scenarios in which he reveals to the world the true facts of Soyaan's life and death, the radio or television repeatedly breaks in with celebrations of Soyaan, the hero of the revolution who died praising the general, its architect. In the end, Loyaan is sent out of the country. He recognizes the implicit threat behind his new assignment, thinly veiled as a promotion. Later in the trilogy, his absence is referred to as exile. Departing against his will, Loyaan bitterly recognizes his own failure in the essence of the proverb: "Who loses one thing has a better chance of finding another thing long lost and abandoned. You must lose something in order, while searching for that very thing, to find another thing long lost and abandoned."

Critics have pointed out that *Sweet and Sour Milk*, which won the English Speaking Union Literary Award in 1980, evokes Franz Kafka in its vision of totalitarianism relying on silence and betrayal for its survival. But Farah's stylized, figurative language also echoes his lifelong training in Somali poetry and supports his belief that literary art can pose effective opposition to tyranny. A writer like Farah must constantly face the challenge of giving equal weight to the story while conveying a political message. In the best scenario, that message is fully integrated into the plot of the novel. Few writers manage to bring off such a wedding with great success, and Farah himself has a tendency to subjugate plot for the sake of his message in some books. But in *Sweet and Sour Milk*, the most artfully constructed novel in his first completed trilogy, Farah has created a major political novel of lasting value.

SARDINES

In the early 1980s Farah lived in West Germany and taught at the University of Bayreuth, where he completed work on *Sar-*

dines (1981), the second novel of his trilogy. *Sardines*, the title of which is taken from a popular children's game, moves farther away from the more traditional plot construction and storytelling devices found in *From a Crooked Rib* and *Sweet and Sour Milk*. The novel, Farah's most open, unrelenting feminist work—Farah has said that his female characters are symbolic of Somalia itself—is really the story of Medina's resistance.

As a journalist, Medina represents the better-educated, more sophisticated class of Somali women. The story begins as she awaits the arrival of her brother, Nasser, who has been abroad. From sentiments in his letters to her, such as "Tell them you are African; tell them the General is a fascist and prove it to them" (p. 22), and "Politics in Africa and the Third World ... is but an insipid goulash of western and eastern ideologies" (p. 21), a pattern of dissent is quickly established. Medina's own activism emerges from her decision to defy the Somali custom that calls for clitoral excision and infibulation (commonly called female circumcision) to be performed on her eight-year-old daughter, Ubax. Medina's decision provokes a firestorm of criticism and pressure, especially from the older women in her family. Under attack, Medina leaves her husband and domineering mother-in-law to raise Ubax on her own and to create and live in what can be called Virginia Woolf's room of one's own.

Ubax, an only child, is oblivious to the controversy swirling around her. Like most children her age, she is primarily interested in feeling secure and having the undivided attention and affection of those who maintain her care. In one respect, however, Ubax differs markedly from other eight-year-olds. Her verbal expression is extraordinary. There are times during the exchanges between mother and daughter when the reader may find it necessary to pause to remember that Ubax is a child, not one of Medina's interesting female friends. In doing so, one realizes that Ubax is being raised as an adult. Only her occasional

hysterical fits, when she does not understand a situation or does not get her way, seem utterly appropriate behavior for her age. Medina's approach to child rearing takes on an ironic significance when one considers that, at the time of the novel's story, three hundred thousand children were dying in Somalia every year.

Ubax's father, Samater, like the male protagonists of other Farah books, holds a government position. As a result, he lives in frustrating opposition to his true beliefs. He must also contend with the fact that his wife's clan is better off financially than his own. Medina, for example, owns their house, which humiliates Samater's mother, who lives with them and wields this fact over him like a club. To Samater's credit, he is not overly concerned about ownership of real estate, but he is less successful in accepting Medina's decree that Ubax not undergo the circumcision ritual. "He was inarticulate with self-questioning," the narrator tells us at one point; he must struggle mightily to hold a useful debate with himself in order to ascertain his motives and positions and to determine a course of action. He knows that to refuse the circumcision ritual will cast himself and his family under greater government scrutiny, perhaps even jeopardize his position. This conflict disrupts the family and leaves Medina in a "barbecue of nerves" (p. 83). Estrangement becomes the family's dominant characteristic. Even the intimate relationship between Medina and her mother suffers as the latter unwittingly argues for a family managed, in effect, as the government manages the country. When in exasperation Medina's mother insists that children, after all, are not equals with adults, Medina counters that General Barre relies on the same faulty assumptions to impose his will on Somalia. The stifled structure of the family mirrors the nation's corrupt political structure.

The greatest of all institutional evils, the one at the root of the corruption of the family, is the complete subjugation of women. The two grandmothers in this story are cast as aggressive mouthpieces espousing the doctrines of the state; theirs is a deadly conformity born of tradition, a conformity that brings its pressure to bear on every member of the next generation, including the women of Medina's inner circle. Sagal, a young athlete and Medina's protégé, must choose between complicity in a farce (her two principal swimming competitors are detained by police for questioning on the eve of an important meet) and open rebellion by refusing to participate in the meet herself; Atta, an African American, views Somalia's culture and struggle through a dangerously naive lens; Sandra, an Italian journalist, has made her bed with the devil, accepting favors and access to the government's highest levels in exchange for stories with a positive spin on the general's revolution; and Dulman, the tragic singer-entertainer and "Lady of the Revolution," presents the most poignant case. The government insinuates itself in her life to the point where it, in effect, becomes her professional manager. Her career may continue as long as she performs in the manner prescribed by her keeper, the state.

Essentially, *Sardines* is the story of how these women deal with the tremendous pressures the state brings to bear on them. In a series of extended conversations and domestic encounters, they resist or succumb to society's aggressive tradition.

Early in the novel, Medina demonstrates her courage and clearheadedness. "The General," she says, "is primitive (to use another aggressive, violent term) in thinking that women are not worth taking seriously, which all the more proves that he is backward and fascist and, worse still, an uneducated imbecile" (p. 45). It is dangerous to hold, much less express, an opinion like this in a totalitarian state. Medina's writing has already been censored, her mobility curtailed, yet she perseveres, insisting not only on survival, but on accepting responsibility for taking her place in the free community of which she dreams. She

will protect her daughter, thereby interrupting the chain of servitude passed down from generation to generation, and she will act as a sounding board and adviser to other women contemplating acts of defiance. In the process Medina takes her place beside Ebla in *From a Crooked Rib* and Soyaan's lover in *Sweet and Sour Milk* as one of Farah's most memorable women, and as one of the most important feminist characters to appear in late-twentieth-century fiction.

Farah realizes this noteworthy accomplishment even as he moves progressively away from traditional strategies of the novel, eschewing plot development and action in favor of poetically textured, multilayered meditations and conversations. Though he writes these segments extremely well and composes meticulously scenes in which the characters busy themselves with the rituals of ordinary maintenance (preparing meals, shaving, washing hands and faces, cleaning house), Farah suffers occasional lapses in accuracy. Two examples stand out in *Sardines*. In the first, Farah refers to Loyaan, three months after his brother Soyaan's death, as being in prison when in fact he is in exile; in the second he describes a photo of Sagal in action at a swim meet: "It was the instant she broke the ribbon, the very instant which won her a bronze medal" (p. 226). In international competition the bronze medal signifies third place; the first-place finisher would be a gold medalist, and no "ribbons" are used in swim meets. Such incidents no doubt occur as a result of poor editing and the difficulty of composing in English. Still, these lapses are relatively minor, especially when measured against Farah's larger themes.

CLOSE SESAME

The international issues of feminism and political oppression lend themselves to dramatic interpretation, and Farah has written on occasion for the theater. In 1976 as resident writer at the Royal Court Theatre in London, he composed plays for the British Broadcasting Corporation. Then in 1982, while teaching at the University of Jos in Nigeria, he wrote and guided into production *Yussuf and His Brothers*, which examines the complexities of exile. This theatrical experience sharpened Farah's sense of pacing and helped him to understand and manipulate the dramatic potential of monologues, which increasingly propel his novels. It also exposed his views and artistry to a larger, sophisticated audience, which increased the critical attention paid to his fiction. This, of course, further enhanced his stature as an international writer.

The self-confidence that accompanies such stature can be seen in the third novel of Farah's first completed trilogy, *Close Sesame* (1983). In a departure from his strategy in the earlier volumes, Farah dispenses with the short, poetic descriptions of weather preceding the book's chapters. From the beginning it is apparent that this story will be Farah's most concentrated effort.

The reader is quickly insinuated into the consciousness of an old man, Deeriye, a vantage point that does not change throughout the novel. Deeriye, as patriarch of a large family and as a political figure of some distinction, is an eerily balanced creation in his fragility, pious strength, and wisdom. A chronic asthmatic, he spends much of his time in bed, meditating, praying, listening to tapes of prayers and classical music, and talking with his relatives. His extended recollections of the past create a most poignant empathy in the reader with both Deeriye and his country as it struggled toward a twentieth-century identity. Deeriye broods at length on his incarceration in the 1940s, a consequence of defying the Italian colonizers. The term of his imprisonment consumed more than a dozen years and was marked by solitary confinement and psychological torture. Spiritual development sustained him then, as it does in the present, but nothing eases the guilt he suffers when he faces

the fact that taking political action made him an absentee father when his children were growing up. Still, the high esteem in which family members hold Deeriye, and the devotion with which they administer to his needs, reinforces Farah's belief in the importance of resiliency in families. Its most tangible representation in Farah's earlier work came with the family's reconciliation at the end of *Sardines*; in *Close Sesame*, virtually every scene reaffirms the affection, respect, and caring at the core of Deeriye's extended family, which includes three generations.

A roll call of family members sets the essential cast: Deeriye's son, Mursal; his grandson, Samawade; his daughter, Zeinab (who serves as her father's doctor and has two children of her own); and his daughter-in-law, Natasha, an American Jew whose parents' families fled Nazi Germany. There is also Deeriye's closest friend, Rooble, whom Deeriye met in prison and who is treated as a family member. Through his long meditation on his relationship with the weaker, naive Rooble, Deeriye reveals his great capacity for loyalty and friendship.

One step removed from this family, existing as a midway point between the most intimate social unit and the impersonal, imposing state, are the neighbors. In *Close Sesame*, Deeriye spends a lot of time trying to understand the breaking up and polarization of community. He regrets that neighbors increasingly act in unneighborly ways. Many spy on those next door, and by such hostile, distancing behavior collectively contribute to upholding—even creating—a corrupt government.

Cigaal, who lives with his young grandson, Yassin, is a typical neighbor in this story. A collaborator when the Italians occupied Somalia, he is Deeriye's ideological polar opposite. In one of the book's most dramatic scenes, Farah suggests that the communal sickness typified by Cigaal and his kind is passed on to succeeding generations. As Deeriye stands at a window in quiet reflection, the pane explodes and he is struck in the face by a rock and shards of glass. The rock thrower is Cigaal's grandson, Yassin, who later concocts an obviously symbolic, preposterous story in which he intended to throw the rock at an owl perched above the window. Everyone, even Cigaal, understands that the wise old owl, Deeriye, was the boy's intended target.

Though hospitalized, Deeriye quickly recovers. From his bed he graciously tolerates the customary reconciliation ritual in which Cigaal brings his grandson before his victim to apologize and beg forgiveness. Deeriye gives his blessing, knowing the boy is unrepentant, and refuses Cigaal's offers of remuneration for the injury and medical expenses. Deeriye's position, a difficult one, transcends the understanding of all other participants in the drama. Though his act of forgiveness may, in this instance, be futile, it offers an example of tolerance that cannot but impress those involved. On a larger scale, it also contradicts the endless messages pounded into the populace by the state.

As Deeriye ponders the state-proclaimed "suicide" of Mukhtaar, a coconspirator in a presidential assassination plot that also involves Deeriye's son, Mursal, he eloquently articulates his despair over the destruction of an ancient way of life:

> These unneighbourly neighbours: a world stood on its head, he reflected, a world whose inhabitants live, like ants, in societies of total exclusiveness from one another, busy eating away at one another's foundation. . . . Traditionally, one had but the best welcome for one's neighbours. It was your neighbours who were first intimated of your ill health; it was your neighbours whose fire lit your hearth; it was your fire's ember which hid the secrets of your neighbour's cold fears when you buried it at night, just before you went to sleep. And one referred to as one's neighbour anyone, man, woman or child, whose dwelling fell within a forty-house radius of yours—in all seven directions. One played

cards with them; one shared a few whispers of gossip with them. . . . It seemed that the Somali rationalism nowadays shared space with the materialistic cynicism of the urban citizenry anywhere: a materialistic cynicism based in fear of one another and suspicion. When Somalis meet, their encounters are tinged with false smiles which alter the emphasis of their unspoken thoughts. Neighbours spying on one another. God forbid!

> (pp. 150–151)

In this way Deeriye acknowledges the despair that encourages inactivity and isolation among people. His personal history of rebellion and lengthy incarceration give him unusual insight into Somalia's nationalist gains and defeats in the twentieth century, and Farah's distilled, relentless depiction of this elder's point of view encourages the reader to consider related struggles in Ireland, Eastern Europe, South America, and elsewhere in Africa. Much of *Close Sesame* concerns the dawning awareness of the younger generation surrounding Deeriye of their limited options. Their capacity for carrying out any meaningful response to government tyranny shrinks with the mysterious disappearance, death, or exile of one comrade after another.

One theme Farah consistently explores in this novel, given this situation, is the responsibility incumbent on the older generation to demonstrate inspired leadership. Unfortunately, rather than act in courageous ways that would improve the nation's quality of life and alleviate a great deal of pressure on younger people, most members of Farah's elder generation are implicated as collaborators and informers, opportunists who willingly bow to any authority that promises immediate personal rewards.

It is made clear early in *Close Sesame* that Deeriye conducts himself differently. If his moral behavior deepens his isolation, it also intensifies his spiritual quest and expands his capacity for wisdom and worldly knowledge. He sees, with more clarity than most, how the general controls the government and the people:

> Keep the populace underinformed so you can rule them; keep them apart by informing them separately; build bars of ignorance around them, imprison them with shackles of uninformedness and they are easy to govern; feed them with the wrong information, give them poisonous bits of what does not count, a piece of gossip here, a rumour there, an unconfirmed report. Keep them waiting; *let them not know;* let them not know what you are up to and where you might spring from again ... tell them the little that will misguide them, inform them wrongly, make them suspect one another so that they will tell on one another.
>
> (p. 74)

Farah repeatedly suggests that the majority of the population, the Cigaals of the country, have been quickest to adapt to this insecure condition. The rank and file become potential informers, betrayers in collusion with authorities whose purpose is to monitor and terrorize the community. In that way the community is divided and rendered ineffectual as a formidable, unified political force. Hence protest and reaction, while effectively blunted among larger groups, become the sole charge of the individual.

In *Close Sesame* the politically aware individuals, despite their loyalties, understand this challenge. Deeriye belongs to the few who not only understand, but are willing to take action and run the risk of losing everything. The torture and murder of his son, Mursal, for his part in the ill-fated assassination attempt become the catalyst for Deeriye's last brave though futile act. At a meeting with the general, Deeriye pulls out a revolver. His intention—to exact revenge and succeed where younger men have failed—is thwarted when the gun becomes hopelessly entangled in his prayer beads. The general's bodyguards destroy Deeriye on the spot. In doing so, they remove a long-standing irritation, yet they also create another martyr for the opposition.

This last consequence gives Deeriye's decision a deeper resonance, for he goes to his death spurred by the knowledge that what he is about to do is not an isolated act. The lessons learned in prison have primed him:

> Were it not for that period of detention, I might never have known what it was like being a Sayyidist, a Somali nationalist and a Pan-Africanist all at the same time. I am not saying that the Italians did me a favour by imprisoning me because that taught me who I was—although that's true too. But I am saying that once in prison and alone my mind set to work and I reasoned that I had not been detained to teach me who I was, a low-breed of a black man anywhere—a fact I hadn't known: I had thought I was an aristocrat born and bred, and a Muslim at that: and no son of an infidel could ever think he was superior to me.
>
> (p. 230)

Deeriye recognizes and accepts his role in this group, this community of the oppressed, and in doing so he succeeds in giving up his personal possessions—even his life—to feed the life force of a just opposition. This constitutes the ultimate charitable act for a believer. One may also justifiably argue that although Deeriye's final act proves a failure in the short run, it provides one of the many stories sustaining opposition in the long run, eroding tyranny's blunt facade and eventually surviving its downfall. In this sense Deeriye's death has more meaning than the consul's in Malcolm Lowry's *Under the Volcano* (1947) or that of Kafka's confused, terrified lawyer in *The Trial* (1925). Unlike these characters, who meet their ends in depressed, chaotic states of mind, Deeriye is at peace with himself because he is convinced that he is contributing to the survival and eventual renewal of his nation's pride and freedom. Thus, his death takes on much greater social significance than the death of either of his literary forebears. This aversion to alienation and isolation, this rejection of a late-modern, antisocial solution to societal problems, accounts in part for Farah's international appeal. He is among the very few writers of whom it can be said that the power of his subject far outweighs the limitations of his style (which, in his case, are caused by his writing in a nonnative language).

MAPS

After completing this trilogy, Farah spent four years in restless travel, working as a teacher and lecturing on human rights and feminist issues. As a result of the stature his books had won for him, he was a guest speaker at several international conferences. During this period of intense activism Farah also conceived plans for a new trilogy. The first novel, *Maps*, appeared in the United States and Great Britain in 1986. *Gåvor* (Gifts), the second novel, appeared in a Swedish translation in 1990 but had not yet been published in English in the mid 1990s. In a 1992 interview Farah said that he was working on the third novel, to be titled "Letters."

As he has done in every new book, Farah in *Maps* stretches and reshapes his uncanny, elastic capacity to empathize with and speak for the chronically disadvantaged. Springing from his all-encompassing attention to a very old man, Deeriye, Farah launches *Maps* through the earliest perceptions of an infant. In his most compressed, poetic composition, Farah constructs his opening chapter in the difficult second person: "You are a question to yourself. It is true. You've become a question to all those who meet you, those who know you, those who have any dealings with you. You doubt, at times, if you exist outside your own thoughts, outside your own head, Misra's or your own" (p. 3).

The narrator is Askar, whom we meet as he lies helpless in a dark, dank room, his dead mother nearby. Misra is the village woman who discovers and cares for him. More than that, she is the world, the cosmos itself. "By touching me," she tells another villager, "he knows he is there" (p. 6).

Thus begins a marvelous account of an orphaned child's discovery of maternal love. United by circumstance amid the brutality of war along the Ethiopia-Somalia border, Misra and Askar represent the backbone of the community—the stay-at-homes and the workers, the young and abandoned, the feminine and abused—who suffer oppression yet ultimately survive their oppressors. These two characters also represent the child and woman in all of us. It is remarkable to experience the way Farah tunnels into these characters' consciousnesses:

> In her company, you were ecstatic—there was no other word for it.... And you were noisy. You displayed your pleasures with the pomp and show one associates with the paranoid among kings. But then you could be quiet in her embrace too, reflective and thoughtful—so thoughtful that some of the neighbours couldn't believe their eyes, watching you pensively quiet, your eyes bright with visions only you could see. It was when she wasn't there, when you missed her presence, when you couldn't smell her maternal odour, it was then that you cried and you put your soul into crying.... Upon returning from wherever she had gone, she would dip you wholly in water, scrub you and wash you with the same devotion as she might have used when cleaning the floor of her room....
>
> When agitated, you stretched out your hands in front of you like a blind man in search of landmarks and if you touched someone other than Misra, you burst instantly into the wildest and most furious convulsive cry. But if Misra were there, you fell silent, you would touch her and then touch yourself.
>
> (p. 5)

Askar remains with Misra in the Ogaden (a region of Ethiopia that borders Somalia) until the age of seven, when he moves to Mogadishu to live with his uncle, Hilaal, and Hilaal's wife, Salaado. Adjusting to urban life in the capital, Askar develops a genuine affection for Hilaal and Salaado, yet is tormented by the mystery of his birth—was his mother actually alive when he was born; if so, how long after his birth did she live?—and by the plight of his tribespeople detained in the border conflict. As he reaches adulthood his agony settles on two options: either to remain in the city and complete his education or to return to the Ogaden to look for the answers to the mystery of his birth and join the Western Somali Liberation Front, which sought to detach the Ogaden from Ethiopia.

Like Loyaan and Deeriye before him, Askar is a brooder, spending much of the narrative in contemplation of the root meaning of life, the specter of death. Early in the story Askar's state of mind is consistent with the obsessive, egotistical morbidity so often found in any culture among teenagers. But in Askar's case, the additional factor of war lends to both his state of mind and his story a tragic dimension not usually found in the coming-of-age struggles of most teens. From his earliest recollection, Askar is on the defensive, interpreting existence as a very real life-and-death struggle, in which the first chapters of his own oblivion consist of the circumstances of his birth and the particulars of his life as an orphan in a besieged village.

Askar's wrestling with the terms of his increasing awareness takes up much of the novel, though the story's final resolution is ambiguous at best. In this regard Askar represents a thoroughly displaced, anxiety-afflicted new generation. The members of this generation, nostalgic for a more ordered past, accept that their development as individuals is linked in every way to political developments. Their future is a paradox. It seems full of limitless possibilities yet appears to be remote, too, a better life that lies far away and, for most, out of reach.

"THE SOUL IS A WOMAN"

Throughout his writing Farah has probed the issue of generational conflict, and in *Maps* he continued his investigation of the plight of women. In novel after novel Farah has pondered woman's difficult condition, in Africa especially. At one point he bluntly and eloquently summarizes that condition and in the process makes a bold claim. Askar ponders the many stories of Ethiopian atrocities:

> And not in all of them were the raped women maids, mistresses or whores. In all of them, man was "taker," the woman the victim. "Why, if she isn't your mother, your sister or your wife, a woman is a whore," said a classmate of his. How terribly chauvinistic, thought Askar. Women were victims in all the stories he could think of.... The soul is a woman—victimized, sinned against, abused.

> (p. 52–53)

"The soul is a woman": Farah's entire oeuvre exists to honor, understand, and assist in the release of that soul, for this is the universal, feminine identity; it is, in part, the author's, and the work's soul, too. For Farah, the act of writing is spiritual comprehension and growth. In that spiritual record, that map, the prototypical male narrator is a confessor whose inherent, masculine limitations of perspective prevent him from attaining wholeness through knowledge and belief. Desperately seeking truth, he is doomed to gather fragments of truth's scissored map. Only the aged male, such as Derriye, may through relentless practice and devotion to things spiritual finally attain lasting peace, which Farah identifies as feminine in nature.

The perfect female character in a typical Farah story is a victim whose pride and intelligence still breathe despite tyranny's best efforts to snuff them out. Like Misra, she is without guile. She understands her tribal role and her role in the modern, emerging community. Acknowledging that society casts women in the roles of servant and brood mare, she cares for and clings to a private spiritual identity that forms the backbone of an independence beyond the brutality and fear meted out by human institutions. The state may, in the course of its business, shackle her, even kill her, but ultimately it fails in its attempts to fragment her spiritual wholeness. It is, in fact, the spiritual wholeness of women that keeps alive the rebellious struggle for equity and eventually topples corrupt institutions. It is the woman's soul that forges the soul of a nation. Though Misra is publicly disgraced, though she is murdered and her body mutilated, her influence on the boy is profound, so much so that the best Askar can do in making sense of his own life is to tell himself the story of Misra over and over.

In much the same way, Farah tells himself the haunting, echoing stories of injustice in underprivileged nations, and in his own country especially. One may recognize in his style of composing by repetition and embellishment an increasingly static, narrative world in which drama and story development almost always take place offstage, outside the reader's attention. Often the narrative consists of interior monologues and, on occasion, intense dialogues between two characters. Yet even Farah's dialogues seem extensions of monologues rather than spontaneous expressions of differing points of view. This internalization of story alters the pacing and plot expectations of readers of conventional fiction, and as has been pointed out by several interpreters, contributes to the evolution of the psychological thriller. Remarkably, Farah also overcomes the awkwardness that arises as a result of writing in a language not native to him. The consistency and clarity of his political outrage allow him to do so, as does the regional setting of his stories in what was, until recently for the west, an obscure though distinctive country.

In the 1990s, Farah continued to travel widely; he lived part of the year in Kaduna, Nigeria, with his second wife.

Selected Bibliography

SELECTED WORKS

Why Die So Soon? Mogadishu, Somalia: Somali News, 1965.
From a Crooked Rib. London: Heinemann, 1970.
A Naked Needle. London: Heinemann, 1976.

Sweet and Sour Milk. London: Allison & Busby, 1979; London: Heinemann, 1980; St. Paul, Minn.: Graywolf Press, 1992.
Sardines. London: Allison & Busby, 1981; St. Paul, Minn.: Graywolf Press, 1992.
Close Sesame. London: Allison & Busby, 1983; New York: Schocken, 1983; St. Paul, Minn.: Graywolf Press, 1992.
Maps. London: Pan, 1986; New York: Pantheon, 1986.
Gåvor (in Swedish). Stockholm, Sweden: Bonniers, 1990.

RADIO PLAY

A Spread of Butter. British Broadcasting Corporation, 1978.

PLAY PRODUCTIONS

A Dagger in Vacuum. Mogadishu, Somalia, 1969.
Yussuf and His Brothers. Jos, Nigeria, University Theatre, 2 July 1982.

ESSAYS

"Do You Speak German?!" In *Okike* 22 (September 1982).
"The Creative Writer and the African Politician." In *Guardian* (Lagos) (7 September 1983).
"In Praise of Exile." In *Third World Affairs* (1988).
"Why I Write." In *Third World Quarterly* 10 (October 1988).
"Childhood of My Schizophrenia." In *Times Literary Supplement* (23 November 1990).

INTERVIEWS

Aiyejina, Funso, and Bob Fox. "Nuruddin Farah in Conversation." In *Life Studies in African Literature and the Arts* 2 (1984).
Jussawalla, Feroza, and Reed Way Dasenbrock. "Nuruddin Farah." In their *Interviews with Writers of the Post-Colonial World.* Jackson: University Press of Mississippi, 1992.
"Just Talking: Chinua Achebe and Nuruddin Farah." In *Artrage* 14 (fall 1986).
Kitchener, Julie. "Author in Search of an Identity." In *New African* (December 1981).
Moss, Robert. "Mapping the Psyche." In *West Africa* (1 September 1986).

Nazareth, H. O. "In the Land of the General." In *City Limits* (11 November 1983).

CRITICAL STUDIES

Adam, Ian. "Nuruddin Farah and James Joyce: Some Issues of Intertextuality." In *World Literature Written in English* 24 (summer 1984).
————. "The Murder of Soyaan Keynaan." In *World Literature Written in English* 26 (fall 1986).
Bardolph, Jacqueline. "Time and History in Nuruddin Farah's *Close Sesame.*" In *Journal of Commonwealth Literature* 24, no. 1 (1989).
Cobham, Rhonda. "Misgendering the Nation: African Nationalist Fictions and Nuruddin Farah's *Maps.*" In Andrew Parker et al., eds., *Nationalisms and Sexualities.* New York: Routledge, 1992.
Lessing, Doris. "Oppressor." Review of *Close Sesame.* In *New Society* 66 (10 November 1983).
Mnthali, Felix. "Autocracy and the Limits of Identity: A Reading of the Novels of Nuruddin Farah." In *Ufahamu* 17, no. 2 (1989).
Rushdie, Salman. "Nuruddin Farah." In his *Imaginary Homelands.* London: Granta, 1991.
Sparrow, Fiona. "Telling the Story Yet Again: Oral Traditions in Nuruddin Farah's Fiction." In *Journal of Commonwealth Literature* 24, no. 1 (1989).
Wright, Derek. "Parents and Power in Nuruddin Farah's Dictatorship Trilogy." In *Kunapipi* 11, no. 2 (1989).

Athol Fugard
1932–

VICTOR I. UKAEGBU

HAROLD ATHOL Lannigan Fugard was born on 11 June 1932 in Middelburg in Great Karroo, Cape Province, South Africa. He was the second of his parents' three children. His Anglo-Irish father, Harold Fugard, a former jazz pianist and the son of Catholic immigrants from England, and his mother, Elizabeth Magdalena Potgieter, the daughter of an Afrikaner family with deep roots in South Africa, owned and operated a small general-goods store. The family's economic circumstances at the time of Athol Fugard's birth were close to poverty, and in 1935, the Fugards moved to Port Elizabeth. The economic situation was exacerbated when his crippled father became an invalid during a prolonged period of ill health, which forced his mother to take over management of the St. George's Park Tea Room between 1941 and 1970. Between 1938 and 1945, young Hallie, as Athol Fugard was then known, was a pupil at the Roman Catholic Marist Brothers College. Beginning in 1941, he and his brother and sister assisted their mother at the tea shop, where Fugard observed racism and its destructive effects on the lives of the black and Colored (that is, of mixed-race origins) members of South African society at first hand. This period left him with the deep and scathing impressions that later shaped his commitments, views, and writings.

From 1946 to 1950 Fugard studied motor mechanics at the Port Elizabeth Technical College. In 1950 he was awarded a scholarship to study for two years for a bachelor of arts degree in philosophy with social science, social anthropology, and French at the University of Cape Town. He won two class medals for academic achievements at the end of the first year. During his enrollment, Fugard wrote some poems and the draft of a novel about his mother's life, which he never published. Two months before his final examination in 1953, Fugard left the university with his poet friend Perseus Adams and hitchhiked to Port Sudan, where he left Adams and signed on as "captains's tiger" and the only white crew member aboard the S. S. *Graigaur*, a British tramp steamer bound for Pacific Asia. Although he did not obtain a degree, his university study under Professor Martin Versfeld had introduced him to the existentialist belief that personal ethics should be founded on individual experiences and choices rather than on the unquestioned acceptance of traditional faiths and dogmas; this philosophical view, enhanced by his two-year sojourn and cohabitation among people of many races and creeds on the S. S. *Graigaur*, had a profound effect on his life and his decision to remain in South Africa under apartheid. Fugard returned to South Africa in May 1954 after his around-the-world trip and began to write free-lance articles for the Port Elizabeth *Evening Post,* which entailed active participation in the unfolding drama of his country's politics.

Between 1955 and 1957 he worked as regional news reporter for the *Evening Post* and was transferred to Cape Town, where he married the actress Sheila Meiring in 1956. Fugard had known Meiring at university, and the two met again when he came to see her in a performance with the famous South African actress Yvonne Bryceland. The three formed the African Theatre Workshop, also known as the Circle Players, and began performing Fugard's one-act plays with Sheila directing most of them. This collaboration later blossomed into cooperative work involving a long association with black actors and theater practitioners. In 1958 Fugard worked briefly as the stage manager and publicity agent for the South African National Theatre Organisation, and his *No-Good Friday* had its premiere at the African Theatre Workshop. This was followed by *Nongogo* in 1959. For six months after that he worked as a clerk in the Native Commissioner's Court (later renamed Bantu Commissioner's Court), where cases involving blacks arrested for contravening the "pass laws," or "reference books," were tried. Pass laws—regulations that restricted blacks and Coloreds to specific parts of the country and permitted them to enter whites-only areas only with passes and only for a specified period of time—were employed by the authorities of the conservative Afrikaner Nationalist Party, which had ascended to power in 1948, to ensure the racial segregation of South Africa and the sociopolitical emasculation of blacks and Coloreds. Through this work Fugard came into close contact with the effects of apartheid on individuals, and he forged friendships with some members of the underprivileged groups. He has remarked that his work in the court was "the ugliest thing I've ever been part of" ("Afrikaner Humanist," *Observer,* 18 July 1971).

In 1960 Fugard and his wife traveled to Europe, where they staged some of his plays. During the trip Fugard and the New Africa Group performed in the prizewinning entry at the Festival of Avant-Garde Theatre in Brussels, Belgium. Amid the international clamor that attended the horrifying massacre of seventy-two Africans who were demonstrating against the pass laws (an event later known as the Sharpeville Massacres), Fugard returned to South Africa and focused his plays and theater on the plight of individuals instead of groups and institutions.

The 1961 performance of *The Blood Knot*, in which Fugard and Zakes Mokae played Morris and Zachariah, two brothers of mixed race, presented South Africa with its first mixed cast. Morris, the lighter-skinned of the pair, succumbs to the temptation to "pass for white," but he is rejected and so resigns himself to his fate. Zachariah, less educated, and more African in appearance, suffers the indignity of the pass laws and can only dream. This play made a powerful statement for racial cohesion and established Fugard's theater as an instrument for its investigation.

By 1963 the government effort toward emasculation of blacks and other opponents of apartheid had intensified, and the white regime banned all opposition and criticism. Many writers and political figures left South Africa; others were thrown into jail for attempting to exercise artistic and creative freedom. Against this background a group of amateur African theater artists from New Brighton, an African township, sought Fugard's help, which initiated his long association with the Serpent Players and other black actors in Port Elizabeth. The Serpent Players consisted of gifted Africans who sought creative outlets to circumvent the restrictions of apartheid, which denied them permits to rehearse and stage their plays. The group (initially made up of Norman Ntshinga, Welcome Duru, Fats Bokholane, and Mike Ngxcolo) lost some of its members to arrest and imprisonment. Later, John Kani and Winston Ntshona joined the group and initiated a period of improvisation.

Fugard's rapport with the Serpent Players brought prodigious developments in his theater and new experimentations with the creative potential of actors. The group produced adaptations of plays by Wole Soyinka, Jean Genet, Samuel Beckett, Niccolò Machiavelli, Bertolt Brecht, Sophocles, and Albert Camus. Fugard's own enduring legacies of this period include *The Coat* (1967), *Sizwe Bansi Is Dead* (1972), *The Island* (1973), and *A Lesson from Aloes* (1978). Incidents in Fugard's life during these years directly influenced his experiments and improvisations in the theater. For instance, during a visit to court with the wife of an arrested member of the group, Fugard observed an imprisoned old man draw the woman aside and hand her a coat to deliver to his family. The improvisations built around this incident yielded *The Coat*. This period also marked for Fugard a span of creative theater productions in which actors dealt more with their own life experiences and social contexts and less often relied on ready-made plays that neither reflected South African society nor made much impact on audiences there. At the same time the government stepped up its official attention to Fugard's work in the theater and withdrew his passport from 1967 until the end of the decade.

One of the greatest influences on Fugard's life and writings is traceable to the underprivileged circumstances of his birth, which exposed him to the harsh deprivations of a life low on the economic ladder and thrust him into contact with the poorer and more deprived black citizens of his country. His close-knit family influenced his fascination and concern with the nexus of family relationships. This and the mixed heritage of his parents led to early exposure to different artistic influences and a respect for other races. Both parents were storytellers: from his father he inherited a command of the English language, and from his mother, a sense of roots and the textural undertones of South African society. His respect for people of other races was reflected in his friendship with Sam Semela, an older Basuto waiter in his mother's tea shop. Fugard felt a deep sense of shame and guilt over his inhuman treatment of Semela earlier in life, and he comes to terms with his youthful behavior in *"Master Harold" ... and the Boys* (1983), in which Fugard may be identified as the seventeen-year-old Hally. The philosophical perspectives that grew out of his childhood experiences, his education, and his mixed parentage combined to produce Fugard's compelling sensitivity and his desire to explore the inner consciousness and deeper feelings of the disenfranchised. For Fugard the theater is a laboratory for the exploration of human feelings and relationships, and the characters in his plays are the specimens.

The influence of dramatists such as Beckett and Camus and of theater directors such as Peter Brook and Jerzy Grotowski also helped to shape Fugard's theatrical style and his preoccupation with the lives of common people. As Dennis Walder points out in *The Varied Scene,* Fugard's friends Barney Simon and Mary Benson exposed him to Grotowski in 1970 when they sent him a copy of Grotowski's *Towards a Poor Theater* (1969) along with notes from Grotowski's productions and lectures, which they were attending in New York.

The desegregation of South African theaters in 1979 brought more collaborations between the races. Fugard's work grew in stature among blacks and Coloreds as both groups saw the theater as a medium for making strong statements on conditions inside South Africa. By 1991 Fugard had written many stage plays, two television plays, three feature films, the novel *Tsotsi,* and hundreds of newspaper articles. He also had discussed his work and his liberal politics in countless radio, television, and magazine interviews. Some of his works were collaborative efforts. Some works—*The Cell, Klass and the Devil, The Last Bus,* and *Friday's Bread on Monday*—remain unpublished. The published plays and dates of their premier performances follow: *No-Good Friday* (1958); *Nongogo* (1959); *The Blood Knot* (1961); *Hello and Goodbye* (1965); *The Coat* (1967); *People Are Living There* (1968); *Boesman and Lena* (1969); *Orestes* (1971); *Statements After an Arrest Under the Immorality Act* (1972); *Sizwe Bansi Is Dead* (1972); *The Island* (1973); *Dimetos* (1975); *A Lesson from Aloes* (1978); *The Drummer* (1980); *"Master Harold"* . . . *and the Boys* (1982); *The Road to Mecca* (1984); *A Place with the Pigs* (1987); *My Children! My Africa!* (1990); and *Valley Song* (1995). His two television plays are *The Occupation* (1964) and *Mille Miglia* (1968). His feature films, which were directed by Ross Devenish, are *Boesman and Lena* (1974), *The Guest: An Episode in the Life of Eugène Marais* (1977), and *Marigolds in August* (1980). His two prose works are *Tsotsi* (1980) and *Notebooks* (1983), an autobiographical work.

Fugard's literary output and his contribution to South African political discourse have attracted accolades and cooperative ventures from outside South Africa. In 1969 he was elected man of the year by the Johannesburg newspaper *Star*. In 1980 he secured a six-month fellowship at Yale University; for about the next decade he was a familiar face in the Yale drama community. He has participated extensively in his own theater—as actor, producer, and director—and in other people's productions. He was often at the core of the experiments and improvisations from which most of his works evolved. Since early 1980 the premieres of his plays have been presented at Yale, the National in London, and the Market Upstairs theater in Johannesburg. His literary stature in South Africa and the English-speaking world was recognized in a 1989 *Time* magazine profile calling him "the greatest active playwright in English" (Henry, pp. 56–58).

FUGARD'S THEMES

Politics

In most of his writings Fugard uses politics as a subterranean theme. Although the lives of common people have been his main subject matter, apartheid and the politics of institutionalized racism are the powerful forces that frame his work. As Julian Mitchell points out, the truth being told is so saturated in politics that politics never has to be mentioned. Characters and their speeches, the settings of plays, and costumes are all laced with unspoken but evident political statements about life in South Africa. As a result, these works are spared the burden of propaganda and have been enriched with images and symbols that speak powerfully and effectively through their presence and silence.

In *Statements After an Arrest Under the Immorality Act* (in *Statements: Three Plays*, 1974), the sexual encounter between a white woman, Frieda Joubert, and a married black man, Errol Philander, immediately loses its stigma in comparison to the contemptuous attentions of Mrs. Buys's snooping, the harsh glare and flash of Detective-Sergeant J. du Preez's camera, and the callousness of the police report. These interferences are supported fully by the laws of racial segregation. Because the discovery and arrests are not motivated by truly moral concerns—but, rather, by the law of racial purity, which robs people of their basic humanity—apartheid earns our censure, and the guilty pair are clearly victims, not criminals. Politics makes the sexual act immoral by controlling people's private lives. Errol's remark that "there's no tomorrow, just today" (p. 87) is enough indictment for the system.

The same political machinery condemns Zachariah to a life of dreams and pain in *The Blood Knot* (in *Three Port Elizabeth Plays*, 1974) and keeps Boesman and Lena in *Boesman and Lena* (in *Boesman and Lena and Other Plays*, 1980) perpetually on the move with their ragged belongings. As Boesman puts it: "We're whiteman's rubbish. That's why he's so *beneukt* [mad, fed up] with us. He can't get rid of his rubbish. He throws it away, we pick it up. Wear it.... We're made of it now. His rubbish is people.... We've been thrown away" (p. 277). The lot of Boesman and Lena confronts all nonwhites in South Africa, as Johnnie and Hester Smit painfully discover in *Hello and Goodbye* (1966). Hester laments: "We weren't just poor. It was something worse. Second-hand! Life in here was second-hand ... used up and old before we even got it. Nothing ever reached us new. Even the days felt like the whole world had lived them out before they reached us" (p. 52).

In *A Place with the Pigs* (1988), Fugard explores the damaging effects of excessive political control on the lives of individuals; Pavel, a Soviet army deserter, dwells in hiding among pigs for forty-one years because of his fear of the authorities. Politics infiltrates the social and family problems of the characters in *People Are Living There* (in *Boesman and Lena and Other Plays,* 1980) and the life-shattering incarceration and ostracism of the Afrikaner Piet Bezuidenhout (a situation that pushes his wife, Gladys, toward insanity) in *A Lesson from Aloes* (1981); but Fugard's most illuminating examinations of politics occur in *Sizwe Bansi Is Dead* (in *Statements: Three Plays,* 1974) and *My Children! My Africa!* (1990).

Confronted by an official restriction to King William's Town, an impoverished area with few opportunities in the black homeland of Ciskei, Sizwe Bansi is determined to remain in Port Elizabeth to earn a living for his family. So he robs a dead man of his identification papers and living and working permit. Sizwe thus becomes a "ghost," forced to live in the shadows after he writes to his wife with the announcement of his own "death" and his resurrection as Robert Zwellinzima. The law inevitably catches up with him, but Sizwe can experience no greater loss than that of his

identity. Sizwe's manliness, his humanity, and his concern for the dead man all retreat in the face of the apartheid system, which forces people to prey on others, even on the dead, and robs people of their capacity for feeling and conscience.

In *My Children! My Africa!* Mr. M, a black schoolteacher, moderates a debate practice between Thami, his favorite student and the black representative of Zolile High School, and Isabel, the chief spokesperson of Camdeboo Girls' High, a visiting white school. The practice itself turns into a debate about the country's political system and a questioning of the morality and justice behind the inferior separate Bantu eduction. The three characters are inextricably linked by their destinies, and a move from any of them threatens to tear the fabric of their society. The three are equally sincere in their quest for justice and peace, but their contrasting approaches make collision inevitable. In the face of black anger, the teacher is accused of betrayal and is killed by his students and people. Thami goes into exile, and Isabel is left to provide the teacher's epitaph. In this powerful and evocative work, words become dramatic experiences, and the three characters engage and stimulate the audience in the manner of Brecht. Clad in their school uniforms and framed by other paraphernalia of the school, the students represent the future of South Africa struggling to escape the debilitating effects of the past and present. The characters in this drama are brutalized, and their desires for freedom and for a fulfilling life are tortured by fear and suspicion, but their innocence is touching and their resilience remains a beacon of hope. This is Fugard's most ambitious political experiment and is almost prophetic in instigating a debate among the peoples of South Africa. Discussing the play in a 1990 interview, Fugard reflected, "In an overall sense I would like to believe there has been a refining process at work. I don't slap as many colours on the canvas" (quoted in Gray, *File on Fugard,* pp. 69–70).

Religion

While politics is at the base of the suspicions that destroy the relationships between races and individuals, Fugard displays a deep disappointment in religion, especially the Christianity of the Dutch Reformed Church, which he blames for encouraging apartheid. In *The Road to Mecca* (1985), the widow Miss Helen rejects the peace and light offered by the sanctimonious Reverend Marius, who pretends to be concerned for her well-being but regards her presence in New Bethesda as capable of diverting and misleading people from the Christian faith. She holds on to her own truth, which points the way to Mecca instead of Jerusalem, Mecca being the religious and symbolic opposite of the Jerusalem epitomized by Marius. Hally in *"Master Harold"... and the Boys* ridicules the pope and the Catholic church for teaching people to obey ethical precepts without giving them any real belief in justice; he likens the church to the United Nations, which he describes as a dancing school for politicians. Fugard's sardonic perspective is also suggested in the title of his play *No-Good Friday* (in *Dimetos and Two Early Plays*, 1977).

In *Friday's Bread on Monday*, Nomhle Nkonyeni's husband finds it impossible to continue the charade of saying the Lord's Prayer on an empty stomach as his son leaves to purchase the previous Friday's stale bread for the family's use on Monday. In a flashback, the man's journey through prison, his evasion of the police over nonpossession of a pass, and the hunger and suffering inflicted upon him because of his race are played out to underscore his loss of faith in prayer. For Errol and Frieda in *Statements After an Arrest Under the Immorality Act*, the Lord's Prayer is no better than the meaningless words of a game played to relieve boredom. Zach and Morris in *The Blood Knot* parody the Bible and reshape the Lord's Prayer with excuses and explanations. Fugard sees religion as an enduring excuse for accepting the status quo;

he records its weakness as an instrument for healing the racial and social cleavages that apartheid has inflicted on South African society. Hester in *Hello and Goodbye* sums up the feelings of the suffering people of South Africa and their disillusion with religion when she emphatically states: "THERE IS NO GOD! THERE NEVER WAS! We've unpacked our life . . . and there is no God" (p. 62).

The Common Person

Fugard's work also explores the futility of living in the dream of a better tomorrow when hopes are certain to be destroyed by a harsh and unrelenting present. All his underprivileged characters share in this dream: some wake up to or die in the rude reality, and others prefer the surreal comfort of such dreams. The family in Styles's photographic studio in *Sizwe Bansi Is Dead* indulges its dreams in smiling portraits that mask its pain. In *Boesman and Lena*, Lena believes that because she is alive she still has a chance. In *The Island* (in *Statements: Three Plays*, 1974), John and Winston retain their sanity through games, flashbacks to their days of freedom, and the hope that their performance of *Antigone* can be a powerful tool of political expression. Zachariah dreams of being white or of having a relationship with someone white in *The Blood Knot*.

By contrast, Morris is aware of his limitations and has stopped dreaming; Styles only helps dreamers to realize the dreams that he shed when he set up his photography studio, the "house of dreams." The reality of the Immorality Act dawns rudely on Errol and Frieda in *Statements After an Arrest Under the Immorality Act*. In *A Lesson from Aloes*, Piet learns the difference between political idealism and its betrayal when his former friends treat him like a traitor; Steve Daniels, Piet's one hope for understanding, places his family above the political cause and leaves on a one-way exit permit. In a simplistic belief in the conversion from evil to good and the erasure of the past, Johnny and Queeny in *Nongogo* (in *Dimetos and Two Early Plays*, 1977) seek to flee an ugly past. The past follows them like a shadow, however, and their putative attempts at a new beginning are destroyed by the evil schemes of Sam and Patrick.

Fugard conveys the themes of racial politics, the failure of religion, and the discrepancy between illusion and reality through the pain and deprivation of common people. Common people on both sides of the color line are painfully affected by the socioeconomic policies of apartheid. In exploring their lives, Fugard exposes the internal feelings that shape external actions and responses. These people are forced to walk the roads, live in poor areas designated for them, and endure a precarious existence where peace and joy are found only in distant dreams and frozen memories of the past. They adopt false attitudes to survive and prey on their fellows in an endless cycle of pain and violence, as in *Nongogo*, *No-Good Friday*, and *Tsotsi*. Evil is thus perpetuated, and the problems of society are identified as resting in and with the people who alone can bring enduring changes. Fugard thus presents characters whose small efforts are doomed to failure in the face of overwhelming evil. In *No-Good Friday*, Willie is an ordinary man who has decided to confront Shark, the extortionist who has been victimizing the people of his township. The township's white liberal priest has seen no reason to get involved, and the township representative prefers to discuss the issue in the assembly. Willie's friends and neighbors rationalize their victimization and abandon Willie to fight alone. Willie's disappointment leads to resignation, and as he waits for death at Shark's hands, he laments that the world is the way it is, not in spite of but because of weaknesses of individuals in the face of evil and injustice.

Fugard's plays are powerful because he presents himself as an expositor, not a champion. He locates the power for change in the individual and, like an exorcist, requests the cooperation of the victims. Fugard's solution lies in the acceptance of society's collective guilt and in the need for collective action. In portraying common people, he brings the internal and the external together and creates endearing characters who remain deeply etched on our consciences. As Dennis Walder points out in *Athol Fugard*, "Without the coincidence of 'external' and 'internal' in an image, Fugard's plays could not be written. For all the 'external,' even documentary detail of his work, it always demonstrates a deeply personal concern for the fate of the 'ordinary,' anonymous, *little* people with whom he most closely identifies" (p. 5).

LITERARY STYLE:
AN AUDIENCE-CENTERED APPROACH

Fugard's concern for common people in South Africa and his desire to record the moments in their struggle to survive the vicissitudes of life make his work an artistic interpretation and record of the history of his country. His style captures the country's pains and hopes by portraying the lives of individuals, who are the real heirs of history. The subject matter and themes of his work are based on true incidents involving identifiable people in the society. This unique style makes his work relevant to his immediate society, where one would expect it to elicit positive responses. Fugard wastes no time on political propaganda and concentrates instead on the people who are the victims of the system and the subject of his art. According to John Kani and Winston Ntshona, two actors who have collaborated with Fugard, in an interview by Peter Rosenwald: "Athol taught us that we need our art, not propaganda" (Gray, p. 50). For Fugard one incident and a few people are enough to provide insight into the pervading situations of society. So, apart from *No-Good Friday*, which has twelve characters, Fugard's works come alive with as few as two or three people. These characters are usually common people or families whose destinies are tied together by the destructive political system. The families and friends prey on one another, and evil thrives on the weakness of the people.

His concern with people requires Fugard to explore the internal feelings of his characters. He achieves this interiority through flashbacks and long explanatory speeches in which characters struggle to find a purpose and meaning, as in *Boesman and Lena, Statements, Sizwe Bansi Is Dead,* and *The Island.* This self-reflection shapes the characters' dreams and their external actions of fawning, fear, and suspicion. Sets are bare or sparse, and the plays are set in the most unlikely places—where such characters are found in real life. Fugard uses dim and solitary lighting to mirror the poor and shadowy world of his characters, and his extensive, detailed stage directions reveal that his plays are "created to be seen and heard rather than read," as Russell Vandenbroucke has observed (p. 11). Recalling an introductory note to a published extract from *The Blood Knot*, Fugard writes, "this experience belongs to the audience. He is my major concern as a playwright" (introduction to *Statements: Three Plays*). The plays begin at critical points in the lives of the characters and use flashbacks and plays-within-the-play to fill the gaps in their lives and emphasize the hopelessness of their dreams of a better future. This technique results in characters shaped by circumstances that they appear incapable of changing.

The radicalism and revolution inherent to Fugard's work also manifest themselves in the theatrical evolution of the plays through improvisation. They thus build bridges between art and life; for instance, John Kani and Winston Ntshona play themselves in *The Island* and *Sizwe Bansi Is Dead,* where their names and those of the Serpent Players are interwoven into those of the characters. This interplay creates a special relationship between the actors and members of the audience, who see the actors telling their own stories. The shabby settings, scanty props, and contemporary themes are evidence of the influence of Grotowski, Brook, and Brecht on Fugard's theatrical style.

Fugard has also experimented with myth, but he is not very accomplished in this mode. Although he successfully integrates and adapts Sophocles' *Antigone* in *The Island*, his modern interpretation of the classical tale of Clytemnestra and Agamemnon—as the anti-apartheid protest bombing in the Johannesburg station concourse by John Harris in the 1960s—is unsuccessful. Fugard seems more efficient in exploring his own sociopolitical environment for the tools, form, and content of his art.

In resolving conflict in his works, Fugard has sometimes left his audiences confused. His inability to identify political solutions perhaps betrays the weakness of political liberalism, which offers token hope without providing a real and lasting solution to the problems of society. All the great dreams and hopes championed by Fugard's characters end in failure. The failings are of such magnitude that the hapless protagonists and their would-be followers are left with the clear message that goodness and hope have no place in South Africa. In *Tsotsi*, Tsotsi turns from evil to good but is crushed to death by a bulldozer as he attempts to save the life of a child that fate thrusts into his hands. In *Hello and Goodbye*, Hester's searching the past for a reason to desire a noble spirit and worthy life succeeds in unearthing more reasons for continuing her life of debauchery. A similar feeling of emptiness arises when Milly and her lodgers, Don, Shorty, and Sissy, are left at the end of *People Are Living There* still lamenting their lots. On the other side of the racial fence is Piet, the Afrikaner in *A Lesson from Aloes* who throws his weight and convictions on the side of equity, racial accommodation, and the black cause, but loses his economic power, social position, and friends. To resolve this play Fugard saddles Piet with an unstable wife and an aloe crop that yields harsh lessons and warnings rather than hope. In his feature film *Marigolds in August*, Fugard reveals his belief that the time for change and a better society in South Africa has not come. Society, like the marigolds planted early in August during the hot African spring, is bound to be scorched by the heat of hatred and bitterness.

These unedifying resolutions are partially addressed in *My Children! My Africa!* In this play Thami's exile and Isabel's survival after the death of Mr. Myalatya suggest some hope for the future. This hopeful resolution is denied Queeny and Johnny, the victims in *Nongogo*, just as Willie's death in *No-Good Friday* destroys the basis for individual and collective action against evil and oppression.

IMAGES AND SYMBOLS: A MIRROR ON SOCIETY

Fugard enriches his ideas with subtle but effective images and symbols that he draws from the material and spiritual worlds of his characters. The images leave profound and concise impressions on the minds of his audience and readers. From nature come butterflies and moths, aloe and marigolds, and birds. In *A Place with the Pigs*, butterflies symbolize the freedom and fragile hope, the beauty and innocence, that Pavel dreams about and desires. While butterflies are part of the sunrise that Pavel has been waiting for but is unable to capture at the critical moment, moths symbolize for Zach and Morris in *The Blood Knot* the painful, fatal attractions and loss of identity associated with aspiring to pass for white in South African society. Birds symbolize the freedom these two seek from their skin, even as they represent the social dislocation of all nonwhites, as in *Boesman and Lena*. A flower such as aloe symbolizes the tough and enduring qualities that any

peace strategy must possess to survive in South Africa. As the local species of a flower known for its endurance in the velds and impoverished farmlands, the aloe is used by Fugard as a symbol to warn that only an internally derived political solution will survive in the country. Marigolds do not survive the August heat and so must not be planted before September if they are to blossom. Although *Marigolds in August* is centered around the dilemmas and poverty imposed on people by the racial law and the difficulties encountered by an African male growing to manhood in this system, Fugard explores the need for all parties in the South African conflict to be sensitive to the timing of peace initiatives. By using marigolds to show that such a time has not yet come and that the future will be scorched by the fire of bitterness, Fugard indirectly calls for the change of heart needed for any lasting transformation.

Fugard has developed symbols that place the South African situation in a spotlight from which it cannot disappear. These symbols have created images that mirror a life of pain and deprivation. The road that appears so often in his writing is not simply the route that takes Morris to and from his journey of self-discovery and that threatens to expose Zach's precarious dreams, or the paths that Boesman and Lena have walked all their lives with their few belongings on a constant flight from one bulldozed shelter to another. It is not only the hunting ground for Tsotsi and his gang or the path that leads Tobias in *No-Good Friday* to death and causes Sizwe Bansi to destroy his identity and become a ghostly shadow. The road, like the precarious path that Errol walks to make his statement for the crime of bridging the sexual divide between whites and nonwhites, signifies the meaninglessness of life and the checkered existence that apartheid inflicts on its victims. For them the road of life is the road to pain and poverty.

For these victims of apartheid, poverty is a companion, and "house" is a terrifying word and an invitation to the bulldozer. A house for white South Africans symbolizes the stability and racial purity that apartheid champions, but for nonwhites it is a dream and a constant index of their oppression. A bulldozer symbolizes the weight, heartlessness, and monstrous capacity of apartheid to uproot and destroy the lives of its victims. While in other circumstances bulldozers might symbolize development, in South Africa they stand for destruction and the kind of terror that kills Tsotsi and sends Boesman and Lena on another search for a temporary shack. The poverty and sparse stage property that Fugard presents in his works go beyond dramaturgy and theatrical convenience. They symbolize the spiritual poverty of South Africa and the material poverty of its victims. This spiritual malaise and destructive capacity are most prominent in symbolic form in Eugène Marais's self-destruction and addiction to drugs in *The Guest*. A great Afrikaans poet and naturalist, Marais as a human being was potential destroyed by the allure of drugs in the manner that South Africa's potential was nearly destroyed by apartheid.

Fugard often uses shadow and darkness to symbolize the dehumanizing effects of apartheid. In *Hello and Goodbye*, Johnnie lives in the secure shadow of his poor dead father, and in *The Blood Knot*, Morris cannot venture outside the shadowy confines of Zach's life and shack. Shark and Tsotsi operate in the shadows and sleep in the day, while for Errol and Frieda, in *Statements After an Arrest Under the Immorality Act*, light is anathema to their relationship, which they conduct in the surreptitious world of darkness. In *A Place with the Pigs*, Pavel lives in the darkness of the pigsty and flees from light; Helen in *The Road to Mecca* shuts out the light of the outside world as she illuminates her dark rooms. Shadows symbolize unreality, anxiety, and terror, yet these characters find security in them. Fugard's characters are frightened of external light, which only brings more pain

and suffering, and they find reassurance in illusory worlds.

Sizwe Bansi's story reflects this conflicting desire for freedom from a life that can only be lived in the shadows, while it literalizes the idea of an illusory world through its focus on photographs. In *Sizwe Bansi Is Dead*, Styles's photography studio becomes a house of dreams where people can temporarily hold a smile; because such a smile is necessarily transient, it needs to be captured in a photograph. The promise of preserving a smile brings in characters, from young children to grandparents, who dream of that single moment of fulfillment when illusions become reality. As a faithful dreamer, Sizwe poses for a photograph to be sent to his wife. Ironically, the photograph is the symbol of his ghostly existence and the reality of his dream. Similarly, Hester returns home in *Hello and Goodbye* and searches for a photograph to remind her of a beautiful time in her life. She fails, and the emptiness that engulfs her awaits other dreamers, as Styles has discovered. Fugard's use of photographs embodies the dual symbolism of a comforting lie and a dream.

FUGARD'S THEATER: A SMALL CANVAS, MIXED BROAD STROKES

Despite the influence of Brook, Brecht, and Grotowski on his work, Fugard's theater has evolved as a distinct form with unique characteristics. From the production of scripted classics and adaptations as well as from direct involvement in varying capacities in his plays, he has created a theater dictated by his exploration of the many possibilities in the theater to contribute, act, and write within the context of apartheid South Africa. Working and experimenting under unflattering conditions, Fugard passed through a phase of improvisations and collaborative efforts in which the ultimate aim was to integrate the actor, the performance, and the stage. Again recalling his introductory notes to *The Blood Knot*, Fugard explains:

> The ingredients of this experience ... are very simple. ... They are: the actor and the stage, the actor *on* the stage. Around him is space, to be filled and defined by movement and gesture; around him is also silence to be filled with meaning, using words and sounds, and at moments when all else fails him, including the words, the silence itself. ...
>
> In other words the full and unique possibility of this experience needs nothing more than the actor and the stage, the actor in space and silence. Externals, and in a sense even the text can be one, will profit nothing if the actor has no soul.
>
> (introduction to *Statements: Three Plays*)

In Fugard's theater the text is secondary to the actor and the performance. The actors must realize the highly symbolic subtexts wherein lies the essence of his theater. Fugard regards his "completed text as being only a half-way stage to my ultimate objective—the living performance and its particular definition of space and silence" (introduction to *Statements*). Coupled with his experiences and experimentations is his desire to record the lives of the common people, which Styles in *Sizwe Bansi Is Dead* sums up in the following way: "This is a strong-room of dreams. The dreamers? My people. The simple people, who you never find mentioned in the history books, who never get statues erected to them, or monuments commemorating their great deeds. People who would be forgotten, and their dreams with them" (*Statements: Three Plays*, pp. 12–13).

In working with actors during improvisations and rehearsals, in creating roles and characters, Fugard is in a process of exploration and documentation in which he becomes a witness to the emotions and feelings of the common lives expressed in the plays. He points out in *Notebooks*, "My life's work was possibly just to witness as truthfully as I could, the nameless and destitute (desperate)

of this one little corner of the world. This is what could be lost ... those little grey bushes in the shifting sands of the dune" (p. 172).

The hallmarks of Fugard's theater are a small cast, makeshift stage, austere props, and characters drawn mainly from outcasts and the impoverished. His plots are simple and present family or social relationships that reflect the tensions and sociopolitical cleavages of life in apartheid South Africa. As Dennis Walder has pointed out: "It is his great strength to move us deeply by showing the plight of ordinary people caught up in the meshes of social, political, racial and even religious forces which they are unable to understand or control. It is his weakness that he cannot reflect upon or analyse these forces himself" (1984, p. 3).

Fugard brings an audience face-to-face with itself through the intense and passionate sharing of the characters' experiences. His theater probes beneath the surface to unearth complex relationships between the individual and society and the influence each has on the other. His theater thus avoids glib generalizations, propaganda, and the application of strokes in only black and white. He prescribes no solutions, and in his characters and resolutions the external and internal merge. His theater is a small canvas with mixed broad strokes. His style is to peer through the microscope for intimate details that comment on larger issues.

POSTAPARTHEID RESPONSE: STIRRING HOPE IN THE VALLEY

The end of apartheid in 1993 did not end Fugard's fascination with his society. In an interview with Heather Neill before the London premiere of *The Valley Song*, Fugard said, "Now we have to find a new motor to drive us" ("Fugard Returns to Face the New South Africa," [London] *Times*, 30 January 1996, p. 37). This impetus and response were tentatively initiated in *My Children! My Africa!*, a work that, in retrospect, prophesied the political dialogues that led to the collapse of apartheid. *Valley Song* (1996) extends the dialogue to the postapartheid era as Fugard returns to his familiar style of peeping into individual circumstances and to his usual subjects, the common victims of society. Set on the dawn of peace in the semidesert Karoo region of central South Africa, the play explores the reactions of three former victims of apartheid, two of whom now stand to benefit most from its collapse: the Colored tenant farmer Abraam Jonkers (Buks) and his seventeen-year-old granddaughter, Veronica. Abraam is afraid of hoping for too much too soon and of leaving and losing his farm and house, which he clings to as his only tangible reality. Veronica desires a move to Johannesburg to seek musical stardom. They approach postapartheid South Africa differently: Abraam with trepidation, Veronica with radiant optimism.

The third major character is "the Author," who comments on the play to the audience as the play goes along. Yet the Author also plays a part in the plot: he turns out to be the white man who is thinking about buying the land on which Abraam lives. (In the play's initial productions in Johannesburg, New York, and London, Fugard appeared as both the Author and Abraam. He also directed all three productions.)

In *Valley Song,* Fugard again presents a small and closely knit family unit and plays on the family members' conflicting desires and responses to one event. Abraam's cautious optimism, borne out by the impact of past atrocities, cannot dampen the hopes of the young woman and others who joyously reach out to the future. In the gentle and warm dialogue, the necessary dislocations that the new South Africa presages are articulated amid a background of trepid caution and unmitigated hope. The play explores both options and presents them as legitimate concerns that must be addressed by all South Africans. The past robbed the people of so

much hope that Abraam finds it difficult to be brave about a change involving a lot of letting go. The past, with some of its structures and systems still in place, is not finished yet. Fugard recognizes the problems of a transition from fear and bondage to freedom; in the Neill interview he describes the play as a "transitional piece." The huge task involved in the transition is what Buks fears and precisely the reason Veronica wants to waste no time in leaving the famished past and valley behind.

Valley Song is Fugard's most optimistic statement on South Africa. While he, like Abraam, is almost too afraid to join in the euphoria, the play—whose title suggests both the hopeful ring of a happy ending and the necessary travail in walking up a valley to reach the mountaintop—does point to a better future.

CONCLUSION

Fugard is South Africa's foremost playwright writing in English, and his works constitute the most significant theater to come out of South Africa. Determined to live and work in South Africa when other artists chose exile or were imprisoned, Fugard is one of the few white South African artists to collaborate successfully with black compatriots.

In his pre-1990 plays, Fugard shies away from overt political discussion of his society and fails to present the advantaged sector of apartheid with the same passion that informs his portrayal of common suffering people. The surrender or feeble opposition of his characters to the sociopolitical situation in South Africa is unedifying. The white dissenting voice is an ineffectual whisper among the few liberals in his writings, and other whites are silent stereotypes. Apartheid remains faceless and acts only through its anonymous surrogates and victims. Not until *My Children! My Africa!* did Fugard actively engage with a fully developed political dialogue.

Fugard's strength lies in his convincing portrayal of characters and events and in his deep probe beneath the surface to explain the pain and anguish caused by racism. He presents his society's historical episodes with an artistic focus that sharpens his ideas and endears his characters to an audience. The endurance and patience of characters such as Willie, Johnny, Myalatya, Thami, Isabel, and Miss Helen are refreshing and hopeful signs for society, and the future for Veronica is more hopeful than ever. Through his writings, Fugard makes a powerful indictment of apartheid. His works detail the plight of the people and society he respects and loves; if his aim was to let the world hear their anguished cries, he has succeeded. Fugard's work is an enduring legacy in both South African and world theater and has confirmed the possibility of a shared artistic and social heritage for the peoples of South Africa.

Selected Bibliography

BIBLIOGRAPHY

Read, John, comp. *Athol Fugard: A Bibliography.* Grahamstown, South Africa: National English Literary Museum, 1991.

SELECTED WORKS

Hello and Goodbye. Cape Town, South Africa: Gothic, 1966. Play.
Statements: Three Plays. With John Kani and Winston Ntshona. London: Oxford University Press, 1974. Includes *Sizwe Bansi Is Dead, The Island,* and *Statements After an Arrest Under the Immorality Act.*
Three Port Elizabeth Plays. London: Oxford University Press, 1974. Includes *The Blood Knot, Hello and Goodbye,* and *Boesman and Lena.*
Dimetos and Two Early Plays. Oxford, U.K.: Oxford University Press, 1977. Includes *No-Good Friday* and *Nongogo.*
The Guest: An Episode in the Life of Eugène Marais. Johannesburg, South Africa: Donker, 1978. Screenplay.
Orestes. In Stephen Gray, ed., *Theater One: New South African Drama.* Johannesburg, South Africa: Donker, 1978. Play.

Boesman and Lena and Other Plays. Cape Town, South Africa: Oxford University Press, 1980. Includes *The Blood Knot, People Are Living Here,* and *Hello and Goodbye.*
Tsotsi. London: Collings, 1980. Novel.
A Lesson from Aloes: A Play. Oxford, U.K.: Oxford University Press, 1981.
Marigolds in August. With Ross Devenish. Johannesburg, South Africa: Donker, 1982. Screenplay.
"Master Harold" ... and the Boys. Oxford, U.K.: Oxford University Press, 1983. Play.
Notebooks 1960–1977. Ed. by Mary Benson. London: Faber and Faber, 1983. Autobiography.
The Road to Mecca. London: Faber and Faber, 1985; New York: Theatre Communications Group, 1988. Play.
A Place with the Pigs. London: Faber and Faber, 1988. Play.
My Children! My Africa! London: Faber, 1990. Play.
Selected Shorter Plays. Johannesburg, South Africa: Witwatersrand University Press, 1990. Includes *The Coat, Orestes, The Drummer, The Occupation,* and *Mille Miglia.*
Valley Song. New York: Theatre Communications Group, 1996. Play.

ARTICLE

"Afrikaner Humanist." In *The Observer* (18 July 1971). Repr. in Stephen Gray, comp., *File on Fugard.* London: Methuen Drama, 1991.

CRITICAL STUDIES

Gray, Stephen, ed. *File on Fugard.* London: Methuen Drama, 1991.
Henry, William A. Profile on Fugard. *Time* (7 August 1989).
Mitchell, Julian. "Athol Fugard in London." In *African Literature Today* 8 (1976).
Pieterse, Cosmo, and Donald Munroe, eds. *Protest and Conflict in African Literature.* London: Heinemann Educational, 1969.
Vandenbroucke, Russell. *Truths the Hand Can Touch: The Theater of Athol Fugard.* Craighall, South Africa: Ad. Donker, 1986.
Walder, Dennis. "Athol Fugard's *Sizwe Bansi Is Dead.*" In *The Varied Scene: Aspects of Drama Today.* Milton Keynes, U.K.: Open University Press, 1977.
———. *Athol Fugard.* London: Macmillan, 1984.

Nadine Gordimer
1923–

SONYA RUDIKOFF

NADINE GORDIMER is a white African writer, but she is as much a daughter of Africa as the black and Colored (that is, of mixed-race origins) African writers and artists who are well known in the west: Zoë Wicomb, Ellen Kuzwayo, Miriam Tlali, Bessie Head, and Noni Jabavu. Born in the town of Springs, near Johannesburg, in South Africa on 20 November 1923 to a Lithuanian father and an English mother, she has lived in South Africa all her life. She has traveled widely in Africa, Europe, and the United States, but has never gone into exile or really left the country of her birth.

The recipient of the 1991 Nobel Prize for literature, Gordimer is representative of her country and its literature, and she is international in her appeal and significance, speaking beyond the limits of origins. Her subjects are South African, but she writes in the language of her times and with a consciousness of social and intellectual life in the world community. Her novels, short stories, and essays have been translated into twenty-five languages. She is also known for her social and political activism on behalf of black liberation and a multiracial society. For many readers she stands as the conscience of her country.

CONTEXT: SOUTH AFRICAN HISTORY

To see Gordimer as a daughter of Africa requires some knowledge about the white settlers who held power in Africa for nearly four hundred years and about the black tribes surrounding them. Throughout most of the twentieth century, in one African country after another, the legal and moral base of white minority rule was under attack, and movements for independence spread over the continent. But South Africa was different from the rest.

Unlike French, Portuguese, and British colonies in the rest of Africa, the four southernmost states became provinces in a republic that was ruled by the prominent white minority of Afrikaners, who are descendants of the sixteenth- and seventeenth-century Dutch pioneers. Also unlike the settlers of other African lands, the Dutch, Huguenots, and British in South Africa were not the agents or representatives of a home country. The Afrikaners considered themselves natives of South Africa and tried to cast off British rule in the South African War, also known as the Boer War, of 1899–1902. They were the supposedly heroic and symbolic *Voortrekkers* (those who

277

travel ahead), who sought biblical justification for their hegemony. Although they lost the war, they were granted self-government shortly afterward. Others came to this land, including Indians, other Asians, Germans, and Lithuanian Jews, making South Africa a land of immigrants mixed with the native black tribes. But the Dutch—who had settled in South Africa to flee religious persecution—had established their small theocracy and were not hospitable to those who came after them. Even among the miners and adventurers in the early settlements, there were divisive designations of *Uitlanders*, or foreigners, and restrictions on citizenship and voting.

South Africa is a society of many races and languages, but its dominant culture was not always shared by all, nor were all citizens entitled to it. Under apartheid, which was instituted in 1948 when the Afrikaner National Party won the general election, blacks were excluded from much of the culture and furnished only with that small part of it that the rulers thought suitable for them. The Bantu Education Act of 1953 officially restricted education for black South Africans to only that which would prepare them for certain forms of labor. The late-arriving English settlers brought their own language, but Afrikaans, which developed from seventeenth-century Dutch, was the founding and official language. Although its native speakers cherish its delicate and vivid expression, it is a dying language, no longer supported by young Afrikaners. To black South Africans, Afrikaans, which was forced upon them, was the language of their oppression. In Gordimer's work, English predominates, but Afrikaans is used also for narrative effect.

LITERARY CAREER AND
THE POLITICS OF APARTHEID

A knowledge of this history is important in understanding Gordimer because her work is so infused with the situation of her country. At the beginning of her career, she might have seemed a descendant of the European and English modernist tradition, showing the influence of E. M. Forster, Marcel Proust, James Joyce, and Virginia Woolf. But her first novel, *The Lying Days* (1953), even with its title's echo of William Butler Yeats's poem "The Coming of Wisdom with Time," is not just a bildungsroman (a novel that traces the moral and psychological development of the main characters and that belongs to a genre pioneered by German writers of the late eighteenth century). Her subject matter in this novel is not only aesthetic, personal, and developmental; racial, Jewish, social, and political issues are also powerfully present. When the white heroine goes to Europe, she makes the classic journey of young white South Africans seeking identity, but her journey is different from that of young English or American women on a similar quest. Although Gordimer's writing has international appeal and she can be read as a citizen of the world without the South African context, she never writes as if she were other than a white African of a particular time and place.

As of the mid 1990s Gordimer had published fourteen collections of short stories and eleven novels, as well as other prose works. The tone and subject matter set by her early work continued to characterize her creative effort. Imaginatively, she looked at the situation of her country from all sides and wrote of blacks, whites, Coloreds, English, and Afrikaners, and less frequently of Jews. Urban and rural settings attracted her, as did the lives of those living a banned or underground existence and the lives of politically active and politically naive people. She did not explicitly write political fiction and instead insisted that human life is her subject. But in her South African settings, political crises reveal the human life that interested her.

As a native-born South African, Gordimer elected to stay in a country ruled by a single political party, whose policies violated all her beliefs and feelings, and she experienced the consequences of that choice. Several of her books were banned, and she was closely watched by the police but never imprisoned or silenced. She wrote movingly of the inhibiting force of the South African regime's surveillance of writers and artists, notably in her 1963 essay "Censored, Banned, Gagged," which is reprinted in her collection of essays *The Essential Gesture: Writing, Politics, and Places* (1988). A lifelong interest in politics led Gordimer through modifications of an essentially liberal and leftist position. When the Black Consciousness movement rejected the involvement of whites, she registered her reaction in the essay "Where Do Whites Fit In?" which was originally published in 1959 and appears in *The Essential Gesture*.

Successive phases of Gordimer's beliefs can be seen in her fiction from Toby Hood's friendships with blacks and whites in *A World of Strangers* (1958), which was banned in South Africa for twelve years after publication, to *My Son's Story* (1990), with its complex mingling of the sexual and political as the prohibitions of apartheid change and disappear. In the fiction she wrote between these two novels, she explores the relations of whites to the world of the black townships and of the blacks to the white world with imaginative perceptions of compelling interest.

There is no aspect of the complicated life of black and white South Africans that Gordimer has not touched during her writing career. In *A Guest of Honour* (1970), a retired British civil servant returns to the African country where he had been an adviser before independence. *The Conservationist* (1974) recreates the world of an Afrikaner whose ties to his personal history and whose shared responsibility for the Afrikaner world and its denials and deceptions lead to tragedy. *Burger's Daughter* (1979) presents the world of mixed Afrikaner and radical heritage in which the young woman of the title grows up. Rosa Burger's involvement in real historical events and her effort to define her identity under this weighty responsibility are the subject of the novel. *A Sport of Nature* (1987) traces a young white woman's emotional and sexual relations with blacks against a background of political events in Africa, Europe, and the United States, and ends with the young woman as consort to the new black dictator. *My Son's Story* presents the intricacies of life for sophisticated whites and blacks involved in underground movements, including political betrayal and self-betrayal in a family.

LIFE

What is especially interesting about Gordimer's work is the complexity and density she evokes, despite having lived all her life in or around Johannesburg in privileged circumstances. Born in the small mining town of Springs in the Reef, a ridge of land southeast of Johannesburg known for its gold deposits, Gordimer attended a convent school and spent a brief period at the University of the Witwatersrand in Johannesburg. She married twice and had a child in each marriage. She lived the comfortable life of the white suburbs, which was buttressed by black servants and supported by an impoverished, disempowered black population. Although her fiction grows out of her deeply felt experience, it is not autobiographical, even—or especially—when the story is told in the first person.

Gordimer was born not in the city, or in the romantic countryside, at Cape Town, or within sight of Table Mountain, or along the Durban coast. Springs was a dreary and uncultured mining town in the Transvaal with an unlovely landscape of "gold" mountains—the mine dumps—in a small settlement, where some white families administered the mine and others served the commercial needs of miners. Gordimer's father, Isidore Gordimer, a watchmaker, owned a jewelry shop. He had come to South Africa as a boy from Lithuania, to escape the pogroms that threatened Jews living there and to make his fortune. Her mother, Nan Myers Gordimer, was Jewish also, but of English lineage. She had a sister and relatives in the Orange Free State, but Nadine felt alienated from this family and soon began to live her life away from them, at first in her fantasy life and later moving away. Many of her early stories were about Jews and Jewish families, but this theme disappeared from her fiction as the racial divisions of South African society became more prominent. This theme returns, however, in the character of Hillela in *A Sport of Nature*, who is named for a Lithuanian rabbinical grandfather.

If Gordimer uses other aspects of her life in her fiction, she has modulated them in order to avoid direct identification. In 1954, as a young divorced woman with a child, she married Reinhold Cassirer, a German Jew of the culturally influential—and wealthy—Cassirer family, with its many branches in various European cities and its many notable and gifted members. With the advent of Hitlerism, many of the Cassirers emigrated to Holland, Sweden, the United States, and England. Reinhold Cassirer became an art dealer and later the South African representative of Sotheby's art and auction house, which opened in Johannesburg in 1969. Gordimer and her husband live in Parktown, one of the comfortable older suburbs of Johannesburg.

SOURCES OF FICTION

Nothing comparable to the treasure trove of material that D. H. Lawrence found in his wife, Frieda von Richthofen Weekley, and her exotic German baronial family occurs in Gordimer's fiction. No family like the Cassirers appears directly in any of her novels or stories. Nor are its members—among them the

philosopher Ernst Cassirer, the art dealers and publishers Bruno and Paul Cassirer, and the neurologist Richard Cassirer—used explicitly as models for Gordimer's characters, although people in many of her fictions work in publishing, medicine, or art. Like Lawrence, she could well have been affected imaginatively by an alliance with a family so different from her own—larger, powerful, wealthy, intellectual, and creative. The Cassirers represented a lost European tradition of culture, professional knowledge, and innovation and sponsored important aesthetic movements of their time, such as the "Berlin secession" in the early twentieth century. It is fitting, therefore, that Reinhold Cassirer headed the South African office of Sotheby's, the international auction house for antiques, fine art, and objets d'art. Nothing could better express the European heritage that shadowed South Africa but was also remote from it.

Immigrants, like Gordimer's parents, came to South Africa before the Boer War and built the country. They were followed by refugees from Europe, like the Cassirers, who fled from the turmoil of the Old World and sought the sanctuary of a rich, modern country with a beautiful landscape. Perhaps a slight echo of a social group such as the Cassirers can be found in the Van Den Sandts in *The Late Bourgeois World* (1966), who have a mixed French, Belgian, and Afrikaner heritage, lead the large busy life of a powerful political family, and create a whole world in their comfortable house in the country. There is also perhaps another echo in *A World of Strangers*, when Toby Hood, the young man from a large family involved in publishing, is sent to South Africa from England to represent his family's firm. A few refugees can also be found in *Occasion for Loving* (1963), where Jessie Stilwell's stepfather is European; *A Guest of Honour*, where a character recalls his youth in Germany; "Town and Country Lovers: One," which features an Austrian geologist (in *A Soldier's Embrace*, 1980); and "Home," which features a Swedish ichthyologist (in *Jump*, 1991).

Of course, a writer's experiences can have different and even contradictory effects on the imagination. Toby Hood distances himself from the ideas and habits, and the social concerns and aesthetic passions, of his English upper-middle-class educated milieu and finds in South Africa not a family but separate groups of black and white friends, a "world of strangers." In *The Late Bourgeois World*, a deftly imagined representation of the decay of bourgeois life, the Van Den Sandt's son, Max, is not able to come into his legacy, is alienated from his family and wants to destroy them, but ends by destroying himself.

Gordimer has spoken of her childhood as culturally meager. Springs was limited and impoverished, and she wanted to escape. So she went to Johannesburg, where she met writers, artists, medical students, revolutionaries, Jews who were unlike her own family, black intellectuals, and white women unlike her mother and sister; in other words, she found a lively cosmopolitan atmosphere. This escape from the world of her childhood can be seen in the different experiences used in her fiction. Although several early stories are concerned with the mine location—the stores there, the owners, and their families—Gordimer's later work did not look back to that childhood world with nostalgia, and it seems to disappear from her consciousness. It is the other world that has superseded it, the world of her young womanhood that followed upon her move to Johannesburg. Such material and experiences are obviously processed by the writer's imagination in complicated ways largely inaccessible to critical scrutiny.

Gordimer's marriage to a refugee from Germany may have strengthened her South African identity as a native-born daughter of the beautiful and tortured land. When the political situation began to deteriorate after the ascendancy of the Afrikaner National Party in 1948 and after the South African revolution began in 1960, perhaps Gordimer became *less* willing to leave the country of her birth. One senses in her an indomitable refusal to be silenced or exiled, as the German Jews were, or to be deprived of her heritage or destroyed, either by horrors performed in the name of the white minority or by fleeing to secure her own safety, leaving the horrors for others.

LITERARY MILIEU

Gordimer once thought of emigrating to Zambia, but there she would have simply felt like a European, which she was not, and the prospect of this emotional as well as geographical displacement did not suit her. Although in her essays she ranges through the literatures of various European countries, citing Jean-Paul Sartre, Anton Chekhov, Roland Barthes, Albert Camus, Bertolt Brecht, Virginia Woolf, and Günter Grass as if she were a European writer too, she remains a white African and feels a special kinship with fellow African writers, black and white, who share in the life of that continent and share a concern for its future. Her position was necessarily different from that of the black writers for the South African journal *Drum*, which seemed to her so advanced and exciting when she first came to know its writers, and the later journal, *Staffrider* (see Bazin, pp. 249–251). She was associated with both journals and with every effort of the Congress of South African Writers and other groups that sponsored the creative work of black writers and artists.

The South African literary environment is important to Gordimer's own history. *Drum* was a publication of the 1950s; *Staffrider*—whose name refers to black riders on trains going into Johannesburg, hanging from doors and windows because the trains were so full—was founded in 1978 in response to the Soweto revolt and was still being published in the late twentieth century. The increased number of publishing houses, writers' groups, journals, critical essays, conferences, and public literary occasions developed a complex literary world in South Africa since Gordimer first began to write. Plays, poetry, and fiction were produced for new audiences; there were new kinds of dramatic and musical groups and a sense of creative ferment among blacks finding a new voice. Gordimer's work must be understood within this context.

Es'kia Mphahlele was Gordimer's first black friend when she was a young writer; later she met Nathaniel Nakasa, Can Themba, and other black and Colored writers. She was energetic in disseminating awareness of writers ranging from Sol T. Plaatje to Herbert I. E. Dhlomo to Lewis Nkosi, and writers in exile, such as Alex La Guma and Mandla Langa. Like Njabulo Ndebele, she addressed the questions of a new South African literature in a liberated society and of the languages that might emerge. Like Mbulelo Mzamane, who wrote an essay for *Staffrider* entitled "Cultivating a People's Voice in the Criticism of South African Literature," a review of a book on black South African unity (in vol. 9, no. 3, 1991), she probed with great sensitivity the question of a people's literature and a people's voice, particularly in her essay "Who Writes? Who Reads? The Concept of a People's Literature." Beginning in the mid 1980s, *Staffrider* provided a forum for the discussion of these issues, and Gordimer was an active participant. As a white South African, she was not subject to the same constraints as her black sisters and brothers. Not only was a more privileged life her lot, but an easier access to the gifts of culture and a warmer welcome from the publishing community as she entered literary life. Unlike her fellow writers on *Staffrider*, she did not experience deprivation, neglect, oppression, the harsh poverty of the townships, and limited possibilities. The privileges of this position brought her criticism and hostility as well as solidarity.

Gordimer stated her convictions about the social and human costs of apartheid in essays, statements, and responses to questions asked of her at lectures and readings. After the institution of apartheid and as one brutal measure succeeded another, it was remarkable that Gordimer was not silenced. Others went into exile, or were forced into it. She was invited abroad for professional purposes and permitted to speak, write, and publish (except for several instances of banning). She was able to travel abroad and return, unlike some writers, such as Breyten Breytenbach, who were given exit visas with no possibility of returning. She was not arrested for her activities, held without charges, or brutalized by interrogation, like so many of her fellow South Africans. The freedom granted her seemed a hypocritical effort by the apartheid regime to display its liberality. Gordimer, not deceived, made the most of her liberty to speak and travel and never withheld her criticism and plain speaking.

ISSUES OF SEXUALITY

As a white African, Gordimer has been especially conscious of the writer's public responsibility and of the moral issue of apartheid. She makes no special claim as a *woman* among writers and does not express identification with feminism as a political movement. According to her, the life of almost any white woman, despite the rigid patriarchy of Afrikaner culture, must be counted a privileged one compared with the indignities that all black women have suffered simply because of their color. Feminism in a country that has prevented the overwhelming majority of its people from finding even minimal self-realization because of their color is almost a distraction. Helen Suzman, for example, as an opposition member of the South African parliament for thirty-six years, was subjected to the most vicious antifeminist and sexist attacks by her Afrikaner colleagues in parliament, but she always responded politically, interpreting such attacks as directed at her liberal views, not her gender (see Suzman's *In No Uncertain Terms*, 1993). Had she responded to the antifeminism exclusively, the racist views of Suzman's political foes would have escaped censure.

So the explicit consciousness of gender in South Africa perhaps seemed an indulgence in a society that thrived and survived because of its institutionalization of racial difference. When the great majority of South Africans had no vote, voice, or freedom to enter the universities or compete for society's rewards, it seemed premature to isolate the disempowerment of women. Gordimer makes no effort to use gender-neutral pronouns or other locutions of nonsexist language that have become standard. Also, it is striking that she so rarely refers to women as writers. Yet, although Gordimer's apparent indifference to feminism as a political movement can be accounted for in this way, she is imaginatively sensitive to the consciousness of gender as it reveals itself in her characters.

Thus, both Maureen Smales in *July's People* (1981) and Elizabeth in *The Late Bourgeois World* feel their sexuality linked to the political situation. The women who write to political prisoners or take as lovers the underground people who stray into their comfortable lives, as in "Safe Houses" (in *Jump*), express their sexuality as an aspect of their politics. Foreign settings, which serve as contrasts to the South African political situation, are often used for this purpose, as when Rosa Burger goes to France, Hillela and her first husband go to Lusaka, in Zambia, or Hillela's sexual adventures take her to other African countries and the United States. A subtle sensitivity to the sexual dimensions of social and political life characterizes Gordimer's conception of her female characters.

On the other hand, Gordimer's skill in creating male characters, whether they are black or white, is also quite remarkable. She has a gift for empathically portraying these characters—who often occupy the central position in her short stories and novels—from within their own consciousness, and their sexual and emotional imagination is stressed, as in "Safe Houses" and "Keeping Fit" (also in *Jump*). In *My Son's Story*, as another example, Gordimer probes the inwardness and sexual consciousness of a father and son and captures the complexities of their lives. Her range of male characters is wide, including an unusual and startling choice—given her political views—of an Afrikaner farmer named Mehring, a middle-aged, intelligent, capable man, for the protagonist of *The Conservationist*.

At the same time, Gordimer's treatment of the sexuality of her female characters is equally varied. Elizabeth, in *The Late Bourgeois World*, thinks of her sexual life with her doomed young husband, Max, and later with her sober grown-up lover, Graham, in a different way from the adventurous Hillela of *A Sport of Nature* or Rosa of *Burger's Daughter*, who is burdened by history.

Sexuality is an aspect of the self, but Gordimer is not always dealing with the same self. Sexuality, like the politics with which it is intertwined, is seen freshly and individually in each character.

IMAGINATION, NOT PROPAGANDA

Gordimer uses figurative examples with an immediacy and vividness that vary from one novel to the next. Her imaginative devices for telling a story are unusual and unpredictable. Her material is necessarily political and often reflects the details of facts, conditions, and events in South Africa, known to its inhabitants intimately and often tragically. For example, the Sharpeville riots of 1960; conditions created by the pass laws, the Group Areas Act of 1950, the Terrorism Act of 1967; consequences of the defiance campaign (when Indian, African, and other leaders banded together in 1952 against the unjust laws of the white authorities); the banning of the African National Congress in 1960; the Black Consciousness movement; and the Soweto riots of 1976–1977 have all found their way into Gordimer's fiction in different forms. But she works as an imaginative writer who invents and proposes imaginary situations with believable persons, compelling issues, and palpable dangers in them.

Gordimer's refusal to write propaganda is clear from her numerous statements on the subject, her concern with the effect of political orthodoxy on literary expression, and her creation of characters in their ambiguous actions. Particularly in her portrayals of black characters, Gordimer avoids resorting to propaganda and instead describes the wide range of responses they have to complex situations. Some of these characters are highly verbal and elusive, like Luke Fokase in *The Late Bourgeois World*, Steven Sitole in *A World of Strangers*, or Steven's very different, more stolid friend, the musician Sam Mofokenzazi. Some are more remote, such as the black characters in the short stories and *July's People*. Others overtly reject the stereotypical image of blacks inherent to political propaganda, such as the young black wife who betrays her husband's revolutionary friends in "'A City of the Dead, a City of the Living'" (in *Crimes of Conscience*, 1991).

The political positions that Gordimer takes in her public life, essays, and statements are not to be equated with fictional presentations, which often seem to contradict her public stance. Indeed, the vivid and often beautiful re-creation of Afrikaners in *The Conservationist* surely comes out of imaginative freedom, even if their love of the land ignores the costs of that love to themselves and others. The love of the land is genuine but can lead to terrible consequences, which are reinforced with the image of the dead black man found on the Afrikaner's land and finally buried there as if to suggest that it is *his* home and not the home of the temporary Afrikaner occupant.

In *Conversations with Nadine Gordimer* (1990), a collection of interviews edited by Nancy Topping Bazin and Marilyn Dallman Seymour, Gordimer makes distinctions between her obligations as a citizen and the demands of her writer's conscience. The position is a difficult one: the writer must separate her ambiguous, ironic, and complex imagination from her political and social beliefs.

She invents fictive people and situations that go beneath politics to uncover human experience in the form of insoluble problems, desires that cannot be realized, implacable forces of body or spirit, and crises that cannot be resolved. The political activist looks for opportunities, policies, remedial action, control, or confrontation; the writer's powers of observation present these moments differently, and perhaps less optimistically. This contrast between art and politics has absorbed Gordimer in all her essays and interviews concerned with how fiction is written, especially those collected in *Writing and Being* (1995).

Gordimer never wavered in her commitment to black liberation and a multiracial society, but her portrayals of black revolutionaries and white terrorists are not always what might be expected. In *A Sport of Nature* and *July's People*, for example, the future is not hopeful: the violent disruption and destruction that the future brings are inevitable, even if these consequences can be attributed to the events that precipitated them. Gordimer frequently said that no statement she makes about politics will be as true as what she has said in a story or novel. This recalls D. H. Lawrence's advice to trust the tale, not the teller of the tale. It suggests that the writer's imaginative sense of the complexity and ambiguity of life and of human conflict may grasp something that eludes his or her political opinions.

In her collection of essays *The Essential Gesture*, Gordimer clarifies and refines these views, especially in the title essay, which identifies the writer's responsibility toward society. Borrowing a phrase from Barthes, she asserts that "a writer's 'enterprise'—his work—is his essential gesture as a social being'" (p. 286). She elaborates on this idea in observations on the historical and social nature of language: "Created in the common lot of language, that 'essential gesture is individual" (p. 286). It may be this individuality of gesture that accounts for the varying ways the writer acknowledges and expresses responsibility. This "essential gesture" takes many forms, from Camus's view of the need for a writer to be "more than a writer," to the demands writers feel from within and without: the responsibility for social activism, the synthesis of social responsibility and creativity, and the seeming divorce from social responsibility represented by purely aesthetic or formal "essential gestures."

Gordimer takes special note of the demand to be "more than a writer," the urgency to write politically, so often felt by black African writers; it is not an urgency imposed on whites. Some black writers among her friends, she says, willingly accept "a kit of emotive phrases, an unwritten index of subjects, a typology" ("Living in the Interregnum" p. 276). Black writers will assent to a definition of their work and mission that is unacceptable to her, despite her awareness of the conditions of black existence. White writers, necessarily standing to one side of the black struggle for self-definition, may not respond to the blacks' imperative. A white writer like Gordimer may feel that this highly politicized black writing is a kind of agitprop, but she acknowledges that these writers may be the first and only true historians of their culture (p. 276).

The historical situation in South Africa cannot be ignored or even temporarily forgotten; it is deep within every life. Gordimer deftly distinguishes this consciousness from the seeming indifference or remoteness of aestheticism, the effort to transform the world by style, which is in its way a response to social demand. There remains the writer's essential gesture, the lifting out of a limited category something that reveals its full meaning and significance only when the writer's imagination has expanded it. In this expansion and elaboration, there is no black or white, there is only fidelity to experience and perception. "So conceived, the white writer's responsibility is as solemn as that of the black writer," she concludes, in *Essential Gestures*, in affirmation of the value of the white writer's imaginative position.

APARTHEID AS SUBJECT

The years after 1948, when the Afrikaner National Party enforced apartheid through terrorism and deprivation of rights, saw Gordimer's major development and maturity as a writer. Apartheid has been her main subject throughout her career. She explored not merely its cruelty and dehumanizing effects on blacks, but also the costs of that cruelty and dehumanizing for the whites who superficially benefited from it by law. She also examined the corrosive effects of apartheid even on those who opposed it, such as white liberals, who dedicated themselves to destroying it, the white revolutionaries, who gave their lives to this mission and were destroyed by the brutality engendered in their struggle against brutality. Apartheid has provided so much material for her fiction that the stories trace the variations in historical attitudes accompanying the changing features of state terrorism.

The Group Areas Act, the Immorality Act, and other laws that governed the social behavior of blacks and whites shaped emotional and sexual relations. Particularly in her short stories, Gordimer explores the ramifications of these laws for black couples who are unable to live together in the city: for interracial couples, when the black partner fears being caught in the apartment of the white lover in "Town and Country Lovers: One"; for the relationships between young Afrikaner farmers and black girls and young women on the farm, which may result in the birth of mixed-race children, in "Country Lovers" (in *Crimes of Conscience*) and "The Moment Before the Gun Went Off" (in *Jump*).

In *A World of Strangers*, the difficulty of blacks and whites meeting for lunch in Johannesburg because of the racial prohibitions is not merely part of the action but is itself the action. This vivid image of the lived situations engendered by the color bar is expressed in another story with its compelling title, "Is There Nowhere Else We Can Meet?" (in *Face to Face*, 1949). The determination of the state authorities to hunt down and entrap political dissidents is depicted in numerous stories about living a nomadic existence underground, such as "Safe Houses." In "A Correspondence Course" (in *Something Out There*, 1984), a young woman begins writing to a political prisoner. As a consequence of racial policies, a whole village is forced into a long trek in the story entitled, with bleak irony, "The Ultimate Safari" (in *Crimes of Conscience*), which is narrated by a child.

NARRATIVE TECHNIQUE

Gordimer's stories may be narrated in several voices or from the point of view of someone not directly involved in the action. They may begin at the end or middle of a situation. Stories sometimes unfold or open out from an indirect perspective, which gives a sense of distance to her writing, a quality that has been often described as cold, because she does not portray heroic figures as unblemished and untouched characters who command intense identification. This is especially true of stories about new African countries, where the government is often a shambles, the revolution needs to be stabilized, and those who made the revolution may not be the ones best able to make a nation. This situation characterizes "A Soldier's Embrace" (in *A Soldier's Embrace*) and "At the Rendezvous of Victory" (in *Something Out There*), and occupies much of the novel *A Guest of Honour*. The young heroine of *A Sport of Nature*, Hillela, who is adventurous and picaresque yet singularly unreflective, lacks a compelling nobility in behavior and ideals. Sometimes a story is presented, often confusedly, from several perspectives, as in "A Journey" (in *Jump*), in which a woman with small children returns to her husband in an unnamed African country that is just recovering from its revolution.

Gordimer uses interior monologue frequently and a style of slightly ironic narration, as in "Spoils" (in *Jump*) and "A Hunting Accident" (in *Soldier's Embrace*), where privileged whites go to country lodges to shoot zebras, lions, elands, and other animals. In the shooting parties in "A Hunting Accident," a photographer's interest in photographing the animals is compared to the interests of the hunters, of the African who takes some fresh zebra meat for his family, and of the buzzards and other scavengers. The photographer's "shooting" is more civilized and cultured, but just as predatory because he methodically photographs a dying animal that is gurgling blood, while the hunters look away, then leaves the scene when his aesthetic pursuits are completed, indifferent to the fate of his subject matter. The even more distant narrator of "Once Upon a Time" (in *Jump*) tells of a young mother, father, and boy living in their beautiful suburban house with its protective steel gate. However, the intricate and lethal steel razor wire, which is supposed to protect them against intruders, does not protect their son when he gets caught in it.

In all these stories, incidents and their details prefigure or represent the story itself, and no details are gratuitous. These incidents are not artificially symbolic and do not stand for experiences to which they are abstractly related, but their concentration of meaning links the narrative with its larger significance. Moreover, whether the characters are Afrikaner farmers, urban whites, or black Africans, each is individually conceived as well as being representative of a class or racial group; and each character's fate, like each story's situation, is equally specific, personal, and imagined. For example, in *The Conservationist* the body of the black man found on Mehring's land is at the end buried on the land and in a profound sense is the land's true owner. The histories of characters such as Mehring are developed through incidents at critical moments in their lives. It is Gordimer's great gift to present each of these characters "with an equivalent centre of self," to borrow George Eliot's phrase.

FAMILY IN GORDIMER'S FICTION

Gordimer's fiction may be placed more precisely by noting that although her characters range widely through the classes and gradations of black township life, white suburban life, and Afrikaner farm life, her portrayals of South African life are limited. In Gordimer's South Africa, family seems to be associated with the country's turbulent history, and both are broken and fragmented. For example, there are few old people in Gordimer's work who play an active part. They are frail and representative of a past that cannot provide any guidance to life in the tortured South African world. Most of the older characters are pathetic suffering onlookers, like Elizabeth's grandmother in *The Late Bourgeois World*, who lives in an old people's home, useful only for her ample bank account, which will be exploited by Elizabeth's black activist friends. Or they are the equally pathetic elderly blacks who are helpless to alter events. In Gordimer's fiction, the elders seem to have disappeared.

In addition, Gordimer's central characters tend to have limited family associations. There are families and surrogate families, but many characters have no sister or brother. Hillela in *A Sport of Nature* has a cousin and two aunts, but others have neither aunts nor uncles. In *A World of Strangers*, Toby Hood has a powerful uncle and a family, but they are far away in England, and his lack of close family ties is contrasted with his South African friends, many of whom have lovers, spouses, or children. Likewise, Toby's girlfriend, Cecil, has no visible parents or other relatives, and her child is not much more than an inconvenient parcel to her. In *The Late Bourgeois World*, Elizabeth Van Den Sandt's child is away at boarding school, partly because she fears her close destructive attachment to him. His dead father, the rebellious Max, used to scream at him when he was a crying baby—an intense discordant image of the disruption of generations.

If in other novels and stories the family has not disappeared, it is a heavy burden, like Rosa Burger's family in *Burger's Daughter*, or a trove of scandals, such as the story Hillela uncovers involving her mother, who ran off with her lover. Avoiding sentimentality, Gordimer does not depict black characters as rooted in family life either. The loyalty and dignity of black mothers, like Aila in *My Son's Story* and the grandmother in "The Ultimate Safari," are compelling, but the lives of these women are broken. In this brokenness, Gordimer finds her subject.

In *A Sport of Nature*, Hillela's young womanhood captures the modern experience of white South Africa in its lifelong, unacknowledged intimacy with blacks and in its dislocated, precarious political moment. Especially in Hillela's liaisons with black lovers—one is a revolutionary, and another is a powerful, charismatic political leader—which Hillela begins and ends without any goal or direction, Gordimer points toward an uncertain future. Throughout the novel, Gordimer uses different perspectives to present this young woman and her adventures, sometimes recounting the story from an impersonal distance and at other times moving closely into her experiences. Less reflective than Rosa Burger, Hillela treats her ancestry with less care but with curiosity, as when she searches out her mother, who has fled to Lourenço Marques, Mozambique. She may be more prepared than almost all of Gordimer's other characters to take on the future in South Africa. Perhaps this nation's terrible history, and the destructive divisions among its people, can be healed only through forgetting, through the careless insouciance of those who have abandoned or renounced the past.

CONCLUSION

Gordimer's accomplishment has been honored around the world, and she has received many prizes besides her Nobel Prize: in England, the James Tait Black Prize in 1972 for her novel *A Guest of Honour*, and the Booker Prize in 1974 for her novel *The Conservationist*; in the United States, the Modern Language Association Award in 1982, the Common Wealth Award in 1981, and the Bennett Award of the *Hudson Review* in 1987; in South Africa, the Central News Agency (CNA) Prize in 1974, 1975, 1976, 1980, and 1991. She was also awarded the Grand Aigle d'Or Prize in France in 1975, the Nelly Sachs Prize in Germany in 1986, and many others. She is an honorary member of the American Academy and Institute of Arts and Letters and of the American Academy of Arts and Sciences and an officier de l'Ordre des Arts et des Lettres. She has received honorary degrees, taught and lectured at many universities, and been interviewed and written about extensively. Numerous bibliographies of her work have been compiled, and she has been the subject of critical commentary throughout the world. She has been active in the International Association of Poets, Playwrights, Editors, Essayists, and Novelists (PEN), as well as in South African literary organizations.

Gordimer has often described herself as a "natural" writer, by which she appears to mean that she does not write in response to specific social situations but would have been a writer no matter what her surroundings were. Perhaps this is true, and like other great writers, she would have brought her formidable novelistic intelligence to bear on any situation. Certainly her work does not illustrate a distinct political point of view or prescribe a course of action. After the Soweto revolt of 1976, the plight of well-meaning whites was often tragic, as was the pathos and disorientation of young Africans who stopped going to school, which Gordimer illustrates in the story "Comrades" (in *Jump*). It would be difficult to glean from her fiction what social policies should be followed. And the tumultuous events of the 1990s—the freeing of Nelson Mandela, the dismantling of apartheid, the joint peace efforts of white government and black leaders, the planning for a constitution, elections, a multiracial parliament, the multicultural society, the yearning for democracy, the loosening of old bonds, dissension among blacks, armed resistance among whites, and accompanying it all the incessant violence—almost defied thoughts of social policy.

In her 1994 novel, *None to Accompany Me*, Gordimer presents the new world in South Africa, in which apartheid is over. The repressions, the cruel laws and persecutions, the campaigns of resistance, the exiles, the detentions, the bannings and brutalities—all these horrors of the past are finished. What remains is the damage done to society and to personal relations. In the consciousness and conscience of Vera Stark, a white lawyer engaged in planning and reconstruction, Gordimer confronts the new conditions: people who have returned from exile or have surfaced from living underground, emotions that reveal the broken old life and the new situation. For Vera and her black friends, the story now includes their children's generation. Vera's legal group investigates black squatters' rights on an Afrikaner farm, which brings her into a new relation with a black colleague; in the new arrangement, she is living alone as his tenant. This fiction expresses succinctly some of the reversals to be encountered in the new South Africa. The novel, with its title derived from the work of the Japanese poet Basho, suggests an identity without the protection of caste, class, and privilege.

In an increasingly transformed South Africa, Gordimer, who turned seventy in 1993, seemed to be at a new stage in her long and productive career. Obviously, her subject did not disappear with the new constitution and the enfranchisement and empowerment of black Africans; the fictions that deal with the future make that clear. The erosion of the color bar proposed new ideas for fiction. Life underground, life in banned organizations, the harboring of banned persons, and all that followed from those fragile conditions disappeared; the life of the shebeens and the black townships certainly changed. People who had been forced into silence now had a legitimate voice.

The role of white South Africans is being transformed once more, diminished further. But the self-development of black South Africans and their increasing entrance into modern democratic experience are observed and encouraged by one who worked and hoped for these changes when they were forbidden or unthinkable. The newly empowered black South Africans have to deal with rural poverty, lack of skills and educational deficits among their fellow citizens with new opportunities, a new franchise. Social and economic advances produce a larger, more educated black South African middle class, with its consequent explorations of taste and intellectual judgment, luxuries that had been denied them by their poverty and segregated status.

Those infused with the spirit of Black Consciousness would insist that development following a western pattern is not necessary for the new South Africa, that African democracy would develop its own forms to guide South Africans to their destiny, as the ill-fated Max Van Den Sandt believes in *The Late Bourgeois World*. Others, equally loyal to the new South Africa, would see this advance in the light of the social progress of the middle class throughout history. The story of the poor, ambitious, and previously deprived entering the middle class is a story that French, English, and Russian literature has recounted again and again, whether in Molière's *Le Bourgeois gentilhomme* (1671), George Eliot's *Middlemarch* (1871–1872), or the works of Ivan Turgenev or Jean La Fontaine.

This story engages black South African writers once they could stay in their own country, no longer required to choose exile or silence, and it interests observant writers among their white South African sisters and brothers. Gordimer, the daughter of Africa who has remained faithful to her roots, responds with her own "essential gesture" in new essays, novels, and statements. Gordimer's essays published in 1995 as *Writing and Being*, which were first given as the 1994 Charles Eliot Norton Lectures at Harvard University, address many of her familiar themes, but there

is a different emphasis. She writes now as an *African* writer, close to the South African blacks she always claimed as brothers, but now among writers of larger Africa and the Middle East—the Egyptian Najīb Maḥfūẓ, the Nigerian Chinua Achebe, and the Israeli Amos Oz. With them, she stands on the stage of the world, joining Albert Camus, Roland Barthes, Italo Calvino, Marcel Proust, William Butler Yeats, and Anton Chekhov. From Achebe, she adopts the cry: "What must a people do to appease an embittered history?" The final essay, "That Other World That Was the World," takes up the cry and explores the question of belonging—from the racial alienation of her youth and the decadence of the late phase of colonization, through the tortuous unravelling of apartheid, to a new sense of home that could allow her to say not only "my country" but, more poignantly, "my people."

Selected Bibliography

BIBLIOGRAPHIES

Cooke, John. "Nadine Gordimer: A Bibliography." *Bulletin of Bibliography* 36 (1979).

Driver, Dorothy, Ann Dry, Craig MacKenzie, and John Read. *Nadine Gordimer: A Bibliography of Primary and Secondary Sources, 1937–1992*. London: Hans Zell, 1994.

Green, Robert J. "Nadine Gordimer: A Bibliography of Works and Criticism." *Bulletin of Bibliography* 42, no. 1 (1985).

Nell, Racillia Jillian. *Nadine Gordimer: Novelist and Short Story Writer: A Bibliography of Her Works and Selected Criticism*. Johannesburg, South Africa: Department of Bibliography, Librarianship, and Typography, University of the Witwatersrand, 1964.

NOVELS

The Lying Days. London: Gollancz, 1953; New York: Simon & Schuster, 1953.

A World of Strangers. London: Gollancz, 1958; New York: Simon & Schuster, 1958.

Occasion for Loving. London: Gollancz, 1963; New York: Viking, 1963.

The Late Bourgeois World. London: Gollancz, 1966; New York: Viking, 1966.

A Guest of Honour. New York: Viking, 1970; London: Jonathan Cape, 1971.

The Conservationist. London: Jonathan Cape, 1974; New York: Viking, 1975.

Burger's Daughter. London: Jonathan Cape, 1979; New York: Viking, 1979.

July's People. London: Jonathan Cape, 1981; New York: Viking, 1981.

A Sport of Nature. London: Jonathan Cape, 1987; New York: Knopf, 1987.

My Son's Story. London: Bloomsbury, 1990; New York: Farrar, Straus & Giroux, 1990.

None to Accompany Me. London: Bloomsbury, 1994; Farrar, Straus & Giroux, 1994.

SHORT STORIES

Face to Face: Short Stories. Johannesburg, South Africa: Silver Leaf Books, 1949.

The Soft Voice of the Serpent and Other Stories. New York: Simon & Schuster, 1952; London: Gollancz, 1954.

Six Feet of the Country. London: Gollancz, 1956; New York: Simon & Schuster, 1956.

Friday's Footprint and Other Stories. London: Gollancz, 1960; New York: Viking, 1960.

Not for Publication and Other Stories. London: Gollancz, 1965; New York: Viking, 1965.

Livingstone's Companions. New York: Viking 1971; London: Jonathan Cape, 1972.

Selected Stories. London: Jonathan Cape, 1975; New York: Viking, 1975.

Some Monday for Sure. London: Heinemann, 1976.

A Soldier's Embrace. London: Jonathan Cape, 1980; New York: Viking, 1980.

Something Out There. London: Jonathan Cape, 1984; New York: Viking, 1984.

Crimes of Conscience. London: Heinemann, 1991.

Jump and Other Stories. New York: Farrar, Straus & Giroux, 1991; Cape Town, South Africa: David Philip, 1991.

Why Haven't You Written? Selected Stories, 1950–1972. London: Penguin, 1992.

ESSAYS

On the Mines. With David Goldblatt. Cape Town, South Africa: Struik, 1973.

Lifetimes: Under Apartheid. With David Goldblatt. London: Jonathan Cape, 1986.

The Essential Gesture: Writing, Politics, and Places. Ed. and intro. by Stephen Clingman. London: Jonathan Cape, 1988; New York: Knopf, 1988.

Writing and Being. Cambridge, Mass.: Harvard University Press, 1995.

INTERVIEWS

Bazin, Nancy Topping, and Marilyn Dallman Seymour, eds. *Conversations with Nadine Gordimer.* Jackson: University Press of Mississippi, 1990.

CRITICAL STUDIES

The Beat of Drum: *The Story of a Magazine That Documented the Rise of Africa.* As told by *Drum*'s publisher, editors, contributors, and photographers. Johannesburg, South Africa: Ravan Press in association with *Drum* magazine, 1982.

Chapman, Michael, ed. *The* Drum *Decade: Stories from the 1950s.* Pietermaritzburg, South Africa: University of Natal Press, 1989.

Clingman, Stephen. *The Novels of Nadine Gordimer: History from the Inside.* London: Allen & Unwin, 1986. 2d ed. Amherst: University of Massachusetts Press, 1992.

Dubbeld, Catherine Elizabeth. *Reflecting Apartheid: South African Short Stories in English with Socio-Political Themes 1960–1987: A Select and Annotated Bibliography.* Johannesburg, South Africa: South African Institute of International Affairs, 1990.

Head, Dominic. *Nadine Gordimer.* Cambridge, U.K.: Cambridge University Press, 1994.

King, Bruce, ed. *The Later Fiction of Nadine Gordimer.* London: Macmillan, 1993.

Newman, Judie. *Nadine Gordimer.* London and New York: Routledge, 1988.

Sampson, Anthony. Drum: *An African Adventure—and Afterwards.* London: Hodder & Stoughton, 1983.

Smith, Rowland, ed. *Critical Essays on Nadine Gordimer.* Boston: G. K. Hall, 1990.

Woodson, Dorothy C. Drum: *An Index to "Africa's Leading Magazine" 1951–1965.* Madison: African Studies Program, University of Wisconsin, 1988.

Tawfīq al-Ḥakīm
1898–1987

PAUL G. STARKEY

TAWFĪQ AL-ḤAKĪM is assured of a lasting place in the history of modern Arabic literature, not only as the founder of modern Egyptian theater but also as a major contributor to the development of the Arabic novel. Born in Alexandria, probably on 9 October 1898, to Ismāʿīl, who was employed in the Egyptian legal service, and a mother of partly Turkish origins, he seldom attended any one school for more than a year because of his father's frequent changes of post in the Egyptian Delta. Al-Ḥakīm's enthusiasm for the arts, however, was quickly apparent: he fell in love with the stories of *The Arabian Nights*, developed a fondness for music, and began to learn to play the lute under the instruction of the singer Ḥamīda; most significantly, perhaps, he was taken by his reluctant father to see a performance of *Romeo and Juliet*, probably staged by the troupe of the famous Egyptian actor Salāma Ḥijāzī. This passion for the arts was reinforced when he moved to Cairo in 1915, taking up residence with his uncles and aunt and entering the Muḥammad ʿAlī Secondary School to prepare for his school intermediate certificate; this domestic arrangement provides the background for the events of his first full-length novel, ʿAwdat al-rūḥ (1933; *The Return of the Spirit*), one of the most influential of his mature works.

EARLY LITERARY EFFORTS

Forbidden by his parents to view films in Cairo, al-Ḥakīm instead attended theater performances whenever possible and quickly moved from spectator to participant. He began by improvising plays with friends and soon started writing; every Thursday afternoon a sketch was performed in one of his companions' guestrooms. When the 1919 revolt — the first modern demonstration of Egyptian national consciousness and solidarity — broke out, al-Ḥakīm composed patriotic songs, some of which gained wide currency, before he was arrested and briefly jailed. But he had little enthusiasm or aptitude for lyric poetry, and before long his nationalist feelings expressed themselves in a full-length play, "Al-Ḍayf al-thaqīl" (The unpleasant guest). Although the play was never printed and was soon lost, a summary given later by al-Ḥakīm shows that the plot revolved around a guest who continually extends the length of his stay and exploits his lawyer host's hospitality, using his host's absences to pass himself off as the house's owner and collect his clients' fees — an unambiguous reference to the British occupation of Egypt.

Having passed the school-leaving certificate, al-Ḥakīm bowed to his father's wishes and entered law school in Cairo in 1921.

Again, however, he was unable to resist the distractions of his artistic interests and failed his first-year exams. Annoyed by his academic failure, his family made him spend the summer improving his French. Ironically, this failure probably helped to shape his development as a writer, for his father arranged for him to study at the Berlitz School, where he was encouraged to read French literature written in a simple style: he became acquainted with the works of Alphonse Daudet and Anatole France (whom he continued to admire) and with the plays of Alfred de Musset and Pierre Marivaux. From this point on, though he successfully completed his law course, his main intellectual interest was the theater.

The five plays dating from his time in law school between 1921 and 1925—*Amīnūsā, Al-Mar'a al-jadīda* (The new woman), *Al-'Arīs* (The bridegroom), *Khātim Sulaymān* (Solomon's ring), and *Al-Khaṭīb* (The suitor) —are for the most part of little interest in themselves and, were it not for al-Ḥakīm's subsequent career, would probably have received little attention. So low was the status of the theater in Egypt then that al-Ḥakīm was forced to write under the name Ḥusayn Tawfīq to escape the attention of his family, and for a long time he concealed the existence of these early efforts. The themes of these plays, written in colloquial Arabic for the popular theater of the 'Ukāsha brothers, do however give an early indication of his versatility. *Al-Mar'a al-jadīda* (1923), the only one of these plays to have been published in full, echoes the earlier "Al-Ḍayf al-thaqīl" in its combination of serious political and social comment with the elements of comedy and melodrama found in most popular Egyptian drama of the period. Taking its title from a book by the Egyptian feminist writer Qāsim Amīn, it is a powerful assault on the movement for the unveiling of women, a major social issue of the day; in its misogyny, the play foreshadows an attitude that al-Ḥakīm, partly by design, later utilized as one of his hallmarks. By contrast, the other four plays followed more conventional patterns of contemporary Egyptian theater with music and songs playing a significant part; in most of them al-Ḥakīm follows the common practice of setting his play in Egypt, even when adapting the work from a western original.

THE INFLUENCE OF PARIS

Although al-Ḥakīm received a law degree in 1925, he was not one of the more successful candidates and failed to obtain a government post. On the advice of the influential intellectual Luṭfī al-Sayyid, al-Ḥakīm's father dispatched him to France with the intention that he earn a doctorate, and from 1925 to 1928 al-Ḥakīm studied in Paris. While his father intended to remove him from the artistic influences of Cairo, his time in Paris had the opposite effect. Al-Ḥakīm returned to Egypt in 1928 without receiving his doctorate. In the meantime, however, he had become acquainted with western culture, an acquaintance that radically altered the course of his literary development. He frequented artists' cafés, concert halls, and art galleries, acquired a taste for intellectual and avant-garde authors such as George Bernard Shaw, Maurice Maeterlinck, and Luigi Pirandello, and devoted whole days to a single hall of the Louvre museum. At the same time, like other Arabs studying in the west, he found himself challenged both by the material superiority of the west and by the difficulties of adapting to a different social structure, particularly in his sexual relations. For a time, he lived in a Paris suburb with a French family, whose down-to-earth advice on the conduct of his love affairs he consistently rejected, before leaving them for a more bohemian existence; an idea of his lifestyle during this period may be gained not only from the novel *'Uṣfūr min al-sharq* (1938; *Bird of the East*), which is closely modeled, like all of his novels, on his own experience, but also from the collection of letters to his friend André, which were written after his return to Egypt in 1928 and subsequently published under the title *Zahrat al-ʿumr* (1943; The flower of life).

Beginning in the 1920s the relation between eastern and western culture and the nature of the Egyptian identity became dominant concerns in al-Hakīm's writing. While in Paris, he wrote the short play *Amāma shubbāk al-tadhākir* (1926; In front of the box-office window), originally in French, in which a young man nervously tries to obtain a date with a girl who is a ticket seller. Although the play is of little significance in itself, its careful but tortuous dialogue indicates the extent to which al-Hakīm had already begun to leave behind him the theatrical world of the ʿUkāsha brothers in his quest for more serious modes of expression.

Al-Hakīm's efforts were not, however, confined to such small-scale works. After toying for some time with the idea of writing a history of art, he decided to embark on a novel of Egyptian life. The resulting work, *The Return of the Spirit*—originally begun in French and eventually published in two parts in 1933—marked the beginning of a realistic trend in the Arabic novel and represented a major advance in the establishment of the novel as a modern Egyptian literary form. Closely modeled on al-Hakīm's experiences in Cairo during World War I, the work depicts the life and frustrated loves of an Egyptian family and culminates in the 1919 popular revolt. This ending has been responsible for the novel's being regarded as a "nationalist" work, attracting the admiration, of, among others, ʿAbd al-Nāṣir, who later became president. Like most of al-Hakīm's works, the novel may be read on several levels: lengthy sections in the second part are devoted to a debate about the nature of the Egyptian *fallāhīn* (peasant farmers), whom al-Hakīm regarded as direct descendants of the builders of the pyramids. Of equal interest for the western reader is its picture of life in contemporary Egypt.

RETURN TO EGYPT

In 1928 al-Hakīm was recalled to Egypt by his father. It was a traumatic homecoming, for not only did he have to contend with his family's disappointment over his failure to earn a doctorate, but he was also afflicted by an overwhelming sense of loneliness, feeling that Egypt was an intellectual wilderness after the artistic paradise of France. Lacking any other practical alternative, he entered the Egyptian legal service and for two years was employed in the Alexandria courts. He was then appointed a deputy public prosecutor and served in this capacity in a number of towns in the Egyptian Delta until 1934. It is probably no accident that this period, in which al-Hakīm was at last brought face-to-face with reality, provided the inspiration for what many regard as his finest work, the novel *Yawmiyyāt nāʾib fī al-aryāf* (1937; *Maze of Justice: Diary of a Country Attorney*). Cast in diary form, the work revolves around a murder investigation. Al-Hakīm presents a damning picture of conditions in the Egyptian countryside and of the Egyptian legal system, which was based on the Napoléonic Code and afforded few concessions to the *fallāhīn*, to whom it was applied. Those administering it were grossly overworked and weighed down by a host of bureaucratic restrictions; justice itself, as P. H. Newby observes in the foreword to Abba S. Eban's English translation, was of no importance to those in power.

The six plays from 1928 to 1934 formed a transitional phase between al-Hakīm's early productions and the more intellectual plays of his mature period. *Hayāh tahattamat* (1930; A shattered life) and *Al-Zammār* (1932; The piper), both written in colloquial Egyptian Arabic, draw on the same background of the

Egyptian countryside that provided the setting for *Maze of Justice. Raṣāṣa fī al-qalb* (1931; A bullet in the heart), also written in colloquial Arabic, revolves around a love triangle, depending for its main effect on a conventional case of mistaken identity. Two other plays, however—*Al-Khurūj min al-janna* (1928; Exit from paradise) and *Baʿda al-mawt* (1929; After death)—use standard rather than colloquial Arabic, are more introspective, and provide a first glimpse of one of the main themes running through al-Ḥakīm's later work: the relation between fantasy and reality. In *Al-Khurūj min al-janna* the influence of Pirandello is readily apparent: the play explores the relationship between a writer and his wife and takes an unexpected twist in the final act with the revelation that the writer has sublimated his experience into a play itself entitled *Al-Khurūj min al-janna*. In *Baʿda al-mawt* an aging doctor, convinced that a girl's suicide was due to her frustrated love for him, is apparently rejuvenated and embarks on a life of pleasure until he becomes disillusioned by the news that it was not he but his namesake, Maḥmūd the chauffeur, whom the girl loved.

FIRST MATURE PLAYS

Interesting as these plays are, writing them appears to have done little either to alleviate al-Ḥakīm's inner conflicts or to satisfy his literary ambitions. His family was urging him to marry, and he was at the same time oppressed by a fear that his artistic impulse might be crushed by the humdrum nature of his legal employment. While in Paris, he had conceived the idea of writing a specifically "Egyptian" tragedy, replacing the Greek idea of the struggle against fate with what he regarded as a more Egyptian concept, the struggle against time and place. The resultant play, *Ahl al-kahf* (1933; The people of the cave), had been written in Alexandria soon after his return to Egypt, but al-Ḥakīm de-

layed publication, fearing the ridicule of his colleagues and worried that the work might not live up to the artistic perfection to which he aspired. In 1933, however, the play appeared and was accorded an enthusiastic reception.

The publication of *Ahl al-kahf* is a decisive date both in al-Ḥakīm's career as a writer—it was his first published work—and in the history of modern Arabic drama, for the use of a Qurʾanic story (a tale known in the Christian tradition as "the sleepers of Ephesus") as the basis for an intellectual drama was unprecedented. The publication enjoyed a spectacular success, going through two editions in its first year, and when the government-sponsored National Troupe was established in 1935, the company opened with this play.

Although *Ahl al-kahf* provoked widely differing interpretations among critics, al-Ḥakīm intended to relate the Qurʾanic story to contemporary Egypt, which appeared to be awakening from centuries of stagnation to face the challenge of the twentieth century and western civilization. As al-Ḥakīm admitted later, however, the play's roots lay neither in ancient nor in Islamic Egypt but in the European tradition of intellectual drama that he encountered in Paris. Indeed, the play is permeated with the confusion between fantasy and reality that characterizes the works of Pirandello. As the sleepers return to their cave to resume their slumbers, they are unable to tell whether their experience has been real or whether they have been dreaming all along. There are several ironic twists in the dialogue, as when one sleeper's story about a Christian who slept for a month is dismissed as a "feeble legend." The play, unlike most of al-Ḥakīm's work for the popular theater, is written in standard modern rather than colloquial Arabic and contains many passages of delicate and subtle writing; at the same time, it is marred by undramatic philosophical discussions that at times detract from the unity of the work. This flaw is also evident in the novel *The Return of the Spirit*, which was also published in 1933, and in many of his subsequent works.

Ahl al-kahf and *The Return of the Spirit* were followed in 1934 by a second full-length play, *Shahrazād*, and by a volume titled *Ahl al-fann* (Artistes), which includes a one-act play and two short stories. While the works in *Ahl al-fann* are of little significance, *Shahrazād* continues the exploration of the relation to time and space begun in *Ahl al-kahf*, with an increasing use of symbolism—the uncertain relation between dream and reality explored in *Ahl al-kahf* is even more apparent here. Although al-Hakīm later claimed to have been trying in *Shahrazād* to break down the divisions between serious and popular drama, he in fact makes little use of the story of Shahrazād from the Arabic popular literary tradition. At the beginning of al-Hakīm's play, the 1,001st night has already ended. Al-Hakīm turns Shahrazād into a symbol of the unknowable, a "mysterious woman" who is interpreted by the other main characters according to their own dispositions but whose true nature remains a mystery to the end of the play. For Qamar, the king's vizier (chief minister), she is an ideal of beauty; for the slave, she embodies sensual gratifiction; for the king himself, she represents pure intellect. Although, as with *Ahl al-kahf*, a number of different interpretations have been proposed by critics, there is general agreement that the play is one of the author's most successful and that the theatrical techniques al-Hakīm employs are excellently wedded to the subject and create an atmosphere of mystery that runs through the entire play.

Al-Hakīm's forebodings about his colleagues' attitude toward his literary activities proved well-founded: summoned before his superiors, he was asked to explain the commotion caused by the publication of *Ahl al-kahf* and advised that in the future he would do better to publish books on law. He countered by requesting a transfer, which was granted, and from 1934 to 1939 served in

Cairo in the Ministry of Education. In 1939, after another literary storm caused by the publication of *Maze of Justice*, he was again transferred and from then until 1943 served in the newly established Ministry of Social Affairs before resigning from government service to become a full-time writer.

Considering the demands of his official employment, al-Hakīm's output during this period is remarkable for both its quantity and variety. In 1936 he collaborated with his friend Tāhā Husayn on a lighthearted novel, *Al-Qasr al-mashūr* (The enchanted castle), which marked a reconciliation between the two men after a disagreement over the character of Shahrazād. The same year saw also the publication of *Muhammad*, an attempt to chronicle the life of the Prophet that mirrors in dramatic form a number of restatements of the Islamic heritage by leading contemporary Egyptian intellectuals. These works were followed—in addition to a number of short stories and articles—by two major novels, *Maze of Justice* and *Bird of the East*, which were in turn followed by the shorter *Rāqisat al-maʿbad* (1939; The temple dancer) and *Himār al-Hakīm* (1940; Al-Hakīm's donkey).

INTELLECTUAL PLAYS

Not until 1942, however, did al-Hakīm produce another full-length, intellectual play, *Pygmalion*, of the type for which he became so well known. Although his introduction to the work makes clear that he was at least partially inspired by George Bernard Shaw's play of the same name, the two plays are in fact quite different. In al-Hakīm's play, social commentary is entirely absent, and he develops his ideas within the original framework of the legend. The central theme—the relationship of the artist to the artistic work—represents another facet of the fantasy/reality motif from al-Hakīm's earlier plays. Tired of his own creation, the sculptor Pygmalion implores the goddess Venus to breathe life into his statue, but no sooner has his prayer been answered than he longs for the ivory Galatea again. Pygmalion's dilemma, however, torn as it is between the real and the ideal, between life and art, is incapable of rational solution, and the play is brought to a close with Pygmalion smashing the ivory statue with a broom, declaring he has wasted his life in a futile struggle with art and fate.

This series of intellectual plays was continued in 1943 with the rather disjointed *Sulaymān al-ḥakīm* (Solomon the wise), which explores the relationship between wisdom and power, and in 1949 with *Al-Malik Ūdīb* (Oedipus Rex), which al-Ḥakīm described as an attempt to rework the Oedipus story in accordance with Islamic beliefs. The latter play develops an idea prominent in *Shahrazād* — the futility of the quest for "truth." Although al-Ḥakīm cannot be said to have been successful in writing an Islamic *Oedipus* and the play closes with many questions of guilt and responsibility unanswered, it remains an important statement of his views on the relationship between thought and feeling. In al-Ḥakīm's play, Oedipus' downfall comes about primarily because of the king's reliance on his intelligence rather than his heart as a guide to action. In this respect the play presages in dramatic form his later extended essay *Al-Taʿāduliyya* (1955; Equilibriumism), an attempt to provide a comprehensive philosophical definition of his attitude toward art and life. In the essay al-Ḥakīm provides an explicit statement of many of the ideas and attitudes implicit in his imaginative works.

FORAYS INTO POLITICAL ISSUES IN DRAMA AND NONFICTION

After resigning from government service in 1943, al-Ḥakīm published only two full-length works in the next few years: the play *Al-Malik Ūdīb* and his last novel, *Al-Ribāṭ al-muqaddas* (1944; The sacred bond). Like his earlier novels, *Al-Ribāṭ al-muqaddas* is closely related to the author's own experiences, examining the idea of marital fidelity and the clash between duty and feeling through a complex plot that owes something to Anatole France's *Thaïs* (1890). At the same time, the work provides one of the most glaring examples of al-Ḥakīm's tendency to introspective, philosophical rambling, which at times threatens to destroy the novel's unity; realizing that his true talents lay elsewhere, he never returned to the full-length novel form.

For the most part, al-Ḥakīm's output during this period was confined to essays and short plays on social themes, the latter originally published in the Cairo newspaper *Akhbār al-yawm* and subsequently reprinted in the collection *Masraḥ al-mujtamaʿ* (1950; Social theater). Unlike many Egyptian writers of his generation, al-Ḥakīm consistently refused to identify himself with any political party, arguing that a writer must maintain independence to preserve moral authority; his articles in the 1930s and 1940s took as their targets Egyptian politicians of all persuasions, accusing them of having abandoned the spirit of the 1919 revolution and attacking corruption and inefficiency in all spheres of public life. The plays of *Masraḥ al-mujtamaʿ*, which are for the most part short, echo this spirit in the context of post–World War II Egypt — a period when, as al-Ḥakīm points out in his preface to the collection, the country was again in a state of social turmoil. His targets include not only "the war profiteer, the man of companies and enterprises" but also Egyptian women who, no longer content to be unveiled, "have been trying to gain a prominent place in politics and public life" (pp. 6–7).

The plays of *Masraḥ al-mujtamaʿ* vary greatly in interest and quality. Al-Ḥakīm's concern with the movement for the emancipation of women is evident in *Urīd hādhā al-rajul* (I want this man), in which a young woman, Nāʾila, challenges the traditional system of arranged marriages. The plot advances by a series of witty and fast-paced conversations as her challenge moves to a successful conclusion. The aspirations of contemporary Egyptian feminists are also the inspiration for *Al-Nā'iba al-muḥtarama* (Honorable member), which revolves around a female member of Parliament (MP), whose influence is sought by the minister in an attempt to persuade her party to drop its opposition to the government's plans. Tensions develop between the MP and her husband, who resents his inferior status, and eventually the MP resigns. The moral is clear: a woman cannot devote herself to both politics and the family, and a choice must therefore be made. This piece also serves as a comment on the corruption of political life in postwar Egypt—a theme treated more explicitly in other plays in the collection. In *Miftāḥ al-najāḥ* (The key to success), for example, a solitary official swims against the tide of the Egyptian bureaucratic system and is eventually dismissed, while in *Li-Kull mujtahid naṣīb* (A share for all who work hard), a ministry official is at a loss to understand his failure to gain promotion, in spite of his great efficiency. Advised by a colleague that it is precisely his industriousness that is holding him back, he changes his ways, and the play ends with the announcement of promotions for everyone in his division.

The most successful of the plays of *Masraḥ al-mujtamaʿ*, *Ughniyat al-mawt* (The song of death), however, is concerned not with corruption in Cairo but with the conflict between traditional and modern values in the Egyptian countryside—a theme that recalls the setting of the earlier novel *Maze of Justice*. Like *Maze of Justice*, moreover, *Ughniyat al-mawt* has some claim as one of the most effective of al-Ḥakīm's works. The play takes its inspiration from the system of family feuds and vengeance widespread in the Egyptian countryside, centering on the return of a young man, ʿUlwān, to his native village after several years away. Although his purpose in returning is to preach a program of social reform, his family believes that he has come to avenge the killing of his father. A series of misunderstandings ensues, leading to ʿUlwān's death at the hands of his family, who cannot bear the disgrace of his remaining alive without having done his duty. The different interpretations of the purpose of ʿUlwān's return allow al-Ḥakīm considerable scope for fast-moving dialogue between characters talking at cross-purposes, and the dramatic unity of the piece is reinforced by the introduction of a song—from which the play takes its name—at crucial points in the action.

In 1951 al-Ḥakīm returned to the Egyptian civil service as director of the National Library, a post he held until his appointment in 1956 to the Supreme Council for Literature and the Arts. His output during this period was as prolific and varied as before: in addition to another collection of short plays, he wrote several volumes of essays and articles, a book of short stories with a philosophical flavor *Arinī Allāh* (1953; Show me God), and a collection of reminiscences from his period as a district attorney.

Al-Ḥakīm's detached attitude toward party politics during the 1930s and 1940s enabled him to find a position of comparative favor with the regime that came to power after the 1952 coup, and in the succeeding period he received many honors and appointments while refusing to act as spokesman for the new regime. In 1954 he was elected to the Arabic Language Academy in Cairo; in 1958 he was awarded the Order of the Republic and in 1959 was appointed the Egyptian delegate to UNESCO (United Nations Educational, Scientific, and Cultural Organization) in Paris. In 1961 he received the First State Literature prize. Two years later his contribution to Egyptian and Arabic literature was again officially recognized with the founding of the al-Ḥakīm Theater in Cairo.

LATE PLAYS

Two main trends can be seen in al-Ḥakīm's work after 1952. First, though like most Egyptian writers he continued to produce regular essays and articles for the press, his major works during this period were for the theater. The only significant exceptions are a volume of autobiography titled *Sijn al-ʿumr* (1964; *The Prison of Life*), *Al-Taʿāduliyya*, and the extended essay *ʿAwdat al-waʿy* (1974; *The Return of Consciousness*), in which he describes his attitude toward the republican regime changing from hope to disillusion. The second main feature of his writing during this period is that, in parallel with a dizzying variety of themes, he began to show a renewed fondness for technical experiment, with a view both to narrowing the gap between the theater and the general public and to enriching the Egyptian theater by importing ideas and techniques from contemporary western playwrights, most obviously Samuel Beckett and Eugène Ionesco.

Al-Ḥakīm's attitude toward the abolition of the Egyptian monarchy in 1953 was at first conciliatory. His play *Al-Aydī al-nāʿima* (1954; Smooth hands) revolves around the need to work for reconciliation and the restoration of harmony among the various classes of Egyptian society, with a strong element of social criticism in the repeated emphasis on work rather than wealth as the basis for social order. He continued this generally conciliatory tone in *Al-Ṣafqa* (1956; The deal), which revolves around an attempt by a group of peasants to secure a land deal in the face of almost insurmountable difficulties. The play is also notable for its innovative use of language; in response to the old dilemma of whether to use classical or colloquial Arabic for dialogue, al-Ḥakīm creates a "third language" that could be read either way. Although he returned to this "third language" ten years later in *Al-Warṭa* (1966; The dilemma), the experiment found little favor among other Egyptian writers, and al-Ḥakīm eventually abandoned it.

In *Īzīs* (1955; Isis) al-Ḥakīm for the first time turned directly for his inspiration to an ancient Egyptian myth. The myth tells how the goddess Isis, wife of Osiris, discovered and reunited the pieces of her murdered husband's body, and through her power brought him back to life. The central problem of *Īzīs* is whether the end justifies the means, but through the characters Mastat and Tut, al-Ḥakīm also develops a more specific argument about the function of the artist in society and the relative merits of the opposing perspectives of "art for art's sake" and "art for life." As such, the play continues the concerns of the series of philosophical plays beginning with *Ahl al-kahf*. A somewhat similar question forms the theme of *Al-Sulṭān al-ḥāʾir* (1960; The sultan's dilemma), in which al-Ḥakīm directs his attention to the relationship between law and force. Although the play is set in the Egypt of the Mamluk period (1250–1517) it is clear from al-Ḥakīm's introduction that it is intended to have contemporary relevance. The concern for world peace in this play also finds expression in *Ashwāk al-salām* (1957; The thorns of peace), a play marred however by an excessively idealistic outlook.

Al-Ḥakīm's period in Paris during 1959–1960, like his earlier stay in the 1920s, reinvigorated his theatrical technique, and the plays written after his return to Egypt show the influence of the theater of the absurd and the more didactic theater of Bertolt Brecht. The first play, *Yā ṭāliʿ al-shajara* (1962; *The Tree Climber*), is also the most successful. Central to the play is the relationship between a man and his wife and the investigation that follows her disappearance. Eventually the wife reappears, but her obstinate refusal to disclose where she has been drives her husband to kill her. Rational communication between the couple seems to have broken down, as each is entirely wrapped up in his or her own concerns; in a curious way, however, they succeed in understanding each other, each picking up the other's phrases and applying them to their own fixations. Although the work is clearly indebted to absurdist theater for its rejection of stage conventions and for its picture of aggression in the face of the unknowable, it lacks the starkness and brutality associated with the works of Beckett or Ionesco.

The Tree Climber was followed by shorter plays in the absurdist tradition and by experiments that betray influences of other theatrical movements. In *Riḥlat ṣayd* (1964; A hunting trip), for example, al-Ḥakīm combines theatrical with cinematic techniques by employing a screen to represent the images passing through a man's mind. *Bank al-qalaq* (1966; The anxiety bank) is a curious attempt to combine the novel and play in a hybrid form, while *Hārūn al-Rashīd wa-Hārūn al-Rashīd* (1969; Harun al-Rashid and Harun al-Rashid) is an experiment utilizing material from *The Arabian Nights* and exploring the motif of fantasy versus reality familiar from al-Ḥakīm's earlier works in a piece of improvised theater designed to break down the barriers between actors and audience while satisfying the requirements of state censorship. *Al-Ṭaʿām li-kull fam* (1963; Food for every mouth) uses a domestic situation to reflect al-Ḥakīm's concern about the problems of world hunger and is characterized by a somewhat didactic, Brechtian tone — though, as in *Ashwāk al-Salām*, the solutions proposed in the play are romantically idealistic. Brecht's influence may perhaps also be seen in *Majlis al-ʿadl* (1972; Council of justice), in which al-Ḥakīm employs an allegorical technique to comment on the situation in the Middle East after the 1967 war between Egypt and Israel, when attempts to resolve the Palestine problem had become bogged down in wrangling at the United Nations; the piece is unusual among his works for its direct relevance to contemporary events.

CONCLUSION

Toward the end of his life, al-Ḥakīm came to be regarded as a sort of elder statesman among Egyptian writers. Like most Egyptian writers, he continued to produce articles for newspapers and periodicals on a variety of topics, retaining to the end his capacity to surprise. Despite his initially conciliatory attitude to the new regime, he did not go out of his way to avoid friction with President Anwar al-Sādāt. In 1973, for example, he was briefly barred from publishing after joining other writers in presenting a petition to the president; in June 1974 he published *The Return of Consciousness*, and the following year he produced a book titled *Wathāʾiq fī tārīkh ʿawdat al-waʿy* (Documents on the history of the return of consciousness), which contains the actual record of interrogations of various Egyptian intellectuals following a letter al-Ḥakīm sent to President ʿAbd al-Nāṣir about a ministerial appointment. He found himself at odds with some of his fellow writers for his favorable view of the Camp David peace accords with Israel and with Muslim fundamentalists for his opposition to extremist religious views. On a personal level, his final years were less than happy, marred by poor health and by the death of his wife and only son. He died of heart failure and associated pneumonia in Cairo on 26 July 1987.

The bewildering variety of themes and influences in al-Ḥakīm's work makes it difficult to evaluate his overall contribution to modern Arabic literature. His work is further marked by inconsistent quality and outlook. Although the language of both his plays and his narrative works is characterized by an admirable simplicity, many of his works are marred by structural faults — most obviously, a lack of unity and a tendency to rambling, philosophical digression. Where he succeeds in avoiding this defect, however, he is capable of producing works whose potential appeal extends far beyond the Middle East. In the field of the novel, the realism and immediacy of *Maze of Justice* make this work a masterpiece of universal relevance, although *The Return of the Spirit*, which succeeds in capturing the mood of his compatriots at a crucial point in their history, may well strike a more obvious chord in the heart of the average Egyptian. It is less easy to judge which of his plays are likely to retain popularity. Many of them lack dramatic qualities and were, on his own admission, written to be read rather than acted. A few, such as *The Tree Climber* and *Ughniyat al-mawt*, are conspicuous, however, for their freshness and consistency of tone. Al-Ḥakīm's influence will certainly extend far beyond our judgments on his individual works, for although he was in no sense the founder of a dramatic school, his continual innovation over half a century has proved a constant stimulus to the development of the theater in Egypt. As such, he is assured of a lasting place not only in the history of modern Arabic literature but also in the affections of the Egyptian people.

Selected Bibliography

PLAYS

Ahl al-kahf. Cairo: Maṭbaʿat Miṣr, 1933.
Shahrazād. Cairo: Maṭbaʿat Dār al-Kutub, 1934.
Muḥammad. Cairo: Maṭbaʿat Lajnat al-Taʾlīf wa-al-Tarjama wa-al-Nashr, 1936.
Masraḥiyyāt. Vol. 1. Cairo: Maṭbaʿat al-Iʿtimād, 1937. Vol. 2. Cairo: Maṭbaʿat Lajnat al-Taʾlīf wa-al-Tarjama wa-al-Nashr, 1937.
Praxagora. Cairo: Maṭbaʿat al-Tawakkul, 1939.
Nashīd al-anshād. Cairo: Maṭbaʿat Miṣr, 1940.
Pygmalion. Cairo: Maṭbaʿat al-Tawakkul, 1942.
Sulaymān al-ḥakīm. Cairo: Maṭbaʿat al-Tawakkul, 1943.
Shajarat al-ḥukm. Cairo: Maktabat al-Ādāb, 1945.
Al-Malik Ūdīb. Cairo: al-Maṭbaʿa al-Namūdhajiyya, 1949.
Masraḥ al-mujtamaʿ. Cairo: al-Maṭbaʿa al-Namūdhajiyya, 1950.
Īzīs. Cairo: al-Maṭbaʿa al-Namūdhajiyya, 1955.
Al-Masraḥ al-munawwaʿ. Cairo: Maktabat al-Ādāb, 1956.
Al-Ṣafqa. Cairo: al-Maṭbaʿa al-Namūdhajiyya, 1956.
Riḥla ilā al-ghad. Cairo: Maktabat al-Ādāb, 1957.
Laʿbat al-mawt. Cairo: Maktabat al-Ādāb, 1957.
Ashwāk al-salām. Cairo: al-Sharika al-ʿArabiyya, 1957.
Al-Sulṭān al-ḥāʾir. Cairo: Maktabat al-Ādāb, 1960.
Yā ṭāliʿ al-shajara. Cairo: Maktabat al-Ādāb, 1962.
Al-Ṭaʿām li-kull fam. Cairo: Maktabat al-Ādāb, 1963.

Riḥlat al-rabīʿ wa-al-kharīf. Cairo: Dār al-Maʿārif, 1964.
Shams al-nahār. Cairo: Maktabat al-Ādāb, 1965.
Al-Warṭa. Cairo: Maktabat al-Ādāb, 1966.
Bank al-qalaq. Cairo: Dār al-Maʿārif, 1966.
Maṣīr ṣirṣār. Cairo: Maktabat al-Ādāb, 1966.
Majlis al-ʿadl. Cairo: Maktabat al-Ādāb, 1972.
Al-Dunyā riwāya hazaliyya. Beirut, Lebanon: Dār al-Kitāb al-Lubnānī, 1974.
Imsik ḥarāmī. Cairo: al-Duwaliyya li al-Intāj al-Thaqāfī, 1981.

ESSAYS, LETTERS, NOVELS, AND SHORT STORIES

ʿAwdat al-rūḥ. Cairo: Maṭbaʿat al-Raghāʾib, 1933.
Ahl al-fann. Cairo: Maṭbaʿat al-Hilāl, 1934.
Al-Qaṣr al-mashūr. With Ṭāhā Ḥusayn. Cairo: Dār al-Nashr al-Ḥadīth, 1936.
Yawmiyyāt nāʾib fī al-aryāf. Cairo: Maṭbaʿat Lajnat al-Taʾlīf wa-al-Tarjama wa-al-Nashr, 1937.
Taḥta shams al-fikr. Cairo: Maktabat al-Ādāb, 1938.
Taʾrīkh ḥayat maʿida. Cairo: Maṭbaʿat Lajnat al-Taʾlīf wa-al-Tarjama wa-al-Nashr, 1938.
ʿUṣfūr min al-sharq. Cairo: Maṭbaʿat Lajnat al-Taʾlīf wa-al-Tarjama wa-al-Nashr, 1938.
ʿAhd al-shayṭān. Cairo: Maṭbaʿat Lajnat al-Taʾlīf wa-al-Tarjama wa-al-Nashr, 1938.
Rāqiṣat al-maʿbad. Cairo: Maṭbaʿat al-Tawakkul, 1939.
Ḥimār al-Ḥakīm. Cairo: Maṭbaʿat al-Tawakkul, 1940.
Sulṭān al-ẓalām. Cairo: Maktabat al-Ādāb, 1941.
Taḥt al-miṣbāḥ al-akhḍar. Cairo: Maṭbaʿat al-Tawakkul, 1941.
Min al-burj al-ʿājī. Cairo: Maktabat al-Ādāb, 1941.
Zahrat al-ʿumr. Cairo: Maṭbaʿat al-Tawakkul, 1943.
Al-Ribāṭ al-muqaddas. Cairo: Maṭbaʿat Saʿd Miṣr, 1944.
Ḥimārī qāl lī. Cairo: Maṭbaʿat al-Maʿārif, 1945.
Qiṣaṣ Tawfīq al-Ḥakīm. 5 vols. Cairo: Dār Saʿd Miṣr, 1949.
Fann al-adab. Cairo: al-Maṭbaʿa al-Namūdhajiyya, 1952.
ʿAdāla wa-fann. Cairo: Maktabat al-Ādāb, 1953.
Arinī Allāh. Cairo: al-Maṭbaʿa al-Namūdhajiyya, 1953.
Min dhikrayāt al-fann wa-al-qaḍāʾ. Cairo: Dār al-Maʿārif, 1953.

Madrasat al-mughaffalīn. Cairo: Dār al-Hilāl, 1953.

ʿAṣā al-Ḥakīm. Cairo: Dār al-Hilāl, 1954.

Taʾammulāt fī al-Siyāsa. Cairo: Dār Rūz al-Yūsuf, 1954.

Al-Taʿāduliyya. Cairo: Maktabat al-Ādāb, 1955.

Adab al-ḥayāh. Cairo: al-Sharika al-ʿArabiyya li al-Ṭibāʿa, 1959.

Sijn al-ʿumr. Cairo: Maktabat al-Ādāb, 1964.

Laylat al-zifāf. Cairo: Maktabat al-Ādāb, 1966.

Qālabunā al-masraḥī. Cairo: Maktabat al-Ādāb, 1967.

Qult ... dhāta yawm. Cairo: Muʾassasat Akhbār al-Yawm, 1970.

Tawfīq al-Ḥakīm yataḥaddath. Cairo: Maṭābiʿ al-Ahrām al-Tijāriyya, 1971.

Aḥādīth maʿa Tawfīq al-Ḥakīm min sana 1951–1971. Ed. by Ṣalāḥ Ṭāhir. Cairo: Dār al-Kitāb al-Jadīd, 1971.

Ḥadīth maʿa al-kawkab. Beirut, Lebanon: Dār al-Kitāb al-Lubnānī, 1974.

ʿAwdat al-waʿy. Beirut, Lebanon: Dār al-Shurūq, 1974.

Ṣafaḥāt min al-taʾrīkh al-adabī min wāqiʿ rasāʾil wa-wathāʾiq. Cairo: Dār al-Maʿārif, 1975.

Al-Amīra al-baydāʾ aw Bayāḍ al-Nahār. Cairo: al-Hayʾa al-Miṣriyya al-ʿĀmma lil-Kitāb, 1978.

Malāmiḥ dākhiliyya. Cairo: Maktabat al-Ādāb, 1982.

TRANSLATIONS

Bird of the East. Trans. by R. Bayly Winder. Beirut, Lebanon: Khayats, 1966.

A Conversation with the Planet Earth; The World Is a Comedy. Trans. by Riad Habib Youssef. Cairo: General Egyptian Book Organization, 1985.

The Fate of a Cockroach and Other Plays. Trans. by Denys Johnson-Davies. London: Heinemann, 1973.

Maze of Justice: Diary of a Country Attorney. Trans. by Abba S. Eban. London, Harvill Press, 1947. Repr. with new preface by P. H. Newby. London: Saqi, 1989.

Muhammad. Trans. by Ibrahim Hassan El-Mougy. Cairo: Supreme Council for Islamic Affairs, 1964.

Plays, Prefaces and Postscripts of Tawfiq al-Hakim. Trans. by William Hutchins. 2 vols. Washington, D.C.: Three Continents, 1981–1984.

The Prison of Life. Trans. by Pierre Cachia. Cairo: American University in Cairo Press, 1992.

The Return of Consciousness. Trans. by R. Bayly Winder. New York: New York University Press, 1985.

The Return of the Spirit. Trans. by William Hutchins. Washington, D.C.: Three Continents, 1990.

The Tree Climber. Trans. by Denys Johnson-Davies. London: Oxford University Press, 1966.

CRITICAL STUDIES

Baadawi, M. M. *Modern Arabic Literature and the West*. London: Ithaca, 1985.

———. *Modern Arabic Drama in Egypt*. Cambridge, U.K.: Cambridge University Press, 1987.

———, ed. *Modern Arabic Literature*. Cambridge, U.K.: Cambridge University Press, 1992.

Cachia, Pierre. "Idealism and Ideology: The Case of Tawfiq al-Hakim." In *Journal of the American Oriental Society* 100 (1980).

Fontaine, Jean. *Mort-résurrection: Une Lecture de Tawfiq al-Hakim*. Tunis, Tunisia: Éditions Bouslama, 1978.

Francis, Raymond. *Aspects de la littérature arabe contemporaine*. Beirut, Lebanon: Dar al-Maaref, 1963.

Ismaʿil, ʿAbd al-Munʿim. *Drama and Society in Contemporary Egypt*. Cairo: Dār al-Kātib al-ʿArabī, 1967.

Kilpatrick, Hilary. *The Modern Egyptian Novel*. London: Ithaca, 1974.

Long, Richard. *Tawfiq al-Hakim: Playwright of Egypt*. London: Ithaca, 1979.

al-Shetawi, Mahmoud. "The Treatment of Greek Drama by Tawfiq al-Hakim." In *World Literature Today* 63 (winter 1989).

Starkey, Paul. "Philosophical Themes in Tawfīq al-Ḥakīm's Drama." In *Journal of Arabic Literature* 8 (1977).

———. *From the Ivory Tower: A Critical Study of Tawfīq al-Ḥakīm*. London: Ithaca, 1987.

———. "Tawfiq al-Hakim (1898–1987): Leading Playwright of the Arab World." In *Theater Three* 6 (1989).

Tomiche, Nada. "Un Dramaturge égyptien: Tawfiq Al-Hakim et l'avant-garde." In *Revue de littérature comparée* 45 (1971).

Bessie Head
1937–1986

ANDREW PEEK

BESSIE HEAD made an extraordinary contribution to the literature of her continent in her relatively short literary career. Her work, including three novels, two collections of short stories, an oral history, a historical narrative, and a collection of articles on her life and writing, panoramically reconstitutes patterns of experience in southern Africa during the nineteenth and twentieth centuries. At the same time, Head established and explored connections between her own autobiography and these larger patterns so that, as her work documents the personal textures of historical experience, so too history is embodied in processes of psychic breakdown and renewal within the individual.

Head's fictional narratives are often framed in terms of a struggle between the forces of good and evil. The most dramatic example of this conflict can be found in her third novel, *A Question of Power* (1973), which has been described as "the first metaphysical novel on the subject of nation and national identity to come out of Southern Africa" (interview by Marquard, p. 59). Early in her career, she represented the struggle between good and evil as one between education, liberal values, and the modern on the one hand, and tribalism, racism, and unquestioning adherence to traditionalism on the other. Later, as she studied the history of the village of Serowe in

eastern Botswana, where she spent the second half of her life, this antithesis came to seem too simplistic and she significantly modified her position.

Although southern Africa and Botswana in particular provide the settings for Head's work, she saw herself as a contributor to world, rather than merely African, literature, and she resisted classification of her work in terms of nation, race, or color. Asked in an interview in 1985 about the audience she wrote for, she replied: "I like what a black professor has said about me: 'It is difficult to know which audience she is addressing,' and I like to leave it vague like that. I don't see myself declaring myself passionately pro-black, I just want to work at a story the way I want to work at it. To feel I'm telling the truth. I wouldn't like a book like *Serowe, Village of the Rainwind* [1981] to be regarded as a nationalistic work" (interview by Peek, p. 11).

Although, as with other writers in anglophone Africa, Head's early education dealt extensively with the literature of Victorian England, the writers Head identified as of great importance to her all shared this internationalist approach. They include Bertolt Brecht, D. H. Lawrence, Boris Pasternak, Leo Tolstoy, and the Irish mystic Æ (George Russell). Favorite quotations from Pasternak and others were pasted up around her small two-room house in Serowe so that they could be continually enjoyed.

Head also repudiated identification with literary groups or styles of writing. She resisted being called a feminist writer, even though her writing deals intimately with the female experience, the position of women in patriarchal societies, and the theme of women taking responsibility for themselves. She was proud of Lewis Nkosi's comment that, though she worked for Drum Publications — an innovative organization famous for *Drum* magazine, which pioneered black investigative journalism and writings by blacks for blacks — she was never part of the *Drum* group. As she put it in the 1985 interview: "I was never one of them, I was unique and alone in everything I did" (p. 8).

Head was a free spirit in circumstances that militated absolutely against freedom, as the details of her life make terribly clear. Her writing demonstrates both the cost at which this freedom was obtained and her insistence that the benefits be open to all to share. As she put it in the 1985 interview: "I have a kind of horror of belonging to camps but not a horror about caring for my fellow man" (p. 9). Looking back over everything she had written, Head described her work as "a kind of defining of goodness," and the paradoxical lines she went on to quote from Pasternak capture the note of redemptive humanity in every book she published:

> In me are people without names, children,
>   stay-at-homes, trees,
> I am conquered by them all and that is my
>   only victory.

BIOGRAPHY

Bessie Head, née Bessie Amelia Emery, was born in a mental hospital in Pietermaritzburg, a city in the Natal Province of South Africa, on 6 July 1937. After a marital breakdown, her mother, an "unknown, lovely, and unpredictable woman" from an affluent white Scottish–South African background, returned to the family home in Johannesburg and fell in love with one of the black stable hands employed to look after the family's race horses. Bessie Head was the child of this union. She was given to an Afrikaner family, who returned her after a week because, in her own words, she "appeared to be black and they could not accept a baby like this" (Marquard, p. 49). Afterward she was given to a Colored couple. (*Colored* in South Africa means people of mixed-race origins.) Her foster father died when she was six; Bessie Emery, her own mother, whose existence she did not know of at the time, had committed suicide around the same time. Head's foster mother continued to care for her. Although Head later found out about her biological mother, her foster mother was a woman whom, Head wrote, "I became deeply attached [to] and accepted as my mother" (*A Woman Alone*, 1990, p. 3).

However, conditions at home began to deteriorate. During World War II, Head's foster mother started selling beer as a means of support. Servicemen and their consorts were always around. According to *A Question of Power*, "hours and hours" of Head's childhood were spent "sitting under a lamp-post near her house, crying because everyone was drunk and there was no food, no one to think about children" (pp. 15–16). She was "secretly relieved" when child welfare authorities decided to transfer her to St. Monica's Home in Hilary when she was thirteen years old.

It was at this point that Head was informed of the circumstances of her birth by the principal of the mission school where she was enrolled. Head was given the following version of her origins: "Your mother was insane. If you're not careful you'll get insane just like your mother. Your mother was a white woman. They had to lock her up as she was having a child by a stable boy who was a native" (*A Woman Alone*, p. 4). Head wrote that "for years and years after that I harboured a terrible and blind hatred for missionaries and the Christianity which they represented" (p. 4), although she also observed that "in some parts of my heart I bow down to the King of the Jews" (p. 44). In an article published a year before her death, she stated, "I value that vivid, great short story teller, Jesus Christ, and the foundation he laid for such terms as mankind, the human race and love of one's neighbour" (p. 96).

Whatever ambiguities Head had toward Christianity and missionaries, there is no question of the shattering impact of the school principal's revelation on her. Already coping with a combination of confusion, relief, and perhaps guilt at being taken from a woman who she had just discovered was a foster mother, the adolescent Head also had to deal with the fact of a biological mother who had a history of mental illness that had led to suicide. Though she subsequently discovered that her maternal grandmother had attempted to keep some contact with her, Head was left feeling that she had no connection with family or even race.

As Craig MacKenzie has written in *Bessie Head: An Introduction* (1989), it is not surprising in these circumstances that Head "struggled her whole life for a sense of identity and a sense of self-worth." He fleshes out this description with two quotations from Head herself: "I have always just been me, with no frame of reference beyond myself," a quotation that dates from 1982, and from an interview the following year, "As you get older, the loneliness takes a terrible toll on you. It is as though there should be some human there to compensate for some things, and some love you've given to life. It's like you've only given and there's nobody to give you anything" (pp. 6–7). In his introduction to *A Woman Alone*, MacKenzie has also suggested links between Head's mother's "progressive psychosis" and her acute awareness throughout her life of the "fragility" of her own mental balance (p. xi).

In spite of the traumatic introduction, Head made the most of her time at her new school,

and she came to value the ideal of service to one's people and community that was a part of "the general atmosphere of the mission school: that we are being given something and now we should serve our people" (interview by Peek, p. 7).

Head went on to gain a teaching certificate in 1955 and worked for two years as a teacher, although she also continued to educate herself through extensive reading in a library for nonwhites in Durban. The library had been endowed by a wealthy Muslim man and reflected his interest in Asian biography and philosophy in general. As a result of the library's emphasis on these areas, Head became interested in Buddhism, reincarnation, and the Hindu practice of "sannyasi," according to which individuals suddenly abandon worldly ways and take up the life of a wandering ascetic. All of these eastern influences find a way into Head's fiction. In particular, there are clear parallels between sannyasi and the sudden, dramatic transformations that often send her characters off in completely unexpected directions, from her first novel, *When Rain Clouds Gather* (1968), to the last book published before her death in 1986, *A Bewitched Crossroad: An African Saga* (1984).

In 1957, Head took another job as schoolteacher. Looking back on her teaching years, she felt that she "didn't have the talent for communicating with young minds" and was "so unhappy in the profession" (interview by Peek, p. 7). Two years later, she began working in Johannesburg for *Golden City Post*, part of the Drum Publications. In 1960 Head moved to Cape Town, where she "lived in a hotel room in District Six [a district famous for its cosmopolitan, bohemian atmosphere] on bread and beer supplied by friends while she worked on a novel that was never published" (MacKenzie, *Bessie Head: An Introduction*, p. 4). She subsequently published articles in the *New African* and *Drum* alongside such prominent figures as James Matthews, Richard Rive, Dennis Brutus, and Ezekiel (Es'kia) Mphahlele.

Journalism, Head believed, offered the potential to travel and meet people, and though she distanced herself from other *Drum* writers, the experience was valuable to the development of her writing: "You produce everyday short stories under great pressure. It sharpens your style. You have to be precise and accurate.... Writing for *Drum* was a useful discipline. I'm not loose and baggy, when I tell a story I tell it as tautly, concisely and economically as I can" (interview by Peek, p. 8).

The first four years of the 1960s were momentous ones for Bessie Head, and the events in those years resonated through everything she subsequently wrote. In addition to her efforts to establish herself as a novelist, she married Harold Head, a journalist—although *A Question of Power*, an autobiographical novel, describes the protagonist's husband as a promiscuous "gangster" (p. 18). She moved temporarily to Port Elizabeth, returned to Cape Town, gave birth to her son, Howard, became estranged from her husband, and in March 1964 moved with Howard to Serowe, a settlement in southeastern Botswana on the edge of the Kalahari Desert. She took up a post as a primary school teacher, though she had already left the profession once and was soon to do so again.

These events went hand in hand with Head's cumulative experiences as a Colored woman in urban South Africa, an environment she described as a "choking, throttling, death-like kind of world" in an interview with Linda Susan Beard (p. 44). Botswana may have seemed an ideal alternative at the time. About to gain independence from Great Britain, which came in 1966, Botswana was home to many political refugees from South Africa. Moreover, unlike Europe and the United States, the usual destinations of nonwhite South African writers, Botswana offered traditional cultures that had the potential to find a new sense of black identity.

However, there were other, less favorable, factors in the choice of Botswana as a place to live. Because Head had been unable to obtain a South African passport, she arrived in Botswana as a refugee and was to remain one for fifteen years. It was only in 1979 that the Botswanan authorities, recognizing Head's literary status and the prestige attached to it, granted her citizenship. Furthermore, she had always been a city dweller and was of mixed-race origin, a journalist and writer, by any standard a liberated person, possessed of a utopian streak, and a woman. Her new home, Botswana, especially the rural areas, struck her as patriarchal, hierarchical, and tribal. The authorities treated her with suspicion; she believed they intercepted and read all her mail. She never learned to speak Setswana, the local language. In every way she was thrown back on her own resources after an early life already characterized by profound dispossession.

Just a few months after she arrived, Botswana went into a major drought. In 1966, Head left Serowe to move to Francistown, approximately a hundred miles to the north. In 1968 her first novel, *When Rain Clouds Gather*, was published in New York. In 1969 she returned to Serowe and went through a period of serious mental illness, culminating in her hospitalization in a psychiatric institution in Gaborone, the Botswanan capital. She recovered in the following year, and in 1971 a second novel, *Maru*, was published in London. Head's third novel, *A Question of Power*, published in London in 1973, reconstructs her mental illness in an extended narrative. As a succession of critical articles has shown, the novel has become one of the great enigmas of modern African writing and is widely considered her finest book.

In the years after she felt settled and secure in Serowe, Head came to describe it as a place where she was able to heal and regenerate. She wrote in *Serowe, Village of the Rainwind*: "It was by chance that I came to live in this village. I have lived most of my life in shattered little bits. Somehow, here, the shattered bits began to grow together. There is a sense of wovenness, a wholeness in life here; a feeling of how strange and beautiful people can be—just living" (p. x). Passages in her fiction and in *Serowe* contain many lyrical descriptions of the place and its people. At the same time the novels and the details of her mental breakdown indicate that the move to Botswana was a profoundly unsettling and challenging one. As she had done earlier, Head made courageous and constructive use of the experiences that came her way.

Serowe is a huge village with a semi-itinerant population of more than forty thousand. Although relatively distant from Gaborone, Serowe is famous in Botswana for the Bamangwato leaders who settled, ran, and sometimes fled from the village, including Khama the Great (who ruled the Bamangwato from 1875 to 1923), his son, Tshekedi Khama, and grandson, Seretse Khama. Head wrote about them in her historical works. Serowe is also known for its highly successful cooperative projects and international aid programs. These include the Swaneng scheme started by the South African Patrick van Rensburg in 1963. Van Rensburg, one of the people to whom Head dedicated her first novel, appears to be a model for the character Eugene in *A Question of Power*. Swaneng initially involved the setting up of a secondary school but ultimately led to a variety of rural development projects designed to employ graduates of the school, who worked alongside international volunteers, in order to help meet the cost of developing and running the school. One of the projects involved a market gardening collective. Head assisted in the day-to-day production of fruits and vegetables that were sold to the villagers and used to stimulate local industries such as jam making.

THE AUTOBIOGRAPHICAL NOVELS

Head described *When Rain Clouds Gather*, *Maru*, and *A Question of Power* as all "definitely . . . autobiographical. Everything that was of value to my development and my ex-

perience went into the first three novels" (interview by Peek, p. 12). Each focuses on outsider figures who move to a large village in Botswana on the fringes of the desert during the 1960s, making use of the experience to renew themselves and find a new belief in humanity. *When Rain Clouds Gather* may well have incorporated personal stories picked up from other refugees in Serowe and Francistown. *Maru* mixes autobiographical and fictional elements. *A Question of Power* by all accounts includes material directly from Head's life—of the main character Head once observed, in a 1989 interview by Michelle Adler and others, "Elizabeth and I are one"—and crosses into territory that seems closer to autobiography than fiction. Head felt there was enough commonality about the three novels to describe them as a trilogy.

These novels also have didactic elements that perhaps evolved from Head's experience as a journalist, who had a "slant" on whatever story she was telling. In *When Rain Clouds Gather* and *Maru*, prejudice, black racism, corrupt tribal leaders, and witchcraft are portrayed as having the power to manipulate and terrorize the common people. Education and a new worldview can work against the old order, and the three novels embrace the innovative forces unequivocally, unlike Nigerian writer Chinua Achebe's novels, for example, where they have a complex and disintegrative effect on the individual, family, and community. In Head's view, inspired and innovative leadership can transform perceptions, though the processes of social change will take place within individuals rather than as a result of being imposed upon them.

The three novels also include a considerable amount of detailed practical information about horticulture, agriculture in general, and the setting up and running of cooperatives, all of which Head had seen and become involved with in Serowe. In addition to putting together an authentic historical record, the many passages dealing with planting, growing, and harvesting carry symbolic meanings for individual characters and for the community as a whole.

At the same time, as they focus on material reality, these novels also explore subjectivity, fantasy, and the immaterial. It is the ability of the characters to dream, to be utopian, to think in terms of nothing less than the cosmos and eternity (they become gods, the sun, moon, earth, and stars) which distinguishes and ennobles them. Romantic love can raise men and women to transcendent states. Indeed, all three novels enact, in very different ways, the fulfillment of relationships between the central male and female characters.

In 1973, Ronald Blythe wrote in the British *Sunday Times* that Head's first three novels "have a way of soaring up from rock bottom to the stars, and are very shaking." These novels display Head's remarkable ability to combine narrative and stylistic diversity with an overall unity of effect.

When Rain Clouds Gather

In this, the simplest of Bessie Head's novels, Makhaya Maseko, a young Zulu on the run from the South African security forces, crosses into Botswana and begins life in the village of Golema Mmidi, which means "to grow crops" (Heinemann edition, p. 28). He meets an old man called Dinorego, who has been instrumental in establishing a cattle cooperative in the village, and Gilbert, an agriculturalist who is running away from bourgeois England and is galvanized by the challenge of farming in the village. With the help of a British colonial administrator, Makhaya is able to begin a new life, helping Gilbert introduce farming innovations to the villagers, in particular the women. Paulina Sebeso, a young widow with great strength of character and another outsider who has established herself in the community, acts as a liaison between Gilbert and the village women.

Makhaya arrives in Botswana with the warning that he may simply be exchanging the white "tribalism" of apartheid in South Africa for the destructive black tribalism of the Batswana. However, as independence approaches, the hold of the vicious village chief, Matenge, becomes progressively weaker. Paulina's son dies of tuberculosis on a distant cattle outpost during a drought, and, to compound her suffering, Matenge attempts to punish her for her involvement in an agricultural project set up by Gilbert and Makhaya. His plan to destroy Paulina is the last straw for the village people. They rally against him, and he commits suicide. Meanwhile, Gilbert has married Dinorego's daughter, Maria, and as the novel ends Makhaya is finally ready to propose to Paulina.

There are some inconsistencies in Head's handling of the main characters. Themes such as Gilbert's utopianism and Makhaya's guilt and self-torture sometimes seem to be imposed on, rather than dramatized within, the characters' behavior. Nevertheless, the novel presents an original reading of a postcolonial situation.

Maru

The short opening section of *Maru* is seen primarily through the eyes of the eponymous hero, who runs a tiny farming community with his wife, Margaret, and three followers, Ranko, Moseka, and Semana. Maru is a visionary and born leader acting out his "strange inner perceptions" (Heinemann edition, pp. 5–6), never doubting the "voices of the gods in his heart" (p. 8). An innovator, resistant to prejudice, Maru nevertheless has his own secret agenda. He has a loving relationship with his wife, though he believes she loves another man at the same time: "There were two rooms. In one his wife totally loved him; in another, she totally loved Moleka" (p. 8).

The point of view then shifts to Margaret before her marriage to Maru. Margaret Cadmore is a Masarwa, one of the "Bushmen" of the Kalahari Desert, an indigenous people subjected to prejudice and enslavement and treated as "untouchables," like those of the lower-caste Hindus, by the Batswana tribespeople. Margaret was adopted as an orphan and raised by an inspirational educator who was married to the local missionary and after whom she was named. The young Margaret is a "brilliant student" and eventually becomes a primary school teacher (p. 19), but as a child she suffers an acute lack of personal identity—there was a "big hole in the child's mind between the time that she slowly became conscious of her life in the home of the missionaries and conscious of herself as a person" (p. 15)—that worsens when her foster mother leaves her to return to Britain.

At her first teaching position in Dilepe, a remote inland village, Margaret declines the easier option of being called Colored and stirs up a storm of protest at school when it is discovered that she is a Masarwa. However, she is befriended by Dikeledi, a fellow teacher and Maru's sister. Dikeledi is in love with Moleka, who happens to be a close friend to Maru. By birth, Maru will inherit the position of paramount chief, head of the village's tribal hierarchy, when the incumbent dies.

Margaret's entry into this triangle of characters has dramatic consequences for all of them. When Moleka and Maru both decide they are in love with Margaret, Maru, who manipulates and controls everyone around him, ensures that he gets her, even though he is aware that he will transform his relationship with Moleka from intimacy to antagonism. He takes Margaret as well as Ranko, Moseka, and Semana off to his new farming settlement, but he continues to feel jealous of Margaret's perceived affection for Moleka and uncomfortable about what he has done.

Although Margaret, Maru, and his three followers leave the village, the fact of a marriage between a Masarwa woman and a man who would otherwise have been paramount chief will permanently change the perceptions of the Masarwa left behind. A "door silently opened on the small, dark airless room in which their souls had been shut for a long time. The wind of freedom, which was blowing throughout the world for all people, turned and flowed into the room. As they breathed in the fresh, clear air their humanity awakened" (p. 126).

Head regularly emphasized the importance of the liberation of racial minority groups through this process of education by example, demonstrated at the close of her novel. It should also be noted that *Maru* is a work of considerable technical flair, notable for the way in which conventional notions of "character" in fiction are questioned and challenged. All the major characters are "doubled" by name or motif, so that, though the temperament and behavior of these characters may be quite distinct, the reader is encouraged to see ironic parallels and connections between them. There are two Margaret Cadmores, for instance, and Arthur Ravenscroft has suggested that we are teased by the question of whether the sagacious Maru and the fiery Moleka "are indeed two separate fictional characters or ... symbolic extensions of contending character-traits within the same man" (p. 179).

A Question of Power

A Question of Power dramatically expands the theme of South African refugees who move to rural Botswana. The refugee in this case is simply called Elizabeth. The novel describes events in Elizabeth's life in South Africa that lead up to her move to her adoptive home, and it invites the reader to interpret Elizabeth's traumatic experiences in Botswana in the light of her South African ones.

Elizabeth has moved from South Africa with her young son to Motabeng, "the place of sand" (Heinemann edition, p. 19). Acute loneliness and alienation, anxiety about her son, and unhappiness with her job as a schoolteacher all increase the tensions in her life to an unbearable level until she begins to show signs of mental instability. She directs a stream of abuse at a local shop assistant— "Oh, you bloody bastard Batswana!! Oh, you bloody bastard Batswana!!" (p. 51)—and chooses to leave her job rather than, at the school principal's request, obtain a certificate to prove her sanity. Eugene, the South African principal of a senior high school, helps Elizabeth obtain a job in the village gardening project. Elizabeth finds growing vegetables restorative to her health. Through her job she meets overseas aid workers such as Camilla, who is from Denmark, and Tom, a friendly and supportive young American, as well as local villagers, including Kenosi, who all offer support to her.

Elizabeth was effectively orphaned after birth, and her deprived Colored South African background continues to provoke unresolved feelings in her. At one point, for instance, she lives in an area in Cape Town where "nearly all the Coloured men were homosexuals" (p. 45). Although she accounts for this in terms of the emasculating effect of racist subjugation by a white regime, under which African men are reduced both in name and status to "boys," Elizabeth is disturbed by a blend of empathy and guilt that causes her to "identify with the weak, homosexual Coloured men who were dying before her eyes" (p. 47). Though she has been damaged by white racism, she also feels profoundly threatened by the Batswana and their practice of witchcraft, and remarks to Tom, "If you saw the soul of the black man the way I saw it, you'd feel afraid" (p. 134).

She verbally attacks an old white woman called Mrs. Jones. In a jealous rage, she posts a note on the wall of the post office, vilifying a married man to whom she is attracted: "SELLO IS A FILTHY PERVERT WHO SLEEPS WITH HIS DAUGHTER" (p. 175). Sent to a mental hospital, she protests, "I'm not an African. Don't you see? I never want to be an African" (p. 181). Later, though, she is able to describe her experiences to Tom as "a strange journey into hell and darkness" (p. 190). Finally, Elizabeth establishes herself in her new home. In the novel's closing lines, "as she fell asleep, she placed one soft hand over her land. It was a gesture of belonging" (p. 206).

This, at any rate, is a synopsis of the events of Elizabeth's life as seen from the outside. From early after her arrival in Motabeng, Elizabeth also leads an extraordinary inner life, constructed out of an elaborate, eclectic blend of world mythologies—Buddhist, Jewish, Hindu, Greek, Roman, Christian—and focused on two local men. The first, Sello, is a married crop farmer and cattle breeder, "a wonderful family man" who "keeps order in his house," according to a young Motswana nurse (p. 29). Dan, the second man, "one of the very few cattle millionaires of the country" (p. 104), has megalomaniac tendencies: "He had not yet told the whole of mankind about his ambitions, like Hitler and Napoleon, to rule the world" (p. 14). He also leads a promiscuous sex life, a fact he uses to harry and dominate Elizabeth.

The first part of the novel portrays the first phase of Elizabeth's relationship with Sello and includes imaginary exchanges involving Elizabeth, Sello, and a series of incarnations. Fragments of dialogue and reported experiences are interspersed with surreal visions to indicate how Elizabeth's mental state mediates and modifies her distressed state at the time. This includes the evocation of different versions of Sello and a Medusa figure who is finally reduced to a pile of ashes on the floor of Elizabeth's room. This phase of the relationship is characterized by overdependency, sexual jealousy, and a debilitating, soulful intensity that is reminiscent of the work of D. H. Lawrence, whose poem "God" provides the epigraph for *A Question of Power*.

In the second part, Elizabeth enters a fiercely destructive relationship with Dan, supposedly a friend of Sello's, and has vivid visions of his seventy-one sexual consorts, including Miss Sewing-Machine, Miss Wriggly-Bottom, Madame Make-Love-on-the-Floor,

The Sugar-Plum Fairy, Body Beautiful, Madame Squelch Squelch, and The Womb. By the end of this hellish relationship, Elizabeth has learned enough about herself and her own feelings to be ready to establish a new and more meaningful relationship with Sello. She now sees him as someone offering the "thread of coherence" that allows her to resolve her questions about human suffering. When she hears his criticism of her dealings with Dan—"Love isn't like that. Love is two people mutually feeding each other, not one living on the soul of the other like a ghoul" (p. 197)—she is ready for a new relationship with Sello. This time he will be her eternal friend and brother.

A Question of Power is about love, creativity, degradation, and the power of good and evil to influence the way people deal with each other. These universal issues are treated through the experience of a woman who, though in crisis, continues to negotiate everyday events and to draw meaning and succor from them: finding work in a gardening project, caring for her son, and appreciating sympathetic individuals and beautiful things around her.

In certain respects, Sello, Dan, and Elizabeth rework the sexual triangle of Maru, Moleka, and Margaret in *Maru*. However, the exhaustive and harrowing evocation of Elizabeth's inner world expands the possibilities of character development allowed Margaret Cadmore and dramatically extends the novel's potential for psychic and mythic resonance. *A Question of Power*, published only five years after Head's first novel, demonstrates the remarkable progress in her narrative techniques and also marks the end of the first phase of Head's literary career.

HISTORICAL AND SOCIOLOGICAL NARRATIVES

If the cooperative projects for which Serowe became famous are written into Head's first three novels, the village's other major claim to fame, the Bamangwato leadership from Khama the Great to Seretse Khama, occupies an increasingly important position in her next three books: *The Collector of Treasures and Other Botswana Village Tales* (1977), a collection of short narratives; *Serowe, Village of the Rainwind* (1981), an oral history; and *A Bewitched Crossroad: An African Saga* (1984), a historical narrative with fictional elements. These books mark an abrupt movement away from subjectivity, introspection, and fantasy, concentrating instead on the people and institutions of Serowe, including its nineteenth- and twentieth-century leaders.

Khama the Great, also known as Khama III, was the most significant of these leaders. Born the eldest son of Sekogma I in 1837, Khama lived at a key juncture of time and place. In his early twenties, Khama converted to Christianity and with his generation began a program of modernization that promoted western liberalism and the rights of the individual, along with more down-to-earth practices like wearing European clothing. He was threatened with witchcraft and assassination by the old order but subsequently assumed leadership of his people (1875–1923) and led them to found their present center at Serowe in 1902. *Serowe* details a variety of practical reforms Khama instituted to promote the rights of the individual, remove the secrecy and fear often accompanying traditional ritual, and end human sacrifice. He suppressed *bogadi,* the practice of paying a bride-price, opposed the slavery of the Masarwa, and modified tribal coming-of-age rituals.

Head describes Tshekedi Khama, who ruled from 1926 to 1959, as a realist and a pragmatist. He introduced the two areas of education and self-help that were later taken up by van Rensburg. Seretse Khama became the first president of independent Botswana in 1966, having previously been forced to flee from Serowe because of his unsanctioned marriage to an English woman, Ruth Williams, in 1948.

Khama and Tshekedi Khama are presented as leaders of considerable genius in *Serowe.*

They are visionary and utopian figures epitomizing the liberating impact of the new. From the eulogistic tone of the comments on Khama in *Serowe*, one senses that Head both upholds and identifies with this historical figure. He is presented as someone who, like Head herself, "fought battles of principle on all sides against both white and black" (p. 70), was "touched by personal insight into human suffering as opposed to group acceptance of tradition" (p. 8), and had been sensitized by early loneliness. All these characteristics have clear connections with Head's autobiographical narratives and the self-image that they construct.

Similarly, the migration theme, which *Serowe* identifies with the Bamangwato leaders, applies to Khama, Tshekedi Khama, and Seretse Khama at different times in their lives and to Head's own individual flight from South Africa to Botswana. Head wrote of the Bamangwato leaders: "The drama was always the same: in a large clan, hostilities of an intolerable nature would develop. One of the clan leaders would pack up house and home and a whole section of the people would move off with him" (p. 66).

However, Khama's major social reforms were by no means an unbridled success, and this had become particularly evident during Head's residence in Serowe. Getting rid of bride-price to give women more dignity, for instance, had the unintended result of undermining marriage and, from what Head could observe around her, of destroying the family as an effective unit. (In *Serowe*, she claims that 97 percent of children in Serowe are illegitimate.) The old tribal laws and ethos that suppressed the individual, the identity of women, and qualities such as compassion and tenderness had, at the same time, provided an external discipline that helped maintain social cohesiveness.

The second phase of Head's writing brought into clear view what the first phase had suggested: that change and external modernizing influences should be unequivocally endorsed in the face of the evils of tribalism and unthinking adherence to tradition. "The discipline people now had to impose on themselves was internal and private," Head explains in the introduction to *Serowe* (p. xiv), and it was the exploration of how this new system could work, in conjunction with retaining the redemptive and in her own word "holy" communality of tradition, that stimulated some of the best writing of Head's career, especially in *The Collector of Treasures, and Other Botswana Village Tales.*

The Collector of Treasures

This collection of thirteen short narratives is subtitled *Botswana Village Tales*. As Gillian Stead Eilersen has pointed out in her introduction to Head's *Tales of Tenderness and Power*, it was assembled with considerable care; Head aimed "to shape the individual stories in such a way that one trailed into the other" (p. 11), despite the fact that a number of them had appeared individually in *Ms.*, *Encounter*, the *Magazine for Black Women*, *Black World*, and other journals. All the tales are presented as fiction, though they derive from a variety of oral and written historical sources as well as what are evidently observations and anecdotes gathered from Head's life and research in Serowe.

The first tale, "The Deep River: A Story of Ancient Tribal Migration," serves as a prologue. Set in a timeless era, it reworks the theme of tribal migration following conflict. The conflict involves a chief whose open love for one of the wives of his dead father defies tribal laws. Upholding the values of romantic love, the leader leaves, accompanied by those villagers who respect his decision. The tale, ironically framed by old men who complain that "they lost their place of birth over a woman" (p. 6), is a paradigm of the coming of the modern to a traditional community.

The next eight stories examine institutions and forces that shape the lives of villagers in Botswana, including the rigid imposition of mission Christianity ("Heaven Is Not Closed"), the power and limitations of witchcraft ("Looking for a Rain God," "Witch-craft"), and the forum for village discussion ("Kgotla"). The final four stories place special emphasis on the role of women in situations where men have been progressively weakened by the colonial and then postcolonial experience and women have had to take responsibility for themselves. The story entitled "The Collector of Treasures" describes how a woman is impelled to murder her brutal husband by cutting off his genitals and finds solace in prison among women who have done the same thing. Head said the story was prompted by a series of newspaper reports of similar incidents in rural Botswana.

There is no room for sentimentality or stereotype in the way these tales present characters whose relationships, values, and even lives are often threatened by "vampire" presences of self-appointed prophets, holy men, and supposed do-gooders. The stories portray village women and some men as being capable of adapting to their changing environment and at the same time of becoming part of the "ancient stream of holiness" in the place they inhabit (p. 11). In this community, discussion has a special dignity and meaning: "It wasn't so important to resolve human problems as to discuss around them, to pontificate, to generalize, to display wit, wisdom, wealth of experience or depth of thought" (p. 62). In the acknowledgements, Head records her debt to C. L. S. Nyembezi's "beautiful interpretations" of Zulu proverbs in his *Zulu Proverbs*, an indebtedness that indicates Head's scholarly and research-oriented approach to the writing of narrative (p. x). In addition to the many passages of beauty and grace, it should also be emphasized that the collection is especially memorable for the fluency with which it transposes the subtleties and delicacies of an oral culture into the written format of the short story.

Serowe, Village of the Rainwind

The Collector of Treasures, together with *Serowe, Village of the Rainwind*, brought Head into a different relationship with her adoptive village home. She was now a custodian of the history of Serowe and its people who brought together community resources in her writing, a process of literary cooperation comparable to the cooperative rural development projects in *Serowe*. She continued to use Serowe to construct models of change and development in Africa while at the same time looking back to missionary histories, for it was the missionary who "produced the first written records of African history, and one is forced to refer to them when doing any research into the past. This hurts, because their writings are a desecration of human life. They keep an eye on the audience back home who will be titillated by the sensational material" (*Serowe*, p. 27). As is often the case in this book, Head promptly qualifies what she has said with an example that counters it: "John Mackenzie's *Ten Years North of the Orange River* stands quite apart in quality and value from the general run of missionary writings, for in Mackenzie, God and humility were wonderfully blended" (p. 27).

Originally conceived in the spirit of Ronald Blythe's well-received portrait of an English village, *Akenfield*, *Serowe* presents a series of oral histories gathered from more than one hundred of Serowe's inhabitants, together with selective quotations from missionary histories and statements by Khama, Tshekedi Khama, and van Rensburg. Since this is the history of a community and its people, Head begins with short oral histories by the oldest members, those men and women immediately influenced by and involved in Khama's social reforms, in Part One, "The Era of Khama the Great." As editor and interviewer, Head provides helpful introductions that contextualize and clarify each account. Although her construction of Khama is an idealized portrait of a charismatic individual, there is a lively discussion of what it was like to live through and after his reforms.

In Part Two, "The Era of Tshekedi Khama," Tshekedi is presented as the leader who carried on the spirit of Khama's reforms by converting them into reality. A number of histories in this part record the disgruntlement of Tshekedi's generation, who contributed extensively to his communal projects and subsequently considered that they had been given little recognition in postindependence Botswana. Part Three offers an impressionistic account of the Swaneng Project and Patrick van Rensburg, who is described in a short section titled "Patrick van Rensburg" and is presented as in essence a continuation of the inspired traditional leadership.

Serowe, Village of the Rainwind captures the spirit of a remarkable community. It contains many voices, reverential, humorous, disappointed, grumpy, inspired, passionate; and the most passionate and lyrical of all of these is Head's own voice in her introductory notes and her gentle epilogue, "A Poem to Serowe."

A Bewitched Crossroad: An African Saga

The title of Head's next book, *A Bewitched Crossroad: An African Saga*, conveys the perception of the Bechuanaland Protectorate, the colonial name for Botswana, as a geographical intersection between major colonial and indigenous forces that somehow escaped the destructive experience of the rest of southern Africa. The book is devoted to exploring possible answers to the question posed in its penultimate chapter: "What made the British Bechuanaland Protectorate a land of 'peace and rest' under direct rule from London?" (p. 196).

To give the broadest perspective (and this is certainly the most panoramic of Head's works), a colonial narrative begins with a brief history of the first European settlement at the Cape (in what was to become South Africa) in 1652, including terms made with the local Khoikhoi that were quickly broken. A second, indigenous narrative begins in 1816 with the beginning of Shaka's rise to power, the period of Mfecane or "the Wars of Calamity," and the style of government adopted

afterward by the Basotho chief Moshoeshoe, which set a precedent for later African leaders, including Khama.

The main historical characters in *A Bewitched Crossroad* include Khama and his father, Sekogma; John Mackenzie, a missionary who later became a colonial administrator and worked hard to safeguard the protectorate's interests, eventually losing his job in the process; and J. D. Hepburn, another missionary who is presented a good deal more sympathetically in *A Bewitched Crossroad* than he is in *Serowe*. We also share the experiences of the Sebina family, who migrate from their traditional homeland to join the Bamangwato tribe under Khama in 1882, as well as the experiences of other villagers who support or criticize their leader. In her author's note Head points out that "the characters of Sebina and the boy Mazebe were erected from an essay, 'History of Makalaka,' by Peter Mazebe Sebina," though the novel "is not intended to be an accurate history of the Sebina clan" (p. vii).

The main historical event in the later stages of *A Bewitched Crossroad* is the attempt by Cecil Rhodes to transfer Bechuanaland to his British South Africa Company. Khama, together with two fellow chiefs, sailed to England to protest to the government about the transfer and toured the nation to promote his case. *A Bewitched Crossroad* suggests that Khama's vision, resourcefulness, and a readiness to embrace liberal western values equipped him to deal effectively with the British government. The novel also makes reference to the Jameson raid, an abortive attempt by Rhodes and Leander Starr Jameson to overthrow the Boer government in Transvaal, South Africa. The failure of the raid discredited Rhodes, who, among other things, was prevented in his plans to gain control of Bechuanaland. Head's novel suggests that this was fortunate for Bechuanaland, and subsequently for Botswana, which benefited from the British colonial presence and was protected from the full force of the destructive trauma experienced elsewhere in southern Africa.

In *A Bewitched Crossroad*, Khama represents the melioristic possibilities when tradition and the modern meet; but even when a leader possesses vision and purpose, serendipity and a beneficent "bewitchment" still have a role to play in transforming a well-intentioned leader into a successful one. Head's final publication before her death celebrates an unusual combination of forces: humanitarian political commitment that cuts across race and creed, faith in a benign higher power, and roots that connect, as she put it, "to the old tribal way of life and its slow courtesies" (Beard, 1986, p. 41).

A Bewitched Crossroad: An African Saga synthesizes material from a range of historical sources, which are noted in an extensive bibliography. Head's book offers an ambitious, engaged piece of historical reconstruction even though it is, as the subheading makes clear, a "saga" rather than a novel in a conventional sense.

POSTHUMOUS COLLECTIONS

Tales of Tenderness and Power

Gillian Stead Eilersen, the editor of *Tales of Tenderness and Power* (1989), brings together twenty-one of Head's short narratives to convey a sense of the pattern of her life and to suggest her developing engagement with history and politics. The title of the collection celebrates Head's enduring preoccupation with the redemptive quality of tenderness and with power and politics, all of them central to the human condition.

The first four pieces, among the earliest Head wrote, vividly evoke black urban life in Cape Town and outside Johannesburg in the 1950s and early 1960s. This group is introduced by "Let Me Tell a Story Now . . . ," a parable about Head's genesis as a

writer that was published in 1962. The next seven pieces, as Eilersen points out, were written during the early period of Head's time in Serowe. They reflect Head's journalistic skills, as exemplified by the bold, opening sentence to "Village People," "Poverty has a home in Africa—like a quiet second skin" (p. 41), and the eye for the event in "Chibuku Beer and Independence." More important, they generate a sense of dignity that broadens and extends the anecdotes they relate. Four later stories in the collection, "A Power Struggle," "A Period of Darkness," "The Lovers," and "Son of the Soil," represent a group of historical tales that Head worked on after *The Collector of Treasures* and that confirm her, according to Eilersen in the introduction, as a "genuine teller of tales, part of an ancient African tradition" (p. 10). "Son of the Soil" reflects Head's admiration for the two writers mentioned in a footnote: the pioneering black writer and journalist Sol Plaatje and the missionary and politician John Mackenzie.

The final five stories bring the collection to the present. "The Coming of the Christ—Child" beautifully but also sardonically pays tribute to the Pan-Africanist Robert Sobukwe, though he is never mentioned by name in the text. "The Prisoner Wore Glasses," anthologized a number of times and translated into Danish, Dutch, and German, develops a story Head heard from a refugee in Francistown about a set of prisoners who humanized a prison officer. It celebrates the relationship between tenderness and power in a way that is toughly affirmative and entirely without sentimentality.

A Woman Alone

Rather than focusing on Head's body of work, *A Woman Alone* (1990) deals, according to its editor, Craig MacKenzie, with "the life of a South African–born woman who happened to become an internationally recognised author" and consists of "a mosaic of sketches, essays and personal notes" (p. x). The sequence of the collection—a third of whose articles had appeared in *Tales of Tenderness and Power*—is chronological, reflecting three phases: Head's early life in South Africa (1937–1964), her exile in Botswana (1964–1979), and her life as a Botswanan citizen (1979–1986).

The autobiographical aspect of Head's three novels supports MacKenzie's selection of Head's writing dealing with her life experiences, including her contact with work of fellow South African artists. Furthermore, *A Woman Alone* contains striking personal testimonies of life in Cape Town ("A Gentle People") and Serowe ("For Serowe: A Village in Africa") and also of Head's visit to Iowa in the United States ("Some Happy Memories of Iowa"). The essay "God and the Underdog" indicates the complex relationship Head had with Christianity, while "Makeba Music" and "Foreword to Ellen Kuzwayo's *Call Me Woman*" record the special meaning that the work of other South African women writers had for her. However, the subsection entitled "Notes on Novels" and "Writing Out of Southern Africa," which refer directly to Head's literary career, contain some of the most substantial and interesting material in this collection.

A Gesture of Belonging

In 1991, Randolph Vigne published *A Gesture of Belonging: Letters from Bessie Head, 1965–1979*, a selection of letters he received from Head from 1965 until their correspondence essentially came to an end in 1979. During the early 1960s, Vigne had actively campaigned against the racist policies of the ruling National Party. Because of his political activities and also because of his role as editor of the monthly journal *New African*, which published six stories and articles by Head between 1962 and 1964, Vigne came into contact with Head and her husband, Harold. Vigne fled to Britain in 1964 to avoid arrest by the South African security forces shortly after Head had moved to Botswana. In the following October,

she wrote to him in London reestablishing contact. For Head, it was valuable to have an editor connected with the literary world in London. She was also prepared to share thoughts and (often choleric) feelings with him in letters that try to assuage the frustration, anxiety, and loneliness of a good deal of her early life in Botswana.

Vigne's book includes 107 letters, divided into six sections, grouped according to date and place. The letters in the final section mention her stay in Iowa as a participant in the International Writers' Program. Vigne describes Head as "a superb correspondent" who always wrote "vividly and with passion" (p. vi). His selection of Head's letters offers insights into the evolution of characters in *When Rain Clouds Gather* and *Maru* and documents initial uncertainties surrounding the publication of *A Question of Power*. There are shorter references to *Serowe, Village of the Rainwind*, *The Collector of Treasures*, and a historical narrative about Khama the Great that became *A Bewitched Crossroad*. The letters reveal Head's swiftness to judge, and in time to reevaluate, the behavior of those she felt had betrayed her. Prominent themes from the novels—including the impact of black, as well as white, racism and the challenge to cope with acute loneliness and sexual brutalization in a migrant situation—indicate how directly Head was prepared to draw on her own experiences to furnish the core of her fiction.

The Cardinals, with Meditations and Short Stories

The Cardinals, in the collection *The Cardinals, with Meditations and Short Stories* (1993), is a novella that presents a vivid, disturbing view of Colored experience in South Africa. Miriam, or Mouse, who was abandoned by her mother, educates herself and is able to find work as a newspaper reporter. She meets a fellow reporter, Johnny, with whom she falls in love. Incest is a prominent theme, expressed through episodes of attempted child molestation by a foster father, Johnny's love for his own sister, and the fact — though they do not know it — that Johnny is Mouse's biological father. The symbolism of a father figure who dominates, exploits, and yet is intimately linked with his victim reflects the historical evolution of Colored people as a result of clandestine and illicit sex between blacks and whites.

The book also contains shorter pieces. "Where Is the Hour of the Beautiful Dancing Birds in the Sun-Wind?" for example, deals with the situation of African women and with the narrator's passionate and deep-seated feelings about her homeland, Africa. *The Cardinals* is the earliest work by Head to appear in print and, like the other pieces in this collection, allows a view of the continuities in her literary career as a whole.

CONCLUSION

In the last thirteen years of her life, Bessie Head's writing attracted mounting interest and recognition. *A Question of Power* was nominated for the Booker Prize in Britain, and Head accepted invitations to attend the Iowa International Writing Program in 1978, the Horizons '79 Africa Festival in Berlin, and Writers' Week at the 1984 Adelaide Festival in Australia. In April 1986 she contracted hepatitis and after three days in a coma, died in Serowe on 17 April. She was forty-eight years old. A collection of her archival material was begun by the Khama III Memorial Museum in Serowe.

Head's is a unique voice in world literature in English. Some of the many articles on her writing have attempted to appropriate her writing for particular political causes, but the wide scope, eclecticism, and ever-changing narrative style of the texts resist this type of classification. Her writing cannot be called "feminist," "black," or "African" without simplifying or distorting what it says.

"I have found that the novel form is like a large rag-bag into which one can stuff anything — all one's philosophical, social and romantic speculations. I have always reserved a special category for myself, as a writer — that of a pioneer blazing a new trail into the future," she wrote in "Some Notes on Novel Writing," which was first published in 1978 and reproduced in *A Woman Alone* (p. 64). In her writing and in her life, Bessie Head overcame tremendous pressures and deprivations to find a sense of belonging and, at the same time, the right to be called a free spirit.

Selected Bibliography

BIBLIOGRAPHY

Gardner, Susan, and Patricia E. Scott. *Bessie Head: A Bibliography.* Grahamstown, South Africa: National English Literary Museum, 1986.
Giffuni, Cathy. "Bessie Head: A Bibliography." In *Current Bibliography on African Affairs* 19, no. 3 (1986–1987).

NOVELS

When Rain Clouds Gather. New York: Simon & Schuster, 1968; London: Victor Gollancz, 1969; New York: Bantam, 1970; Harmondsworth, U.K.: Penguin, 1971; London: Heinemann Educational Books, 1972.
Maru. London: Victor Gollancz, 1971; New York: McCall Publishing, 1971; London: Heinemann Educational Books, 1972; Harare: Zimbabwe Publishing, 1985.
A Question of Power. London: Davis-Poynter, 1973; London: Heinemann Educational Books, 1974; New York: Pantheon, 1974.
A Bewitched Crossroad: An African Saga. Craighall, South Africa: Ad. Donker, 1984.

SHORT FICTION

The Collector of Treasures and Other Botswana Village Tales. London: Heinemann Educational Books, 1977; New York: Africana Publishing

Co., 1977; Cape Town, South Africa: David Philip, 1977.

Tales of Tenderness and Power. Intro. by Gillian Stead Eilersen. Craighall, South Africa: Ad. Donker, 1989; Oxford, U.K.: Heinemann Educational Books, 1990.

The Cardinals, with Meditations and Short Stories. Intro. by M. J. Daymond. Cape Town, South Africa: David Philip, 1993.

HISTORY

Serowe, Village of the Rainwind. London: Heinemann Educational Books, 1981.

AUTOBIOGRAPHICAL WRITINGS AND LETTERS

A Woman Alone: Autobiographical Writings. Ed. by Craig MacKenzie. Oxford, U.K.: Heinemann Educational Books, 1990.

A Gesture of Belonging: Letters from Bessie Head, 1965–1979. Ed. by Randolph Vigne. London: Heinemann, 1991; Portsmouth, N.H.: SA Writers, 1991.

INTERVIEWS

Adler, Michelle, et al. "Bessie Head Interviewed by Michelle Adler, Susan Gardner, Tobeka Mda and Patricia Sandler." In Craig MacKenzie and Cherry Clayton, eds., *Between the Lines: Interviews with Bessie Head, Sheila Roberts, Ellen Kuzwayo, Miriam Tlali.* Grahamstown, South Africa: National English Literary Museum, 1989.

Beard, Linda Susan. "Bessie Head in Gaborone, Botswana: An Interview." In *Sage* 3 (1986).

Franklin, Betty McGinnis. "Conversations with Bessie." In *World Literature Written in English* 17 (November 1978).

Marquard, Jean. "Exile and Community in Bessie Head." In *London Magazine* 18 (December 1978–January 1979).

Peek, Andrew. "Bessie Head in Australia." In *New Literature Review* 14 (1985).

CRITICAL STUDIES

Abrahams, Cecil, ed. *The Tragic Life: Bessie Head and Literature in Southern Africa.* Trenton, N.J.: Africa World Press, 1990.

Achufusi, Ifeyinwa. "Female African Writers and Social Criticism: A Study of the Works of Bessie Head and Grace Ogot." Ph.D. diss., University of Wisconsin, 1991.

Bazin, Nancy Topping. "Feminist Perspective in African Fiction: Bessie Head and Buchi Emecheta." In *Black Scholar* 17 (March–April 1986).

———. "Venturing into Feminist Consciousness: Bessie Head and Buchi Emecheta." In Cecil Abrahams, ed., *The Tragic Life: Bessie Head and Literature in Southern Africa.* Trenton, N.J.: Africa World Press, 1990.

Beard, Linda Susan. "Bessie Head's *A Question of Power*: The Journey Through Disintegration to Wholeness." In *Colby Library Quarterly* 15 (1979).

———. "Bessie Head, Cape Gooseberry and the Question of Power." In *ALA Bulletin* 12, no. 2 (1986).

———. "Bessie Head's Syncretic Fictions: The Reconceptualization of Power and the Recovery of the Ordinary." In *Modern Fiction Studies* 37 (fall 1991).

Bruner, Charlotte H. "Bessie Head: Restless in a Distant Land." In Carolyn A. Parker et al., eds., *When the Drumbeat Changes.* Washington, D.C.: Three Continents Press, 1981.

Campbell, Elaine. "Bessie Head's Model for Agricultural Reform." In *Journal of African Studies* 12 (summer 1985).

Chase, Joanne. "Bessie Head's *A Question of Power*: Romance or Rhetoric?" In *ACLALS Bulletin* 6 (November 1982).

Chetin, Sarah. "Myth, Exile, and the Female Condition: Bessie Head's *The Collector of Treasures*." In *Journal of Commonwealth Literature* 24, no. 1 (1989).

Clayton, Cherry. " 'A World Elsewhere': Bessie Head as Historian." in *English in Africa* 15 (May 1988).

Daymond, M. J. "Bessie Head, *Maru* and a Problem in Her Visionary Fable." In J. Bardolph, ed., *Short Fiction in the New Literatures in English: Proceedings of the Nice Conference of the European Association for Commonwealth Literature and Language Studies.* Nice, France: Faculté des Lettres et Sciences Humaines de Nice, 1989.

Dovey, Teresa. "*A Question of Power*: Susan Gardner's Biography Versus Bessie Head's Autobiography." In *English in Africa* 16 (May 1989).

Drake, Ellen. "Bessie Head Dies." In *New African* 225 (June 1986).

Eilersen, Gillian Stead. "Social and Political Commitment in Bessie Head's *A Bewitched Crossroad*." In *Critique* 33 (fall 1991).

Eko, Ebele. "Beyond the Myth of Confrontation: A Comparative Study of African and African-American Female Protagonists." In *ARIEL* 17 (October 1986).

Flewellen, Elinor C. "Assertiveness vs. Submissiveness in Selected Works by African Women Writers." In *Ba Shiru* 12, no. 2 (1985).

Gardiner, Susan. "Bessie Head: Production Under Drought Conditions." In Cherry Clayton, ed., *Women and Writing in South Africa: A Critical Anthology*. Marshalltown: Heinemann Southern Africa, 1989.

Gardner, Susan. "'Don't Ask for the True Story': A Memoir of Bessie Head." In *Hecate* 12, no. 1–2 (1986).

Geurts, Kathryn. "Personal Politics in the Novels of Bessie Head." In *Présence africaine* 140 (1986).

Heywood, Christopher. "Traditional Values in the Novels of Bessie Head." In D. Massa, ed., *Individual and Community in Commonwealth Literature*. Papers of European Association of Commonwealth Language and Literature Conference. Msida: University of Malta Press, 1979.

Johnson, Joyce. "Metaphor, Myth and Meaning in Bessie Head's *A Question of Power*." In *World Literature Written in English* 25 (fall 1985).

———. "Structures of Meaning in the Novels of Bessie Head." In *Kunapipi* 8, no. 1 (1986).

———. "Proper Names and Thematic Concerns in Bessie Head's Novels." In *World Literature Written in English* 30 (spring 1990).

Katrak, Kety H. "From Pauline to Dikeledi: The Philosophical and Political Vision of Bessie Head's Protagonists." In *Ba Shiru* 12, no. 2 (1985).

Kemp, Yakini. "Romantic Love and the Individual in Novels by Mariama Bâ, Buchi Emecheta and Bessie Head." In *Obsidian II* 3 (winter 1988).

Lorenz, Paul H. "Colonization and the Feminine in Bessie Head's *A Question of Power*." In *Modern Fiction Studies* 37 (fall 1991).

MacKenzie, Craig. *Bessie Head: An Introduction*. Grahamstown, South Africa: National English Literary Museum, 1989.

———. "Bessie Head's *The Collector of Treasures*: Modern Story-Telling in a Traditional Botswanan Village." In *World Literature Written in English* 29 (fall 1989).

———. "Short Fiction in the Making: The Case of Bessie Head." In J. Bardolph, ed., *Short Fiction in the New Literatures in English: Proceedings of the Nice Conference of the European Association for Commonwealth Literature and Language Studies*. Nice, France: Faculté des Lettres et Sciences Humaines de Nice, 1989. Also in *English in Africa* 16 (May 1989).

———. "Alienation, Breakdown, and Renewal." In Robert Ross, ed., *International Literature in English: Essays on the Major Writers*. New York: Garland, 1991.

Matsikidze, Isabella P. "Toward a Redemptive Political Philosophy: Bessie Head's *Maru*." In *World Literature Written in English* 30 (fall 1990).

Menager-Everson, V. S. "*Maru* by Bessie Head: The Dilepe Quartet; or, From Drought to Beer." In *Commonwealth Essays and Studies* 14 (spring 1992).

Ogungbesan, Kolawole. "The Cape Gooseberry Also Grows in Botswana." In *Journal of African Studies* 6 (1979).

Ola, Virginia U. "Women's Role in Bessie Head's Ideal World." In *ARIEL* 17, no. 4 (October 1986).

Pearse, Adetokunbo. "Apartheid and Madness: Bessie Head's *A Question of Power*." In *Kunapipi* 5, no. 2 (1983).

Peek, Andrew. "Bessie Head and the African Novel." In *SPAN* 21 (October 1985).

Ravenscroft, Arthur. "The Novels of Bessie Head." In C. Heywood, ed., *Aspects of South African Literature*. London: Heinemann, 1976.

———. "African Novels of Affirmation." In D. Douglas Jefferson and Graham Martin, eds., *The Uses of Fiction: Essays on the Modern Novel in Honour of Arnold Kettle*. Milton Keynes, U.K.: Open University Press, 1982.

Sam, Agnes. "Bessie Head: A Tribute." In *Kunapipi* 8, no. 1 (1986).

Sample, Maxine. "Landscape and Spatial Metaphor in Bessie Head's *The Collector of Treasures*." In *Studies in Short Fiction* 28 (summer 1991).

Sarvan, Charles P. "Bessie Head, *A Question of Power* and Identity." In *African Literature Today* 15 (1987).

Severac, Alain. "Beyond Identity: Bessie Head's Spiritual Quest in *Maru*." In *Commonwealth Essays and Studies* 14 (fall 1991).

Thorpe, Michael. "Treasures of the Heart: The Short Stories of Bessie Head." In *World Literature Today* 57 (summer 1983).

Tucker, Margaret E. "A 'Nice-Time Girl' Strikes Back: An Essay on Bessie Head's *A Question of Power*." In *Research in African Literatures* 19 (summer 1988).

Uledi-Kamanga, Brighton. "Alienation and Affirmation: The Humanistic Vision of Bessie Head." In *Journal of Humanities* 1 (April 1987).

Vanamali, Rukmani. "Bessie Head's *A Question of Power*: The Mythic Dimension." In *Literary Criterion* 23, no. 1–2 (1988).

Visel, Robin. "'We Bear the World and We Make It': Bessie Head and Olive Schreiner." In *Research in African Literatures* 21 (fall 1990).

Wilhelm, Cherry. "Bessie Head: The Face of Africa." In *English in Africa* 10 (May 1983).

Luís Bernardo Honwana
1942–

DAVID BROOKSHAW

LUÍS BERNARDO HONWANA was born Luís Augusto Bernardo Manuel in Lourenço Marques (now called Maputo), the capital of Mozambique, in November 1942. Honwana was the fourth of nine children of Raúl Bernardo Manuel Honwana and Nally Jeremias Nhaca. He was brought up in Moamba, a small town in the rich agricultural belt along the valley of the River Incomáti, where his father was an official interpreter. The senior Honwana wrote *Memórias* (Memoirs; Rio Tinto, Portugal: Edições Asa, 1989), an invaluable eyewitness account of life in colonial Mozambique between 1905 and 1975. He also illuminates the lives of the Honwanas as members of an *assimilado* family (that is, a black African family that had assimilated into white settler society) of the type described in some of the stories in the younger Honwana's *Nós matámos o cão-tinhoso* (1964). At the age of seventeen, Luís Bernardo Honwana returned to the capital and became involved in various types of journalistic activity, including writing stories for the young people's page of the newspaper *Notícias*. It was at this time that he first met the poet José Craveirinha, who recognized his talent.

As a supporter of Frente de Libertação de Moçambique (FRELIMO, or the Mozambique Liberation Front), the guerrilla movement for independence founded in 1962, Honwana was jailed by the colonial authorities in 1964. After his release in 1967, he studied law at the University of Lisbon and later lived in Switzerland, Algeria, and Tanzania. After the coup that brought down the Portuguese dictatorship in Mozambique on 25 April 1974, Honwana returned and joined the transitional government leading up to independence on 25 June 1975. After that, he held a number of political posts, serving as head of the cabinet office during the presidency of Samora Machel and then as secretary of state for culture. In the early 1990s Honwana became his country's cultural and educational representative to the United Nations. He has made several documentary films, has exhibited paintings, and is a highly rated photographer.

Honwana's one collection of short stories, *Nós matámos o cão-tinhoso*, was first published in Lourenço Marques in 1964. Since then, it has appeared in a Brazilian edition and has had several Portuguese editions. It is required reading in Mozambican secondary schools. Furthermore, it has been translated into English, under the title *We Killed Mangy-Dog and Other Mozambique Stories* (1969), by Dorothy Guedes, the South African wife of a Portuguese architect living in Lourenço Marques, Pedro Guedes. Pedro Guedes, along with other white liberal intellectuals like Eugénio Lisboa and Rui Knopfli, as well as Craveirinha, encouraged Honwana in his writing.

According to Russell Hamilton, Honwana's work "set a direction for the modern prose fiction of Mozambique" (p. 213). One could go so far as to say that his collection of short stories is now commonly regarded as a classic of African literature in Portuguese. Most critics agree that the abiding literary qualities of Honwana's stories lie in their rich combination of western literary models and local African influences. In his social concerns and his often profoundly lyrical descriptions of nature, there are echoes of Portuguese and Brazilian neorealists such as Fernando Namora and Graciliano Ramos, and even of North American fiction writers of the 1930s such as Erskine Caldwell. On the other hand, some have discerned in Honwana's writing the presence of resources tapped from the African oral tradition. Hamilton has noted the descriptive refrains in the first part of the title story, which give the narrative a particular rhythm akin to African storytelling techniques (p. 214). Specifically, the repeated references to Mangy-Dog's eyes "like someone asking for something without wanting to say it" not only emphasize the creature's humility but also give the narrative the quality of an oral lament. At the same time, the narrator's voice occasionally halts the flow of the story to apparently address the audience directly by means of section headings capitalized in the text for greater impact: "Senhor Administrador spat at the two of us and said that about Mangy-Dog, but it was only because he and his partner had taken a licking" (p. 82), "There were twelve of us when we went to the abattoir road with Mangy-Dog" (p. 92). Similarly, "As mãos dos pretos" ("The Hands of the Blacks") is clearly modeled on oral culture. The dramatization of this story by the Mozambican theater group Mutumbela Gogo at the 1993 International Iberian Theatre Festival in Portugal fully demonstrated its debt to oral culture. However, Honwana's use of animal symbols most vividly and consistently communicates the African quality of his work.

The collection consists of the extended title story and six shorter pieces. They are all set in the type of rural, small-town environment in which the author grew up. Most of them revolve around the same family and juvenile narrator. In some stories, such as the title story, the purely descriptive "Inventário de imóveis e jacentes" ("Inventory of Furniture and Effects"), and "The Hands of the Blacks," this narrator adopts the stance and even the deadpan expression of a preadolescent schoolboy; in others, such as "A velhota" ("The Old Woman") and "Nhinguitimo" ("Nhinguitimo"), he is clearly a sexually aware older teenager already confronting the brutal social and political realities of the adult world. This common thread running through *We Killed Mangy-Dog and Other Mozambique Stories* almost lends it the atmosphere of a loosely structured novel.

SOCIAL CRITICISM

Most of the stories in the collection focus on the daily tensions and humiliations suffered by the native African population in a colonial environment. While a concrete change for the better is never achieved as a result of their experiences, the protagonists usually gain a greater awareness of their predicament. The story often involves a clash between an older generation that has been conditioned to accept humiliation and the youths who are disappointed by their elders' inability to react against daily tyranny.

In the title story, the young narrator, Ginho (also called by his nickname, Toucinho, meaning "bacon"), is urged by his school companions to collaborate in the destruction of a sick dog. The killing of the dog, a symbol of Ginho's soul, turns into a ritual of violence and a rite of passage into manhood. Ginho's sympathy for the creature succumbs to his underlying desire and need to be accepted by his peers.

In "Dina" ("Dina") a respected old peasant, Madala, witnesses his daughter prostituting herself to the overseer of the plantation on which he labors. He does nothing about it, to the disgust of a young worker who is also aware of the incident. Honwana skillfully engineers the tension that escalates as the story reaches its climax: the overseer's realization that Madala is the girl's father; a heavy-handed attempt at reconciliation by offering the humiliated Madala his bottle of wine; and the potential for violent uprising as the other workers await Madala's command to kill the overseer. By choosing to have the characters avoid a violent uprising, Honwana shows his ability to increase the power of a story through understatement.

In "Papá, cobra e eu" ("Papa, Snake & I"), Ginho, the boy narrator of the title story, recounts another incident of daily humiliation suffered by his father from his white neighbor, Mr. Castro. Mr. Castro has demanded compensation for his dog, killed in Ginho's family's backyard. After witnessing the incident, Ginho asks his father why he waited until Mr. Castro was out of earshot to express his anger. Not receiving an answer, Ginho later asks his father why he prays when he is angry. When his father tells him that the only way to get through the petty humiliations that occur every day is to have hope, Ginho learns something about the difficulties that may face him in later life. Father and son are drawn together in a shared secret that excludes the mother, and this new bond serves to redefine their relationship. Ginho has moved imperceptibly away from the domestic embrace of the mother, with her concern that he should eat up his food and take a purgative when told, to the adult world of the father.

In "The Old Woman," a youth, beaten up in a bar, returns home to his mother and younger siblings. Honwana depicts with great subtlety the mother's concern that her son may be hungry, while his hunger, it is implied, is of another kind: a hunger for self-esteem. At the same time, both mother and son, much like one father and son in "Papa, Snake & I," are committed to keeping his humiliation a secret, out of a desire to protect the younger children from knowledge of the outside world. This touching story illustrates the type of helpless comfort that an impoverished family may offer, as mother and son speculate on the future and on whether the situation will have changed by the time his younger siblings come of age.

"Nhinguitimo" documents the humiliation of an ambitious peasant, Vírgula Oito, whose plot of land is usurped by Rodrigues, his white boss. The peasant's loss of his land leads to an anarchist act and implied self-destruction. Although Vírgula Oito has aspirations to make his fertile allotment productive and to become a prosperous farmer, he is blind to the warnings of his companions that, as a black man, he will not be allowed to realize his ambitions. When Rodrigues persuades the local administrator to hand over the tribal land to extend his own property, Vírgula Oito goes berserk and shoots his companions. The story ends as the settlers prepare to go and deal with Vírgula Oito before he kills anyone else; however, at the closing paragraph the unnamed youthful narrator suddenly realizes that something is wrong and that the situation must change.

ANIMAL SYMBOLISM

A crucial element in Honwana's stories is the presence of animal symbols, which may be ambiguous but also throw into relief aspects of the human society around them. The most exhaustively studied of these symbols, and one that has generated a certain amount of debate, is the mangy dog of the title story. The critical debate has centered on the local and wider implications of the symbol.

Mangy-Dog walks clumsily like a "rickety old cart" (p. 75), an image that is a painful reminder of the rural backwardness of Mozambique. The dog has tearful blue eyes, which could mark its physical sickness but which are just as likely intended as a symbol of the creature's moral purity and spiritual pathos. They look, as Honwana writes, "like someone asking for something without wanting to say it" (p. 75, Heinemann edition). Shunned by the other dogs of the village— canine counterparts of their settler masters, with suitably masculine and imported names such as Leo, Lobo (Portuguese for "wolf"), and Mike—Mangy-Dog has only one friend, a mentally retarded black girl, Isaura, to protect it. Of the schoolboys, only Ginho feels any sympathy for Mangy-Dog; significantly, he too is black. Honwana clearly intends an affinity between the sick creature, whose skin beneath the crusts of his scars is also black, and the colonized African. It follows that all the other participants in the story are symbolic embodiments of different elements in the social hierarchy of colonial Mozambique.

At the top of the pyramid are the adults, with the Senhor Administrador at its pinnacle, followed by his card-playing cronies, the village postmaster and the veterinary doctor. Fittingly, it is the Senhor Administrador who decrees that Mangy-Dog must be destroyed, although the execution order is passed down the chain of command, eventually arriving at the boys. The excuse is that the dog is sick, but in fact the order is given on a whim, after the Senhor Administrador has been beaten in card games and, irritated, notices the dog watching him. The other adult characters in the story are distant figures representing varying degrees of colonial authority; most directly affecting the children is the Senhora Professora, who represents the rigid hierarchy and authority of the colonial education system. The schoolboys are the colonial residents, each representing one of the ethnic components of Mozambican society. This intermediate hierarchy is headed by Quim, who is Portuguese; to some extent, Quim is the group's link with the outside world, since he is privileged enough to have been to the cinema in Lourenço Marques. Information, even distorted information, is power in this colonial backwater, and Quim is able to tell the others that Mangy-Dog's scars are the result of exposure to an atom bomb explosion.

The trading of racist insults between Quim and Gulamo, the East Indian (the largest group in settler society after the Portuguese and therefore their rivals), reveals animosity among the ethnic groups. Faruk and Changai represent the smaller Islamic and Chinese presences, respectively. At the bottom of this hierarchy is Ginho, representing the African assimilated into settler society, who has to prove himself continually in order to be accepted by the group as a whole. The relationship between Quim and Ginho is one of exploitative dependency, a meeting of egotistical self-confidence and bravado on the one hand and low self-esteem on the other. In order to be accepted, for example, Ginho allows Quim to copy his work.

Ginho's divided loyalty—between the dog he seeks to save and the group that the adults have delegated to execute it—demonstrates most clearly his predicament as a black boy. Unable to stop the inevitable murder of Mangy-Dog, Ginho is obliged to prove his manhood by taking it to the designated spot for execution and then firing the first shot. Although he takes no further part in the slaughter, his role in the destruction of his African identity, symbolized by the dog, cannot be reversed. Yet if Ginho's sense of fear and guilt is strong, it is ultimately not absent in Quim himself. In some way, all the elements of colonial society, as symbolized by these schoolboys, are as ashamed of what they have done as Ginho. It is at this point that the dog's more universal significance may be extrapolated.

Gregory McNab explains that the dog's function in the story is that of a prototypical *pharmakos*, or scapegoat, by drawing our attention to both the popular Portuguese designation of Satan as the "Mangy-Dog" and the inoffensive character of Honwana's dog. Thus, the creature is not evil, but a reminder of evil; the ritual of cleansing society of evil and assuaging guilt inevitably requires the dog's extinction. Honwana's pathetic creature therefore brings together two intertwined symbolic strands. On the one hand, this outcast dog symbolizes on a more universal level that which society, in its conformity and hatred of difference, regards as evil. On the other, it incarnates the very real evil that has been visited upon Africa as a result of colonialism. Mangy-Dog does not symbolize Africa by virtue of its close link with Isaura and Ginho but represents what the colonizer has done to Africa and to the African. Hence, the supreme irony: the disease the dog has contracted is western civilization. By killing it, the westerners are destroying the values they have brought to Africa, which constitute the raison d'être for their presence there.

In "Dina," Madala watches a scorpion as he works in the field and recalls his companion Pitarossi who had died of a snake bite and whose wife had been forced into prostitution as a result. Here, the scorpion and the snake underline the cheapness of human life when faced with the hazards of the natural environment. Madala's fear that he would not be able to stand up to a scorpion's sting reflects his own weakness and enhances the story's message of alienation and enslavement.

A mamba (a type of poisonous African tree snake) is the central animal motif of "Papa, Snake & I." Ensconced under a pile of junk behind the house where Ginho and his family live, it kills hens when they stray into its lair. Hearing his mother upbraiding his father for not doing anything about it, Ginho uncovers the snake and watches, mesmerized, its confrontation with Lobo, the dog that belongs to his white neighbor, Mr. Castro. In a moment of bravado, Lobo, like Quim when he confronts Mangy-Dog in the first story, confronts this symbol of evil, while Toto, the African family's dog, looks on from a safe distance.

This time, however, bravado does not pay, and Lobo is bitten and dies. The incident culminates in the father's humiliation at the hands of Mr. Castro, who demands compensation for the loss of his dog.

The snake as a symbol of evil is as common to traditional African folklore as it is to European culture. Yet it is difficult to ascertain the nature of this evil in the story. Like Mangy-Dog, the snake draws together more than one suggestive element: it symbolizes the potentially fatal force of African nature and simultaneously throws into relief the foreignness of the European presence in Mozambique.

Yet Ginho's family suffers as a consequence of the snake's invasion of its premises. It is significant that the father appears to tolerate this poisonous presence in the midst of the family. This is a family of assimilated Africans, who as a class occupy the bottom rung of bourgeois society. They practice Christianity, speak Portuguese, and, like other colonials, have a maid. It may be that the snake, with the chaos it causes, represents a warning against complacency. The biblical association of the snake with loss of innocence renders particular significance to the fact that the snake is discovered by the adolescent Ginho in the throes of an awakening sexuality (he likes to gaze at the maid's legs as she washes the clothes); as a consequence of the incident surrounding the snake, Ginho receives his first lesson in political and social education. More important still, after the incident, Ginho admits to his father that he could have stopped Mr. Castro's dog from being bitten but chose not to, proving that Ginho has crossed the threshold from childhood innocence to an adult consciousness of the world.

"Nhinguitimo" begins with a detailed account of the activities and tactics of pigeons, the great parasites of agricultural land in southern Africa. Pigeons devastate crops in the period leading up to the "Nhinguitimo," the name given to the southerly wind that ushers in the cold and rain. The pigeons behave like colonizers, with organization and military precision, arriving some weeks before harvest time. They represent the antithesis of nature's poetry and harmony: avaricious, prosaic, and destructive. In turn, their greed is reflected in the ambitions of the white settler, Rodrigues, who wishes to expand his agricultural holdings and take over the fertile land of the tribal community, starting with Vírgula Oito's own allotment. It is also mirrored in the equally ambitious aspirations of Vírgula Oito himself. Indeed, it is precisely the latter's success that leads Rodrigues to pressure the Senhor Administrador into allowing him to usurp the African's holding and so ironically bringing about Oito's downfall.

The greed of Rodrigues is no different from that of the pigeons. References to their migratory tendencies, their alienation from the natural environment, and their fatter and darker appearance with the passing of time equate the pigeons with settlers, who become more prosperous and more deeply tanned under the tropical sun. Yet this is not only a story about the exploitation of Africa and Africans by the Portuguese, but also a more general warning of the potentially destructive nature of ambition. When Vírgula Oito recounts his plans to his companions, the narrator remarks on the similarity between the sound of his voice and the self-absorbed cooing of the pigeons. Vírgula Oito is no less avaricious for being a native; he aspires to be a boss, like the whites, and pays dearly for trying to follow their example.

THE INFLUENCE OF THE FOLKTALE

The idea that blacks are the equal of whites before God and the Devil, implicit in "Nhinguitimo," is also the subject matter of "The Hands of the Blacks," one of the shorter pieces in the collection. Taking as his base folktales about the creation of the races, products of the colonial experience, Honwana satirizes the smugness and prejudice of settler society and demonstrates the inherent absurdity of stereotypes.

Once again, the narrator is a young boy, perhaps the same one as in the other stories. The village priest tells him and his companions after catechism that blacks were better than whites because blacks are always praying; this explains why the palms of their hands are lighter than the rest of their body. The narrator then recalls his schoolteacher's claim that the palms of the blacks were white because until recently they used to walk around on all fours. His curiosity provoked, he decides to ask the adults he knows to confirm the stories. Each one gives him a different version, some versions more humorous than others, but all of them underlining in some way the inferior status of blacks as well as the ignorance of the person giving the explanation. The child is convinced only by his mother. After wiping away the tears of laughter induced by her son's account of what he has heard, she explains that God caused blacks to have white palms as proof that all mankind is equal in its labor and as a reminder to whites who are convinced of their own superiority.

THE PORTUGUESE LANGUAGE AND THE ASSIMILATED AFRICAN FAMILY

Unique among African writers in Portuguese of his time, Honwana displayed considerable sensitivity in his treatment of the language problem in Mozambique and in his rendering of black speech patterns. No doubt his father's experience as an interpreter helped Honwana gain a sensitivity toward the problem of language. While Honwana may imitate the speech patterns of Africans when using Portuguese, he does not do so in the way colonial writers were prone to do in rendering black speech for comic or folkloric effect; rather, he aims to demonstrate the vulnerability of those whose command of the language of power is rudimentary. This is why he only uses black speech when the native is confronting the white and never when blacks are talking among themselves.

Command of the language, or rather lack of it, is a key symptom of Vírgula Oito's weakness in the face of the Senhor Administrador and Rodrigues, a weakness that disappears when he is able to describe his dreams and ambitions to his friends in his own language. Indeed, the mutual understanding of each other's greetings in different local vernaculars underscores the foreignness of the language of the colonizer. Language also defines the relationship of power between Quim and Ginho. The former's assumption of superiority is expressed in his insult to Ginho that the latter does not seem to understand Portuguese, even though Quim's own capacity for explaining things cogently is limited. In "Dina," the daughter's lack of language skills is, in no small measure, responsible for her inability to fend off the overseer within sight of her father.

"Papa, Snake & I" most effectively depicts both the prestige of Portuguese in colonial society and the cultural dualism of an assimilated family. Portuguese policy toward native language in its African colonies differed considerably from British colonial policy: while the British actively encouraged the publication of books and tracts in the local vernaculars, the Portuguese, like the French, promoted the colonizer's language as the only one with any value or prestige. The system of assimilation, whereby certain Africans could obtain some of the privileges of Portuguese citizenship, merely reflected this prejudice, for candidates were submitted to an examination in Portuguese and were visited by inspectors to ascertain whether their domestic habits were sufficiently Portuguese. Local languages were therefore despised at an institutional level, and no efforts were made to encourage their use in print.

Such a system invited and even required assimilated Africans to turn their backs on their own language and culture. In "Papa, Snake & I" Honwana demonstrates with dexterity the attitude of assimilated Africans to-ward their language: while the mother speaks to the maid in Ronga, a local language, to her children, for whom she has aspirations of further social advance, she speaks in Portuguese. On the other hand, Honwana shows how the emotional pull of the mother tongue can make itself felt at moments of crisis. When the mother gets irritated, she speaks in Ronga; after the incident with Mr. Castro, the father prays in the local vernacular.

"Inventory of Furniture and Effects," a child's description of his family's home, succinctly and implicitly highlights the twin pressures of poverty and social pretension. The narrator takes us around the limited confines of the house and focuses, as if with a camera, on the petty signs of poverty. These include cramped sleeping arrangements; dining room walls blackened by the proximity of the cooking stove, whose recent removal to the backyard signals modest social improvement; and a motley and insufficient collection of chairs. That the curtains in the mother's bedroom were used to make a skirt for one of the daughters while the father was imprisoned typifies the family's financial vulnerability, while the father's imprisonment suggests the recent political repression experienced in the country. The five shelves of books in the tiny corridor and the boxes of more books and magazines under the father's bed not only illustrate the maximum use of space in this crowded environment, but also pinpoint the family's social position: the father is at the very least a man of some education.

On the other hand, the kapok, as opposed to straw, mattress in the mother's bedroom signals a degree of social pretension. So do the foreign magazines laid out on the table in the sitting room for visitors. That the father considers the arrangement of the foreign magazines rubbish is another hint, like his imprisonment, that he is a nationalist. The passing reference to one of the children having pencilled the name "Elvis" on the cupboard locates the description in time and indicates the strength of western popular culture in this corner of rural Africa. The mention of the houseboy, Madunana, who also appears in "Papa, Snake & I," is another indicator of the relative social privilege that this family paradoxically enjoys. Honwana's description is as concise and economic as the family dwelling itself: form matches content perfectly, and the title of the piece is as ironic as the description is straightforward and childlike.

Honwana is, of course, not alone in rising to fame on the basis of one book. It was a characteristic of his generation and the vitality of the period in which he grew to intellectual maturity: he was inspired by the moment, the injustices of the colonial system, and the changes that were taking place in Mozambique during the 1950s and 1960s. When that period came to an end and Honwana was called upon to serve the new regime, literary activity became less easy to reconcile with his political duties. After *We Killed Mangy-Dog*, Honwana published one more short story, "Rosita, até morrer" (Rosita, till death do us part), in the Portuguese magazine *Vértice* in 1971. Written in the form of a letter from an uneducated woman to her beloved, who has run away to the city and taken up with an *assimilada* woman, the piece exploits not only the relationship between language, power, and social status, but also the contrasts between rural and urban culture and society. Despite the paucity of Honwana's literary production, and notwithstanding his known modesty, the book that brought him to international recognition stands the test of time. *We Killed Mangy-Dog* constitutes a watershed in African literature in Portuguese.

Selected Bibliography

SELECTED WORKS

Nós matámos o cão-tinhoso. Lourenço Marques, Mozambique: Tribuna 1964; Porto, Portugal: Afrontamento, 1972, 1988, 1992; Lourenço Marques, Mozambique: Académica, 1975; São Paulo, Brazil: Editora Ática, 1980.
"Rosita, até morrer." In *Vértice* 31 (1971).
"The Role of Poetry in the Mozambican Revolution." In *Lotus* 8 (1971).
Papá, cobra e eu. Lobito, Angola: Capricórnio, 1975.

TRANSLATIONS

"Dina." Trans. by Dorothy Guedes. In Ezekiel Mphahlele, ed., *African Writing Today.* Harmondsworth, U.K.: Penguin Books, 1967.
"The Hands of the Blacks." Trans. by Dorothy Guedes. In Ulli Beier, *Political Spider.* London: Heinemann Educational Books, 1969.
We Killed Mangy-Dog and Other Mozambique Stories. Trans. by Dorothy Guedes. London: Heinemann Educational Books, 1969. Publ. as *We Killed Mangy-Dog and Other Mozambican Stories.* Harare: Zimbabwe Publishing House, 1987.
"The Old Woman." Trans. by Dorothy Guedes. In Paul A. Scanlon, ed., *Stories from Central and Southern Africa.* London: Heinemann Educational Books, 1983.
"The Hands of the Blacks." Trans. by Dorothy Guedes. In *Being Here: Modern Short Stories from Southern Africa.* Cape Town, South Africa: David Philip, 1994.

CRITICAL STUDIES

Burness, Donald. "Luís Bernardo Honwana and Lives of Humiliation." In *Fire: Six Writers from Angola, Mozambique and Cape Verde.* Washington, D.C.: Three Continents Press, 1977.
Dal Farra, Maria Lúcia. "A identidade de um certo olhar infantil." In *Les Littératures africaines de langue portugaise: A la recherche de l'identité individuelle et nationale.* Paris: Fondation Calouste Gulbenkian, 1985.
Ferreira, João. "O traço moçambicano na narrativa de Luís Bernardo Honwana." In *Les Littératures africaines de langue portugaise: A la recherche de l'identité individuelle et nationale.* Paris: Fondation Calouste Gulbenkian, 1985.
Hamilton, Russell G. *Voices from an Empire: A History of Afro-Portuguese Literature.* Minneapolis: University of Minnesota Press, 1975.

Harland, Mike. "Children Across Africa: The Theme of Education in the Works of Honwana and Luandino Vieira." In T. F. Earle and Nigel Griffin, eds., *Portuguese, Brazilian, and African Studies.* Warminster, U.K.: Aris & Phillips, 1995.

McNab, Gregory. "Porque mataram o Cão-Tinhoso." In *África* 14, no. 9 (1986).

Medina, Cremilda de Araújo. "Herdeiros e arrimo da dignidade conquistada." In her *Sonha mamana Africa.* São Paulo, Brazil: Edições Epopeia, 1987.

Moser, Gerald M. "Luís Bernardo Honwana's Place Among the Writers in Mozambique." In Bruce King and Kolawole Ogungbesan, eds., *A Celebration of Black and African Writing.* Oxford, U.K.: Oxford University Press, 1975.

Seixo, Maria Alzira. Review of *Nós matámos o cão-tinhoso.* In *Colóquio letras* 16 (November 1973).

Christopher Hope
1944–

DAMIAN GRANT

CHRISTOPHER HOPE, a South African who moved to England in 1975, is one of a number of non-British-born writers who have contributed significantly to English fiction in twentieth-century Britain. He joins Doris Lessing, Salman Rushdie, Kazuo Ishiguro, and Timothy Mo in this category of cultural import. But Hope's contribution has not been only to fiction. Besides six novels, a novella, and a volume of short stories, Hope has published three volumes of poetry, an autobiographical memoir, and a travel book, as well as two books for children and five plays broadcast on BBC radio or television. Almost paradoxically, he has became a fixture on the British literary scene; he was elected a fellow of the Royal Society of Literature in 1990 and frequently lectures in England and abroad for the British Council.

These non-British-born writers have brought a greater sense of political urgency to English fiction than is often found in the homegrown product. Their situation recalls George Orwell's comment, in 1944, that there has been nothing resembling Arthur Koestler's *Darkness at Noon* (1941) in English fiction "because there is almost no English writer to whom it has happened to see totalitarianism from the inside" (in *The Collected Essays, Journalism, and Letters of George Orwell*, 1968, vol. 3, p. 235). The political urgency in Hope's writings comes from his having lived for the first thirty years of his life in South Africa, a country that has remained the dominant focus of his work. Like the exiled James Joyce writing obsessively about Dublin, Hope lives in England but resides imaginatively in South Africa, reworking his formative experiences.

Hope's upbringing in a small Irish Catholic community gave him a particular insight into the racial issues of South Africa, and racial definition and discrimination in all its forms remained his permanent subject. Before 1994, Hope had returned to South Africa only once, in 1987, to observe and write about that year's all-white general election, which was won by the National Party. Little did he know then that this would be the last all-white election, and it was surely with great satisfaction that Hope was back in South Africa in 1994 to share at close quarters in the election of the first black president, Nelson Mandela.

Travel has always enticed Hope, in part because of the difficulty of arranging it in the darker apartheid years, when at best travel involved a one-way ticket that rid the regime of another unwelcome liberal critic. It is as if the writer has to leave the claustrophobic atmosphere of the country in order to see it —and himself or herself—more clearly. Hope's fiction reflects this need. Only his first novel, *A Separate Development* (1980), takes place wholly in South Africa; the later novels have an international itinerary. Both his prizewinning second novel, *Kruger's Alp* (1984), and *The Hottentot Room* (1986) begin or are rooted in South Africa and then move abroad, first to England and then to another part of Europe. *My Chocolate Redeemer* (1989) is set in France, although political interaction with an unspecified black African country is fundamental to the plot. *Serenity House* (1992) begins in Britain before traveling geographically and in time to Germany and the United States. *The Love Songs of Nathan J. Swirsky* (1993) returns to South Africa, and the ten-year-old narrator stays put; but Swirsky, who establishes the imaginative space of the book, has always just come from or is about to depart for somewhere else.

The critical consciousness that Hope formed in South Africa, therefore, informs these fictions and provides their moral motivation. But yet another awareness lies behind this: the sense of Africa as a continent beyond the imagination of its European settlers.

> That was something the Europeans knew nothing of, that long downward precipitation, that long fall, the plunge into the gulf of indifference. ... People were not anchored by history or by the heavy dead or by the pressures of population.... In regions like Africa the geological scale was so much greater; you had to travel much further before you noticed the difference. History in Africa was no compulsive force, it held nothing together.
>
> (*The Hottentot Room*, p. 98)

Behind the unsparing analysis and exposure of the evils of apartheid lies an acute sense of the strangeness, the absurdity even, of life in what was for three centuries a white man's country perched unconvincingly at the southern tip of Africa. Hope also touches on this theme in his poems, especially the colonial story told obliquely in *Englishmen* (1985). When Hope eventually travels to England, he misses the physical reality of Africa, and there are many passages unfavorably contrasting the small, damp, northern country at which

he has arrived with the hot, rich, and fertile continent he has left behind.

Politics is not the exclusive preoccupation of Hope's novels, however; rather, it is the frame for personal relationships. He treats the subject of adolescence with great sensitivity in the early novels and in his memoir. In the later novels he enters with equal confidence into the field of family life—as seen from a series of special perspectives. In each case, he locates the immediate experience in a larger, ultimately political scheme.

This is especially true of Hope's treatment of sex. All of his novels contain explicit accounts of sexual experience. Very often this takes the form of a man being sexually "serviced" by an adept and experienced, but not necessarily involved or reliable, woman. As a consequence, Hope emphasizes the material and alienating aspects of this human activity. The reader is soon forced to ask, especially of a writer so much a master of metaphor as Hope, what these repeated, almost formulaic encounters signify. Once more the clue lies in the political. The idea of private sexual behavior reflecting the public morality of political life has been explored by other writers in the twentieth century; it dates back to the Homeric epics. Such novelists as William Golding and John Updike have recycled the theme, as have poets like Tony Harrison and Tom Paulin, and a similar preoccupation features, appropriately enough, in Derek Walcott's reworking of Homer in *Omeros* (1990). Likewise, the sexual adventures of Hope's characters reflect the political realities they inhabit. Ultimately, "sex in the modern world," as one character observes, "is another word for power" (*The Hottentot Room*, p. 137).

EARLY LIFE AND WRITING

Hope was born in Johannesburg on 26 February 1944. His maternal grandfather had come to South Africa from Ireland at the beginning of the century. Hope's father, an

Irishman named Dennis Tully, was killed in a World War II battle over North Africa shortly after his son was born. Hope was brought up in the house of his grandfather and eventually took the name of his mother's second husband. On her remarriage the family moved from the Johannesburg suburbs to Pretoria, where Hope was sent as a boarder to the Christian Brothers College from 1952 to 1960. Here he learned not only the harsh discipline of the lay brothers (oddly anticipatory of the ways of the regime in the world outside), but also the reality of being an unpopular minority (the Catholics) within an English-speaking community that was in turn "locked in the iron embrace of the Afrikaner nationalists who ruled the country." He served in the South African Navy in 1962 and then enrolled as an undergraduate at the University of the Witwatersrand in Johannesburg. He worked during his university years as an underwriter, copywriter, editor, and reviewer and completed his studies with an honors degree at the University of Natal in 1970 and a master of arts degree back at Witwatersrand in 1973. He married Eleanor Klein, a music administrator, in 1967, and they have two sons.

Hope's first publication was a privately printed volume of verse (with Mike Kirkwood) titled *Whitewashes* (1970), which earned him the Pringle Award from the English Academy of South Africa in 1972. *Cape Drives*, another volume of poems, followed in 1974; for this work Hope received a Cholmondeley Award from the British Society of Authors in 1977. Meanwhile, in 1975, Hope moved from South Africa to Britain, where he worked first as a teacher and then in 1978 as a writer in residence at Gordonstoun School in Elgin, Scotland. Just as Alan Paton had begun writing *Cry, the Beloved Country* (1948) in Norway in 1946 with the cold northern air sharpening and clarifying his vision, so the experience of exile confirmed Hope's career as a novelist. In 1981 *A Separate Development* won the David Higham Prize from Britain's National Book League and an award from the University of Natal for outstanding contri-

bution to the arts and humanities; but it was banned by the authorities in South Africa. *Kruger's Alp* brought Hope to general notice when it won Britain's Whitbread Award for Fiction in 1984. Since 1984, Hope has published novels at regular intervals and earned an admiring and discriminating readership.

WHITE BOY RUNNING

Hope's twelfth publication, the autobiographical *White Boy Running* (1988), both fleshes out the details of his early experience in South Africa and locates the origins of the central preoccupations of his fiction. Ostensibly the book is an account of a journey around South Africa in 1987 to assess the political atmosphere before the general election (a whites-only election that was won, like every election from 1948 until 1994, by the National Party). Although he is perceptive, even prescient, about contemporary politics, the re-creation and reassessment of his formative years, first in the small town of Sandringham, near Johannesburg, and later in a suburb of Pretoria, provides the real heart of the books, just as "bitter memories are the real heart of politics" (p. 35). It is as if Hope can only understand what is happening in South Africa in the 1980s by locating himself in his own past, which, even for a schoolboy in a surreal Dickensian establishment, was ineluctably political.

In *White Boy Running*, Hope describes his Irish grandfather, Daniel McKenna, "a poor lad from Waterford, . . . an incandescent Irish Nationalist" (pp. 17, 18), who came to South Africa during the Boer War of 1899–1902, fought between the Boers (descendants of Dutch settlers) and the British. He also describes his schooling at the hands, often literally, of the Irish Christian Brothers. We learn a lot about Hope's reading (he was precocious and started to read at four years old) and about the dawning of his ambition to be a writer. At first, he simply recorded his personal experiences for the benefit of his school friends (sometimes in rhyming couplets), but later he became determined to record specifically and purposefully those experiences that distinguished South African reality: "It was as if the place was so absurd, so incredible, so terrifyingly funny that it was only by putting it into story form that you could believe in it" (p. 104).

According to Hope, "South African politics are ... very Irish" (p. 52), so much so that he records his dawning "failure of faith ... in the existence of my country as a real place" (p. 82). This imaginative detachment—or moral refusal—becomes a major theme of the second half of the book. South Africa is "a theory unsupported by the facts" where "life ... goes in contraries" (pp. 126, 150); "South Africa does not exist as a place, it is only the expression of policy; it is not a country, it is a *condition*" (p. 241); it is "a country more bizarre than anything a writer could dream up" (p. 261). The fictional character of "true" history is a theme that recurs in Hope's world, and South Africa seems to have been the best introduction to the idea: "South Africa is a place where grotesquely disparate elements are found in horrible, homely juxtaposition. Open your eyes and your head flies apart" (p. 218).

Living in and administering such an environment involves "evasions, prevarications and coded warnings [that] are among the true delights of South African political life" (p. 108). Hope provides many examples of these, such as the official list of changes of color category as sanctioned by a government department in 1986 and the list of banned people, books, ideas, and forms of behavior. The book ends with the predictable Nationalist victory and a depressing vision of a South Africa—where "it is always yesterday" (p. 16) —once again turning to the past: "they have chosen to be governed by the dying or the dead" (p. 271). With the momentous dismantling of apartheid in the political process culminating in 1994, this situation changed, but the process of recording and understanding that past remained problematical.

PRIVATE PARTS AND OTHER TALES AND *LEARNING TO FLY*

The publication details of Hope's short stories are somewhat complicated. The volume *Private Parts and Other Tales* (1981) contains ten stories. The later volume, *Learning to Fly* (1990), republishes seven of these (omitting the title story, "Whites Only," and "Maggie Running") and adds five new ones. The metaphor of sexuality as freedom had been explored in the three omitted stories with a directness that was meant to be disturbing, if not actually reproachful, to a white readership. But the dozen stories in *Learning to Fly* are sufficiently representative of what Hope can do in this genre. Most of these stories were written during the late 1960s and early 1970s in South Africa and might be thought of as exercises for his novels, developing the themes and metaphors that give such a strong sense of identity to his work.

One of the earliest stories, "The Problem with Staff," is a sustained exercise in metaphorical imagination: the new hotel that is so difficult to manage represents Africa; and the disgruntled, dying Mrs. Whitney represents the imminent death of the old, ignorant, anachronistic white attitudes. The longest of the stories, "Ndbele's People," carries a similar metaphoric weight, as the papier-mâché figures made by the despised native priest, Ndbele, return, like the dumb and dispossessed tribes, to claim their inheritance. "Learning to Fly," a caustic account of the security torturers of the old regime, provides some premonitory consolation when the chief interrogator, Colonel du Preez, pitches to death from his eighth-floor window, which is left open for his victims to take their only and anticipated escape.

The finest of the stories is the last, "Whatever Happened to Vilakazi?" which relates the mysterious appearance and disappearance of an African boy on the grounds of a Pretoria parish church. Part of the reason for the success of this story is that it revisits the intense atmosphere of church and school from

Hope's childhood at the "dark, devouring time" of the Lenten ceremonies when Christ's suffering, death, and resurrection are ritualized. This context illuminates the appearance of Vilakazi dressed incongruously in priestly robes, as described by the child narrator:

> I was about to leave when I saw him. He came out of the door leading to the vestry. At first I thought I was having a dream or vision. He wore a cope. It seemed from where I was green, dark green with gold markings, and he walked very slowly and quietly. Of course he had no shoes on, I remembered, and this slowness and silence gave him a strange and frightening dignity.
>
> (p. 180)

Vilakazi is also the name of a character in *Kruger's Alp*, Horatio Vilakazi, who is clearly an allusion to Mandela. The sufferings of this boy at the hands of the unsympathetic German sacristan, Brother Musel, who gasses badgers in his spare time, allude not only to the long suffering and imminent resurrection of the blacks, but also to the Jewish suffering in the Holocaust, introducing a parallel that recurs throughout Hope's fiction. The clean and scrupulous Brother Musel throws Vilakazi's picture of a priest into the furnace, saying "What picture?" and tyrannical ignorance triumphs for the moment. But at the story's end, the child narrator looks at his face in the sacristy mirror "for signs of the knowledge I knew I carried within me" and finds there, "faintly darkening my forehead, the last minute flakes of what had been my cross of ash" (p. 182). "Whatever Happened to Vilakazi?" is a moving and richly metaphoric story, anticipating the best of Hope's more mature and more extended fiction.

A SEPARATE DEVELOPMENT

Hope has described *A Separate Development* (1980) as "a kind of joke-book," in that "if apartheid is cruel it is also ridiculous, and the most cheering thing about its victims is their well-nourished sense of the ridiculous" (in *Contemporary Authors*, vol. 106, 1982, p. 250). The novel is the narrative of Harry Moto, a young man of indeterminate race and ambiguous gender (he has an unnaturally developed chest) whose unstable identity exposes him first to personal embarrassment and eventually, after he is accused of having sex with a white woman, to persecution by the regime. The story opens with Harry's statement: "Let's say it began that afternoon when I exposed myself to Mina Meintjies" (p. 5). Hope's very first fictional sentence establishes the link between the sexual and the political that returns throughout his work. The second paragraph moves into the heart of the South African subject, as Harry meditates in his cell on the obligation that has been laid upon him to write his story:

> A country which has based itself absolutely on the sacred belief in sundered, severed, truncated, fractured, split, divided, separate selves now craves a detailed account of my development in the deluded hope that once all the facts are known the odd case that I am will swim into focus, there will be an intermingling, an intermeshing of parts and their insanity will be miraculously proved to be wise policy.
>
> (p. 5)

Harry's adventures are absurd—they include serving as a "before-and-after" model for a man who sells skin-lightening creams—but he is a political, if low-grade, victim; he is dismissed from his job as a dishwasher for talking politics at work, and by the end of his narrative the racist persecution of the police state is real enough.

After his arrest and "questioning," Harry is persuaded by his interrogator, Dekker, to write his story. "While I write I'm safe" (p. 109); like Scheherazade, the storyteller in *The Arabian Nights*, he must narrate for his life. Naively, Dekker expects Harry's story to empower him—"Dekker saw himself controlling the universe on the information I was going to give him"—and somehow help to vindicate the system; in Dekker's words, "It could be an unique document. Life on the edge of our multi-ethnic society. A glimpse of the undeniable richness of our racial divisions. Living proof that oil and water won't mix." But of course Harry's exposure actually rebounds on his interrogators, much as Colonel du Preez is projected from his own window in "Learning to Fly." Not surprisingly, the real authorities in South Africa banned the novel soon after its publication. Hope also provides a metaphor of the novelist at work as Harry labors in his cell at his autobiography. "I am the beginning and the ending," the novel ends; "Very well then, begin" (p. 177). With Proustian effect, the novel reflects its own process of composition. This formal awareness — a permanent feature of Hope's work — distinguishes his fiction from partisan documentary, or the kind of ideological gossip that cost Harry Moto his dishwashing job.

KRUGER'S ALP

In his second novel, published in 1984, Hope unveils the myth of South Africa more formally and to more devastating effect. Given the extraordinary assurance of this work and its moral and imaginative maturity, it is not surprising that *Kruger's Alp* established Hope's career as a writer or that it is thought of as his most characteristic work.

From the short focus of his first novel, which dwells mainly on the personal experience of one essentially comic character, Hope moves here to a deep focus that includes the whole of South African history, especially the history of its collective illusions, upon which the politics of the 1980s were predicated. Hope achieves this depth partly by adopting a formal device from John Bunyan's *The Pilgrim's Progress* (1678): the moralized dream. *Kruger's Alp* opens: "As I walked through the wilderness of what remained of the world of Father Lynch and his 'little guild,' I saw much to disturb me" (p. 1). Hope introduces the familiar setting of the church and school, the moral and educational, spiritual and secular

seeding grounds of his experience. But this time the "destroyed church with the gaping roof" takes on a larger significance (p. 1). Under the tree where the radical Irish priest named Father Lynch had taught his rebellious boys, "I lay down around noon and slept. And while I slept I dreamed. In my dream I saw Theodore Blanchaille" (p. 2). Protégé of the indefatigable Father Lynch, Blanchaille is the Colored priest whose mixed-race origins (recalling Harry Moto) and priestly status give him a unique vantage point on the successive revelations that make up the novel. The anonymous dreamer accompanies Blanchaille through twenty-five chapters as the latter reviews South African history and then travels abroad on the one-way ticket reserved for critics of the regime. First he goes to England, and afterward to Geneva, ostensibly in search of the Kruger millions, the portable gold mine supposedly carried abroad by Paul Kruger, founder of the Boer state, when he went into exile in October 1900. (This gold mine is the "alp" of the title, which has served as a mythical focus for believers in white supremacy.)

If Bunyan provides Hope with the formal structure for his novel — the focalization, the angle on reality — Jonathan Swift is Hope's master in satire and sets his stylistic example. Bunyan could excoriate the abuses of his time, and this tone is frequently reproduced as Hope confronts categories of depravity. But from Swift, Hope learned to perceive South Africa as a kind of "Flying Island" and the South African regime from 1948 to 1994 as not only repugnant but absurd. Hope presents this world in a series of vignettes that are simultaneously appalling, because of the reality disclosed, and exhilarating, because of the exercise of moral intelligence that is capable of such disclosure. "Last week I saw a woman flayed, and you will hardly believe how much it altered her appearance for the worse": the matter-of-fact registration of moral horror in Swift's famous sentence in *Gulliver's Travels* is recycled in Hope's unflinching presentation of the moral infamy of apartheid.

Hope shows the evil of apartheid incarnated in the detention camps—which are repeatedly compared to Nazi concentration camps—in the brutality of the townships, and especially in the fear and hypocrisy of those who operate the system. All of this evil is related in anecdotes of the system's misfits, failures, and obliging jailbait women. Another novelist of oppression, Aleksandr Solzhenitsyn of Russia, said that the anecdotal novel was the true epic of our time, and his *Gulag Archipelago* (1974) certainly fulfills this panoramic, pointillistic intention. But something different and more formally unsettling happens with Hope's anecdotal structure. Toward the end of the quest, Blanchaille's friend Kipsel expresses his impatience with the endless storytelling to which they are subjected: "'And what do you do here?' Kipsel was bold enough to ask. 'What do we do? We tell stories, of course.' 'More stories!' Kipsel protested. 'I'm tired of stories. Will we never get to the end of stories?'" (p. 267). But the matron reproves him: "Stories have brought you this far. From the most powerful member of the Regime to the lowest gardener, cook or nanny, we all need stories. We owe our lives to stories" (p. 267). Hope's narrator comes to realize, before waking from his dream, that his characters have been travelers in a fiction; the novel has been generated by their hopes, fears, and desires: "and I wished, as the curtains closed one by one, that I too was inside with that strange company of story tellers before I woke from my dream to find myself, as of course I knew I would find myself, alone in Father Lynch's ruined garden beneath the Tree of Paradise" (p. 278). Of course he is— we all are. The "strange company of story tellers" is a valid description of ourselves as we make our way through the interwoven fictions of our world.

THE HOTTENTOT ROOM

The Hottentot Room (1986) is Hope's novel of exile, the work that draws most immediately on his experience as a self-exiled South Afri-can living by force of circumstance rather than mere personal preference in London. The central character, Caleb Looper, is, like Hope, a writer, but he is "a journalist who overstepped the mark [and] had been jailed and deported" (p. 13). Looper soon gravitates to a run-down club for his fellow South Africans, the "Hottentot Room." Hope describes this place and its dozen regulars with all the bitterness of familiarity. It is "a seedy hole where sentimental exiles played silly games of let's pretend" (p. 56), where each has his or her own self-validating version of the master story. In Chapter 4, Hope introduces Buffy Lestrade, who at one time was "quite simply the most famous Marxist in the Southern Hemisphere" and has now "moved into the field of militant nutrition" (pp. 40, 43); Mona May, the "brilliant young high-jumper from the Bushveld" whose career closely resembles that of the South African athlete Zola Budd (p. 45); Mr. Govender, "president of the Congress of Allied Democrats" (p. 46), with his suspiciously beautiful daughter, Anagupta; and Morris Morrison, the former priest. In these anecdotal details, Hope's novel achieves lightness, an imaginative buoyancy.

Meanwhile, these people are living nowhere, a reality of which they are reminded by Rose, the caustically clear-sighted daughter of Frau Katie, owner of the club. Provoked by the self-styled Soweto Knights "arrayed in leopard skins, their bodies shining with oil," Rose shrieks: "This is Britain, you know! We are living in *Bri-tain!*" (p. 93). Rose is even more severe on her mother's illusions:

The Room remains because my mother preserves it by an act of will. It's an old-fashioned museum where she locks up her dreams. Her curious imaginings about Africa. In the Room there are only two realities: old Berlin and the new Africa. They are totally unconnected and quite false. They have no historical link. This place is built on illusions. Her memories of old Berlin are distorted by time, sentimentalised, romanticised.... Her visions of Africa are based on nothing more than ignorance.

(p. 55)

It may at first seem incongruous that the club is owned by a German woman who has never been to Africa. But for Hope, the two are far from being "totally unconnected"; indeed, the connection is one of the main lines of the novelist's imaginative network. Frau Katie is the relict of another, more cataclysmic refugee crisis: that of the Jews from Germany in the 1930s. As the wellborn wife of a German general, Katie was implicated in the Nazi regime, but she suffers from it, too: her husband abandons her to an underground existence and gives her a pistol with which to shoot herself. This pistol is crucial to the plot. Back in Berlin, Katie used it to kill a Gestapo officer who was tailing her, and midway through the novel she shoots herself in her room above the club, stalked this time by cancer, old age, and ambiguous memories. One of her illusions is that she will one day elope to Berlin with Looper, who truly loves her as he loved his mother. Looper's feelings for Katie are much more significant than his sexual relationship with Rose, which fits Hope's pattern as a mere "business arrangement." Looper fulfills his promise, and Hope his theme, by taking Katie's ashes to Germany and scattering them in woodland near her home. The ends of these two exiles coincide; for Looper, shadowed by the sinister Zulu from back home, gives himself, half voluntarily and half under protest, to death in the snow.

In the last three chapters, Hope meditates on the destructive place of racial hatred in history and unlocks a powerful and moving elegiac note that is far removed from his typical satirical inflection. The satirical brilliance is much on display earlier in the novel when Hope analyzes the sliding scale of illusion, self-deception, and compromise, and the steepening slopes of cynicism, selfishness, cowardice, and outright corruption. But this is played against the novel's darker undertow, its exploration of Hope's own heart of darkness: not that which the white man has conveniently located in Africa, but the darkness of the heart that will overtake any society founded upon racist principles.

MY CHOCOLATE REDEEMER

My Chocolate Redeemer (1989) is an anomaly among Hope's novels, which may explain its less enthusiastic response from his admirers. In the first place, the imaginative axis is between France and central Africa rather than England and South Africa, and Hope therefore grafts his perennial themes onto less familiar ground. Instead of the ghosts of the Boers and their descendants, the shadowy figures of Jean Bédel Bokassa (the self-proclaimed "Emperor" of Central Africa Republic) and Valéry Giscard d'Estaing (French president) stalk this novel; the implicit reference is to the melodramatic, and grotesque, history of postcolonial French Africa and to the dubious, collusive counterpoint of French politics of the time. In the second place, the narrator is, for the first and only time in Hope's works thus far, a woman, Bella Dresseur, the daughter of a French diplomat who has been murdered in the mythical country of Zanj.

The detective-story plot concerns the relationship between Bella and the exiled black leader of Zanj, who may be identified with Bokassa and who, under the less threatening name of Brown, is tamed by Bella. Her childhood obsession with chocolate matures into another narrative metaphor in her commitment to the beleaguered Monsieur Brown, the "chocolate redeemer," who knew her father and unravels that story with his own. But as usual with Hope, the elaboration and detail count for more than the plot. Apart from her errant and unreliable mother, who sends banknotes rather than letters from the United States, Bella's circle includes André, a reformed stockbroker and owner of the hotel where Brown has taken refuge; Monsieur Cherubini, leader of the PNP, a populist right-wing political party with dubious associations; Father Duval, the obligatory priest and reactionary chaplain to the party; Clovis, a crippled young addict; and Uncle Claude, a man given to abstract thought about the universe, pure mathematics, and what he calls TOE, his "Theory Of Everything."

These characters constitute Bella's circle in that she is at the center inventing them all, conferring on them the gift or grace of being. She functions as a metafictional device, the projection of the novelist's own creativity. What her uncle complains of as Bella's "allergy to the truth" — that is, to "facts, figures, details, accuracy" (p. 114) — is actually an allegiance to another kind of truth: the personal, validating truth of emotion and imagination. This is the truth that Laurence Sterne's narrator, Tristram, defends in *Tristram Shandy* (1759–1767) against the wild theorizing of his father, Walter, and the painful empiricism of his Uncle Toby, and it provides a valuable insight into Hope's sense of history that he joins with Sterne in this enterprise. Hope creates the sense that history will only yield its meaning to those equipped with the sensibility and intelligence to be wounded by it. Otherwise, the cells of the Gestapo in Lyons (filled, it turns out, with the complicity of André's father) will remain as soundproof as the deep freezes where Emperor Bokassa allegedly deposited his jointed victims.

For all its intellectual ambition, which is backed up by thorough research, *My Chocolate Redeemer* lacks some of the lightness Hope has achieved elsewhere. The "fictive covering," in Wallace Stevens' phrase, remains a patchwork, and there is too much historical documentary for comfort: "To answer that I must tell you something more of the history of my country," says Monsieur Brown to Bella (p. 123), and he proceeds to do so at some length. In Shakespeare's *The Tempest*, Prospero had the same problem in telling Miranda her story; some facts are simply necessary. This novel continues Hope's ongo-ing commitment to redeeming history through the imagination.

SERENITY HOUSE

From his earliest writings, Hope has underlined the link between the racist policies of the former South Africa regime and those of Hitler's Nazi Party. For Hope this is not imaginative juxtaposition, but a matter of historical fact, which is noted with disgust by the disillusioned Colonel Visser in *Kruger's Alp*: "The Kaiser had supported Paul Kruger against the British in the old days and that was a pretty good precedent for his descendants to do the same.... *Ergo* — the later liaison between the Austrian housepainter and the hairy little rockspiders who run our country. A marriage of true minds" (p. 109). Hope's descriptions of detention camps and townships in that novel deliberately evoke Nazi death camps; in his perception, such aberrations imply an analogous moral universe. It is perhaps the fulfillment of a deeper logic, therefore, that in his novel *Serenity House* (1992) Hope turns directly to the Holocaust, as if this ultimate and terrifying subject had lain in waiting all the time, daring him finally to confront it. The novel takes a complex and circuitous route — with a series of ritual unveilings — to reach its destination in the Polish killing fields.

Serenity House is Hope's most consciously experimental novel, and it was a finalist for Britain's prestigious Booker Prize (although many people thought it deserved the prize itself). The plot concerns an anglicized German, Max Montfalcon, who after a career at Oxford University returned to Germany and played his part as a scientist in the atrocities of the Nazi years, emerging from the death camps with grotesque mementos: gold teeth, skulls, and eyes in formaldehyde — the materials of his genetic research. He took up residence in England again after the war, assumed an English identity, became an English teacher (the pedantic accuracy of his own English owing much to an intimate knowledge of *Fowler's Modern English Usage*, which provides an epigraph for the novel), married, had a daughter, became a successful property developer, lost his wife to cancer and his daughter to indifference (and marriage to a member of Parliament), and grew old.

The novel begins with Max in the nursing home where he has been moved by his family. His daughter, Lizzie, and his busy son-in-law, Albert, have given up; only his granddaughter, Innocenta, loves and tries to protect him. There are echoes of Shakespeare's *King Lear* and *The Tempest* at work here; at one level, Max is a more deeply compromised Prospero figure. In the sinister Serenity House, he meets Jack, an American who has learned of Max's secret past from the Polish woman Marta, who raised him and turns out to have been Max's personal assistant in the camps. Jack, who is variously identified as Everyman Jack, the oedipal Jack from the Beanstalk, and Jack the Ripper, is a truly terrifying conception. Raised in a trailer in Ohio after his mother's desertion, product of junk food and violent videos ("Jack needed to watch people being killed," p. 166), he is the embodiment of everything destructive and depraved in society. In terms of the novel's larger metaphor, Jack represents the American contribution to history and, in this respect, is allied with Max's half-American mother's family, which made its money from the slave trade.

Max blames the fact that "people knew little history" for the consequence that we cannot make sense of contemporary experience (p. 128). This irony is intentional on Hope's part, since it is Max himself, in his earlier incarnation as Maximilian von Falkenberg with his fateful calipers and micrometer, who represents the monomaniac scientist of the Frankenstein myth. Even in old age he is unrepentant, clinging to his own version of history: "Retrospective moral judgements in historical matters were vulgar" (p. 134). But retrospection cannot be ruled out, as his son-

in-law is alerted to the researches of a Commons Committee on War Criminals that has Max in its sights. Max manages to escape both in the end, thanks to the intervention of Innocenta. Meanwhile, in a subplot that again brings to mind *The Tempest*, Innocenta (as Miranda) is brutally raped by Jack.

By a further loop of imaginative logic, the unraveling leads to Disneyland, Jack's backyard and the fulfillment of the visual, packaged, regimented junk culture that lies at the center of this book. The cinematic narrative technique of the novel—with flashbacks, crosscuts, ellipses, fades, and dissolves, its iconic solidity embodied in Max's hideous Holocaust artifacts, its motifs, its measured buildup of tension, and its final brilliant visual denouement—enables Hope to establish not just a link but a strict synchrony between the moral and imaginative death of Nazi Germany, modern cash-and-carry Britain, and the ultimate American theme park that is run very much like a concentration camp. The happy ending contemplated by Max as he plans to abort Innocenta's monstrous fetus—although he is tempted to let her carry the fetus to term for scientific experimentation—is surely one of the most blackly ironic in contemporary fiction, subversive of all traditions of romance in its fearful iteration of historical horror stories.

THE LOVE SONGS OF NATHAN J. SWIRSKY

The Love Songs of Nathan J. Swirsky (1993) consists of a dozen linked short stories set in a deprived suburb of Johannesburg in the depressed early 1950s. Like Joyce's *Dubliners* (1914) or Charles Dickens' novels, *The Love Songs of Nathan J. Swirsky* has a young narrator, the ten-year-old Martin, who lives on an estate and whose innocent commentary on the absurd behavior of his parents—the behavior being itself a reflection of the idiotic measures of the government—enables Hope to infuse his moral analysis with a rare blend of detached humor. A precondition of success in this mode is an understanding of the child's mind, and here Hope is totally convincing:

> Much later, I grew sleepy and it seemed to me that the men in the garden were not men at all. They were planes and tanks moving across the sand in the desert war in North Africa. While, in the yard next door, Tamburlaine keened and whimpered. His long chain, which had been tied to the steel pole that held the washing line, clashed like the waves of a metal sea.
>
> ("Maundy," p. 139)

The British novelist Graham Greene remarked that a writer is someone who never forgets his or her childhood; clearly, Hope fits the definition, and this novel gains from the curiously intense perceptions mediated by Martin. The case that comes to life in this "light vessel of consciousness" includes Martin's friends, his parents, a miscellaneous group of neighbors who move in and out of focus, and Tamburlaine, the menacing Doberman pinscher next door. There is the deftest account of a child's pristine sexual feeling in his description of the girl Sally and a movingly unelaborated description of the death of a young friend in a collapsed tunnel. Martin's father is a sympathetic liberal who expresses such sentiments as "Since this damn government of dyed-in-the-wool fascists came in, in '48, it's been like living in a bloody great prisoner-of-war camp" ("Love Songs," p. 169). His mother is a woman of the most inveterate prejudice.

Most spectacularly, there is Swirsky himself, a Jewish Pied Piper who entrances the children while he appalls the adults with his larger-than-life behavior, his pharmacist's shop that is more like an Aladdin's cave, his real and imaginary travels, his stories, and his temporary English wife, Ruthie, from Wimbledon. Hope uses the Dickensian device of concentrating Swirsky's moods in his mustache, which goes from being a bat, an axe, or a stiletto in his prime to "not very well pegged washing on the line" after his wife's desertion with a baritone named Wolfgang Christ ("Love Songs," p. 170). On Swirsky's final disappearance, this mustache is adopted as a symbol on the banner raised by the Black Zionists whom Swirsky has bizarrely baptized into his faith.

The detail is delightful, the comedy captivating. But the superficial charm is deceptive; the novel does not represent Hope's retreat into anecdote and whimsy. His permanent themes break the surface of the child's consciousness like a sinister shark's fin: war, imprisonment, punishment, and death; sexuality and unhappiness; ignorance and prejudice, especially that arising from the poisoned well of racist feeling. At the end of it all we have a sense of the intimidating power of the African continent itself. "I want my Africa raw" ("Bravo!" p. 116), announces Ruthie on arrival from Wimbledon, but she cooks up all kinds of trouble during her brief stay, and Gus Trupshaw draws the appropriate moral for her: "You can't mess around with Africa" ("Maundy," p. 135). Not even Nathan J. Swirsky, for all his stories, could get away with that.

MOSCOW! MOSCOW!

Just as Hope's first travelogue, *White Boy Running*, traces the roots of his life and artistic themes, his fascinating account of his visit to Mikhail Gorbachev's Russia in 1989 provides a natural summary of many of his preoccupations. *Moscow! Moscow!* (1990) is first of all a celebration of Russia for being so like South Africa. The inveterate politics, the surreal bureaucracy, the depth of disillusion, and above all the Moscow circus of official lies make Hope feel at home there. The book has a curiously nostalgic flavor; Russia is, he finds, "all very strange and yet wonderfully familiar" (p. 1). In six chapters that move (like Joyce's *Ulysses*, 1922) from the maternity hospital to the morgue, from Shakespeare's *Hamlet* to the whorehouse, Hope enjoys the randomness and unreliability of his host country. Like South Africa, Russia is not a place one can hope to understand; it has to be believed like any other improbable but persuasive fiction.

It is a place reproached by its past, haunted by ghosts. Old photographs of the city assail him with a sense of a "vivid energy ... long departed" (p. 69). Rather like Looper in Berlin in *The Hottentot Room*, he feels in Red Square "the ghosts of the place crying aloud, like Hamlet's father, for vengeance" (p. 15). More sinister than the ghosts, however, is the sense Hope has, quickened by his own experience, of the "tribal hatred" now resurgent in Russia: "Through the Russian empire the tribes are growing restless and the hot winds of change are blowing as they did once in Africa" (p. 65). What impresses Hope, time and again, is the truthfulness and integrity of ordinary Russians condemned to live in these deprived and demoralized circumstances: "I learnt again that nothing a foreigner can say about Moscow begins to compare with the devastating honesty of its inhabitants" (p. 139). The interpreter Nadia is a heroic example of the resistant Russian consciousness:

> Nadia had the eye of a surgeon and the heart of a sceptic. She denied being a nihilist but she was the purest pessimist I have ever met. Her pessimism was dark and deep and of a refined sort, compounded of fury, grief and despair, forced through the filter of her crushed expectations until it became so terribly clear you forgot how deep it was.
>
> (p. 155)

The Russians he meets don't seem to believe in language any more. Well versed in *Hamlet*, they are only too aware of the "words, words, words" that have been used to lie to them for years. "In Moscow words frequently fail, perhaps because they have failed so many so often; the currency is almost valueless" (p. 77).

Just as in his earliest schoolboy compositions Hope valued writing as a way to preserve the past and prepare for the future, he continued to look to language as a way to contend with circumstance, a way to maintain the truth in a world of lies. There are some positive signs to be found, even in Russia: "The new freedom is to be found in talk, words: they are *freer*, without being absolutely free" (p. 3); ordinary people are "at last discovering the joys of plain speaking"; "the true achievement of glasnost and perestroika has been the slow opening up of language; a closer relationship between words and their meanings is being encouraged for the first time since the Revolution" (p. 38). If the currency has been debased, Hope suggests that we must take to irony, acting like black marketeers of language, searching out — at whatever cost in disillusion — the real human values that cannot be falsified, even by money, power, and sexual relations. For the writer, it is a great responsibility, and it is the mainspring of Hope's commitment to his craft.

Selected Bibliography

NOVELS

A Separate Development. Johannesburg, South Africa: Ravan Press, 1980; New York: Scribner, 1981.

Kruger's Alp. London: Heinemann, 1984; New York: Viking, 1985.

The Hottentot Room. London: Heinemann, 1986; New York: Farrar, Straus & Giroux, 1987.

Black Swan. London: Hutchinson, 1987; New York: Harper & Row, 1987.

My Chocolate Redeemer. London: Heinemann, 1989.

Serenity House. London: Macmillan, 1992; Boston: Little, Brown, 1992.

The Love Songs of Nathan J. Swirsky. London: Macmillan, 1993; Boston: Little, Brown, 1993.

Darkest England. London: Macmillan, 1996; New York: Norton, 1996.

SHORT STORIES

Private Parts and Other Tales. Johannesburg, South Africa: Bateleur Press, 1981; London: Routledge & Kegan Paul, 1982.

Learning to Fly. London: Minerva, 1990.

NONFICTION

White Boy Running. New York: Farrar, Straus & Giroux, 1988.
Moscow! Moscow! London: Heinemann, 1990.

POETRY

Whitewashes. With Mike Kirkwood. Durban, South Africa: privately printed, 1970.
Cape Drives. London: London Magazine Editions, 1974.
In the Country of the Black Pig and Other Poems. London: London Magazine Editions, 1981.
Englishmen. London: Heinemann, 1985.

CHILDREN'S LITERATURE

The King, the Cat, and the Fiddle. With Yehudi Menuhin. New York: Holt, Rinehart, & Winston, 1983.
The Dragon Wore Pink. London: A. & C. Black, 1985; New York: Atheneum, 1985.

ARTICLES

"Out of the Picture: The Novels of Nadine Gordimer." In *London Magazine* 15, no. 1 (1975).

"On Breyten Breytenbach's Recantation." In *Contrast* 10, no. 4 (1976).
"Poetry and Society." In Peter Wilhelm and James A. Polley, eds., *Poetry South Africa: Selected Papers from Poetry '74.* Johannesburg, South Africa: Donker, 1976.
"A Warning to Others." In *Index on Censorship* 5, no. 4 (1976).
"Visible Jailers." In *Index on Censorship* 11 (August 1982).
"A View from the Hills." In M. J. Daymond, J. U. Jacobs, and Margaret Lenta, eds., *Momentum: On Recent South African Writing.* Pietermaritzburg, South Africa: University of Natal Press, 1984.
"The Political Artist in South Africa." In *English in Africa* 12 (May 1985).

CRITICAL STUDIES

Horn, Peter. "Post-War Jo'burg Blues." Review of *The Love Songs of Nathan J. Swirsky.* In *South Africa Review of Books,* no. 38 (July/August 1995).
Maltz, Harold P. "Narrative Mode in Christopher Hope's *Kruger's Alp.*" In *English in Africa* 14 (October 1987).

Yūsuf Idrīs

1927–1991

SABRY HAFEZ

YŪSUF IDRĪS was the most influential and prolific of the Arab writers who started their careers in the 1950s, amid the euphoria of independence. He achieved instant fame and attracted the admiration, even adulation, of readers and critics throughout his career. Although his desire to remain in the public eye was not without complications, he used his popularity to advance the cause of freedom and to enhance his ability to shock readers and political authorities out of complacence. This was the era of Jean-Paul Sartre's *littérature engagé* (literature taking a stand on contemporary events) and of the artist as public figure. Idrīs was as committed to his writing and the freedom to experiment in theme and form as to social concerns and national causes. He wrote with vigor and intensity and brought a fresh approach to realistic narrative after a long period of stagnation by opening the short story to the lives of real people in real situations. He introduced a new language of everyday expression that often bordered on the vernacular yet reverberated with poetic resonance.

Idrīs was born in a small Egyptian village, al-Bayrūm, in the district of Sharqiyyah, on 19 May 1927, four months after the last issue of *Al-Fajr* (The dawn), the pioneering journal that put the short story as a new and distinctive literary genre on the cultural map of Egypt and the Arab world. Some twenty years later, he provided this new literary genre with its greatest accomplishment in Arabic and widely extended its popularity.

LIFE AND CONTEXT

Idrīs was born into a middle-class farming family in the Egyptian Delta and spent his early childhood in a small village. His family led an unsettled life, for the economic crisis of the 1930s forced his father to move constantly. In addition, his family was haunted by the deaths of a number of male children, and Idrīs was the first boy to survive. Yet this did not guarantee him a happy childhood. He was deprived of his mother's love and attention, given to a wet nurse, and brought up by his grandmother, a sharp-tongued woman with a quick temper who lashed out at him at the slightest misdeed. In his grandmother's home he was the only child in a world of adults and was expected to act like a grown-up. At five years old, he walked several miles a day to the nearest primary school, in the small town of Fāqqūs, where he was the only child among adolescent schoolmates. This situation forced him into contemplative silence, which he fed on a diet of folktales and popular lore. Upon completing primary school, he was sent to

345

Damietta to live with an elderly uncle, 'Abd al-Salām, and begin his secondary education. His uncle had an endless reservoir of stories, proverbs, popular narratives, and the tales of *The Arabian Nights*. Forced into a sedentary life by age, poor health, and rheumatism, his uncle earned a living by knitting and dressmaking. Female customers confided in him and filled the house with gossip and stories that nourished Idrīs' budding talent for storytelling.

With the outbreak of World War II Idrīs had to move again and spent the war years in a chain of secondary schools in Mansūral, Zaqāzīq, and Tanṭā. He spent his adolescence in these unsettled years, which reinforced his contemplative nature and isolated him from his fellow students. The end of the war coincided with his school-leaving exams. His academic record exempted him from university fees, and he enrolled in the Faculty of Medicine at Cairo University. At the time, the leadership of the student movement relocated from the Faculty of Law to the Faculty of Medicine and Engineering. The Faculty of Medicine was the center of the students' national movement during this turbulent time in Egypt and the cradle of the influential Al-Lajnah al-Waṭaniyyah liʾl-Talabah waʾl-ʿUmmāl (The national committee for students and workers). Participating in this movement provided Idrīs with a cure for his isolation, for he found himself in the crucible of political struggle and social polarization. The university was rife with political activities, and idealistic students were drawn into alternative political groups that articulated the country's dissatisfaction with the corrupt monarchy and a political establishment that was subservient to Great Britain. Although Egypt was nominally independent, the ubiquitous presence of British troops in the capital gave the lie to this. The traditional, popular, liberal, and patriotic Wafd party was discredited during the war, and the university became a recruiting ground for newly emerging alternatives, such as the Muslim Brotherhood and leftist groups.

Idrīs quickly was attracted to leftist groups, and his national zeal and his talent enabled him to rise instantly to the position of secretary of the faculty's student union. Throughout his university years he continued his public and political activities and edited a magazine, *Majallat al-jamīʿ* (Everyman's magazine), which was banned by the police and led to his arrest and university disciplinary action. As a result, he expressed his views in other left-wing publications, such as *Al-Kātib* and *Al-Malāyīn*, which increased his contact with left-wing circles and sharpened his social and political awareness. Because of his political activities, by the age of twenty he had directly experienced the tyranny and political intimidation of the minority governments that ruled Egypt throughout the late 1940s. His friendship with the sensitive Chekhovian writer Muḥammad Yusri Aḥmad led him to literature.

Like Aḥmad Khayri Saʿīd, a medical doctor and editor of *Al-Fajr*, who inspired new writers and offered them his patronage, Muḥammad Yusri Aḥmad was one of those indolent but talented writers whose greatest aptitude is for sparking talent in others. In Idrīs, Aḥmad discovered that beneath the exterior of the professional medical man and ardent political orator and activist there lay an ingenious and gifted writer: he persuaded Idrīs to begin reading literature, especially folktales and Russian fiction, and encouraged him to try his hand at short-story writing. In 1950, Idrīs published his first short story, "Unshūdat al-ghurabāʾ" (The ode of strangers), in *Al-Qiṣṣah*, where Aḥmad was an established writer. At this time a group of medical students, including Ṣalāḥ Ḥāfiz and Muṣṭafā Maḥmūd, were also writing short stories, and Ibrāhīm Nāji, a medical doctor, well-known literary figure, and regular contributor to *Al-Qiṣṣah*, encouraged and supported them. A wave of young writers took up the short story as their favorite medium. The vigor of the early years (1948–1959) of this wave put the short story in a prominent position on the cultural map, silenced speculation about its death or triviality, and saved it from the lower ranks of entertainment and sentimentality. Ṭāhā Ḥusayn's *Al-Muʿadh-dhabūn fī ʾl-arḍ* (1949; *The Sufferers: Stories and Polemics*) was also highly influential in the the new trend of realistic short stories. The stature of Ḥusayn compensated for the rudimentary structure of some of his short narratives and enabled this book to change the course of the short story by establishing a new way of writing about the poor. The powerful tableaux of the life, suffering, and tribulations of Egypt's underdogs provided many writers of the younger generation with a literary outlet for their social and political anger.

THE EARLY SHORT STORIES

This anger found its supreme expression in Idrīs, whose talent eclipsed that of his contemporaries. His work was not only rich in form and subject matter, but also abundant and constantly developing. After the publication of his first story, he continued publishing in some of the leading periodicals of the period, such as *Rūz al-Yūsuf*, *Al-Miṣri*, and *Al-Taḥrīr*, until his first collection, *Arkhaṣ layālī* (*The Cheapest Nights*), appeared in 1954. He then published twelve more collections of short stories and several novels and plays. Although Idrīs' contribution to the Egyptian novel and drama is considerable, his major achievement lies in his short stories. At the beginning of his literary career, Idrīs was not aware of his predecessors' accomplishments in the field. He was more focused on social and political issues and the need to give shape and form to the dreams of Egyptians who yearned for a place in this new and long-awaited world. In 1952, two years after the beginning of Idrīs' literary career, the Egyptians' hopes rose when the army seized power. Some of the dreams for which, as a student and political activist, he had fought seemed to be approaching fulfillment and needed just a little push to materialize.

At this early stage, Idrīs treated the short story as an extension of his political activities and as a tool to prove the correctness of his political and ideological views. But he steadily grew more aware of his role as an artist and moved toward a more subtle approach to depicting reality. His short stories fall into three categories: the first includes the five collections published in the first ten years of his career; the second consists of the four collections published during the 1960s; and the third includes his last four collections. The works of the first stage poured out in rapid succession, almost annually as if to assert his talent and secure his place in literary life. During the second stage the intervals were longer, and there were four years of silence (1962–1966), or rather of a search for new modes of expression to convey the change in his artistic sensibility.

He wrote and published his first five collections— *Arkhaṣ layālī, Jumhūriyyat Farāḥāt* (1956; Farāḥāt's republic), *A-Laysa ka-dhālik* (1957; Isn't it so?), *Al-Baṭal* (1957; The hero), and *Ḥādithat sharaf* (1959; A question of honor)— before the age of thirty, at a time of great social and political aspirations. The issues were crystal clear in this period, or at least appeared so to writers; equally clear were the goals and identity of friends and enemies. During these years the old order collapsed dramatically, and the fulfillment of dreams of an almost utopian dimension seemed a possibility. Idrīs' stories were a significant element in this fervent atmosphere, for they gave concrete form to nationalist aspirations. They articulated the concerns of the voiceless underprivileged and the protest of the desolate poor against the literature of entertainment. In contrast to sentimental short stories situated in luxurious places, lofty villas, and elegant cars, Idrīs' stories portrayed the world of the poor and the simple space of their joy and suffering.

In his first five collections, Idrīs created an artistic world unique in its breadth, depth, richness, and authenticity. The realm in which his characters move — despite their belonging mostly to the lower strata of society — is wide. Idrīs depicts town life with the same sure-footedness and ease as he depicts the village. He refrains from dwelling on characters or locations he has previously treated, and when he does revisit an experience or characterization, he modulates the tone and alters the quality until it appears as if he were embarking on a fresh type of discourse. In these five collections, Idrīs does not limit his themes or bind himself to one oppressed group of people; he moves freely through the social spectrum and across a wide range of locations. When he narrates village life, he endeavors to present all possible variations on the rural scene. He presents the average-size village, the small kafr and the marginal 'izbah, alongside the coastal village and remote rural places. His favorite rural location is the village in lower Egypt, and particularly in his native province of al-Sharqiyya. He also covers a range of urban space, from the capital, Cairo, to the small provincial town. The important factor in this diversity of setting, however, is his ability to create a strong sense of reality, as if he has had firsthand experience of each location.

The diversity of characters is as rich as that of locations and space. In *The Cheapest Nights*, for example, Idrīs creates characters from a variety of occupations, ages, classes, and temperaments. In the other four collections, he expands this range and continues to break new ground in theme and characterization. Although he focuses chiefly on the lower classes and different strata of the middle class, he moves through the whole spectrum of Egyptian society. Simple peasants sparkle with wit and humanity and the stagnant corners of Egyptian society reveal richness and vitality, profound conflicts, and stimulating ideas. Unlike some of his predecessors, he treats workers and peasants with care and respect. But Idrīs' major artistic achievement lies in characterization and his ability to illustrate complicated issues without perplexing

the reader. His lively and realistic characters are not recapitulations of the morally impeccable cardboard figures of social-romantic stories, incorrectly called works of social realism. They come across as real people in whose trials and tribulations, joys and pleasures the reader sees his or her own situation. The stories of this period also prove that Idrīs is adept at obiter dicta, or incidental observations, which provide the narrative and dialogue with insight, depth, and vitality.

The great variety of Idrīs' world also extends to time. Nocturnal activities particularly interest him. Unlike Yaḥyā Ḥaqqi, who associates night with loneliness and grief, Idrīs conceives of the night, particularly in the village, as a time of intimacy, casual gatherings, frank conversation, relaxation, and contemplation; the nocturnal atmosphere not only lends the action mystery and ambiguity but also harmonizes with the underlying tone of suffering and grief in the lives of his wretched and sensitive characters. In stories like "Al-Baṣra" ("Snap"), "Maẓlūm" ("Wronged"), and "Fī al-layl" ("At Night"), nighttime becomes an integral part of the action and an important component of the situation. It would be impossible to depict these stories in the daytime, yet the nocturnal setting gives the reader an insight into the daytime life of characters.

Unlike many of his contemporaries, Idrīs avoids sentimentalizing and exaggerating the suffering of the poor. On the contrary, he accentuates the humorous elements in sad and distressing situations as a way to moderate grief. He does not, however, superimpose a naive optimism on a tragic situation; rather he demonstrates how people endure what seems beyond endurance. For him, the important aspect of endurance is the way people overcome difficulties and preserve their dignity and humanity, how they cope with oppression and poverty, and how they find or create joy in the midst of tragic situations.

Idrīs concentrates on the external elements of a fictional situation, sometimes at the expense of the interior aspects of a character. At this stage, he is mainly concerned with the conflict between people and society, a society that appears as an abstraction. At the same time, he emphasizes the sensuality and beauty in the daily activities of the poor and deals with external experiences as if they were fascinating rituals. He portrays few voluptuous moments in this gloomy, rough, and constricted world and goes into raptures over rare instances of pure sensation, treating them as a form of sublime sensual worship.

Although Idrīs presents a wide variety of characters in these five collections, one type is dominant: the frustrated person full of dreams and projects that are often larger than life and therefore unlikely to be fulfilled. A character's craving for life with all its sensual pleasures is as great as the insurmountable obstacles that stand between him and his aspirations. His characters live in a world that seems enveloped in a miasma of oppression, failure, insecurity, and lack of fulfillment. Even when a flash of joy appears on the horizon of this closed and gloomy atmosphere, it is always dim and fleeting. Failure is common in the life of Idrīs' characters, although it is never complete because at the lowest ebb of defeat there always appears a possibility of advancement. This limited victory, which can be accompanied by no real exultation, is the only feasible attainment in a closed and unjust world. Idrīs depicts life as an amalgam of small victories and heroic failures, like those of the indomitable hero of Ernest Hemingway's story *The Old Man and the Sea* (1952), who conquers the huge fish but returns, at the end of his fabulous adventure, with nothing but its skeleton.

To present this atmosphere of frustration in which a character's dreams never come to fruition, Idrīs treats his material as if it were part of a nightmare, dreadful but transient. Details of setting, situation, and action turn, through human discoveries and suffering, into the components of a bad dream. The world narrows to a confined space; for social and economic reasons, most alleviating elements are eliminated. In "Arkhaṣ layālī" ("The Cheapest Nights"), for example, the nocturnal world of the village narrows before its protagonist, who is encumbered by a large family. He is fully aware of the causes of his distress and tries to avoid the vicious circle that aggravates his poverty. But in his attempt to escape, he entangles himself in a web of distress. Idrīs excludes all possible sources of relief. With the mentality of a besieged individual, the protagonist finally resorts to the very solution from which he has dissuaded everyone at the opening of the story—a desperate solution that implies a desire to squeeze some little rapture or sensual delight from his narrowing world.

The nightmarish atmosphere is not confined to nocturnal scenes. In "Ḥādithat sharaf" (A question of honor), the action takes place in the bright light of morning, yet the progression of events and the accumulation of details envelop the scene in desperation and grief, especially when the ordeal of the heroine reaches its climax. In this story, as in many others, Idrīs accentuates the interaction between the individual and the dreary surroundings, between the powers that attempt to defeat a person and his or her heroic resistance and never-ending ability to extract small and often significant victories from destructive powers. This pattern is enhanced by the circularity of the stories. Idrīs' technique emphasizes cyclical continuity and stresses the main action of the story as temporary, but also animating and pervading the whole cycle in a way that affects the next revolution. He therefore avoids sudden endings and denouements. When the course of action demands such an ending, he often continues to elaborate with an overinsistent authorial presence that occasionally jeopardizes the artistic effect. But when the story contains an element of structural irony and is out of keeping with the closed circular form, Idrīs transforms the circle into a spiral: a subsequent cycle of events takes place at another level on which the influence of the previous cycle can still be felt.

The content of these forms emphasizes the transient nature of the nightmare and the interrelationship between illusion and reality, a theme that reaches its peak in "Laylat ṣayf" (A summer night). Here Idrīs juxtaposes the coarse, realistic world of manual work with the vivid sexual extravaganza conjured up by a group of adolescent peasants. They relax at night by listening to the stories of their friend Muḥammad, who has traveled to the city and experienced urban life. For these young villagers, the city is a paradise of sensuality and carnal pleasures, a place where a young man has a chance to prove his virility and fulfill his sexual desires. As Muḥammad tells them a story about a sexual encounter he had in the city with a woman, who symbolizes the dreams of his audience, his audience becomes absorbed in the story and participates fully in its creation. By the end, his listeners have become completely overwhelmed by the colorful extravaganza that they have created and in which Muḥammad has become merely a catalyst. He tries to recall them to reality when they ask him to take them to the woman's house in the city; they finally convince him to take them and set off. Idrīs' description of their trip to the city, walking through the farms at night, is highly significant. He not only shows how the nightmarish atmosphere is conjured, but he also illustrates the power of illusion and, consequently, the difficulty of returning to reality. These qualities are particularly evident when the young men realize that they have gone too far and are forced by the impending rise of the sun to return to their village physically weary, psychologically frustrated, and unable to come to terms with their discovery.

In other stories, the oppressive condition ceases to be transient. Instead of the simple social pressures that a character manages to overcome in earlier stories, in the later stories of this stage, Idrīs introduces a host of new subjugating factors without dispensing with the social ones. In "Ḥādithat sharaf" the pressure is mainly psychological, while in "Rama-ḍān" it is metaphysical, and in "Khams sāʿāt" (Five hours) the metaphysical element is accompanied by political intimidation and fear. In all these stories, social and economic factors are major components of the oppressive atmosphere that can be coupled with other factors but not eliminated. The importance of the psychological, metaphysical, absurd, and political elements becomes vital and more pronounced in the short stories of the 1960s.

STORIES OF MODERN SENSIBILITY

The four collections of the 1960s — *Ākhir al-dunyā* (1961; The end of the world), *Al-ʿAskarī al-aswad* (1962; The black policeman), *Lughat al-āy āy* (1966; The language of pain), and *Al-Naddāhah* (1969; The siren)—contain some of Idrīs' finest short stories. By 1960, the euphoria of the early 1950s was over and most of Idrīs' comrades in the struggle for independence and a better future were behind bars. Idrīs himself was imprisoned for a few months in 1955. The years had gone by, and far too few of the dreams had been realized. Then came the 1960s, a decade of confusion, contradictions, and crises that were important catalysts for the early changes in artistic sensibility and literary conventions, especially in the genre of the short story.

Idrīs' works in the 1960s were substantially different from those in the 1950s, despite some continuity. As his early work managed to bring a breath of fresh air to the realistic short story and put it back in vogue, his work in the 1960s played an important role in shaping and crystallizing modern sensibility. Although his production of short stories slowed down in this period, his range of locations and characters remained, yet his depiction of the human experience tends to be more concentrated and revolves around fewer themes. For example, in his collection *Lughat al-āy āy*, all the stories harbor two main themes: the central character's discovery of the futility and absurdity of life; and perpetual feelings of loneliness, of a lack of fulfillment, and of being the quarry in a mysterious pursuit. The discovery of the futility and absurdity of life, coming too late, places characters at the mercy of self-reproach, exposes them to censure, and fills them with bitterness and despair. The quarry of the unjust hunt is unable to pin down or identify the pursuer. This character is also incapable of rationalizing the ambiguous hunt and hence becomes defenseless against its reckless power.

The elimination or reduction of the element of transient nightmare is an important change in this period of Idrīs' work. What survives is only a pessimistic strand of gloom, for in this second stage Idrīs tends to water down the nightmarish elements and lean toward abstract structures and a dreamlike progression of action that involves unrealistic images or details. In "Al-Awūrṭi" (The aorta), Idrīs takes as his point of departure a myth that cannot be vindicated, yet still convinces the reader. The direct, sharp, rhythmic sentences play a vital role in hypnotizing the reader into the inner logic of the story's make-believe world, in which a haunted man, the quarry of a mysterious pursuit, is running in the streets without bowels or an aorta. He is accused without evidence, convicted without trial, and denied the very essence of life, his aorta. Yet he is still dressed in layer upon layer of ligature, like an Egyptian mummy in its papyrus bandages. The description of the chase and seizure of the central character and the unwrapping of his bands has the quality of a slow-motion picture because of its freezing effect and highly controlled economy of gaze.

In "Al-Luʿbah" (The game), Idrīs creates abstraction not by resorting to the unreal, but by using a dreamlike progression of action. The dream here is not synonymous with the nightmare of the previous stage, but is its antonym, for nightmares are associated with reality while dreams achieve their effect by a complete detachment or withdrawal from reality. Ironically, the action in the dreamlike sequence seems plausible. In "Al-Luʿbah" it concerns a man who goes to a party and participates in a game. The quiet, direct account of the action in its general effect and without any attempts to clarify or justify what seems improbable, or rather with a deliberate intention to stop short of any explanation, widens the scope of the action and opens it to several interpretations. Under the apt description and slow-motion narrative technique, the game ceases to be a single game at a party and becomes the game of life; the player is never a specific person but a symbol of humanity, and the silent conniving crowd reflects social conformity and collective apathy.

In the stories written in the 1960s, Idrīs creates characters who leave a state of oppression and heroic failure for its opposite. These characters become enigmatic and miraculous and these qualities are neither rare nor confined to a particular class or group. Idrīs abandons simple and schematic development of a character and uses repetitive forms based on a succession of images and actions. The stories' departure from a schematic and syllogistic progression reflects a unique logic in which the quality of a character dictates the appropriate style of characterization. The miraculous character is an individual who stands alone in confrontation with obstacles. He challenges collective submissiveness and is capable of defeating, in a subtle and unique manner, those who attempt to terrorize him. In "Muʿjizat al-ʿAṣr" (The age's miracle), a story reminiscent of Jonathan Swift's writings, Idrīs uses satire to present his enigmatic and miraculous character. Exaggeration is employed in two directions: to minimize the physical size of the hero and thus aggrandize his achievements; and to reduce the people's awareness of the hero's potential and intensify the effect of their rejection upon him so that the evidence of his talent contrasts starkly with their mental blindness. Idrīs deliberately makes the hero very small in order to ridicule the norm and prevent any identification with him, for the reader must identify with the narrator and those who victimize the hero.

In terms of situation and action, Idrīs accentuates the enigmatic, miraculous aspect of the individual's confrontation with the group, which represents the order of society. Frequently, the hero reacts by withdrawing from reality. Although this tendency to withdraw seems to contradict the new rebellious quality of the individual, it underlines the pervasiveness of corruption, which the individual seeks to escape, and imbues his rebellion with tragedy. As for those who are not rebellious, withdrawal from reality is a result of the disintegration of reality and the inability of the individual to accept its corrupt order. Withdrawal indicates that collective submissiveness and group connivance in the existing order have perpetuated a perverted scale of social and moral values, within which the innocent individual suffers. Even in the stories that convey extraordinary aspects of humanity, Idrīs portrays withdrawal to demonstrate that he has not neglected elements of frustration and failure. The amalgam of greatness and misfortune is a basic ingredient of many characters. Shawqī, the hero of "Al-ʿAskarī al-aswad" ("The Black Policeman," included in *Rings of Burnished Brass*, 1984), although a victim of brutal political intimidation, is a unique and concrete example of greatness entwined with frustration and defeat. His withdrawal does not vindicate the effectiveness of political terror, for those who inflicted it upon him are now in the same boat, but it indicates how vision becomes blurred and issues confused.

THE LAST COLLECTIONS

The confusion and inversion of values are among the main themes of the stories in Idrīs' last four collections: *Bayt min laḥm* (1971; House of flesh), *Anā sulṭān qānūn al-wujūd* (1978; I am sultan, the law of being), *Uqtulhā* (1982; Kill her), and *Al-ʿAtab ʿalā al-naẓar* (1987; Sight is to blame). These collections were written in the period when confusion reigned and the political project of the 1960s was dismantled. The small gains that had been achieved in raising the standard of living of the poor suffered a devastating setback from the greed and corruption of Anwar al-Sādāt's *infitah* (open door) policy, and Egypt, once the leader of the Arab world, was ostracized by Arab countries after his Camp David peace accords with Israel. It was also a period of poor health and of conflict with the political establishment for Idrīs. At the beginning of the 1970s, he was severely ill and was suspended from his job, and at the end of 1980s his health worsened. These difficulties influenced his writing and affected his productivity; as a result he published only four collections in twenty years. The stories of these last collections vary in aesthetic quality and thematic concerns; they present a different world marked by the inversion of a number of his earlier themes.

The stories in *Bayt min laḥm* illustrate the the sociopolitical changes taking place and the formation of a counterculture of irregularity, corruption, transgression, and evil beneath the natural order of logic, rationality, freedom, and morality. This underworld starts with a few permissible exceptions, but their accumulation dislodges the natural world, sacrifices its rules and values, and negates its ethos through a carefully controlled game of replacement and changing roles. Gradually, exceptions become the rule, consolidate their grip on reality, and turn society into a mere "house of flesh" with no values, responsibilities, or morals. The inversion of old social values results in the alienation of the individual who still believes in the logical and rational laws of the natural world. This individual is viewed as either a neurotic or fool, for he or she still believes that it is possible to escape the new laws of inversion. The silencing of such individuals is vital for the preservation of the new order. In these stories darkness is the leitmotif and is not confined to the night, for it attacks people in the middle of the day and envelops them.

Idrīs demonstrates the depressive nature of this inverted world by contrasting it to the natural or physical one. In "Ummuh" (His mother), he creates a powerful contrast between the hero's relationship with the social world and his affinity with the natural one, represented by a tree. The social world is corrupt, dismissive, and cruel, violating the boy's dignity, body, and soul, while the tree, acting as mother and womb, offers him warmth and protection. In this and similar stories, Idrīs reestablishes life on a purely biological plane in order to show the difference between the laws of nature and those of society and posit a return to the natural order.

One of the major themes of Idrīs' early collections is the importance of the father's role in a patriarchal society. The father represents ultimate authority; he offers his children protection and tenderness, but also causes oppression and fear. He is the axis of family life, thus when he disappears, life loses its enjoyment, spontaneity, and purpose. The undermining of patriarchal authority disturbs the order of life and upsets its delicate balance. Idrīs inverts this theme in the later stories to hint at the disintegration of patriarchy and the weakening of central authority in society long before it actually took place in Egypt or in any Arab country. In "Al-Riḥlah" (The journey), the father is no longer the source of authority and power, but rather he is frail, helpless, dependent on his son, and eventually a useless burden. The son is then free from the oppressive grip of the father and enjoys his freedom, but is still emotionally attached to the decaying father. The journey of the title is one of liberation from the oppressive presence of the father whose uselessness and decay attract the scorn of others.

The same inversion can be seen in the conflict between the group and the individual, which reaches a high degree of sophistication and richness in the early stories. The group is presented not as a faceless crowd or a reckless mob, but as a humane and almost sacred cluster of lovable individuals. In the first five collections, the individual comes into conflict with the group for two main reasons: an attempt to exploit the group or overcome its will, and a lack of understanding of the group's logic, ethos, or culture. The wrongdoings are always on the side of the individual, never on that of the group. Though oppressed or frustrated, the group is always right. In the final collections the group is aimless, irrational, or actively involved in the corruption that afflicts individuals. It becomes part of the dynamics of oppression, apathy, and despotism that hypnotize its members into submission. Unlike the groups of the early stories, which resist tyranny or transcend their failures and griefs through collective dreams, the groups of the last stories are lost or entangled in the perpetuation of their own misery. The group is no longer sacred and infallible; it is stupid, hostile, immoral, conniving, and submissive. It is an accomplice of the status quo and suppresses any attempt to defy it. A comparison between the behavior of the group and the individual in the early stories and the later ones reveals a complete change of roles: the subdued individual becomes a rebel, and the resisting and indomitable group becomes submissive. In "Snobism," a powerful satire of collective submissiveness, the group becomes the basic tool of oppression and perceives the individual's attempt to challenge the existing corrupt order as a danger to its stability. Even in the stories where the group is neither protagonist nor antagonist, it plays a negative role for it is completely assimilated to the surrounding milieu against which the individual reacts.

In Idrīs' last stories, the individual is transformed from the indomitable hero of the early stories or the miraculous, enigmatic figure of the middle phase to a defeated antihero who is void of honor or resistance. Two stories in his last collection, "Abu al-rijāl" (The leader of men) and "Al-Rajul wa'l-namlah" (The man and the ant), offer the ultimate examples of the collapse and undoing of the individual, whose defeat and humiliation occur before a large audience; in "Anā sulṭān qānūn al-wujūd" (translated as "Sultan, the Law of Existence" in *Modern Egyptian Short Stories*, 1977), Idrīs graphically portrays the crushing of an individual in front of a large audience at a circus. This public dishonor is curiously embraced by the humiliated individual as his only course of action, and this acceptance eliminates any resistance. The ultimate disgrace is achieved only through the quasi-voluntary cooperation of its victim. In "Ḥam-māl al-karāsī" (The chairs' carrier), Idrīs gives this feature a mythic dimension in order to pose some basic questions about the ethos of millennium Egypt, the basic attitudes of Egyptians, and the role of the writer in helping them to shake off their apathy.

The humiliation of the alienated individual reaches the level of annihilation in the story "19052," where the hero becomes a worthless creature who is not seen, heard, or acknowledged in a world that is becoming increasingly unrecognizable. Only when he commits suicide by jumping from the tenth floor is he noticed. Blood is one of the main features of Idrīs' later stories, a mark of death but also a sign of life. The stories of the previous phases have little or no blood in them, while none of the stories in his last collections are free of it. Indeed, in some of the stories ablution with blood is a purification ritual that leads to a new beginning. In *Uqtulhā*, Idrīs portrays killing as the purgatory that removes the obstacles to realization of the new utopia. The only hope is a new beginning liberated from the mistakes, oppression, and apathy of the past, but such a beginning is only possible by going through baptism by blood.

In "Sultan, the Law of Existence," Idrīs presents the spilling of the blood of a lion tamer as the necessary prelude to establishing the law of nature. This story, which describes a lion's accidentally killing its tamer in Cairo's circus, becomes a metaphor and prophecy of the 1981 assassination of Sādāt, which took place several years after the publication of the story. By setting the story not on the night of the killing, but on the previous night, Idrīs draws from the incident the ruler's loss of legitimacy as a result of violating the social contract between the ruler and the ruled, between the tamer and the lion. Idrīs achieves this effect by creating a fictional time with its own logic and duration, almost stagnant and unreal, but possessing supreme authority over its dreamlike world. Within this particular time, Idrīs presents the fictional situation in slow motion, which allows him to account for the minutest detail and to ponder the slightest movement. As in film technique, he freezes some scenes, focuses on their totality at the beginning, then zooms in on tiny details. This method magnifies moments in the action and turns them into opportunities for examination and discovery, magic mirrors that reflect the essence of life.

Multiple levels of meaning, sensitive observation, poetic language, and impressive characterization are the hallmarks of Idrīs' short stories.

THE EARLY PLAYS

In addition to short stories, Idrīs wrote plays, novels, and novellas. Drama is his second most important medium and is closely linked to his short stories; three of his eight plays are based on short stories and a fourth is loosely connected to one of his short stories. He wrote two one-act plays—*Malik al-quṭn* (1956; Cotton's king) and *Jumhūriyyat Fara-ḥāt* (1956; Farahāt's republic), the latter of which is based on the title story of his second collection—and six full length plays—*Al-Laḥzah al-ḥarijah* (1958; Critical moment), *Al-Farāfīr* (1964; The flip flaps), *Al-Mahzalah al-arḍiyyah* (1965; The farce of the world), *Al-Mukhaṭaṭīn* (1969; The striped ones), *Al-Jins al-thālith* (1971; The supermen), and *Al-Bahlawān* (1983; The clown), two of which are based on previously published short stories. *Al-Mahzalah al-arḍiyyah* is based on the short story "Fawq ḥudūd al-ʿaql" (Beyond reason) in his collection *Lughat al-āy āy* and *Al-Jins al-thālith* is based on "Hiyā" (She) from *Bayt min laḥm*. In addition *Al-Laḥzah al-ḥarijah* is loosely based on the short story "Al-Jurḥ" (The wound) from *Al-Baṭal*. The close link between the plays and short stories suggests a shared typology, but since Idrīs wrote only one play in the 1980s, it is more logical to divide the plays into two groups: the one-act plays and *Al-Laḥzah al-ḥarijah*; and the rest of the plays.

The one-act plays represent Idrīs' dramatic debut and are marked by economic structure and rich characterization. *Malik al-quṭn* takes place in a village at the time of harvesting the major cash crop, cotton. The play's conflict is between the peasant Qamḥāwi, who is a sharecropper, and the wealthy landowner, Sunbāṭi, who wants to minimize Qamḥāwi's share in order to pay his bank loan, expand his land, and buy more jewelry for his wife. Qamḥāwi, who has worked the land for eight months, is waiting to sell cotton so he can repair the roof of his house and marry off his oldest son. The contrasting needs of the two protagonists are matched by their attitudes toward the cotton, which Sunbāṭi sees in terms of its cash value and Qamḥāwi views with pride and affection as the fruit of his labor. In an attempt to protect his share from the tricky calculations of Sunbāṭi, Qamḥāwi, an illiterate, brings the educated Hajj Shawādifi to check the accounts. Ironically, the dubious Hajj allies with Sunbāṭi in an effort to swindle Qamḥāwi of most of his share. The conflict between the two protagonists is enriched by a host of subplots in which their wives and children are involved in a network of relationships. The play reaches its climax when Kamal, Sunbāṭi's son, inadvertently sets fire to the cotton while hiding behind the cotton sacks to smoke a cigarette. Although this happens after Qamḥāwi knows that he has been, once again, deprived of most of the fruit of his toil, he rushes to extinguish the fire, thereby simultaneously demonstrating his strong affinity to the cotton and his superior humanity.

In *Jumhūriyyat Faraḥāt*, Idrīs depicts a city police station in an ostensibly realistic manner. He creates a nightmarish setting through the nocturnal atmosphere of melancholy, the timeless tunnel of a room, the black walls, the sticky floor, the peculiar nauseating smell, the dim light imprisoned in lamps rather than radiating from them, the shadows and darkness, the people moving as if hypnotized, a heap of broken boxes and chairs, the exhausted suspects, and the policemen in black uniforms. The details create a sense of siege that necessitates flight into the utopian dream of the title: the bright republic envisioned by Faraḥāt, with its honesty, social justice, order, full employment, and happiness. The political prisoner, whose only crime is dreaming of a better future, an earthly utopia, is the only one who can appreciate Faraḥāt's dream. But his presence leads Faraḥāt to realize how stupid he has been to build castles in the air, and sadly he returns to reality. The return to reality is not as easy as the departure from it, for in Idrīs' world, the character slips easily into dream and illusion, but struggles, often with significant loss, to return because the dream is a means of discovering or rediscovering reality.

Al-Laḥzah al-ḥarijah, Idrīs' first full-length play, was inspired by the Suez war of 1956 and investigates that war's vital impact on the country's ethos, attitudes, psyche, and politics. M. M. Badawi, a historian of modern Egyptian drama, says it differs radically from the bulk of ephemeral plays churned out as propaganda, glorifying the struggle of Egyptian patriots against imperialist aggression. In this play, Idrīs focuses on death and the threat of death in order to enhance a concern for life. A physical death occurs and the metaphorical death of a family's hopes and dreams is used to accentuate the value of life that reveals itself in moments of danger and to exorcise the apathy for the country's future. The play deals with a lower-middle-class Egyptian family living in Port Said. The family has worked hard to rise from the squalid conditions of the poor and to send one of the sons to university. This son puts his loyalty to his larger family, Egypt, before his duty to his immediate one and volunteers to join the National Guard after the nationalization of the Suez Canal and the threat of war.

Idrīs articulates the tension between the parents' concern for their son and the son's patriotism and desire to prove himself. The conflict is entirely within the family, which serves as a microcosm of Egyptian society, for despite an appearance of unity the members of the family are very different from one another. The conflict between the parents and the son erupts when war breaks out and he is called up. It offers a study in fear, loyalty, the meaning of patriotism, the nature of commitment, and the conflict between words and deeds. In this critical moment of reckoning the arguments of the first act are substituted by action; deeds speak louder than words and give them new meaning. The older generation, which was shaped under the old regime, is reluctant to embrace the new regime, let alone sacrifice for it, and is entangled in fear and self-interest. The father is only concerned with the safety of his family, unable to realize that his family cannot be safe when the country is unsafe. He believes that the country does not belong to him, yet he has built his business in it and sacrificed everything for his family's future there. Ironically, he is shot at the very moment he thinks he has saved his family.

Similarly, the son's cowardice and fear reveal that the new regime has not yet won over the younger generation or motivated it to defend the country. On the fated night, he deliberately makes enough noise to wake up his parents. As expected, the father prevents him from leaving the house and locks him up behind a door that even his little sister knows has a faulty lock and can easily be opened. When war comes to the house, as British soldiers searching for fedayeen (members of an Arab commando group), the son takes off his uniform and hides his gun. Through the contrast between the verbal bravado of the hero and his cowardice in war, Idrīs reveals the failures of the new regime. When it appeared, the play was severely criticized for its lack of patriotic fervor, but it qualifies as a serious drama with convincing characterization that reveals the truth of the historical moment, the nature of its characters, and the reality of the political events that remained shrouded in deceit throughout the following decade.

AL-FARĀFĪR AND LATER PLAYS

Idrīs' next play, *Al-Farāfīr*, is a milestone not only in his dramatic career but also in the history of modern Arabic theater. The play consciously abandoned the traditional or Aristotelian form of drama and encouraged a new type of dramatic presentation based on indigenous theatrical forms. In *Al-Farāfīr* Idrīs uses the dramatic form of popular theater with its episodic structure, impersonation, improvisation, and character types. He introduces the play with a lengthy theoretical treatise, "Naḥwa masraḥ miṣri" (1964; Toward an Egyptian theater), in which he elaborates the affinity of his new theatrical endeavor with the semidramatic tradition of popular comedies, which are similar to commedia dell'arte: the village *sāmir*, the *qaraqōz* (puppet shows), *muḥabbaẓīn* (popular entertainers), and the more literary type of dramatic spectacle known as *khayāl al-ẓill* (shadow play). Idrīs' attempt to root his play in the Egyptian theatrical tradition is inseparable from his desire to widen the scope of its theme and enhance the audience's rational response to its issues. It enabled him to use the popular form of criticism by mockery and derision to violate some of the taboo issues of his time and elevate some aspects of the play to the realm of political allegory. In addition, by using popular theatrical strategies, he aims at creating an Egyptian version of the Brechtian principle of destroying dramatic illusion, *Verfremdungseffekt*. In this respect alone, the play's theoretical claims are justified because they induce a more rational and less emotional response in the audience, which is essential for a play that is highly critical of social norms, political practices, hypocritical conduct, intellectual mediocrity, and formalities.

In its published form, the play includes a lengthy metatext in which Idrīs elaborates his conception of drama, the function of masks, and the characteristics of the protagonist, *farfūr*. Although those ideas can be extrapolated from the play itself, the metatext emphasizes the interaction between the audience and actors, the elimination of psychological distance between them, the fluidity of the performative act, and the need to expunge theatrical illusion from the play. In addition, the technique of the play inside a play deconstructs the dramatic as a prelude to deconstructing the dynamics of power and authority. It starts with a character calling himself the author, who introduces his characters to the audience, outlines the rudiments of the plot, and asks his characters to improvise an entertaining evening. He also asks for audience participation.

The author, a tall, dignified man wearing spectacles, a starched white shirt, bow tie, and elegant dinner jacket, is first framed at his lectern as the sole source of power, the originator of characters and the prime mover of the action. But as he leaves the lectern, the audience discovers that beneath his immaculate upper half, he is wearing brief shorts that expose his long, thin legs and his feet, with shabby shoes but no socks. The inevitable audience laughter, which is commented upon irritably by the author, is but the first act of undermining the author's absolute power. This is immediately followed by the entrance of *farfūr*, who interrupts the author's introductory remarks. The author asks him to go backstage to allow the author to complete the introduction. *Farfūr* refuses and starts to deride the author, thus aligning himself with the audience and providing them with further opportunity for ridicule. Then *farfūr* asks the

author to get out and leave him to get on with the play, but he soon discovers that the author has not provided him with the characters necessary to commence the performance. As the hierarchy of power is reversed, the scene ends with the author urging *farfūr* to help him to make the play a success.

The themes suggested in this first scene, the shifting nature of power and the need for liberation from authority, are worked out in the play, through the relationship of master and servant, improvised development, and dramatic scrutiny of common social types. The servant, or *farfūr*, is a resourceful character, full of energy and wit. In the first act, his method of finding a job for his master exposes the rigid structure of power relations and its inherent contradictions. The search develops in two opposing but complementary directions: it descends the social hierarchy of jobs, but ascends in terms of the degree of violence in each job. The master finally selects the job of grave digger after rejecting many decent and respectable jobs and proceeds to kill in order to provide work for himself. The first killing whets the master's appetite for more, and the spiraling brutality leads *farfūr* to rebel against the master-servant relationship. The crescendo of the first act reveals that violence is inherent in the very structure of the exploitative master-servant relationship and inevitably leads to destruction and bloodshed.

The master's insatiable urge for violence and *farfūr*'s defiant reaction prompt Idrīs, in the second act, to probe questions of authority and freedom, the hierarchical structure of society, and the tendency of power to generate evil. Though not free from wordiness, digression, and repetition, this search symbolizes humanity's ceaseless quest for freedom and is the zenith of the play's dramatic achievements. The shift from the sociopolitical to the politico-philosophical sparks a change in dramatic strategies that pushes the play toward the techniques of the theater of the absurd. This is consistent with the play's desire to treat power as social, political, and metaphysical and to undermine its hold on society. The structure of the play, with its horizontal juxtaposition of contrasting conditions and conflicting qualities instead of vertical development, subverts the very concept of hierarchical power. It is worth mentioning that questions of freedom and political tyranny were among the taboo subjects of the period, which to some extent explains the play's wordiness and repetition.

None of the plays written after *Al-Farāfīr* attained its popularity or its influence on writers, audiences, and critics, yet in all of them Idrīs continued his search for a new form of theater and fresh areas of dramatic expression. *Al-Mahzalah al-arḍiyyah* contributes to this search through an amalgam of fantasy, symbolism, dreamlike scenes, and the absurd. The equivocal nature of the play both enhances and obscures its philosophical dimensions as a comment on the human condition — on the nature of greed, reason, truth, the meaning of human relationships, and love. In this play Idrīs investigates the validity of a man committing his brother to a lunatic asylum and his motivation for doing so. In order to eliminate any realism, Idrīs gives the three brothers the same name with different numbers, Muḥammad I, II, and III, and calls the nurse of the clinic Ṣifr (Zero). This device enhances the abstract nature of the action, which is further reinforced by the constant shift between illusion and reality, the worlds of the living and the dead. The play continually cancels out what it has just established in a manner that creates a labyrinth of conflicting accounts of the human condition and confirms its lunatic nature. In this respect, the structure of the play reflects the human condition it portrays. The vision that emerges from the play, which ends with the doctor pleading to be taken to the mental asylum, is depressing and pessimistic.

This pessimism reappears in most of Idrīs' subsequent plays with varying degrees of intensity. Despite its political orientation, his next play, *Al-Mukhaṭaṭīn*, is also a gloomy statement on the human condition. Its title, a double entendre meaning "the striped ones," "the planned ones," or even, if pronounced differently, "the planners," alludes to the ruling establishment and roots the play in 1969, the tenth anniversary of the Five-Year Plan launched in 1959. The play is a political allegory, and Idrīs uses abstract rendering, caricature, exaggeration, black humor, a theater within a theater, and some elements of *Verfremdungseffekt* to demonstrate the nightmare of totalitarian rule. In this play Idrīs defends freedom by demonstrating how the monopoly on truth and the obsession with absolute ideas and power are achieved by sacrificing people, including the originator of the idea. Curtailing the freedom of others destroys the humanity of jailers and erodes their freedom, too. Idrīs is also concerned with the ease by which the striped ones, despite their mediocrity, control power, which is provocatively reflected in the very structure of the theater in which the play takes place. Among the play's many nightmarish qualities, only its transience offers the audience a faint glimmer of hope.

The following play, *Al-Jins al-thālith*, is the antidote to *Al-Mukhaṭaṭīn* and is loosely linked to Idrīs' one-act play *Jumhūriyyat Faraḥāt*; it moves away from the narrow and stifling world of politics and offers the audience a different type of utopia. Unlike the social utopia of Faraḥāt, which is based on honesty and justice, the utopian dream in this play is cosmic and philosophical and based on love, life, and human will. The play is structured along the dialectical relationships between dream and reality, good and evil, fantasy and fact, utopia and society. The hero of the play, significantly named Adam, is an aspiring young microbiologist experimenting with DNA to find the secret of life and death. The contrasting nature of life and death is analogous to that of utopia and reality. Thus the journey to the counterworld of dream, good, beauty, and superbeings sharpens the hero's insight into his world. Like the bird in

Manṭiq al-ṭayr (*The Conference of Birds*) by the twelfth- and thirteenth-century Sufi writer Farīd al-Dīn al-ʿAṭṭār, who has to travel the world in order to discover what is at his doorstep, Adam responds to the irresistible enigmatic call of Hiyā (She) and travels to her mysterious world of hybrid creatures, talking trees, and surrealistic beings to discover that the love he was looking for is that of his beautiful young assistant, Narāh. Despite the happy ending to this complex and elaborate play, its vision is tinged with gloom and despair.

Idrīs' final play, *Al-Bahlawān*, is a light social satire dealing with the world of the media and the degeneration of Egyptian society in the 1970s and 1980s as a result of Sādāt's *infitah* policy. Its hero, Hasan al-Muhayli, is the editor in chief of the most influential daily newspaper in the country and playing the clownish role of justifying the contradicting views of the political establishment and perpetually moving in the world of power and hypocrisy. The duplicity of the declared open policy and democracy and an undeclared despotic control over the media and society weighs heavily on the hero's conscience. In the evenings, he furtively practices his hobby of playing a clown in the circus, and his long absence from the office complicates his career and entices his rivals at the newspaper to replace him. In the circus, Mirvat, the beautiful acrobat, is attracted to him, and the sincerity of her feelings contrasts starkly to the world of social lies in which he is one of the pillars. After a series of comic complications during which Idrīs reveals that the owner of the newspaper is also the owner of the circus, the hero chooses to remain in the circus and solve the duplicity of his life.

THE NOVELS AND NOVELLAS

Idrīs' first novel, *Qiṣṣat ḥubb* (Love story) appeared in 1956 and his last novella, *New York 80*, in 1980. In between he published four novels—*Al-Ḥarām* (1959; The sin), *Al-ʿAyb* (1962; Shame), *Rijāl wa thīrān* (1964; Men and oxen), and *Al-Bayḍāʾ* (1970; The white woman)—and four novellas—*Qāʿ al-madīnah* (1957; The bottom of the city), *Al-Gharīb* (1961; The stranger), *Al-ʿAskarī al-aswad* (1962; The black policeman), and *Al-Sayyidah Vienna* (1962; Mrs. Vienna). With the exception of *New York 80*, most of his novels and novellas were written in the early part of his literary career and have more affinity with his early work in the short story than with his later work.

His first novel, *Qiṣṣat ḥubb*, was published with four short stories as his second collection, *Jumhūriyyat Faraḥāt*, and can be read as the story of the political prisoner to whom Faraḥāt outlines his social utopia in the first story of the collection. Unlike Faraḥāt, the protagonist of *Qiṣṣat ḥubb*, Ḥamzah, does not confine himself to dreams or utopian projects but works for a just and independent Egypt. In his student days in the 1940s, he joined the struggle against the British, and has been subjected to imprisonment and surveillance by the secret police. By 1951, the time of the armed struggle in the Canal region and of the narrative, he has joined the armed movement and is setting up a training camp on the outskirts of Cairo. There he meets Fawziyyah, a zealous young schoolmistress who organizes a collection at her school in support of the armed struggle. A week later Cairo burns in the great fire of January 1952, and martial law is declared. The training camp is neglected, and Ḥamzah becomes a fugitive, hiding from the secret police who successfully hunt down most of his colleagues.

The novel is the story of Ḥamzah's hiding, his growing dependence on Fawziyyah, and their falling in love. But it is also the story of Egypt and the new type of liberating love that it craves. Idrīs demonstrates how the emergence of this new healthy love is inseparable from the struggle for the country's independence, changing outmoded attitudes about class and gender and the discovery of the collective potential of the people. Idrīs inscribes the gradual process of education and liberation into the texture of the narrative. He begins the novel from Ḥamzah's perspective and gradually moves toward a more balanced polyphonic narrative that reflects the process of transformation. The narrative device of hiding from the police reverses the power relations that were established in the camp, curtails Ḥamzah's unlimited power, and enables the heroine to have more control over the process of mutual development.

The happy ending and optimistic tone of *Qiṣṣat ḥubb*, which Idrīs wrote while imprisoned for his political views, are in clear contrast to the following three novels written after his release. His finest novel, *Al-Ḥarām*, is set in the countryside and deals with one of the more complex themes in his work, sex, to demonstrate how relating individual experience involves telling the collective narrative of the oppressed. The story of the unfortunate sin of a poor peasant woman is delicately constructed through a combination of first- and third-person narratives that allows Idrīs to elaborate the social and psychological elements of the action. It is a complex study of the individual's psychology and the collective psyche of rural Egypt in which the interplay of class, gender, and power is aptly expressed. It also constitutes a major step in Idrīs' quest to define the nature of the Egyptian concepts of sex, sin, and shame. In Egyptian society, sex is regarded as 'ayb (shame) and ḥarām (sin) and hence becomes taboo, but the Islamic Egyptian concept of sin, Idrīs maintains, is radically different from its Judeo-Christian counterpart and is coded in highly complex social modes.

This difference is graphically illustrated in the structure of the novel. The plot appears to focus on the sin of an individual woman, 'Azīzah, but beneath this simple story Idrīs exposes the social nature of the individual conscience. The stark difference between the order of the narrative and that of the story, in which the telling of 'Azīzah's sin, her pregnancy, and the birth and killing of her baby is delayed to Chapter 14, reveals how the social aspects of the Egyptian concept of ḥarām take priority over individual ones. Delaying the story of the individual's sin allows Idrīs to elaborate on the reactions of the various groups and centers of power in the village after the discovery of the murdered newborn. In the first thirteen chapters, Idrīs presents the villagers' responses to sin in order to show the social nature of the individual's sense of guilt and how these collective responses constitute the specificity of the concept of ḥarām that infiltrates every aspect of social life. The last three chapters, which follow the telling of 'Azīzah's tale, interweave the perspective of the individual with that of society and reveal the hidden dynamics of ḥarām and how it is tinged with hypocrisy. Her act is strongly condemned in public but intensely desired in secret, collectively rejected but individually craved.

In *Al-'Ayb* Idrīs continues to explore the paradoxical nature of the social-sexual code by bringing a bureaucracy and its structured groups into the equation and moving the action from the village to the city. Through the story of an innocent, idealistic, and naive young woman, Sanā', who goes to work in a highly corrupt, governmental licensing office, Idrīs reveals the dynamics of the interaction between the concepts of 'ayb and ḥarām. In addition to the themes of innocence and corruption, the novel deals with the intrusion of women into a world that has been the exclusive preserve of men. With the arrival of Sanā', both the fragile coexistence of conflicting codes of morality and old group dynamics are severely threatened. All the men in the office are contaminated by bribery and corruption. They retain their sanity by making a distinction between their public world of evil and their private world of honor and morality. Idrīs posits the solidarity of the group and its elaborate justification of its conduct against the vulnerability of the isolated individual, armed only with moral values that have no exchange value.

But the obstinate individual's refusal to participate in the fraudulent activity of the group turns the small office into a living hell. One of the remarkable textual strategies in this novel is the manipulation of social and geographical space around the heroine and the group. The conflict between the two comes to a head when Sana' faces a severe economic crisis as a result of her family responsibilities, the very excuse used by men for their vices. The novel is a study of the context and process that lead from innocence to corruption, from social and moral good to evil through the stifling of value judgments and the conflict of economic and social values. As in his other novels, Idrīs uses the individual to reveal the dynamics of the group; the gloomy end of the novel foreshadows the pervasive corruption that prevailed in the following decades.

Apart from *Rijāl wa thīrān*, a light and structurally problematic novel about bull-fighting in Spain, *Al-Bayḍā'* is Idrīs' most troubled novel. It suffered from censorship, self-censorship, and rewriting in response to unfair accusations from political groups. Written and serialized in 1959, the year of the mass arrest of leftist intellectuals and political activists, the novel was accused of betraying the left and being an exercise of political repudiation. It was not published in book form until 1970, yet it remained one of the important documents of the period and is of great significance to students of politics and the sociology of literature because of its hero's refusal to abandon his critical attitude toward the historical events the story treats and because of its subtle psychological analysis.

Unlike *Al-Bayḍā'*, most of Idrīs' novellas are of exquisite literary quality with fine analyses and a sensitive balance of psychological and social issues. In *Qāʿ al-madīnah*, Idrīs explores both the lower strata of the city and the middle class's fixed attitudes toward sex, class, and gender. The hero's departure from his comfortable flat in a wealthy quarter and his trip, for the first time, to the poorest part of the city constitute a departure from a state of being and of thinking, and from a comfortable perception of his identity to a searing state of doubt and questioning. In *Al-ʿAskarī al-aswad*, Idrīs examines the dynamics of tyranny and the lasting impact of political intimidation and torture on a victim and his jailers. In *Al-Gharīb*, sex is no longer ʿayb or ḥarām, in spite of its sinfulness, but is an act of fulfillment, of proving the self and confirming its hold on reality. It is also associated with the Oedipus complex on the one hand and with illegal clandestine activities on the other. Idrīs expands a son's Oedipal relationship with his mother to include a father figure and introduces fear and frustration into the already complex nexus. *Al-Sayyidah Vienna* and *New York 80* represent Idrīs' contribution to a perennial theme of modern Arabic literature: contact and interaction with the west. Their contrasting visions demonstrate how the changing perception of the "other" is indicative of a similar change in the perception of the self and illustrate the vital role of this interaction for the changing national as well as individual self.

In addition to his creative works, Idrīs was a prolific essayist and contributed in succession to *Al-Shaʿb*, *Al-Jumhūrriyah*, and *Al-Ahrām*. Many of his essays have been collected in books, and others are scattered in these three newspapers. In the last fifteen years of his life, his prolific journalistic output was achieved at the expense of his literary productivity. One reason for this shift was his aversion to repeating his literary discoveries or dwelling on old themes and characters. Another more cogent reason was the changing nature of Egyptian society and economy on the heels of the *infitah* and Sādāt's policies, which devastated old values and demanded bolder and more direct treatment that was not conducive to literary subtleties. In the 1970s and 1980s, the era of Egypt's dependence on U.S. policies in the region, Idrīs, the commited writer of the age of *littérature engagé* and the artist as public figure, kept his faculty of revolt very much alive. He engaged in relentless battles against rampant corruption, declining living standards, growing political apathy, the erosion of national independence, the dwindling of secularism and patriotism, and the rise of religious fundamentalism. These battles lent themselves more readily to journalism, and his essays are marked by bold and provocative ideas, lucid presentation, and persuasive argumentation. He used this medium to enhance his public role and encourage the younger generation to practice and defend its freedom.

Idrīs died on 1 August 1991.

CONCLUSION

Idrīs' enduring popularity results primarily from his ability to bring fresh insight into the most familiar situations, characters, and locations. Although he wrote fine novels and plays, he made a lasting impact on the genre of the short story. He is the rare poet of the Arabic short story and its most visionary writer because he did not confine himself to documenting his society but worked actively to transform it. His preoccupations with the social are aided by his insight into the aspirations of the individual and the role of human will. He forged a new language to articulate his vision and liberate narrative fiction from the shackles of traditional and archaic *fuṣḥā* by injecting the poetry of the vernacular into its arthritic syntax.

The work of Idrīs was so powerful and popular in both Egypt and the rest of the Arab world that it not only overshadowed that of many writers of his own generation but also eclipsed the work of those slightly older and those slightly younger than he. From the 1960s, through the change of literary sensibility toward modernist writing, he played a leading role in encouraging the younger generation and developing with them new ways of writing and textual strategies. With the passage of time, the force of his writing endures and reveals new layers of meaning because of his ability to rejuvenate narrative and integrate contemplative elements into concrete representation.

Selected Bibliography

BIBLIOGRAPHIES

Jones, Marsden, and Ḥamdi al-Sakkūt. "Bibliu-grāfyā Yūsuf Idrīs." In *Adab wa Naqd* 34 (December 1987).
Kurpershoek, P. M. *The Short Stories of Yūsuf Idrīs: A Modern Egyptian Author*. Leiden, Netherlands: Brill, 1981.

COLLECTED WORKS

Naḥwā masraḥ ʿArabi. Beirut, Lebanon: al-Waṭan al-ʿArabī, 1974.
Al-Riwāyāt. Beirut, Lebanon: Dār al-Shuruq, 1987.
Al-Qiṣṣah al-qaṣīrah. 2 vols. Cairo: Dār al-Shuruq, 1988–1989.
Al-Masraḥiyyāt. Cairo: n.p., 1990.

SELECTED WORKS

Arkhaṣ layālī (*The Cheapest Nights*). Cairo: Dār Rūz al-Yūsuf, 1954.
Jumhūriyyat Faraḥāt (Faraḥāt's republic). Cairo: Dār Rūz al-Yūsuf, 1956. Contains four short stories and the novel *Qiṣṣat hubb* (Love story).
Jumhūriyyat Faraḥāt. Cairo: n.p., 1956. A one-act play.
Malik al-quṭn (Cotton's king). Cairo: al-Muʾassasah al-Qawmiyyah lī ʾl-Nashr, 1956.
A-Laysa ka-dhālik (Isn't it so?). Cairo: Markaz Kutub al-Sharq al-Aswaṭ, 1957.
Al-Baṭal (The hero). Cairo: Dār alā Fikr, 1957.
Al-Lahẓah al-ḥarijah (Critical moment). Cairo: al-Kitāb al-Fiḍḍī, al-Shirkah al-ʿArabiyyah lī ʾl-Ṭibāʿah, 1958.

Ḥadithat sharaf (A question of honor). Beirut, Lebanon: Dār al-Ādāb, 1959.

Al-Ḥarām (The sin). Cairo: al-Shirkah al-ʿArab-iyyah lī ʾl-Ṭibāʿah, 1959.

Ākhir al-dunyā (The end of the world). Cairo: Muʾassasat Rūz al-Yūsuf, 1961.

Al-ʿAskarī al-aswad (The black policeman). Cairo: Dār al-Maʿrifa, 1962.

Al-ʿAyb (Shame). Cairo: Muʾassasat Rūz al-Yūsuf, 1962.

Al-Farāfīr (The flip flaps). Cairo: Dār al-Taḥrīr, 1964.

Rijāl wa thīrān (Men and oxen). Cairo: al-Muʾas-sasah al-Miṣriyyah al-ʿĀmmah līʾl-Taʾlīf, 1964.

Al-Mahzalah al-arḍiyyah (The farce of the world). Cairo: Majallat al-Masrah, 1965.

Lughat al-āy āy (The language of pain). Cairo: Muʾassasat Rūz al-Yūsuf, 1966.

Al-Mukhaṭaṭīn (The striped ones). Cairo: Majallat al-Masrah, 1969.

Al-Naddāhah (The siren). Cairo: Muʾassasat Dār al-Hilāl, 1969.

Al-Bayḍāʾ (The white woman). Beirut, Lebanon: Dār al-Ṭalīʿah, 1970.

Al-Jins al-thālith (The supermen). Cairo: ʿĀlam al-Kutub, 1971.

Bayt min laḥm (House of flesh). Cairo: ʿĀlam al-Kutub, 1971.

Mufakkirat (Idris' diaries). 2 vols. Cairo: Maktabat Gharīb, 1977, 1980.

Anā sulṭān qānūn al-wujūd (I am sultan, the law of being). Cairo: Maktabat Gharīb, 1978.

New York 80. Cairo: Maktabat Miṣr, 1980.

Uqtulhā (Kill her). Cairo: Maktabat Miṣr, 1982.

Al-Bahlawān (The clown). Cairo: Maktabat Miṣr, 1983.

Al-ʿAtab ʿalā al-naẓar (Sight is to blame). Cairo: Markaz al-Ahram līʾl-Tarjamah waʾl-Nashr, Muʾassasat al-Ahram, 1987.

TRANSLATIONS

Modern Egyptian Short Stories. Trans. and intro. by Saad al-Gabalawy. Fredericton, Canada: York Press, 1977. Includes "The Wallet," "Farahat's Republic," and "Sultan, the Law of Existence."

The Cheapest Nights. Trans. by Wadida Wassef. London: Heinemann; Washington, D.C.: Three Continents Press, 1978; Cairo: American University in Cairo Press, 1990.

In the Eye of the Beholder: Tales of Egyptian Life. Ed. by Roger Allen. Minneapolis: Bibliotheca Islamica, 1978.

Rings of Burnished Brass. Trans. by Catherine Cobham. London: Heinemann, 1984; Washington, D.C.: Three Continents Press, 1984; Cairo: American University in Cairo Press, 1990. Includes the title story, "The Stranger," "The Black Policeman," and "The Siren."

The Sinners. Trans. by Kristin Peterson-Ishaq. Washington, D.C.: Three Continents Press, 1984; Colorado Springs, Colo.: Three Continents Press, 1995.

A Leader of Men. Trans. by Saad Elkhadem. Fredericton, Canada: York Press, 1988.

Selected Stories. Trans. and intro. by Dalya Cohen. Exeter, U.K.: Ithaca, 1991.

Three Egyptian Short Stories. Trans. by Saad al-Gabalawy. Fredericton, Canada: York Press, 1991. Includes "Farahat's Republic," "The Wallet," and "Abu Sayyid."

The Piper Dies and Other Short Stories. Trans. and intro. by Dalya Cohen-Mor. Potomac, Md.: Sheba Press, 1992.

ESSAYS

Biṣarāḥah ghayr muṭlaqah (Frankly speaking). Cairo: Dār al-Hilāl, 1968.

Iktishāf qārrah (Discovering a continent). Cairo: Dār al-Hilāl, 1972.

Al-Irādah (The will). Cairo: Dār Gharīb, 1977.

"Jabarti" al-sittīnāt (Jabarti of the sixties). Cairo: Maktabat Miṣr, 1984.

Ahammiyyat an natathaqqaf—yā nās (The importance of culture). Cairo: Dār al-Mustaqbal al-ʿArabī, 1985.

Faqr al-fikr wa fikr al-faqr (Poverty of thought and the thinking of poverty). Cairo: Dār al-Mustaq-bal al-ʿArabī, 1985.

Inṭibāʿāt mustafizzah (Provocative ideas). Cairo: Markaz al-Ahram liʾl-Tarjamah waʾl-Nashr, 1986.

Al-Abb al-ghāʾib (The absent father). Cairo: Maktabat Miṣr, 1988.

Al-Idz al-ʿArabī (Arabic AIDS). Cairo: Dār al-Mustaqbal al-ʿArabī, 1989.

Islām bilā ḍifāf (Islam without boundaries). Cairo: al-Hayʾah al-Miṣriyyah al-ʿĀmmah līʾl-Kitāb, 1989.

Madīnat al-Malāʾkah (City of Angeles). Cairo: al-Hayʾah al-Miṣriyyah al-ʿĀmmah līʾl-Kitāb, 1989.

CRITICAL STUDIES

Abdel-Salam, M. "The Longer Stories of Yūsuf Idrīs." Master's thesis, American University, Cairo, 1973.

Abū ʿAwf, ʿAbd al-Raḥmān. *Al-Baḥth ʿan ṭarīq jadīd līʾl-qiṣṣah al-qaṣīrah al-miṣriyyah* (Toward a new direction for the Egyptian short story). Cairo: al-Hayʾah al-Miṣriyyah al-ʿĀmmah, 1971.

al-ʿĀlim, Maḥmūd Amīn. *Al-Wajh waʾl-qinaʿ fī masraḥinā al-ʿarabī al-muʿasir* (Mask and reality in Arabic theater). Beirut, Lebanon: Dār al-Ādāb, 1973.

al-ʿĀlim, Maḥmūd Amīn, and ʿAbd al-ʿAẓīm Anīs. *Fiʾl-thaqāfah al-miṣriyyah* (On Egyptian culture). Cairo: Dār al-Fikr al-Gadīd, 1955.

Allen, Roger. "Egyptian Drama After the Revolution." In *Adabiyyat* 4, no. 1 (1979).

———. "The Artistry of Yūsuf Idrīs." In *World Literature Today* 55 (winter 1981).

———. *The Arabic Novel: An Historical and Critical Introduction.* Manchester, U.K.: University of Manchester, 1982.

al-ʿAshri, Jalāl. *Thaqāfatunā bayn al-aṣālah waʾl-muʿāṣarah* (Our culture between tradition and modernity). Cairo: al-Hayʾah al-Miṣriyyah al-ʿĀmmah līʾl-Taʾlīf waʾl-Nashr, 1971.

ʿAwaḍ, Louis. *Dirāsāt fī adabinā al-ḥadīth* (Studies in modern Arabic literature). Cairo: Dār al-Maʿrifah, 1961.

———. "Problems of the Egyptian Theatre." In R. C. Ostle, ed., *Studies in Modern Arabic Literature.* Warminster, U.K.: Aris and Phillips, 1975.

ʿAyyād, Shukri. *Tajārib fīʾl-adab waʾl-naqd* (Experiments in literature and criticism). Cairo: Dār al-Kātib al-ʿArabī, 1967.

Aziza, Mohamed. *Regards sur le théâtre arabe contemporain.* Tunis, Tunisia: Maison Tunisienne de l'Édition, 1970.

Badawi, M. M. *Modern Arabic Drama in Egypt.* Cambridge, U.K.: Cambridge University Press, 1987.

al-Banna, Hassan. "Language Levels in Yūsuf Idrīs's Writings." Master's thesis, American University, Cairo, 1982.

Beyerl, Jan. *The Style of the Modern Arabic Short Story.* Prague, Czechoslovakia: Charles University, 1971.

Cobham, Catherine. "Sex and Society in Yūsuf Idrīs: ʾQaʿ al-Madīnaʾ." In *Journal of Arabic Literature* 6 (1975).

Cohen, Dalya. "Symbolic and Surrealistic Features in the Short Stories of Yūsuf Idrīs." *Dissertation Abstracts International* 50 (January 1990).

Duwwārah, Fuʾād. *Fī al-naqd al-masraḥi* (On dramatic criticism). Cairo: al-Dār al-Qawmiyyah, 1965.

Faḍl, Ṣalāḥ. *Shafarāt al-naṣṣ* (The codes of the text). Cairo: Dār al-Fikr līʾl-Dirasat waʾl-Nashr waʾl-Tawziʾ, 1990.

Farag, Nadia Raouf. "Yūssef Idrīs and Modern Egyptian Drama." Ph.D. diss., Columbia University, 1975.

Hafez, Sabry. "Innovation in the Egyptian Short Story." In R. C. Ostle, ed., *Studies in Modern Arabic Literature.* Warminster, U.K.: Aris and Phillips, 1975.

———. "The Rise and Development of the Egyptian Short Story." Ph.D. diss., University of London, 1979.

———. "The Modern Arabic Short Story." In M. M. Badawi, ed., *Modern Arabic Literature.* Cambridge, U.K.: Cambridge University Press, 1992.

Jad, Ali. *Form and Technique in the Egyptian Novel: 1912–1971.* London: Ithaca 1983.

Ketman, Georges. "The Egyptian Intelligentsia." In Walter Z. Laqueur, ed., *The Middle East in Transition.* London: Routledge and Kegan Paul, 1958.

Kilpatrick, Hilary. *The Modern Egyptian Novel: A Study in Social Criticism.* London: Ithaca, 1974.

———. "The Egyptian Novel from *Zaynab* to 1980." In M. M. Badawi, ed., *Modern Arabic Literature.* Cambridge, U.K.: Cambridge University Press, 1992.

Kurpershoek, P. M. *The Short Stories of Yūsuf Idrīs: A Modern Egyptian Author.* Leiden, Netherlands: Brill, 1981.

Mahmoud, Fatma Moussa. *The Arabic Novel in Egypt: 1914–1970.* Cairo: Egyptian General Book Organization, 1973.

Makaruis, Raoul. *La jeunesse intellectuelle d'Egypte au lendemain de la Deuxieme Guerre Mondiale.* Paris: Mouton, 1960.

Mikhail, Mona N. *Studies in the Short Fiction of Mahfouz and Idrīs*. New York: New York University Press, 1992.

Najīb, Naji. *Al-Ḥulm wa'l-ḥayah fī ṣuḥbat Yūsuf Idrīs* (Dream and life with Yūsuf Idrīs). Cairo: Dār al-Hilāl, 1985.

al-Naqqāsh, Rajā'. *Fī aḍwā' al-masraḥ* (The lights of theater). Cairo: Dār al-Maʿārif, 1965.

al-Nassāj, Sayyid Ḥāmid. *Ittijāhāt al-qiṣṣa al-miṣriyyah al-qaṣīrah* (Trends in the Egyptian short story). Cairo: Dār al-Maʿārif, 1978.

———. *Banūrāmā al-riwāyah al-ʿarabiyah al-hadithah* (An overview of the Arabic novel). Cairo: Dār al-Maʿārif, 1980.

Prockazka, T. "Treatment of Themes and Characterization in the Works of Yūsuf Idrīs." Ph.D. diss., University of London, 1972.

al-Qiṭṭ, ʿAbd al-Ḥamīd ʿAbd al-ʿAzim. *Yūsuf Idrīs wa'l-fann al-qiṣaṣi* (Yūsuf Idrīs and the art of narrative). Cairo: Dār al-Maʿārif, 1980.

al-Qiṭṭ, ʿAbd al-Qādir. *Qaḍāyā wa mawāqif* (Questions and situations). Cairo: al-Hay'ah al-ʿĀmmah li'l-Ta'līf, 1971.

Rāghib, Nabīl. *Fann al-masraḥ ʿinda Yūsuf Idrīs* (The art of theater in Yūsuf Idrīs' work). Cairo: Maktabat Ghurayyib, 1980.

al-Raʿi, ʿAli. "Some Aspects of Modern Arabic Drama." In R. C. Ostle, ed., *Studies in Modern Arabic Literature*. Warminster, U.K.: Aris and Phillips, 1975.

———. "Arabic Drama Since the Thirties." In M. M. Badawi, ed., *Modern Arabic Literature*. Cambridge, U.K.: Cambridge University Press, 1992.

Ryberg, Birgitta. *Yūsuf Idrīs: Identitätskrise und Gesellschaftlicher Umbruch*. Beirut, Lebanon: Orient-Institut der Deutschen Morgenlandischen Gesellschaft, 1992.

al-Ṣabūr, Ṣalaḥ ʿAbd. *Hattā naqhara al-mawt* (To conquer death). Beirut, Lebanon: Dār al-Talīʿah, 1966.

al-Sayyid, Shafīʿ. *Ittijāhāt al-riwāyah al-Miṣriyyah mundhu al-Ḥarb al-ʿĀlamiyyah al-Thaniyyah ilā sanat 1967* (Trends in the Egyptian short story from World War I to 1967). Cairo: Maktabat al-Shabab, 1976.

Shalabi, Khayri. *Fi'l-masraḥ al-miṣri al-muʿāṣir* (On contemporary Egyptian theater). Cairo: Dār al-Maʿārif, 1981.

al-Shārūni, Yūsuf. *Namadhij min al-riwāyah al-miṣriyyah* (Types of Egyptian novels). Cairo: al-Hay'ah al-Miṣriyyah al-ʿĀmmah li'l-Kitāb, 1977.

Sherif, Nur. *About Arabic Books*. Beirut, Lebanon: Beirut Arab University, 1970.

Somekh, Sasson. *Dunyā Yūsuf Idrīs: min khilāl aqāṣīṣih* (The world of Yūsuf Idrīs through his short stories). Tel Aviv, Israel: Dār al-Nashr al-ʿArabī, 1976.

Sūmīkh, Sāsūn. *Mabnā al-qiṣṣah wa mabnā al-masraḥiyyah fī adab Yūsuf Idrīs* (The structure of narrative and drama in the work of Yūsuf Idrīs). Tel Aviv, Israel: Jamiʿat Tel Aviv, 1981.

———. *Lughat al-qiṣṣah fī adab Yūsuf Idrīs* (The language of fiction in the literature of Idrīs). Acre, Israel: Maktabat wa Matbaʿat al-Suruji, 1984.

ʿUthmān, Iʿdad Iʿtidāl. *Yūsuf Idrīs: 1927–1991*. Cairo: Matabi al-Hay'ah al-Miṣriyyah al-ʿĀmmah li'l-Kitāb, 1991.

al-Waraqi, al-Saʿīd. *Mafhūm al-waqiʿiyyah fī'l-qiṣṣah al-qaṣīrah ʿinda Yūsuf Idrīs* (The concept of realism in Yūsuf Idrīs' short stories). Alexandria, Egypt: Dār al-Maʿrifah al-Jamiʿiyah, 1990.

Wiet, Gaston. *Introduction à la littérature arabe*. Paris: G.-P. Maisonneuve et Larose, 1966.

Yūnān, Ramsīs. *Dirāsāt fī'l-fann* (Studies in art) Cairo: Dār al-Kātib al-ʿArabī, 1969.

al-Zayyāt, Laṭīfah. *Min ṣuwar al-mar'ah fī'l-qiṣaṣ wa'l-riwāyāt al-Arabiyyah* (The portrayal of women in the Arabic narrative). Cairo: Dār al-Thaqāfah al-Jadīdah, 1989.

Festus Iyayi
1947–

OBI MADUAKOR

FESTUS IYAYI is one of the young radical Nigerian writers whose work began to make an impact on the literary scene in the 1970s. His novels complement the work of the dramatists of radical theater, such as Femi Osofisan, Tunde Fatunde, and Akanji Nasiru, and the popular poetry of Odia Ofeimun and Niyi Osundare. These writers are passionate critics of a social and political system that encourages concentrating the wealth of a nation in the hands of a privileged few. They highlight the injustice of a situation in which the producers of labor, the peasants, are exploited and excluded from the profits of their work. They heighten social awareness among workers and encourage them to fight for their rights through group action. In this respect, the radicals differ from such earlier writers as Chinua Achebe, Wole Soyinka, and their literary disciples, who merely express unease toward social decadence without tracing it to its roots or hazarding a solution to the problem.

LIFE

Iyayi was born in 1947 at Benin, Nigeria, to peasant parents. He was educated from 1969 to 1975 at the Kiev Institute of National Economy, Ukraine, where he obtained a master of science degree in economics, and from 1977 to 1980 at the University of Bradford, England, where he earned a doctorate in economics. Between 1974 and 1977 he worked first as a journalist and then as an industrial training officer in Bendel State, Nigeria. In 1980 he was appointed lecturer in economics in the Department of Business Administration at the University of Benin, Nigeria, and became senior lecturer in the same department in May 1987.

As an academic, Iyayi was an active member of the Academic Staff Union of Universities, a trade union known for its radical stance. He was president of the University of Benin branch of the union from 1982 to 1986 and was the union's national president from 1986 until 1988. Under his leadership the union became increasingly confrontational and was banned in 1988. Iyayi was detained from 10 July to 10 August 1988 on charges of treasonable felony, and after his release he was dismissed from his university post. After this dismissal he worked as a managing consultant to private business.

Iyayi, a member of the Association of Nigerian Authors (ANA), has been honored with many awards. He has written three novels: *Violence* (1979), *The Contract* (1982), and *Heroes* (1986); *Heroes* won the ANA award in 1987 and the Commonwealth Writers' Prize in 1988.

VIOLENCE

Iyayi's first novel, *Violence*, was acclaimed upon publication as a pioneering experiment in social realism in the Nigerian novel. The novel was inspired by the author's outrage at the widening gap between the rich and the poor. While the rich revel in an abundance of wealth, the poor are left in misery, poverty, and disease. Iyayi portrays representative characters from these two categories of society. Among the rich are the ever-present prostitute, Queen, and her husband, Obofun (a name easily associated with *buffoon*), who has made his fortune on kickbacks from his involvement in awarding government contracts. They own a fleet of cars, chains of supermarkets, and several landed properties, part of which they rent out at exorbitant rates to government agencies. Queen wins a contract through dubious connections to build low-cost houses for the government, but she invests the mobilization fee in the expansion of her personal estate.

Among the poor are Idemudia and his wife, Adisa, who are miserable and unemployed. Idemudia has to sell his blood to hospital blood banks in order to feed his family. He is later hired by Queen with three other laborers to unload fifteen hundred bags of cement from three trailers at the meager wage of five naira per person. Not only is the labor terribly underpaid, but the wage is exacted with difficulty from the employer. At the end of the assignment Idemudia becomes sick, is hospitalized, and incurs a medical bill of twenty-three naira, which must be paid before he can be discharged. Iyayi shows how the system is designed to undercut the poor at every turn. Obofun cashes in on the situation by sexually exploiting Idemudia's wife. Because Adisa's mind and body are not in the sexual act, which earns her one hundred naira, Obofun is described as "a vulture picking at the flesh of a dead prey."

In the hospital episode, Iyayi captures the hopelessness of the thousands of patients who besiege the hospital daily in search of medical care. The hospital itself is "a market of patients" (p. 64). The din of weeping children and wailing women rends the air. This scene of hopelessness can move an onlooker to tears: "It was evident that these were people who had been engaged by life in a terrible and fierce struggle and that they had come out of each bout worse and still more badly battered" (p. 64). Iyayi even criticizes the nurses, who are shown to lack kindness: "There was no pity in [their] eyes" for the sick (p. 120); yet the nurses stage plays to honor the memory of Florence Nightingale, whom they acclaim as the "Mother of Nursing" (p. 170).

Queen's second assignment for Idemudia and his friends is as taxing as the first. This time they work under very poor conditions to speed up construction of the low-cost houses contracted out to Queen. Because of the urgency of the assignment the men have to work long hours and on Sundays, with their break time cut from forty-five to fifteen minutes. The men see their task as slave labor, and when they protest, Queen tries unsuccessfully to break their solidarity, first by offering Idemudia cash (he will be paid three hundred naira if he can persuade the workers not to strike) and second by offering him her body. Idemudia's temptation scene brings to mind Adisa's trials before Obofun, but Idemudia heroically resists Queen's attempt to seduce him.

Between the rich and the poor lies a gap that can only be bridged through physical and psychological violence. Idemudia reflects on the situation and blames his suffering on societal violence:

"What kind of life is this?" . . . A man gets a job and he cannot protest. He cannot ask for higher wages, the period of his leisure is cut down arbitrarily and he must come out to work when he is told. This was slavery, this was . . . violence. . . .

. . . His unfinished education, his joblessness, his hunger, his poverty, all these he found out were different forms of violence. It consisted not of physical, brutal assault but of a slow and gradual debasement of himself, his pride as a man.

(p. 251)

Iyayi endows his peasant characters with an exaggerated, superhuman moral probity: Adisa at first resists Obofun's advances on the ground that adultery is a sin against God and against her husband. Idemudia more successfully makes the same point when confronted with Queen's naked body: "I cannot do what you want me to do.... You have a husband and I have a wife.... It would be adultery" (p. 306, 307). Obofun, Queen, and her chain of lovers, however, are uninhibited by such moral sensitivity as they luxuriate in adultery.

In addition to the problematic issue of the moral superiority of the poor over the rich, Iyayi posits that violence ensues when the gap between rich and poor widens. In one of the plays staged at the hospital, also titled "Violence," the lawyer defending four men charged with armed robbery states somewhat crudely the novel's moral point of view:

Acts of violence are committed when a man is denied the opportunity of being educated, of getting a job, of feeding himself and his family properly, of getting medical attention cheaply, quickly and promptly. We often do not realise that it is the society, the type of economic and hence the political system which we are operating in our country today that brutalises the individual, rapes his manhood. We often do not realise that when such men of poor and limited opportunities react, they are only in a certain measure, answering violence with violence.

(p. 193)

Iyayi's language is occasionally uncouth — for instance, when the lawyer states, "and may I add that my client has taught betters than you"—but he is at his best when depicting men at work. The truck pushers plying their trade on Sunday morning, their bodies wet with the sweat of labor, and the men throwing themselves body and soul into their work at the construction site are episodes that celebrate the dignity of labor: "The men came again and again and each time they brought the wheelbarrows, and headpans and the buckets. Their chests glistened with sweat, their faces glistened with sweat, their backs were bathed in sweat. They worked in subdued silence like prisoners, coming and going in the intense light of the sun" (p. 252).

When *Violence* appeared in 1979, the Nigerian reading public encountered a new kind of fiction, one that speaks boldly against the social divide between the rich and the poor, using a working-class character, Idemudia, both as its hero and the focus of its moral vision. This is a new development in the history of the Nigerian novel, and it made the work popular. Idemudia stands his ground as an honest man and as a reliable trade-union leader. At the end, he forgives his wife's adultery because he realizes she did it for him.

THE CONTRACT

Iyayi's second novel, *The Contract*, highlights the racket in contract inflation and the greed of contract brokers. In this form of corruption, the percentage paid to members of contract-award committees is officially built into the value of a contract. The novel opens with a vast panorama of environmental chaos reflected in the madding crowds at airports, traffic confusion on the roads, and mountains of refuse on the streets. Ogie Obala, the protagonist just back from the United Kingdom, is assaulted at the international airport by a sea of battered and hungry faces. At the domestic airport, where he goes to make a local connection, no sense of order or decorum exists as evidence of civilized behavior: boarding passes are sold by scalpers, and the desperate, angry confusion escalates into physical violence when broken bottles fly about the vast hall. As Ogie drives into the city from the airport, he is depressed by the squalid houses and the gigantic heaps of rubbish at the road-side: "Everywhere there was dirt and filth and chaos. Chaos was there in the way the houses stood, in the way the refuse spilled into the roads" (p. 7).

Traffic disorder exacerbates the confusion. People deliberately drive on the wrong side of the road, blocking each other's way and driving into each other. "There was nothing but abuse and curses and the blaring of horns and the screeching of brakes and then more abuse and finally, swift physical violence and then death" (p. 7). The chaotic setting provides the backdrop for the theme of social decadence in this novel. Ogie returns to a Nigeria in which corruption has been institutionalized. When he becomes assimilated into the system he is able to recognize the filth and vomit as external manifestations of the people's inner decay: "Inwardly the people were as rotting garbage, full of worms, beetles and mice. Yes, we are an indecent people. We are vomit" (p. 66).

Since Ogie is unfamiliar with the new surroundings, the old hands reinitiate him into the morality of "business," a euphemism in the Nigerian context for theft and robbery. Mallam Mallam, Ogie's former schoolmate, is now a successful businessman who owns a Mercedes Benz worth seventy thousand naira. His business is to cash checks for dubious deals in behalf of top government officials. His profit each week on this spurious enterprise amounts to several thousand naira. "It is easy cash," boasts Mallam Mallam, but to make it you must first "rule out morals. There are no morals in this country.... You must be a realist because only realists have the potential to succeed in this country.... You steal from your friends, they steal from you. You go to bed with their wives, they go to bed with yours" (pp. 18–19).

Ogie is shocked by the absolute lack of conscience in the new Nigeria and thinks that he will not be corrupted. His girlfriend, Rose Idebale, takes up Ogie's social education where Mallam Mallam leaves off: "All our people are now caught up in this intense craze for money. Money and women" (p. 24). Still, Ogie the idealist is convinced that he will be untainted by the general epidemic of sexual immorality and greed. But already he is vulnerable to one of the two social temptations, women. In an instant of manic passion Ogie pounces on Rose, demanding sex. No amorous preliminary leads to the attack. On count one Ogie is showing signs of weakness, and his fall on the second count, money, is inevitable.

The ubiquitous Chief Ekata plays an important part in educating Ogie about economics in the new Nigeria. As pragmatic as Queen in *Violence*, he is a man of many parts and many faces. Name any business and Chief Ekata and his construction company are involved. His impressive credentials include being "a general contractor, an importer and exporter, a transporter and supplier of general equipment, building materials, cement, rice, stockfish, lace material and general textiles" (pp. 79–80).

Chief Ekata is bidding for a multimillion-naira contract from the city council in Ogbe, a project that is under the direct jurisdiction of Ogie Obala in his capacity as officer charged with special projects. As a practical realist, Chief Ekata holds a few home truths. One is that "woman was the greatest weakness of the Nigerian male. He was a living example" (p. 72). Eunice Agbon, whom Chief Ekata sends to entice Ogie, is successful in her mission; Ogie succumbs instantly to her charms. When he has eaten the apple, he begins to see percentage ethics in a new light: he will accept the percentages, but he will invest the profit in local business. But as his conscience warns him, using stolen money locally rather than salting it away into foreign banks does not make the original crime less offensive. So Ogie recognizes himself for what he is, a hypocrite: "It is wrong to be idealistic. ... I have to work within the system.... I want all my money here. Not outside the country" (p. 87). Thus, it does not take long before Ogie not only joins the veteran adepts of the system, but endeavors to outdo them. He keeps Eunice Agbon as his regular girlfriend, Rose Idebale as a potential fiancée, and the receptionist Tessy, his latest conquest, as a girlfriend on reserve.

Meanwhile, the Ogbe contract has been inflated from the original value of 100 million naira to 500 million, 90 percent of which is to be shared among the members of the award committee. Ogie's share of the booty amounts to millions. Now fully integrated into the system, he begins to boast of his kickbacks from contracts. He speaks the language of the veterans of the system, such as Mallam Mallam and Chief Ekata. Proposing to Rose, Ogie says: "Most people do not marry those they love.... Love is not as important in marriage as other things...money for instance" (p. 110). Through the meteoric fall of Ogie's idealism, Iyayi makes the point that the state of decadence within the nation is beyond salvation.

With Mallam Mallam and Chief Ekata, Ogie Obala plans to forestall his father's intention of freighting the looted millions to Switzerland in behalf of the looters. They storm Chief Eweh Obala's strong room at night to cart away Ogie's portion of the booty. Chief Obala shoots at the robbers and kills one of them, who turns out to be his son.

Ogie's death is twice foreshadowed. Insisting that he will defend unto death his way of life, his father has waved a gun at Ogie on previous occasions, warning him to make up his mind because "the undecided die first" (p. 125). Also, Rose and Eunice, whom Ogie has used and dumped, hate him so much that they regard him as someone who is "gone, dead and buried" (p. 194).

The only somber humor in this gloomy story occurs when Major Alafia, the state administrator nicknamed Major Chop-Chop for his gluttonous appetite, chairs a board meeting in between mouthfuls of jollof rice and chicken, splashing his face and army uniform with chicken fat as he cracks the bones. Some of the food escaping his mouth as he talks lands on the dishes of other board members to the disgust of Ogie, who is still exuding a false sense of moral superiority.

Iyayi devotes much of the space of the novel to the disagreement between father and son on how to dispose of the loot, a disagreement that is not one of principle but of procedure. Since Ogie is aware that the purpose for which stolen money is used does not mitigate his crime, it is futile for Iyayi to make this issue the focus of narrative conflict. Meanwhile, the real victims of the looting, the poor, are forgotten. On this point *The Contract* falls short of the expectations created by *Violence* because it focuses on official corruption to the exclusion of the workers' role in the struggle. The workers and their sympathizers are largely anonymous in *The Contract*. Iyayi mentions the activities of radical intellectuals like Onise Ine and of student activists, such as Oniha Obala, but these are not foregrounded. Their activities are but echoes of the vigorous class war depicted in *Violence*.

Iyayi also downplays his portrayal of the ghettos, which are more prominently highlighted in *Violence*, where we follow Idemudia to the slums of Owode Street. An allusion is made in passing to the existence of two cities—the government reserved area and the ghettos—but for the most part, the poor merely pass through the thoughts of the central characters like anonymous ciphers. In Chapter 17 Iyayi mentions lean men in "cheap trousers and shirts" who walk the streets aimlessly. At night "such a man entered his burrow and he was empty. He had nothing before him, nothing with him and the day behind him had yielded nothing. And when he slept with his wife with this same emptiness, with this same nothingness, small children, black and tiny like the faeces of dogs were eventually excreted into this cycle of misery" (p. 130).

In their interior soliloquies Chief Oloru and Chief Ekata express their hatred toward the slums while dreaming of their contract potential: "If only he would be given the contract to demolish" the mean and squalid houses that stood on the other side of the street. "How much would such a contract amount to?" (p. 72). In *Violence* the predicaments of the poor are integrated into the structure of the narrative; in *The Contract* they seem a super-imposition.

HEROES

In *Violence* and *The Contract*, Iyayi presents contractors, businessmen, and top govern-ment officials as enemies of the people. In *Heroes* he adds another group of exploiters to the list: army generals and officers. In *The Contract*, Mallam Mallam had allayed Ogie Obala's fears about the possibility of a mili-tary coup and revolution by assuring him that there would be no revolution because the army officers who plan and execute coups belong to the ruling class. They subscribe to the philosophy of this class, which places emphasis on money and values individual material well-being. Thus Iyayi portrays the army as a bourgeois establishment that par-ticipates in the bourgeois conspiracy against the people. In *Heroes*, he pursues this idea further.

The historical background to the novel is the Nigerian civil war, which began in 1967 with the declaration of independence by the Igbo-led republic of Biafra and ended in 1970 with Biafra's defeat by the federal government. The novel was published sixteen years after the war and is Iyayi's imaginative reconstruc-tion of that conflict based on history and personal observation. Major actors in the event are mentioned by name—Yakubu Gowon, Chukwuemeka Odumegwu Ojukwu, Patrick Chukwuma Kaduna Nzeogwu, Ayo Banjo, and Olușẹgun Ọbasanjọ—and real episodes from the war fronts are given fic-tional interpretation. In the article "How the Present Shapes the Past: Festus Iyayi's *Heroes* —The Nigerian Civil War Revisited," Firinne Ni Chréacháin relates some of the episodes in

the novel to their historical analogues, using General Ọbasanjọ's account of the civil war in *My Command* (1980).

Iyayi reappraises the war from a class per-spective. As he imagines it, the real motive behind the war from the Nigerian side is not "to keep Nigeria one," but greed. The war is a business enterprise prosecuted for the profit motive at the expense of the poor. The bene-ficiaries are politicians and generals, and the losers are peasants whose children are killed and whose houses are destroyed by bombs and grenades.

Like George Bernard Shaw, Iyayi examines the concept of military heroism and finds the generals and officers cowardly, despite their boastful memoirs. The real heroes are the common soldiers, such as the unknown sol-diers who lost their lives in an ambush in which the commanding officer carefully or-ganized his escape to safety. Iyayi shows that some of the risks to which soldiers are ex-posed by their officers are deliberate acts of betrayal. The brigadier Otunshi sends his men on poorly planned missions right before pay-day, then collects the paychecks of dead sol-diers. For his betrayal of his men on various occasions, he has been rewarded with a pro-motion to the rank of general. Similarly, the major whose tactical error cost three hundred lives in his company is promoted to lieutenant colonel, whereas the sergeant who disagreed with him is demoted to corporal.

The story is told from the perspective of a daring, often conceited, war correspondent, Osime Iyere, who naively thinks of the federal troops as heroes until he is manhandled and humiliated by them. This experience is the first stage in a process of reeducation, which leads him to recognize that soldiers are sol-diers whether they are Biafrans or Nigerians. What distinguishes both is their addiction to brutality. Osime originally thinks in black and white: the Biafran soldiers are devils and the Nigerian soldiers angels. When Osime's landlord is gunned down in cold blood by federal troops, at the command post where

Osime has persuaded him to go to present himself, Osime is completely disillusioned. The truth painfully dawns on him that there is in every human being "*a sadist, a rapist, a fascist and a murderer . . . who wait for war and army uniforms to give them expression*" (p. 62).

Acts of cold-blooded murder follow one another in quick succession. At Benin, the so-called heroic federal troops murder Igbo civilians in the house of a Bini Good Samaritan who has hidden them in the ceiling. What is most dastardly about this episode is the callousness of the soldiers as they sport with the hot blood of their victims.

Osime steals his way from camp to camp subverting the troops, which for him means telling them the truth: "I want you to know the truth and knowing the truth helps until there are so many who know the truth that you can do something about it" (p. 132). The first truth is that the soldiers' real enemy is not the soldier on the other side but the generals on both sides. Generals in opposing armies have a way of making up quarrels among themselves. "*Ten years from now,*" Osime predicts, "*the generals on both sides will be sitting round the same table, planning how to deal with the working class*" (p. 214). Osime's observation here is drawn from history. Ojukwu, the Biafran leader, was granted a state pardon in 1982, and soon afterward the press flashed a reconciliatory handshake and warm embrace between him and General Gowon. Both belonged to the same political camp during the second republic.

Osime tries to persuade the rank and file to recognize their common bond of poverty: "the ordinary Igbo has a great deal more in common with the ordinary Hausa and the ordinary Yoruba than he has in common with the Igbo businessman and general and politician" (p. 168). The slogan "to keep Nigeria one" is a meaningless cliché as far as the poor are concerned, for whether the country remains one or is divided nothing really changes for them: "*the farmer and the worker will continue to live in mud houses and starve and be ignorant and sick and yield up their children for senseless wars*" (p. 64). Osime proposes a "third army," similar to what Wole Soyinka calls the "Third Force" in *The Man Died* (1972). The third army is the people's army made up of recruits from both sides. It will kill all the generals on both sides and reunite the country. Osime's idea, however, does not go down well with most of the rank and file; only a few of them, like Sergeant Kesh Kesh, buy the idea. Iyayi realizes that even though the idea is good, the time is not yet ripe for such a proposition.

In this novel Iyayi again evokes environmental decay, pointing to mountains of refuse on the roads and the infested markets with people like vermin feeding on vomit, and he spells out their symbolic import: "The dirt is a reflection of the character of the times" (p. 23). The huge gluttonous appetite of the ruling class is mirrored in the image of the Oba who spends hours at stool because "*he has the food of hundreds of millions of others in his stomach*" (p. 97).

Having survived the risky Asaba Bridge operation and the war, Osime returns to his girlfriend, Ndudi, at the end of the war, still firm in his belief that the real heroes of the war are the common soldiers, not the boastful generals.

WOMEN IN IYAYI'S NOVELS

Perhaps the people hardest hit in this society of exploitation are women. "Women are among the most cruelly and callously used," says Rose Idebale in *The Contract* (p. 25). The case of Queen, who in *Violence* uses her "bottom power" to secure contracts and other economic advantages for herself, might be different. Iyayi's women are at a double disadvantage, as members of the working class and as sex objects to be exploited both by the rich and by members of their own class. In *Heroes*, the head of state and the governor of Bendel State spend a week at a holiday resort in

Ubiaja. Theresa, one of the women who are violated on this escapade, is abandoned after she becomes pregnant, and when she threatens to expose these high officials, they arrange to have her and her unborn baby killed in a car crash.

Generally the women characters in Iyayi's novels come from a peasant background. They are poor and uneducated. They inhabit the ghettos and are used and abused by men. Rose uses the metaphor of the "slaughter house" to describe the rendezvous houses where women are raped. They value their jobs for the income, which becomes their families' main source of support. For this reason women tend to put up with some of the ignominious errands imposed on them by their employers.

But Iyayi anticipates the emergence of the new woman in Rose Idebale, the virtuous, calculating, and sensitive woman who refuses to be dazzled by an outward show of affluence or by prosperous suitors such as Ogie Obala. Rose rejects them all, resolving to stick to what endures, the enrichment of the mind guaranteed by education, even if her pursuit of this ideal condemns her to poverty: "The quality of a person counts. A foolish man and his money are soon parted but education remains, it stays and as long as the person who has it is alive, you cannot take it away. That is the more important thing,... the quality of the person, not the amount of money he has" (p. 156).

CONCLUSION

Iyayi is one of the first Nigerian writers to conceive of the art of the novel from a class perspective. His dedication to the cause of the common people leads him to see their position in relation to their bourgeois exploiters as one of slavery. In all his novels, the slave motif emerges. Idemudia and his friends see themselves working under hard conditions as slaves. In *The Contract*, two workers talking about their exclusion from such amenities as water supply, electricity, roads, and hospitals see themselves as "slaves in our own country" (p. 116). In *Heroes*, Iyayi makes the point that "the ordinary Igbo man will be as much a slave, a servant, in the new Biafra as he was in the old Nigeria" (p. 168). This goes also for the ordinary Hausa and the ordinary Yoruba in Nigeria.

Iyayi has made a name for himself as the pioneer of socialist realist fiction in Nigeria. But after the 1986 publication of *Heroes*, he has not written much fiction. The Nigerian economy took a dramatic plunge in the 1980s; the naira was devalued by more than 500 percent. Salaried workers suddenly discovered that their wages could only provide necessities of life. Nigerian intellectuals from all walks of life found it economically expedient to leave the country in search of greener pastures. The "brain drain" continued into the 1990s, and those who were unable to escape were entrapped in an economic, social, and political chaos that hindered, among other things, creativity. Iyayi was one of those who were entrapped, and this might explain his creative silence since 1986.

Selected Bibliography

NOVELS

Violence. London: Longman, 1979, 1987; Washington, D.C.: Three Continents, 1979.
The Contract. Harlow, U.K.: Longman, 1982.
Heroes. Harlow, U.K.: Longman, 1986, 1989.

ARTICLE

"The Freedom and Responsibilities of a Writer." In *Landfall: A New Zealand Quarterly* 44 (December 1990).

CRITICAL STUDIES

Dunton, Chris. "The Comrade-Enemy." Review of *Heroes.* In *West Africa* (28 September 1987).

Fatunde, Tunde. "Images of Working People in Two African Novels: Ouologuem and Iyayi." In Georg M. Gugelberger, ed., *Marxism and African Literature*. London: James Currey, 1985.

Maja-Pearce, Adewale. "Darkness Visible." In his *A Mask Dancing: Nigerian Novelists of the Eighties*. London: Hans Zell, 1992.

Ni Chréacháin, Firinne. "Festus Iyayi's Heroes: Two Novels in One?" In *Research in African Literatures* 22 (spring 1991).

———. "How the Present Shapes the Past: Festus Iyayi's *Heroes*—The Nigerian Civil War Revisited." In *Journal of Commonwealth Literature* 27 (August 1992).

Olaniyan, Tejumola. "Festus Iyayi." In Yemi Ogunbiyi, ed., *Perspectives on Nigerian Literature 1700 to Present*. Vol. 2. Lagos, Nigeria: Guardian Books, 1988.

Solanke, Adeola, and Dulue Mbachu. "Iyayi: Commonwealth Prize Winner." In *West Africa* (12 December 1988).

Taylor, Sarah. "A Radical Message." Review of *Violence*. In *West Africa* (22 February 1988).

Dan Jacobson
1929–

SHEILA ROBERTS

DAN JACOBSON was born in Johannesburg, South Africa, on 7 March 1929 to Liebe and Michael Jacobson, first-generation Jewish immigrants from eastern Europe. When he was four years old, the family moved from Johannesburg to Cape Province and settled in Kimberley, an unremarkable city in those days but famous for its once-rich deposits of diamonds. The city's drabness, flatness, and lack of identity (though its citizens are proud of the city's role in the history of South Africa), reappear in many of Jacobson's fictional settings. He received primary and secondary education in Kimberley, then earned a bachelor of arts degree in English from the University of the Witwatersrand in Johannesburg in 1948. Thereafter he traveled to Israel and England and taught in a Jewish boys' school in London in 1950. He returned to South Africa in 1951, worked at several jobs, and in 1953 began writing fiction. In 1954 he married Margaret Pye, a Rhodesian woman with a young son from a previous marriage, and returned with her to England. There he became a freelance writer and journalist; however, within two years he was acclaimed as an impressive young novelist on the literary scene. Apart from sojourns of varying durations to the United States, Israel, South Africa, and eastern Europe, he remained in London with Margaret and their children.

Jacobson described his desire to leave South Africa as "quite imperious: the political dispensation and cultural terrain in South Africa were depressing and stifling: to become a writer seemed an easier ambition to fulfill elsewhere" (interview by Gray, 1989, p. 77).

Jacobson held a chair in English at the University College of London until the end of the 1993 academic year, when he retired from teaching. He published in journals many of the literary-critical essays that grew out of his university teaching, a collection of which appeared in 1988 under the title *Adult Pleasures: Essays on Writers and Readers*. Throughout his writing life he published fine, thoughtful essays on the places he visited, essays that differ from the typical travelogue in their profundity and respect for "otherness." In 1994 he published his first full-length work on traveling in southern Africa, titled *The Electronic Elephant: A Southern African Journey*.

THE EXPATRIATE IN LONDON

Jacobson has written most tellingly about what it meant to him to arrive in England in the early 1950s, both in autobiographical essays and from the perspectives of fictional characters. About his own experiences he writes: "It was as though some part of my

377

imagination had been dry before, deprived of nourishment it did not even know it needed; now, immersed in the English medium, it slowly filled itself and expanded" (*Time and Time Again: Autobiographies*, 1985, p. 88). In one sense, Jacobson was a visitor to London, an exile, and yet in many ways very much at home. Of course, as exile or expatriate he inevitably had two worlds competing in his imagination. Thus in his fiction he frequently intertwines experience and knowledge gained from both places in fascinating and subtle ways. Another South African expatriate, Denis Hirson, writes: "We belong to no single place, ours is the history of those who cross over." However, the cultural critic Edward Said has stated that the expatriate has the advantage of a "contrapuntal" awareness. Whatever the griefs and losses of expatriation were for Jacobson, he used these aspects as well as more positive ones to great effect in his fiction.

LOOKING HOMEWARD: *THE TRAP* AND *A DANCE IN THE SUN*

Jacobson's first book-length publications were *The Trap* (1955) and *A Dance in the Sun* (1956). These novellas initiated what were to become ongoing preoccupations in his fiction: the influence of landscape and environment on character; the unthinking racist fears and preoccupations of most people around the world, not only white South Africans; and the mystery that lies at the core of so much human behavior. He was also intrigued by people's propensity for subterfuge and treachery as a means to gain personal power. These novels and everything else that Jacobson has written were influenced by a religious skepticism and distrust of ostensible goodness and human motive that he acquired in a South Africa that was rationalizing its brutal racism from Parliament, the pulpit, and the press. To emphasize his interest in the mysteriousness of

human behavior, both early novels, in his own words, sent him in search of solutions to puzzles he had created in the texts; he has undertaken such searches in different ways in all his subsequent books, not only the novels. Jacobson has stated that the writer cannot "hope to surprise the reader if he has not succeeded in surprising himself" (preface to the 1988 Oxford edition of *The Trap; and, A Dance in the Sun*, p. 6).

For the first fifteen years of his career as a novelist and short-story writer, Jacobson availed himself of familiar South African settings: the semidesert of the Great and Little Karroos; Kimberley in the northern Cape; and Johannesburg in the Transvaal. *The Trap* and *A Dance in the Sun* are set in the barren scrubland of the Karroo, a landscape that seems to infuse its white colonial inhabitants with aridity and harshness and to hold in terrible subjugation its powerless black and Colored (a legal designation in South Africa for people of mixed-race origins) workers.

The Trap explores the horrible ease with which people betray one another. Willem, a black farmhand, has been stealing his employer's sheep and selling them clandestinely and cheaply to Maclachlan, an English-speaking white butcher. Setole, a fellow worker, discovers what Willem is doing and so is beaten by Willem. When Willem lies to their Afrikaner employer, Van Schoor, that Setole is a homosexual and harasses young boys on the farm, Van Schoor fires Setole. Meanwhile, Willem has made the mistake of taunting Maclachlan with the possibility that they both might be discovered. Maclachlan makes short shrift of Willem by reporting him immediately to the police. Willem is trapped, beaten, and arrested; the word of Maclachlan, the white man, is never doubted as the truth. The novella ends on two disturbing notes: the police drag the beaten Willem to Van Schoor, who immediately goes against his better nature by beating the black man again; and Van Schoor's half-crazed wife, seeing the depth of brutality to which Van Schoor has been reduced, taunts him and is threatened with bodily harm.

The Trap is both powerful and saddening in the depiction of one poverty-stricken black worker beating and betraying another and the events involving Van Schoor's wife, a woman driven almost to madness by hardship and her husband's repeatedly failed farming ventures. It is not known whether Jacobson had read Doris Lessing's *The Grass Is Singing* (1950) before writing *The Trap*, but Mrs. Van Schoor is reminiscent of Mary Turner in Lessing's novel, as is Mrs. Fletcher in Jacobson's *A Dance in the Sun*. All three take their places among the many female characters in South African literature who have been reduced to insanity by poverty, powerlessness, and isolation.

Mrs. Fletcher in *A Dance in the Sun* has a more prominent role to play than does Mrs. Van Schoor in *The Trap*. Mrs. Fletcher greets two young student hitchhikers who come to her house hoping to rent a room for the night. The boys immediately notice her large, ungainly hands and her awkward and suspicious manner. Although they were told earlier that the house is a "private hotel"—a private home whose owners sometimes take in paying guests—the boys feel uneasy there; the house is cluttered with heavy furniture, neglected books, and the horns of deer. The many shutters are closed and do not appear to have been opened for some time. Whereas Mrs. Fletcher is as thin and dry as a starveling, her husband, who talks incessantly, is blond and pink. The mystified boys soon find themselves witnesses to a family drama.

Some three years earlier, Mrs. Fletcher's younger brother, Nasie Louw, had fathered a child with the sister of Joseph, a black worker on the farm. The Fletchers were fearful that criminal charges would be brought against Nasie for his violation of the Immorality Act, which prohibits interracial relationships, so Mr. Fletcher paid the young woman to leave

with her child and paid Nasie to give up his claims to the farm and leave. On the night the students arrive, Nasie is expected to return, and Mr. Fletcher is afraid of him. Joseph has meanwhile stayed on at the Fletcher's place, hoping one day to discover the whereabouts of his sister and her child.

Nasie does arrive, a plump, relaxed young man who has an air of vigor. He is like a breath of fresh air blowing into the moribund house and its occupants, and the hitchhikers take a liking to him. After a night of tension and conflict between him and his sister and brother-in-law, Nasie systematically smashes much of the useless furniture and then leaves, refusing to take his sister with him when she begs him to do so. She is left to her dry, futile life, with its absurd sense of reality. Joseph has still not found out where his sister is, but he remains to haunt the Fletchers with his unrelenting presence. Jacobson's interest in the satirical first emerges in the final scene of *A Dance in the Sun*, where a madly frustrated Fletcher, unable to rid himself of the tenacious Joseph, dances in the dust of the path, gnawing at his knuckles, pulling at his ears, and shaking his fists at the heavens. Odd, eccentric, and grotesque characters continued to walk, dance, shuffle, and gambol through Jacobson's fiction in the years to come.

In an essay titled "Olive Schreiner: A South African Writer" (1971), Jacobson wrote about English-speaking South Africans: "They have mined much gold; established impressive industrial enterprises; bought many motor cars; excavated many swimming pools in the gardens of their houses. But, time and money notwithstanding, they have remained a nation of lower middle class philistines. Blankness rules; blankness perpetuates itself" (p. 6). Jacobson certainly had the blankness and the lower-middle-class narrow-mindedness and lack of compassion in view when he drew the character of Mr. Fletcher, an English speaker. Furthermore, both Fletcher and Maclachlan in *The Trap* are dishonest, vicious, and pitiably disloyal men. They will also never be at home in the country colonized by their people. This is epitomized in the closed shutters of the Fletcher house, which keeps out the pale blue luminosity of the sky and the wide landscape. In later novels set in South Africa, Jacobson continued to depict white English-speaking South Africans as mean-spirited and cowardly, but these later characters are secondary ones rather than protagonists. While his treatment of Van Schoor in *The Trap* and other characters of Afrikaner stock (that is, the Afrikaans-speaking population, who largely descended from Dutch settlers) in later fiction was marginally more sympathetic than that of Fletcher and Maclachlan, both English speakers, Jacobson offered a complex yet finally damning portrait of an Afrikaner in *Hidden in the Heart* (1991).

MINING MAGIC WITH DANGER: *THE PRICE OF DIAMONDS*

Jacobson's next work, a short novel titled *The Price of Diamonds* (1957), deals in a manner that is part realism and part fabulation with the plight of Fink and Gottlieb, two small, elderly Jewish business partners in Kimberley who became involved in handling illicit diamonds. The events flow from Gottlieb's inadvertent acquisition of a packet of uncut diamonds and move toward cancellation of that mistake when he flings the stones into an old, disused mineshaft. The reader derives a certain amusement from Jacobson's inventive pleasure in writing the novel and from the charming combination of affability and irascibility of the two old men, caught in a series of events that are just serious enough to lend tension to the comic ambience.

Although the novel was generally well received on publication, for some readers it is unsatisfactory, perhaps because of the seemingly unresolved ambivalence in Jacobson's intention. He seemed to want to embed the events in the harshness of the South African political as well as economic system, which is exemplified, in Renee Winegarten's description, by "the unproductiveness, sordid decay and moral corruption caused by the diamond industry" (p. 71). But he also seemed to want to lift the story out of these systems and restrict it to the private interaction between the partners, as well as to color it with the magical and dangerous presence of the diamonds. The combination is not quite successful. What is engaging, however, is the Dickensian element in the novel: the eccentric and incompetent Fink and Gottlieb; the sad, comical Detective Groenewald; and the puddinglike secretary, Maisie Scholtz. These madcap characters fit nicely in Jacobson's satirical world.

TRANSGRESSING THE SOUTH AFRICAN IMMORALITY ACT: *EVIDENCE OF LOVE*

The subject of interracial sex (seemingly de rigueur for authors in the worst years of apartheid, the official policy of racial segregation), and the crux of the family drama in *A Dance in the Sun*, receive full treatment in Jacobson's next novel, *Evidence of Love* (1960). This book, his first full-length novel, moves broadly over space and time, first depicting the separate early lives in South Africa of Isabel, a white woman, and Kenneth, a light-skinned man from a mixed-race family. In young adulthood they meet in London—where Kenneth is a law student and Isabel, like many South Africans of her generation, is sojourning in London to escape from the nullity of a place like Kimberley and hoping to get a clearer perception of what it is she wants from life—and they fall in love. When Isabel finds out that Kenneth is Colored, she temporarily leaves him. They are later reconciled and marry, but then, in defiance to the Immorality Act, they return to South Africa and, as expected, Kenneth is arrested and sentenced to prison.

In *Evidence of Love* Jacobson creates a memorable sense of place, perhaps more memorable than his treatment of interracial love. His description of life in the "Colored Camp" in Lyndhurst — the flat, dusty mining town where the characters live initially — is powerful and shocking and strongly contrasts with not only the mansion in town where the moneyed spinster, Miss Bentwisch, lives among objets d'art, but also with the scenes in London. These scenes demonstrate Jacobson's sharp attention to the sights, sounds, and smells of London and to its impact on "colonials" who try to live there. The omniscient narrator muses about what England means to people from the colonies: "England is truth, and it is dream; England is reality, and it is pure vision. England is like a mirror in which they see their deepest selves reflected, the selves they have sought for and never found, and have known only by the sense of incompleteness that haunted all their previous days" (p. 131).

If Jacobson was influenced by Charles Dickens in minor ways in his earlier fiction, in *Evidence of Love* his debt to the master of rich pathos and bizarre comedy is obvious. The plot follows the Dickensian model in its depiction of a young man offered great expectations by a powerful but destructive old woman (Miss Bentwisch), the purveyor of illusions; and in the chance meeting, separation, and reunion of the lovers. The names of many of the characters are symbolic; some of the secondary characters are eccentric in looks and behavior and are identifiable by their idiosyncratic and crazily poetic speech. But what relates *Evidence of Love* not only to Dickens but to the tradition of English fictional realism — and what distinguishes it from Jacobson's three earlier works — is the passage of time that it records, the processes of growth and change that the two protagonists undergo, and the critique it provides of the social and personal exploitation of the poor and the vulnerable.

MOVING BETWEEN WORLDS: *THE BEGINNERS*

Evidence of Love, with its realism and its larger scope, led to *The Beginners* (1966), a longer work that has been praised for its Tolstoyan breadth and realism. It is the saga of three generations of a Jewish family as they immigrate to and emigrate from South Africa. The events encompass thirty years, depicting the lives of Benjamin and Sarah Glickman and their three children, Joel, Rachel, and David. The main character, Joel, returns to South Africa in 1954 from serving in the armed forces and is faced with a country that seems about to remake itself along democratic lines but reverts to a right-wing ideology reminiscent of the Nazis, whom he has risked his life to fight against.

After much searching for a worthy occupation and a new home, Joel ends up in London. He falls in love with a married woman, Pamela Curtis, who leaves her husband to marry him. The settings range from Russia to South Africa, Israel to England, and then back to South Africa. There is a wealth of fascinating secondary and peripheral characters in the book. In spite of his compelling descriptions of other settings, Jacobson embeds much of his own experience in his portrayal of London, which remains the most memorable location in the novel. *The Beginners* brings to epic culmination Jacobson's career as a South African writer and one who had been perceived as belonging largely to the mainstream of traditional fiction writers.

Few English-language novels from or about South Africa compare with *The Beginners*. Stuart Cloete's *The Turning Wheels* (1937), Francis Brett Young's *They Seek a Country* (1937), and James Michener's *The Covenant* (1980) all deal with South African settlers in epic proportions, but none have the literary quality or the richness of setting and character of *The Beginners*. In fact, one has to go outside the South African literature to find a work—for example, Patrick White's *The Tree of Man* (1956), an epic set in the Australian wilderness—that is comparable in scope, quality, and authorial intention. Both novels explore the lives of two generations of settlers to a new country and end on an auspicious note with a third generation in innocent early childhood. But there is an essential difference between them: whereas the settlers in *The Tree of Man* do not need to uproot themselves again, their counterparts in *The Beginners*, affected by the openly racist government that comes to power in South Africa in 1948, are forced to become aliens in their new homeland and most of them leave, some for Israel, others for England. In addition, most of the characters in *The Beginners* are Jewish and torn between the urge to assimilate as settlers in a developing gentile world and the need to extricate themselves from the narrow, racist assumptions of that world and seek their identity elsewhere.

The epic nature of *The Beginners* allows the reader to become acquainted intimately with several families and gain an awareness of the great continuum of human life, with its wars, migrations, catastrophes, and old age. After this grand fictional enterprise, Jacobson diverged his art into paths of formal and technical experimentation. *The Beginners* seemed to release him from his preoccupation with South Africa and its people: a disengagement process that he had started geographically in his own life in the early 1950s was now completed artistically. He stated, "When I found I *could* no longer write about South Africa, one of the reasons I felt liberated was that I was no longer working under external obligations of any kind" (Hamilton, p. 27). Or, as V. S. Naipaul has said, he found himself "in a free state" (Gurr, p. 11).

GOING "AROUND THE COURSE TWICE"

Jacobson's later novels are not set in South Africa in any recognizable sense, though the implications of the South African political and social systems survive in them as subtexts or as an unstated but ever-present influence. In *The Rape of Tamar* (1970) and *Her Story* (1987) he invents the landscape and mores of ancient Judea and Roman-occupied Judea, respectively, while allowing a subtle and ambivalent late-twentieth-century consciousness to infuse the narratives. In *The Wonder-Worker* (1973) and *Hidden in the Heart* (1991) he draws on his extensive experience of Britain and his satiric awareness of what he considers English snobberies. *The Confessions of Josef Baisz* (1977) is set in the mythical Republic of Sarmeda, and the events of *The God-Fearer* (1992) play themselves out in a small town called Niedering, which "lay in the most westerly region of the land of Ashkenaz" (p. 1).

The geographic liberation Jacobson experienced also found expression in the growing flexibility of his plot structures and in his seemingly effortless adoption of the self-reflexive or metafictional modes of postmodernism. Awareness of artifice is an intrinsic part of all successful storytelling, and Jacobson understood this from the beginning, as his early successes attest. Later he exploited artifice to its limits while maintaining the integrity of character and causality in his plots. Jacobson has stated that he went "around the course twice as a novelist: first as a South African writer; then... writing fiction which is not only *not* about South Africa, but is also a different kind of fiction from what had gone before" (interview by Hamilton, p. 25).

THE LUST FOR POWER: *THE RAPE OF TAMAR*

The Rape of Tamar is a brilliant reconstruction of the terse and ambiguous story in 2 Samuel 13:1–39 of the rape of King David's daughter Tamar by her half-brother, Amnon. The narrator in Jacobson's retelling of the story is Yonadab, a friend of Amnon and nephew of King David. Yonadab's cynical perspective reveals King David's guile, piety, and careful grasp on power; Amnon's self-indulgence, cruelty, and cowardice; Amnon's half-brother Absalom's ambition to supplant his father; and Tamar's hopeless attempts at self-preservation and revenge. In Jacobson's revision of the biblical account, Yonadab contrives the plan whereby Amnon gains private access to Tamar. Then from a hidden vantage point, Yonadab observes the rape without a thought of coming to the rescue of the fearful and frantic Tamar. Because Yonadab is the instigator of the action and a close observer of all events, he is a plausible narrator. But he is also someone who "utterly lacked the capacity to believe in the worth, or even the veracity, of anything" (p. 11). Thus the reader, though fascinated by him and entranced by his supple, evocative prose, must reject him as a judge of human value and an interpreter of motive.

The Rape of Tamar is intrinsically engrossing and mysterious; indeed, its mysteries remain unsolved because of Yonadab's unreliability as a witness. He is Kantian insofar as he relies only on sense perception for his knowledge of the world he resides in. But Yonadab's voice makes the novel much more than a historical reconstruction. He speaks with a hard, bright, urban voice and has the alienated consciousness of a citizen of the late twentieth century. Jacobson, via Yonadab, manipulates his readers quite openly. If we dare to allow ourselves to become immersed in this story of David's court, we are jolted back to an awareness that we are *reading* a story. The tale draws our attention to those very aspects that have governed its creation and to the material characteristics of the book as an object. Thus we are forced to pose questions about the relationship between fiction and reality. However, we never escape from the fascination with treachery and the disenchantment with human motive.

Jacobson has explained why he, as a South African, felt a special affinity with some as-

pects of this moment in King David's reign: "Well, in relation to the empires and metropolitan powers of his time, he was a provincial, a man on the margins. Yet, thirty centuries later, it was his life, not that of any of the greater kings contemporary with him, which was still feeding my own fantasies" ("The King and I," *Adult Pleasures*, p. 140).

MAGICAL REALISM: *THE WONDER-WORKER*

The apparent narrator of *The Wonder-Worker* (1973) is an unnamed sick young man undergoing treatment in a Swiss clinic. He is writing a story about Timothy Fogel, a strange being whose mother cried out in terror at the moment of his conception and who develops the capacity as a young child to submerge his consciousness into the substance of various objects: wood, stones, gems. In a most evocative way, he can participate in the texture of all matter. But this narrator eventually transforms himself into his own creation, and his wealthy parents into Timothy's parents—a junk-shop dealer and his wife. The novel is so cunningly constructed, however, that for the most part the reader has the impression that Fogel is the creator of events and the primary consciousness. Of course, Jacobson is the creator of both Fogel and the young man in the clinic, but he entwines the two characters so tightly around each other that they form a gemlike labyrinth. Ultimately, all is revealed to be fabrication and illusion, designed first to solicit sympathy with the characters and then to call attention to the fictional conventions of the novel itself.

Whereas Yonadab's voice is hard-edged and taunting, the narrator of *The Wonder-Worker* is dryly humorous, sometimes comic and absurd, but always exuberant. This voice describes in loving detail the intricate facets of the lives of the characters, as well as, most poetically, the substance and textures of the external world. *The Wonder-Worker* offers a verbal feast and an enchanting, surreal vision of the world. It constitutes a sort of hiatus between the cynicism and the enjoyment of human weakness and treachery of *The Rape of Tamar* and *The Confessions of Josef Baisz*.

POLITICS FOR POWER'S SAKE: *THE CONFESSIONS OF JOSEF BAISZ*

In *The Confessions of Josef Baisz* (1977) Jacobson returns not only to his early preoccupation with the inherently treacherous character but also to a harsh, dry landscape reminiscent of the South African Karroo. He again explores the nature of those who hunger after personal power. The country in the novel, the Republic of Sarmeda, is the site of all totalitarianisms; the critic C. J. Driver terms it "Africa-sur-Volga," referring to the river in the former Soviet Union (p. 50). *The Confessions of Josef Baisz* examines the effects on the individual of living in a totalitarian state similar to South Africa before the dismantling of apartheid in the 1990s. The situation is postrevolutionary; the rightists have destroyed a once-revolutionary movement and established an oppressive system of control.

Josef Baisz is "bodyguard, police spy, kidnapper, murderer and favored son of the regime" (p. 4), a conniver in unfolding events whose political philosophy can be summed up as follows: "To wound and to love; to love what I wounded; to betray and look pityingly upon the consequences of my treachery; and to do it again—and again—and again" (p. 125).

Jacobson introduces the narrative, Baisz's written confessions, with a "translator's preface" that informs the reader that the confessions were smuggled out of Sarmeda in mysterious circumstances and entrusted to the translator. The confessions are written in a spare, ironic conversational style, expressive of the tension between Baisz's ostensible desire to tell all about his career of political opportunism and treachery yet to leave out what suits him. Thus, again Jacobson creates an unreliable narrator, a character who, on the eve of his suicide, manipulates interpretations of his motives. And again Jacobson deliberately exposes the artifice of his fiction, not through Brechtian alienation devices, which he uses in *The Rape of Tamar* and *The Wonder-Worker*, but through his depiction of Sarmeda as a setting and a political situation that are familiar from countless newspaper reports of totalitarian states. This familiarity helps to expose the deliberateness and transparency of Jacobson's disguises.

RECOVERING THE PAST: ESSAYS

In the ten years that followed the publication of *The Confessions of Josef Baisz*, Jacobson devoted himself largely to writing nonfiction. In 1982 he produced *The Story of the Stories: The Chosen People and Its God*, an investigation into the Hebrew scriptures and into the appeal of the belief that a people is special to God. This volume offers a brilliant literary critique of the Hebrew Bible. It also delves into the nature of the Hebrew god—a god so mysterious that Jacobson's pursuit of him has the excitement and tension of a detective's search for a missing person who has scattered extensive clues about himself. While much of Jacobson's fiction has taken its impetus from his fascination with the Bible and with mystical religious phenomena, in *The Story of the Stories* he demonstrates his extensive knowledge of biblical scholarship. Indeed, the book elicited serious responses from biblical scholars such as Jonathan Sacks and Hillel Halkin. In a review of *The Story of the Stories*, David Lodge compared Jacobson's work with Robert Alter's prestigious study, *The Art of Biblical Narrative* (1981).

In 1985 Jacobson brought together a series of personal and autobiographical essays under the title *Time and Time Again* on topics ranging from his boyhood and family life in

Kimberley to his adjusting to life in London and his experiences as a parent. He includes touching accounts of both his meeting with the literary critic F. R. Leavis and a visit to Kimberley more than twenty years after having left it. The long central essay, "Time of Arrival," in which Jacobson describes his arrival in London and the wondrousness of being in such a place, as well as the confusion in acclimating to it, appeared in an early collection of essays, *Time of Arrival and Other Essays* (1962). This essay has universal relevance to the expatriate experience of so many colonials seeking a mythical "home." Jacobson's essays are well worth reading. His skill as a novelist infuses his nonfiction with a wonderment. His memories of scenes, people, and events are always sharp and lucid; his prose is supple, graceful, and full of striking images. Jacobson has also written scores of reviews, topical essays, and commentaries.

THE VOICES OF WOMEN: *HER STORY* AND *HIDDEN IN THE HEART*

Jacobson could not stay long away from writing novels. *Her Story*, structured as a novel within a novel, appeared in 1987 to great acclaim. In this futuristic narrative, which opens in the twenty-third century, a female Japanese historian, Naoko Kamikatazawa, discusses the recently discovered work of a certain Celia Dinan who lived and died mysteriously 250 years earlier. Among Dinan's papers is a novel set in A.D. 1–33 that deals with the pain and distress of the mother of one of the thieves who died on the cross with Jesus. (At first the reader is led to believe that the mother is Mary because of the similarities between the two women.) This mother's eldest son disappeared when he was twelve years old, and she could not forget him or cease searching for him. Some twenty years later, the mother discovers someone whom she believes to be her son. He is a faith healer and charlatan, and only a short time elapses be-

fore she loses him again. Later he is arrested and sentenced to death, and she witnesses the horror of his cruel execution.

Dinan, the author of this Judaic tale, also lost her son. Dinan was the child of a silent, passive mother and an unfeeling, domineering father. Her husband was the leader of a cult. During a police raid on the cult's compound, her baby son was killed. By the year 2296, when Kamikatazawa is writing, Britain has become a fundamentalist Islamic society, and women's freedoms are drastically curtailed. *Her Story* is, therefore, very much a novel about women's experiences throughout the ages: inadequate parents, the pain of motherhood and loss, and cruel societal judgment and oppression. The novel is sensitively wrought, particularly the core Judaic story, which is narrated in the second person with stark passion and feeling. As Jennifer Uglow states in her review, "*Her Story* is not self-conscious but self-aware... drawing on springs of thought and feeling which make it a novel of stirring power" (p. 896). If Jacobson had been open to criticism in the past for not creating many major female characters in his work, he more than redeemed himself in *Her Story*.

In *Her Story*, Jacobson intentionally raises many unresolved questions. Why did the boy in the core story run away in the first place, when his parents were so good and loving? Why could his mother not forget him and devote herself to her other children, who needed her so much? Why did the boy become a half-crazed thief and faith healer? What happened to transform Britain into a fundamentalist Islamic society? Searching for the answers to these questions inevitably draws the reader back into the intense human dramas it describes.

In *Hidden in the Heart* (1991), Jacobson again availed himself of the framing device of a female narrator who undertakes to tell a story not her own: she translates from the Afrikaans the surviving narrative of Adrian Bester, who, we discover, had briefly been her lover. The first-person narrator, a young woman who, like Kamikatazawa, is sitting at a computer, controls and structures the story, told in third-person narration, of Bester, a young Afrikaner living in London. Bester, ashamed of his background and nationality and hoping to hide them by assuming a form of English heard on BBC television, among other types of "protective coloration," falls in love with a woman eighteen years his senior, the wife of a major English poet. Although the plot of the novel seems simple, the motives of Bester, who seeks out the poet and pursues his not very attractive wife, are convoluted. What appears to be a novel of adultery and subterfuge becomes one of subtle, inexplicable hatreds leading to the wife's mysterious death. (Later it is revealed that Bester has allowed her to drown without attempting to save her.) With *Hidden in the Heart*, Jacobson returns to the kind of world that Fletcher, Yonadab, and Josef Baisz inhabit, one where subterfuge and treachery are commonplace, human beings act against one another out of diseased egocentricity, and the voices explaining events are hard, cynical, and disillusioned. Jacobson's skepticism of anything that looks like overblown goodness, or even simple, sincere emotion, again comes to the fore. Here, as in some of his earlier novels, he does not introduce admirable or lovable characters or unilaterally punish evil and reward goodness.

UNIVERSAL INTOLERANCE: *THE GOD-FEARER*

In the same way that Jacobson dwells on the deep recesses of parental love and pain in *Her Story*, he explores the experience of sincere repentance in *The God-Fearer* (1992). As a skeptic and rationalist, Jacobson implicitly asserts in his work that no one is impervious to weakness, cowardice, or dishonesty—not the otherwise decent Van Schoor or the great King David. Similarly, no religious group is free of intolerance, and no group is exempt from the appeal of mass action and mass hysteria. In *The God-Fearer*, the dominant religious group in the fictitious country of Ashkenaz is the Yehudim, and the despised minority, forced to live in ghettos and subjected to pogroms, is the Christers. In his youth, Kobus, the narrating consciousness of the novel, is a friend of Malachi, a heavy, slovenly young man. Both men are Yehudim. When Malachi inexplicably becomes crazed, the marginalized Christer community is blamed for bewitching him, and a fifteen-year-old Christer servant girl, Sannie, is arrested along with some other children.

The otherwise well-meaning Kobus has a chance to save Sannie during her trial but chooses not to. When she commits suicide in prison, the Yehudim lose their scapegoat. Frustrated, they again violently attack the Christer community. Thereafter the Christers move away. In essence, the novel explores the ease with which a demented person like Malachi can stir the prejudiced townspeople to irrationality and violence. Following the disasters Kobus recalls the cowardly part he played in events, feels remorse, and then attempts to understand the ghostly apparition of two Christer children who haunt him for most of his subsequent life. Kobus cannot undo his deeds and is left to mourn "not only their unlived lives, but the lives of all others like them; and his own unlived life too, the possibilities he had never taken advantage of" (p. 156).

Their beauty and sweetness remind him of what might have been—the children the poor Sannie might have given birth to—and personify his striving for self-understanding and repentance. When Kobus, now an old man, collapses in pursuit of the children who haunt him and dies at the side of the road, the moment is not tragic but somehow fitting: he is a wiser man who has learned to understand his own twisted motives and weaknesses and to accept that nothing in life is simple and that not everything can be explained rationally.

SMALLER CANVASES: THE SHORT STORIES

Throughout his career Jacobson has written short fiction. He has published three collections, *The Zulu and the Zeide* (1959), *Through the Wilderness and Other Stories* (1968), and *Inklings* (1973), and many stories in magazines and journals. Whereas many of his early stories have the same South African and British settings as his novels, his later short fiction explores other realms of consciousness and existence. "The Circuit" (1986) depicts the trapped and circular existence of a mechanical hare used in dog races, as well as the complex and speculative consciousness of the hare, a poor creature who reminds the reader of Franz Kafka's Joseph K. There is a similar Kafkaesque tone to "Amazed" (1987), in which a cat confined for experimental purposes addresses himself to "Dear God." An earlier story, "My Life" (1983), is also narrated by an astute cat. The animal protagonists in these stories represent the voice of late-twentieth-century humanity bewildered by a universe of multiplying technological power and helpless in the face of senseless personal disasters.

CONCLUSION

As a novelist, Jacobson has "gone around the course twice." He began writing largely naturalistic fiction set in South Africa during the formative years of apartheid, incorporating trenchant criticism of that institution. In the many ways that the characters of his novels subvert or evade the restrictions of apartheid, Jacobson created a sense of the system's vulnerability to change and implied a prophecy of its demise. In the early 1970s his work took a new direction into structural and thematic experimentation, and he produced novels that lent themselves to analysis under such categories as self-reflexivity, metafiction, and postmodernism. His output over the years was not only prolific but also consistently complex in thought and original in design and craftsmanship. He made a place for himself as one of the foremost writers working in London, and South African readers proudly claimed him for their own while scholars wrote extensively on his work. Neither his imagination nor his powers of creativity has diminished over time: he has a solid, prestigious place among late-twentieth-century writers.

Selected Bibliography

FICTION

The Trap. New York: Harcourt, Brace, 1955. Repr. in *The Trap; and, A Dance in the Sun.* Oxford, U.K.: Oxford University Press, 1988.

A Dance in the Sun. New York: Harcourt, Brace, 1956.

The Price of Diamonds. New York: Knopf, 1957; London: Weidenfeld and Nicolson, 1957.

The Zulu and the Zeide: Short Stories. Boston: Little, Brown, 1959.

Evidence of Love. Boston: Little, Brown, 1960. Rev. ed. London: Allison and Busby, 1992.

The Beginners. New York: Macmillan, 1966; London: Weidenfeld and Nicolson, 1966.

Through the Wilderness and Other Stories. New York: Macmillan, 1968.

The Rape of Tamar. London: Weidenfeld and Nicolson, 1970; Middlesex, U.K.: Penguin, 1973.

Inklings: Selected Stories. London: Weidenfeld and Nicolson, 1973.

The Wonder-Worker. London: Weidenfeld and Nicolson, 1973.

The Confessions of Josef Baisz. New York: Harper and Row, 1977; London: Secker and Warburg, 1977.

"Patient — Part One." In *London Review of Books* 5 (17 February–2 March 1983).

"Patient — Part Two." In *London Review of Books* 5 (19 May–1 June 1983).

"My Life." In *London Review of Books* 5 (1–14 September 1983).

"The Circuit." In *London Review of Books* 8 (6 February 1986).

"Amazed." In *London Review of Books* 9 (10 December 1987).

Her Story. London: Andre Deutsch, 1987; London: Flamingo, 1988.

Hidden in the Heart. London: Bloomsbury, 1991.

The God-Fearer. London: Bloomsbury, 1992.

NONFICTION

A Long Way from London. London: Weidenfeld and Nicolson, 1958.

No Further West: California Revisited. London: Weidenfeld and Nicolson, 1959.

Time of Arrival and Other Essays. London: Weidenfeld and Nicolson, 1962.

The Story of the Stories: The Chosen People and Its God. New York: Harper and Row, 1982.

Time and Time Again: Autobiographies. London: Andre Deutsch, 1985; Boston: Little, Brown, 1985.

Adult Pleasures: Essays on Writers and Readers. London: Andre Deutsch, 1988.

The Electronic Elephant: A Southern African Journey. London: Hamish Hamilton, 1994.

ARTICLES

"Settling in England: Reflections of a South African Jew." In *Commentary* 29 (January 1960).

"Return to South Africa." In *Commentary* 30 (July 1960).

"Olive Schreiner: A South African Writer." In *London Magazine* 10 (February 1971).

"Among the South Africans." In *Commentary* 65 (March 1978).

"A Way of Seeing." In Margaret Daymond, Johan Jacobs, and Margaret Lenta, eds., *Momentum: On Recent South African Writing*. Pietermaritzburg, South Africa: University of Natal Press, 1984.

"About *The God-Fearer*." In *London Review of Books* 14 (9 July 1992).

INTRODUCTION

The Story of an African Farm, by Olive Schreiner. Harmondsworth, U.K.: Penguin, 1971.

INTERVIEWS

Gray, Stephen. "In Conversation with Dan Jacobson." In *Contrast* 16 (December 1986).

———. "The Private Landscape of Meaning: Or, The Public Landscape of Politics: Stephen Gray Interviews Dan Jacobson—2." In *Kunapipi* 11, no. 2 (1989).

Hamilton, Ian. "Interview with Dan Jacobson." In *New Review* 4 (October 1977).

Hayman, Ronald. "Dan Jacobson in Interview." In *Books and Bookmen* (February 1980).

Mindlin, Meir. "A Talk with Dan Jacobson." In *Jewish Affairs* (August 1959).

CRITICAL STUDIES

Alvarez, A. "The Difficulty of Being South African." In *New Statesman* 59 (4 June 1960).

Baxter, Con. "Political Symbolism in *A Dance in the Sun*." In *English in Africa* 5 (September 1978).

Blythe, Ronald. "Gem-like." Review of *The Wonder-Worker*. In *Listener* 90 (1 November 1973).

Christie, Sarah, Geoffrey Hutchings, and Don Maclennan. "Dan Jacobson: *A Dance in the Sun* (1955)." In *Perspectives on South African Fiction*. Johannesburg, South Africa: Ad. Donker, 1980.

Decter, Midge. "Novelist of South Africa." In her *The Liberated Woman and Other Americans*. New York: Coward, McCann and Geoghehan, 1971.

Driver, C. J. "A Somewhere Place." Review of *The Confessions of Josef Baisz*. In *New Review* 4 (October 1977).

Girling, H. K. "Provincial and Continental: Writers in South Africa." In *English Studies in Africa* 2 (September 1960).

Gurr, Andrew. *Writers in Exile: The Identity of Home in Modern Literature*. Atlantic Highlands, N.J.: Humanities Press, 1981.

Halkin, Hillel. "The Wheel of History." In *Commentary* (September 1982).

Lodge, David. "Readings and Lessons." Review of *The Story of the Stories*. In *Times Literary Supplement* (5 November 1982).

Parker, Kenneth, ed. *The South African Novel in English: Essays in Criticism and Society*. New York: Africana Publishing Co., 1978.

Roberts, Shelia. *Dan Jacobson*. Boston: Twayne, 1984.

———. "*Tamar* and After: A Glance at Dan Jacobson's Recent Work." In Margaret Daymond, Johan Jacobs, and Margaret Lenta, eds., *Momentum: On Recent South African Writing.* Pietermaritzburg, South Africa: University of Natal Press, 1984.

―――. "At a Distance: Dan Jacobson's South African Fiction." In Michael Chapman, Colin Gardner, and Ezekiel Mphahlele, eds., *Perspectives on South African English Literature.* Parklands, South Africa: Ad. Donker, 1992.

―――. "'The Mother's Space': Dan Jacobson's *Her Story.*" In *Current Writing* 5 (April 1993).

Symons, Julia. "Intolerance." Review of *The God-Fearer.* In *London Review of Books* 14 (8 October 1992).

Uglow, Jennifer. "Leaves from a Triptych." Review of *Her Story.* In *Times Literary Supplement* (21 August 1987).

Wade, Michael. "Apollo, Dionysus, and Other Performers in Dan Jacobson's South African Circus." In *World Literature Written in English* 13 (April 1974).

Winegarten, Renee. "The Novels of Dan Jacobson." In *Midstream* 12 (May 1966).

Kateb Yacine
1929–1989

CHARLES BONN
TRANSLATED BY JOHN FLETCHER

KATEB YACINE was the pseudonym of Yacine Kateb, who chose to invert his first name and patronymic. The practice in Arabic cultures is to address individuals by their first names, whereas the French custom is to use the patronymic. Kateb's inversion of his names was a kind of play on these conflicting practices and a recognition of his chosen profession; *kateb* means "writer" in Arabic. He was born in Constantine (now Qacentina), in Algeria, on 6 August 1929, the son of Mohamed and Jasmina Kateb. After attending Qurʾānic school he went to the French school at Sédrata and from there to the French lycée in Sétif. Later he performed various jobs, including reporting for the Communist Party paper *Alger républicain* from 1948 to 1950, before becoming a full-time writer.

NEDJMA

Unlike his compatriot Mohammed Dib, who over time developed a more personal style, Kateb Yacine became a kind of living symbol of literature itself in its most provocative and elusive aspects; he challenged both geographical and formal boundaries. At the heart of his work stand the novel *Nedjma* (1956) and its associated cycle of plays, *Le Cercle des représailles* (1959; The circle of reprisals).

Nedjma is the tragedy of a "sacrificed generation," a generation that lost all political hope after the repression of the 8 May 1945 demonstration. But above all this text overturns the tradition of French realism that until then had been dominant in Maghrebian, or North African, literature. Through a complex relationship with tribal mythology, the novel poses the politically essential question of whether it is possible to express oneself in nontraditional narrative. In these senses, *Nedjma* can be considered as a foundation text, an indispensable point of reference for later Maghreb authors.

In his childhood Kateb traveled around eastern Algeria with his father, a lawyer, and the region provides the setting for the wanderings of the characters in the novel. The myth that haunts the whole work is that of the *keblouti* tribe, made up of the descendants of Keblout, the mythical tribal chief of the Islamic conquest of the Maghreb; Kateb belonged to the scholarly branch of this tribe. The *keblouti* practiced Islamic scholarship, but Kateb's father, who transmitted tradition and the law to his son in Arabic, "thrust him into the mouth of the wolf," as we read at the end of *Le Polygone étoilé* (1966; The star-shaped polygon, p. 181), by sending him to the French school. By choosing a French rather than an Arabic school, Kateb's father was breaking with tradition, but by educating his son he was also respecting his family's scholarly tradition and was perhaps instrumental in turning his son into the French writer that the world came to know.

The decisive step of sending Kateb to the lycée at Sétif was the occasion of much grief. It represented a symbolic second cutting of the umbilical cord as Kateb bade farewell to the oral tradition and to the "intimate childhood theater" he had shared with his mother; as such it was probably one of the major sources of his later writing (*Le Polygone étoilé*, p. 181). Another fundamental break occurred when Kateb, a brilliant high school student, was expelled from the lycée at Sétif for his part in the demonstration of 8 May 1945. The violent suppression of this demonstration for civic equality between the Algerians and the French in colonial Algeria marked the start of a series of atrocities in which a hundred or so Europeans and many thousands of Arabs perished. Kateb was also held in jail a few weeks. The author later said that it was in prison that he really discovered himself as a writer in contact with his people; his handful of earlier adolescent poems were still those of a good pupil in the humanities class.

Soon afterward Kateb experienced a third break, this time with his mother, who went mad after the death of her husband (in 1950) and several of her children. In losing her sanity, Kateb's mother became a latter-day Keltoum, the original "wild woman." In the *keblouti* tribal legend Keltoum, the wife of Keblout, became deranged after killing her husband. The "wild woman" resurfaces in Kateb's fiction in the characters of Mustapha's mother and Nedjma herself in *Nedjma*. Shortly after mourning his father's death and his mother's loss of sanity, Kateb had his first meeting in Bône (later Annaba), Algeria, with the cousin who served as the model for Nedjma, making *Nedjma* a semi-autobiographical work, albeit obliquely.

The novel's four central characters, Rachid, Lakhdar, Mourad, and Mustapha, can be read as different facets of the author, who lends each of them episodes from his own life, a life perpetually intermingled with the writing. Indeed, from the time that Rachid is enclosed in his jail cell and he dreams about Keblout and the *keblouti*, the whole work seems to spring from the meeting between the deserter, Rachid, and the mythical ancestor, Keblout. The character Lakhdar represents another facet of Kateb's own experiences, that of the demonstration, jail, the arrival in Bône, and the meeting with Nedjma.

Nedjma consists of not one story but several stories that echo each other, and it lacks a central character. While this approach may cast doubt on any apparent unity of plot or character, it is precisely from the encounter between several strands of narrative that the meaning springs: the novel offers the "present tense" narrative in which the friends Rachid, Lakhdar, Mourad, and Mustapha are employed as laborers on a building site near Bône, where their unattainable cousin Nedjma lives; the story of the 8 May 1945 demonstration and its repression told first by Lakhdar and then by Mustapha; the account of Rachid's journey to Mecca with his uncle Si Mokhtar (who may be Nedjma's and Rachid's real father), an account that includes in its turn the tribal legend which all the characters share; the story of a half-imaginary, half-real visit to Le Nadhor, the birthplace of the *keblouti* tribe; the account of the characters' childhoods; and other stories that are incorporated into the text.

The meaning in *Nedjma* is never conveyed by an omniscient narrator speaking to the reader. Rather, the stories' settings convey a mythic dimension that is more important than their realistic or psychological dimension. Even more important than the novel's message is the very fact that the mythic narrative of the Maghreb people exists at all. A people's identity is bound up with its capacity to "tell itself": collective identity is, all things considered, only the accumulation of narratives that make up a national history, for example, or a holy book. It is a collection of shared stories through which the members of a group recognize themselves. A people without history, real or mythical, does not exist.

The colonial grade school in Algeria, the "mouth of the wolf" constituted by the French language in which Kateb writes, had claimed the right to tell the history of Maghreb society. Faced with this alien control of the discussion of Maghreb identity, the two traditional discourses of selfhood, Islam and tribal myth, are rendered ineffectual because they cannot conceive of the idea of "nation" in the secular sense of the term. But Kateb's work shows that dialogue with the occupier can be fruitful; the major contradiction of nationalism in formerly colonized nations is that it relies on a concept that can only be expressed in the language of the occupier.

Kateb transforms these two bases of Maghreb identity in *Nedjma*. The novel is savage about Islam; in *Nedjma*, the pilgrimage that is intended to give the faith concrete form becomes a burlesque epic, and a failed one at that. Islam is represented by a grotesque pilgrim, Si Mokhtar, who is often drunk and talks nonsense, and this pilgrimage, failing to bring about Islamic identity, is doomed from the outset. It is also doomed because, their papers not in order, the two pilgrims must stay in the ship's hold, where they narrate the tribe's history: implicitly Islam is itself reduced to tribal history, a blasphemous suggestion considering the extent to which tribalism is despised by Muslim orthodoxy.

The tribal story arising from the collapse of the pilgrimage is ultimately more fascinating to the pilgrims than Islam is. The tribal story's echoes are the musical backdrop that gives the whole novel its unique tone. But a search for tribal origins in another journey— Rachid's utopian journey to Le Nadhor, the tribe's birthplace—is a failure, too. Rachid, the character most haunted by the story of the tribe's origins, is probably the most likeable and complex of all. But at the same time his journey ends in dream and illusion, lost in an opium den high above a ravine that contains the mysterious cave of origins and of confusion, the cave where Nedjma was conceived.

Nedjma's father was one of the four Muslim lovers that her mother, a French Jew, had. The lovers include Si Mokhtar and Rachid's father, who was found dead, killed with his own gun, in the cave the morning after Nedjma was conceived. Nedjma's confused origins can be seen as representative of Algeria's own confused identity. The fact that Rachid's search for the tribal origins leads him to this cave of confusion could mean that he is mistaken in his approach. Rather than searching for his identity in his origins, he should search for his identity in his actions, as does Lakhdar, who creates his identity through his political actions.

The quest for origins simply gets lost in its own unreality, in foggy conjecture; none of this seeking leads to any progressive engagement that would liberate the country—and thereby confer on the protagonists an identity forged in revolutionary action. Among the four main characters who take turns narrating the stories that weave through the novel, Rachid the city dweller, made ineffectual by the weight of his ancestral culture, is counterbalanced by his opposite, Lakhdar, who like Mustapha is a peasant. These characters take part in the 8 May 1945 demonstration, and it is Lakhdar who finally wins Nedjma's hand; in *Le Cercle des représailles*, she goes on to bear their child. Lakhdar's success suggests that the Algerian revolution was primarily a rural one.

In the novel *Nedjma*, however, Lakhdar becomes jealous without cause and loses Nedjma. Some critics hold that Nedjma represents Algeria. *Nedjma* means "star" in Arabic, and the star is used to symbolize the nation on the flags of many countries. She alone among the leading characters in the novel never acts as narrator, suggesting that the future nation has not yet found its own language or learned to master the narrative upon which identity depends. At the heart of the novel is Nedjma's absent speech, speech that never does occur.

Some readers have tended to see in the name Nedjma an allusion to the Étoile Nord-Africaine (or North African Star), the first

Algerian nationalist party to which Kateb belonged (before he joined the Communist Party). But this is not the only interpretation possible—and toward the end of his life Kateb added his voice to that of others protesting violently against the cover illustration of an Arabic translation of *Nedjma* that showed a woman freedom fighter waving the Algerian flag. (Furthermore, it is by no means certain that the many speeches following his death which ignored the complexity of the work in order to emphasize political meanings would have been at all to Kateb's taste.)

The essence of the novel is the representation of the painful emergence of stories, of the laborious reconquest of memory, and of the need to free oneself from memory in order to invent the language of a nation and of writing. It could be said, too, that just like the French language, the novel itself as a genre is part of the colonial heritage. The gap at the center of *Nedjma* where the heroine's words should be has an obvious connection with the nascent Algeria's lack of a unified language: the official Arabic language differed from the Arabic spoken by the people, and French and Berber were also present in everyday Algerian life.

A common language of liberation seems subsequently to have been found, since Algeria freed itself from colonialism by force of arms. The plays that Kateb was writing at the same time as *Nedjma* in fact depict characters who finally commit themselves to the liberation struggle, but at the same time they are riven by infighting and rushing headlong toward disaster. Thus, while Kateb calls for a new language for the nation, his voice retains a terrible, tragic lucidity. While the novel sometimes seems to encourage an ideological interpretation such as the anticolonial one here proposed, it will also repudiate such an interpretation, as if constantly on its guard against any form of political takeover. In fact, the author never gives any explanation or any interpretive lead. The raw stories are there, raising questions that no interpretation can answer.

If within this fictional domain the tribal narrative betrays its inability to take up the challenge of modernity, both politically in terms of offering an alternative to colonial power and artistically in terms of replacing inherited narrational models, it nonetheless disrupts these dominant discourses. *Nedjma* upsets the traditional French fictional model largely through the orality of the tribal narrative, which does not quite fit into traditional fictional forms. The unusual construction of the novel relies on the dizzying effect of Chinese boxes. Stories are contained within each other, and it is not always possible at first reading to identify the narrator of each enclosed narrative.

What results is a kind of whirl, reminiscent of the effect that the *meddahs*, professional storytellers operating in public places in the Maghreb, have on their audience, or—to take an example more familiar to western readers—the effect of *The Arabian Nights*. In the case of *Nedjma*, the oral tale literally imprisons the fictional narrative, while Rachid's fascination with it causes him to lose the very object of his quest. So before all else subversion in *Nedjma* is very much at the level of the story.

The essence of Kateb Yacine's entire career is located in *Nedjma*'s chanson de geste (understood here as a collection of epic tales), in all the characters and stories that make it up, and in all the rhythms and symbols that attach to it. This epic impulse feeds not only into *Nedjma* but also into the plays written in 1957 and 1958, into *Le Polygone étoilé* of 1966, into the plays of 1970, and finally into the plays written in Algerian dialect (as opposed to classical Arabic) from 1971 onward. This phenomenon whereby the same story is echoed obsessively from one text to the next enables Kateb's work to transcend the limits of time, of literary genre, and of particular languages.

Kateb's work is driven first and foremost by the fertile encounters—with each other and with biographical and national reality—of seemingly heterogeneous genres. Both the genre of the novel and the genre of tragedy (inspired by Greek drama through the example of Bertolt Brecht, whom Kateb met in 1954) are transformed in Kateb's hands by the genre whose demise they are supposed to have brought about: the mythic tale. In a way, it is from the meeting between different kinds of story that the work's dynamic arises. This essential freedom enables Kateb's writing to move with perfect naturalness from one literary genre to another and to use at will, for example, a fragment from a poem in a play or in a novel that lends it new meanings.

The novel *Nedjma* and *Le Cadavre encerclé* (The encircled corpse), the first tragedy in the cycle *Le Cercle des représailles*, were written at about the same time, and the tragedy can be considered as a response to the characters' stymied commitment in the novel. But in the second tragedy of the cycle, *Les Ancêtres redoublent de férocité* (The ancestors strike back), this commitment ends with the death of the heroes, just as the first play opens with Lakhdar's corpse. The drama and the novel are obviously complementary, and if the move from one genre to another occurs quite naturally, the play of responses and echoes from one to another introduces into Kateb's work a particularly rich level of meaning.

The play of different genres and languages recurs in the relationship between Kateb's work and that of other writers in his circle. Although Kateb shows a fundamental independence from these writers, the reader can mine new meanings if his texts are considered alongside those of his fellow Algerian writers.

By virtue of its publication date, 1956, *Nedjma* invites comparison with other first novels by contemporary Algerian writers, of whom the best known are Mouloud Feraoun, Mouloud Mammeri, and Mohammed Dib. Kateb met Dib when the two of them worked for the newspaper *Alger républicain*. Another friend from this period was Malek Haddad, with whom in 1950 he embarked upon a long period of wandering. These years took him first around France and later to other parts of the world; he did not finally return to Algeria until 1972. Kateb had read little when he began writing *Nedjma*, which took ten years to complete, and he certainly had no feeling at the time of working within a francophone Algerian literary tradition; in any case, such a tradition had hardly begun to exist.

Seen from the perspective of the late twentieth century *Nedjma* stands out as the foundation text of modern Algerian fiction. Unlike more realistic works that follow the French fictional tradition to highlight the dignity and tragedy of a dominated society—and to show, as Mouloud Feraoun, one of the most important Algerian writers in this tradition, puts it, that "the Kabyles are men too"—Kateb's novel first and foremost massively undermines the fictional model inherited from the French nineteenth century. In fact, after the publication of *Nedjma*, Algerian writers abandoned this purely descriptive style of fiction.

For example, *Nedjma* and the Algerian fiction influenced by this work contain few if any realistic, emotive, or exotic descriptions; few passages have even a noticeable political content. The most politically explicit technique in modern Algerian fiction is the occasional reversal of the descriptive point of view: the object of a particular description is no longer the "native" caught up in a fictional discourse that is not his own—as it would be in colonial French writing about Algeria—but rather the "colonist." In Kateb's narrative, the colonist becomes the exotic personage, for example, in the cruelly mock-heroic episode of the marriage of Monsieur Ricard, which reveals the ridiculous aspects of French colonial society in Algeria.

The power relationship in fictional realism, denounced at the time by Alain Robbe-Grillet and other theorists, between on the one hand the subject who constructs or reads the novel within a dominant value system bound up with the control of writing and reading, and on the other the object interpreted by that value system, is here turned on its head. In a colonial situation such a reversal makes sense.

The particular political context of *Nedjma's* publication is inseparable from the fundamentally eruptive, indeed anarchic, nature of Kateb's creativity, and creates other levels of meaning in his writing that are distinct from the concerns of the western "New Novelists" such as Robbe-Grillett whose theories he nonetheless shared.

Other formal aspects of *Nedjma* reflect Kateb's willingness to destabilize the novel genre: he dispenses with the single narrator dear to nineteenth-century novelists; he refuses to engage in psychological analysis, as the writers of the early twentieth century had done; and he shatters conventional chronology, instead turning to the proliferation of stories, one unfolding inside the other. It is clear that disconcerting the reader as Kateb does through these techniques is to some extent a significant political act in itself. Kateb uses the structure of the text to produce political meaning, and this mechanism for the production of meaning makes *Nedjma* a determinedly modern novel.

Because it is formally so innovative, so in tune with the most confidently avant-garde tendencies in French writing, *Nedjma* is the bedrock of a new Algerian literary identity. For Kateb grasped at the outset that contrary to what some dogmatic and paternalistic critics have asserted, an emergent literature cannot, any more than others, confine itself to what Kateb himself called "production for illiterates." Writing that is not demanding cannot be revolutionary. In any case, the "difficulty" in reading *Nedjma* is encountered only by those looking for facile exoticism and unsophisticated expression, and the novel contains neither.

DRAMATIC WORKS

The stage plays written at the same time as *Nedjma* can be read as a kind of counterpoint to the novel's hollowed-out structure. Questions raised in *Nedjma* are answered in the plays. Nedjma, silent in the novel, speaks in the plays, and the protagonists are engaged with the war of liberation. The stage cycle *Le Cercle des représailles* (1959) is laid out in a tetralogy. Although each play stands alone and is staged separately, the plays are linked in the manner of ancient Greek drama. It consists of the tragedy *Le Cadavre encerclé*, followed by *La Poudre d'intelligence (Intelligence Powder)*, a comic interlude recalling the pranks of Djeha, a popular hero in the oral literature of the Maghreb. A second tragedy, *Les Ancêtres redoublent de férocité*, and a long dramatic poem, *Le Vautour* (The vulture), close the cycle.

The novel turned on the fact that Nedjma's love for Lakhdar could not be consummated. In the drama, Ali, her son by Lakhdar, appears suddenly at the end of *Intelligence Powder* dressed in guerrilla uniform. The future seems to be taking shape, and time is following a development marked by history. However, the cycle is primarily a tragedy, as *Le Cadavre encerclé*, the first play in the cycle, shows. In this first tragedy, Lakhdar becomes a political activist only through his death; his passing means that Nedjma's newfound and seemingly historicized speech becomes a funeral lamentation.

In the third play, *Les Ancêtres redoublent de férocité*, Nedjma joins Lakhdar in the death of an entire generation, those young Algerians who on 8 May 1945 fell victim both to the curse of the ancestors and to their own internecine disputes, as represented by their rivalry over Nedjma. All that remains is the voice of the Vulture, who is at once the Ancestor's representative and Lakhdar's double. The tragic beauty of the Vulture's long dramatic speech stems from the fact that it is a lonely monologue.

LE POLYGONE ÉTOILÉ

The question arises whether tragedy has not got the better of history, and it is perhaps one of the lessons to be learned from the apparent disorder of *Le Polygone étoilé* (1966), a sort of novel that appeared ten years after *Nedjma*. Its form, which is essentially "terrorist" in nature, is an ambiguous medley that produces unexpected or ludicrous meanings. These meanings suddenly become savage by reasons of their very ambiguity, and also because of the author's seeming refusal to incorporate any logical construction in the book.

Nedjma may have challenged purely uni-vocal meanings, but its epic register did hold out the possibility of inventing future signification. However, the terrorist form of *Le Polygone étoilé*—the difficulty and ambiguity of the text—excludes the possibility of the epic, which is never ambiguous. It above all records a loss of meaning, or a meaning too obvious to be detected in its textual polyphony. The leitmotif sentence "Each time the plans are overturned" has a double meaning; it could refer to either the plans of the French leaders in the colonial era or the plans of the leaders of independent Algeria. The meaning of this sentence is reiterated by the comic poem that states "in a cat's world/there are no straight lines" (p. 86–87). The double meaning is furthered by the absence of any reference to a date. The "camps" to which the heroes are hurriedly sent as early as page 1 could exist in either colonial or independent Algeria. This double meaning emerges gradually from the unexpected juxtaposition of fragments.

As the denunciation is never made explicit, the playfulness of the writing becomes pro-gressively more ironic and subversive and more like political terrorism: absence of mean-ing is still the cruelest meaning of all. In designating the text at the same time as it is signified in an iconoclastic confusion, the car-nival of *Le Polygone étoilé* can also be read as implicitly mocking all attempts at finding a meaning, perhaps especially so after *Nedjma* had adumbrated that absence. And yet one of the most pleasurable aspects of reading *Le Polygone étoilé* is its parody of the preceding novel. This unusual text, considered by its

author as the culmination of the works that preceded it, can also be used as a reading system for *Nedjma* in that it gives new mean-ings to some of the same characters.

THE POPULAR THEATER

From 1971 onward, Kateb began experiment-ing with plays in Algerian dialect that would have mass appeal. First he headed the Drama Group in the Workers' Cultural Program under the auspices of the Ministry of Labor; he then took over management of the Bel-Abbès Theater. He was engaged in a form of agitprop drama, propagandistic theater that has usually been seen as an act of political commitment. Kateb returned to ideological coherence: some twenty years of writing in the French language and of immersion in formal experimentation presented a danger of alien-ating Kateb from the people for whom he had always intended to write. He certainly showed faith and courage in undertaking the enter-prise and in persevering with it despite diffi-culties of all kinds. Although Kateb was too prominent a writer to ban outright, the politi-cal powers in Algeria, who found themselves the target of the plays' increasingly audacious criticism, stifled his theater group by such bureaucratic ploys as limiting the places the group could play and making it difficult to find spare parts for its truck.

Nonetheless, the shift in focus between Kateb's agitprop drama and the work that preceded it reflects more than a straightfor-ward linguistic and ideological choice: the polyphony of *Nedjma* and the mockery of *Le Polygone étoilé* are replaced by an explicit probing statement. The question has to be asked: why this shift?

The ideological project and the choice of the more difficult lifestyle inherent in this theatrical work are obvious and in full accord with the ideal of instability (including instabil-ity in the status of a writer) that has always been the source of Kateb's greatness. But at the same time there is a link between this theater work and the career leading from *Nedjma* to *Le Polygone étoilé*. The link is emphasized by the recurring presence in the agitprop plays of characters familiar from Kateb's mythology, even if here their explicit meanings often seem far removed from their earlier fertile ambiguity.

Any continuity, however, is blocked by the oral nature of the theatrical project and of collective improvisation, and by the fact that none of these plays has been published even where a French text exists in typescript alongside a recording in Algerian dialect. It could therefore be said that these texts represent a sort of culmination of the tragic side of writing that at the end of *Le Polygone étoilé* suddenly revealed Kateb's most intimate biographical details: his fall, at the end of childhood, into the "mouth of the wolf" of the French language and into the career of a wandering writer.

The popular theater work put Kateb back in touch with his people, rectifying an alienation he had experienced since childhood. This sense of alienation is exemplified by the poem that appears in *Nedjma* (pp. 53–54). In this poem Kateb mocks his own idealism as a young student as compared with the reality of a peasant's hunger. His reconnection was achieved through writing in the service of ideas—turning away from a mockery of Algeria that sometimes appears in *Nedjma*, and putting aside the quarrel with *Alger républicain* over the boundaries between art and propaganda—but it did not for all that manage to become truly effective politically. This was not because of literary failure, but because writing and reality are perhaps by nature incompatible, and because writers can only become revolutionary in their writing if they avoid well-trodden paths and condemn themselves to loneliness. This secret isolation was perhaps one of the most important dimensions of Kateb, a man who was always the center of attention.

CONCLUSION

Kateb was not the first North African author to write in French; he had a few prestigious forerunners. But the symbolic founding role he played in Maghreb literature is widely recognized today; even if his work is less important than Mohammed Dib's, for example, Kateb represents a kind of mythical point of reference in the shadow of which his successors produce their work. Their texts frequently hark back to Nedjma's saga, as if to act on its authority and in order to develop in their turn their characteristic ferocity, which they sometimes seem reluctant to assume without referring to the first in this arena, iconoclastic Kateb.

The question arises whether Kateb was a political activist at all. His relations were notoriously stormy with *Alger républicain*, the Communist Party newspaper that provided him with a livelihood from 1948 to 1950 but against which he always fiercely defended the independence of the writer's calling. "What I balk at in Bertolt Brecht," he said in an interview in *L'Action* (Tunis, 28 April 1958), even though in his own drama of the 1950s he was often in harmony with the German playwright, "is the way he, a poet, continually subordinates poetry to the preaching of a doctrine." Kateb kept his literary activities to some extent separate from his party friendships and from the definite stands he took on political issues, but even so, too many hurried readers, perhaps finding the richness of the work beyond them, mistakenly reduce the writer to the political activist.

Kateb was able to evade what had become a cliché about his career: "at the heart of trouble the constant troublemaker." There was a grain of truth in it, but Kateb could also confuse people by letting himself be recruited for apparently contradictory causes with which he cheerfully expressed total agreement, especially around the issue of communist orthodoxy. Much has been made of the quarrels that he as a writer had with the party, but even in his last years he was quite happy as an individual to use communist turns of phrase. The walls inside his house at Ben Aknoun were ostentatiously covered with political slogans and in what could be considered a rather eccentric form of heckling he added "Stalin" to the forename of one of his children.

The plays in Algerian dialect contain ideological oversimplifications whose enormity, on the part of such a subtle writer, is curiously puzzling. Puzzling too is the role he assumed in championing the rights of the Berber people, a cause he took up in his later years, stressing his own Berber origins, which were probably less than genuine. He was perhaps playing with origins, in the manner of *Nedjma*, or thumbing his nose at readings that concentrate exclusively on the ethnic dimension in postcolonial writing while still believing every word of it. Perhaps the "troublemaking" least noticed by Kateb's critics is this tendency to embrace rival ideologies with equal enthusiasm and to remain quite untroubled by the resulting contradictions.

A further paradox is that the man who had become a symbol of total dedication to the writer's craft had himself largely given up writing. When the top French literary prize, the Grand Prix National des Lettres, was awarded in 1987 to Kateb, he had published nothing of substance for the past seventeen years. In order to be able to focus an interview with Kateb for a French television program about books dealing with Algeria on something fairly recent, the producer had to dig up a collection of long-forgotten pieces edited by the critic Jacqueline Arnaud.

On the other hand, a play (originally performed in Algerian dialect) about the French revolutionary leader Robespierre entitled *Le Bourgeois sans culotte* (The bourgeois of the common people), produced in France at the Avignon Festival in the summer of 1989 (shortly before Kateb's death), went es-

sentially unnoticed. This was perhaps because it did not provoke the energetic protests that greeted the premiere of an earlier play by Kateb, *L'Homme aux sandales de caoutchouc* (The man in rubber sandals), put on in Lyons in 1971 by the famous producer and actor Marcel Maréchal. The play may also have been disregarded because the Avignon players were less well known than other companies that had put on Kateb's earlier French plays. Indifference to the play no doubt rested even more in the fact that for Kateb's Avignon audience the revolution he presents symbolically in *Le Bourgeois sans culotte* was not the revolution that occurred in France in 1789 but that of Algeria in 1954, and more generally that of the entire third world in the throes of decolonization. Above all, though, lack of interest in the play was because for most people Kateb will always be, as he said of himself, "a one-book man," that book being *Nedjma*.

Kateb was original in the contradictions that his very excess in all things—even gentleness—necessarily entailed. His profound and liberating influence arose from the mythical literary dimension achieved by such paradox. He had a lasting impact on other North African writers, such as Rachid Boudjedra, Nabile Farès, and Mourad Bourboune, by virtue of his power and daring. His many imitators play subtle variations on his themes and even adopt his stylistic mannerisms. Indeed, the fact that all defer to him, as if there were no other indigenous models around, is striking in itself. In a rather touchy nationalistic environment, he alone had the audacity and therefore the authority to make the use of an assumed literary language, French, acceptable, something that did not need to be apologized for. At the time of Kateb's death in Grenoble, France, on 28 October 1989 (from the aftereffects of leukemia treatment), he had achieved for Algeria a literary identity in a credible francophone tradition.

Selected Bibliography

SELECTED WORKS

Nedjma. Paris: Seuil, 1956.
Le Cercle des représailles. Paris: Seuil, 1959.
Le Polygone étoilé. Paris: Seuil, 1966.
L'Homme aux sandales de caoutchouc. Paris: Seuil, 1970.

COLLECTED WORKS

L'Oeuvre en fragments. Ed. by Jacqueline Arnaud. Paris: Sindbad, 1986.

TRANSLATIONS

Nedjma. Trans. by Richard Howard. New York: Braziller, 1961.
Intelligence Powder. Trans. of *La Poudre d'intelligence,* from *Le Cercle des représailles,* by Stephen J. Vogel. New York: Ubu Repertory Theater Publications, 1985.

BIOGRAPHICAL AND CRITICAL STUDIES

Aresu, Bernard. *Counterhegemonic Discourse from the Maghreb: The Poetics of Kateb's Fiction.* Tübingen, Germany: Günther Narr, 1993.
Arnaud, Jacqueline. *La Littérature maghrébine de langue française: Le Cas de Kateb Yacine.* Paris: Publisud, 1986.
Aurbakken, Kristine. *L'Étoile d'araignée: Une lecture de* Nedjma *de Kateb Yacine.* Paris: Publisud, 1986.
Bonn, Charles. *Kateb Yacine,* Nedjma. Paris: Presses Universitaires de France, 1990.
Gontard, Marc. Nedjma *de Kateb Yacine: Essai sur la structure formelle du roman.* Paris: L'Harmattan, 1985.
Sbouai, Taieb. *La Femme sauvage de Kateb Yacine.* Paris: L'Arcantère, 1985.

Alex La Guma
1925–1985

ROSEMARY COLMER

THE NONWHITE South African writers of the 1950s and 1960s were in a peculiar situation: legally designated inferior beings, they lived in an oppressive police state that their works were committed to exposing abroad. Working within a repressive society, the writers had to establish to the outside world the value of their very existence—and this in a country that was culturally as well as politically dominated by white values.

South African fiction of the period does not merely reflect the nature of the society, but inevitably criticizes it. Even the least politically didactic novel cannot avoid mentioning the social conditions under which nonwhites have lived in South Africa for most of the twentieth century. Merely to describe the daily existence of the nonwhite communities of South Africa is to criticize implicitly the policies of the former administrations, which dictated that human beings should live under these conditions, and such a description stands as an indictment of the sensibilities of the white South Africans who until the 1990s lived within and supported this system.

For Justin Alexander—known as Alex—La Guma, born into a working-class "Colored" (that is, of mixed-race origins) family in the Cape Province on 20 February 1925, fiction was a channel for his criticisms of a way of life he found intolerable. Under the influence of his mother, Wilhelmina Alexander, a worker in a cigarette factory, and his father, Jimmy La Guma, a trade-union organizer, he grew up conscious of the economic as well as political reasons for the development of increasingly separatist policies by the South African government, and of the role of the left-wing labor movement in fighting racist practices. After leaving school in 1942 to work in a factory (completing his schooling at night classes), La Guma was drawn to the Communist Party and became a member in 1948, two years before the party was declared illegal in South Africa.

On 13 November 1953, La Guma married Blanche Valerie Herman. He began working as a journalist, but from 1955 on, he was continually harassed by arrests on various charges and by detention without trial; in December 1962, his works were banned, and he was placed under house arrest. Since the ban meant that nothing he wrote could be published or mentioned in print, this was the end of La Guma's career as a journalist and is the reason that all of his major fiction has been published outside South Africa, for a foreign audience. When it was clear that the ban would continue for five more years, La Guma and his wife, whose income as a nurse maintained the family through many difficult times, decided that there was no future for their family in South Africa. They and their two sons obtained an exit visa and left for London at the end of 1966.

At first as a journalist for *New Age* (1955–1962), and later as a writer of short stories and longer fiction, La Guma used detailed description of the conditions under which nonwhite South Africans lived as the subject of his work, in an attempt to rouse the conscience of the white readers and to stir the nonwhite readers to action. His authorized biographer, Cecil A. Abrahams, a perceptive critic and ardent promoter of his work, records that when he died in Havana on 11 October 1985, he was still writing fiction, although his role as official Caribbean representative of the African National Congress formed another important expression of his commitment.

In a very real sense politics is the main reason why the South African writers of La Guma's generation write. They write in order to communicate their awareness of the political situation to outsiders and in some cases to offer their own solutions. For writers like La Guma, the beginning of hope lies in the African workers' recognition of their own ability to act, to lead, to be equal to or above their white compatriots, yet the writers find themselves forced to write for an audience outside South Africa. To a certain extent this role of writer as a literary ambassador dictates a structuring pattern of cumulative meaningful episodes that is commonly found in novels by such writers: these novels concern the political education of the central character or the exposure of a politically aware central character to events that bring him or her to a crisis point of action. It is a useful narrative pattern when writing for an audience unfamiliar with the social realities of South African life. The foreign reader, no less than the character, is progressively exposed to a series of events and led toward a conclusion in terms of political awareness or political action.

La Guma's *A Walk in the Night*, for example, utilizes a detached, descriptive approach that is wholly convincing in its portrait of the dehumanization of South African society. *The Stone Country* and *In the Fog of the Seasons' End* are subjective; they lack the superficially objective tone that makes *A Walk in the Night* so compelling. Instead, they involve the reader in the central character's total conviction of the worth of his political work, particularly in the case of Beukes, the hero in *In the Fog of the Seasons' End*. Occasionally, as in *In the Fog of the Seasons' End*, we are offered the view of a man already politically aware and active, but more often, as in *The Stone Country*, even political activists have something to learn about human relationships and the extent to which the white race's model of human relations is reflected in all hierarchical, power-based structures within the society.

What La Guma asserts constantly, in each of his novels, is the need for collective action. Individual suffering and individual action are less meaningful and fruitful than action taken by and on behalf of a group working toward the same ends. Except perhaps in *In the Fog of the Seasons' End*, where the political work itself occupies center stage, La Guma is always concerned to present the alienated individual as, however little he may realize it, a member of a society with whose communal life his individual efforts are inextricably bound up. Whether this wider society is the slum of District Six in Cape Town or the rain-sodden shantytown where the Pauls family lives, the prison or the drought-stricken country village, its life reverberates through the narrative as the background to the life of the individuals who exist within it.

EARLY WORKS—THE SUFFERERS

The Heinemann edition of *A Walk in the Night* (1967) collects six stories and the novella *A Walk in the Night* (1962). *And a Threefold Cord* (1964), written in 1963, belongs to the same period of La Guma's writing, when he deals with the lives of slum dwellers whose consciousness of political issues is limited to their anger and resentment about the way their own existence is affected by particular policies and practices.

A Walk in the Night

Many of La Guma's short stories present the hopeless moment when the central character is brought to realize the strength of the forces of racism that deny any possibility of happiness or even of dignity. Facing the immediate future of brutal violence ("The Lemon Orchard"), vilification ("Slipper Satin"), or ostracism ("A Glass of Wine"), the characters nevertheless reaffirm their own values, in opposition to those imposed by the state. The individual suffers but does not give up.

A Walk in the Night describes with lavish atmospheric detail the events of one night in the lives of four men who live in a decaying slum area, District Six in Cape Town. Each thinks of himself as an individual, but La Guma shows that together they represent the life of a whole district. The first, Michael Adonis, loses his job, accidentally murders an old man in a fit of drunken rage, and decides to join a gang of thieves. Willieboy, a "skolly" (a South African term for a young hoodlum) who prides himself on never having worked in his life, is mistakenly identified as the murderer of the old man. When he ventures into the street after a brawl in an illegal bar, he is spotted by the police, chased, shot, and left to die in the back of the police wagon. Meanwhile, in the same block of flats where the old man was murdered, Franky Lorenzo learns that his wife is going to have a sixth child. His dismay is overcome by his love for his wife and his bitter recognition that children are the riches of the poor.

The fourth figure, young Joe, who lives off what he can find in the sea around the docks, repays Michael's casual handout with real friendship. When he realizes that Michael is about to accept an offer to join the gang in a planned robbery, Joe pleads with him to change his mind. When that fails, Joe runs after Michael in the street to renew his plea: "'Please, Mike,' Joe said. He looked as if he was going to cry. 'I'm your pal. A man's got a right to look after another man. Jesus, isn't we all people?'" (p. 75, the Heinemann edition). The individual has rights, and these are not just the right to earn a living and the right to walk the streets without harassment, or the marital rights Franky Lorenzo shouts about when he discovers he has the responsibility of another mouth to feed. The individual also has the right to assume responsibility for fellow human beings.

Police Constable Raalt, who follows Willieboy across the roofs and shoots him in cold blood for the satisfaction of the hunt, is the story's prime example of the individual who has reneged on not only his ordinary human responsibilities, but also, as his prim fellow officer notes, his responsibility to uphold the public image of the whites. Raalt is a parasite on the community that he is supposed to protect, as his extortion of bribes demonstrates. Yet it is not always clear where one's responsibility lies: the person who identifies Willieboy as the murderer claims to be acting in good faith, yet he acts alone and is reproached by his neighbors for cooperating with the police; even the police officer sneers at him.

A Walk in the Night is an evocation of mood rather than a prescription for action. No political conclusion is drawn in *A Walk in the Night*; one is simply left with the picture of a society in which those responsible for the maintenance of law and order are the most irresponsibly violent people in the community. After reading about how Raalt shoots Willieboy simply because he fits the description of the murderer, who was wearing a yellow shirt, one may have a nightmare vision of police vans converging on the police station from every direction, each bearing a dying man—a kinky-haired man wearing a lemon, ocher, or canary-colored shirt. The squalor of living conditions for the nonwhites and the dehumanization of the white police officers by their own power say enough about the state of South Africa without La Guma or any of his characters openly drawing conclusions.

La Guma is interested in showing the interdependence between rights and responsibilities in a functioning human community, as well as the way that the inhumane political system denies individuals' sense of responsibility along with their rights. If he does draw a conclusion, it is verbalized in Joe's words: "A man's got a right to look after another man."

And a Threefold Cord

And a Threefold Cord leads toward a similar conclusion, though it is expressed only in the narrow domestic setting of a single relationship, when Charlie Pauls awkwardly attempts to comfort Freda for the loss of her children, burned to death in a shanty fire: "People can't stand up to the world alone, they got to be together.... Is not natural for people to be alone. Hell, I reckon people was just *made* to be together" (p. 168).

Charlie's family holds together, except for his brother Ronald, who rejects Charlie's offer of help. As the novel ends, a few yards from the shanty where she was born, their sister Caroline has just given birth to a child, helped by her mother and the neighbors who band together in times of joy or trouble. "You better go and call Missus Nzuba to give a hand. She'd want to he'p. She he'ped with Ca'line's wedding, and she'll be cross if I don't ask her to he'p," Caroline's mother says (p. 108). "[Nzuba] always he'p with these things" (p. 148). The dead are helped out of the world, and the living into it.

The title and the epigraph (from Ecclesiastes 4:9–12) reiterate the insight toward which Charlie is groping: that there is strength in numbers. Those who insist on standing alone, as Ronald does, will suffer and fall alone; those who stand together have the strength of a supportive community to sustain

their efforts, just as a threefold cord binds more strongly than a single one. So far, Charlie's sense of solidarity has been expressed only in terms of his own family, but his resentment of the inequities in society is already leading him to ask awkward questions. His attack on a police officer is one anonymous, unpremeditated blow, but the novel presents a country in which the racist foundations of society are as unstable as the foundations on which the Pauls' shanty rests. A few more storms may bring the whole structure down.

THINKERS AND ORGANIZERS

The Stone Country

La Guma's third novel, *The Stone Country* (1967), explores the world of the prison, the country of stone, from the inside, and finds it a microcosm of South African society. Those prison guards who are white bullies enforce the law of power that protects them, and those who are Colored men are caught in the dilemma of wanting more power and respect than their skin color entitles them to in their society. Below the guards are the cell bosses, the "big men" whose power is measured by their strength and by their ability to bully and terrify; but their power is nothing compared with that of the guards, and even among their own henchmen there may be a sly knife awaiting the right moment to strike. Around the cell bosses are the toadies and supporters who give them their power. And the rest, rank on rank, are the ordinary inmates: the powerless, the sufferers, the underdogs.

This picture reflects the nature of South African society as portrayed by La Guma elsewhere. The white guards might be any white man—and in La Guma's fiction most whites are police. The Colored guards and the cell bosses are two sides of the same coin: the tough guy who survives in the city, as in the prison, by knowing how to obtain power and how to wield it. Yusef the Turk, a variation on this theme, is the knowing crook, the wheeler-dealer whose power lies less in muscle than in his instinct for the moment when a challenge must be made and in his knack for the timing necessary to win a physical confrontation. Outside the prison, beyond the criminal life, he represents the shopkeeper and exploiter.

Into this prison, as into all walks of South African life, comes the intruder, the one who does not fit, the one who questions. George Adams is no less a stranger in the streets, to the people of his everyday life — landlady and nonpolitical friends — than he is in the smaller society of the prison. Yet his alien nature, his failure to take the place assigned to him among the downtrodden, breaks the whole pattern. His questioning of the system leads to a challenge to the cell boss's authority by Yusef the Turk and ultimately, though indirectly, to the death of the cell boss at the hands of one of his own followers.

The incident in which the prison cat plays with a captive mouse and distracts the guards from their duties is central to the novel. While artistically it may be overstated, it demonstrates that concern with the helpless victim which is embodied in many South African novels. The mouse, in its terrified bid for freedom, acts alone. The passage is striking, unsubtle, even at times clumsy — "The three guards were watching, with fascination, the punishment of the mouse, chuckling, as if they felt a natural association with the feline sadism" (p. 124), for instance — but undeniably it is effective in underlining the points La Guma is making about life in prison and life outside.

The parallel is not merely between the mouse and the prisoners who are planning to escape (the byplay between cat and mouse distracts the guards long enough for hacksaw blades to change hands), but also between the mouse and all the people oppressed by those with the physical power to dominate: the ordinary prisoner under cell bosses and guards; the ordinary man in the street under gang bosses, police, and a vicious social system. It is important, too, that like the mouse, the men are prisoners but not convicts. They are being held awaiting trial. The "punishment" of the mouse is for no crime but that of existence, and this obviously throws the scope of reference beyond the prison, beyond even the section for those awaiting trial, to the life of all nonwhites in South Africa.

Further, the incident operates with an inverse dramatic irony. Because the mouse succeeds in escaping from the cat through a drainpipe, we expect Gus, a burglar who is masterminding an escape with two fellow inmates, to succeed as well. Instead, just when freedom seems within reach, Gus's nerve fails him, and he and Morgan are recaptured. Ironically, it is Koppe, the third and most reluctant participant in the scheme, who gets away.

> "Got away," Morgan hiccoughed. "Got away. *Ou* Koppe got away. *That* fairy." He shook with laughter that hurt him all over. "Why man, that little basket didn't even *want* to go."
>
> Morgan lay there and filled the darkness with his crazy and painful laughter.
>
> (p. 162)

La Guma is fond of the ironic ending, particularly the kind that plays tricks with the reader's expectations. In the story "Tattoo Marks and Nails" from *A Walk in the Night*, for example, the reader does not know which, if either, of the two damning tattoos Ahmed the Turk is about to reveal: the one that will expose him as the coward and cheat of his own story, or the one that will condemn him as a killer.

Each of the many embedded stories in *The Stone Country* has a similar ironic ending. La Guma makes effective use of his wry humor by showing how Yusef's protestations of his innocence in the murder of the cell boss end with the admission that he was caught because "it happen that we didn't tie the watchman up so good when we get into the facktry.

So he get loose and phone the Squad" (p. 41). In a grim subplot, Toffy Williams is hanged for murdering his wife's supposed lover; at the same time, his wife takes up with the man who has wrongly accused her of infidelity in the first place. In another bitter subplot, The Casbah Kid conceals his knowledge that his mother had not been murdered by his father but had killed herself in despair, a revelation that might have saved his father's life. Afterward, in a conversation with George Adams, he recalls how his father has pleaded with him to tell the truth:

"'My son, my own son,' my father cried. 'Now you will save me. You will tell them all.'

"I smile at him.

"So when they brought him back into the court, he is wild with joy, see. He stood there in the dock, gabbling out the story what I told him. He was innocent. I would tell them everything. He turn on me, shouting at me to tell them what he was telling was the real truth. He was innocent, he babbled, and *I can prove it*."

"And what did you say?" asked George Adams, horrified, as The Casbah Kid ground a finger-nail between his teeth.

"I stood there in the court, mister, and it was as if I saw my mother's ghost rising up behind the Judge. I look at him and I shake my head. 'I don't know what he mean,' I say."

"So they hanged your father?" George Adams whispered. He did not know whether to look upon The Casbah Kid with astonishment, contempt or pity.

"The Judge say he don't accept drunkenness as excuses," the boy scowled.

"But-but," George Adams asked, stuttering. "Is this story true?"

The Casbah Kid looked at him and chewed a thumb-nail.

(p. 145)

The Casbah Kid has taken it upon himself to judge his father guilty, in spirit, of his mother's suicide. When given a death sentence himself, for a murder thoughtlessly committed in the course of a robbery, The Casbah Kid accepts it without question. He subscribes to the principle of an eye for an eye, an idea alien to George Adams, with his concepts of human dignity and cooperation.

George Adams is "everybody's friend." His commitment to a political cause makes him capable of disinterested generosity and gives him a dignity and courage in standing up for his rights that is unknown in the prison, where the inmates are too narrowly concerned with survival, and too busy seeking protection and favors, from their respective bosses, to see beyond their own self-interest. In this they resemble the whole population of the macrocosmic "Stone Country," South Africa: beleaguered, taking shelter behind her stone walls from a critical world, and in the process creating a society of prisoners and jailers, a nation of the condemned.

In the Fog of the Seasons' End

In the Fog of the Seasons' End (1972) prescribes action by showing it working at the most basic level. The novel centers on Beukes, who works full-time for an underground movement, and the events of a few days during which his controller, Elias Tekwane, is arrested and one of his recruits, Isaac, leaves the country to be trained as a guerrilla fighter. This novel explores the injustices of ordinary life to a far smaller extent than does *A Walk in the Night*. Partly, and paradoxically, this is because Beukes is so quick to point them out when he encounters them, and partly it is because his own hunted life is abnormal. Instead, this novel focuses on the lot of the active worker: the loneliness, the fear, and the rewarding knowledge that one is doing something useful. A series of flashbacks dealing with Beukes's own life and the lives of his colleagues fills in our sense of the narrow margin between hope and fear in which most people must live in the police state. For political activists, danger is closer than for most other people. A routine police check can find them with their passes out of order, and the leaflets hidden in a case may mean a death sentence if they are discovered. In a nerve-racking episode, Beukes smuggles such illegal documents:

> Beukes stood for a moment on the sidewalk outside the house and watched the street. Where the evicted old woman had sat amid her belongings, there was only an empty cardboard box toppled into the gutter. Satisfied that there was nothing unusual about the surroundings, he walked down the street, taking his time, casually carrying the case stuffed full of handbills. Endangered life was crowded between walls of cheap cardboard: the penalty for urging the armed overthrow of the government could be death. But with his everyday brown suit, the anonymous hang of the shoulders, he was just somebody going somewhere.
>
> (p. 61)

In this tense atmosphere, when the security police may be only moments away and any life may end at the hands of the police torturers, those who continue in the movement must have a very special kind of grim courage. Beukes's impatience with Arthur Bennett's cowardice and subservience to his wife springs from a full knowledge of the risks he himself is running all the time and from the memories of his own wife and child. He cannot visit his family for fear that he might implicate them.

Isaac's sense of powerlessness under a system that enforces his inferiority finds release in his drawings of fantastic weaponry. When the police come for him, he leaves behind a paper covered with sketches of guns, ranging from a submachine gun adapted from the drawing of a rifle to "a weapon which looked like a cross between an old-time blunderbuss and a ray-gun" (p. 117). His escape from the police means the end of his life of impotence, and he heads for the border and life as a fighter. His real knowledge of weapons is far more practically oriented than his drawings suggest:

> Isaac had taken a keen interest in regular and irregular warfare. He had read history books and the smuggled handbooks on guerrilla fighting, he had examined pictures and drawings of small arms of every sort. Theoretically he knew much about Magnums, and about Uzi submachine guns manufactured in Israel.... Corners of his mind were stored with the accumulated knowledge out of technical books and he longed like a lover for the time when he would be able to turn from theory to practice. With his new air of cockiness, the work-a-day jacket and unpressed trousers, the scuffed shoes and the permanent look of surprise, he appeared more like an unsuccessful young man who had just received news of an inheritance than like a potential partisan fighter.
>
> (p. 119)

Elias Tekwane, too, is drawn by an interest in weaponry into reassessing the possible relations between whites and blacks in South Africa. He has discovered, through boyhood reading, that not so many years ago the whites, too, fought with spears and shields, and he has concluded that the whites' power can be conquered. His vision of the Zulu warriors of old strengthens his spirit while the police torture his body:

> The ghosts waited for him on some far horizon. No words came, only the screaming of many crows circling the battlefield. *Wahlula amakosi! Thou hast conquered the Kings!* The far figures moved along the far horizon. *He! Uya kuhlasela-pi na? Yes, where wilt thou now wage war?* Far, far, his ancestors gathered on the misty horizon, their spears sparkling like diamonds in the exploding sun.
>
> (p. 175)

Unlike the lonely individuals of La Guma's earlier fiction, Tekwane works for a cause— and for a people.

TAKING ACTION—ALONE OR WITH THE PEOPLE?

Time of the Butcherbird

In *Time of the Butcherbird* (1979) La Guma moves for the first time into a rural setting and, again for the first time, uses a white man (an English salesman) as one of his central characters, who also include an elderly Afrikaner landowner and his grandson. The focalization through a number of characters in short passages, which works well in *A Walk in the Night*, tends in this novel to dissipate the tension. Instead of creating a sense of individuals fatefully gathered in one place, the action tends to split into unrelated segments.

As in *And a Threefold Cord*, La Guma examines the way in which individual actions (Charlie Pauls's unpremeditated attack on the police officer in *Threefold Cord* and the private vendetta of Shilling Murile against Hannes Meulen for the murder of his brother in *Butcherbird*) relate to broader community aims. Mma-Tau's attempts to get the people to resist their forcible relocation from the mineral-rich site where they have lived for several generations will have less dramatic immediate results than Murile's removal of the single parasite, but they may have more far-reaching consequences. Thematically and structurally, the two kinds of political action are interrelated in this novel.

Time of the Butcherbird directs the reader's attention away from the committed urban member of the movement to the movement's attempt to establish a popular base in the country. The country people whom Mma-Tau influences are politically naive, but they learn that the only way to assert their humanity is to protest, however vainly, against the system that treats them inhumanely. To understand is to resent and to protest.

Shilling Murile pursues his own personal ends throughout the novel, but his contact with Mma-Tau, the political activist, begins to stir his sense that there is something beyond his own individual concerns worth caring about. Again and again, Shilling Murile claims that his intended action—the execution of Hannes for murdering his brother—is his own affair: "his rage was a personal thing, keeping him away from these people" (p. 41). Again and again he is reminded that he is not alone but is a member of a people: "fatherless children belong to everybody" (p. 20). When Mma-Tau articulates in political terms the

connection between his personal desire for vengeance and the wider cause ("A man with your desire for vengeance belongs with the people"), she is rebuffed by him: "I have no need of people" (p. 80). By the end of the novel, Murile agrees to go with the villagers, although to the shepherd Madonele's question, "Are you coming with our people?" (p. 118), he will answer only in personal terms, agreeing to accompany the shepherd rather than explicitly to join the community.

Within the Afrikaner community, too, there are those who pursue single ends and those who identify with the Afrikaner people. The recognition by English-speaking Edgar Stopes of Afrikaner Hannes Meulen as a fellow traveling salesman helps to illuminate Meulen's roles as both aspiring politician and mineral exploiter and highlights his nature as a parasite on the black people. The way in which Dominee Visser's prayer for rain wanders offtrack to become an impassioned exhortation to preserve racial purity and an exaltation of the privilege of the master race contrasts markedly with the rhetoric of Mma-Tau addressing the dispossessed: "Our people go to prison every day. Are not our leaders in prison? We are all in prison, the whole country is a prison" (p. 80).

Three peoples clash in this novel, and their differences are enhanced by the rhetoric they employ: Mma-Tau speaks of the good of her people, and her vision embraces Murile's rhetoric of vengeance; Visser speaks of the purity of the Afrikaner but encourages Meulen's unrestrained greed; Stopes, the English settler businessman, repeats clichés about seeking his own personal advancement.

CONCLUSION

In his major works of fiction La Guma is concerned to show the process of moral development that leads to the moment of commitment to political action. Characters like Charlie Pauls, Michael Adonis, and Shilling Murile are aware of the political situation but are far too narrowly focused on their own troubles, hatreds, and anxieties to join a group fighting for a larger cause, though both Murile and Pauls are beginning to perceive the need to belong to a supportive community by the end of their respective narratives. Even in *In the Fog of the Seasons' End,* in which Beukes has completed his moral growth before the opening of the novel, a series of flashbacks on the early lives of the characters shows what led them to undertake a commitment to so dangerous a cause; in this novel the focus is not just on what leads a man to commit himself to political action, but also on his reaction to the testing time.

As Lewis Nkosi writes in *Home and Exile* (1965):

> If Alex La Guma tills the same apartheid plot which the other writers have so exhaustively worked up, what distinguishes him as a true novelist is his enthusiasm for life as it is lived. He has the artist's eye for the interesting detail; his stories and novels are sagging under the weight of real people waging a bloody contest with the forces of oppression; and credibly they celebrate their few moments of victory in sex, cheap Cape wine and stupid fights. The rooms they inhabit smell of decay, urine and sweat; they share them with "roaches, fleas, bugs, lice." Their only triumph is that they are human — superlatively human; and this is their sole claim upon our imagination.
>
> (p. 134)

For La Guma it is superlatively human to have the dignity to insist on one's rights, not the least of which is the right to care for one's fellow human beings.

Selected Bibliography

BIBLIOGRAPHIES

Green, Robert, and Agnes Lonje. "Alex La Guma: A Selected Bibliography." In *World Literature Written in English* 20 (spring 1981).

Lindfors, Bernth, comp. *Black African Literature in English: A Guide to Information Sources.* Detroit: Gale Research Co., 1979.
————. *Black African Literature in English: 1977–1981 Supplement.* New York: Africana Publishing Co., 1986.
————. *Black African Literature in English: 1982–1986 Supplement.* London: Zell, 1989.
————. *Black African Literature in English: 1987–1991 Supplement.* London: Zell, 1995.

SHORT FICTION

"Etude." In *New Age* (24 January 1957). Repr. as "Nocturne" in Richard Rive, ed., *Quartet: New Voices from South Africa.* New York: Crown, 1963; London: Heinemann, 1965.
"Out of Darkness." In *Africa South* 2 (October 1957). Repr. in *Quartet.*
"A Glass of Wine." In *Black Orpheus*, no. 7 (1960). Repr. in *Quartet.*
"Slipper Satin." In *Black Orpheus*, no. 8 (1960). Repr. in *Quartet.*
"At the Portagee's." In *Black Orpheus,* no. 11 (1963). Repr. in *A Walk in the Night.* London: Heinemann, 1967.
"Blankets." In *Black Orpheus*, no. 15 (1964). Repr. in Ezekiel Mphahlele, ed., *African Writing Today.* Harmondsworth, U.K.: Penguin, 1967.
"Coffee for the Road." In Ellis Ayitey Komey and Ezekiel Mphahlele, eds., *Modern African Stories.* London: Faber & Faber, 1964.
"Tattoo Marks and Nails." In *Black Orpheus*, no. 14 (1964). Repr. in *A Walk in the Night.*
"A Matter of Honour." In *New African* 4, no. 7 (1965).
"The Gladiators." In *A Walk in the Night*, 1967.
"The Lemon Orchard." In *A Walk in the Night,* 1967.
"A Matter of Taste." In *A Walk in the Night,* 1967.
"Late Edition." In *Lotus* 29 (1976).
"Thang's Bicycle." In *Lotus* 29 (1976).

LONGER FICTION

A Walk in the Night. Ibadan, Nigeria: Mbari, 1962. Repr. with six additional short stories. London: Heinemann Educational Books, 1967; Evanston, Ill.: Northwestern University Press, 1967.
And a Threefold Cord. Berlin: Seven Seas, 1964.

The Stone Country. Berlin: Seven Seas, 1967; London: Heinemann Educational Books, 1974.

Apartheid: A Collection of Writings on South African Racism by South Africans. Ed. by Alex La Guma. New York: International Publishers, 1971; London: Lawrence and Wishart, 1972.

In the Fog of the Seasons' End. London: Heinemann Educational Books, 1972; New York: Third Press, 1973.

A Soviet Journey. Moscow: Progress Books, 1978.

Time of the Butcherbird. London: Heinemann Educational Books, 1979.

SELECTED ESSAYS

"The Third Afro-Asian Writers' Conference." In *Cultural Events in Africa* 29 (1967).

"The Writer in a Modern African State." In Per Wästberg, ed., *The Writer in Modern Africa.* New York: Africana Publishing Co., 1969.

"African Culture and Liberation." In *Journal of the New African Literature and the Arts* 7/8 (1970).

"Literature and Life." In *Lotus: Afro-Asian Writings* 1, no. 4 (1970).

"The Condition of Culture in South Africa." In *Présence africaine* 80 (1971).

"South African Writing Under Apartheid." In *Lotus: Afro-Asian Writings* 23 (1975).

"Culture and Liberation." In *World Literature Written in English* 18 (April 1979).

Memories of Home: The Writings of Alex La Guma. Ed. by Cecil A. Abrahams. Trenton, N.J.: Africa World Press, 1991.

INTERVIEWS

Abrahams, Cecil A. "The Real Picture." In Cecil A. Abrahams, ed., *Memories of Home: The Writings of Alex La Guma.* Trenton: N.J.: Africa World Press, 1991.

Serumaga, Robert. In *Cultural Events in Africa* 24, supp. (1966).

———. In Cosmo Pieterse and Dennis Duerden, eds., *African Writers Talking: A Collection of Radio Interviews.* London: Heinemann, 1972.

CRITICAL STUDIES

Abrahams, Cecil A. "Achebe, Ngũgĩ and La Guma: Commitment and the Traditional Storyteller." In *Mana Review* 2, no. 1 (1977).

———. "The Literature of Victims in South Africa." In *Literary Criterion* 13, no. 2 (1978).

———. *Alex La Guma.* Boston: Twayne, 1985.

———. "The Writings of Alex La Guma." In Hedwig Bock and Albert Wertheim, eds., *Essays on Contemporary Post-Colonial Fiction.* Munich, Germany: Max Hueber Verlag, 1986.

———. "Defiance and Restraint." In Robert L. Ross, ed., *International Literature in English: The Major Writers.* New York: Garland, 1991.

Asein, Samuel O. "The Revolutionary Vision in Alex La Guma's Novels." In *Lotus: Afro-Asian Writings* 24/25 (1975).

Carpenter, William. "'Ovals, Spheres, Ellipses and Sundry Bulges': Alex La Guma Imagines the Human Body." In *Research in African Literatures* 22 (winter 1991).

———. "The Scene of Representation in Alex La Guma's Later Novels." In *English in Africa* 18 (October 1991).

Coetzee, J. M. "Alex La Guma and the Responsibilities of the South African Writer." In *Journal of the New African Literature and the Arts* 9/10 (1971).

———. "Man's Fate in the Novels of Alex La Guma." In *Studies in Black Literature* 5, no. 1 (1974).

Ezeigbo, Theodore Akachi. "'A Sign of the Times': Alex La Guma's *Time of the Butcherbird.*" In *Literary Half-Yearly* 32 (January 1991).

Green, Robert J. "Alex La Guma's *In the Fog of the Seasons' End*: The Politics of Subversion." In *Umoja* 3, no. 2 (1979).

———. "Chopin in the Ghetto: The Short Stories of Alex La Guma." In *World Literature Written in English* 20, no. 1 (1981).

JanMohamed, Abdul R. "Alex La Guma: The Generation of Marginal Fiction." In his *Manichaean Aesthetics: The Politics of Literature in Colonial Africa.* Amherst: University of Massachusetts Press, 1983.

July, Robert W. "The African Personality in the African Novel." In Ulli Beier, ed., *Introduction to African Literature: An Anthology of Critical Writings from* Black Orpheus. London: Longman, 1967.

Kibera, Leonard. "A Critical Appreciation of Alex La Guma's *In the Fog of the Seasons' End.*" In *Busara* 8, no. 1 (1976).

Lindfors, Bernth. "Form and Technique in the Novels of Richard Rive and Alex La Guma." In

Journal of the New African Literature and the Arts 2 (1966).

Maughan-Brown, David. "Adjusting the Focal Length: Alex La Guma and Exile." In *English in Africa* 18 (October 1991).

Obuke, J. Okpure. "The Structure of Commitment: A Study of Alex La Guma." In *Ba Shiru* 5, no. 1 (1973).

Rabkin, David. "La Guma and Reality in South Africa." In *Journal of Commonwealth Literature* 8, no. 1 (1973).

Riemenschneider, Dieter. "The Prisoner in South African Fiction: Alex La Guma's Novels *The Stone Country* and *In the Fog of the Seasons' End*." In Daniel Massa, ed., *Individual and Community in Commonwealth Literature*. Msida: University of Malta Press, 1979.

Santos, D. G. "Alex La Guma: Revolutionary Intellectual." In *Black Scholar* 17 (July–August 1986).

Scanlon, Paul A. "Alex La Guma's Novels of Protest: The Growth of the Revolutionary." In *Okike*, no. 16 (1979).

Wade, Michael. "Art and Morality in Alex La Guma's *A Walk in the Night*." In Kenneth Parker, ed., *The South African Novel in English*. New York: Africana Publishing Co., 1978; London: Macmillan, 1979.

Camara Laye
1928–1980

JOHN D. CONTEH-MORGAN

CAMARA LAYE'S reputation as one of Africa's foremost — as well as one of its earliest — French-language novelists is firmly established, but his achievement continues to be the subject of debate. It has never completely emerged from the cloud cast over it in the early 1950s, and sporadically since then, by the ideological assaults of radical critics. Laye's artistry has never been in doubt, and he is widely recognized as a *maître de la parole* (a master craftsman of the word), to use his description of the verbal artists of his traditional Malinke culture of West Africa. His distinction as a prose stylist is especially evident in his first novel, *L'Enfant noir* (1953; *The Dark Child*), an autobiographical work whose sensitivity to the materiality of language (a quality he partly attributes to the influence of Gustave Flaubert's *L'Education sentimentale*, 1869) and whose intense lyricism have contributed to its enduring literary success. What has been at issue, however, is the vision that Laye uses this finely crafted language to express.

ARTISTIC VISION AND CRITICAL RESPONSE

Laye's last work, *Le Maître de la parole* (1978; *The Guardian of the Word*), is a translation and adaptation of an epic song as performed to him by the griot Babou Condé. Like Condé and Laye's other traditional Malinke predecessors and sometimes contemporaries — indeed, like his blacksmith/goldsmith father — Laye had a deeply religious view of the function of the artist. Just as he interpreted his father's work as a goldsmith as mediating the realms of the sacred and the profane, so he conceived the function of the modern writer as giving concrete expression to religious and spiritual truths.

Laye eschewed the dreary depiction, associated with nineteenth-century realism, of dry historical, social, or political facts. He believed that such depictions could only rise to the level of art if they were invested, in the tradition of symbolist writing, with religious meaning; if, in other words, the facts, events, and situations conformed to or illustrated a supernatural scheme. Adele King has described Laye's vision of the artist as "a priest giving form to the mystery beyond daily life, expressing the supernatural" (p. 116).

To Laye, the natural and social world, and our experience of it in dreams and wakefulness, is like a "forest of symbols," a field of hieroglyphics whose necessarily religious meanings wait to be deciphered by the artist-priest. Examples of this decipherment, or projection of the symbolic and the spiritual

413

onto the natural and the factual, abound in his work. Let us take the case of the narrator's departing in *The Dark Child* from his home in rural Kouroussa and neighboring Tindican for urban Conakry and then moving to France. To a secular and realist imagination, such a trajectory, though emotionally wrenching, can be understood and explained as the consequence of a French colonial policy that located few, if any, institutions of educational and economic opportunity in the colonies, and thereby made migration to France for ambitious colonial subjects of Laye's generation seem socially logical. While Laye was aware of such explanations, his religious cast of mind configures his exile in *The Dark Child* as the expression, in individual human terms, of a separation that is superficially geographic and cultural but in essence metaphysical: that of man's estrangement from the roots of his spirituality—from the "ground of his being," as Paul Tillich put it—in short, from God. Thus, the sociological phenomenon of migration from a deprived colonial periphery to an endowed metropolitan center, well known to colonial and postcolonial subjects, is transmuted into the symbol of a higher truth. The logic of exile is no longer immanent, social, and historical, but transcendental, spiritual, and ahistorical. Laye's essentially religious vision of the world has been at the heart of the controversy over his achievement.

To many of Laye's western readers, caught in the "dilemma of a modernity" that is at once efficient and alienating, his spiritual vision and lyrical evocation of Africa were instantly appealing. But to many 1950s "radical" African readers, it posed problems. To focus on spiritual essences, they argued, or to present Africa from the angles of rural simplicity, carefree innocence, and festivals carried serious practical implications. It meant opting out of the raw actualities of history—in this case, French colonial rule in Africa—and pandering to the folkloristic colonial stereotypes of eternal Africa. The Cameroonian writer Mongo Beti, whose

widely quoted remarks made under the pseudonym Alexandre Biyidi are representative of this argument, observed: "Laye closes his eyes stubbornly on the most basic reality.... Could he possibly have seen nothing but a peaceful, beautiful and motherly Africa? Is it imaginable that he did not once witness a single exaction by the colonial administration?" Further on, he characterizes Laye's Africa as "an idyllic universe of endlessly stupid feasts, carnivalesque initiation rites, circumcisions, excisions, superstitions and Uncle Mamadous whose lack of political consciousness is only equalled by their unreality" (1954, p. 420).

Laye, it is true, was not an overtly political writer. But to portray him as one who colluded in his people's subjugation (because his work is silent on it) is both to practice bad and dangerous logic and to misconceive the radical, even subversive, character of his creative output.

Laye was concerned not so much with colonialism—the fact of foreign political domination—as with the Enlightenment project of a civilizing modernity inscribed in colonialism's heart and heralded by it in the empire. The issue for him, in other words, was not one of hostility (in the tradition of other African writers like Beti or Sembène Ousmane) to a colonialism that failed to deliver on its otherwise beneficent modernizing promises. It was, rather, one of profound disagreement with those very promises, whose results he had witnessed and experienced in France. In this respect, it is no coincidence that Laye wrote his two most religiously oriented novels, *The Dark Child* and *Le Regard du roi* (1954; *The Radiance of the King*) while in France. The traumatic phase that Laye experienced and describes in the chapter "A Sleepless Night" in *Dramouss* (1966; *A Dream of Africa*)—a phase that the Palestinian-American literary critic Edward Said calls, in another context, the "negative apprehension" of French modernity—no doubt inspired in Laye the urge to create a countervailing social and individual reality that he posited as distinctly and essentially African.

Rather than interpret Laye's religious vision and essentialized portrayal of Africa as tantamount to opting out of history, they should be understood as the response of a man who recoiled in horror at what he saw as a dehumanizing and materialistic French society. Laye proceeded to postulate an original, premodern African society that is in every way oppositional to the colonialist project of society, as distinct from its methods and contradictions, and that alone is truly civilized and civilizing. In his rejection of science and technology and their impact on social organization—a stance that calls to mind the English poet William Blake's propensity toward mythology—Laye subscribes to romantic conservatism, and his ideal society seemingly corresponds to the negative stereotypes of colonialist literature on Africa. However, Laye places positive values on these images, which is partly explained by the traditional nature of his family background.

THE WRITER AND HIS BACKGROUND

The essentials of Laye's life are contained in his autobiographical novels *The Dark Child* and *A Dream of Africa*, and in interviews he accorded such scholars as Jacqueline Leiner. Born on 1 January 1928 in the town of Kouroussa in what was then French (Upper) Guinea, Laye was the eldest of twelve children in the Camara household. (Camara is Camara Laye's family name.) He was Malinke, one of the largest ethnic groups in West Africa and among the three most important in Guinea. The Malinke have a long and illustrious history that stretches back to the thirteenth century, the time of the "Mansa" or Emperor Soundjata Keita, founder of the Empire of Mali. Although they have been Islamized for over a millennium, their culture retains strong elements of pre-Islamic African beliefs. Laye

provides an example of this syncretism in his references in *The Dark Child* to his father's appeals both to the Qur'ān and to nature spirits.

Laye's father, Komady Camara, was descended from a family of blacksmiths, a profession that is both respected and feared in an agrarian culture such as the Malinke's. The blacksmith is perceived as both the provider of life, through the agricultural implements he makes, and the purveyor of death, through the weapons he forges. If, like Laye's father, the blacksmith doubles as goldsmith, he also meets the community's needs for ornamentation. A fine craftsman and mystic, two qualities he passed on to his son, Komady is portrayed by Laye as an "open-handed" man, a "lavish giver" whose solicitude went beyond his immediate family to encompass the village community. The task of educating Laye in the traditional values and etiquette of culture fell to his mother, Dâman Sadan, to whom he dedicated *The Dark Child*. She was the daughter of a blacksmith and a native of the neighboring village of Tindican.

Although Laye's parents were traditionalists, they differed greatly in their attitudes toward western civilization, which, in the form of the French school, was a reality that could not be ignored. Dâman refused to acknowledge the inevitability of the modernization that was gnawing away at ancestral beliefs and practices. Komady, however, bowed to it and encouraged his son to be part of that process by sending him to school.

Laye's early schooling was in Kouroussa, where he showed an aptitude for literature. On completion of his elementary education in 1942, he went to Conakry to attend the École Georges Poiret. After an initial period of resentment over being sent to a technical institute, which trained mere "laborers," and not to the more prestigious École Camille-Guy, which produced "clerks," he settled down to his work and earned a scholarship in 1947 to pursue advanced studies in France in automobile engineering.

Laye's stay in France was crucial to his later development. He received an education but also experienced great hardship in that country. After his scholarship was not renewed by the French government, presumably to force him back home after his first diploma, he was often penniless and homeless. He had to abandon his studies to take up a variety of manual jobs in Paris, first in the Halles markets and later at the Simca car factories. But Laye's stay in France also provided great opportunities. He took advantage of the cultural treasures of Paris not only to learn more about French culture but also to initiate himself at the Musée de l'Homme into a more systematic study of his African culture, especially its arts. He became closely associated with the Paris-based movement for African cultural and artistic renaissance known as Négritude. Indeed, his first two novels — *The Dark Child* and *The Radiance of the King*, which were published within a year of each other — were a substantial contribution to that cause.

Laye lived in France for nine years and only visited Guinea briefly in 1954. He finally left France in 1956, but he did not return immediately to his country. He took various positions, first in Dahomey, which later became Benin, then in President Kwame Nkrumah's Ghana, where he taught French and wrote a French news column for the *Evening News*. He returned to Guinea in 1958 on its gaining independence under the radical nationalist leader, Sékou Touré. In a dramatic vote, Guineans rejected a French referendum proposal that would have granted limited autonomy to the colonies within a broader Franco-African community.

The break in diplomatic, economic, and cultural ties with France that ensued from this vote, and the difficulties it created for the young republic, put enormous strain on its limited human resources. Laye quickly emerged as a key player in the new Guinea and became within a few years ambassador to Ghana, then head of the Division of Eco-

nomic Agreements in the Ministry of Foreign Affairs, and later associate director of the National Institute for Research and Documentation. He clearly had little time during this period for writing. His literary endeavors between 1958 and 1965 were limited to papers presented in March and April 1963 at the African literature conferences held in Dakar, Senegal, and Freetown, Sierra Leone, respectively; to writing a few radio plays; and to interviewing traditional sages.

By the mid 1960s, however, Laye had become disillusioned with his country's leadership. Deteriorating economic conditions had led to a restless and sometimes conspiratorial population. The massive and brutal repression with which Sékou Touré reacted to this threat, and the populist and anti-intellectual character of his regime, convinced Laye, by now fearful for his physical safety and in need of medical treatment, to go into exile. He left in 1965. Until his death from kidney disease on 4 February 1980, he lived in Dakar, Senegal, where he was a researcher at the Institut Fondamental d'Afrique Noire, which later became the Institute Cheikh Anta Diop. He also traveled frequently to Ivory Coast, partly because he considered its president, Felix Houphouët Boigny, a model of enlightened leadership.

At the time of his death, Laye had published a few short stories and essays; three novels, *The Dark Child*, *The Radiance of the King*, and *A Dream of Africa*; and a transcription and translation of an oral epic, *The Guardian of the Word*. In her introduction to *The Writings of Camara Laye*, King mentions the existence of a novel in manuscript form, "L'Exil" (The exile), which Laye compiled in 1971 but did not publish.

THE DARK CHILD

Laye's first novel, *The Dark Child*, for which he is best known, was hailed a classic upon its publication in 1953. Crafted as a novel, it is an autobiographical account of Laye's growth and development from childhood to maturity, and his corresponding loss of innocence. It divides into two parts. The first, which consists of Chapters 1 to 5, is devoted to the narrator's childhood in rural Kouroussa. The second, Chapters 9 to 12, depicts his adolescent and mature experiences in urban Conakry. Separating the two is a transitional section of three chapters that partakes of both worlds.

A formal aspect of the first section of *The Dark Child* could be called its anthological character. The events described in it do not follow chronological order. They are not causally linked, unrepeatable events but recurring or habitual experiences: the narrator's father's activities as a goldsmith, the narrator's visits to Tindican, the harvesting season, and so on.

In this section, existence is repetitive or circular, and all human activities—even the most mundane—are integrated into cosmic cycles. An example of such integration occurs in Chapter 2, where the crafting of gold is understood by the community not as an ordinary exercise in individual skill but as partaking in the primordial act of creation. It is not a singular event, in other words, but the sacred reenactment of what Mircea Eliade calls in *The Myth of the Eternal Return* (1954) an "archetypal action," an action "consecrated in the beginning ('in those days,' *in illo tempore, ab origine*) by gods, ancestors or heroes" (p. 4). This quality of sacredness associated with the activities described by Laye—harvesting, circumcision, gold smelting—explains the elaborate acts of ritual purification, the incantations and appeals to nature spirits, that accompany them.

The apprehension of time as circular in the first part of the novel is suggested not only by the narrator's predominant use of the imperfect tense—the time of habitual action—but also, and more strikingly, by the absence of temporal references, a device that lends to the world evoked a mythical timelessness charac-

teristic of the legends, epics, and folktales of African oral tradition.

The first five chapters of *The Dark Child* also emphasize the importance of social bonding. Human interaction in Kouroussa and Tindican, the villages that define the territorial boundaries of the narrator's community, is organic. Relationships are based on a shared social consciousness and communal experience. The most striking example of this is provided in the narrator's descriptions of the annual harvest in Tindican:

> My uncle Lansana or some other farmer—for the harvest threw people together and everyone helped everyone else—would signal that the work was to begin. Immediately, the black torsos would bend over the great golden field, and the sickles begin to cut....
>
> The movement of the sickles as they rose and fell was astonishingly rapid and regular....
>
> The long line of reapers hurled itself at the field and hewed it down.... They sang and they reaped. Singing in chorus, they reaped, voices and gestures in harmony. They were together!—united by the same task, the same song. It was as if the same soul bound them.
>
> (pp. 57, 61)

This passage celebrates a collectivity whose cohesion and togetherness are conveyed by a cluster of verbs and adjectives ("sang," "reaped," "same") and the evocation of choral singing. Awareness of being part of a whole and the need to remain so is such an integral part of the ethics of these farmhands that when one of them, Uncle Lansana, breaks off from the group and stands out as an individual far ahead of the others, he slows down, remarking to his nephew: "'Don't forget that I must not get too far ahead of the others; it would offend them'" (p. 62).

This section of the novel also conveys an atmosphere of wonder and fantasy. The universe of Laye's childhood is peopled not only by loving and admirable humans but also by a variety of both beneficent and evil spirits that must constantly be courted or kept at bay through religious ceremonies. It is an enchanting and poetic world in which work is holy and humans commune with animals and the sun-drenched natural world.

In the second part of the novel, the narrator is torn from this stable and harmonious universe. From his arrival in Conakry until his departure for France, events in his life are no longer the reenactment of archetypal acts. Whether it is his enrollment at the École Georges Poiret, his awareness of his sexuality, or the death of his friend Check, they are all individualized and irreversible events, indicative of a linear progression. In symbolic terms, the narrator's departure for Conakry can be interpreted as a fall from the timeless world of grace and mythical experience into the time-bound universe of suffering and historical experience. Stylistically, the predominantly poetic prose of the first five chapters gives way to the more descriptive language of Chapters 10–12, as the sacred world of myth yields to the profane universe of rationality. The narrator sums up the transformation in mental attitude when he observes of the traditional healers trying to cure his friend Check: "I don't know whether Check had any great confidence in the medicine men. Probably not. By now we had spent too many years in school to have real faith" (p. 175).

Corresponding to this new experience of temporality and its attendant problems is that of infinite physical space. In physical terms, Kouroussa and Tindican represent bounded, finite space. Outside this region, and particularly in Conakry with its vast ocean, the narrator discovers unbounded space. This is how he contrasts the two regions:

> The great plain where I had lived until now, that plain so rich, so poor, so sunburnt—yet so familiar and friendly—was giving way to the foothills of the Fouta Djallon. . . .
>
> This country, new to me, too new and too rugged, disturbed rather than enchanted me.
>
> (p. 145)

About Conakry, he observes:

> I walked into town. It was different from Kouroussa. . . . The houses were all embowered in flowers and foliage. Many looked *submerged* in all the greenery, *drowned* in a frantic proliferation. And then I saw the sea. . . .
>
> I stood a long time observing its vastness, watching the waves roll in, one after another, to break against the red rocks of the shore.
>
> (pp. 148–149; emphasis added)

Beyond the new and unfamiliar physical landscape, the narrator discovers something hitherto unexperienced: suffering and evil. For the first time in his life, he is lonely; he experiences frustration at being unable to go to the school of his choice. In his metal workshop class, he sustains a wound that turns ulcerous and necessitates hospitalization. Above all, in terms of the symbolic economy of the novel, he discovers in Conakry, in Check's fate, the supreme evil: death.

Of course, the narrator's "fall" from grace is not strictly simultaneous with his arrival in Conakry. Although he experiences it most intensely in Conakry, signs of a gradual fall are already present in the last three chapters of his period in Kouroussa—the transitional chapters. In two of these, Chapters 7 and 8, the narrator is initiated into *kondén diara* (the ceremony of the lions) and is ritually circumcised. These ceremonies are rites of passage, marking a transition from childhood to adulthood within traditional Malinke society—a point underscored by the fact that after his circumcision, the narrator, now an adult, can no longer share sleeping accommodations with his mother.

What makes his coming of age dramatic, however, is that it is a growth not into the fullness of traditional Malinke adulthood, on the threshold of which he stood after *kondén diara*. With his almost simultaneous initiation into the French school—a western *kondén diara*—his development becomes instead one into the fullness of western, and more specifically French, adulthood. To put it differently, the narrator's growth into adulthood — like that of Africa to which he stands in a metonymic relationship — is a growth into western modernity.

Such individual and national development is hailed by cultural evolutionists as progress. While Laye acknowledges its inevitability — one of the dominant themes in the book — he strongly contests its desirability. Indeed, by making the narrator's ascension to modernity coincide with his experience of spiritual and emotional impoverishment, of a burdensome consciousness and of physical suffering, Laye subverts modernity's civilizing claims.

THE RADIANCE OF THE KING

If Laye's critique of modernity remains muted and implicit in *The Dark Child*, in his second novel, *The Radiance of the King* (1954), it is most explicitly formulated. A richly allegorical novel, *The Radiance of the King* tells the story of Clarence, a white European who finds himself in Africa and becomes involved in a series of adventures that are as comic as they are nightmarish.

Shortly after he arrives in the imaginary northern African city of Adramé, Clarence is ruined by gambling debts and stays in a run-down inn after being thrown out of a hotel. In despair, he seeks an audience with the local king, hoping for a job. On the day of the king's appearance on the esplanade, however, Clarence is unable to get close to him because of the dense crowd. Quite unexpectedly, a beggar offers to help him meet the king. At first incredulous that such a poorly clothed and presumably worthless individual would even make such a gesture, but desperate for a job and willing to clutch at any straw, Clarence reluctantly accepts the offer. But his hopes are soon dashed when the beggar returns with a story of failure. He suggests, however, that Clarence travel south with him, as that is the king's next destination.

Increasingly reliant on the beggar, Clarence accepts his suggestion. Before their departure, Clarence invites two urchins, Noaga and Naoga, whom he has met at the esplanade, and the beggar to accompany him to his inn for a meal. The visit to the inn ends in total humiliation for Clarence, who is stripped of his jacket by the innkeeper because he cannot settle his bill. But this is just the beginning of his strange adventures. In the streets of Adramé, on their way south, he is accused of stealing the jacket he is wearing, which had in fact been stolen by the two urchins, and is arrested. Despite his protestations of innocence, he is dragged through an arbitrary trial in a courtroom, which he reaches through a maze of corridors and rooms. Just before his sentencing, he is advised, again by the beggar, to escape.

Clarence manages to flee the courtroom, only to find himself in the building's labyrinthine corridors, facing the prospect of being caught again. However, a chance encounter with a bare-breasted dancer saves him from recapture; she leads him out of the maze to an area of town where he is reunited with the beggar, Naoga, and Noaga. They are carousing with the dancer's father, who turns out to be the judge whose court he has just fled. The judge, however, seems not to recognize Clarence; in fact, he offers him drinks and accompanies him and the rest of the party to the outskirts of town as the four men resume their journey south.

Clarence and his friends travel only a few miles before they encounter a new obstacle. This time they lose their way in a dense tropical forest with an overwhelming fragrance that assaults Clarence's senses to the point of making him unconscious. After an unspecified period of time, during which Clarence, in his entranced state, feels as if he were going around the forest in circles, the party finally reaches its destination, the village of Aziana.

The travelers are hospitably received by the local ruler, the Naba, who is the grandfather of the two urchins. He invites Clarence, whose request for a job has been relayed to him, to wait in Aziana for the king. Meanwhile he gives him a house and, in the Azianan tradition, a wife, Akissi. Although Clarence is totally bewildered by his experiences, he rapidly settles down in his new environment and sheds his European identity.

What Clarence does not realize is that the hospitality he enjoys is not without a price. He has been sold off by the beggar as a stud, and each night, while he lies inebriated by the fragrance of flowers left by his bedside, a new "wife" from the Naba's harem is smuggled into his room to share his bed. Clarence's dim suspicions that such a trick is being played on him are later confirmed by the indiscretions of a character named the Master of Ceremonies and by his own observation of the high proportion of half-caste children in the population since his arrival.

This shattering discovery, coupled with his awareness of his sensuality, a feature of his character he has always repressed, induces intense feelings of guilt and self-disgust in Clarence. He longs for death and drifts toward a river. But stranger things happen to him there. In an experience that appears to him both real and imaginary, he sees creatures resembling mermaids, with opulent breasts, emerge from the water. After this frightening episode, he rushes to the old woman Dioki so she can prophesy the future for him. She reassures him that the king is on his way to Aziana. But, feeling sinful and worthless, Clarence shuts himself up in his house and decides not even to attempt to see the king. At this point, when he least expects it, he feels the radiance and the eyes of the king shining on him: "'Didn't you know that I was waiting for you,' asked the king. . . . Then the king slowly closed his arms around him and his great mantle swept about him and enveloped him forever" (p. 283).

The Radiance of the King has often been interpreted as the story "of the lone traveler lost in a strange land, illustrating the eternal nature of the spiritual quest" (Lee, p. 52). Its protagonist, Clarence, is an Everyman searching for salvation. That he is European is immaterial to critics like Sonia Lee, for whom—and rightly so—race is not the issue. This identity is important only to the extent that it constitutes "the perfect metaphor for man's unjustified arrogance and complacency" (Lee, p. 52). Otherwise, his story "tells of the search for God, and God has no denomination" (Lee, p. 52).

In this regard, Clarence's journey—journey being a frequent motif in traditional oral narrative—from Adramé to Aziana is given symbolic meaning. It is not just geographical. With its innumerable physical and psychological obstacles—also features of traditional myths of quest—it is a journey from ignorance to truth, from a state of ungodliness to one of spiritual redemption. The phases of his quest have been compared to those of the mystic who goes through successive stages of "renunciation of reason, then of the senses, to reach the annihilation of the ego in which divine grace, even unity with God, can be achieved" (King, p. 44). Adele King sees another dimension to the novel, that of a "man attempting to adjust to an alien culture whose customs and ways of thought he must learn to understand" (p. 40).

While readings of the text as mystical allegory or critique of cultural absolutism fit the particulars of the plot and are persuasive, they seem too decontextualizing and in danger of obscuring the work's more immediate polemical significance. Stated simply, in *The Radiance of the King*, Laye challenges the humanist optimism of Enlightenment modernity, its triumphalist and, in its colonial phase, conquering claims and assumptions of constituting a superior form of civilization, of providing the tools, in rationality and human will, for a life of material fulfillment, unlimited progress, and moral perfection. Laye's strategy in the novel is simple: he pits those claims as embodied by Clarence—modern European and therefore symbol of this spirit—against his own experiences of reality and exposes them as incapable of making sense of that experience.

In this manner, the novel's mode of narration is reminiscent not only of the questing tales of the African oral tradition but also of modern stories like Voltaire's *Candide* (1759), in which the hero, possessed of an optimistic vision of the world, is put through difficult adventures and trials, at the end of which he emerges wiser for having been forced by experience to recognize the shortcomings and dangers of his assumptions. Like Candide, Clarence is inducted — indeed, initiated in the ceremonial sense of the word — into a higher order of truth.

The truths that the two protagonists attain differ and, in fact, are opposed. In *Candide*, which is in many ways an expression of Enlightenment modernity, the eponymous hero moves from a view of truth that derives from unquestioned authority and metaphysical speculation to one that proceeds from observation and the evidence of the senses. But more important, for this comparison, he moves from a conception of human salvation that is dependent on divine reason to a view of it that is linked to the modest cultivation of human effort, notably of reason and will. The idea of divine providence, Candide concludes, is, if not a false notion, then at best an unknowable one. Reliance on such an empirically unverifiable belief can lead to quietism — a mystical quest for union with God, which correspondingly suggests a retreat from the world — if not to complicity with evil and suffering.

In *The Radiance of the King*, Clarence evolves in the opposite direction: he moves from a view of human rationality and enterprise as necessary and sufficient for happiness to a discovery of religious transcendence and providence, knowledge of which cannot be acquired, as he had confidently believed, by rational procedures of thought and inquiry or by acts of the individual will. Reliance on these beliefs can only lead to frustration, dereliction, and angst.

Clarence arrives at this insight painfully. In the early pages of the novel, he emerges as a character confident in his ability to control his destiny. He is looking for a job that will make him independent, and his status as a European in colonial Africa should, he believes, guarantee him rights — not least the right of automatic audience with the local ruler to whom he wishes to convey his request for a job. He explains: "I came here to speak to the king" (p. 10). Informed by one of the black men in the crowd at the esplanade that such a demand is "absolutely unheard of," Clarence thunders: "I am not 'just anybody'... I am a white man" (p. 10). But he rapidly discovers the futility of his efforts. Beset with innumerable problems, including his inability to see the king, his wrongful arrest, and his trial, he discovers not a well-ordered and rational universe but a world of chance and arbitrariness, a surreal place where the most basic laws of everyday causality in the social and physical realms seem inoperative. In the African country where Clarence finds himself, dreams and reality are inseparable; nature is intoxicating; characters, such as the beggar and the king, take on multiple, even contradictory, qualities; social status, material wealth, and skin color are poor indexes of human worth.

What appears arbitrary and incoherent to Clarence, however, is so only in appearance. For beneath what his rational mind perceives as chaos lies a divine design. Only when he gives up all pretense of being able to make rational sense of his experience and lies prostrate and humble, defeated and gnawed by feelings of unworthiness — when, in short, he divests himself of his Promethean spirit, to a bare state symbolized by his near nudity — does he discover the plenitude of divine grace.

By making Clarence's salvation coincide with the moment of his total surrender to the values associated with traditional Africa, Laye asserts the superiority of those values and challenges not only the meliorist assumptions of modernity that the world can become better through human intervention, but also the vehicle through which they were introduced into Africa, colonial rule. The progress of the mystical pilgrim in *The Radiance of the King* is also a statement on cultural nationalism.

A DREAM OF AFRICA

Laye's third novel, *A Dream of Africa* (1966), is essentially a continuation of *The Dark Child*. It tells the story of the return to Guinea from France, after an absence of six years, of the dark child, now called Fatoman, who narrates the story; of his marriage to Marie, who has been the narrator's girlfriend in Conakry in *The Dark Child*; and of his thoughts on and experiences of Guinea in the period immediately preceding and following its independence.

Although it contains autobiographical elements, *A Dream of Africa* is not an autobiography in a strict sense. Not only do protagonist-narrator and author have different names, but the central focus in *The Dark Child* and *A Dream of Africa* is different. In *The Dark Child*, Laye explores issues of personal identity and growth. In *A Dream of Africa*, he emphasizes external social and political events and not their impacts on the development of Fatoman's personality; as a result, Fatoman's reflections on the sociopolitical condition of Guinea in the mid 1950s take precedence over the re-creation of personal experience. The autobiographical writing of *The Dark Child* creates a mood of joy tinged with sorrow; an outright sadness dominates the relatively impersonal thoughts of *A Dream of Africa*.

The emphasis on sociopolitical reflections is evident in the first chapter of the novel, with debates for and against colonial rule and detailed descriptions of the changed face of Conakry, which has new avenues and boulevards, big warehouses and bauxite mines, but also many unpaved roads on the outskirts of town. In the subsequent chapters, the narrator dwells, between recollections of his stay in Paris, on the threat posed to ancient Guinean practices and life by the forces of vulgar commercialism sweeping across the country. He sees this trend particularly in the displacement of artisanal products by cheap industrial goods and in the emergence of men like Bilali, the narrator's diamond-trader friend, for whom "there's nothing on this earth you can't get with money" (p. 90).

The novel's French title, *Dramouss*, derives from the central episode in the narrator's experience: his frightening dream in which a giant wreaks death and destruction on a hapless community of people who have become his prisoners. The narrator is freed from this hell by a beautiful woman named Dramouss who, taking the form of a flying snake, lifts him to safety. The dream ends with the destruction of the giant by a black lion.

In the context of the narrative's time frame (1954–1956), this dream foretells the tyranny into which Guinea was to sink shortly after independence in 1958. But, according to Sonia Lee, the novel was actually written in 1963, well after the Guinean government had turned repressive. Therefore, in writing of the prophetic dream Laye probably benefited more from hindsight than from the kind of prophetic wisdom displayed by the Nigerian writer Chinua Achebe, who in *A Man of the People* (1966) predicted for Nigeria a military coup that indeed took place in 1966.

Although *A Dream of Africa* is devoted to issues of society and politics, personal moments are not altogether absent. Fatoman's reunion and conversation with Marie and his discussions with his parents are not unlike similar episodes in *The Dark Child*. The difference lies in the emotions evoked in connection with these experiences. In *The Dark Child*, the narrator's innocence—in his relations with Marie, for example—is totally credible. In *A Dream of Africa*, however, it seems false, even childish, such as when his aunt Awa advises him and his wife on their marital obligations: "You should talk and amuse yourselves, and not turn your backs on one another" in bed (p. 33). Also, the sense of protectiveness conveyed in *The Dark Child*, where the protagonist is constantly being fussed over by loving aunts and uncles, is unconvincing in *A Dream of Africa*. Here, Uncle Mamadou emerges as a bully with such orders to Fatoman and Marie as "I hereby command you to live, from this night on, as man and wife.... This...is the pleasant surprise which I have felt it my right and duty to reveal unto you" (p. 26).

Significantly, by incorporating traditional African narrative techniques into its structure, *A Dream of Africa* makes one of the earliest attempts in French African literature to Africanize the novel form. The traditional device that Laye uses, apart from the premonitory dream, is the oral tale. Critics, such as Lee and King, have pointed to the value of this device, explaining that insofar as the recited tale about the Imam Moussa explores a resolution to problems similar to those preoccupying Fatoman and Marie—problems of jealousy, trust, divine omnipotence, and so on—it serves as a practical lesson to them.

An important function of this device, which is rarely discussed, is that it endows the narrative with the quality of an oral performance. The tale of the imam is not meant to be flatly narrated. With its accompanying *cora* (African harp) music, its dramatizations, and its audience participation—especially from Marie, who is constantly questioning the storyteller and engaging in brisk exchanges with him at a live performance in Kouroussa—it constitutes a theatrical interlude from the high seriousness characteristic of the narrative not only for Fatoman and his wife, but also for the reader, for whom the spectacle has been so vividly described.

THE GUARDIAN OF THE WORD

Laye's attempt to preserve in print a rapidly declining oral art form is pursued in his last work, *The Guardian of the Word* (1978), which is a transcription and translation of the epic of Soundjata, the founding hero of Laye's Malinke people. His version of the epic includes the sequences into which the hero's life is conventionally structured: his noble ancestry and miraculous birth; his exile from home; his military exploits against Soumaoro, the king of the Susu people; and, finally, his triumphant return.

That Laye should have been attracted to translating this epic is no surprise. It is the national charter of his people, a chronicle of great achievement and an embodiment of their cherished values. It also illustrates many of the themes that concerned Laye in all his imaginative works: childhood, destiny, exile, the supernatural, and so on. Indeed, it has been persuasively argued that the inordinate emphasis Laye puts on Soundjata's childhood and on his relationship with his mother— inordinate when compared with the treatment of this subject in, say, the version of the same epic written by another Guinean writer, Djibril Tamsir Niane—is a reflection of Laye's own lifelong preoccupation with these themes.

But more than just a convenient peg on which to hang his own concerns, the Soundjata epic is for Laye a festival of language and of the verbal arts of his people, combining myth, folktale, praise poetry, and legend. Its very title suggests, if not a shift from the exploits of Soundjata—the traditional concern of the narrative's translators—then an awareness of the custodians of that narrative and their creative gifts. In *The Guardian of the Word*, Laye celebrates not just the wisdom and values of an ancient civilization, but artistic creation itself.

Selected Bibliography

NOVELS

L'Enfant noir. Paris: Plon, 1953. Repr. Paris: Presses Pocket, 1976.

Le Regard du roi. Paris: Plon, 1954. Repr. Paris: Presses Pocket, 1975.
Dramouss. Paris: Plon, 1966. Repr. Paris: Presses Pocket, 1976.
Le Maître de la parole. Paris: Plon, 1978.

SHORT STORIES

"Les Yeux de la statue." In *Présence africaine* 13 (1957).
"Prélude et fin d'un cauchemar." In *Fraternité-Matin* (17 December 1976).

TRANSLATIONS

The Dark Child. Trans. by James Kirkup and Ernest Jones. New York: Noonday, 1954. Repr. London: Collins, 1955; New York: Farrar, Straus & Giroux, 1969; New York: Hill & Wang, 1987.
The Radiance of the King. Trans. by James Kirkup. London: Collins, 1956. Repr. New York: Collier, 1965, 1971.
"The Eyes of the Statue." Trans. by Una Maclean. In *Black Orpheus* 5 (1959). Repr. in Charles Larson, ed., *More Modern African Stories*. London: Fontana-Collins, 1975.
"The Black Lion." In *Black Orpheus* 14 (1964). Repr. in Gerald Moore, ed., *African Literature and the Universities*. Ibadan, Nigeria: Ibadan University Press, 1965.
"The Soul of Africa in Guinea." In G. D. Killam, ed., *African Writers on African Writing*. Evanston, Ill.: Northwestern University Press, 1973.
A Dream of Africa. Trans. by James Kirkup. London: Fontana-Collins, 1968. Repr. New York: Collier, 1971.
The Guardian of the Word. Trans. by James Kirkup. London: Collins, 1980. Repr. New York: Vintage, 1984.

CONFERENCE PAPERS AND ESSAYS

"Premier contact avec Paris." In *Bingo* 14 (1954).
"Et demain?" In *Présence africaine* 14–15 (1957).
"L'Âme de l'Afrique dans sa partie guinéenne." Paper presented at Colloque sur la Littérature Africaine d'Expression Française. Dakar, Senegal, March 1963.

"L'Afrique et l'appel des profondeurs." Paper presented at Fourah Bay College Conference, University of Sierra Leone, April 1963.
"The Black Man and Art." In *African Arts* 4 (fall 1970).
"Le Rêve dans la société traditionnelle malinké." Paper presented at the Conference on Manding Studies, School of Oriental and African Studies, London University, 1972.

CRITICAL STUDIES

Azodo, Ada Uzoamaka. *L'Imaginaire dans les romans de Camara Laye*. New York: Lang, 1993.
Bernard, Paul R. "Individuality and Collectivity: A Duality in Camara Laye's *L'Enfant noir*." In *French Review* 52, no. 2 (1978).
Bertrand, Brenda. "Gender and Spirituality: Initiation into the *Koré* in Camara Laye's *Le Regard du roi*." In *French Review* 67, no. 4 (1994).
Biyidi, Alexandre [Mongo Beti]. "*L'Enfant noir*," in "Trois écrivains noirs." In *Présence africaine* 16 (1954).
———. "Afrique noire, Afrique rose." In *Présence africaine* 1–2 (1955).
Blair, Dorothy. "Camara Laye." In her *African Literature in French*. London: Cambridge University Press, 1976.
Brière, Eloise A. "*L'Enfant noir* by Camara Laye: Strategies in Teaching an African Text." In *French Review* 55 (May 1982).
Gikandi, Simon. "Character and Consciousness in the Novels of Camara Laye and Ayi Kwei Armah." In his *Reading the African Novel*. London: James Currey, 1987; Portsmouth, N.H.: Heinemann, 1987.
Harrow, Kenneth W. "The Margins of Autobiographical Literature of *Témoignage*: Camara Laye, *L'Enfant noir*." In his *Thresholds of Change in African Literature: The Emergence of a Tradition*. London: James Currey, 1994; Portsmouth, N.H.: Heinemann, 1994.
King, Adele. *The Writings of Camara Laye*. London: Heinemann, 1980.
Lee, Sonia. *Camara Laye*. Boston: Twayne, 1984.
Leiner, Jacqueline. "Interview avec Camara Laye." In *Présence francophone* 10 (spring 1975).

Miller, Christopher. "*L'Enfant noir*, Totemism and Suspended Animism." In his *Theories of Africans: Francophone Literature and Anthropology in Africa*. Chicago: University of Chicago Press, 1990.

Mortimer, Mildred. "Camara Laye in Quest of a Vanishing Self." In her *Journeys Through the French African Novel*. London: James Currey, 1990; Portsmouth, N.H.: Heinemann, 1990.

Obumselu, Ben. "The French and Moslem Backgrounds of *The Radiance of the King*." In *Research in African Literatures* 2 (spring 1980).

Olney, James. "Ces Pays lointains." In his *Tell Me Africa: An Approach to African Literature*. Princeton, N.J.: Princeton University Press, 1973.

Palmer, Eustace. "Camara Laye: The African Child." In his *Introduction to the African Novel*. New York: Africana, 1972.

Sellin, Eric. "Alienation in the Novels of Camara Laye." In *Pan-African Journal* 4 (1971).

Doris Lessing
1919–

LORNA SAGE

DORIS LESSING is among the most inventive, prolific, and many-sided writers
in the English language. For her English is
more than one language—a vital, quarrel-
some, sometimes cacophonous mixture of
voices and registers—a habit of hearing she
undoubtedly acquired during her formative
years in southern Africa. Her heritage, however, was very British. Her parents were part
of a generation of restless, middle-class Britons
displaced after World War I: she was born in
Persia (now Iran) and brought up in Southern
Rhodesia (now Zimbabwe), where her father
became a settler and farmer when she was five.
Southern Rhodesia, which had been settled by
British colonists led by Cecil Rhodes in 1890,
became a largely self-governing white protectorate—though still British, still marked out
in pink on the world map—in 1924, just
before her family moved there. Lessing's parents and her brother lived out their lives in
Africa; but she left for London in 1949 and,
after a visit "home" in 1956, was declared a
"prohibited immigrant" and banned from returning, on political grounds. After the country had been reborn as Zimbabwe in 1980 she
returned in 1982, the first of a series of visits
described in her book *African Laughter: Four
Visits to Zimbabwe* (1992).

In the many years between, there had been
desperate conflict. White Southern Rhodesia's
racial-segregation policy toward black Africans was very like—and much influenced
by—the policy of apartheid in neighboring
South Africa. In 1965 the white minority,
under the leadership of Ian Smith and
threatened by London with the prospect of
black majority rule, issued a unilateral declaration of independence from Britain. There
followed in the 1970s a war of liberation in
which two groups—the Zimbabwe African
National Union (ZANU), led by the Marxist
Robert Mugabe, and Joshua Nkomo's Zimbabwe African People's Union (ZAPU)—
played a major part in overturning white rule.
It was a bitter and untidy struggle. Black
policemen and troops fought on the side of
the government; white Southern Rhodesians
were involved, along with South Africans, in a
wider strategy of destabilizing black rule in
various adjoining states—backing Renamo
guerrillas in Mozambique, for example.

On independence, Mugabe was voted into
power, supported mainly by small farmers,
and began to implement a policy of returning
land to the people. Many whites stayed on,
however, and certain reconciliations that once
had looked impossible were effected. A hundred years from the beginning of settlement,
white domination had ended, and Zimbabwe
had a substantial measure of democracy and
a level of infant mortality substantially lower

than that in most African countries. However, the difficulties of its neighbors—particularly Mozambique, with its vital railway and oil pipeline linking landlocked Zimbabwe to the sea—were a daily drain on resources, and the prospects of stability and prosperity remained linked with the agonizing, long-resisted process of change in the continent's last white-ruled stronghold, South Africa, where white minority government ended in 1994.

Lessing's ties with the country where she grew up and married twice before she left at thirty were at once intimate and, as she herself saw it, limited and partial. Influenced by her reading and by the refugees and servicemen who came to the colony during World War II, bringing with them ideas from Europe, Lessing early dissociated herself politically from most of the white settler world, including her parents, her first husband, and her brother. She joined a Communist-inspired group: "It must have been blessed by Lenin from his grave, it was so pure.... If we had been in any other part of the world, where in fact there was a Communist Party, the beautiful purity of the ideas we were trying to operate couldn't have worked" (Howe, p. 425). But she later saw orthodox ingredients of contemporary progressive thinking as blinkered and inadequate: for instance, the dismissive doctrine that nationalism, including black nationalism, was anachronistic and irrelevant.

Lessing was a utopian to begin with, but by the time she became a writer (her first novel, *The Grass Is Singing*, was published in England in 1950), she was already hesitant about "representing" black points of view in her fiction. She became an un-settler, an anti-settler, someone alert to the false consciousness involved in putting down roots and speaking "for" others. In her preface to the first volume of her *Collected African Stories* (1973), she wrote that her "biggest regret" was that she could not write about the tribal life that predated white settlement and was ignorantly supplanted by the settlers:

The breakup of that society, the time of chaos that followed it, is as dramatic a story as any; but if you are a white writer, it is a story that you are told by others.

All the stories here are set in a society that is more short-lived than most: white-dominated Africa cannot last very long.

But looking around the world now, there isn't a way of living anywhere that doesn't change and dissolve like clouds as you watch.
                    (Triad/Panther edition, pp. 11–22)

One of the main legacies of Lessing's African life was this hypersensitivity to processes of change at work. It often made her seem uncannily prescient and helps to account for the authority she could wield in fiction and nonfiction alike, less as a spokeswoman for the oppressed than as an analyst of the divided consciousness of the postimperial cultures.

African themes in this sense surface throughout Lessing's writing. In the science fiction series Canopus in Argos (the first volume of which appeared in 1979), for example, issues of empire figure large, even though Earth is seen from the distance of space: "A grid had been stamped over the whole continent...a map, a chart, a certain way of thinking...made visible...the mind of the white conquerors" (*The Sirian Experiments*, 1981; Jonathan Cape edition, p. 277). *African Laughter* expresses Lessing's intense interest and pleasure in the new Zimbabwe and its people; yet at the same time she returns to the moral about mutability that she had drawn long before: "There are more and more people who have had to leave, been driven from, a country, the valley, the city they call home, because of war, plague, earthquake, famine. At last they return, but these places may not be there...there are gaps and holes or a thinning of the substance, as if a light that suffused the loved street or valley has drained away" (Panther edition, p. 13).

In 1994 she published *Under My Skin: Volume One of My Autobiography, to 1949* (1994), in which she once more revisited the land of her early life, meditating on the relations between fiction and fact: "when I wrote *Martha Quest* [1952] I was being a novelist and not a chronicler. But if the novel is not the literal truth, then it is true in atmosphere, feeling, more 'true' than this record.... *Martha Quest* and my African short stories are a reliable picture of the District in the old days. That is, from a white point of view" (London edition, p. 162). Her account is remarkably free of nostalgia while giving full weight to the enduring influence of childhood: "In the story of a life, if it is being told true to time as actually experienced, then I'd say seventy per cent of the book would take you to age ten" (p. 109). Lessing's imaginative resilience and the bleakness that often dominates her vision both derive from her sense of the transience of home, never being able really to go back.

LIFE

Doris Lessing's father, Alfred Cook Tayler, was born in 1886; his father was a bank clerk in Colchester, Essex, in England, and Alfred and his older brother also worked in a bank when they left school. The brother became a manager and prospered; Alfred led a carefree bachelor life, leaving home to live and work in Luton until he enlisted in the army in 1914. He served first as a regular soldier and later as an officer. His leg was shattered at Passchendaele, Belgium, in 1917; while he was in England, recovering from the ensuing amputation and shell shock, he met Emily Maude McVeagh, a nurse, and they married in 1919. She had been born in London and was the granddaughter of a bargeman on the river Thames.

Their first child, Doris May, was born on 22 October 1919, while they were living in Kermanshah, Persia, where Captain Tayler worked for the Imperial Bank of Persia. When Doris was two and a half, they moved to Tehran. In 1926, on leave in London with his family (according to his daughter's later ac-

count), her father attended the Empire Exhibition. One display promised that fortunes could be made farming in Southern Rhodesia: "So on an impulse, turning his back forever on England...my father collected all his capital, £800, I think, while my mother packed curtains from Liberty's, clothes from Harrods, visiting cards, a piano, Persian rugs, a governess and two small children" (*A Small Personal Voice*, 1974; Vintage edition, p. 90). They settled in Mashonaland, in the Banket district: "Lomagundi—gold country, tobacco country, maize country—wild, almost empty. (The Africans had been turned off it into reserves.)" (*A Small Personal Voice*, p. 90). There they lived in a colonial version of genteel poverty, for her father, though sustained by government loans and able to employ nearly limitless numbers of Africans very cheaply, was never able to make a profit from the farm. Over the years he became dreamy, irascible, hypochondriac, and genuinely ill with diabetes, and her mother again became his nurse.

The cigar-shaped house of thatch and mud where the piano went out of tune and the Liberty's curtains faded was meant as temporary accommodation but became their only home, a magical place as well as a claustrophobic one during the years their daughter was growing up. Her stories and the early novels (particularly the Children of Violence sequence, 1952–1969) describe the house, the farm, and the wild landscape she and her brother roamed in childhood again and again. Writing in 1968 about another woman writer from southern Africa, Olive Schreiner, Lessing distilled many of her speculations about the origins of her own vocation in the imaginative economy of family life:

To the creation of a woman novelist seem to go certain psychological ingredients; at least, often enough to make it interesting. One of them, a balance between father and mother where the practicality, the ordinary sense, cleverness, and worldly ambition is on the side of the mother; and the father's life is so weighted with dreams and ideas and imaginings that their joint life gets lost in what looks like a hopeless muddle and failure, but which holds a potentiality for something that must be recognised as better, on a different level, than what ordinary sense and cleverness can conceive.

(*A Small Personal Voice*, p. 108)

Variants on this picture of her background are used in stories as well as in the semi-autobiographical earlier novels: father the dreamer; mother the manager, conventionally ambitious for her children. Mother comes off much the worse, of course. It wasn't until her speculative dystopian novel *The Memoirs of a Survivor* (1974), which Lessing described as "an attempt at autobiography," that she replayed the family scenario with a significant difference: the mother figure ("the large cart-horse woman, her tormentor, the world's image") is also imagined as a small child, repressed in *her* mother's image, and so on, possibly even back to infinity.

Although her mother wanted her to go to university, Lessing left school at fourteen—"I felt some neurotic rebellion against my parents who wanted me to be brilliant academically. I simply contracted out of the whole thing and educated myself" (*A Small Personal Voice*, p. 49). She took a series of stopgap jobs in the Southern Rhodesian capital, Salisbury, before marrying Frank Wisdom, a civil servant, in 1939; they had two children—a son, John, and a daughter, Jean—before separating in 1942. The children stayed with their father following the divorce in 1943, and in 1945 Doris married Gottfried Lessing, the leading member of the Communist group with which she had been involved for some time. With Gottfried Lessing she had one son, Peter, who moved with her to London in 1949, the year her second marriage ended in divorce. (Gottfried Lessing went to East Germany after the war; in 1979, when he was East German ambassador to Uganda, he was killed in the revolt that overthrew Idi Amin.) "Let's put it this way," she told Roy Newquist in an interview in the 1960s, "I do not think that marriage is one of my talents" (p. 46). She did

not marry again. She did, however, informally adopt another child, Jenny Diski, who became a novelist. Lessing's childhood, adolescence, and marriages form the basis for the first three novels of the Children of Violence sequence and the "Black Notebook" sections of *The Golden Notebook* (1962).

Since 1949, Lessing has lived in London. This changing city, once the hub of an empire, was blitzed in World War II and not yet rebuilt when she arrived, and has been continuously demolished and developed ever since. For her it became at once a home base and a city of exiles and refugees, people passing through. Lessing rapidly found a publisher, Michael Joseph, for the manuscript she brought with her—her first novel, *The Grass Is Singing*—and so was launched on her career as a writer. In 1952 she joined the British Communist Party, and left it, along with many others, in 1956, in reaction to the Soviet invasion of Hungary. In 1958 she helped to organize the first Campaign for Nuclear Disarmament (CND) march. Looking back, Lessing told an interviewer: "An epoch of our society, and of socialism, was breaking up at that time. It had been falling apart since the Bomb was dropped on Hiroshima. . . . Slowly, it began to sink into our consciousness. . . . I feel as if the Bomb has gone off inside myself, and in people around me" (*A Small Personal Voice*, p. 65). During the 1960s Lessing became a scathing critic of the progressive, rationalist, and socialist-realist assumptions that had been main props of her mental universe, and her new interest in, for example, the antipsychiatry of R. D. Laing and in Sufism is increasingly evident in her work. She put herself through a comprehensive course in "nonlinear thinking," and as a result, middle age became the second great formative period of her life.

Her personal experience was no longer supplying the materials for Lessing's fiction. Or, rather, the quality of her personal life, and of her understanding of her own and other people's "characters," had changed. From then on, she played out her role as woman of letters—*The Golden Notebook* had established her as a major figure on the international literary scene—in a variety of ways, using a diversity of forms and approaches and voices. In 1979 she began her series of speculative science fiction novels, Canopus in Argos; in 1983 and 1984 Lessing published two realist novels, *The Diary of a Good Neighbour* and *If the Old Could*... under the pseudonym Jane Somers and was gratified to note that they received very little attention (although a reader at Michael Joseph, the company that had published her first works, did recognize the style as reminiscent of the early Doris Lessing and accepted the manuscripts). Also in the 1980s she espoused the cause of the mujahideen struggling against Soviet rule in Afghanistan (*The Wind Blows Away Our Words*, 1987). She viewed that war against a technologically advanced invader as a version of instinctive resistance to the many threats to global ecological balance and to the survival of the planet, and she saw herself as a species of Cassandra:

> Cassandra, daughter of Priam, who was King of Troy, warned, "her hair streaming loose" of the forthcoming disastrous war, but no one took any notice.
>
> (Picador edition, p. 13)

> Once upon a time, there were the special, talented-for-prophecy individuals. Then, a few people in every palace, settlement, farmstead. But now, a multitude.... Cassandra is a shout of warning coming from everywhere.
>
> (p. 16)

Also in 1987, Lessing published a series of lectures she had given two years earlier for the Canadian Broadcasting Corporation, under the title *Prisons We Choose to Live Inside*. Again she mused on the role of writers: "I see writers, generally, in every country, as a unity, almost like an organism, which has been evolved by society as a means of examining itself.... Its most recent evolution has been

into space and science fiction.... The world is becoming one, and this enables us to see our many different societies as aspects of a whole" (Jonathan Cape edition, p. 17). Her communist internationalism had survived, but in a very different guise.

During the 1980s, Lessing also revisited the new Zimbabwe and compiled the materials that became *African Laughter*. Here the scenes of her early life resurfaced behind the scenes of the present. Her son John had become a tobacco farmer in Zimbabwe; her daughter Jean was married to a law professor and lived in South Africa (where Lessing was still prohibited and thus could not visit her grandchildren). In 1982 Lessing was reunited with her brother, Harry (they had corresponded sporadically over the years), who had a factory making pictures from feathers, and horn buttons and key rings. He could not accommodate himself to black rule and was about to "take the gap," that is, leave for South Africa. Over a decade, in the course of four visits, Lessing registered not only the contrasts with the country of her youth but also the continuing processes of change in the present—immersing herself in all the improbable reconciliations, the disillusions, the hopes, and the corruption. Empathizing with the people's burgeoning energies for good and ill, and with the ongoing struggles against drought and AIDS and poverty, in the world of Zimbabwe but not of it, she was in her element.

EARLY WORK

Doris Lessing did not take long to establish a reputation on the 1950s British literary scene. Although her fortunes when she arrived were "at their lowest," she proved rich in imaginative currency. For a start, she had a novel in her suitcase—the product of the long-cherished and confident vocation that was the real story underlying her dead-end jobs and marital digressions:

I always knew I would be a writer, but not until I was quite old — twenty-six or -seven — did I realize that I'd better stop saying I was *going* to be one and get down to business. I was working in a lawyer's office at the time, and I remember walking in and saying to my boss, "I'm giving up my job because I'm going to write a novel." He very properly laughed, and I indignantly walked home and wrote *The Grass Is Singing*. I'm oversimplifying; I didn't write it as simply as that.

(*A Small Personal Voice*, p. 46)

It was, however, a most convincing debut. Her writing, though recognizably realist — and realism was the dominant mode of postwar fiction — had a distinctive vividness and energy, as well as a distinctive subject matter that can be crudely summed up as "female" and "African." The fiction and drama associated with "angry young men" from the British provinces set the tone at the time. In this context Lessing was at once strikingly unparochial and (though she regarded sexual equality as only one item, probably rather low down, on the progressive agenda) angry from a different angle, on women's account.

But *The Grass Is Singing* is not autobiographical. It is a slice of collective colonial psychohistory, the inside story of the murder of a white woman by her black houseboy on a remote farm — a crime of mutual violence, as it turns out, one that epitomizes racism's denial of shared humanity. Mary Turner visits on Moses all the frustrations of her relations with her dead father and her dreamy husband. His face bears the scar of her whip, and he becomes the focus of her neuroses: "her feeling was one of a strong and irrational fear, a deep uneasiness, and even — though this she did not know, would have died rather than acknowledge — of some dark attraction" (p. 190). This obsessive bond (expressed as hatred and rejection) culminates in the murder, an act that hints at forbidden intimacy and intensity of feeling between black and white. And so the white community instinctively closes ranks, "by means of a kind of telepathy" (p. 10), with

the banal cover story of a thieving servant. Lessing frames her novel with an account of the process of suppression. The effect is savagely ironic, since she, too — as author — is in her very different way closed off from her character Moses; it is the whites whom she analyzes with such penetration.

In the African short stories this same pattern emerges again and again, though less violently. Lessing chronicles the myths and neuroses and dreams and general bad faith of the settlers — which she felt were writ large before she went to work on them — exaggerated by the isolation in which so many lived, "all outsize and fit for tales and epics, because the white farmers lived at distances from each other" (*African Laughter*, p. 302). Nearly all of these stories are set before World War II and so relate to the period of Lessing's childhood and adolescence, a rich vein of material she mined for many years. There is in fact a cruel but creative tension at work between her deep, sensuous knowledge of the landscape and the subsequent awareness of her inevitable disinheritance ("a society that is more short-lived than most: white-dominated Africa cannot last very long"). Africans are noticeable by their omnipresence and their social, human absence ("the native problem," to her white characters). Very seldom does Lessing try to enter into a black consciousness.

The major exception — the novella "Hunger" (published in *Five: Short Novels*, 1953), about a young man who makes his way to the city and is corrupted in its underworld — was written, it seems, as a kind of experiment in socialist-realist aesthetics. Lessing was aiming, for once, to be the writer who worked with a broad brush and invented "typical" characters on the model of the great nineteenth-century novelists whom Marxist theoreticians such as George Lukacs admired. "After all, there was Dickens, and such a short time ago, and his characters were all good or bad. . . . There I was, with my years in Southern Africa behind me, a society as startlingly unjust as Dickens's

England" (*Collected African Stories*, vol. 2, preface; Triad/Panther edition, p. 10). "Hunger" does have echoes of *Oliver Twist*, incongruously enough, and through contrast highlights the subtlety and assurance of her settler stories. Lessing is at her best as a version of that characteristic figure of the later twentieth century, the alternative anthropologist who is turning back on her own culture the curious, analytical gaze with which earlier generations had regarded "primitive" peoples.

When writing about the physical landscape, however—this goes for the Children of Violence novels, too—Lessing is speaking from her primitive self. She relaxes her vigilance and allows herself back into paradise lost. Her documentary descriptions in *Going Home* (1957) of the night sky, the smells and sounds and spaces of the bush, and the thatched mud house where she grew up share this same quality of meticulous memory, and yearning too strong to be labeled nostalgia:

> I knew the geography of that wall as I knew the lines on my palm. Waking in the morning I opened my eyes to the first sunlight, for the sun shot up over the mountain in a big red ball just where my window was. The green mosquito gauze over the window had tarnished to a dull silver; and my curtains were a clear orange; and the sun came glittering through the silver gauze and set the curtains glowing like fire. The heat was instant, like a hot hand on your flesh. The light reached in and lay on the white wall, in an irregular oblong of soft rosy red. The grain of the wall, like a skin, was illuminated by the clear light.
>
> (Grafton edition, pp. 51–52)

Her parents' house was never meant to be permanent, so it decayed and was patched up year by year, becoming a sort of permeable shelter, open to the elements: hence its idyllic aspect, like the tree houses children build in less magical lands. This is Lessing's motherland, each day a birth. However, once she populates her world with adult characters from her white tribe, it becomes a claustrophobic place. People's body language—all twitches and tics and graceless, contradictory signs—betrays at every turn their lack of naturalness; and the plots are all about bad faith and self-deception.

CHILDREN OF VIOLENCE

The first three Children of Violence novels—*Martha Quest* (1952), *A Proper Marriage* (1954), and *A Ripple from the Storm* (1958)—chart the entry of Lessing's alter ego, Martha Quest, into this small world. They look like bildungsromans: Lessing was laying her own past life on the line, testing her capacity to reinvent herself as a character for the record, finding her personal place in a wider history. But this means, as it turns out, chronicling a series of false starts and failed resolutions. Marriage—which as a plot device had long symbolized not only the individual's entry into community but also, by analogy, the bridging of cultural and class divisions—is such a shaky, temporary affair that it has lost its power to confer the sense of an ending. Even before she marries Douglas at the end of the first of these novels, Martha is aware she wants something else and something more; her divorce at the end of the second novel is a gesture in this direction, but already compromised by the prospect of remarriage; and her second marriage, in the third novel, is in nearly perfect bad faith—an investment in party comradeship that is a personal and sexual disaster. So the ritual that used to stand as an emblem of wholeness (Lessing is obviously thinking back with bitterness to sexual mythmaking in the novels of D. H. Lawrence) becomes an ironic shadow of its former self. The sign of continuity is hollowed out into sameness, mere repetition. And this of course was—and remains—the paradoxical strength of these novels: that they find so much wanting.

Repetition—"the great bourgeois monster, the nightmare *repetition*" (*A Proper Marriage*, Panther edition, p. 90)—looms especially large in the colony, where so much psychic energy is devoted to defusing the prospect of change and passing on a version of middle-class privilege that Europe can no longer afford. Martha's generation, growing up in the 1930s, appears remarkably free, for the colony's social and sexual mores have a flavor of experiment and indulgence about them; but this, like serial monogamy, is a license for straying as long as one doesn't disrupt the social order. Martha lies to herself systematically, like a moral sleepwalker, acting out her role in the script (the shorthand for this is "turning into mother") while denying it:

> this the nightmare, this the nightmare of a class and generation: repetition ... a series of doomed individuals, carrying their doom *inside* them ... Nothing could alter the pattern.
>
> But inside the stern web of fatality did flicker small hopeful flames. . . . She had decided not to have a baby; and it was in her power to cut the cycle.
>
> (*A Proper Marriage*, p. 109)

But Martha is already pregnant, reproducing the "line," and somewhere at the back of her consciousness, she knew it all along. This is one of the most disturbing and ludicrous examples of her alienation from the "self" she keeps trying to give birth to. Her only real remaining strength—and this is what made Martha so recognizable to the women's movement some years later—is her refusal to be seduced by the pieties of either marriage or, more shockingly, motherhood (what Betty Friedan called the "feminine mystique" in 1963). Instead we get—through her eyes, for the most part—a set of descriptions of sexual intimacy, domesticity, pregnancy, and childbirth, with the values and conviction taken out. Lessing is writing a fictionalized history, a chronicle, a record, even a confession—but not classic realism.

For that, the writer must sustain a symbolic distance between the narrative and the world —a space where a germ of the universal can flourish. These opening volumes of Children of Violence hollow out the realist formula and discredit it. Nicole Ward Jouve, in an excellent essay, "Of Mud and Other Matter—The Children of Violence," put it thus:

> Martha, because she is questing for some kind of truth or freedom or self or whatever it is, because she is *voyaging*, becomes a tourist of life; she discards more and more, needs more and more people, experiences, to burn through. ... The novels as they proceed become aware of something false, a vacuity, which is the falsity of their own fictional mode.
>
> (Taylor, p. 130)

It is a particularly uneasy shift into self-consciousness because at the same time Lessing stays convinced of the primacy of those values—to do with wholeness, the transcendence of difference, shared ground—which were at the heart of realism's project. Martha is given rare moments of vision and painful ecstasy:

> There was a slow integration during which she, and the little animals, and the moving grasses, and the sun-warmed trees, and the slopes of shivering silvery mealies, and the great dome of blue light overhead, and the stones of earth under her feet, became one, shuddering together in a dissolution of dancing atoms.
>
> (*Martha Quest*, Panther edition, p. 62)

At these times out of time she finds her place, dissolves into the landscape:

> Martha allowed herself to be held upright by the mud, and lowered her hands through the resisting water to the hard dome of her stomach. There she felt the crouching infant, still moving tentatively around in its prison, protected from the warm red water by half an inch of flesh.
>
> (*A Proper Marriage*, p. 153)

But other people dispel this conviction—even the baby, when she comes, dispels it—and the idea of human unity, in historical time, becomes abstracted, utopian, and infinitely problematic. At this point Lessing turned away from the Children of Violence and wrote *The Golden Notebook*.

THE GOLDEN NOTEBOOK

The Golden Notebook (1962) is a novel of reluctant, even agonized, reflexiveness. Writing about writing was for Lessing a symptom of defeat and a sign of one's loss of the real world. So although it is a text of impressive formal inventiveness and ingenuity, *The Golden Notebook* has little of avant-garde experimentalism about it: not the nausea-cum-narcissism of the French *nouveau roman* or the bleak euphoria of the fiction of Samuel Beckett, let alone the playfulness of metafictionists like Jorge Luis Borges or Vladimir Nabokov. Nonetheless, with this book Lessing placed herself in the company of the self-conscious, which, as it turned out, was the hallmark or stigma of contemporaneity.

For her, the sense of loss was foregrounded because her political convictions had led her to associate great writing with the practice of an almost classical mimesis—a universalizing impulse rendered, one suspects, all the stronger by her desire to transcend the barriers of gender, as well as those of class and race. Thomas Mann was the Marxist critics' favorite example, and Lessing's character Anna cites him in *The Golden Notebook* in exactly the same spirit: "Thomas Mann, the last of the writers in the old sense, who used the novel for philosophical statements about life" (Granada edition, p. 79). She goes on:

> I am incapable of writing the only kind of novel which interests me: a book powered with an intellectual or moral passion strong enough to create order, to create a new way of looking at life.... I have only one ... of the qualities necessary to write at all ... curiosity. It is the curiosity of the journalist.
>
> (p. 80)

Lessing's Anna is voicing the same concerns as the British Marxist critic Raymond Williams, at almost exactly the same moment: "Reality is continually established by common effort, and art is one of the highest forms of this process. Yet the tension can be great ... and many kinds of failure and breakdown are possible" (*The Long Revolution*, 1961, pp. 305, 315). Unreality, formlessness, and breakdown acquire a kind of inverted representative function: the shapeless shape of things to come. Lessing's Anna doesn't write like a journalist—she cultivates chaos.

Lessing the author has caught up with herself: the writing self of the present tense, of the 1950s, who lives in London, leaves the Communist Party, comes to the end of a long spell in analysis with a matronly Jungian, and so on. The novel's "form" is that of a box with boxes inside it. Anna has four color-coded notebooks: red for the Party, black for Africa, blue for psychoanalysis, yellow for writing—though they are all about writing. She separates the parts of her life to stave off terminal disorder, but succeeds—perhaps she was plotting this in secret from herself all along—only in courting disintegration. The "frame" or "envelope" (the outside box) is a conventional third-person narrative called "Free Women," a wry story about social survival, that gets written (one gathers) by censoring, subsuming, and denying most of the material from the notebooks. However, this is emphatically *not* the "golden" notebook of the title. The golden notebook is a fifth, "insider" account, in which Anna finally abandons the old duty to establish reality by "common effort," in order to take an overview, to salvage a whole.

This inner narrative—a horrible and raw record of an affair with Saul, an American writer who also is falling apart, in a collusive, violent episode in which they pressure each other into craziness—wraps itself around *The Golden Notebook*, wraps up the "Free Women" box with the other boxes inside and delivers them to the reader. It is like being presented with work in progress—or, rather, in regress—a mass of fragmented, alternative versions of the "same" material, some processed, ironized, narrated, and some not, without hierarchy or principle that will "place" a newspaper clipping or an image from a dream in an orderly set of perspectives.

This writer's "I" becomes representative by virtue of its self-disgusted civil war: "the artist himself," Lessing said later to an interviewer, "has become a mirror of society. The first novelists didn't write about themselves, but now almost every novelist writes about himself" (*A Small Personal Voice*, p. 68). In the novel, Anna and Saul merge in this hell.

> Yes, that was me, that was everyone, the I. I. I. I am. I am going to. I won't be. I shall. I want. I. He was walking around the room like an animal, a talking animal, his movements violent and charged with energy, a hard force that spat out I, Saul, Saul, I, I want.
>
> (p. 605)

The paths to wholeness have been tried and found wanting: The Communist Party has split and split again, riven with witch-hunts and bad faith; remembering her African experience returns Lessing to the fact of her whiteness and exile; analysis privileges the timeless, mythic dimension of experience, leaving out the mess of history (madness is more accurate); and—in the yellow notebook—the marriage plot (as in Children of Violence) will not get itself written except as betrayal and bitter farce, the sex war. A measure of the misery apotheosized in *The Golden Notebook* is this sort of description:

> My body was a thin, meagre, spiky sort of vegetable, like an unsunned plant; and when I touched the hair on my head it was dead. I felt the floor bulge up under me. The walls were losing their density. I knew I was moving down into a new dimension, further away from sanity than I had ever been.
>
> (p. 591)

As they part company, Saul and Anna give each other opening sentences for their novels (he gives her the opening sentence of "Free Women"). Lessing meant her readers to see that there was, in however terrible a sense, still common ground. In fact, however, this ingenious formal device did not contain the book's meanings. Her readers responded to the partial, angry intensities of the book and pro-duced different books for themselves—"about the sex war ... about politics ... the theme of mental illness." The novel's power—and Lessing's authority as an author—were, it seemed, diffused in the very crisis she had addressed. The book's reception dismayed and fascinated her, and confirmed, in the long run, her sense of the author as a kind of tape recorder or lightning rod or Geiger counter.

RETURNING TO CHILDREN OF VIOLENCE CYCLE

Meanwhile, Lessing returned to Children of Violence with *Landlocked* (1965), a hybrid, uneasy novel that carries on Martha's story (divorced again, leaving Africa) but transfers her role as the central consciousness to her former lover, Thomas, a Jewish refugee who goes off into the bush and dies there. Martha inherits a bundle of ant-eaten manuscript, a palimpsest of anthropological notes interleaved with violent voices out of the ether—"notes, comments, scribbled over and across and on the margins of the original text" (New American Library edition, p. 269). "Martha sat holding this extraordinary document, fitting the leaves in between each other, separating them, so that sense and nonsense met each other, as in a dance, and left each other" (p. 272). This is a book that peers over the edge of its world, into self-destruction, and draws back. The fifth and final volume of the sequence, *The Four-Gated City* (1969), dismantles what is left of the realist format and takes off into speculative and savagely deconstructive territory.

In reaction against the package of progressive thoughts she had started with (rationalist, realist, humanist), Lessing now built a deliberately ramshackle countercultural canon of more or less illegitimate "authorities" across the ages. Here are the prophets without portfolio, alchemists, Rosicrucians, gnostics, Sufi teachers, mystics, visionaries, and shamans, who (like the science fiction writers in whom she was becoming interested) chart the mental territory that mainstream western traditions leave out. Her creature Martha, an alien in London, becomes housekeeper for a middle-class family whose history is an allegory of cultural change in the 1950s and 1960s. It is an epic-sized book that is at once spacious and claustrophobic — dealing with the cold war, wars around the world, the desecration of the environment, and, most disturbingly, antipsychiatry and the revaluation of madness. This last theme locks the narrative inside Martha's head — inside anybody's — "it is not a question of 'Lynda's mind' or 'Martha's mind'; it is the human mind, or part of it" (*Four-Gated City*, Panther edition, p. 513). And bodies are hideous — "all soft like pale slugs, or dark slugs, with their limp flabby flesh . . . and the eyes, tinted-jelly eyes which had a swivelling movement that gave them a life of their own" (p. 521) — for they are our ties to the old "real," the hostages we give to the world, which proceeds to domesticate us, locate us, make us at home.

The angry grotesquerie of this writing, and the throwaway crudity of the moves into the future tense, are a scornful commentary on the conventions with which Children of Violence began. Writing about writing had not elevated Lessing into literariness, but it had opened up her work to all sorts of alternative voices and uses, some of which she welcomed, some of which made her impatient (women's liberation, for instance). She had left African materials mostly behind now, but she had not turned into a British writer. Instead, her displacement had become her stock in trade.

BEYOND REALISM

Unlike her heroine Anna, Lessing had not suffered from writer's block in the literal sense. She had been prolific: between the 1950s and early 1970s, apart from the Martha Quest novels and *The Golden Notebook*, she wrote many short stories set in England (collected in two volumes in 1978); as well as a novel, *Retreat to Innocence* (1956), also set in England; the essay "The Small Personal Voice" (1957); and *In Pursuit of the English: A Documentary* (1960). Her hesitation was about what kind of writer she was to be. Lessing reinvented herself in her forties, in fact; *The Golden Notebook* is her "Portrait of the Artist" — a portrait of the artist as a late-twentieth-century Cassandra:

> I'm very much concerned about the future. I've been reading a lot of science fiction, and I think that science fiction writers have captured our culture's sense of the future. *The Four-Gated City* is a prophetic novel. I think it's a true prophecy. I think that the 'iron heel' is going to come down.
>
> (*A Small Personal Voice*, p. 70)

"The Small Personal Voice," about her view of the writer, put it more optimistically. The point is roughly the same, however. Something speaks through the writer:

> We are all of us . . . caught up in a great whirlwind of change; and I believe that if an artist has once felt this, in himself, and felt himself as part of it; if he has once made the effort of imagination necessary to comprehend it, it is an end of despair, and the aridity of self-pity.
>
> (*A Small Personal Voice*, p. 20)

The essay's title is ambivalent and fakes a kind of self-deprecation, for Lessing does not think the personal is personal any longer; she thinks of the personal life as the sounding board of the culture's undercurrents and crosswinds. One may agonize all alone in a separate suburban box, but it turns out that all along everyone was haunted by the wide world's voices.

A short story like "To Room Nineteen," about a wife and mother who turns her back upon the life of feeling, kin, and continuity, and "chooses" solitude, emptiness, and finally suicide, has a superficially documentary air. The technique is not overtly experimental, but the refusal to name and explore the impulses involved is a way of making space for the

shock therapy as the finishing touch, though not before he has recounted his adventures.

It is a dystopian variant on the narrative of human self-definition and civilization: how we learned violence and acquired separate identities and forgot our relations to other species—not only those "below" us but also the visitors from outer space we used to see. This parable of a great chain of being overlaps with the language of the "mad" golden notebook. Watkins is horrified by the machine-gun rat-tat-tat of "I":

> Some sort of a divorce there has been somewhere along the long path of this race of man between the "I" and the "We," some sort of terrible falling away, and I ... feel as if I am spinning back ... into a vortex of terror, like a birth in reverse, and it is towards a catastrophe ... when the microbes, the little broth that is humanity, was knocked senseless ... so that ever since most have said I, I, I, I, I, I, I and cannot, save for a few, say We.
>
> (Panther edition, p. 103)

This language of lost collectivity, psychic communism, involves an authorial change of identity: Lessing becomes storyteller, shaman, maker and unmaker of myth, casting herself in the role of go-between or "medium," impatient of finesse. She told an interviewer in 1969 that because of her determination "to reach people," the form of *Four-Gated City* was "shot to hell," and one gets the same feeling about *Briefing for a Descent into Hell*. The idea of the writer as living in these words, putting a personal signature on them, has gone by the board.

The Summer Before the Dark

The Summer Before the Dark (1973) is superficially more conventional—a woman's book about the crisis summer when forty-five-year-old Kate Brown wakes up from the roles of wife and mother and sexual woman. She wakes in order to dream. The dark side of her consciousness claims her, and she discovers the now familiar Lessing revulsion against ordinary human animals who deny their kinship with the animals. Kate goes to the theater and watches the audience, "covered with cloth and bits of fur, ornamented with stones ... their hair was the worst: mats and caps and manes and wigs of hair, crimped and curled and flattered and lengthened and shortened and manipulated, hair dyed all colours, and scented and greased and laquered" (Penguin edition, p. 149). Kate lets her own hair grow gray while she dreams a serial dream about carrying a seal to the sea. Comparing her world to a theater, she disowns the parts she has played so thoroughly that at the end she can return home, her alienation is so secure. In a most ironic sense, this book makes its peace with life—a kind of guidebook for inner-space travelers who want to "pass" as human.

The Memoirs of a Survivor

This was a transitional period. In 1979 Lessing began her next grand-scale project, the series of (thus far) five science fiction novels Canopus in Argos, which was eventually to match Children of Violence, with realism turned inside out and the theme of colonialism, though this time the empires were intergalactic. Meanwhile, however, she produced *The Memoirs of a Survivor* in 1974. She called it "an attempt at autobiography," and it reworks with a difference the family materials she had used in her African writings. It is a book about rebirth, which is signified by its visions of a childhood located in London—or, rather, behind the walls of a London flat, which are becoming transparent and permeable as the city loses its solidity and its reality. We are in a not-too-distant future of returning barbarism, pollution, vagrancy, and disorder. The narrator finds herself saddled with a homeless girl called Emily, who is billeted on her like an evacuee in World War II; she also finds herself revisiting her own infancy (or Emily's childhood, or her mother's) in the impossible but increasingly convincing country of memory behind the wallpaper. (Emily was one of Lessing's mother's Christian names.) The main motif is the threatened loss of individuality, in terms of both the "outer" world, where people are reverting to the behavior of tribes, or flocks, or herds, and the inner space where pasts converge.

Lessing's imaginative rejection of the notion of individual autonomy is thoroughgoing enough for her to find a sort of bliss in this situation. Traditionally the loss of personal space and a particular history is the stuff of dystopia. But here, though the writing does register the physical horror of losing one's boundaries—"everyone tasting and licking and regurgitating everyone else" (Octagon edition, p. 74)—the pleasure of stepping through the walls of calcified character is irresistible. Lessing's writing recovers subtlety and power as she picks apart the layered metaphorical meanings of home:

> walking through... the essence of woodland brought to life in the effaced patterns of the wallpaper, I moved through rooms that seemed to have aged since I saw them last. The walls had thinned, lost substance to the air, to time ... ghosts of walls, like the flats in a theatre.
> (p. 86)

The Memoirs of a Survivor deconstructs itself before our very eyes: "folding up as we stepped into it ... parcelling itself up" (p. 182). This is a house made of paper, one that will not be needed after the death of the self.

Critics' reactions to Lessing's revision of the author's role were often disappointed and skeptical. Elaine Showalter, in *A Literature of Their Own* (1977), spoke for many (particularly women) readers who had found in Lessing's earlier work a form of self-fashioning, clues to the making of identity:

> Lessing has not yet confronted the essential feminist implications of her own writing.... Kate Brown and the nameless "survivor" of the memoirs discard their female identities because

they are unimportant in the face of impending doom. But this is not a solution; it is the equality that comes at the end of a gun.
(pp. 311, 313)

Lessing concurs with the metafictionist avant-garde in her sense that life and authority have drained away from realist writing. But she does not conform to the recipes for reflexive liberation. In fact, it seems that for her one of the attractions of a genre like science fiction was precisely that its writers and readers were engaged in discussing real-world issues—supposedly not transcending or endlessly deferring them like the authors of self-consciously "literary" fictions. Was she guilty—as she had written mockingly in *Four-Gated City*—of what the world calls "'commitment,' perhaps? 'mysticism?'" Certainly. She was, as she said of Olive Schreiner in *A Small Personal Voice*, "the sort of woman who in an older society would have been made the prophetess of a tribe" (p. 118).

CANOPUS IN ARGOS

"*Shikasta* was started in the belief that it would be a single self-contained book.... But as I wrote I was invaded with ideas for other books, other stories, and the exhilaration that comes from being set free into a larger scope" (Jonathan Cape edition, p. ix). Lessing's prefatory "Remarks" in *Re: Colonised Planet 5, Shikasta* (1979) heralded a sequence of five heterogeneous fictions: *Shikasta, The Marriages Between Zones Three, Four and Five* (1980), *The Sirian Experiments* (1981), *The Making of the Representative for Planet 8* (1982), and *Documents Relating to the Sentimental Agents in the Volyen Empire* (1983). Science fiction writers, she said, "have played ... the role of the despised illegitimate son who can afford to tell truths the respectable siblings ... do not dare" (p. x). Lessing's feelings of release and pleasure are obvious, and though the Canopus in Argos novels are far from uniformly celebratory, they do share a casual, vagrant attitude to forms and conventions—mythic here, ironic there, everywhere provisional and throwaway—that acts as a prophylactic against earnestness.

Lessing had been studying serenity, learning to woo peace of mind. This comes out in her invention of the Canopeans, emissaries and agents of the power that has the overview in these books. Canopeans speak the language of "we" and thus often hardly speak at all, or at least not so as to be heard easily behind the babble of competing local rhetorics in every corner of the cosmos. Canopeans are do-gooders who try to do as little as possible and in the end cannot be distinguished from recording angels, because to do good, one needs to study patiently the laws at work in the universe and fit one's own energies into their operations. The Canopeans spend a lot of time looking on and take occasional vacations to recover from the depressive effects of becoming too immersed in local horrors and fears. They respect other cultures' differences, of course, because they are guardians of difference, taking on the character of the regions to which they are assigned and incarnating themselves as historical individuals. At the same time they are subverters of the politics of difference. Lessing had come to regard the tendency to take the public world personally, by papering the walls of one's own psyche with press clippings, as a disease: "Do you know," she said in a 1992 interview, "it's now a recognisable mental illness . . . people desperate about international affairs. I'm not very far off it. But I've lived through disaster after disaster, and we just go on; it's the history of everybody" (Sage, p. 225). The trick is to pay attention to the public world without being absorbed into it, infected, torn apart—particularly difficult on the planet Shikasta, where energy converts to suffering so routinely that it is as though it is a law of (meta)-physics.

Re: Colonised Planet 5, Shikasta is an alternative Earth epic, drawing on an eclectic body of myths about paradise lost, Manichaean battles between good and evil, falls of various sorts (when we worried about our souls, we were dimly remembering a sense-of-we feeling, SOWF for short, which we catastrophically mislaid millennia ago), and (through disaster after disaster) survivalist mutations:

> Nothing they handle or see has substance, and so they repose in their imaginations on chaos, making strength from the possibilities of a creative destruction. They are weaned from everything but the knowledge that the universe is a roaring engine of creativity, and that they are only temporary manifestations of it.
> (Jonathan Cape edition, p. 203)

Creative destruction is the keynote in the novels that follow—though not always in this oxymoronic balance. The next book, *Marriages Between Zones Three, Four and Five* is picturesquely, concretely imagined in the manner of a medieval illuminated manuscript—a charming romance in which femininity and masculinity are represented as rulers of two separate countries (a matriarchy where people communicate with animals and a martial, hierarchical kingdom) who "marry" for the good of their peoples and because it is the will of the Providers. Then they move on, still like medieval monarchs: he to a new alliance, she—like a weary queen entering a convent—to a cold, high place not named in the title, Zone Two, where you can lose your identity: "What are all these guises, aspects, presentations?" asks a wise bard, and he answers himself: "Only manifestations of *what we all are* at different times" (Jonathan Cape edition, p. 197). This particular novel, though, keeps the metaphysics at bay more than any of the others.

The Sirian Experiments is, by contrast, a dry, bureaucratic book whose central consciousness and narrator is Ambien II, a woman civil servant in the Sirian Empire. Ambien's realization that, for better and worse, "It is not possible for an individual to think differently from the whole he or she is part of" (Jonathan Cape edition, p. 272), is the book's—and, it could be argued, the whole series'—moral. To make this flat axiom work, however, the reader has to understand that the collective consciousness is layered. Ambien, for example, decides that the "rival" empire of Canopus is in the right. She looks for the moment like a traitor to her government but is actually a prosaic and boringly reasonable prophet, whose views will become accepted over time. Sirius has been a technocracy, plagued by unemployment, existential doubt, all the diseases of the redundant individual. However, the unofficial line, the decentered, dispersed consciousness, will triumph in the end as surely as death. In *The Making of the Representative for Planet 8*, death is another name for cultural dispersal. In this novel, a whole planet's people are reduced, by means of ice-age adversity and consciousness-raising tutorials from Canopean visitors, into one freeze-dried, collective, nearly anonymous voice, thus levitating into a kind of immortality. It is perhaps a measure of the thinness and abstraction of this book in particular that avant-garde composer Philip Glass based an opera with the same title (first performed in 1988) upon it: Glass, too, has been accused of, and praised for, his repetitiousness, and admires the "panoramic vision" of Lessing's Canopus series.

The final volume to date, *Documents Relating to the Sentimental Agents in the Volyen Empire*, addresses the inadequacy of mere words, especially political words. A Canopean observer in a lesser, disintegrating empire describes the style of the revolutionaries: "Shedding the Rhetoric of Empire, which they are prepared to analyse with acumen and to reject with scorn and contempt, they become prisoners of the Rhetoric of oppositional groups" (Jonathan Cape edition, p. 32). Yet another generation is conned and conscripted by the armies of words. It became crystal clear in this novel that Lessing sees group mentality as a travesty of and barrier to thinking "whole." We have a rich vocabulary for naming difference: "races, kinds, types, nations,

classes, sorts, genders, breeds, strains, tribes, clans, sects, castes, varieties, grades, even species" (p. 161). However, we fail to see that differing, partiality, is what we have in common. Lessing's Canopeans have all along spread the repetitious word that cross-influences and interactions are at work all the time, undermining difference: "'Our Empire isn't random, or made by the decisions of self-seeking rulers or by the unplanned developments of our technologies.... Our growth, our existence, what we are is a unit, a unity, a whole'" (*Planet 8*, p. 80). The rhetorical device used in this sentence—synecdoche, the part for the whole—is the structuring conceit of the Canopus series. The result is an extraordinary equivocation: a writing at once authoritarian and decentered, a doublespeak that appropriates the voices of others (see Lorna Sage, *Women in the House of Fiction*, 1992).

"JANE SOMERS"

Lessing's imaginative wanderlust was not satisfied with the space offered by science fiction, and she expressed her frustration with characteristic literalness and mischief. She had, from around the time of the third Canopus book (1981), been plotting a literary hoax. She invented "Jane Somers," who after several rejections, including one from Jonathan Cape, which has published most of her writing since 1971, published a first novel, *The Diary of a Good Neighbour*, in 1983, and a second, *If the Old Could...*, in 1984, both with Lessing's first publisher, Michael Joseph. Lessing then revealed herself as Jane's inventor. The two books, which had attracted very little attention, were published together under her name as *The Diaries of Jane Somers* (1984): it all went to show, she said in her preface to the collected volume, what is in a name, how hidebound and reputation-minded the literary world was. However, Jane Somers in fact read more like a loyal imitator of what Lessing once was (a documentarist, a realist) than like Lessing "herself." With hindsight it is of course possible to trace the signs of her ruling preoccupations: the decay of metropolitan life, relations between the generations—or, rather, the distortions, neuroses, and sheer mutual ignorance that pass for continuity.

In the first book, a middle-aged Jane finds herself taking on an old woman, a dying, garrulous stranger, who becomes her guide to changing her life, living by a different timetable; in the second, she falls in love with a man her own age—but this is not the "real" theme, which has to do with their ties to the young—his children and her niece, a shapeless, hopeless teenager adrift in the city. The claims of others are Lessing's theme: not so much in the charitable or even social-worker sense as in terms of our frightening lack of relation to our own pasts and futures as mirrored in those on the margins of society. That she was reviving a style from her past had its own ironic appropriateness. She was breaking her sequence, as she had done with *The Golden Notebook* twenty years before, though this time it was to go back to a kind of realism. The tangled impulses at work here—to discard an identity? to add one? to reassert a continuity?—reveal Lessing as a true outsider, a writer not content to break the rules inside the text.

THE GOOD TERRORIST AND THE FIFTH CHILD

The children who won't grow up return in Lessing's major single book of the 1980s, *The Good Terrorist* (1985), a finalist for Britain's Booker Prize in 1985 and winner of the W. H. Smith Award, also in Britain, the following year. The novel is a black comedy about a tiny militant political group, the Communist Centre Union (C.C.U.), with a core of half a dozen ill-assorted comrades who are squatters in a rambling London house. At their center is thirty-six-year-old Alice, the good terrorist of the title. The novel is very much a story

about good housekeeping. Alice, who looks after Jasper, the leading inspiration of the C.C.U. who almost never lets her touch him (he is gay, if anything), is a daughter of the bohemian middle-classes, with a gift for nannying, caring, serving, fixing up houses, and large-scale catering that enables her to make one nest after another for the wandering revolutionaries devoted to pulling the whole system down. She deals marvelously with housing officials, people from the electricity board, and the police. She loves fixing things up, making rooms clean and warm and comfortable, saving discarded but good furniture, unclogging lavatories, and feeding stray cats. And in the book's climactic episode she is a party to a bomb attack on a West End hotel that leaves five people dead. For Alice is emotionally retarded (there seems no other way to put it), racked with resentments and hatreds and fears that remain unresolved from childhood and now issue in a love affair with violence and an ecstatic hatred of the middle class to which she so patently belongs.

The gross contradictions in Alice's character are presented descriptively and in close-up, moment by moment, so that the competent nanny shades plausibly into the little girl who actually welcomes Jasper's sexual rejection and finds his cruel bullying reassuring. Perhaps the most impressive effects come from concentrating on the how rather than the why of things: how she gets the electricity switched back on, how she steals money from her father's office, how she, without going to a doctor, deals with a woman who has slashed her own wrists. Lessing contrives to immerse the reader in Alice's world to the point where the reader can begin to share the myopia that enables her to enjoy her own competent busyness, on the way to murder. Thus the "feel" of the book is documentary, but only in a sense: there is an overload of obsessive detail concerned with rubbish, detritus, and filth, both metaphorical and literal. One of the commune's favorite swearwords is "shit," and Alice's most impressive and memorable achievement on taking over the house is to remove bucketfuls of stinking excrement from the attics and bury it in the garden.

Lessing is echoing *The Memoirs of a Survivor*, where the baby behind the wall is traumatized and damaged when she is punished for playing with her own feces, and also the first "Jane Somers" book, in which bathing the incontinent old lady is one of the narrator's conversion experiences. There is a mixture of Swiftian disgust (Gulliver among the Yahoos) and punitive carnival comedy in all this that is impossible to disentangle. Lessing is trespassing on forbidden territory— society's sewage. Talking about this book, she claimed kinship with her main character:

> I'm convinced that we are all boxes containing various personalities and these are what my characters are: aspects of my own personality. The prominent ones like the detached story teller, the sensible practical woman, and the rather crazy girl, all recur. I'm not too pleased to think that the nasty Jasper in *The Good Terrorist* is a part of me, but the infantile creature who keeps turning up, Alice in this case, I think I rather like her.
> (interview by Simon Banner, *Times*, London, 15 May 1986)

Lessing's final novel of this prolific decade —in which she also published her plea for Afghanistan, *The Wind Blows Away Our Words*, and her Canadian Broadcasting Corporation lectures, *Prisons We Choose to Live Inside* (both in 1987)—was *The Fifth Child* (1988). It is a slighter book, but also a shocking one—and again she explodes the image of "home." David and Harriet, a couple who set their faces against 1960s sexual mores, create a marital household that is a microcosm of order and fertility, until their fifth child is born. He is a changeling, a throwback, an anarchic hobgoblin, and he destroys the whole happy, well-meaning edifice single-handed. There is a good deal of the genre of fable about this book, which is cruelly stylized. Jeanette Winterson, a British novelist who emerged in the mid 1980s and who is much interested in fairy tales, fantasy, and the grotesque, reviewed *The Fifth Child* with enthusiasm as an antimoral tale:

> Lessing is acutely aware of society as an artificial gesture. She is also committed to its potential. David and Harriet, by preferring the artificial gesture and refusing to admit to the importance of social change, however painful or confusing, unleash on themselves and their immediate community a living image of the suppressed self. The suppressed self that the 1960s, however clumsily, was trying to get to grips with. What Lessing shows is that no one knows what evolutions are necessary for the development of the psyche, we only know that movement is the key.
> (*Sunday Times*, London, 17 April 1988)

This startlingly cool, didactic reading seems right. Lessing is more interested in change than in progress, or regress.

LATER WRITINGS

London Observed

London Observed (1992) collects eighteen short stories, many of them hardly fictionalized, seen through the eyes of a veteran watcher of the city's manners and mores. Having been at times one of the more visionary and afflicted critics of the horrors of the metropolis, Lessing here displays a protective—even tender —attitude toward "polyglot and casually mannered London" (Flamingo edition, p. 89). It has changed its character spectacularly since the 1940s, when, at least in the minds of Londoners, it was all "pinko-grey as [George Bernard] Shaw said":

> in that other London there were no foreigners . . . for the Empire had not imploded, the world had not invaded, and while every family had at least one relative abroad administering colonies or dominions, or being soldiers, that was abroad, it was there, not here, the colonies had not come home to roost.
> (p. 84)

And yet London has in a way stayed, for Lessing, see-through—"the solid wall had the fluidity of dancing atoms" she wrote in *In Pursuit of the English* (1960, Panther edition, p. 79), about the bomb-damaged, traffic-battered house in which she lived when she arrived. That is the language she uses to describe her early formative intuitions of integration in the African landscape (compare *Martha Quest*: "a dissolution of dancing atoms"), and it is of course a version of creative destruction. (For Lessing, "atoms" would inevitably have been shadowed by the Bomb.)

Lessing has become the type and exemplar of the woman writer with her ear to the wall of received ideas, the one who hears rumors of the future behind the buzz of the present. She is streetwise in imagination, a citizen of the rebuilt and riven city she describes these days with such pleasure:

> I have such a good time in [London].... I like just wandering about and watching things. And the surrealism of the place is amazing. I see a *vast* lorry which should really be carrying loads of—I don't know what—of bricks, but on it are two little bay trees with pink ribbons round them, destined for a restaurant.... I suppose I see the place as a kind of theatre.
>
> (interview by Sage, p. 169)

African Laughter

The Zimbabwe visits chronicled in *African Laughter*, published in 1992, also address the genius of place, Lessing's once-upon-a-time "myth country." The book is built out of blocks of very different kinds of writing: personal pain, old scores, and buried affection; documentary quotations; portraits of individual Zimbabweans, from comrades in the government to lost hitchhikers dreaming of making a fortune in the capital, Harare (called Salisbury when Lessing left the country); lists of lost wildlife, sacrificed to farming; bitter monologues and propagandist catechisms and poems and snatches of conversation that

strive to net the country's spirit in passing. On her first (1982) visit she registers the scars of civil war, both visible and invisible—"Something has been blasted or torn deep inside people" (Panther edition, p. 16). There is always a new generation of children of violence. Already, however, there is "a shimmer in the air, like mental heat waves" (p. 17), produced not only by her recognition of dizzying contrasts with the past but also by the energy released under the new dispensation. Lessing does not, as visits go by, downplay the flourishing corruption (she jokes that she may be banned yet again for writing about it), but the emphasis falls, still, on the vitality with which people are confronting their formidable tasks. One realizes, with hindsight, that in the last Canopus in Argos novel to date, *Documents Relating to the Sentimental Agents in the Volyen Empire*, which is in part about coping with the end of empire, she was reflecting on Zimbabwe. Its preoccupation with the evils of jargon and rhetoric are echoed in *African Laughter*: "A United Nations report: 'All of Africa is bedevilled with rhetoric. There is no connection between what is going on and how it is described. And Zimbabwe is the worst of them all'" (p. 330).

In fact, the role Lessing is playing in this book is not entirely unlike that of one of her Canopean undercover agents, holding back from judgment but alert to false notes—changes of pace, tone, language, and body language—that register people's underlying fears and hopes. She puts off her personal pilgrimage "to the old farm" until her 1988 visit:

> This business of writers' myth-countries is far from simple.... All the people I know from former dominions, colonies, or any part of the earth they grew up on before making that essential flight in and away from the periphery to the centre: when the time comes for them to make the first trip home it means stripping off new skin and offering exposed and smarting flesh to—the past.
>
> (p. 301)

In the event, despite the horrible bungalow that has replaced the house, and despite the disappearance of the bush, she finds herself reconciled to the inevitable grief: "Well, every day there are more people everywhere in the world in mourning for . . . lost landscapes . . . you could say this is an established part of the human mind, a layer of grief always deepening and darkening" (p. 318). One can see from this writing how thoroughly Lessing has found her place in the world through losing it. The babble of voices on the page—where she can thread her own voice in and out of them—is for her the sound of hope and drowns out official politics. She has a gift for moving on, emotionally and imaginatively. In *Under My Skin: Volume One of My Autobiography, to 1949*, she describes her passionate commitments to people and to causes and, with equal candor, her saving genius for falling out of love:

> It took me four or five years from my first falling in love with Communism, or rather, ideal Communism, in 1942, to become critical enough to discuss my "doubts" . . . but it was not until the early 1960s I ceased to feel residual tugs of loyalty, was really free. . . .
>
> I was able to be freer than most because I am a writer, with the psychological make-up of a writer, that sets you at a distance from what you are writing about. The whole process of writing is a setting at a distance.
>
> (London edition, p. 397)

Lessing has been looking back and taking stock a good deal in recent years, but, true to form and to her restless imagination, she has also been exploring new directions.

Love, Again

In *Love, Again* (1996), her first novel in eight years, the central character, Sarah Durham— "A good sensible name for a sensible woman," (Flamingo edition, p. 3)—undergoes a most painful reawakening, assailed in her sixties by obsessive love for a man young enough to be her grandson. They both belong to a theater company—"How easily, how recklessly, we join this group or that, religious, political, theatrical, intellectual" (p. 81)—and the book's whole atmosphere is permeated by the backstage drama surrounding the impending production of a play Sarah has created out of the journals and music of a late-nineteenth-century French–West Indian woman. This figure, Julie Vairon, was (people argue) born before her time, a female genius (and partly black too, from Martinique); as her life is re-created she becomes a focus and a foil to the passions of those involved in the re-creation. The company breeds intrigue: not only does Sarah fall in love with Bill, the young actor who plays Julie's first lover (and who probably loves men), but the play's backer, Stephen, turns out to have a fatal passion for long-dead Julie herself. Much of the action, and of the acting, takes place against lush country backdrops in England and Provence, France, for the play is produced outdoors in the summer. The theme is love across time: Stephen's love for a woman dead for ninety years, Sarah's love for an unattainable man, from a different generation. Lessing tells the story through Sarah, in the third person, and we watch Sarah watching herself, as if from a great distance, with "compassion that was not tenderness but as dry and as abstract as the eye of Time" (p. 155).

It is a theme Lessing had touched on before, though never with such sustained scrunity: the longing, incredulity, and pain with which we approach the gulf between generations. Her character Sarah enters a labyrinth of selves and discovers she is still a stranger to herself, even in old age. In *African Laughter*, too, Lessing describes eloquently the paradoxes she has discovered in being the same person throughout life. Looking back at her younger self in Southern Rhodesia, she writes:

> I lived in different places, with different people. I *was* different people. Between the efficient young housewife of my first marriage, and the

rackety "revolutionary" of 1943, '44, '45 there seems little connection. Even less between those two and the young woman who—still always in crowds of people who changed, came from everywhere in the world, were always on the move—was developing the habit of privacy, writing when she could. . . . And yet we all know what the connection was: it is the sense of self, always the same—and that is the consoling, the steadying thing, that whether you are two and a half, or twenty, or sixty-nine, the sense of yourself, who you are, is the same. The same in a small child's body, the sexual girl, or the old woman.

(pp. 72–73)

This living tension, the vital fable Lessing has made out of the agonies and embarrassments and euphoria of change, is the key to her place in the world of English writing—writing that reflects the spread and history of the language, that is, writing from the heart of the imploded empire of English.

Selected Bibliography

COLLECTED WORKS

A Small Personal Voice: Essays, Reviews, Interviews. Ed. by Paul Schlueter. New York: Knopf, 1974; New York: Vintage, 1975.

Collected African Stories. 2 vols. London: Michael Joseph, 1973; St. Albans, U.K.: Triad/Panther, 1979; London: Paladin, 1982. Vol. 1, *This Was the Old Chief's Country.* Vol. 2, *The Sun Between Their Feet.*

Collected Stories. 2 Vols. London: Jonathan Cape, 1978; London: Grafton, 1979; St. Albans, U.K.: Triad/Panther, 1979. Vol. 1, *To Room Nineteen.* Vol. 2, *The Temptation of Jack Orkeney.*

The Doris Lessing Reader. London: Jonathan Cape, 1989; New York: Knopf, 1989; London: Paladin, 1991.

SEPARATE WORKS

The Grass Is Singing. London: Michael Joseph, 1950; New York: Crowell, 1950; London: Paladin, 1989.

This Was the Old Chief's Country. London: Michael Joseph, 1951; New York: Crowell, 1952.

Martha Quest. London: Michael Joseph, 1952; New York: Simon & Schuster, 1964; St. Albans, U.K.: Panther, 1966; London: Paladin, 1990. The first vol. of Children of Violence.

Five: Short Novels. London: Michael Joseph, 1953; London: Paladin, 1990.

A Proper Marriage. London: Michael Joseph, 1954; New York: Simon & Schuster, 1964; St. Albans, U.K.: Panther, 1966; New York: New American Library, 1970; London: Paladin, 1990. Second vol. of Children of Violence.

Retreat to Innocence. London: Michael Joseph, 1956.

Going Home. London: Michael Joseph, 1957; New York: Ballantine, 1968; London: Flamingo, 1992; New York: HarperCollins, 1996. With drawings by Paul Hogarth.

The Habit of Loving. London: MacGibbon & Kee, 1957; New York: Crowell, 1957; London: Grafton, 1985.

A Ripple from the Storm. London: Michael Joseph, 1958; St. Albans, U.K.: Panther, 1966; New York: Simon & Schuster, 1966; New York: New American Library, 1970; London: Paladin, 1990. Third vol. of Children of Violence.

Each His Own Wilderness. In E. Martin Browne, ed., *New English Dramatists: Three Plays.* Harmondsworth, U.K.: Penguin, 1959.

Fourteen Poems. Northwood, U.K.: Scorpion, 1959.

In Pursuit of the English: A Documentary. London: MacGibbon & Kee, 1960; New York: Simon & Schuster, 1961; St. Albans, U.K.: Panther, 1980; London: Flamingo, 1993.

Play with a Tiger. London: Michael Joseph, 1962; London: Davis-Poynter, 1972.

The Golden Notebook. London: Michael Joseph, 1962; New York: Simon & Schuster, 1962; London: Granada, 1973; London: Paladin, 1989.

A Man and Two Women. London: MacGibbon & Kee, 1963; New York: Simon & Schuster, 1963; London: Paladin, 1992.

African Stories. London: Michael Joseph, 1964; New York: Simon & Schuster, 1965.

Landlocked. London: MacGibbon & Kee, 1965; New York: Simon & Schuster, 1966; New York: New American Library, 1970; London: Paladin, 1990. Fourth vol. of Children of Violence.

Particularly Cats. London: Michael Joseph, 1967; New York: Simon & Schuster, 1967.

The Four-Gated City. London: MacGibbon & Kee, 1969; New York: Knopf, 1969; St. Albans, U.K.: Panther, 1972; London: Paladin, 1990. Fifth vol. of Children of Violence.

Briefing for a Descent into Hell. London: Jonathan Cape, 1971; New York: Knopf, 1971; St. Albans, U.K.: Panther, 1972.

The Story of a Non-Marrying Man and Other Stories. London: Jonathan Cape, 1972. Also publ. as *The Temptation of Jack Orkeney and Other Stories.* New York: Knopf, 1972; London: Paladin, 1990.

The Singing Door. In Alan Durband, ed., *Second Playbill Two.* London: Hutchinson, 1973.

The Summer Before the Dark. London: Jonathan Cape, 1973; New York: Knopf, 1973; Harmondsworth, U.K.: Penguin, 1975; London: Paladin, 1990.

The Memoirs of a Survivor. London: Octagon Press, 1974; New York: Knopf, 1975; London: Picador, 1976.

Re: Colonised Planet 5, Shikasta. London: Jonathan Cape, 1979; New York: Knopf, 1979; London: Grafton, 1981. First vol. of Canopus in Argos.

The Marriages Between Zones Three, Four and Five. London: Jonathan Cape, 1980; New York: Knopf, 1980; London: Grafton, 1981. Second vol. of Canopus in Argos.

The Sirian Experiments. London: Jonathan Cape, 1981; New York: Knopf, 1981; London: Grafton, 1982. Third vol. of Canopus in Argos.

The Making of the Representative for Planet 8. London: Jonathan Cape, 1982; New York: Knopf, 1982; London: Grafton, 1983. Fourth vol. of Canopus in Argos.

Documents Relating to the Sentimental Agents in the Volyen Empire. London: Jonathan Cape, 1983; New York: Knopf, 1983; London: Grafton, 1985. Fifth vol. of Canopus in Argos.

[Jane Somers, pseud.]. *The Diary of a Good Neighbour.* London: Michael Joseph, 1983; New York: Knopf, 1983.

[Jane Somers, pseud.] *If the Old Could . . .* London: Michael Joseph, 1984; New York: Knopf, 1984.

The Diaries of Jane Somers. London: Michael Joseph, 1984; New York: Vintage, 1984; Harmondsworth, U.K.: Penguin, 1985. Contains *The Diary of a Good Neighbour* and *If the Old Could . . .*

The Good Terrorist. London: Jonathan Cape, 1985; New York: Knopf, 1985; London: Paladin, 1990.

Prisons We Choose to Live Inside. Toronto: Canadian Broadcasting Corporation Enterprises, 1986; London: Jonathan Cape, 1987; New York: Harper & Row, 1987.

The Wind Blows Away Our Words. London: Picador, 1987; London: Pan, 1987; New York: Vintage, 1987.

The Making of the Representative for Planet 8: An Opera in Three Acts. Bryn Mawr, Pa.: Dunvagen Music, 1988. Written with Philip Glass.

The Fifth Child. London: Jonathan Cape, 1988; New York: Knopf, 1988; London: Paladin, 1989.

African Laughter: Four Visits to Zimbabwe. London and New York: HarperCollins, 1992; London: Flamingo, 1993.

London Observed: Stories and Sketches. London: HarperCollins, 1992. Also publ. as *The Real Thing: Stories and Sketches.* New York: HarperCollins, 1992; London: Flamingo, 1993.

Under My Skin: Volume One of My Autobiography, to 1949. London and New York: HarperCollins, 1994.

Love, Again. London: Flamingo, 1996; New York: HarperCollins, 1996.

INTERVIEWS AND PROFILES

Barker, Paul. "A Golden Notebook of 70 Years of Dreams." *Independent* (16 October 1989).

Bergonzi, Bernard. "In Pursuit of Doris Lessing." *New York Review of Books* (11 February 1965).

Fathers, Michael. "An Englishwoman Abroad." *Independent* (16 March 1987).

Howe, Florence. "A Conversation with Doris Lessing (1966)." *Contemporary Literature* 14 (fall 1973).

Landreth, Amy. "£20 in Her Handbag. . . ." *Daily Graphic* (28 February 1950).

Newquist, Roy. "Interview with Doris Lessing." Repr. in Paul Schlueter, ed., *A Small Personal Voice.* New York: Knopf, 1974; New York: Vintage, 1975.

Raskin, Jonathan. "Doris Lessing at Stony Brook." Repr. in Paul Schlueter, ed., *A Small Personal Voice.* New York, Knopf, 1974; New York: Vintage, 1975.

Sage, Lorna. "Lessing Observed . . ." *Vogue* (London) (May 1992).

Tomalin, Claire. "Mischief: Why a Famous Novelist Played a Trick on the Literary World." *Sunday Times* (London) (23 September 1984).

BIOGRAPHICAL AND CRITICAL STUDIES

Bertelsen, Eve, ed. *Doris Lessing.* Johannesburg, South Africa: McGraw-Hill, 1985.

Brewster, Dorothy. *Doris Lessing.* New York: Twayne, 1965.

Drabble, Margaret. "Doris Lessing: Cassandra in a World Under Siege." *Ramparts* 10 (February 1972).

Draine, Betsy. *Substance Under Pressure: Artistic Coherence and Evolving Form in the Novels of Doris Lessing.* Madison: University of Wisconsin Press, 1983.

Fishburne, Katherine. *The Unexpected Universe of Doris Lessing: A Study in Narrative Technique.* Westport, Conn.: Greenwood, 1985.

———. "Wor(l)ds Within Words: Doris Lessing as Meta-Fictionist and Meta-Physician." *Studies in the Novel* 20 (summer 1988).

Hardin, Nancy Shields. "The Sufi Teaching Story and Doris Lessing." *Twentieth Century Literature* 23 (October 1977).

Hite, Molly. "(En)Gendering Metafiction: Doris Lessing's Rehearsals for *The Golden Notebook.*" *Modern Fiction Studies* 34 (fall 1988).

Holmquist, Ingrid. *From Society to Nature: A Study of Doris Lessing's Children of Violence.* Götenborg, Sweden: Acta Universitatis, Gothoburgensis, 1980.

Jouve, Nicole Ward. "Of Mud and Matter: The Children of Violence." In Claire Sprague, ed., *In Pursuit of Doris Lessing: Nine Nations Reading.* Basingstoke, U.K.: Macmillan, 1990; New York: St. Martin's Press, 1990.

Kaplan, Carey, and Ellen Cronan Rose, eds. *Doris Lessing: The Alchemy of Survival.* Athens: Ohio University Press, 1988.

———. *Approaches to Teaching Lessing's* The Golden Notebook. New York: Modern Language Association of America, 1989.

Karl, Frederick R. "Doris Lessing in the Sixties: The New Anatomy of Melancholy." *Contemporary Literature* 13 (winter 1975).

King, Jeannette. *Doris Lessing.* London: Edward Arnold, 1989.

Knapp, Mona. *Doris Lessing.* New York: Frederick Ungar, 1984.

———. "Canopuspeak: Doris Lessing's *Sentimental Agents* and Orwell's *1984.*" *Neophilologus* 70 (July 1986).

Maslen, Elizabeth. *Doris Lessing.* Plymouth, U.K.: Northcote House, 1994.

Morgan, Ellen. "Alienation of the Woman Writer in *The Golden Notebook.*" *Contemporary Literature* 14 (fall 1973). The entire issue is devoted to Lessing.

Pratt, Annis, and L. S. Dembo, eds. *Doris Lessing: Critical Studies.* Madison: University of Wisconsin Press, 1974.

Rubenstein, Roberta. *The Novelistic Vision of Doris Lessing: Breaking the Forms of Consciousness.* Chicago: University of Illinois Press, 1979.

Sage, Lorna. *Doris Lessing.* London and New York: Methuen, 1983.

———. "The Available Space." In Moira Monteith, ed., *Women's Writing: A Challenge to Theory.* Brighton, U.K.: Harvester Press, 1986; New York: St. Martin's Press, 1986.

Schlueter, Paul. *The Novels of Doris Lessing.* Carbondale: Southern Illinois University Press, 1973.

Showalter, Elaine. *A Literature of Their Own: British Women Novelists from Bronte to Lessing.* Princeton, N.J.: Princeton University Press, 1977.

Singleton, Mary Ann. *The City and the Veld: The Fiction of Doris Lessing.* London: Associated University Presses, 1977; Lewisburg, Pa.: Bucknell University Press, 1977.

Spilka, Mark. "Lessing and Lawrence: The Battle of the Sexes." *Contemporary Literature* 16 (spring 1975).

Sprague, Claire, and Virginia Tiger, eds. *Critical Essays on Doris Lessing.* Boston: G. K. Hall, 1986.

Taylor, Jenny. *Notebooks/Memoirs/Archives: Reading and Rereading Doris Lessing.* London: Routledge, 1982; Boston: Routledge & Kegan Paul, 1982.

Thorpe, Michael. *Doris Lessing's Africa.* London: Evans Brothers, 1978.

Vlastos, Marion. "Doris Lessing and R. D. Laing: Psychopolitics and Prophecy." *PMLA* 91 (March 1976).

Whittaker, Ruth. *Doris Lessing.* Houndmills, U.K.: Macmillan, 1988.

———. "Doris Lessing and the Means of Change." In Linda Anderson, ed., *Plotting Change: Contemporary Women's Fiction.* London: Edward Arnold, 1990.